Microsoft® Windows® SharePoint® Services Inside Out

Jim Buyens

PUBLISHED BY
Microsoft Press
A Division of Microsoft Corporation
One Microsoft Way
Redmond, Washington 98052-6399

Library of Congress Control Number 2004118210

Printed and bound in the United States of America.

3 4 5 6 7 8 9   QWT   9 8 7 6 5

Distributed in Canada by H.B. Fenn and Company Ltd.

A CIP catalogue record for this book is available from the British Library.

Microsoft Press books are available through booksellers and distributors worldwide. For further information about international editions, contact your local Microsoft Corporation office or contact Microsoft Press International directly at fax (425) 936-7329. Visit our Web site at www.microsoft.com/ learning/. Send comments to *nsideout@microsoft.com*.

Microsoft, Active Directory, ActiveX, BizTalk, FrontPage, Great Plains, InfoPath, JScript, Microsoft Press, MSDN, MSN, OneNote, Outlook, PivotChart, PivotTable, PowerPoint, SharePoint, Verdana, Visio, Visual Basic, Visual C#, Visual Studio, Windows, Windows NT, and Windows Server are either registered trademarks or trademarks of Microsoft Corporation in the United States and/or other countries.

The example companies, organizations, products, domain names, e-mail addresses, logos, people, places, and events depicted herein are fictitious. No association with any real company, organization, product, domain name, e-mail address, logo, person, place, or event is intended or should be inferred.

Acquisitions Editor: Hilary Long
Project Editor: Kristine Haugseth
Project Manager: Steve Sagman
Editorial and Production: Studioserv (www.studioserv.com)
Copy Editor: Gail Taylor
Technical Editor: Mark Harrison
Indexer: Lucie Haskins and Ed Rush

Body Part No. X11-08647

This book is dedicated to the homeless mentally-ill persons of America. Why do we lavish health care dollars on victims of other, less debilitating illnesses while condemning these unfortunates to the streets and gutters?

Contents At a Glance

Table of Contents

Part I
Overview and Concepts

Chapter 1
Introducing Windows SharePoint Services   3

Chapter 2
Introducing SharePoint Portal Server   41

What do you think of this book?
We want to hear from you!
Microsoft is interested in hearing your feedback about this publication so we can continually improve our books and learning resources for you. To participate in a brief online survey, please visit: *www.microsoft.com/learning/booksurvey/*

Part II

End-User Features and Experience

Chapter 3
Using SharePoint Built-In Features   65

Chapter 4
Using SharePoint with the Microsoft Office System 97

Part III
Designing Sites and Pages with a Browser

Chapter 5
Creating SharePoint Sites and Pages 139

Table of Contents

Chapter 6
Designing Lists, Libraries, and Pages

171

Chapter 14
Backing Up, Restoring, and Migrating SharePoint Sites

435

Chapter 16
Managing Site Settings   523

Chapter 17
Administering Your SharePoint Site   539

Acknowledgments

First and foremost, thanks once again to my wife, Connie, who kept the family together while I devoted countless hours to this long, long project. When things got tough she revived me, and when I feared possession she restored my sanity. She's truly my friend, my helpmate, and my life's love.

Thanks as well to my children, Lorrill, Justin, and Lynessa, for their support and for bearing all the antics and absences involved in writing such a book. Thanks as well to my parents, my brothers, and their families: Harold, Marcella, Ruth, Dave, Connie, Michael, Steven, Rick, Jenny, Matt, and Claire.

At Microsoft Press, thanks to Sandra Haynes, the development editor, to Hilary Long, who handled the business details, and to Kristine Haugseth, the project editor, for their ceaseless confidence, encouragement, and assistance.

Support from the Windows SharePoint Services team was outstanding, perhaps unprecedented. Maria Hristova, Mike Ammerlaan, Iyaz Allah Baksh, Gabe Bratton, Ron Curtis, Lana Fly, John Hansen, Erik Heino, David Hua, Neelima Jain, Naganandhini Kohareswaran, Robin Liu, Luis Angel Mex, Maurice Prather, Rohit Puri, Bob Samer, Robert Silver, Matt Swann, Michael VandeKerkhof, Wendy Wenjing Wang, Geno White, Randy Yeh, and Ling Zhong: thanks a million to all of you. The book is better in a thousand ways because of your efforts.

Sincere appreciation is also due the FrontPage team for their invaluable assistance. Thanks particularly to John Jansen, Rob Mauceri, Greg Chan, Ellen Gryj-Rubenstein, Darren Miller, Kevin Morley, and Yuka Sanada, who contributed above and beyond the call of duty. Like the Web itself, this book has benefited thoroughly from your insight and imagination.

Thanks to the entire team at Studioserv Book Publishing Resources, especially Steve Sagman, whose experience and professionalism shined brightly at every moment. Thanks as well to Gail Taylor, the copy editor, and to Mark Harrison, the technical editor, both of whom contributed heavily to the overall quality of the book. Working with such a gifted group of people was a true delight.

Most of all, thanks to you, the readers, who make an effort such as this both possible and worthwhile. I hope the book meets your expectations and that we meet again.

About the CD

The companion CD that ships with this book contains many tools and resources to help you get the most out of your Inside Out book.

What's On the CD

Your Inside Out CD includes the following:

- **Complete eBook**   In this section you'll find the an electronic version of *Microsoft Windows SharePoint Services Inside Out*. The eBook is in pdf format.
- **Insider Extras**   Including all the author's sample files and code. To use the Insider Extras refer to "Using the Insider Extras," below.
- **Microsoft Resources**   A catalog of Windows SharePoint Services resources.
- **Reference Books**   Here you'll find the full electronic versions of the *Microsoft Computer Dictionary, Fifth Edition*; *Microsoft Encyclopedia of Networking, Second Edition*; and *Microsoft Encyclopedia of Security*

The companion CD provides detailed information about the files on this CD, and links to Microsoft and third-party sites on the Internet. All the files on this CD are designed to be accessed through Microsoft Internet Explorer (version 5.01 or later).

> **Note**   Please note that the links to third-party sites are not under the control of Microsoft Corporation and Microsoft is therefore not responsible for their content, nor should their inclusion on this CD be construed as an endorsement of the product or the site.
>
> Software provided on this CD is in English language only and may be incompatible with non-English language operating systems and software.

Using the Insider Extras

To use the following items, simply copy them from the InsiderExtras folder to your hard disk and remove the Read-Only attribute:

- **\utils\ShowStyles**   A Web page that displays sample of each SharePoint style name. This is useful when searching for a standard SharePoint style that has the appearance you want. For more information, refer to Chapter 9.

- **\utils\TagWalker**   An HTML fragment that displays all the CSS styles in effect the for the pixel under the mouse pointer. This is useful when you need to figure out why a SharePoint element looks as it does, and how you can reproduce that appearance in other Web Pages. Again, refer to Chapter 9 for more information.

- **\utils\WssBackup**   This is a WSH (Windows Scripting Host) script that retrieves a list of the top-level sites on a virtual server, and then runs the stsadm.exe -o backup command for each one. For more information refer to Chapter 14.

- **\utils\SPBackup**   This program from the Microsoft SharePoint Products and Technologies Resource Kit backs up each top-level sit that's changed during the previous day or week. Chapter 14 has more information.

- **\utils\Web Part Toolkit**   This folder contains four more utilities from the SharePoint Products and Technologies Resource Kit: InstallAssemblies (an installer for Web Parts), SharePoint Configuration Analyzer (a diagnostic tool that verifies critical settings on SharePoint servers), SharePoint Explorer (a tool that displays Web Part and Web Part Page properties), and Web Part Assembly (two powerful administrative-level Web Parts: GhostHunter and Inspector). Chapter 15 briefly introduces the SharePoint Configuration Analyzer. Chapters 19 and 20 briefly introduce the InstallAssemblies tool. For more information, refer to the help file that comes with the Web Part Toolkit.

The following folders in the InsiderExtras folder contain the Visual Studio .NET projects (including source code) for some simple but illustrative Web Parts. To use them, you would typically copy each folder to your Visual Studio .NET projects folder, clear the read-only attributes, and then open the .sln file in Visual Studio .NET.

- **\WebParts\proseware**   Contains the source code for a Web Part named MsgPara that displays a fixed, one-paragraph message. (Think, "Hello World.") For more information about this Web Parts, refer to Chapter 19.

- **\WebParts\tailspintoys**   Is a simple Web Part named TypicalEvents that demonstrates event handling. Chapter 19 has more information about this Web Parts.

- **\WebParts\WssIso**   Contains a project that include three Web Parts. The first, named Welcome, displays information about the current team member. The SiteLinks Web Parts displays links to parent and child sites of the current SharePoint site. Finally, a ListBrowser Web Part displays a quick listing (OK, a dump) of any list or library in the current site. For more information about these Web Parts, refer to Chapter 20.

- **\WebParts\WssIsoAdmin**   Contains a Web Part named TopSites that displays a list of top-level sites on the current server, and provides a simple form for creating additional top-level sites. An organization might develop such a Web Part for use by Help Desk or other employees responsible for routine upkeep of a SharePoint site. For more information, refer to chapter 21.

System Requirements

Following are the minimum system requirements necessary to run the CD:

- Microsoft Windows XP or later or Windows 2000 Professional with Service Pack 3 or later.
- 266-MHz or higher Pentium-compatible CPU
- 64 megabytes (MB) RAM
- 8X CD-ROM drive or faster
- Microsoft Windows–compatible sound card and speakers
- Microsoft Internet Explorer 5.01 or higher
- Microsoft Mouse or compatible pointing device

Support Information

Every effort has been made to ensure the accuracy of the book and the contents of this companion CD. To correct a missing or damaged CD, call 1-800-MSPRESS in the United States, or your Microsoft Press distributor in other countries.

To connect directly to the Microsoft Press Knowledge Base and enter a query regarding a question or issue that you may have, go to *http://www.microsoft.com/learning/support/*

For support information regarding Windows XP, you can connect to Microsoft Technical Support on the Web at *http://support.microsoft.com/*.

Conventions and Features Used in This Book

This book uses special text and design conventions to make it easier for you to find the information you need.

Text Conventions

Convention	Meaning
Abbreviated menu commands	For your convenience, this book uses abbreviated menu commands. For example, "Choose Tools, Track Changes, Highlight Changes" means that you should click the Tools menu, point to Track Changes, and select the Highlight Changes command.
Boldface type	Boldface type is used to indicate text that you enter or type.
Initial Capital Letters	The first letters of the names of menus, dialog boxes, dialog box elements, and commands are capitalized. Example: the Save As dialog box.
Italicized type	Italicized type is used to indicate new terms.
Plus sign (+) in text	Keyboard shortcuts are indicated by a plus sign (+) separating two key names. For example, Ctrl+Alt+Delete means that you press the Ctrl, Alt, and Delete keys at the same time.

Design Conventions

 InsideOut tips

These are the book's signature tips. In these tips, you'll find get the straight scoop on what's going on with the software—inside information on why a feature works the way it does. You'll also find handy workarounds to deal with some of these software problems.

Tip

Tips provide helpful hints, timesaving tricks, or alternative procedures related to the task being discussed.

Troubleshooting sidebars

Look for these sidebars to find solutions to common problems you might encounter. Troubleshooting sidebars appear next to related information in the chapters. You can also use the Troubleshooting Topics index at the back of the book to look up problems by topic.

Cross-References   Cross-references point you to other locations in the book that offer additional information on the topic being discussed.

 On the CD
This icon indicates sample files or text found on the companion CD.

Caution   Cautions identify potential problems that you should look out for when you're completing a task or problems that you must address before you can complete a task.

Note   Notes offer additional information related to the task being discussed.

Sidebars

The sidebars sprinkled throughout these chapters provide ancillary information on the topic being discussed. Go to sidebars to learn more about the technology or a feature.

Introduction

People working together is a key element in the success of any organization. Only through the cooperation, interaction, and collaboration of its members can an organization multiply its efforts and become stronger and more productive.

Much of this collaboration is, of course, face-to-face—we work together in pairs, in informal groups, in targeted meetings, and even in large assemblies. And when we can't be face-to-face, we speak by telephone, teleconferencing, instant messaging, or by video hookup. Although these methods are personal, immediate, convenient, and efficient, we sometimes need a more permanent record of our thoughts, our preparations, and our statements. For that, we've historically resorted to paper trails and mountains of pages, file folders, and cabinets. More recently, we've used electronic media such as e-mail messages, word processed memos, Excel spreadsheets, PowerPoint presentations, databases, and Web pages.

To be useful, of course, documents of any kind must find their way to the people who need them. Traditionally, they've followed one of four routes:

- **Mail**   Gets the immediate attention of its recipient, but it creates duplicate copies of each document for each recipient; it requires the sender to anticipate who might need a document; and it's awkward for long-term storage.

- **File Systems**   Provide medium-term storage for documents and (usually) a hierarchical scheme for organizing them. Unfortunately, most computer file systems maintain very little data about the documents they store; often just a cryptic filename and the date the file was last updated. Searching for documents by content or by property (such as author, title, keyword, or version) is slow and resource-intensive.

- **Databases**   Provide excellent long-term storage and search capabilities, but only by splitting documents into discrete data elements. As such, they usually store the data content of highly-structured documents, and not the documents themselves.

- **Libraries**   Combine, in many respects, the file system and database approaches. A library stores whole documents, not just their structured data content, and it provides a database of information about the documents it stores. This is a powerful approach but it often suffers from a lack of scalability. Either the library can't accommodate the massive number of documents a large organization can generate, or its indexing, search, and retrieval mechanisms aren't granular enough—for example, they start generating search results in the thousands or tens of thousands.

Taken individually, none of these approaches meets all the requirements for quick, easy, accurate, and efficient collaboration throughout an organization. Vendors, systems integrators, and organizations have therefore tried combining these approaches in various ways, hoping to multiply their benefits and cancel out their deficiencies.

Presenting Windows SharePoint Services

Microsoft's approach to collaboration and document management answers the shortcomings of all past and present approaches. It centers on two products named, collectively, SharePoint Products and Technologies:

- **Windows SharePoint Services**   Is a collection of add-on services bundled with Microsoft Windows Server 2003. Using these services, you or any authorized team member can create specialized *team Web sites* for sharing information, developing group documents, organizing meetings, and generally fostering collaboration among team members. The key components of these Web sites are lists and libraries.

    - A SharePoint *list* contains rows and columns of data, much like a standard database table. SharePoint lists, however, are much easier to create and maintain. They're great for collecting and sharing fielded information such as contact lists, calendars of events, or custom information of any kind.

    - A SharePoint *library* is similar to a list, except that it exists solely to store a collection of documents. Each list item describes one document, providing information such as the filename, the file title, the date last modified, and the person who last modified the document. SharePoint libraries can retain multiple versions of each document, and they support change control through document check-in and check-out. Windows SharePoint Services supports special library types for pictures and for InfoPath forms.

    Organizing these lists and libraries into team Web sites places most administration and content management in the hands of team members who are close to the work and familiar with the subject matter. This avoids the bureaucracy and the waiting times that are typical of strictly centralized administration. But at the same time, Microsoft provides all the tools that centralized administrators need to keep the installation under control and running smoothly.

    Team members can access SharePoint Web sites using either a browser or an Office 2003 application. Individuals in teams can configure lists and libraries to record whatever information they want, and they can easily create shared work areas for documents, projects, and other work in progress. Members can sign up to receive change notifications by e-mail. These features go way beyond anything traditional file-sharing can provide.

    You can also use Windows SharePoint Services as a development platform for creating custom collaboration and information-sharing applications. For example, third-party or in-house programmers can access SharePoint sites using Web services or readily-accessible application programming interfaces. In addition, you can develop custom Web pages using FrontPage 2003, and custom objects using Visual Studio .NET.

- **SharePoint Portal Server 2003**   SharePoint Portal Server 2003 is an application that runs on the Windows SharePoint Services platform. For most organizations, its most important feature is the ability to categorize Windows SharePoint Services Web sites— or even individual documents—into a hierarchy of *areas*. Portal users can drill into this hierarchy to find the information they need.

The portal server can also provide a special, personal Web site for each user. It can search and catalog conventional Web servers and file shares like an Internet search engine, and manage sign-in to additional business applications. It can also match areas to audiences so that, for example, employees with a particular interest can receive notifications of new or changed documents pertaining to that interest.

When you install SharePoint Portal Server, it occupies the root site of a virtual Web server running Windows SharePoint Services. The rest of the server continues to support Windows SharePoint Services, just as it would if the portal site weren't present.

Both of these products integrate smoothly, almost effortlessly, with your existing Microsoft software. The platform is Windows Server 2003; the Web server is Internet Information Server (IIS); security integrates with Windows domains or Active Directory; the run-time environment and development platform are both .NET. All Office 2003 programs function as SharePoint clients. You can send mail to an Exchange public folder and have any attachments appear automatically in a SharePoint library. Microsoft Project Server runs on Windows SharePoint Services, and SharePoint Portal Server integrates with BizTalk. The list goes on and on.

Both Windows SharePoint Services and SharePoint Portal Server make extensive user of Microsoft SQL Server. Small installations running only Windows SharePoint Services can use a special, restricted version called Microsoft SQL Server 2000 Desktop Engine (Windows)—WMSDE. Larger installations, or those using the portal server, require Microsoft SQL Server 2000 SP3 or later.

Scalability is no longer an issue. If usage demands, you can create as large a farm of Web servers as you like, and spread the database load across as many SQL servers as you like. And if you want fault tolerance, SharePoint Products and Technologies can do that too.

Who This Book Is For

This book addresses the needs of anyone who uses, designs, installs, administers, or programs Windows SharePoint Services. It begins with an overview of the product, and ends with an explanation of programming techniques. In between, the material is organized in order of increasing detail and complexity. This means you can read until you learn what you need at the moment, and then continue as the need arises.

Alternatively, you can approach the book randomly, on a sort of "need to know" basis. The index and table of contents will guide you to the specific information you need.

Even in its initial release, Windows SharePoint Services integrates tightly with an extremely wide range of Microsoft software. This includes not only Windows Server 2003 and Microsoft SQL Server, but also Internet Explorer, Microsoft Office System 2003, and Visual Studio .NET.

This book, however, is a complete guide only for Windows SharePoint Services. It presumes that if you're interested in the interface between Windows SharePoint Services and, say, Outlook, then you already know how to use Outlook. The same is true for the other Office programs, for Windows Server 2003, for Microsoft SQL Server, and for Visual Studio .NET

How the Book Is Organized

This book consists of seven parts, organized in order of increasing complexity and specialization. The early chapters, for example meet the needs of the widest and least technically curious audience: team members who use Windows SharePoint Services via Internet Explorer or Microsoft Office System 2003 on a daily basis. Later chapters address the needs of more specialized workers, such as Web designers, administrators, and software developers.

Here are the titles and specific coverages of each part:

- **Part I - Overview and Concepts**   In this part, Chapter 1 introduces the basic features and mindset of Windows SharePoint Services. For comparison, Chapter 2 briefly describes SharePoint Portal Server.

- **Part II - End-User Features and Experience**   This part explains the features that team members are likely to use the most. Chapter 3 explains how to work with SharePoint sites using a browser, and Chapter 4 explains how to access SharePoint sites from Microsoft Office System 2003.

- **Part III - Designing Sites and Pages with a Browser**   This is another part that consists of two chapters. Chapter 5 explains how to create new SharePoint sites and SharePoint Web pages using only a browser. Chapter 6 explains how to create, modify, and manage SharePoint lists and libraries, again using the browser interface.

- **Part IV - Creating and Designing Sites Using FrontPage 2003**   FrontPage 2003 has more SharePoint features than any other Office program: so many, in fact, that it takes six chapters to explain them all.

  Chapter 7 explains how FrontPage 2003 can create, open, add pages to, export, import, backup, and restore SharePoint sites. Chapter 8 then explains how to create and modify Web Part Pages. These are special Web pages that display the output of SharePoint software components called, logically enough, Web Parts. It also explains how FrontPage can create and modify themes that control the appearance of SharePoint sites.

  Chapter 9 explains how various FrontPage features interact with SharePoint sites. This includes site navigation, dynamic Web templates, styles and themes, interactive buttons, and DHTML behaviors.

  Chapters 10 through 12 explain how FrontPage can create pages that leverage the database capabilities of Windows SharePoint Services. Chapter 10 explains how to design, create, and modify SharePoint lists and libraries, and how to establish connectivity with these and external data sources. Chapter 11 explains how to create and configure List View Web Parts, which display the contents of SharePoint lists and libraries, and Data View Web Parts, which can also display data from external databases, XML files, and XML Web Services. Chapter 12 explains how to configure List Views, Data Views, and other Web Parts to interact with each other, and how to display deeply-nested XML data.

- **Part V - Installing SharePoint at the Server**   In this part, Chapter 13 explains how to plan for and then install Windows SharePoint Services in the most common scenarios. Chapter 14 then explains how to backup and restore SharePoint sites.

● **Part VI - Administering SharePoint Services**   An organization running Windows SharePoint Services can delegate administration at the physical server, virtual server, site collection or site level. If your duties fall into any of these categories, this part has something for you.

Chapter 15 explains the administrative functions available through the SharePoint Central Administration server. This is a virtual server that the Windows SharePoint Services setup program creates. To access it, you must be a server or SharePoint administrator. As you might expect, the functions on the Central Administration server are the broadest and most global of all.

Chapters 16 and 17 explain how to administer an individual SharePoint site or site collection. For the most part, these are functions that administrators of individual sites or site collections will use. Such administrators are usually designated team members, and not part of the centralized IT function.

Chapter 18 explains a variety of Web Parts and other design features that require administrative access to install or incorporate. These include some special built-in Web Parts, some .NET Server controls, some Office 2003 Web Parts, and XML site definitions.

● **Part VII - Developing Web Parts in Visual Studio.NET**   This part provides three chapters of interest to software developers who want to develop new components that behave like (and interact with) the Web Parts that come with Windows SharePoint Services. Chapter 19 provides some general guidance, and then Chapter 20 explains how to code three simple but useful Web Parts. Chapter 21 concludes with instructions for creating Web Parts that perform administrative functions, including sample code.

If this strikes you as quite a range of topics, you're right, and it indicates the central position that Windows SharePoint Services occupies among Microsoft products and technologies. All evidence suggests that this central position will grow not only for helping individuals collaborate, but also for integrating software functions and technologies of every kind. With this kind of promise, it's no wonder you're interested in Windows SharePoint Services.

Part I

Overview and Concepts

Chapter 1

Introducing Windows SharePoint Services

If you asked a dozen people to define the term *portal*, you'd almost certainly get a dozen different answers. To some, it means a home page. To others, it means an Internet search site like Microsoft's MSN or Google. To managers and corporate planners, it promises a way for knowledge workers to share documents and collaborate with others. To developers, it means a platform that provides services for developing Web-based systems. To Web visitors of all kinds, a portal offers relief from the confusing array of dissimilar Web sites they encounter every day, even within the same company. It unifies applications and information from many sources.

The Microsoft approach to portals involves two primary components known collectively as SharePoint Products and Technologies. These are Microsoft Windows SharePoint Services and Microsoft SharePoint Portal Server.

Windows SharePoint Services provides a high-function, scalable, and inexpensive platform that can support high function Web sites by the tens of thousands. Windows SharePoint Services comes with a collection of very useful templates for information sharing and collaboration sites, but these only scratch the surface of what's possible. There's almost no limit to the number of applications and the kinds of applications that can run on this platform.

SharePoint Portal Server is an application that enhances a Windows SharePoint Services installation with features like site organization and navigation, content topics, targeted news, personalized sites, content search, organization-wide alerts, and enterprise application integration.

If you're developing a corporate portal site and need multi-layered, hierarchical control over the content and policy of individual Web sites, you should definitely consider SharePoint Portal Server. But if your application isn't a corporate portal, or your administrative needs aren't so complex, then Windows SharePoint Services is probably all you need.

Windows SharePoint Services, all by itself, is amazingly powerful, flexible, and easy to use. The rest of this book, therefore, explains how to make the most of this amazing component that comes free with every copy of Microsoft Windows Server 2003.

The remainder of this chapter provides a brief overview of Windows SharePoint Services, how you can customize and enhance it, how it works with the Microsoft Office System, and how you can develop entirely new SharePoint applications. *Brief*, however, is the watchword. Later chapters will explain these topics in much greater detail.

Neither is this chapter a guide to setting up a SharePoint server; for that, refer to Part V, "Installing SharePoint at the Server."

Presenting Windows SharePoint Services

At a high level, Windows SharePoint Services consists of five primary components:

- A Web delivery mechanism, consisting of one or more Internet Information Services (IIS) Web servers.
- A back-end data store, which is basically a Microsoft SQL Server database.
- A collection of background software and services that provide database services, document management, security control, and administration.
- Software components called Web Parts that execute on the Web server and display output in portions of a Web page.
- Sample Web site templates of which there are seven.

Table 1-1 lists the applications that come with every copy of Windows SharePoint Services. As you can see, they're all oriented toward information workers in a corporate setting. However, you can use the same concepts to create Web sites for sports teams, youth groups, social clubs, schools, churches, professional or charitable organizations, and almost any kind of group. In addition, you can use the same platform to develop information systems of any kind.

Table 1-1. Site Templates Supplied with Windows SharePoint Services

Team Site	A site that helps a group of workers create, organize, and share information. It includes a Document Library, and basic lists such as Announcements, Events, Contacts, and Quick Links.
Blank Site	A site that starts with a blank home page. You can add as many Windows SharePoint Services features as you want.
Document Workspace	A site that a workgroup might use to develop an important document. It provides a document library for storing the primary document and supporting files, a Task list for assigning to-do items, and a Links list for related resources.
Basic Meeting Workspace	A Web site that helps plan, organize and track a meeting. By default it contains an Objectives list, an Attendees list, an Agenda list, and a Document Library.

Table 1-1. Site Templates Supplied with Windows SharePoint Services

Blank Meeting Workspace	A blank Meeting Workspace you can customize to meet your requirements.
Decision Meeting Workspace	A site where co-workers can review relevant documents and record decisions. It contains a Document Library and these lists: Objectives, Attendees, Agenda, Tasks, and Decisions.
Social Meeting Workspace	A planning tool for social occasions. Features include an Image/Logo, a discussion board, a picture library, and four lists: Attendees, Directions, Things To Bring, and Discussions.

At first, it might seem preposterous to create a Web site just to organize a single meeting or collaborate on a single document. In most cases, however:

- The members of a department or project will have authority to create as many of these Web sites as they like, subordinate to a Team Site. Furthermore, the whole site consists of fully-functional template pages. This reduces the time to create or delete such a site to seconds.

- Organizing all the file versions, related files, interested parties, discussions, task lists, agendas, and other pertinent items for a single objective into a single site makes it easy for team members to get the data they need, keep up to date, and collaborate— much easier, in fact, than dumping all these items into (hopefully) one sharename and identifying them with filenames.

- Windows SharePoint Services has no trouble accommodating thousands of such sites, and it controls them with disk quotas and clean-up routines that identify and delete old, inactive sites.

> **Note** In the context of Windows SharePoint Services, a team member is anyone authorized to browse, contribute to, design, or administer a given site.

Introducing Team Sites and Lists

The most all-inclusive sample application that comes with Windows SharePoint Services is the Team Site. This application addresses the needs of a typical department, project, or other small workgroup. Figure 1-1 shows the home page of a new Team Site.

The top navigation bar provides access to the highest-level functions. The shaded Quick Launch area at the left provides rapid access to the pages most often used. The Announcements, Events, and Links areas display the up-to-date content of three corresponding lists. Of course, in a new site, these lists have no significant content.

Microsoft Windows SharePoint Services Inside Out

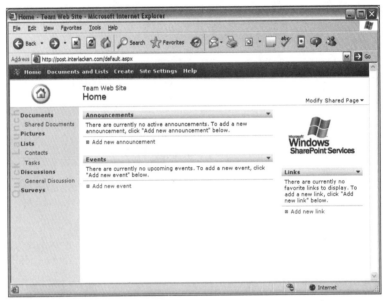

Figure 1-1. This is the default home page for a Team Site running on Windows SharePoint Services.

To add, say, an announcement, a team member would click the Add New Announcement link. This displays the Announcements – New Item page shown in Figure 1-2.

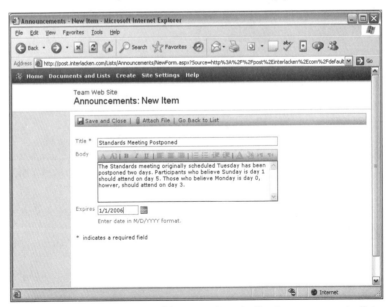

Figure 1-2. This Web page adds a new item to the Announcements list.

Introducing Windows SharePoint Services

If the team member fills in the form fields as shown, clicking Save And Close updates the Announcements list and redisplays the home page as shown in Figure 1-3. The figure also shows new items in the Events and Links lists. The process for creating Events and Links list items is similar to that for adding announcements.

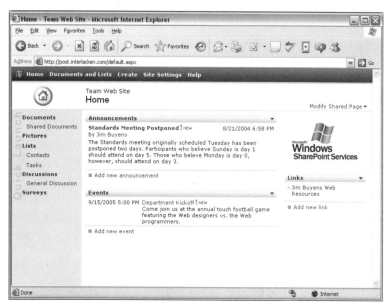

Figure 1-3. The home page now displays a new Announcements item, a new Events item, and a new Links item.

The Announcements, Events, and Links lists aren't just text files or any other sort of mundane objects; they're blocks of records in database tables. A single SharePoint site can have as many lists as you like, and those lists can contain whatever fields you like.

What's more, you can add, modify, or delete lists using nothing more than a browser. And when you create a list, SharePoint automatically creates forms to maintain and display its content. The My T-Shirt Inventory page in Figure 1-4 provides an example of this. A team member created this list, populated it with data, and displayed it, all without leaving the browser.

Microsoft Windows SharePoint Services Inside Out

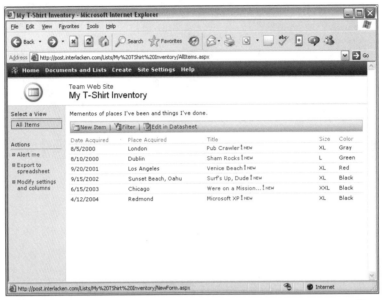

Figure 1-4. A team member created, populated, and displayed this SharePoint list without ever leaving the browser.

Introducing Document, Picture, and Form Libraries

Document libraries and picture libraries are also lists, but they have a document attached to each record. A single SharePoint site can have any number of document or picture libraries.

> **Note** Server administrators can assign quotas that limit the amount of disk space a SharePoint site consumes.

When a team member adds an item to a document library, the team member can either create a new document or upload an existing one.

- If the team member chooses to create a new document, Windows SharePoint Services will download a template file, the team member's PC will start the required Office program, and that program's Save command will upload the completed file into the SharePoint library.

- If the team member chooses to upload an existing document, Windows SharePoint Services displays an HTML form that contains a typical file upload control.

You can store whatever information you'd like about the content of a SharePoint library. Windows SharePoint Services captures some of this information automatically, such as the identity of the team member who uploaded the file and the date and time the upload occurred. The Shared Documents page shown in Figure 1-5 is a typical listing of the default document library.

Introducing Windows SharePoint Services

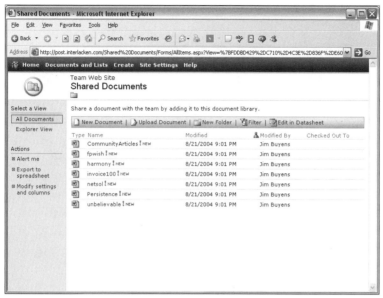

Figure 1-5. A SharePoint site can accommodate any number of document libraries like this one.

If you want to store additional information, such as a project task number, keywords, or a product number for each document, you can add fields for these purposes just as you would for any other list. The Create New Column page shown in Figure 1-6 shows this operation in progress. To display this page, you would click the Modify Settings And Columns link in Figure 1-5, and then, under Columns, click Add New Column.

Like document libraries, picture libraries are basically lists that have a file attached to each record. Of course, in the case of a picture library, the file will be a photograph or drawing. As shown in Figure 1-7, the Web pages that display picture libraries have options to display the library contents visually.

For more information about using a Team Site, refer to Chapter 3, "Using SharePoint Built-In Features."

A SharePoint form library is similar to a document library, but its default template is an electronic form compatible with Microsoft InfoPath. To fill out the form, team members click the form library's Fill Out This Form button. The SharePoint site then downloads the template and starts InfoPath on the member's computer.

To submit the form, the team member saves it from InfoPath into the form library. Each form submission therefore creates one document in the library. Form libraries have special features to extract information from these documents and display it as columns in the library listing. Furthermore, InfoPath has features to download multiple forms and summarize their content.

Microsoft Windows SharePoint Services Inside Out

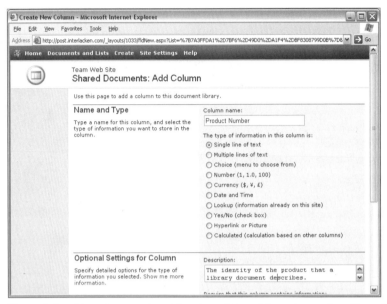

Figure 1-6. It's quite easy to add and configure data columns in a SharePoint list or library.

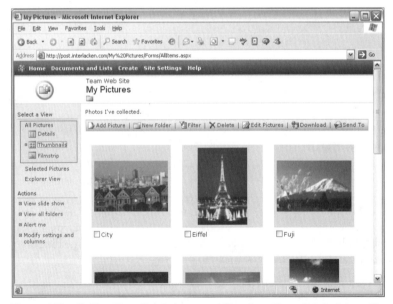

Figure 1-7. Unlike SharePoint document libraries, SharePoint picture libraries offer visual display of their contents.

Introducing Web Parts, Web Part Pages, and Web Part Zones

It should be obvious by now that SharePoint sites contain very little static HTML. Instead, software on the server customizes each page based on the Web site's configuration, each team member's preferences, the content of libraries and lists, and other factors.

Less obviously, much of this software isn't tied to specific Web pages. Instead, it consists of software modules called Web Parts. A Web Part occupies a portion of a page and displays its output in that portion. Windows SharePoint Services comes with a variety of useful Web Parts. If that's not enough, you can download more Web Parts from Microsoft or third-party Web sites, or you can write your own.

> **Note** In Figure 1-1, the areas titled Announcements, Events, and Links are List View Web Parts. An Image Web Part displays the Microsoft Windows SharePoint Services logo.

Web pages that contain Web Parts are called, logically enough, Web Part Pages. The Web Parts themselves are ASP.NET custom controls, and Web Part Pages must therefore be ASP.NET pages. That is, they must have a filename extension of .aspx.

A Web Part Zone is a container that encloses any number of Web Parts. A Web designer can add Web Parts to a page without putting them in Web Part Zones, but this stops team members from adding, removing, or rearranging the Web Parts on their personal view of the page.

> **Note** Some Web Part Pages support a feature called personalization that can store a different arrangement of Web Parts for each team member. On a team site home page, members can switch between the shared (default) view and their personal view by clicking the Modify My Page or Modify Shared Page drop-down arrow and then choosing Shared View or Personal View from the resulting menu.

In Figure 1-7, for example, a team member is modifying his or her personal view of a team site home page. The team member clicked the Modify My Page drop-down arrow on this page, and then chose Add Web Parts and Browse from the resulting submenus. This reveals two Web Part Zones, as shown in Figure 1-8: one named Left, which contains the Announcements and Events Web Parts, and one named Right, which contains the Image and Links Web parts. It also displays an Add Web Parts task pane that partially obscures the Right Web Part Zone.

Microsoft Windows SharePoint Services Inside Out

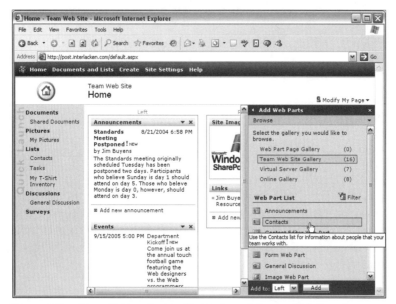

Figure 1-8. After clicking the Modify My Page link on a Web Part Page, you can add, remove, configure, or rearrange its Web Parts.

The Browse section of the Add Web Parts task pane selects one of four Web Part galleries. In the figure, the team member has selected the Interlacken.com – Root Site Gallery. The Web Part List section therefore displays a list of Web Parts available within that gallery. To add any of these Web Parts to an existing Web Part Zone, the team member would:

1 Select a Web Part listed under Web Part List.

2 Specify a Web Part Zone by selecting its name in the Add To drop-down list. (This appears at the bottom of the Add Web Parts task pane.)

3 Click the Add Button.

The combination of Web Parts, Web Part Zones, and Web Part Pages provides a very flexible environment. Consider, for example, that:

● A single Web Part Page can contain any number of Web Part Zones.

● A Web Part Zone can contain any number of Web Parts.

● The same Web Part can appear in any number of Web Part Pages or Web Part Zones.

● Whoever designs a Web Part Page can lock some Web Part Zones so everyone gets the same content, and leave others on the same page open for personalization.

For more information about Web Part Pages, refer to "Configuring Web Parts," in Chapter 5, and to Chapter 8, "Creating and Modifying Web Part Pages."

Reviewing Key Scenarios

The next series of topics explains some of the ways you might use Windows SharePoint Services. These topics are only brief introductions, and they don't pretend to illustrate every possible situation. They should, however, give you a feel for the power of Windows SharePoint Services itself, and for what it can accomplish.

Sharing Information

SharePoint document libraries take file storage to a whole new level, with features far beyond those of ordinary file sharing. For example, SharePoint document libraries can:

- Store whatever information you want about each document.
- Display flexible, customizable views of each document library's contents.
- Lock documents so multiple users can't make simultaneous changes with check-in and check-out.
- Display documents online.
- Manage multiple versions of each document.
- Require that a so-called *list manager* approve changes before they appear for other team members. This is what Windows SharePoint Services calls Content Approval.
- Notify interested parties of document additions, updates, or deletions.

In addition, SharePoint sites can store event calendars, contacts, Web links, discussions, issues lists, announcements, and much more. This is way beyond what you can achieve by dumping files into directories in sharenames. Team members can easily find and share data, with full protection against loss of data.

In short, SharePoint sites are smart places where team members can share information and get work done, and not just a place to save files.

Collaborating within Teams

Every SharePoint library provides options for team members to review documents and post comments online. Figure 1-9, for example, shows a listing of the default document library named Shared Documents. The team member has selected the file readmesp.htm and clicked the resulting drop-down arrow. (The filename extension .htm is apparent from the Microsoft Internet Explorer icon at the beginning of the line.)

Microsoft Windows SharePoint Services Inside Out

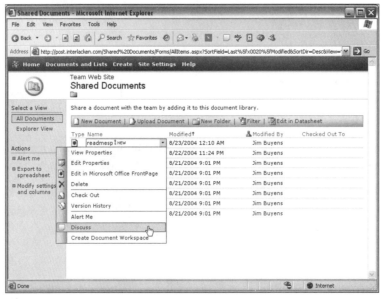

Figure 1-9. To enter discussion comments about a library document, open its drop-down list and select Discuss.

Here are the functions of each command in this drop-down list.

- **View Properties**   Displays a Web page that shows all available descriptive data for the document, even if it doesn't appear in the current library view.

- **Edit Properties**   Displays a Web page where you can modify the descriptive data for the current document.

- **Edit In Microsoft Office FrontPage**   Starts Microsoft FrontPage and tells it to open the current document. This option changes to match the document type. For a document with a filename extension of .doc, the option would read Edit In Microsoft Office Word.

- **Delete**   Removes the current document from the library.

- **Check Out**   Locks the library copy of the document so that no one except you can update it. Once the check-out is in effect, a Check In command appears in this position.

- **Version History**   Displays a clickable listing of all versions that are currently available. This listing includes the version date, the person responsible, and the file size. From this listing, you can view, restore, or delete any version.

- **Alert Me**   Displays a page where you can choose to receive e-mail whenever someone changes any aspect of the document.

Introducing Windows SharePoint Services

- **Discuss**   Displays the document in a browser or in its native application, so that you can record discussion comments.
- **Create Document Workspace**   Creates a new Web site for the sole purpose of working on the current document. The new site will have a document library already containing the document, a tasks list, a members list, and a list of links.

When you choose the Discuss command for a document your browser can display, the document appears as shown in Figure 1-10. The discussion toolbar at the bottom of the browser window has options to insert comments within the document, insert comments about the document as a whole, refresh the displayed comments, set discussion options, and so forth.

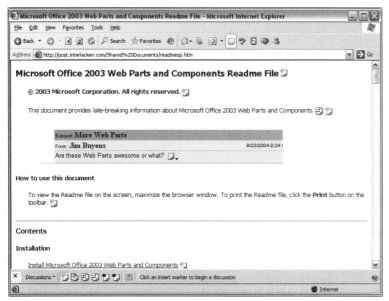

Figure 1-10.   This is how Internet Explorer displays Web documents for discussion. You can attach comments anywhere a document icon appears.

If you choose to discuss a Microsoft Office document the browser can't display, the browser loads a copy of the document's native program and tells it to open the document for discussion. Figure 1-11 shows this in progress for a Microsoft Word document. Note the Internet Explorer icon at the left of the title bar, the Microsoft Word menu bar, and the Internet Explorer Standard Buttons toolbar.

Microsoft Windows SharePoint Services Inside Out

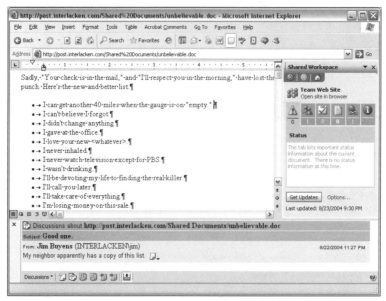

Figure 1-11. For this discussion, Microsoft Word is running within the browser window. The discussion pane is for viewing and entering comments. The Shared Workspace task pane displays information about the SharePoint site that hosts the document.

The Shared Workspace task pane is a new feature of Office 2003 that provides access to the SharePoint site where the document resides. This saves you from switching back and forth between the Office application and Internet Explorer. Table 1-2 explains the row of toolbar buttons near the top of the task pane.

Table 1-2. Toolbar Buttons in the Shared Workspace Task Pane

Icon	Command	Description
	Status	Lists important status information about the document.
	Members	Lists the members of the document's SharePoint Web site.
	Tasks	Displays the Tasks list from the document's SharePoint Web site.
	Documents	Displays the contents of the document library where the current document resides.
	Links	Displays the Links from the document's SharePoint Web site.
	Document Information	Displays the index information for the current document, as recorded in the SharePoint library.

Introducing Windows SharePoint Services

After you click any of these buttons, the results appear in the center of the task pane, and additional commands appear at the bottom. If you click the Tasks button, for example, you get a list of tasks in the current site and commands for adding new tasks and receiving tasks alerts. (A task alert is an e-mail message that informs you of a new, changed, or deleted item in a Task list.)

Clicking the Members, Tasks, Documents, or Links button displays the corresponding list for the entire SharePoint site that contains the document. If this is a general purpose site, these lists could contain a *lot* of information not related to the current document.

To prevent this, you could choose the Create Document Workspace option in the drop-down list that appeared in Figure 1-9. This would create a new SharePoint site dedicated solely to your document discussion.

- The Members would include anyone whose opinion or input you desired.
- The Tasks lists would contain tasks related to the review activity.
- The Links list would contain only those links that pertained to the document.
- The document library would contain your document, of course, but also any supporting or related documents you cared to retain.

The administrative overhead of creating a Document Workspace site is very small, because team members who can update the document library usually have permission to create and delete their own subsites. And if the creator of a document workspace forgets to delete it after the review is over, SharePoint management tools can detect the unused site, send out a warning message, and eventually delete it.

The Shared Workspace task pane is also available in Microsoft Office 2003 versions of Excel, OneNote, PowerPoint, Project, Word, and Visio. OneNote provides a version with only the Members, Tasks, Documents, and Lists options. Microsoft Office Outlook 2003 provides similar task panes for Meeting Workspaces and Shared Attachments.

In Excel, PowerPoint, and Word, SharePoint members can create a Document Workspace site without leaving the program. Here's the procedure:

1. Display the Shared Workspace task pane. For example:
   - If no task pane is on display, press Ctrl+F1.
   - If some other task pane is on display, click the drop-down arrow in the task pane title bar, and then select Shared Workspace.
2. Choose a Document Workspace name and a SharePoint Web site.
3. Click the Create button.

   Team members using only a browser can create Document Workspace sites from any SharePoint document library page.

   This section has mentioned only a few of the ways that Windows SharePoint Services can help team members collaborate. Even this brief introduction, however, makes it clear that SharePoint site and document libraries offer tremendous advantages over traditional file sharing, tag-team e-mail, or (perish the thought) exchanging floppy disks.

17

Integrating with Microsoft Office

The programs in Microsoft Office 2003 all provide a remarkable degree of integration with Windows SharePoint Services. With Office and SharePoint working together, the distinctions among the desktop, the Web, and seamless information sharing have never been so transparent. The following sections will briefly review some of these capabilities.

Opening and Saving Document Library Files

Microsoft Excel, FrontPage, InfoPath, OneNote, Outlook, PowerPoint, Visio, and Word can all directly open and save files residing in SharePoint libraries. Figure 1-12, for example, shows the Save As dialog box in Word accessing a Team Site library.

Figure 1-12. Using this dialog box view, most Office applications can directly open and save documents in a SharePoint library.

The File Open dialog box looks very much the same. To make either dialog box access a SharePoint library, proceed as follows:

1 Click the My Network Places icon in the My Places bar.
2 Select or type the URL of the SharePoint site.
3 Choose WebView from the Views drop-down list.

Checking Documents In and Out from Client Applications

SharePoint members can check out or check in a file from within Excel, FrontPage, PowerPoint, Visio, and Word. Checking out a file puts it under your control, so that other team members can't overwrite or edit the library copy. To use this feature:

1 Open the document as the previous section described.
2 Display the Shared Workspace task pane, and click the Document Information button.
3 Click the Check Out or Check In link near the bottom of the task pane.

You can also check documents in and out by using SharePoint Web pages.

Assigning Document Properties Automatically

When you add Excel, InfoPath, PowerPoint, Visio, and Word documents to a SharePoint library, SharePoint will automatically get the document title and other properties from the document itself. These are the values you enter in Office after choosing Properties from the File menu.

Synchronizing Events and Contacts

When you display a Contacts or Events list on a SharePoint site, the Contacts or Events toolbar has a Link To Outlook button. The Events page shown in Figure 1-13 illustrates this.

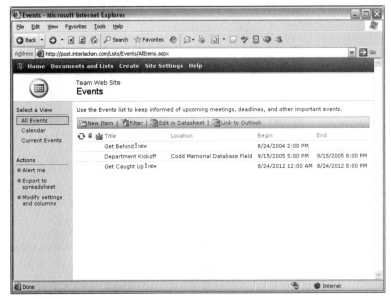

Figure 1-13.   Clicking the Link To Outlook button in this Events list page downloads a copy of the list into Outlook.

Clicking this button transmits (and periodically refreshes) a read-only Contacts or Calendar folder in Outlook. This makes the information available in Outlook even when you're disconnected from the network.

To view a SharePoint site directly in Outlook:

1 Create a new, empty Outlook folder.

2 Right-click the new folder, and select Properties from the shortcut menu.

3 Click the Home Page tab.

4 Enter the URL of your SharePoint site in the Address box.

5 Select the Show Home Page By Default For This Folder check box.

Viewing and Editing Datasheets

When Internet Explorer displays a SharePoint list, an Edit In Datasheet option appears if, and only if, Office is installed on the current team member's computer. Clicking this button opens the list with a spreadsheet-style editor that supports add row, copy, paste, and fill-down commands. It also provides rich options for filtering and sorting. Figure 1-14 shows the facility in use.

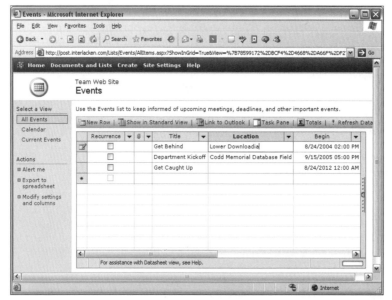

Figure 1-14. This editable view of a SharePoint list is available only if Office is installed on the team member's computer.

If Office isn't installed on the team member's computer, the team member needs to use an HTML form that updates one list item at a time.

Editing List Data with Access and Excel

Both Microsoft Access and Excel can retrieve and store the data in any SharePoint list. In Access, for example, you would:

1 Choose Open from the File menu.

2 When the Open dialog box appears, select Windows SharePoint Services in the Files Of Type drop-down list near the bottom of the dialog box.

3 When the Link To Windows SharePoint Services Wizard dialog box appears, specify the site URL, the List name, and the View name.

4 Click Next until you get to the last step of the wizard, and then click Finish.

Introducing Windows SharePoint Services

Figure 1-15 shows Access displaying the My T-Shirt Inventory list seen previously in Figure 1-4. You could process this table as if it resided in an ordinary Access database.

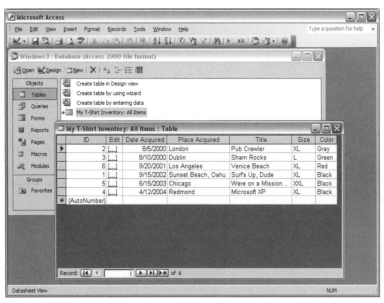

Figure 1-15. In most respects, Microsoft Access can process SharePoint lists as if they were ordinary Access tables.

To copy a list into Excel, display the list in Internet Explorer and click the Export To Spreadsheet link. This downloads a small file that has an .iqy filename extension, and that tells Excel how to access the list interactively. Excel displays a List toolbar that has options to modify the list columns and settings, synchronize data with the SharePoint site, create charts, and so forth.

Editing Pictures

Microsoft Office 2003 users can view and edit the contents of a picture library with a new application called Microsoft Office Picture Manager. This application can receive bulk downloads from a SharePoint picture library, transmit bulk uploads to a SharePoint picture library, and perform global editing such as resizing, rotation, and color correction. Figure 1-16 shows a typical view of this application.

Microsoft Windows SharePoint Services Inside Out

Figure 1-16. Microsoft Office Picture Manager can perform simple editing, bulk uploads, and bulk downloads on files in a SharePoint picture library.

Sharing Attachments

When you create an e-mail message and attach a file, Outlook can treat the file as a shared attachment. This means Outlook won't attach the file itself. Instead, it creates a SharePoint document workspace, places a copy of the file in that workspace, enrolls the sender and all recipients for access, and puts only a link to the document in the e-mail message. The savings in disk space can be huge. Figure 1-17 shows this in progress.

When recipients open the attachment, they receive any updates from the Document Workspace site. If they save the attachment, they update the copy on the SharePoint site. This frees document contributors from attaching and distributing multiple copies of the document. It also frees reviewers from modifying filenames or using other improvised methods to track revisions. If you turn on versioning, you'll never lose thoughts that appeared on intermediate versions. And if you turn on alerts, team members don't even need to inform each other when they save a new version; the SharePoint site will send the necessary e-mails.

Introducing Windows SharePoint Services

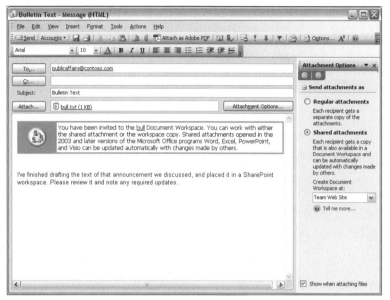

Figure 1-17.   When you designate an Outlook attachment as shared, Outlook doesn't transmit the document with the e-mail message. Instead, it puts the file in a SharePoint document workspace and transmits a link.

Enhancing Coordination with Meeting Workspaces

SharePoint members can create Meeting Workspace sites when they create a meeting invitation in Outlook. Meeting workspaces provide a place for managing meetings and their associated information such as attendees, agendas, documents, decisions, and action items. Outlook automatically propagates attendee status to the SharePoint site. You can also create Meeting Workspace sites from SharePoint Event lists.

Integrating InfoPath and SharePoint Form Libraries

After you've designed a form in InfoPath, you can upload it to a SharePoint form library. To do this:

1   In InfoPath, display the Design Tasks task pane and click the Publish Form link.

2   When the Publishing Wizard appears, click Next to bypass the opening screen.

3   On page 2 of the wizard, select To A SharePoint Form Library. Figure 1-18 illustrates this step.

Microsoft Windows SharePoint Services Inside Out

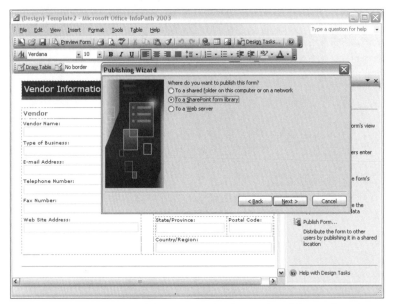

Figure 1-18. Microsoft InfoPath can upload completed forms directly to a SharePoint library.

4 Click Next, and then choose whether to create a new library or use an existing one.

5 Click Next, and then specify the location of your SharePoint site.

6 Satisfy the remaining prompts, and then click Finish.

When you're done, your SharePoint site will contain a library like the one shown in Figure 1-19. The Fill Out This Form button starts InfoPath and tells it to load the form for this library. When the InfoPath user clicks Save, InfoPath will modify or replace the SharePoint library data. Anyone with access to the SharePoint site can then view, sort, filter, modify, and consolidate the data, or integrate it with other applications.

Team members using a SharePoint form library can also start InfoPath for the purpose of autoaggregating multiple InfoPath library files into a single report. For example, the team member could combine the information from many individual status reports into a single rollup status report.

Introducing Windows SharePoint Services

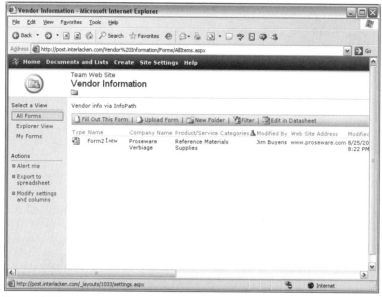

Figure 1-19. Clicking the Fill Out This Form button in this SharePoint library starts InfoPath and loads a blank copy of the form.

Integrating Microsoft Project

When you start a new project using the Microsoft Project desktop software, you can automatically create a SharePoint site for project documents, issues, and risks. This centralizes your project documentation, makes project documents available to team members, and gains the advantages of version tracking and document check-in and check-out.

Microsoft Project Server 2003 is a server-based application that runs under Windows SharePoint Services. Using a browser, team members can enter the time they spend on assigned tasks, report task status, and associate tasks with deliverable documents. With project members using this facility, only the project manager needs the Project desktop software.

> For more information about integrating SharePoint with the Microsoft Office System, refer to Chapter 4, "Using SharePoint with the Microsoft Office System."

Using Additional Development Tools

Windows SharePoint Services is far more than a collection of prepackaged applications and templates. In fact, it's a powerful platform capable of supporting almost any type of application. The topics in this section introduce two development tools you can use with Windows SharePoint Services.

Designing Sites with FrontPage

Windows SharePoint Services automatically provides most features of the FrontPage Server Extensions. This requires no separate installation. If you can open a SharePoint site with a browser, you can open it in FrontPage 2003 (assuming, of course, that you have the necessary permissions).

> **Caution**   Never open a Windows SharePoint Services site in FrontPage 2002 or any earlier version. Because these versions predate Windows SharePoint Services, they frequently corrupt HTML or XML that Windows SharePoint Services needs in order to operate.

The primary FrontPage features that SharePoint sites don't support are those related to databases: Save Results To Database, Database Results Region, and Database Interface Wizard. Fortunately, however, this isn't much of a problem. The SharePoint site provides database features far more capable than those earlier FrontPage components.

Each SharePoint site functions as a FrontPage-based Web site. If you have the necessary permissions, you can add, modify and delete pages and sites at will. For example, you can add pictures or text, refine page layouts, and do all the things that Web designers usually do. In addition, you can create and configure Web Part Pages, Web Part Zones, SharePoint lists, SharePoint libraries, and data sources.

Figure 1-20 shows FrontPage editing the home page of a SharePoint Team Site. The Quick Tag Selector displays the XML tags for Web parts as well as the ordinary HTML tags that give the page its structure. FrontPage provides page templates, menu commands, dialog boxes, task panes, smart tags, and shortcut menu options for creating and working with Web Part Pages, Web Part Zones, and Web Parts as easily as it works with ordinary Web pages and conventional FrontPage components. For example, the List View Options smart tag that appears in the figure configures the properties of the Announcements List View Web Part.

FrontPage can also create new SharePoint lists and libraries, and configure Data View Web Parts to display them. In Figure 1-21, for example, FrontPage is configuring a Data View Web Part to display data from the T-Shirt Inventory list. The Data View Web Part in the FullPage Web Part Zone is configured to display data in tabular form. The designer has created a new blank column, and is now dragging the Color field from the Data View Details task pane and dropping it into the empty column. This will display each list item's Color value in the given column.

Introducing Windows SharePoint Services

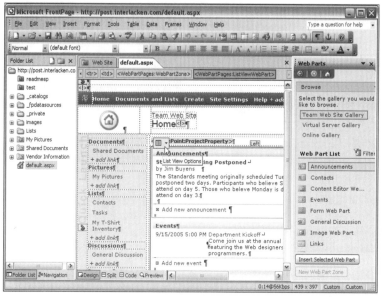

Figure 1-20. FrontPage 2003 provides great flexibility for modifying SharePoint sites.

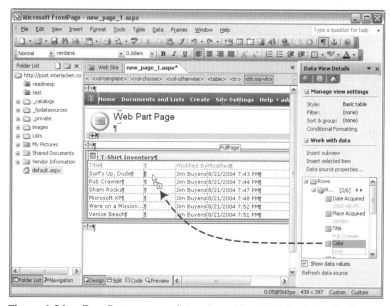

Figure 1-21. FrontPage can configure Data View Web Parts to display any columns you want from a data source.

With FrontPage, you can browse and search Web Part galleries, locate Web Parts of any kind, and use them in Web Part Pages. You can preview these Web Parts in FrontPage, and you can build new user interfaces by creating Web Part connections among Web Parts. This provides a way for mouse clicks, form field changes, and other events in one Web Part to affect the data, visibility, or appearance of other Web Parts. If, for example, you had a Web Part that displayed department numbers, you could connect it to another Web Part that displayed employees. With proper configuration, clicking on a department would then display a list of employees in that department.

FrontPage Themes and SharePoint Themes are not only compatible; they're identical. This means you can use the FrontPage Theme editor to create new or modified Themes for any SharePoint site you want.

FrontPage can also save working or prototypical sites as solution packages that you can distribute throughout an organization. It provides two such packages—Web Log and News and Reviews—right out of the box.

In short, FrontPage provides remarkable power and ease for working with almost any aspect of a SharePoint site.

> For more information about using FrontPage to create and design SharePoint pages and sites, refer to Part IV, "Creating and Designing Sites Using FrontPage 2003."

Creating Web Parts with Visual Studio .NET

Windows SharePoint Services provides remarkable power to create and modify new sites, even if you have nothing but a browser. FrontPage provides even more powerful site creation, page creation, and page editing features. If that's not enough, you can obtain additional Web Parts from Microsoft and from third-party providers.

But what if even that isn't enough? What if you need to create your own Web Parts? This could be for discrete, simple functions, but it could also be for complete business systems that used Web Parts rather than conventional Web pages as the basic unit of display. This is where Microsoft Visual Studio .NET comes in.

With Visual Studio .NET, you can develop Web Parts that perform any custom function you can imagine. To assist you in this, Microsoft provides downloadable Web Part templates that you can add to Visual Studio .NET, and documentation in the form of a Software Development Kit (SDK). This leaves it to you, of course, to fill in the code for your application.

> For step-by-step instructions for creating Web Parts in Visual Studio .NET, refer to Part VII, "Developing Web Parts in Visual Studio .NET".

Introducing Windows SharePoint Services

Customizing Site Settings

Windows SharePoint Services provides broad control over the appearance, content, and access permissions of every SharePoint site. To begin working with these settings, click the Site Settings link at the top of any page. This displays the Site Settings page shown in Figure 1-22.

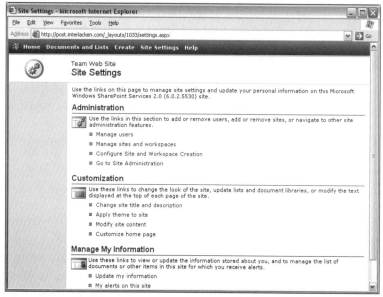

Figure 1-22. Web site administrators can use this page to configure and control access to their sites.

In the Administration section, the following links control access and permissions, add or remove sites, and link to additional administration features.

- **Manage Users**   Displays a list of current team members, and provides links for adding, removing, or configuring users.
- **Manage Sites And Workspaces**   Displays a list of all sites and workspaces that are subordinate to the current site, and that you have permission to access.
- **Configure Site And Workspace Creation**   Displays a list of site groups that can create new sites and workspaces subordinate to the current site.
- **Go To Site Administration**   Links to the Site Administration page shown later in this section.

Note   A site group is a collection of user accounts that receive permissions as a unit. A site group can pertain a single site or to a collection of sites. The predefined site groups are Reader, Contributor, Web Designer, and Administrator.

Microsoft Windows SharePoint Services Inside Out

The links in the Customization section modify the appearance of the site and its contents.

- **Change Site Title And Description**   Displays a page where you can modify the site title that appears on the top of each page and the site description that appears on the home page.

- **Apply Theme To Site**   Provides an assortment of color schemes you can apply to the site.

- **Modify Site Content**   Displays a list of lists, libraries, discussion boards, and surveys in the current site, with a Customize link for each one. Clicking any of these links jumps to a page where you can change the design of the corresponding item.

- **Customize Home Page**   Displays the home page in editable mode, as shown previously in Figure 1-8.

The links in the Manage My Information section provide ways to view or update your personal information and your alert subscriptions.

> **Note**   An alert is an e-mail message that you receive when a change occurs.

- **Update My Information**   Shows your current display name, e-mail address, and notes, and provides links for modifying these settings. It also shows whether or not you're a site collection administrator.

- **My Alerts On This Site**   Displays all libraries, files, lists, and other items for which you receive alerts. To reconfigure or delete any listed alert, click its name.

- **View Information About Site Users**   Displays a list of all users who have participated in or have been added to the current Web site. Clicking any user's display name displays that user's information.

> **Note**   Note: A site collection is a group of SharePoint sites that share a common Web Part gallery, a common list template gallery, a common template gallery, and a set of cross-site groups. The collection includes all sites within the folder tree of a designated Top Level site. Creating a Top Level site requires special administrative permission.

The Top-Level Site Administration page shown in Figure 1-23 provides a means to change permissions, select regional settings, view usage statistics, and manage sites. Some of options on this page won't appear if the current site isn't a top-level site, or if the current user isn't a site administrator.

Introducing Windows SharePoint Services

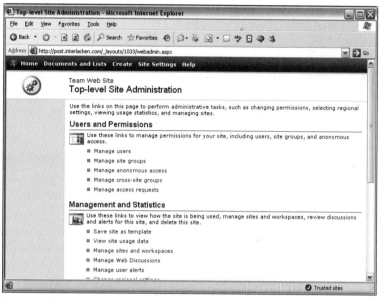

Figure 1-23. Site administrators can use this page to control additional settings for their site. Ordinary sites have fewer options than the top-level site shown here.

The Users and Permissions section manages site permissions such as users, site groups, and anonymous access.

- **Manage Users**   Lists the users in the current Web site and provides options to add new users, remove users from all site groups, or assign users to site groups.

- **Manage Site Groups**   Lists the site groups for the current site and provides options to create new site groups, delete site groups, or change a site group's description and rights.

- **Manage Anonymous Access**   Displays a page where you can grant or deny access to visitors with no logon credentials. You can also grant or deny access to all authenticated users on your network. (An administrator must enable this feature at the server level before you can use it on individual sites.)

> **Note**   Windows SharePoint Services always uses Windows Active Directory accounts for authentication.

- **Manage Cross-Site Groups**   Displays a list of existing cross-site groups and provides options to add, modify, or delete cross-site groups.

> **Note**   A cross-site group is a named collection of user accounts that you can use throughout a site collection, even in sites that don't share permissions with the parent site.

Microsoft Windows SharePoint Services Inside Out

- **Manage Access Requests** Displays a page where you can configure a site to display a request form whenever a user attempts to create a page, add an item to a list, or perform some other operation for which they lack permission. By filling in the form and clicking Send Request, the user sends a Request For Access message via e-mail to a designated administrator.

  The Management and Statistics section has options to view site usage statistics, to manage sites and workspaces, to review discussions and alerts for the current site, and to delete the current site.

- **Save Site As Template** Displays a form for saving a copy of the current site, with or without its data, as a template. Team members can then use the template to create new sites.

- **View Site Usage Data** Displays activity reports for the current Web site, provided a server administrator has activated a feature called Usage Analysis.

- **Manage Sites And Workspaces** Displays a list of sites that you can access, and which lie below the current site in the URL directory structure. This page also provides options to browse, add, or delete sites.

- **Manage Web Discussions** Displays a list of ongoing document discussions. Administrators can delete any or all of these discussions.

- **Manage User Alerts** Displays a list of alerts in effect for any team member and provides options to delete them.

- **Change Regional Settings** Displays a page that specifies the locale, linguistic sort order, time zone, and time format for the site. The locale setting controls the visual format of dates, text, and numbers based on conventions in some region of the world.

- **Delete This Site** Displays a page that deletes the current site.

The Site Collection Galleries section appears only for top-level sites. It provides links to manage the set of Web Parts, list templates, and site templates available to the current site and all sites and workspaces beneath it.

- **Manage Web Part Gallery** Displays a page that controls which Web Parts are available for use in the current site collection. This is typically fewer than the total collection of Web Parts on the server.

- **Manage List Template Gallery** Displays a page that controls the set of templates available for creating lists in the current site collection.

- **Manage Site Template Gallery** Displays a page that controls which custom Web site templates are available for creating sites within the current site collection.

Site Collection Administration is another section that appears only for top-level sites. The options in this section affect not only the current site, but also any sites and workspaces beneath it.

- **View Site Hierarchy**   Displays a list of all sites in the current site collection.
- **View Site Collection Usage Summary**   Displays activity reports for the current Web site collection.
- **View Storage Space Allocation**   Displays disk space reports for the current Web site collection.
- **View Site Collection User Information**   Lists the users in the current Web site collection and provides options remove selected users.
- **Configure Connection To Portal Site**   Displays a form for connecting the current site to a Windows SharePoint Services–compatible portal site. Users can then categorize lists, connect to user profiles, link to portal search, and use other portal site features.

Administering Central Windows SharePoint Services Settings

When you install Windows SharePoint Services on a computer, the setup program creates a so-called SharePoint Central Administration virtual server that manages SharePoint settings for all other virtual servers on the same machine. This section introduces the functions available on this administrative server.

Tip   **Choose Your Installations Options Carefully**

If you install Windows SharePoint Services with all defaults in effect, the setup program installs the WMSDE database engine and extends the default IIS Web server.

If you choose a custom installation, the setup program doesn't extend any virtual servers. Instead, it opens a browser session to the SharePoint Central Administration virtual server, so you can specify which database server to use and which virtual Web server to extend.

The terms, "Add Windows SharePoint Services to a virtual server," and "Extend a virtual server with Windows SharePoint Services," are synonymous.

SharePoint Central Administration functions can affect any Windows SharePoint Services server on the same machine, and generally they have far-reaching effects. For that reason, most organizations will permit only a few centralized administrators to access the central administration server.

The Central Administration page shown in Figure 1-24 is the home page for a SharePoint Central Administration server. It configures virtual server, security, server, and component settings for Windows SharePoint Services.

Microsoft Windows SharePoint Services Inside Out

Figure 1-24. Server administrators use this page to manage the most global settings for a SharePoint installation.

The Virtual Server Configuration section provides options to install Windows SharePoint Services on a virtual server, configure settings across all sites on a virtual server, or create a new top-level Web site.

- **Extend Or Upgrade Virtual Server**   Displays a list of all virtual servers on the administrative site computer that aren't already running Windows SharePoint Services. To add Windows SharePoint Services to one of these virtual servers, click the virtual server's name.

- **Create A Top-Level Web Site**   Displays a list of virtual servers running Windows SharePoint Services. To create a new top-level site, click the server that will host the site, and then fill out the resulting form.

- **Delete Site Collection**   Displays a page that completely deletes a top-level site and any subsites it may have.

- **Configure Virtual Server Settings**   Displays a Server Administration page listing all virtual servers on the local machine.

    - If a server isn't running Windows SharePoint Services or the FrontPage Server Extensions, clicking its name displays a page for extending it.

    - If a server is running the FrontPage Server Extensions, you have two choices, neither of which are simple options that appear on the Server Administration page:

        If you don't need to preserve the server's existing content, remove the FrontPage 2002 Server Extensions and then extend the server with Windows SharePoint Services.

If you do need to preserve the server's existing content, create a new virtual server, extend it with Windows SharePoint Services, and then use a SharePoint command-line tool named smigrate.exe to migrate the content.

■ If a site *is* running Windows SharePoint Services, clicking its name displays a page where you can administer automated Web site collection management, view and update security settings, list, create, delete, or configure virtual servers, and manage additional components installed on the virtual server.

The Security Configuration section updates the security options that impact all virtual servers, and it adds, updates, or changes user information for a single top-level Web site.

● **Set SharePoint Administration Group**   Displays a page where you can specify a Windows security group that will have administrative access to all SharePoint servers on the machine. This is in addition to the local Administrators group, which always has access.

● **Manage Site Collection Owners**   Displays a page where you can specify a primary and secondary owner for a site collection. This also makes these users site collection administrators.

● **Manage Web Site Users**   Grants or revokes access to any SharePoint site on the local computer.

● **Manage Blocked File Types**   Manages a list of file types that users may not save in or retrieve from any SharePoint site on the server. This prevents abuse of the server beyond its intended function. For example, you can block executables, music files, and videos.

● **Configure Antivirus Settings**   Specifies when you want to scan content files for viruses, whether to attempt cleaning infected documents, and how much server resource the virus scanning process can use. This requires that third-party virus scanning software compatible with Windows SharePoint Services be installed on the computer.

The Server Configuration section manages server connections, including e-mail, databases, and Web servers.

● **Configure Default E-Mail Server Settings**   Configures the SMTP mail server and e-mail addresses the server will use for sending alerts, invitations, and administrator notifications.

● **Manage Web Server List**   Displays a clickable list of Web servers in the same server farm as the current server. Clicking any server name displays the Central Administration page for that server.

● **Set Default Content Database Server**   Displays a page where you can specify the name of the default content database server. This is the database that stores all the content files for the current virtual server.

● **Set Configuration Database Server**   Displays a page where you can create or connect to a SharePoint configuration database. This database stores configuration and site mapping information for your physical server, the virtual servers on your physical server, and servers in a server farm.

- **Configure HTML Viewer**   Displays a page for activating or disabling the use of an HTML Viewer service, and for specifying the service location.

> **Note**   An HTML Viewer service translates Word, Excel, and PowerPoint documents to HTML so that team members who don't have these applications can view such documents in their browser. The software for this service comes as a separate download from Microsoft's Web site. For performance reasons, it generally runs on a dedicated server.

- **Configure Virtual Server For Central Administration**   Displays a page where you can change the IIS application pool and security account for the SharePoint Central Administration virtual server.

> **Note**   An application pool is basically a memory space. If two processes are running in the same application pool, they have more opportunity to interfere with each other than if they were running in separate application pools. However, creating too many application pools can degrade overall system performance.

The Component Configuration section manages components that work across all virtual servers, including search, usage analysis, and quotas.

- **Configure Full-Text Search**   Displays a page where you can enable or disable the full-text search and index component.

> **Tip**   You can only enable full-text search and index if your content database is running on Microsoft SQL Server. The default Windows Microsoft Data Engine (WMSDE) database server doesn't support this feature.

- **Configure Usage Analysis Processing**   Displays a page that specifies whether and when a timed process will analyze IIS Web server logs and capture SharePoint statistics.
- **Manage Quotas And Locks**   Displays a page where you can manually lock and unlock sites and place limits on the amount of disk space a site can consume.
    - When SharePoint locks a site for exceeding its storage quota limit, users who attempt to upload new content will receive a "disk full" error message. Site administrators can clear locks of this type.
    - When a server administrator manually locks a site, users who attempt to view the site will see an access denied message. Only a server administrator can clear such a lock.
- **Configure Data Retrieval Service Settings**   Displays a page where you can permit or deny the use of SharePoint-based data sources by client computers. If you permit such access, you can make it read-only or permit updates. You can also configure a maximum response size in bytes and maximum time in seconds.

> **Note**   For more information on administering SharePoint services, see Part VI, "Administering SharePoint Services."

Introducing the Windows SharePoint Services Architecture

The following topics briefly introduce the internal structure of Windows SharePoint Services. The rest of the book will touch and expand on these topics many times over.

Introducing Server Components

At the highest level, the design of Windows SharePoint Services involves two components:

- **A Front-End Communication Service**   This must be Internet Information Service 6.0 (IIS6).
- **A Back-End Data Store**   This must be either Windows Microsoft Data Engine (WMSDE) or Microsoft SQL Server 2000 SP3 or later.

> **Note**   WMSDE is a limited version of SQL Server that comes free with Windows SharePoint Services. It has very few management tools; it doesn't accept network connections except from the local machine, and it doesn't support full-text searching. Nevertheless, it's an economical solution for small sites and system development.

Every SharePoint server makes use of at least two databases. These databases serve quite different purposes.

- A configuration database stores site settings and configuration information.
- A content database serves as the file system for Web pages, pictures files, lists, tasks, contacts, events, document libraries, picture libraries, and all the other types of content that make up a SharePoint site.

> **Note**   A SharePoint site makes very little use of the normal Windows file system. Except for centralized software libraries and template files, everything goes into a database.

Because of the way it uses IIS and SQL Server, Windows SharePoint Services is extremely scalable. If demand warrants, you can provide server farms of IIS servers to handle the communication, and multiple, optionally clustered SQL Servers to handle the data storage. This provides nearly unlimited capacity and fault tolerance.

Windows SharePoint services load-balances SQL Servers by distributing Web sites among them. For example, you can specify that the first 10,000 sites on a virtual server reside on one database server, the next 10,000 sites on a different database server, and so forth. Even running a farm of Web servers, no confusion results because the configuration database directs each Web server to the correct SQL Server for a given site.

Microsoft Windows SharePoint Services Inside Out

If your needs are more modest, a single computer can run Windows SharePoint Services on up to ten virtual servers, even with the database running on the same machine. The best configuration for your company depends on the activity level your users generate. Figure 1-25 shows just a few of the many possible configurations.

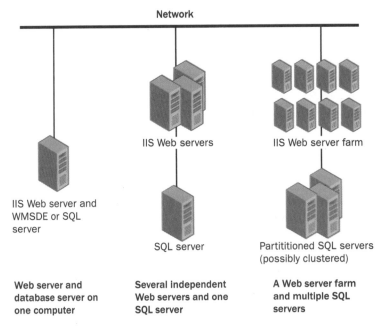

Figure 1-25. The SharePoint architecture provides great flexibility for meeting workload demands.

In a typical installation, you would have one configuration database per IIS physical server or server farm, and one content database for each IIS virtual server. However, in this context:

● You can add as many content databases as you like, and spread sites within a single URL space among them.

● You can run as many Web servers as you like in parallel, all accessing the same content databases and therefore delivering the same content.

By default, a virtual server issues an administrative warning when there are 9,000 sites in a single content database, and stops creating new sites when there are 15,000 in the same content database. If this seems like a lot of sites, remember these facts:

● Each Team site, document workspace, meeting workspace, and so forth counts as one site. Typically, each information worker in your organization will have permission to freely create these kinds of sites.

- A feature called Use Confirmation and Automatic Deletion automatically sends e-mail messages to owners of site collections when no activity occurs for certain period. This message asks them to confirm that the site collection is still in use. For example, you could configure these messages to start once a site collection has no activity for ninety days, and repeat them once a week. You could also configure this feature to delete the site collection if a certain number of consecutive messages go unanswered.

Introducing the SharePoint Object Model

Windows SharePoint Services is obviously more than a collection of Web servers and SQL Servers (or one of each, or both on one physical server). At the next level, it's also a library a fully programmable software objects, all fully compliant with the Microsoft .NET framework and .NET development practices. These libraries contain the software that actually creates and manages the lists and libraries resides, the software that performs site administration resides, the software that merges Web Parts into Web Part Pages resides, and so forth. Together, these objects and their properties, methods, and events form the SharePoint application programming interface (API).

Team Sites, Document Workspaces, and all the other sample applications that come with Windows SharePoint Services obviously use these APIs, but so can applications you develop as Web Parts in Visual Studio .NET. This means that if you can implement a solution in software, you can implement it in Windows SharePoint Services.

> For more information about developing Web Parts, refer to Part VII, "Developing Web Parts in Visual Studio .NET."

Introducing SharePoint Web Services

Windows SharePoint Services exposes many of its internal functions to other programs by means of XML Web services. This is how, for example, all the programs in the Microsoft Office System achieve their integration with SharePoint sites.

In Figure 1-15, for example, Microsoft Access was manipulating the content of a SharePoint list by means of a Web service.

In Figure 1-21, FrontPage is reading and modifying SharePoint list views and Web Parts by means of a Web service. Windows SharePoint Services provides Web services that network clients can use to perform such tasks remotely.

You can also use these Web services in applications you develop yourself.

Microsoft Windows SharePoint Services Inside Out

A Brief Introduction to XML Web Services

Physically, XML Web services work very much like a Web visitor submitting requests to a Web site. However:

- Instead of a browser sending the requests and receiving the responses, custom program code performs these functions.
- Instead of sending query string or form field values to the Web server, the program using a Web service formats its request as XML.
- Instead of receiving HTML, the program using a Web service receives XML.

Using HTTP, the standard protocol of the World Wide Web, to transmit Web requests and Web responses in XML format makes it easy for networked applications to interact in both simple and complex ways. HTTP provides cross-platform connectivity, and XML handles data structures of any complexity.

In Summary...

This chapter introduced Windows SharePoint Services, a new component of Windows Server 2003. Windows SharePoint Services is a powerful, Web-based platform that can bring together information workers and information systems throughout an organization.

The next chapter will explain the features that SharePoint Portal Server adds to Windows SharePoint Services.

Chapter 2

Introducing SharePoint Portal Server

The fact that Microsoft has two products with SharePoint in their names is a frequent source of confusion. This is partly because the two products seem to have overlapping features and partly because, until recently, both products ran on different platforms, addressed different audiences, and didn't fully integrate.

To resolve such confusion, this chapter begins by clarifying the distinctions among the various SharePoint products and versions, and in particular between Windows SharePoint Services and SharePoint Portal Server 2003, which are the current versions.

Next, it briefly explains the major features of SharePoint Portal Server 2003. This builds on the understanding of Windows SharePoint Services you gained in Chapter 1. The wrap-up offers some final thoughts on the relationship between these two products.

Reviewing SharePoint Products and Technologies

Table 2-1 shows the relationships among the four SharePoint products Microsoft has released to date. Subsequent sections will briefly describe each of these products.

Table 2-1. SharePoint Products and Technologies

Version	Team Sites	Portal Sites
Initial	SharePoint Team Services	SharePoint Portal Server 2001
Current	Windows SharePoint Services	SharePoint Portal Server 2003

Looking Back at SharePoint Team Services

SharePoint Team Services, Microsoft's first attempt at supporting SharePoint Team Sites, was basically an addition to the FrontPage 2002 Server Extensions. Each team site was a FrontPage-based Web site, and library documents resided in the same file space as the Web site. A SQL Server or MSDE database stored lists, alerts (then called subscriptions), and document discussions.

Microsoft Windows SharePoint Services Inside Out

This product was limited in flexibility and scale, but it proved the concept and value of Team Sites.

> **Note** The FrontPage Server Extensions are a group of software features that run on a Web server and support various features of FrontPage. Some of these features work with the FrontPage desktop software when a designer is developing a Web site, and some provide services when a Web visitor browses the site.

Looking Back at SharePoint Portal Server 2001

The first release of SharePoint Portal Server was a much larger, more scalable, more flexible, and somewhat distant relative of SharePoint Team Services. It provided software and services that ran on an IIS Web server and that used the Microsoft Web Storage System for storing data. This is the same storage system that a Microsoft Exchange server uses.

This product introduced:

- Web Part Pages, which it called digital dashboards. However, neither the pages nor the Web Parts made any use of .NET technology, which at the time didn't exist.
- Workspaces, which were somewhat analogous to Team Sites, but included content from a variety of sources. However, they didn't interoperate fully with SharePoint Team Services sites.
- Features for grouping and categorizing individual sites, and for categorizing and searching documents on multiple servers of various kinds.
- A Personalization feature that maintained profiles for portal users.

These features clearly positioned SharePoint Portal Server 2001 as an organization-level product. SharePoint Team Services, by contrast, was clearly a workgroup-level product, no matter how many workgroups you had.

SharePoint Portal Server 2001 was more scalable and flexible than SharePoint Team Services, but it wasn't scalable beyond a single server. It was best for small and medium-sized organizations that had small to moderate numbers of documents.

Introducing Windows SharePoint Services

This is a completely new product that replaces (though you might say overwhelms) SharePoint Team Services. Windows SharePoint Services is all-new technology, and it takes maximum advantage of the .NET framework. There's no dependence whatsoever on the FrontPage Server Extensions. In Windows SharePoint Services, Web Parts are ASP.NET custom controls, and Web Part Pages are ASP.NET pages.

As a rule of thumb, a single virtual Web server extended with Windows SharePoint Services can support at least 10,000 sites. These could be Team Web Sites, document workspaces, meeting workspaces, sites built from other standard templates, or custom sites of almost any kind. What's more, a single physical server can run Windows SharePoint Services on ten virtual servers. In total, that's 100,000 Web sites per physical server. If that's not enough, you can add more physical servers and configure them all to work together as one. Web sites by the millions are a distinct possibility.

As always, capacity estimates depend not only on the design of software such as Windows SharePoint Services, but also on hardware capacity, and the amount and type of activity that the user population generates.

> **For more information on capacity planning for Windows SharePoint Services, download the Windows SharePoint Services Administrator's Guide from *http://www.microsoft.com/technet/downloads/ sharepnt.mspx*.**

Because all the configuration data, all the lists and document libraries, and all the Web pages and supporting files reside in SQL Server databases, as many Web servers as you need can work in parallel to deliver the SQL Server content. If you run out of SQL Server capacity, you can expand onto as many SQL servers as you need.

> **Note**   Certain files that appear in every SharePoint site, such as administration pages, actually reside in the server's file system. In such cases, the content database contains only a pointer to the disk file. This avoids needless files duplication. Microsoft calls this technique ghosting.

Unlike its predecessor, Windows SharePoint Services is clearly an enterprise-class product. Nevertheless, even the smallest organization can receive its benefits. It comes free with every copy of Windows Server 2003, and in many cases you can use a free embedded version of SQL Server called Microsoft SQL Server 2000 Desktop Engine (Windows) (WMSDE).

Introducing SharePoint Portal Server 2003

The latest version of SharePoint Portal Server is no longer a monolithic application that catalogs documents, including those in its own small-to-medium sized document library. Windows SharePoint Services now provides the platform and the document libraries. The portal server is simply one of many applications that can run on Windows SharePoint Services.

SharePoint Portal Server 2003 provides features for grouping and organizing individual sites and listings, and for searching across multiple sites. It can also scan and index Windows file sharing locations, conventional Web sites, and third-party document libraries. Personalization services can match portal users to potentially interesting Web sites, list items, and library documents.

Chapter 2

Personalization also supports SharePoint Single Sign-On. This is a new feature that remembers and enters user passwords for external applications. One way of using Single Sign-On, for example, supports integration with Microsoft BizTalk Server. Here's how this works:

- BizTalk, in this context, is a server that retrieves data from enterprise business systems and presents it as XML. BizTalk can also receive XML data and push it into an application.
- A so-called *BizTalk Adapter* for each business system provides the exact translation.
- SharePoint then formats the XML data for presentation to a SharePoint team member.

Of course, this kind of data access needs to be secured, and this is where SharePoint Portal Server 2003's Single-Sign-On feature comes into play.

Once a virtual Web server is running Windows SharePoint Services, it can support at most *one* SharePoint Portal Server 2003 portal site. Furthermore, the portal site must be in the Web server's root folder. All the other Web sites on the same virtual server will function as perfectly ordinary sites running under Windows SharePoint Services.

In volume, SharePoint Portal Server 2003 costs about $4,000 per server plus $70 per portal user. An External Connector License that covers an unlimited number of non-employees costs about $30,000.

The cost of software tends to vary over time, of course, and street prices are generally lower than list prices. Nevertheless, this pricing positions SharePoint Portal Server 2003 as an enterprise product for medium to large organizations. But even in the largest organizations, SharePoint Portal Server will serve mainly to organize and identify Windows SharePoint Services Web sites, and to integrate enterprise applications.

Reviewing SharePoint Portal Server

This section will review the features of SharePoint Portal Server in somewhat greater detail. Screen shots and simple procedures keep the explanations practical and concrete. The explanations assume, however, that SharePoint Portal Server is already installed and running. If you need a full installation guide and comprehensive reference, you'll need to look elsewhere.

> The URL of the Microsoft SharePoint Portal Server home page is http://office.microsoft.com/en-us/FX010909721033.aspx

Figure 2-1 shows the home page of a newly installed SharePoint Port Server 2003 site.

Introducing SharePoint Portal Server

Figure 2-1. This is the home page of a newly installed SharePoint Portal Server 2003 site.

By default, this page contains four Web Parts:

- **News** Is the area that displays Explore The Portal With The Quick Start Guide and Welcome to Microsoft Office SharePoint Portal Server 2003. In a full production portal site, the department responsible for company news would post items to this area.

- **Events** Displays a list of major events.

- **Links For You** Displays a list of useful hyperlinks, matched to your personal interests.

- **Portal Owner QuickStart Guide** Is a sort of welcome screen that appears for new portal sites. It helps new portal administrators find the commands they'll most likely need to use in getting the site ready for production. Clicking any option displays both the Web page and the help page to perform the given function.

  The last link in this Web Part removes it from the home page. You would click this sometime before cutting the portal to production.

The News, Events, and Links For You Web Parts raise an interesting question: What content should these Web Parts display for the thousands of employees in a large organization who, presumably, would make this portal their home page? Not all news articles, event notices, or links are useful for all kinds of employees. To prevent possible information overload, SharePoint Portal Server provides a feature called Audiences. The next section describes this feature.

Microsoft Windows SharePoint Services Inside Out

Targeting for SharePoint Portal Audiences

In the SharePoint Portal Server mindset, an audience is a group of portal users with similar interests. Here are examples of some typical audiences:

- All employees who work in Texas
- All engineers
- All administrative assistants
- Everyone who reports to Alessandro Leoni.
- Everyone in the Windows security group *na-marketing*

Audience rules determine which portal site users belong to each audience. Figure 2-2, for example, shows the configuration of a rule named Engineers. According to this rule, all portal users with the characters *Engineer* in their department name or job title are members of the Engineers audience.

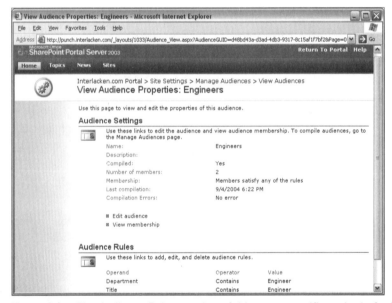

Figure 2-2. The Audience Rules section of this page specifies criteria for including portal users in an audience named Engineers.

Figure 2-3 shows the bottom of the Add Listing page, which adds content to an area such as News. In the Audience section, you can specify which audiences will receive the given listing. In the figure, only the audience named Engineers will receive the current item.

Figure 2-4 shows the completed item. The fact that its location is Home>Targeted Links On My Site means that it will appear in the Links For You Web Part on the portal home page. However, based on the Audience configuration in Figure 2-3, it will appear only for engineers.

Introducing SharePoint Portal Server

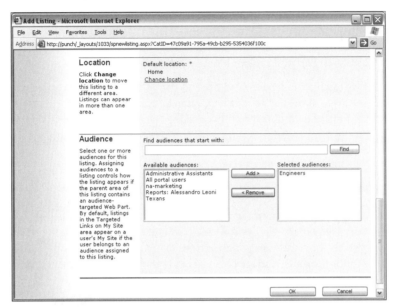

Figure 2-3. This is the bottom of a page that posts listings to content areas such as News. The Audience section specifies groups of portal users for which the listing will appear.

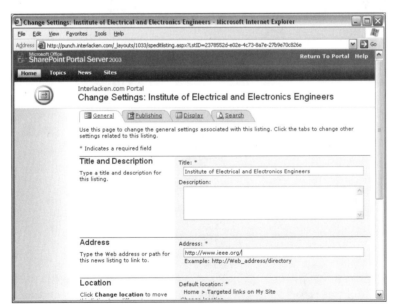

Figure 2-4. Because the Default Location of this targeted link is Home>Targeted Links On My Site, it will appear in the Links For You Web Part on the portal home page. However, based on its Audience configuration in Figure 2-3, it will only appear for engineers.

Microsoft Windows SharePoint Services Inside Out

Audience targeting, by the way, doesn't work for all Web Parts. For example, it *does* work for Web Parts with names that end, "For You," but it doesn't apply to the News or Events Web Parts that appear by default on the portal home page. To get audience targeting, you could delete the News Web Part and replace it with a News For You Web Part.

There's another catch to audiences: you need to compile them after each change. This determines the list of audiences to which each portal user belongs. Unfortunately, if you have a lot of portal users or a lot of rules, this can take a long time. The solution in that case may be to perform the compilation at a scheduled time. This also incorporates any changes that may have occurred to external objects, such as Windows security groups.

Managing User Profiles

The Manage Users page shown in Figure 2-5 manages the user accounts that can access the SharePoint Portal Server site. Except for the two menu bars and the title bar at the top of the page, this is exactly the same page you would see in a Windows SharePoint Services site. The accounts that appear on the Manage Users page are those that have access to the site.

Figure 2-5. If possible, please set Figure 2-5 and Figure 2-6 on the same or facing pages. This Web page lists user accounts authorized to browse the portal.

The View User Profiles page shown in Figure 2-6 manages a different collection of user data: the SharePoint Profile Database. The profiles in the SharePoint Profile Database control the site's features and behavior on a user-by-user basis.

A user account and a user profile are two completely different objects, and one can exist without the other. If a prospective portal user has a Windows logon account but isn't listed as a portal user (in Figure 2-5, for example) access to the site will fail. If a visitor's account is registered as a portal user but has no profile, the visitor will proceed with default profile settings.

Introducing SharePoint Portal Server

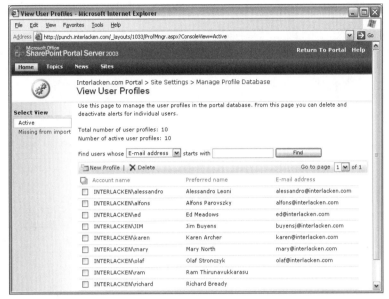

Figure 2-6. This page lists SharePoint Portal Server user profiles.

On the Edit User Profile page shown in Figure 2-7, an Administrator can modify the current values in a user profile. Alternatively, an administrator can import user profile information from an Active Directory service. This, however, overwrites many of the values for properties in the user profile. (The fields that Active Directory won't overlay aren't visible in this figure.)

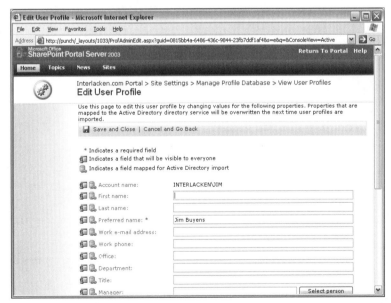

Figure 2-7. This is the top of a page that administrators can use to update user profiles. Importing information from Active Directory overlays any field flagged with a linked disk icon.

Microsoft Windows SharePoint Services Inside Out

Accessing Personal Sites

Every SharePoint Portal Server user can have a personal site. This is a place to keep documents, pictures, links, lists, or whatever else the portal user wants to store. In many ways, it's similar to a user's home directory in a file sharing environment, or the My Documents folder on a Windows computer. To access this site, the portal user simply clicks the My Site link at the top of the portal home page. Figure 2-8 shows the home page of a typical personal site.

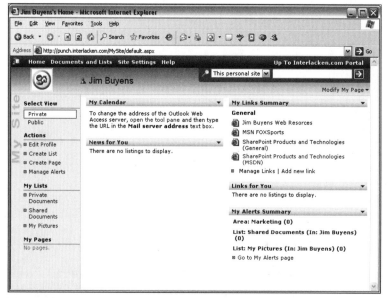

Figure 2-8. This is a typical home page for a new personal site, as the owner himself would see it.

By default, all the Web Parts on the home page of a personal site are, well, personal. They only display content relevant to the owner of the personal site.

- The My Calendar Web Part displays your calendar, as retrieved from an Outlook Web Access server.

- The Links For You and News For You Web Parts target content to audiences.

- The My Links Summary is specific to each personal site. To modify this list, click Manage Links or Add New Link at the bottom of the Web Part.

- The My Alerts Summary displays only alerts that pertain to the owner of the personal site.

Of course you can remove, replace, or reconfigure these Web Parts with others that offer non-personalized views, or that pertain to specific aspects of your job.

Introducing SharePoint Portal Server

Figure 2-9 shows a second view of the personal site home page, namely the *public* view. All portal users other than the personal site owner receive this view. It shows more of the owner's user profile and less of the owner's data. Specifically, it shows only documents, list entries, and other information the owner has marked for public consumption.

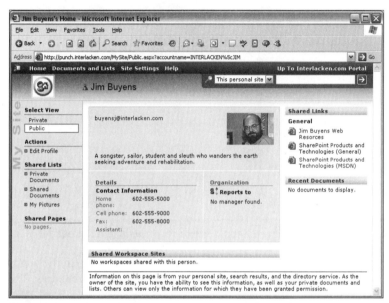

Figure 2-9.   This is the same home page as in Figure 2-8, as other team members would see it.

The owner of a personal site can create and configure Web Part Pages, including both views of the home page. The owner can also create and modify document libraries, pictures libraries, lists, surveys, and even create subsites.

Managing Areas

In SharePoint Portal Server 2003, most pages in the portal site display a Category Navigation Web Part as the second item on the page. This is the toolbar that displays Home, Topics, News, and Sites in Figures 2-2, 2-7, and most of the figures in between. Home, Topics, News, and Sites are each SharePoint *Areas*.

The Portal Site Map page, shown in Figure 2-10, displays an expandable view of all the areas in a portal site. Administrators, Web Designers, and Content Managers can display this page by:

- Clicking the Manage Portal Site link in the Home page's Actions pane.
- Clicking the Site Settings link in any page header, and then, under Portal Site Content, clicking Manage Portal Site Structure.

Microsoft Windows SharePoint Services Inside Out

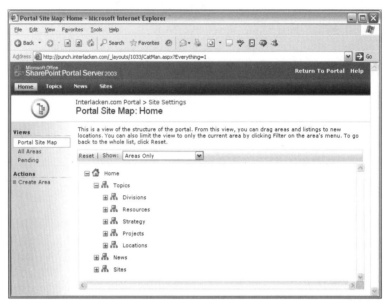

Figure 2-10. This page configures the hierarchy of areas and subareas for a portal site.

The diagram in the Portal Site Map page is, of course, the site map for the portal site. As usual, clicking the Plus icon in front of any area displays that area's children. The Plus also changes to a Minus, and clicking the Minus collapses the view.

If you were to add a new area under Home—such as Products or Standards—it would immediately start appearing in navigation bars throughout the site (provided, of course, it passed audience targeting rules). There are three ways of adding a new area or subarea:

- Move the mouse over any area or subarea in the Portal Site Map diagram. This will change the area name from plain text to a drop-down list. Open the drop-down list and choose Create Subarea.
- Click the Create Area link under Actions in the Portal Site Map page.
- Click the Create Subarea link under Actions on the home page or any Area page.

Any of these actions will display the Create Area page shown in Figure 2-11.

To specify the properties of the new area, fill out the Create Area page as follows.

- **Title**   Enter a short descriptive name that will appear in navigation bars and selection lists.
- **Description**   Optionally enter a one- or two-sentence explanation of the area.
- **Start Date**   Optionally specify the first date that the area should be visible.
- **Expiration Date**   Optionally specify the last date that the area should be visible.
- **Default Location**   Confirm that this field specifies the title of the parent area you want. If it doesn't, click the Change Location link and choose the correct parent from the expandable list that appears. Each area can have only one default location.

Introducing SharePoint Portal Server

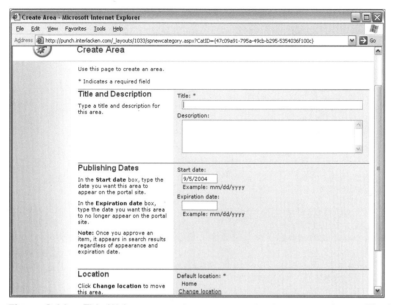

Figure 2-11. This Web page creates a new content area or subarea. The Location section specifies the new area's parent.

You can create as many areas as you want, and nest them to any depth.

Designing Area Structures

There's an art to designing an area structure, or for that matter, a hierarchy of any kind.

- If you create too many areas or arrange them illogically, the portal users will lose their way and never find the content they need.
- If you create too few, each area will contain too much content, and the portal users will end up looking for needles in haystacks.

For these reasons, most organizations assign the task of creating and managing areas to librarians or subject matter experts outside the IT department.

The drop-down list that appears when you move the mouse over an area name in the Portal Site Map page also provides these options:

- **Edit** Displays a page with five tabs of options pertaining to the area: General, Publishing, Page, Display, and Search. With these you can change the area's title, description, dates, approval requirements, display template, display options, inclusion or exclusion from full text search results, and so forth.
- **Delete** Deletes the area from the site map and all navigation bars.

Microsoft Windows SharePoint Services Inside Out

- **Manage Security**   Displays a Manage Security Settings For Area Divisions page where you can specify who can view, update, and administer the area.
- **Filter**   Condenses the site map so that the current area appears as the top area.
- **Add Listing**   Adds a content item to the area.
- **Add To My Links**   Adds a link from the current portal user's personal site to the given area.

Choosing Add Listing displays the Add Listing page shown in Figure 2-12. The bottom of this page appeared previously in Figure 2-3.

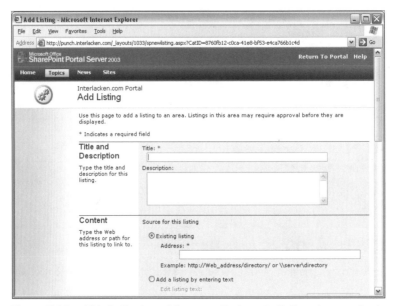

Figure 2-12.   This is the top of the page that posts listings to a content area. The bottom appeared in Figure 2-3.

Here's how to fill out each section of this form:

- **Title and Description**   Enter a title and a description that will identify the listing.
- **Content**   Enter the URL, the file path, or the Web text for the listing.
- **Group**   Assign this listing to a group. The default groups are Highlight, General, and Expert.
- **Image**   If you want a picture to appear with this listing, enter its URL here.
- **Location**   Verify that this field specifies the areas you want. If it doesn't, click the Change Location link, then select or clear any areas you want.
- **Audience**   Select one or more audiences for this listing. The listing will then appear only for portal users who belong to one of the audiences you select.

Introducing SharePoint Portal Server

> **Note**   Groups organize content within an area or subarea
>
> When you add a listing to an area or subarea, SharePoint Portal Server requires that you assign a group name to the listing.
>
> Then, when SharePoint Portal Server displays the contents of an area or subarea, it sorts the listings by group and displays a heading for each group.
>
> The default groups are General, Highlights, and Experts, but you can define as many group names you want.

Once you've added a listing to an area, it will appear on the Portal Site Map page, provided you set the Show drop-down list to All. To review and modify additional settings:

1 Pass the mouse pointer over the new listing, so a drop-down list appears.

2 Choose Edit in the drop-down list.

3 When the Change Settings page appears, click the General, Publishing, Display, or Search tab and set the options you want.

Activating and Training the Topic Assistant

SharePoint Portal Server 2003 has a new *Topic Assistant* feature that attempts to guess the best area for a new listing. However, this requires that you first "train" the Topic Assistant by designating some existing documents as samples. The assistant will then assign new listings to areas based on similarity to the samples.

The first step in using this feature is to activate the Topic Assistant for any areas you want it to consider. To do this, an administrator would follow this procedure:

1 Display the Portal Site Map page shown previously in Figure 2-10.

2 Pass the mouse pointer over the relevant area name. When the name changes to a drop-down list, select Edit.

3 Click the Search tab and then, under Topic Assistant, set Include In Topic Assistant: to Yes.

4 Click OK.

To train the Topic Assistant, an administrator would perform these steps:

1 Click the Site Settings link in the top navigation bar of any page that displays it.

2 Under Portal Site Content, click Use Topic Assistant.

3 Select the Enable Topic Assistant check box.

4 Under Precision, select a precision level from 1 (Highest) to 5 (Lowest).

   ■ A high precision reduces the number of listings that the assistant can categorize, but improves the accuracy of those it can categorize.

   ■ A low precision increases the number of listings that the assistant can categorize, but decreases the accuracy of those it can categorize.

5 Under Training Status, click the Train Now link.

6 Recheck the page until the Status message states Training Is Complete.

Tip In order for training to succeed, the topic must include at least ten documents and two areas.

Topic Assistant training continues for each document you add to an area. To view the assistant's suggestions, follow this procedure:

1 Click the Site Settings link in the top navigation bar of any page that displays it.

2 Under Portal Site Content, click Manage Portal Site Structure.

3 Click on the area you want to know about.

4 Under Actions, click Edit Page.

5 Near the bottom of the page, click Manage Grouping And Ordering.

6 At the left of the page, under View, click Suggestions.

7 The resulting Suggestions page will display any suggested groupings. To add any listing to the suggested area, click its link.

Enabling Single Sign-On

In many organizations, portal users expect the portal system to provide access to corporate information systems just as easily as it provides access to document libraries, news, events, and other kinds of lists. And *easily*, in this case, means without entering additional usernames and passwords.

The Single Sign-On feature of SharePoint Portal Server 2003 supports these requirements. Single Sign-On provides a secure, encrypted database for storing usernames, passwords, and any other logon information that portal users need to enter. These can be either group accounts (meaning one set of credentials for everyone who uses the portal) or individual accounts (meaning separate credentials for each portal user).

When you first install SharePoint Portal Server, the Single Sign-On feature is disabled. To enable it, an administrator must create up to four special service accounts, start the Microsoft Single-Sign-On Service on the portal's Job server, and create an Enterprise Application Definition for each application.

Figure 2-13 shows the Enterprise Application Definition for a fictitious application called Humongous Insurance Policy System.

Introducing SharePoint Portal Server

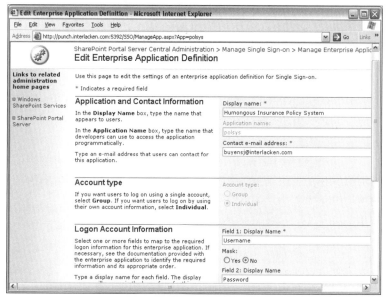

Figure 2-13. An administrator uses this page to define the sign-on fields for an application. The portal server then creates an encrypted database to hold each portal user's credentials.

The definition includes this information:

- **Display Name**   The name of the application as portal users will see it.
- **Application Name**   The name of the application that programmers will specify in their code.
- **Contact E-Mail Address**   The address of a person who can resolve issues regarding the application.
- **Account Type**   Group if all portal users will use the same application credentials. Individual if each portal user will have unique credentials.
- **Logon Account Information**   Five repetitions of the following fields. Each repetition represents one field required for logon. Only the first is mandatory.

  - **Display Name**   The name of the field as portal users will see it.
  - **Mask**   *Yes* to hide input characters for this field as the portal user types them. *No* if typed characters can appear normally.

The next step (and it's a big one) is to obtain a Web Part that uses the Single Sign-On database to access the application. Ideally, the entire application would be available as Web Parts, providing the same look and feel as the rest of the portal. But the initial Web Part must, at least, do whatever is necessary to launch the application and enter the stored logon information.

If your application is a commercial product, the vendor may provide SharePoint Portal Server Single Sign-On support as a built-in or added feature. Otherwise, using Visual Studio. NET, you can develop your own Single Sign-On Web Parts. For more information:

- Browse *http://msdn.microsoft.com* and search for the *Microsoft.SharePoint.Portal. SingleSignOn* namespace.
- Download the SharePoint Products and Technologies 2003 SDK from *http:// www.microsoft.com/technet/downloads/sharepnt.mspx*.

Searching Content Sources

If you install Windows SharePoint Services with the default WMSDE database, it provides no full-text search capability.

If you install and configure Windows SharePoint Services to use a SQL Server 2000 database that has full-text searching installed, then you can enable full-text search and indexing for the entire virtual server. Each site, however, will search only within itself. Windows SharePoint Services can't search the entire server, or even an entire site collection, for documents or Web pages containing given text.

SharePoint Portal Sever 2003, however, can search and index as many Web pages, Web sites, file shares, and Exchange public folders as you like. The Web sites can be running SharePoint Portal Server or Windows SharePoint Services, of course, but they can also be ordinary Web servers located anywhere on the Internet. Portal users can search all these content sources with great precision or with a single command.

> **Note** With third party products, SharePoint Portal Server can also search and index non-Microsoft document formats and non-Microsoft document libraries.

By default, SharePoint Portal Server 2003 indexes its site directory, its user profiles, and all Web pages on the local server. To include more sites, an administrator would:

1 Click Site Settings on the home page of the portal site.
2 Under Search Settings And Indexed Content, click Configure Search And Indexing.
3 Under Other Content Sources, click Manage Content Sources. This displays the Manage Content Sources page shown in Figure 2-14.

On this page, the administrator would click Add Content Source and then enter the location to search. By using additional Web pages, the administrator can also configure the frequency and timing of full and incremental content searches, parts of sites to include or exclude, and so forth.

Introducing SharePoint Portal Server

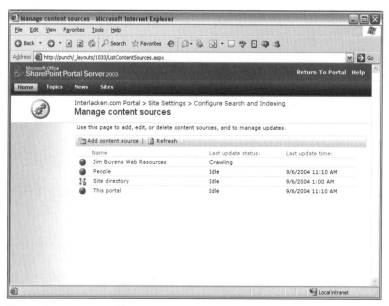

Figure 2-14. This page manages the list of locations that the portal server will index and then include in search results.

To perform a search, the portal user uses a search box like the one below. You can see one of these, for example, in the home page that appeared previously in Figure 2-1.

The drop-down box at the left selects a search scope, and the text box at the right specifies the text to find. Clicking the arrow or pressing Enter quickly returns a list of matching Web pages and document. If the list is too long, the portal user can click an Advanced Search link and submit a more specific request.

Comparing SharePoint Portal Server and Windows SharePoint Services

Beyond any doubt, SharePoint Portal Server enhances Windows SharePoint Services with a wealth of intriguing features. Obtaining these features, however, entails some very real costs. Here are some examples:

- **Software**   Windows SharePoint Services is free. SharePoint Portal Server requires licenses for each server and for each portal user.

- **Hardware**   SharePoint Portal Server features like the Topic Assistant, audience compilations, and external content searching are decidedly resource intensive. In addition, a single, centralized portal site will likely require larger, more fault-tolerant, and more expensive servers than a distributed array of smaller sites.

- **Technical Administration**   Configuring farms of Web servers, application servers, and clustered SQL servers is a complex, high-visibility job. Administering SharePoint Portal Server features isn't much easier. Therefore, an organization running SharePoint Portal Server is likely to need more administrators, and of a higher caliber, than one that's not running it.

- **Content Management**   Organizing topical areas, publishing news and events, and managing audiences are typically jobs for functional areas of the company, and not for IT. An IT department lacks the necessary "touch" with the information itself, with the people who create it, and with the people who use it.

  If content managers and subject matter experts throughout the company aren't willing and able to manage these features—both initially and ongoing—then much of the portal's expected payback will disappear.

For all these reasons, the smaller or more distributed your enterprise, the less attractive SharePoint Portal Server is likely to be.

Windows SharePoint Services, however, remains the base platform for Team Web Sites, document and meeting workspaces, Web sites you obtain as templates from a variety of sources, and custom applications that run on Microsoft's latest and greatest Web platform. For a great many organizations, Windows SharePoint Services is all they need.

And don't forget, even if you do need SharePoint Portal Server, it's only one site that occupies the root of your server farm. All the remaining thousands of sites are running under Windows SharePoint Services and nothing else.

In Summary...

This chapter explained the origins of Microsoft's two SharePoint offerings: Windows SharePoint Services 1.0 and SharePoint Portal Server 2003. It also briefly reviewed the features of SharePoint Portal Server. You can and should compare this information to the overview that Chapter 1 presented about Windows SharePoint Services.

Windows SharePoint Services provides a highly scalable platform and highly functional applications that provide Web sites for information workers. The same platform delivers Microsoft's most advanced technology for Web-based business systems. Whether or not you also need SharePoint Portal Server, Windows SharePoint Services brings impressive features and benefits to your organization.

Part II, which immediately follows this chapter, examines the end-user features and experience of Windows SharePoint Services. For new SharePoint users, this provides a tutorial for the most basic features. For administrators and programmers, it illustrates the working environment Windows SharePoint Services can deliver.

Part II

End-User Features and Experience

Chapter 3

Using SharePoint Built-In Features

This chapter explains how to use the built-in features of a Team Site running under Windows SharePoint Services. These features use Web pages that come with Windows SharePoint Services and require only a browser to use. They're also the features team members use most.

If you're a team member, this chapter will help you get the most out of an existing Windows SharePoint Services installation. If you're an administrator or developer, it will convey the features and mindset of a working site.

This chapter addresses Team Sites exclusively, because all the other site templates that come with Windows SharePoint Services are subsets of a Team Site. If you know how to use a Team Site, you know how to use all the others as well.

The next chapter explains how to use Microsoft Office applications with a Team Site. Chapter 5 explains how to create and configure SharePoint sites, and Chapter 6 presents instructions for creating and configuring lists, libraries, and Web Part Pages. This places the topics in order of increasing complexity and decreasing frequency of use.

Certain features of the Windows SharePoint Services browser interface make heavy use of ActiveX controls and other software that comes with Office 2003. If these components aren't available, the SharePoint pages fall back to simple HTML.

This chapter, like the rest of the book, illustrates an "optimum" environment; that is, one that includes:

- Internet Explorer 6 as the browser.
- A complete installation of Microsoft Office 2003—including FrontPage and InfoPath—on the team member's computer.
- The Windows XP operating system on the team member's computer.
- The presence of SharePoint Portal Server on the network.

65

Because of this optimum configuration, the screen shots in the book may appear richer than the pages that appear in your environment. In almost every case, however, the "fallback" HTML elements will provide a way to accomplish the same results. (The exceptions, by the way, all apply to administrative functions. Administrators should definitely run a Windows version of Internet Explorer 6.)

Introducing Team Site Features

Team Sites provide the following services to anyone with a Web browser, connectivity to the server, and the necessary permissions:

- **Lists**   These are the basic units of storage in a Team Site. Lists can contain announcements, upcoming events, scheduled tasks, team members or contacts, excuses, or anything else you want. The number of lists and the fields they contain are totally at your discretion.

- **Document Libraries**   These are basically lists that have a document attached to each record. The list provides much more information about each document than the directory listing in an ordinary file share. For additional structure, you can organize the contents of a document library into folders. If you wish, you can activate document versioning, check-in/check-out, and content approval.

- **Form Libraries**   This type of library is similar to a document library, but its default document template is a Microsoft InfoPath form. When team members click a Fill Out This Form button, the Team Site downloads the template and starts InfoPath. When the form is ready to submit, the team member saves it into the form library. The form library, in turn, can extract selected fields and display them in the library listing, or download multiple form submissions to InfoPath for aggregation.

- **Picture Libraries**   This type of library is similar to a document library, except that each document is a picture, and the various picture library Web pages display the pictures visually. Built-in features provide several ways of locating, viewing, and modifying pictures. For example, you can display pages that feature clickable thumbnails, full-sized pictures, and slide shows.

- **Discussion Boards**   This is the sort of feature most people call a *threaded discussion group*. Within a Team Site, you can create as many discussion boards as you want, and each board can accommodate an almost unlimited number of threads and messages. You can display messages in threads, or you can select a flat view and then sort the messages any way you want.

- **Surveys**   These are essentially lists with a column for each question you want to ask. Surveys do have some special views, however, that are useful for analyzing the results. Chapter 6 will provide further coverage of surveys.

- **Alerts**   With this feature, team members can ask to be notified whenever a specified document or folder changes. Windows SharePoint Services detects such changes and sends the notifications by e-mail.

● **Web Discussions**   After a Microsoft Office 2000, Office XP, or Office 2003 document is saved to a Web server as HTML or any native Office file format (and remember, this is an integrated, one-step process), team members browsing that document can make comments using a *Discuss toolbar*. Windows SharePoint Services stores these comments separately from the document itself. Then, when the document creator opens the document, all the comments appear seamlessly merged.

For information on Windows SharePoint Services security, refer to Chapter 17, "Administering Your SharePoint Site."

Using a Team Site Home Page

Figure 3-1 shows the home page from a typical Team Site located in the Web server's root folder. This is a Web Part Page. The Windows SharePoint Services logo and the layouts titled Announcements, Events, and Links are each Web Parts that instantly retrieve and display up-to-date information from lists.

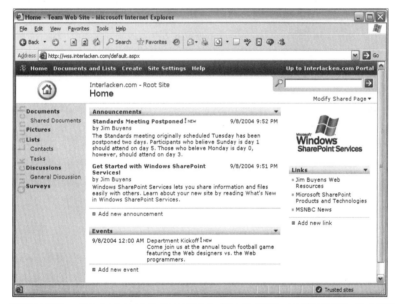

Figure 3-1.   The home page for a Team Site is highly configurable, but this version is fairly typical for a new site.

Functionally, here's what the various elements in a Team Site home page provide:

● The navigation bar at the top of the page provides access to all features in the site. By default, it contains these links.

■ **Home**   Displays the home page for the current Web site.

■ **Documents And Lists**   Displays a clickable list of all lists and libraries in the current SharePoint site.

■ **Create**   Displays a page with links to create SharePoint sites, lists, libraries, Web Part pages, and so forth.

■ **Site Settings**   Displays a menu of options for modifying and configuring the site.

■ **Help**   Opens a new window that provides instructions. Often, these are specific to the current page.

● **Up To**   If the current site is a top-level site configured with the address of a SharePoint Portal Server site, this area contains a link to that portal site.

■ If the current site is a top-level site not configured with the address of a portal site, this area is blank.

■ If the current site isn't a top-level site, this area contains a link to the current site's parent.

● The Quick Launch bar on the left provides hyperlinks to lists and libraries that you designate.

● The Announcements and Events areas are Web Parts. They display recent additions to their respective lists and provide links to more detailed views.

● The Links area is a Web Part that provides hyperlinks that team members might frequently use. This data resides in a list called, logically enough, Links.

● The Modify Shared Page link above the Windows SharePoint Services logo displays an editable version of the page. Team members can then can add, remove, or rearrange the Web Parts that make up their view of the home page.

Using Lists

Team Sites store virtually all information in lists. A SharePoint list is very much like a database table. It contains zero, one, or many records, and each record contains one or more fields. A list can record any combination of fields you configure.

A new Team Site automatically contains the following lists.

● **Announcements**   Records informative messages for display on the site's home page.

● **Contacts**   Records information about people your team works with.

● **Events**   Maintains a list of upcoming meetings, deadlines, and other important events.

- **Links**   Records Web locations that your team members will find interesting or useful.
- **Tasks**   Maintains a list of assignments that your team members need to complete.

Each of these lists starts out with a different assortment of fields, but using only a browser, you can add, remove and modify the fields in any list. In addition, you can create new lists with any fields, and therefore for any purpose, you like.

> Chapter 6, "Designing Lists, Libraries, and Pages," will explain how to create and modify SharePoint lists and libraries.

Viewing Lists and List Content

Clicking the Documents And Lists link on the top navigation bar of any Team Site page displays the Documents And Lists page shown in Figure 3-2. This is basically a list of all the lists in the current site. Each list contains a different combination of fields, serves a different purpose, and provides different views.

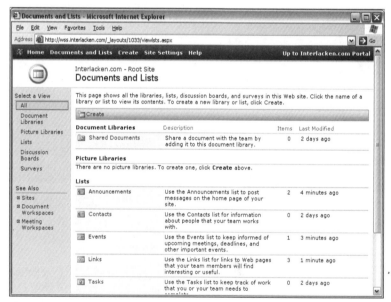

Figure 3-2.   From this page you can select any list in a Team Site.

At the left edge of the page, the choices in the Select A View area filter the list based on type: all lists, document library lists, picture library lists, and so forth. The Lists choice displays all lists that aren't document libraries, picture libraries, discussion boards, or surveys.

To display the contents of a specific list, click its entry in the Documents And Lists page. For ordinary lists, this displays a list view page like the one shown in Figure 3-3.

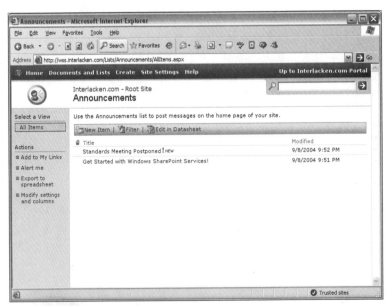

Figure 3-3. The Announcements list is one of the simplest lists in a Team Site.

Here's how the links on this page work:

- **Select A View**   Click any link in this area to display the list in the format you want. By default, the five built-in lists have only one view, such as All Items or All Contacts, but you can create more.

- **Actions**   This area provides the following commands for working with the list:

  - **Add To My Links**   Appears only if the current site collection is configured with a portal connection. In that case, it jumps to an Add Link page on the portal site. Clicking OK on that page updates your Personal Site with a link to the given document library.

  - **Alert Me**   Displays a New Alert page where you can request e-mail notification when someone changes the contents of the list.

> **Note**   Alert is a pervasive feature. You can ask to receive alerts regarding almost any aspect of a Team Site. A later section in this chapter will explain alerts in more detail.

  - **Export To Spreadsheet**   Downloads a Microsoft Excel Web Query file. Such files have an .iqy file extension that, by default, causes Excel to start. Excel then connects to the Team Site database and downloads the data for the list you requested.

- ■ **Modify Settings And Columns** Displays a Customization page that modifies the name of the list, its available views, its assigned template, its presence or absence on the Quick Launch bar, and so forth. Significantly, clicking this link also provides options that add or remove columns (that is, fields) from the list. You can use these extra columns to record any sort of data you want.

- **New Item** Displays a page named New Item Form that adds a new item to the list.

- **Filter** Limits the displayed items based on criteria you specify.

- **Edit In Datasheet** Displays the list in an editable table that resembles a spreadsheet.

Additional options may appear depending on the type of list. A Contacts list, for example, has commands for copying entries between the list and your Outlook address book. If Access 2003 or Excel 2003 is installed on the team member's computer, options for exporting and importing the list data will also appear.

Updating List Content

Windows SharePoint Services has built-in features for deleting, adding, or changing the content of any list. To perform these actions, first display the list, and then proceed as follows.

- To delete a list item, move the mouse pointer over its name, open the resulting drop-down list, and choose Delete Item.

- To add a new item, click the New Item button in the lists's toolbar.

- To modify an existing item, move the mouse pointer over its name, open the resulting drop-down list, and choose Edit Item.

> **Tip** Unless you're running a recent version of Internet Explorer, moving the mouse pointer over an item name won't display a drop-down list. If you encounter this, click the item name to display a Web page that offers the same options.

Choosing either New Item or Edit Item displays a page like the one in Figure 3-4. For a new item, all the input fields will, of course, be blank or default. For an existing item, the item name will replace New Item in the heading, and each input field will contain its current value.

The commands on the list's toolbar will vary, depending on the list's configuration. The Announcements list shown in Figure 3-4, for example, provides these commands:

- **Save And Close** Saves the current input values and returns to the list view page.

- **Attach File** Associates and stores a file along with the list item. An administrator or list manager can activate or block this capability.

- **Delete Item** Removes the current item from the list. (This command appears only when you edit an existing item.)

- **Go Back To List** Returns to the list view page without saving any additions or changes.

71

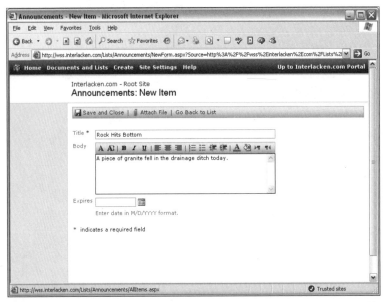

Figure 3-4. This page creates a new item in the Announcements list. The forms for other lists will, of course, offer different input fields.

An Incredibly Brief Introduction to SharePoint Security

Like FrontPage, Windows SharePoint Services organizes pages into sites. A site is a group of Web pages that you initialize from a single template, manage as a unit, and eventually delete as a unit.

Windows SharePoint Services further organizes sites into *site collections*. A site collection begins with a so-called *top-level site*, and includes all SharePoint sites that are within the top-level site's folder tree, and not within any other top-level site's folder tree. The administrators of a top-level site are the administrators of the entire site collection.

Most SharePoint sites don't permit anonymous access. They either use Windows logon accounts to control access, or accounts stored in a designated branch of an Active Directory. An administrator configures the site so that the appropriate team members belong to one of four default groups.

- **Reader** Members in this group have read-only access to the Web site. If anonymous visitors have any access at all, it will probably be as readers.
- **Contributor** Members in this group can add content to existing document libraries and lists.
- **Web Designer** These members can create and configure lists and libraries, and they can customize pages.

- **Administrator** These members have full control of the Web site.

Membership in any group entitles a team member to one or more specific rights. There are twenty-one such rights in all.

The Manage Lists right, for example, entitles the member to approve content in lists, add or remove columns in a list, and add or remove public views of a list. By default, only Administrators and Web Designers receive the Manage Lists right.

Using Content Approval

An administrator or list manager can configure any list so that new items aren't publicly visible until an administrator or list manager approves them. Windows SharePoint Services calls this feature Content Approval.

When Content Approval is in effect, two more options appear in the list's Select A View area.

- **Approve/Reject Items** Sorts the list items into three categories: Pending, Rejected, and Approved. Figure 3-5 illustrates this view (even though there are no rejected items). To change the status or attach an approval comment to any item, the administrator or list manager would choose Approve/Reject as shown in the figure.

- **My Submissions** Displays only those list items that the current SharePoint member has submitted. This view resembles Approve/Reject Items view in format, and displays items in all three status categories. This provides a way for contributors to check on the status of their postings.

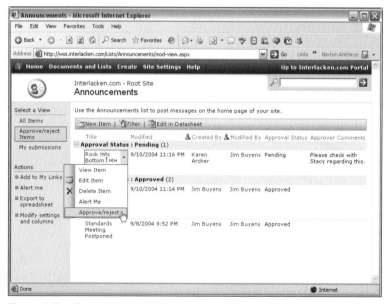

Figure 3-5. Content Approval suppresses the display of new items until an administrator or list manager approves them.

Here are two things to keep in mind if you decide to use the Content Approval feature.

● When an administrator or list manager submits a list item, Windows SharePoint Services immediately marks the items approved. However, any administrator or list manager can change the approved item to pending or rejected.

● If you configure a list to require content approval, it's a good idea to configure an alert for the same list. This reminds you to review the submission.

Using Document Libraries

A SharePoint document library is similar to a list where every item must have an attachment. However, document libraries have some additional capabilities and features particularly suited to the dual jobs of storing and managing documents.

Viewing Document Libraries

To work with a Team Site document library, click Documents And Lists on the top navigation bar of any page in the same site. This displays the Documents And Lists page, shown previously in Figure 3-2. To view a list of document libraries only, click the Document Libraries link in the Select A View area on the left.

The one document library shown in Figure 3-2—Shared Documents—appears automatically in every new Team Site. However, a single site can have as many document libraries as you want.

> **Tip** The top navigation bar of every Team Site page contains a Create link. This link jumps to a Create page that has options to create new document libraries and other Team Site objects.

Click the icon for any library to display a document library view page like the one shown in Figure 3-6. This page lists the documents in the library.

Here are the page's notable features:

● **Select A View** This area in the top left corner selects among all available formats for listing documents in the library. By default, there are two such formats:

 ■ **All Documents** Displays one line of text for each document in the library. Figure 3-6 illustrates this format.

 ■ **Explorer View** Lists the library contents in a format resembling Microsoft Windows Explorer. This is available only on Windows versions of Internet Explorer.

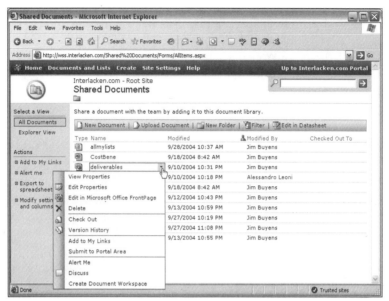

Figure 3-6. To display a list of documents like this, click a library name or icon in the Documents And Lists page (Figure 3-2) or click the Shared Documents link in the site's Quick Launch bar.

- **Actions** This area provides additional commands for working with the library:

  - **Add To My Links** Appears only if the current site collection is configured with a portal connection. In that case, it jumps to an Add Link page on the portal site. Clicking OK on that page updates your Personal Site with a link to the given document library.

  - **Alert Me** Displays a New Alert page. This page tells Windows SharePoint Services to send you an e-mail message whenever someone changes the contents of a document or folder within the library, or adds Web discussions.

  - **Export To Spreadsheet** Downloads an Excel query file that points to the library content list. After opening this file in Excel, authorized team members can download, modify, or export the content list.

  - **Modify Settings And Columns** Displays a Customization page that modifies the name, description, columns, views, and other settings.

Chapter 6, "Designing Lists, Libraries, and Pages," explains how to create and modify SharePoint lists and libraries.

- **Main Document Area** This is the large area that appears in the center of the Web page. It lists all the documents in the current library. To sort this listing on any field, click the field's column heading (that is, click Type, Name, Modified, Modified By, or Checked Out To). It also provides a toolbar with these links:

- **New Document**   Downloads a document template to your computer, which the corresponding application then opens with the current library as the default save location. If the library has no defined template, the default is an empty Microsoft Word document.

- **Upload Document**   Displays an Upload Document page that uploads a document from your computer and adds it to the library.

- **New Folder**   Displays a New Folder page for creating an additional folder within the current library.

- **Filter**   Redisplays the current Web page, adding selection controls above each selectable column heading. These controls limit the list of documents based on criteria you specify.

- **Edit In Datasheet**   Displays the list of documents as an editable table that resembles a spreadsheet. If Access 2003 or Excel 2003 is installed on the team member's computer, this view also provides a task bar for exchanging data with those programs.

Each line in the main document area of a document library view page (Figure 3-6) contains the following clickable fields:

- **Type**   Displays an icon that indicates the document type. Clicking this icon opens the file for viewing. If the file is a type that the browser can display, the browser displays it. Otherwise, the browser treats the file as a download and starts the application on your computer that normally opens the given file type.

- **Name**   Displays the document's file name. Clicking that name displays a drop-down menu with these choices:

  - **View Properties**   Displays all available information about the document.

  - **Edit Properties**   Displays a page where you can modify the document's name or title.

  - **Edit In <application>**   Downloads a temporary copy of the document and opens it in the associated application on your computer.

  - **Delete**   Removes the document from the library.

  - **Approve/Reject**   This option appears only if Content Approval is in effect for the library. In that case, it displays a page where administrators and list managers can set the document's Approval Status to Approved, Rejected, or Pending.

  - **Check Out**   Stops anyone but you from updating the document. (After you choose this option, it changes to Check In.) An administrator or list manager can activate or block this feature.

  - **Version History**   Displays a history of updates to the document. This includes date, time, modified by, document size, and comments. The next section will explain this feature.

■ **Add To My Links**   Appears only if the current site collection is configured with a portal connection. In that case, it jumps to an Add Link page on the portal site. Clicking OK on that page updates your Personal Site with a link to the given document.

■ **Submit To Portal Area**   Appears only if the current site collection is configured with a portal connection. In that case, it jumps to an Add Listing page on the portal site, where you can add the document to a portal area or topic.

■ **Alert Me**   Displays a New Alert page where you can request e-mail notification when someone changes or electronically discusses the document.

■ **Discuss**   Displays the document, including comments from other team members, and a toolbar that you can use to make comments yourself.

> The section, "Using Web Discussions," later in this chapter will explain document discussions in more detail.

■ **Create Document Workspace**   Creates a specialized SharePoint site for the sole purpose of organizing material related to the current document. This site contains a document library for the primary document and supporting files, a task list for assigning to-do items, and a links list for resources related to the document.

> **Note**   The URL path to a document workspace is the path to the Team Site that originally contained it, plus the document's file name base. If a Team Site at *www.fabrikam.com/sales* contained a document named policy.doc, the URL of that document's workspace would be *www.fabrikam.com/sales/policy*.

● **Modified**   Displays the date and time when the last document update occurred.

● **Modified By**   Shows who last updated the document. A hyperlink jumps to one of two locations:

  ■ If the current site collection is configured with the address of a portal site, the link displays the portal's personal page for the team member who last modified the document.

  ■ If the Team Site isn't configured with the address of a portal site, the link displays a Personal Settings page that provides information about the team member who last modified the document.

● **Checked Out To**   Works like Modified By, except that the link will target the team member who checked out the document.

77

Troubleshooting

Explorer View for Document Libraries Is Blank

When you try to view a document library in Explorer view, the body of the library view may remain blank, or may display the words Action Cancelled.

This occurs on Windows XP or later operating systems, and if the WebClient service is disabled. To start this service, proceed as follows.

1 On the computer's Start menu, right-click My Computer, and then click Manage.

2 When the Computer Management window appears, expand Services and Applications, and then select Services.

3 In the right pane, scroll down to the WebClient service, and double-click it.

4 When the WebClient Properties dialog box appears, make sure the General tab is selected.

5 Select one of these options in the Startup Type drop-down list:

  ■ **Automatic** This option starts the WebClient service whenever the computer starts.

  ■ **Manual** This option starts the WebClient service only in response to a manual command.

6 Click the Apply button to save your changes.

7 Click the Start button to start the WebClient service.

8 Click OK to close the dialog box.

Updating Document Libraries

Because each item in a document library must have an attached document, updating a document library requires procedures that are somewhat different from updating an ordinary list. The next five topics describe these procedures.

Creating a New Document and Adding It to the Library

Every SharePoint document library has a default document template. In the absence of any specific configuration, this is a Microsoft Word template, but whoever creates and manages the library can specify any template they want. For example, the default document template could be an Excel Spreadsheet or an InfoPath form.

When you click the New Document button in a toolbar of a library view (such as the one that appeared in Figure 3-6), Windows SharePoint Services downloads this default document template. This starts the appropriate program on your PC and sets the document library as the default save location.

When you save the document into the library, SharePoint will automatically record your name, the date and time, the type of document, and, if possible, the document title from within the document.

Adding an Existing Document to the Library

To add a document that already exists to a SharePoint library, click the Upload Document button on the library's list view toolbar. This displays the Upload Document page shown in Figure 3-7.

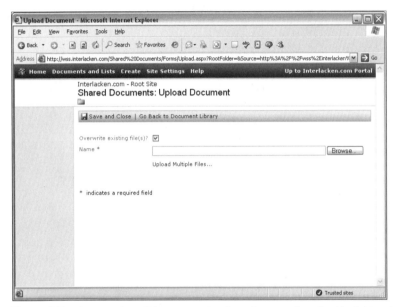

Figure 3-7. In one step, this page uploads a document and adds it to a document library.

Select the Overwrite Existing File(s)? check box if you want any documents you upload to overwrite existing library documents that have the same file name. To guard against overwriting any existing files, clear the check box.

From this point, the procedure varies depending on whether you have a single document to add, or multiple documents.

- To add a single document to the library:
    1. Click the Browse button on the Upload Document page.
    2. When the Choose File dialog box appears, locate and select the file you want, and then click Open.
    3. To add the file you chose, Click Save And Close.
- To add multiple documents to the library:
    1. Click the Upload Multiple Files... link on the Upload Document page.
    2. A Windows Explorer view of your desktop will appear in the Upload Document page. Figure 3-8 provides an example of this. Expand or collapse any folders you like, meanwhile selecting the check box for any file you want to add.
    3. To add all the files you chose, click Save And Close.

79

This facility to upload multiple documents is available only if Office 2003 is installed on your computer, and only if you're using a Windows version of Internet Explorer.

To return to the library view without adding a document, click the Go Back To Document Library toolbar button.

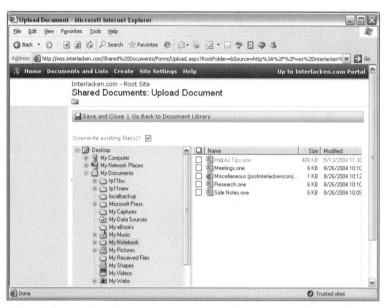

Figure 3-8. In this Explorer view, you can select multiple documents for upload to a SharePoint library.

Updating a Library Document

To change the content of a library document, follow the procedure outlined below.

1 Hold the mouse pointer over the document name until a drop-down list appears.

2 If you wish, open the drop-down list and choose Check Out. This locks the library copy of the document so no one but you can update it.

3 Open the drop-down list again and choose Edit In *<application>*. This will download a temporary copy of the document to your computer and open it in the corresponding application.

4 Change and save the document. This will update the copy in the document library.

5 If you checked out the document in step 2 and are now finished making changes, open the drop-down list, and choose Check In.

Updating the List Information for a Library Document

Here's the procedure for updating the library information for a document. This has no effect on the document itself.

1   Hold the mouse pointer over the document name until a drop-down list appears.

2   Open the drop-down list and choose Edit Properties. This will display a page named with the library name, a colon, and the document title.

3   Overtype the value of any fields you like.

4   Click the Save And Close button.

Deleting a Library Document

To delete a library document, hold the mouse over its title, open the resulting drop-down list, and select Delete.

Using Document Versions

An administrator or list manager can activate Document Versions for any library. With this feature in effect, SharePoint will retain not only the current version of each document, but all historical versions as well. Any team member can then use the following procedure to investigate the version history of a document.

1   In any library view, move the mouse pointer over the document name. The name will then change to a drop-down list.

2   Select Version History in the drop-down list. This will display the Versions page shown in Figure 3-9.

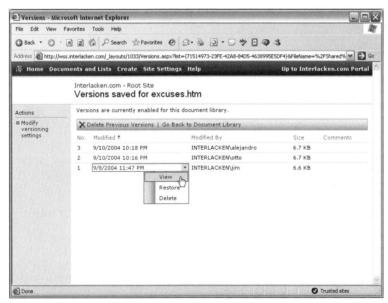

Figure 3-9. Version control stores and manages multiple versions of each document in a library.

The Versions page displays each version of a document that's present in the current library. To work with these versions, move the mouse pointer over any version date, open the resulting drop-down list, and choose one of these commands.

- **View** Opens the document version in its default application.
- **Restore** Creates a new copy of the document version, and makes it the current version. (This will increment the current version number by one.)
- **Delete** Removes the version from the library.

Using Picture Libraries

Typically, most of the deliverable and working documents that teams collect are textual in nature. Some, however, are graphical. Team Sites therefore provide picture libraries to efficiently handle the storage, viewing, and retrieval of graphical information.

Creating Picture Libraries

A new Team Site doesn't contain any picture libraries, but you can easily create as many as you want. Here's the procedure:

1 Open the Team Site in Internet Explorer, and click the Create option on the top navigation bar of any page.

2 When the Create page appears, click the Picture Library link.

3 When the New Picture Library page shown in Figure 3-10 appears, specify these options:

- **Name** Specify a short name that will identify the library throughout the Team Site.

- **Description** Briefly characterize the library's content or purpose.

- **Display This Picture Library On The Quick Launch Bar?** Select Yes if you want a link to this library from the Quick Launch bar of the Team Site home page.

- **Create A Version Each Time You Edit A File In This Picture Library?** Select Yes if you want Windows SharePoint Services to store a backup copy and history record every time someone updates a picture in this library.

4 To create the library, click the Create button at the bottom of the page.

Updating Picture Libraries

At this point, Windows SharePoint Services will display an empty contents page for the new picture library, in a format similar to that of a document library. To begin adding pictures, click the Add Picture link. This displays the Add Picture page shown in Figure 3-11.

82

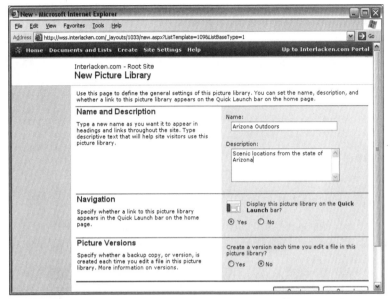

Figure 3-10.   Use this page to create a new Team Site picture library.

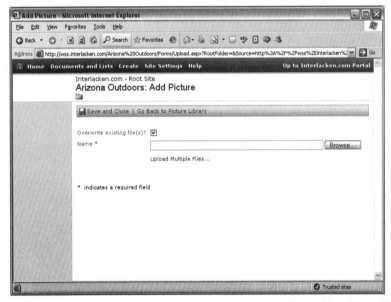

Figure 3-11.   This is the page that adds pictures to a Team Site picture library.

To add pictures to the library one at a time, proceed as follows:

1 If you want to overwrite an existing file, select the Overwrite Existing File(s) check box.

2 Click the Browse button to locate a picture file on your computer.

3 Click Save And Close to upload the file and add it to the library.

If Microsoft Office Picture Manager is installed on your computer, you can use it to upload several pictures at once. Here's the procedure:

1 Display the Add Picture Page shown previously in Figure 3-11.

2 Click the Upload Multiple Files... link.

3 When Office Picture Manager appears, select the pictures you want, and then click the Upload And Close button.

> **Microsoft Office Picture Manager** is a new application that comes with Office 2003. For more information on using this program, refer to "Working with Pictures in Picture Manager" in Chapter 4.

Viewing Picture Libraries

Figure 3-12 shows the contents of a picture library containing seventeen pictures. To display the library in this format, click Details under All Pictures in the Select A View area.

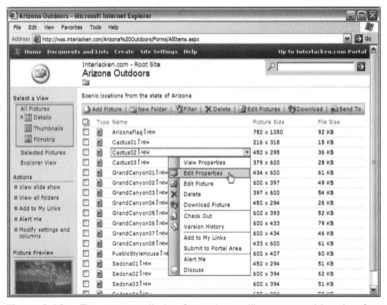

Figure 3-12. The contents listing for a picture library resembles that for a document library, but contains additional controls for working with pictures.

To display the library contents in a different format, click one of these links in the Select A View area:

● **Details**   Displays the list information for each picture in the library, but doesn't show the pictures themselves. This is the view that appears in Figure 3-12.

● **Thumbnails**   Displays a miniature version of each picture in the library, as shown in Figure 3-13.

- Clicking any thumbnail displays a larger version of the picture in a formatted SharePoint page.
- Clicking the larger version displays the full-size picture alone in the browser window.

Figure 3-13. This page lists the contents of a Team Site picture library by displaying thumbnails.

- **Filmstrip**   Displays a horizontal series of thumbnails representing each picture in the library.
    - Clicking any thumbnail loads a larger version of the corresponding picture into the thumbnail page.
    - Clicking the larger version displays the full size picture alone in the browser window.
- **Selected Pictures**   Displays only those pictures whose check boxes you selected in an All Pictures view.
- **Explorer View**   Lists the library contents in a format resembling Windows Explorer. This is available only when you use a Windows version of Internet Explorer.

Here are some common actions you can perform from the Details view. Many of these actions are available in other views as well.

- Clicking the Type icon for any picture displays the full-sized picture—and nothing else—directly in the browser window.
- Clicking the name of any picture displays a larger version of the picture in a formatted Team Web page. Figure 3-14 provides an example.

Figure 3-14. This page displays all current information for an entry in a picture library.

- Moving the mouse over the name of any picture displays a thumbnail in the Picture Preview area in the lower left corner. It also changes the picture name to a drop-down menu with these choices:

  - **View Properties** Displays all available information about the picture.

  - **Edit Properties** Displays a page where you can modify the picture's name or title.

  - **Edit Picture** Starts Office Picture Manager and tells it to open the picture for editing.

  - **Delete** Removes the picture from the library.

  - **Approve/Reject** This option appears only if Content Approval is in effect for the library. In that case, it displays a page where administrators and list managers can set the document's Approval Status to Approved, Rejected, or Pending.

  - **Download Picture** Downloads the picture to your computer.

  - **Check Out** Stops anyone but you from updating the picture. (After you choose this option, it changes to Check In.)

  - **Version History** Displays a history of updates to the picture. This includes date, time, modified by, picture size, and comments.

  - **Add To My Links** Appears only if the current site collection is configured with a portal connection. In that case, it jumps to a page where you can update your personal site with a link to the picture.

- **Submit To Portal Area**   Appears only if the current site collection is configured with a portal connection. In that case, it jumps to an Add Listing page on the portal site, where you can add the document to a portal area or topic.

- **Alert Me**   Displays a New Alert page where you can request e-mail notification when someone changes or electronically discusses the picture.

- **Discuss**   Displays the picture, including comments from other team members, and a toolbar that you can use to make comments yourself.

The Actions area, which appears on the left, provides these additional capabilities:

- **View Slide Show**   Opens a new window that displays the first picture in the library and buttons to display additional pictures automatically.

- **View All Folders**   Displays a selection list of folders in the library.

- **Add To My Links**   Appears only if the current site collection is configured with a portal connection. In that case, it jumps to a page where you can update your personal site with a link to the library.

- **Alert Me**   Displays the New Alert page so that you can request e-mail notification when someone changes or electronically discusses anything in the library.

- **Modify Settings And Columns**   Displays a Customization page with links to change options in effect for the library. This includes the capability to add new columns, reorder existing columns, and create new views. You might use new columns to record who took each picture, when the picture was taken, and so forth. A new view could then filter on those criteria.

Using Discussion Boards

A Team Site discussion board works a lot like an Internet newsgroup or a FrontPage Discussion Web. Team members can post new messages, respond to existing messages, and view messages in their entirety or in condensed lists. Whoever administers the Team Site can purge and correct messages, alter discussion board settings and defaults, and so forth. If security settings permit, team members can initiate and control their own discussion boards, and whoever posts a message can subsequently revise or delete it.

Choosing or Creating a Discussion Board

To display a list of discussion boards in the current site:

1 Click Documents And Lists on the top navigation bar of any page in the Team Site.

2 Under Select A View, click Discussion Boards.

This displays the Discussion Boards view, shown in Figure 3-15, which shows the name and description of each available discussion board. The General Discussion board appears by default as part of every new Team Site.

Chapter 3

87

Figure 3-15. This page provides a selection list of Team Site discussion boards. The single discussion board shown here appears by default in every new Team Site.

To create a new discussion board, click the Create link on the top navigation bar of any Team Site page. When the Team Site's Create page appears, scroll down to Discussion Boards, and then click Discussion Board.

Viewing and Updating a Discussion Board

To view or modify the contents of an existing discussion board, click its icon or title to display a discussion page like the one shown in Figure 3-16.

Here's how to use this page:

- **Select A View**   Click any link in this area (on the left) to display the discussion board in the format you want. Threaded view, the default, is the view shown in Figure 3-16. Flat view displays each message independently, regardless of its relationship to other messages.

- **Actions**   Click any of these links to achieve the corresponding results.

  - **Add To My Links**   Appears only if the current site collection is configured with a portal connection. In that case, it adds a link from your personal portal site to the discussion board.

  - **Alert Me**   Signs you up for e-mail notification whenever someone updates the board.

  - **Modify Settings And Columns**   Reconfigures the board, adds columns, or creates additional views.

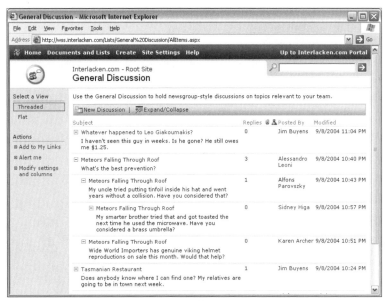

Figure 3-16. Click a discussion board name or icon in Figure 3-15 to display a list of messages like this.

● **New Discussion**   Click this link to create a new top-level message. Figure 3-17 shows the Web page that supports this function. (Remember, to create a new discussion board, click the Create link at the top of the page.)

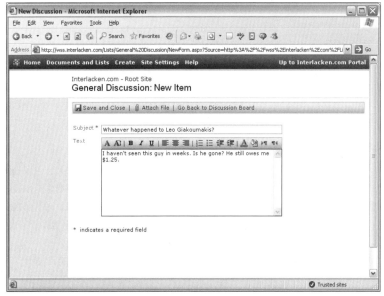

Figure 3-17. This Web page starts a new discussion thread. To display it, click any New Discussion link.

- **Expand/Collapse** This link appears only in Threaded view. Click it to toggle between a display of all messages and a display of top-level messages only.

- **Filter** This link appears only in Flat view. Click it to redisplay the current Web page, adding selection controls above each selectable column heading. These controls limit the list of messages based on criteria you specify.

- **Subject, Posted By, and Modified** In Flat view, click any of these column headings to sort the display on that column.

- **Posted By** Click any entry in the Posted By column to display information about that person.

Clicking on the Subject text of any message displays the message itself and all related details. Figure 3-18 provides an example.

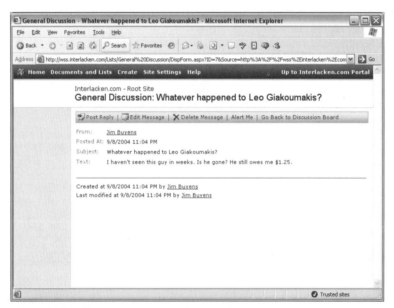

Figure 3-18. This is how a Team Site displays an individual discussion message.

The toolbar on this page contains the following links:

- **Post Reply** Creates a new message that responds to the current one. The page for posting a reply strongly resembles the one shown in Figure 3-17.

- **Edit Message** Modifies the current message. Depending on the settings in effect for the discussion board, this might be possible only for an administrator or the person who originated the message.

- **Delete Message** Deletes the current message. Again, this might be possible only for an administrator or the person who originated the message.

- **Alert Me**   Displays a New Alert page where you can request notification whenever someone changes the current message.
- **Go Back To Discussion Board**   Backs up one screen (usually to the Discussion Board view page, shown in Figure 3-16).

Using Alerts

The Alert feature of a Team Site sends e-mail notifications to interested team members whenever another member changes some aspect of the Team Site. Each member decides which lists, libraries, or documents they want to receive alerts about.

Clicking any Alert Me link on a Team Site page (such as the document library view page shown in Figure 3-6) displays the New Alert page shown in Figure 3-19. On this page, you can ask to receive change notices for the current document or for any document in a specified folder (subject to filters), set notification criteria, specify your e-mail address, and indicate how long Windows SharePoint Services should accumulate changes before sending them.

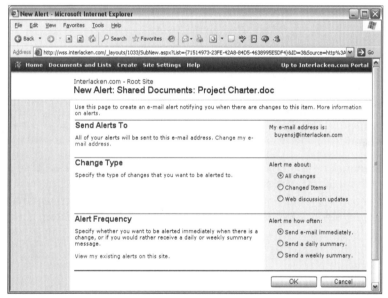

Figure 3-19.   This Web page requests e-mail notification of changes to a given document or folder.

Figure 3-20 shows a typical alert message. Although the message in the figure provides only one notification, a single message can report multiple changes.

The notification process periodically scans a database and combines all notifications to the same recipient. The less often you choose to receive messages, the more notifications each message will contain.

91

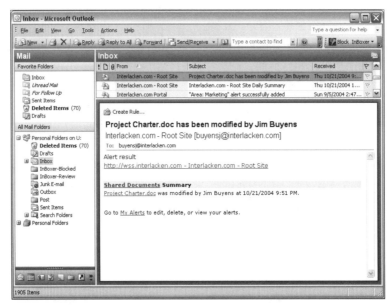

Figure 3-20. A Team Site sent this alert automatically.

Troubleshooting

Members don't receive Team Site alerts

Team Site members who request alerts might not receive the expected mail for any of the following reasons:

- **Not enough time has passed**   Team Sites send notifications at specified intervals, even if a team member selected Send E-Mail Immediately. These intervals apply to the entire Web server and are thus something an administrator must control. The following settings are the defaults, but your server's configuration might vary:

    - **Immediate Notifications**   Every five minutes.

    - **Daily Notifications**   Midnight.

    - **Weekly Notifications**   Sunday midnight.

- **Server settings might be incomplete**   The server administrator must configure Windows SharePoint Services with the name of an SMTP mail server and an address that will appear in the From and Reply To fields of each outgoing message.

- **The Alert feature might be disabled**   The server administrator can turn off the Web Alerts features at the server level. Obviously, this inhibits the transmission of notification messages.

Using Web Discussions

The Discuss option is what most Office applications call *Web Discussions*. Despite the similarity in names, this option has nothing to do with Team Site Discussion Boards. Web Discussions provide a way to add yellow "sticky notes" to a document and to share those notes with others—all without actually updating the document itself. This is possible because the sticky note information resides in a database on a *discussion server*. This is the same database that services the Team Site.

This is a very useful approach, because several people can review and annotate the same document simultaneously, and then the document owner can see all their suggestions merged together. There are no concerns about someone accidentally updating the document itself, because no one can update the document at all.

Figure 3-21 shows Internet Explorer accepting discussion comments for a document.

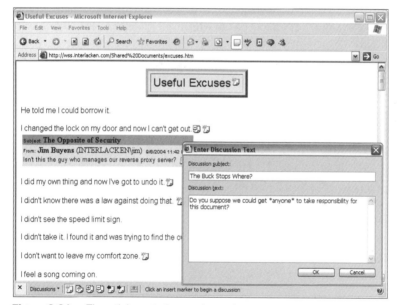

Figure 3-21. The sticky note icons show where you can append comments to the document. Click one to display the Enter Discussion Text dialog box.

> **Tip** To show or hide the Discuss toolbar in Internet Explorer, choose Explorer Bar from the View menu, and then choose Discuss.

In this figure, the team member:

1 Displayed the Shared Documents page shown previously in Figure 3-6.

2 Hovered the mouse over the file name deliverables.

3 Opened the resulting drop-down menu, and chose Discuss.

Because the deliverables file is in HTML format, Internet Explorer directly displays that document and the Discuss toolbar shown at the bottom of Figure 3-21. If the document had been in some other Office format, Internet Explorer would have downloaded the document, started the appropriate Office application, and told that application to display its own Discuss toolbar.

Here's how to use the buttons on the Discuss toolbar. (Note that some buttons might be dimmed, depending on the type of document.)

- **Close**   Click this button to close the Web Discussion bar.
- **Discussions**   Click this button to display a menu containing the following options:
  - **Insert In The Document**   Choose this command to display or hide all possible locations for inline sticky notes (those that appear inline with the document text). There's basically one sticky note location per paragraph. To add text to a new or an existing sticky note, click it.
  - **Insert About The Document**   Choose this command to display an Enter Discussion Text dialog box in which you can enter discussion comments about the document in general.
  - **Refresh Discussions**   Choose this command to retrieve a current set of discussion comments from the discussion server. Your display will then reflect changes other visitors might have made after you first displayed the page.
  - **Filter Discussions**   Choose this command to display discussion comments from only a certain participant, or within a certain time span.
  - **Discussion Options**   Choose this command to select the discussion server and the discussion fields to display.
- **Insert Discussion In The Document**   Click this button to perform the same function as the Insert In The Document menu command just described.
- **Insert Discussion About The Document**   Click this button to perform the same function as the Insert About The Document menu command just described.
- **Expand All Discussions**   Click this button to display the title, text, and all other fields for each discussion comment.
- **Collapse All Discussions**   Click this button to hide the contents of all discussion comments. A sticky note with a plus sign appears in place of each comment. To expand a particular comment, click the plus sign.
- **Previous**   Click this button to display the previous discussion comment.
- **Next**   Click this button to display the next discussion comment.
- **Show/Hide Discussion Pane**   Click this toggle button to display or hide the discussion pane.

Discussion text also appears—in almost identical format—when the document creator opens the file in its native Office application. In fact, all discussion text from all contributors is merged seamlessly into place. (If no discussions appear, choose Online Collaboration from the Tools menu, and make sure that the correct discussion server is specified.)

94

Web discussions are a less granular facility than the comment and change-tracking provided by Microsoft Office programs like Word and Excel. For example, you can't change the document, and you can only attach comments at designated locations. The advantage of Web discussions is that they operate on the Internet and don't require making copies of the document.

In Summary...

Windows SharePoint Services provides a rich array of useful functions for working with lists, libraries, and discussions using only a browser. As a whole, these features are much easier to use and understand than the cryptic file names and other obscure practices that arise in a file sharing environment.

The next chapter explains how Windows SharePoint Services integrates with the applications in Microsoft Office System 2003.

Chapter 3

Using SharePoint with the Microsoft Office System

The previous chapter explained, among other things, how you can start Microsoft Office programs from the Windows SharePoint Services browser interface. For example, you can move the mouse over the name of any file in a document library, open the resulting drop-down list, and choose Edit In Microsoft Word (or whatever the correct application happens to be).

As you might suspect, the reverse is also possible. Starting in any Microsoft Office 2003 program, you can open and save files, view member lists, manage alerts, and otherwise manipulate SharePoint sites without using a browser at all. The Office programs themselves act as Web clients.

This chapter will explain how Microsoft Office 2003 programs act as clients to Windows SharePoint Services. This includes Access, Excel, InfoPath, Picture Manager, OneNote, Outlook, PowerPoint, Project, Publisher, Visio, and Word.

FrontPage interacts with Windows SharePoint Services in an even more powerful way. It can design SharePoint sites, templates, Themes, and Web Part Pages, right down to the bare HTML, XML, and CSS. Part IV, "Creating and Designing Sites Using FrontPage 2003," will explain this in some detail.

Opening and Saving Library Documents

The ever-present File Open and File Save As dialog boxes provide the most universal type of access to a SharePoint site. Here's the procedure:

1 In any Office program, choose Open or Save As from the File menu.

2 Click the My Network Places icon in My Places bar.

3 Double-click the URL of the SharePoint site. This will be an HTTP address such as *http://wss.example.com/mysite.*

If the address you want doesn't appear in the My Network Places list, type it and press Enter.

4 The dialog box may switch into Web View automatically. If it doesn't, choose WebView from the Views drop-down list. The dialog box should then display each library in the site, as shown in Figure 4-1.

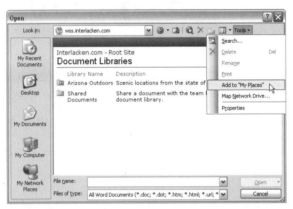

Figure 4-1. All Office file-oriented dialog boxes can directly browse the libraries in a SharePoint site.

5 Double-click the library you want and if this generates a logon prompt, enter your credentials. This will display a list of the documents in that library, much as Figure 4.2 illustrates.

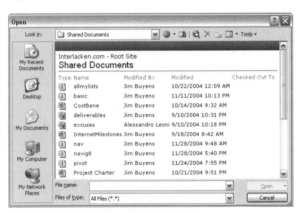

Figure 4-2. This is how the file-oriented dialog boxes in Office programs display the contents of a SharePoint library.

6 If you originally chose File Open, double-click the file you want to open.

If you chose File Save As and want to overwrite an existing file, double-click that file. Otherwise, type the filename you want to assign and then click the Save button.

> **Tip**   If you use a specific SharePoint site often, you can save steps by creating an icon for it in the My Places bar. This is the vertical column of icons that appears at the left of Figures 4-1 and 4-2. To add such an icon, follow steps 1-4 above, then choose Add To "My Places" from the Tools menu. Figure 4-1 shows this in progress.

Accessing SharePoint libraries directly from these dialog boxes is much easier and much more direct than downloading documents to disk, opening them from disk, saving them to disk, and then uploading them to some other portal or document management system.

Using the Shared Workspace Task Pane

Excel, OneNote, PowerPoint, Project, Visio, and Word all provide a Shared Workspace task pane that can create, view, or modify document workspaces for the current document. As a bonus, most of the functions work with other types of SharePoint sites as well. Here's one way to display the Shared Workspace task pane:

- If no task pane is on display, press Ctrl+F1.
- If a different task pane is on display, click the drop-down arrow in the task pane title bar and select Shared Workspace.

Alternatively, choose Shared Workspace from the Tools menu.

An Incredibly Brief Introduction to Document Workspaces

A *document workspace* is very much like a Team Site. It contains a document library named Shared Documents and the usual assortment of predefined lists: Announcements, Contacts, Events, Links, and Tasks. The difference is that a document workspace exists solely to facilitate collaboration on a specific document.

The SharePoint browser interface and the Shared Workspace task pane both provide commands that create document workspaces based on an existing document. By default, the name of the new document workspace will come from the document's filename base. The new site's Shared Documents library will, of course, contain a copy of the document.

At this point, the collaborators start checking the document workspace, updating and annotating the original document, adding and revising supporting documents, having discussions, monitoring tasks, checking deadlines, and so forth. Only one collaborator at a time, however, can have the same document open for edit.

When the document is complete, its owner publishes the final version, usually by copying it to the original library. After a suitable period, the owner deletes the document workspace.

You could do all the same activities in an existing Team Site, of course, but then the Team Site fills up with all those intermediate work results. Using a document workspace keeps that work segregated and makes it easier to clean up after the work is complete.

Chapter 4

99

Whenever you have a document open in one of these programs, and the document doesn't reside in a SharePoint library, the Shared Workspace task pane looks like the one in Figure 4-3.

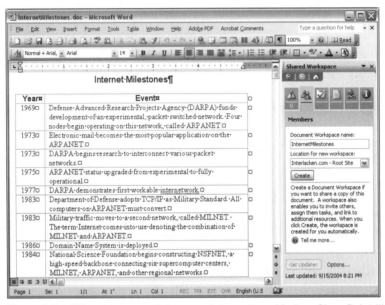

Figure 4-3. When the current document doesn't reside in a SharePoint library, the Shared Workspace task pane offers to create a document workspace and save the document there.

To save the current document in a new Shared Workspace site, proceed as follows:

1 Select either the Members, Tasks, Documents or Links tab in the Shared Workspace task pane.

2 Review the contents of the Document Workspace Name box. This will become the name of the new document workspace. If you want a different name, simply type it in.

3 Review the Location For New Workspace box. This specifies the SharePoint site that will serve as the parent of the new document workspace. The Shared Workspace task pane will suggest a site, but you can choose a different one by opening the drop-down list or by typing a URL.

4 Click the Create button.

Once you've opened or saved a document in a SharePoint site, the Shared Workspace task pane changes to show the content of that site. The next six topics will explain the six views this task pane can present: Status, Members, Tasks, Documents, Links, and Document Information.

Chapter 4

Using the Shared Workspace Status Tab

The Status tab of the Shared Workspace task pane displays document information such as version and check-out status. This tab appears at left in Figure 4-4.

Figure 4-4. Respectively, these are the Status, Members, and Tasks tabs of the Shared Workspace task pane.

The following controls appear near the bottom of every tab in the Shared Workspace task pane.

- **Get Updates** This button retrieves and displays the most recent information from the SharePoint site.
- **Options** This link displays a Service Options dialog box where you can configure settings for the Shared Workspace task pane. A later section in this chapter will explain these options.

Using the Shared Workspace Members Tab

The Members tab displays the names of all team members in the current SharePoint site. A typical display appears in the middle of Figure 4-4. The member names are in three groups:

- **The Current Member** This should be your name.
- **Members Who Are Online With Windows Messenger** Clicking any of these names starts a Windows Messenger conversation with that member.
- **Members Who Aren't Online** Clicking any of these names starts an e-mail message to that member.

Chapter 4

Moving the mouse over any member name displays a drop-down menu that looks like this:

Here are the functions of each command on this menu. Some of the commands, however, don't appear for the current member. This is because, for example, it makes no sense to send e-mail or an instant message to yourself.

- **<*membername*> Is <*status*>**   Reports the Windows Messaging status of the given member: Online, On The Phone, Not Online, Not An Online Contact, and so forth, provided you're signed into Windows Messenger.

- **Schedule A Meeting**   Displays the standard Outlook dialog box for scheduling a meeting. Both you and the member you selected will be attendees. From there you can invite additional attendees, choose a date and time, and even create a meeting workspace.

- **Add Or Edit Phone Numbers**   Displays the Outlook contact form for the member you selected. Enter the phone numbers you want and then click Save And Close.

  If your Outlook contact record for the member already has a phone number, this option changes to Call <*type*> <*phone number*> and displays a submenu. The submenu has commands to call each phone number, and to add or edit more numbers.

  Calling a phone number works only if you can make phone calls through Windows Messenger.

- **Send Mail**   Opens a new Outlook e-mail message to the member you selected.

- **Send Instant Message**   Starts a new Windows Messenger conversation with the member you selected. However:

  - If you aren't signed in to Windows Messenger, this option changes to Sign-In To Messenger.

  - If the member you selected isn't online, the option is dimmed.

  - If the member you selected isn't one of your Windows Messenger contacts, the option changes to Add To Messenger Contacts.

- **Additional Actions**   Opens a submenu of commands other programs on your computer might offer.

- **Remove Member From Workspace**   Revokes the selected member's rights to access the SharePoint site.

- **Edit Site Group Membership**   Displays an Edit Site Group Membership Web page where you can change the security groups to which the selected member belongs.

- **Edit User Information**   Displays an Edit Personal Settings Web page where you can enter or correct the selected member's name, e-mail address, or notes.

- **Open Outlook Contact**   Displays the Outlook contact form for the member you selected. If the member isn't currently one of your Outlook contacts, this option changes to Add To Outlook Contacts.

- **Outlook Properties**   Displays the Outlook properties dialog box for the selected member. This is the dialog box that appears below.

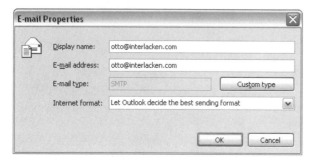

The Add New Members link near the bottom of the tab provides a way of adding members to the site. To use this facility:

1 Click the Add New Members link near the bottom of the Members tab.

2 When the Add New Members wizard shown at top left in Figure 4-5 appears, enter either the e-mail address or the domain account of each member you want to add. Separate member identities with semicolons.

3 Under Choose Site Group, use the drop-down box to select a security group for the new members. After you select any group, the text below the drop-down box will explain the capabilities of that group.

4 Click Next to display the wizard page shown at bottom right in Figure 4-5. If possible, the wizard will look up the new member's e-mail address or domain account (whichever you didn't already specify) and the new member's display name. Fill in any missing values.

5 Click Finish to create the new members. If the SharePoint server is using domain accounts for authentication, it will verify that the accounts you specified are valid.

6 A final prompt will ask whether you want to send mail inviting the new members to start using the site. If you click Yes, the message will appear in Outlook, ready for sending.

The Send E-Mail To All Members link near the bottom of the tab opens a new message in Outlook and addresses it to all members of the current site.

103

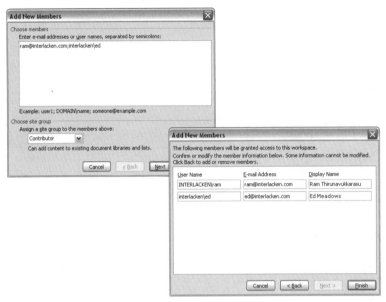

Figure 4-5. This two-step wizard adds team members to the document workspace where the current Office program resides.

Using the Shared Workspace Tasks Tab

The Tasks tab displays a list of tasks recorded in the current SharePoint site. A typical display appears at right in Figure 4-4.

Clicking the Sort By heading opens a drop-down list where you can specify the order in which tasks appear: by creation date, by status, by title, and so forth.

Moving the mouse pointer over any task displays a drop-down arrow that offers these choices:

- **Edit Task**   Displays a Task dialog box where you can change the title, status, assigned member, and other properties of the task. Figure 4-6 illustrates this dialog box.
- **Delete Task**   Deletes the current task.
- **Alert Me About This Task**   Displays a SharePoint Web page where you can sign up to receive e-mail whenever changes occur to the current task.

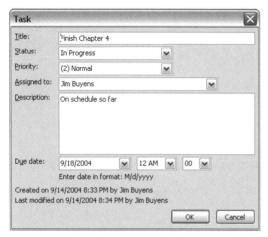

Figure 4-6. Clicking the Add New Task link in a Shared Workspace task pane displays this dialog box, which adds a task to the current SharePoint site.

The Add New Task link at the bottom of the Tasks tab displays an empty version of the Task dialog box shown in Figure 4-6. Enter the information for a new task and then click OK.

The Alert Me About Tasks link displays a SharePoint Web page where you can sign up for e-mail that notifies you of any change to the entire task list.

Using the Shared Workspace Documents Tab

The Documents tab displays the contents of the Shared Documents library in the current SharePoint site. A typical display appears at left in Figure 4-7.

Figure 4-7. These are the Documents, Links, and Document Information tabs of the Shared Workspace task pane.

To sort the list of documents in a particular sequence, click the Sort By column heading and choose the order you want: Creation Data, Modified Date, File Name and so forth. To work with a specific document, pass the mouse over its name, open the resulting drop-down menu, and choose one of these commands:

- **Open In** *<application>*   Opens the document in its usual application.
- **Delete**   Removes the document from the Shared Documents library.
- **Alert Me About This Document**   Displays a SharePoint Web page where you can sign up to receive e-mail whenever someone changes the document.

To add a new document to the Shared Documents library, click the Add New Document link near the bottom of the task pane. This displays a dialog box like the one below. Type or browse for the filename you want, and then click OK.

To create a new folder in the Shared Documents library, click the Add New Folder link, type the folder name, and click OK. To sign up for e-mail notification of any change to the entire Shared Document library, click the Alert Me About Documents link. This displays a New Alert Web page that pertains to the entire library.

Using the Shared Workspace Links Tab

The Links tab displays the contents of the Links list in the current SharePoint site. It appears in the center of Figure 4-7, and requires no new techniques to use. To sort the display, for example, click the Sort By column heading and choose the order you want.

The drop-down commands for each link are Edit Link, Delete Link, and Alert Me About This Link. These commands work very much like those for tasks and documents.

To add a link, click Add New Link near the bottom of the task pane. To receive alerts about changes to any link, click Alert Me About Links.

Using the Shared Workspace Document Information Tab

The Document Information tab displays SharePoint data about the current document, such as the person who created it, the person who last modified it, and the date of the last modification. A typical display appears at right in Figure 4-7. The four links near the bottom of the task pane work as follows:

- **Restrict Permission**   Click this link to control access to the document via Microsoft Information Rights Management. This means anyone who wants to view, forward, print, or otherwise process the document must first authenticate through a Microsoft Content Management Server running either on the Internet or your local network.

- **Alert Me About This Document**   Click this link to display a SharePoint Web page where you can sign up to receive e-mail whenever someone changes the document.

- **Check Out**   Click this link to lock the library copy of the current document so that no one but the current user (you) can change it. This remains in effect until you check the document in.

- **Version History**   Click this link to display a Versions Saved For *<document name>* dialog box. This dialog box displays the version number, date modified, responsible person, and comments for each version of the current document that resides in the SharePoint library.

Setting Shared Workspace Options

If you saved an existing document into a new document workspace by using the Shared Workspace task pane's Create button (shown previously in Figure 4-3), Office maintains an association between the original document and the copy in the document workspace. Then, if you open the original document (as from a file share), Office will, by default, check for document updates or other kinds of changes in the document workspace. This can result in prompts like the one below.

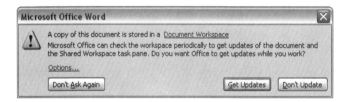

To configure this behavior, click the Options link at the bottom of the Shared Workspace task bar. This displays the Service Options dialog box shown in Figure 4-8.

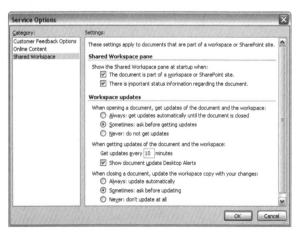

Figure 4-8.   The options in this dialog box configure synchronization between an offline document open in Office and a SharePoint site.

107

Chapter 4

Here's how to configure the options in this dialog box:

- **Show The Shared Workspace Pane At Startup When:**   These options control when the Shared Workspace task pane will appear automatically.

  - **The Document Is Part Of A Workspace Or SharePoint Site.**   Select this check box if you want the Shared Workspace task pane to appear whenever you open a document from a SharePoint site, or a local document that Office is synchronizing with a copy on a SharePoint site.

  - **There Is Important Status Information Regarding The Document.**   Select this check box if you want the Shared Workspace task pane to appear when you open a local document that Office finds is no longer in sync with one on a SharePoint site.

- **When Opening A Document, Get Updates Of The Document And The Workspace:** When you open a local document that Office is synchronizing with a document workspace copy, this option controls whether Office compares the two copies.

  - **Always**   Choose this option if you want Office to compare the two copies every time.

  - **Sometimes**   Choose this option if you want Office to prompt you before comparing the two copies.

  - **Never**   Choose this option if you never want Office to compare the two copies. To check for changes manually, click the Get Updates button at the bottom of the Shared Workspace task pane.

- **When Getting Updates Of The Document And The Workspace:**   These options control how often, during the editing session, Office updates the Shared Workspace task pane with information from the document workspace. This refreshes the content on the various tabs and detects discrepancies between the local and document workspace copies of a document.

  - **Get Updates Every <*n*> Minutes**   Specify the number of minutes between comparisons.

  - **Show Document Update Desktop Alerts**   Select this check box if you want visual notification when a change occurs to the document workspace copy of the current document.

- **When Closing A Document, Update The Workspace Copy With Your Changes:**   This option controls whether Office synchronizes the document workspace copy of a document when you close the local copy.

  - **Always**   Choose this option to update the document workspace copy every time you close the local copy.

  - **Sometimes**   Choose this option if you want Office to prompt you before updating the document workspace copy.

  - **Never**   Choose this option if you never want Office to update the document workspace copy.

Inside Out

Use Check In/Check Out rather than synchronization

The Office feature for synchronizing local and SharePoint copies of the same document is tricky to invoke and easy to misuse.

If you need to work with a SharePoint document offline (when traveling or telecommuting, for example), you should check it out, download it, perform your updates, upload the changed copy, and then check it in.

Integrating with Outlook

A Team Site contains many kinds of data that would also be useful in Outlook: contact names and addresses, events, shared documents, and meetings, just to name a few. Fortunately, Microsoft noticed those similarities as well, and provided a wealth of features for copying and synchronizing data between the two programs. This section will review the entire set.

Importing and Exporting Contacts

A SharePoint Contacts list is a repository where team members can share the names and addresses of co-workers and outside associates. Figure 4-9 shows a typical SharePoint Contacts list.

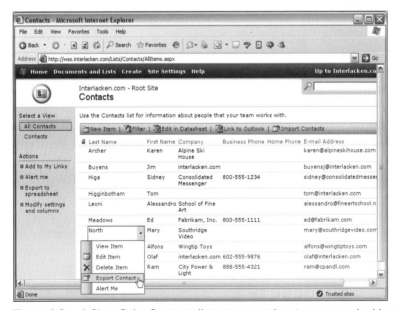

Figure 4-9. A SharePoint Contacts list stores pertinent names and addresses. You can copy contacts from such a list to Outlook, or from Outlook to a Contacts list.

Useful as this information may be, it would be even more useful in Outlook. Windows SharePoint Services therefore provides several ways of exchanging contact information with Outlook 2003. Here, for example, is how you can export a single contact to your Outlook personal address book.

1 Move the mouse pointer over the last name of the contact you want to export, and then open the drop-down list and choose Export Contact.

2 The SharePoint site will download the contact information as a .vcf file. If you receive a security download prompt, choose to open this file.

3 Windows opens the .vcf file in the default application for that filename extension, which is usually Outlook. Outlook, in turn, loads the information into its standard Contacts window. Figure 4-10 illustrates this. Confirm all the details, and then click Save And Close.

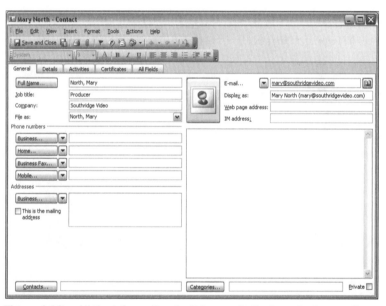

Figure 4-10.   All the information for this new Outlook contact came from an entry in a SharePoint Contacts list.

To export an entire SharePoint Contacts list, click the Link To Outlook button in the Contacts list toolbar. Outlook will display a prompt verifying that you want to add a new Outlook folder, and then it stores your contacts as shown in Figure 4-11.

> **Tip**   Be cautious exporting a large Contacts list to Outlook. Synchronizing a large Contacts list can take a long time, and this is something Outlook does repeatedly.

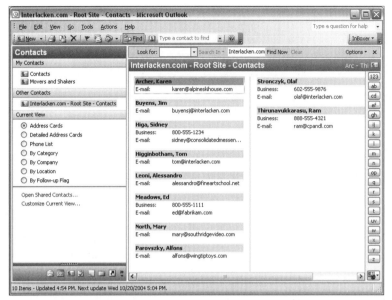

Figure 4-11. Downloading an entire SharePoint Contacts list to Outlook creates a Contacts folder like this. Outlook will periodically refresh this information.

Note that each SharePoint Contacts list you download becomes a different Outlook folder. This is slightly inconvenient when you're sending mail—first you have to select the correct folder, and only then the recipient—but it makes it very easy for Outlook to keep the list up to date. Every ten minutes (or whatever interval you configured in the Service Options dialog box shown previously in Figure 4-8), Outlook checks the SharePoint list for updates and downloads any it finds. This accounts for the following message in the status bar of Figure 4-11.

10 Items – Updated 4:54 PM, Next update Wed 10/10/2004 5:04 PM.

> **Tip**   Be cautious about selecting a short interval between server refreshes. If too many team members choose too short an interval, server performance could degrade. To immediately synchronize the current list, view a different list and then switch back to the one you want.

To copy contacts from Outlook to a SharePoint Contacts list, proceed as follows:

1   Display the SharePoint Contacts list in your browser.

2   Click the Import Contacts toolbar button.

3   If you have multiple Outlook profiles on your computer, a Choose Profile dialog box will appear. Specify the profile you want and then clock OK.

4   When the Select Users To Import dialog box shown in Figure 4-12 appears, select as many names as you want and then click the Add button.

111

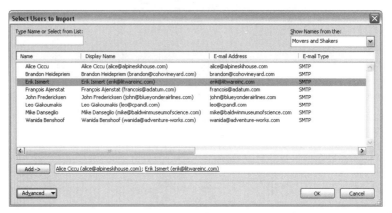

Figure 4-12. This dialog box selects Outlook contacts for inclusion in a SharePoint contacts list.

5   Click the OK button to copy the selected contacts into your SharePoint Contacts list. When the message box shown below appears, click OK.

Exporting Events

Windows SharePoint Services can't exchange individual events with Outlook, but you *can* link an entire SharePoint Events list to an Outlook calendar. The procedure is very much like that for linking contacts. Proceed as follows.

1   Display the Events list you want to link with Outlook. This should resemble Figure 4-13.

2   Click the Link To Outlook toolbar button.

3   When Outlook displays a prompt asking if you want to add a new Outlook folder, click Yes.

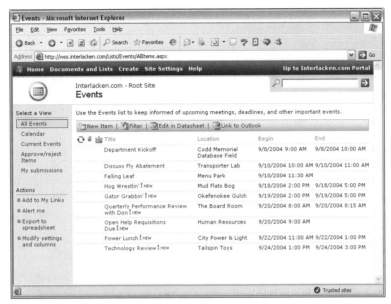

Figure 4-13. The Link To Outlook toolbar button in a SharePoint Events list copies the events to an Outlook calendar.

4 Outlook will display the events in a new calendar, as shown in Figure 4-14.

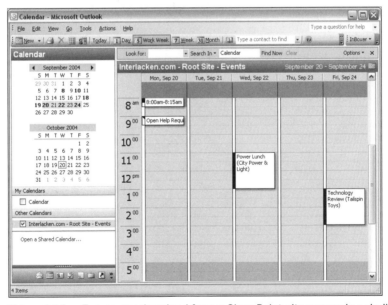

Figure 4-14. Events you download from a SharePoint site appear in a dedicated Outlook calendar like this.

Outlook doesn't merge the SharePoint events into your regular calendar; instead, it creates a new, read-only calendar containing only the SharePoint events. You can view multiple calendars at the same time by clicking their check boxes in the Calendar navigation pane. This isn't as convenient as viewing all the events on one calendar, but it does provide a way of taking a copy of your project events with you when you go off-net.

As with contacts, Outlook periodically checks the SharePoint Events list for updates and downloads any it finds.

Managing Alerts

If you receive very many SharePoint alerts, you'll probably want to filter them as they arrive in Outlook. Fortunately, this is very easy to do. Here's the procedure:

1 In Outlook, choose Mail from the Go menu, or click the Mail icon in the Navigation pane.

2 Choose Rules And Alerts from the Tools menu.

3 When the Rules And Alerts dialog box appears, click the Manage Alerts tab.

Outlook will display a list of alerts currently in effect, much as you see in Figure 4-15.

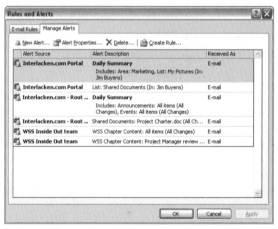

Figure 4-15. This Outlook dialog box displays all SharePoint alerts directed at the current user.

The Manage Alerts tab groups alerts in the same way that they arrive, that is, by SharePoint site and frequency. The listing Interlacken.com Root Site, Daily Summary, for example, includes all the alerts from a SharePoint site named Interlacken.com Root Site that arrive daily. This is because all those alerts would arrive in one message.

To manage these alert listings, use the toolbar buttons on the Rules And Alerts dialog box as follows:

- **New Alert** Click this button to create a new SharePoint alert. Outlook will display a New Alert dialog box listing two groups of SharePoint sites: those currently sending you alerts and those you've recently visited. To continue:

  1 Either select one of the listed sites or type the address of a new site in the Web Site Address box.

  2 Click Open. This will display a New Alert Web page from the site you chose.

  3 The New Alert page will list each list or library in the site. Select the one you want, click Next, and follow the prompts.

- **Alert Properties** Select any listed item and then click this button to display the Alert Properties dialog box shown below.

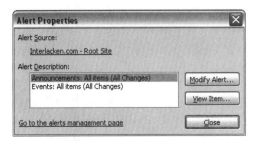

Here's how to use the links and buttons in this dialog box.

  - **Alert Source** Click this link to browse the home page of the SharePoint site that generates the alerts.

  - **Go To The Alerts Management Page** Click this link to browse the My Alerts On This Site page from the SharePoint site. From that page, you can add new alerts, reconfigure existing alerts, and delete alerts.

  - **Modify Alert** Select an item in the Alert Description list box, and then click this button to display the Edit Alert page for the alert you selected. From that page, you can reconfigure or delete the alert.

  - **View Item** Select an item in the Alert Description list box, and then click this button to display the document, list, or item to which that alert pertains.

- **Delete** Click this button to display a Delete Alerts dialog box. Select the check box for each alert you want to delete, and then click OK.

- **Create Rule** Click this button to display the Create Rule dialog box shown in Figure 4-16. Here you can specify whether Outlook will display a visual alert when the message arrives, whether Outlook will play a sound, and whether Outlook should file the message in a special folder. To configure more complex rules, click the Advanced button.

Chapter 4

115

Figure 4-16. Clicking the Create Rule button in Figure 4-15 displays this dialog box, where you can create rules for filing alerts.

Sending Shared Attachments

In many ways, attaching a file to an e-mail message is like starting a game of telephone tag. Consider:

- You send the file.
- The recipient sends it back with changes and a slightly different filename.
- You resend the file with additional changes and yet another filename.
- The recipient makes even more changes and again renames the file.

And so it goes. The problem is even worse if three, four, or twenty people are updating content and changing filenames.

To avoid this, you might choose to send a *shared attachment*. With this approach you would:

1 Compose the message and specify the attached file as usual.

2 Click the Attachment Options button in the Message window.

3 When the Attachment Options task pane appears, click Shared Attachments.

4 In the Create Document Workspace At drop-down list, select the parent site of the new document workspace, or select (Type New URL) and then type in the URL of a SharePoint site. Figure 4-17 shows this selection in progress.

5 Click Send.

Chapter 4

When you send a message with a new shared attachment, Outlook creates a new SharePoint document workspace whose URL is the parent you specified in step 4 plus the filename base of the file you attached. Windows SharePoint Services will consider you the owner of this site, but all other permissions will default to those of the parent SharePoint site. If any recipients of your message need additional privileges to access the document workspace, it's your job to grant those permissions manually.

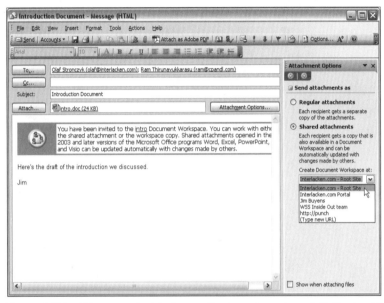

Figure 4-17. When you designate an attachment as shared, Outlook adds it to a SharePoint site and mails only a pointer to that site.

For more information about managing permissions for SharePoint site members, refer to Chapter 17, "Administering Your SharePoint Site."

Meeting Workspaces

When you propose a meeting in Outlook, you can simultaneously create a SharePoint meeting workspace. This is a SharePoint site equipped specifically to organize, prepare, conduct, record, and follow-up from a meeting. As shown in Table 4-1, there are five kinds of meeting workspaces, each with different features.

Table 4-1. Types of Meeting Workspaces

Site Feature	Meeting Workspace Type				
	Basic	Blank	Decision	Social	Multipage
Objectives List	●		●		●
Attendees List	●		●		●
Agenda List	●		●		●
Document Library	●		●		
Tasks List			●		
Decisions List			●		
2 Blank Pages					●
Directions				●	
Image/Logo				●	
Things to bring				●	
Discussions				●	
Picture Library				●	

To schedule a meeting and create a meeting workspace simultaneously, proceed as follows.

1 In Outlook, choose New from the File menu, and then choose Meeting Request.

2 Specify the attendees, subject, location, time, and other details in the usual way.

3 Click the Meeting Workspace button. The Outlook Meeting window should then resemble Figure 4-18.

4 The Create A Workspace section of the Meeting Workspace task pane shows the options currently in effect. If these are what you want, skip the rest of this step and jump ahead to step 5.

If one or more settings are incorrect, click the Change Settings link. This will make the Meeting Workspace task pane look like the one at left in Figure 4-19. If necessary, change the workspace location, spoken language, or type.

Alternatively, click the Link To An Existing Workspace option and choose one of the locations listed. As choices, the list box will include all SharePoint sites located just subordinate to the site under the Select A Location heading.

When you're done making changes, click OK. This returns the task pane to its normal state, shown in Figure 4-18

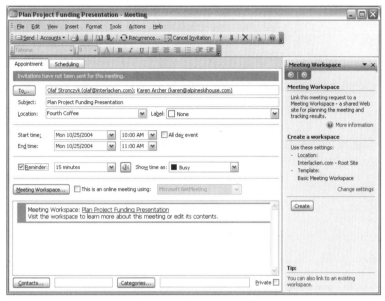

Figure 4-18. When you create a meeting in Outlook, the Meeting Workspace task pane can create a SharePoint workspace based on the same information.

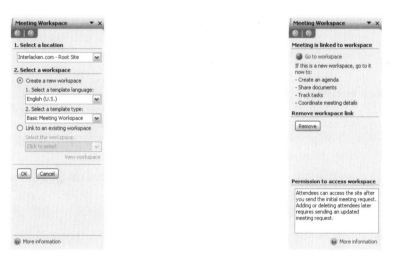

Figure 4-19. These two views of the Meeting Workspace task pane appear before and after you create the workspace, respectively.

5 Click the Create button in the Meeting Workspace task pane. When Outlook finishes creating the workspace, the task pane will appear as shown at right in Figure 4-19.

Figure 4-20 shows the home page of a typical basic meeting workspace. A Site Settings link in the top navigation bar is a notable omission, but you can modify permissions and other settings by clicking the Modify This Workspace link and choosing Site Settings from the drop-down menu.

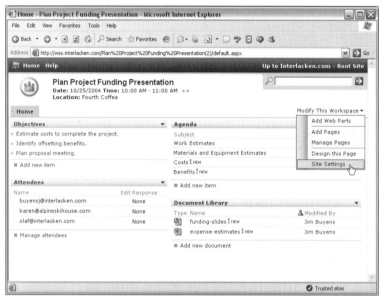

Figure 4-20. This is the home page for a SharePoint Meeting Workspace site.

Creating and Using Lists in Excel

Microsoft Excel 2003 is fully capable of opening and saving files in a SharePoint library. That is, it fully supports the Shared Workspace task pane and the enhanced Open and Save As dialog boxes that earlier sections in this chapter explained.

You can directly access SharePoint libraries from other file operations as well. This includes Insert Picture, Insert File, and so forth. In addition, you can link to cells in other worksheets that reside in a SharePoint library. To try this:

1   Open two worksheets, at least one of which resides in a SharePoint library.

2   Select a cell in the SharePoint worksheet, and then choose Copy from the Edit menu.

3   Select a cell in the second worksheet, and then choose Paste Special from the Edit menu.

4   When the Paste Special dialog box appears, click the Paste Link button.

In addition, Excel 2003 can designate a block of cells as a *list*. The Excel list then behaves much like a SharePoint list, and in fact you can link the two lists together so that changes in one appear automatically in the other. There are two ways of setting up such a relationship: you can either start in Excel or start while browsing your SharePoint site.

Setting Up Linked Lists from Excel

Here's the procedure for designating a range of cells as an Excel list, and then creating a linked copy in a SharePoint site.

1 Open a worksheet in Excel and select the block of cells that contains the data you want to treat as a list. If possible, include a row of column headings as well.

2 Choose List from the Data menu, and then choose Create List.

3 The area you selected will now appear as shown in Figure 4-21. You can sort, filter, and summarize the Excel list in much the same way as you can sort, filter, and summarize lists in a SharePoint site. If the List toolbar doesn't appear, choose Toolbars from the View menu, and then choose List.

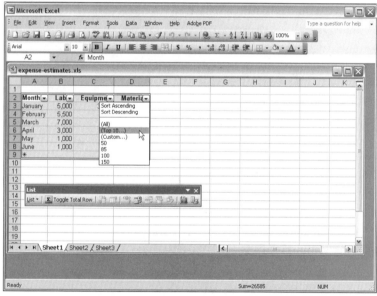

Figure 4-21. In Excel 2003, you can create lists that behave very much like SharePoint lists.

4 With the Excel list still selected, choose List from the Data menu, and then choose Publish List.

5 When the Publish List to SharePoint Site wizard appears, shown at left in Figure 4-22, fill in these fields:

■ **Address** Enter the URL of the SharePoint site that will contain the new list.

■ **Link To The New SharePoint List** Select this check box if you want the Excel list and the new SharePoint list to remain linked (that is, if you want changes in one to appear automatically in the other). To simply copy the data into the SharePoint and not synchronize future changes, clear the check box.

- **Name**   Give the SharePoint list a name.
- **Description**   Enter any text you like that describes the list.

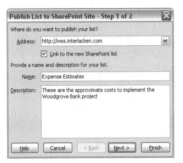

Figure 4-22.   This two-step wizard publishes an Excel list into a SharePoint site. If you wish, Excel will keep the two lists synchronized.

6   Click Next to display step 2 of the Publish List To SharePoint Site wizard, which appears at right in Figure 4-22. Then, examine the data types assigned to each field. Excel guesses these data types based on the data values in each column.

If any of these data types is incorrect (if, for example, the data type is Text but you know the field should be Number), then click Cancel and make sure all the data values in the problem column are correct. Then, restart at step 2.

If all the data types are correct, click Finish. When Excel finishes creating the SharePoint list, it displays a message box like the one below.

If you click the link in this message box, the new SharePoint list appears in your browser as shown in Figure 4-23.

To verify that the lists are linked, try these actions:

- Change a value on the Web page, switch to Excel, and click the Synchronize List button on the List toolbar.
- Change a value in Excel, switch to the Web page, and click the Refresh Data toolbar button.

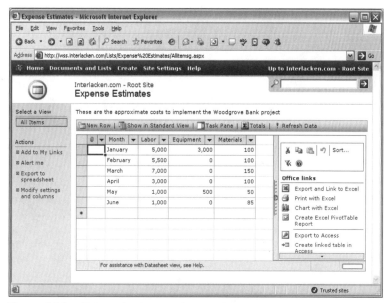

Figure 4-23.   This is the SharePoint list that corresponds to the Excel list in Figure 4-21.

Setting Up Linked Lists from a SharePoint Site

If your data already resides in a SharePoint list and you want it to appear in an Excel worksheet, proceed as follows.

1   Display the SharePoint list in your browser.

2   Under Actions, click the Export To Spreadsheet link. (Alternatively, click Edit In Datasheet, Task Pane, and Export And Link To Excel.)

3   If you receive a download prompt with the choices Open, Save, or Cancel, click Open.

4   If you receive an Opening Query dialog box asking whether to open the query, click Open.

5   When the Import Data dialog box shown at left in Figure 4-24 appears, choose where you want the Excel list to appear.

- **Existing Worksheet**   Select this choice if you want the list to appear in the current worksheet.

- **New Worksheet**   Select this choice if you want the list to appear in a new worksheet within the current workbook (that is, within the current .xls file).

- **New Workbook**   Select this choice if you want the list to appear in a new, blank workbook.

Chapter 4

123

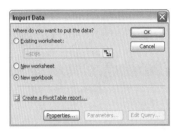

Figure 4-24. When you export a SharePoint list to Excel, the dialog box on the left prompts for the Excel location. The dialog box on the right controls additional properties.

6 To specify additional options, click the Properties button. This displays the External Data Range Properties dialog box shown at right in Figure 4-24. Change the options you want, and then click OK.

7 Click the OK button in the Import Data dialog box. This will create an Excel list, much like the one shown previously in Figure 4-21.

Creating and Using Lists in Access

SharePoint lists and Microsoft Access database tables are so alike in structure that exchanging data between them is very easy. There are just a few simple terms you need to understand first.

● The words *export* and *import* refer to *copy* operations. They result in two physical copies of the data, which you can then change independently.

● The word *link* refers to a second pathway for accessing the same physical data. So, for example, if you link an Access table to a SharePoint list and then update the Access table, members browsing the SharePoint site see the change immediately.

● In a SharePoint list, a *lookup column* is one whose only valid values are those in another list. Suppose, for example that:

■ You have a SharePoint list named Departments, and it contains a column named Dept Num.

■ You create another SharePoint list named Employees.

■ Within the Employees list, you define a lookup column named Empl Dept, and specify that this column get its value from the Department list's Dept Num column.

With this lookup column in place, the SharePoint site will prevent any addition of or change to any Employee record unless its Empl Dept value matches a Dept Num value in the Department list. (Access calls this a Relationship. Database experts call it a foreign key constraint.)

Lists that use lookup columns don't actually store the values of those columns in each record. Instead, they store the ID of the corresponding row in the lookup table. So, for example, the Employees table wouldn't contain a department number like 123. Instead; it would contain the ID of the Departments record for 123.

- A SharePoint *list* is the full representation of the data. It includes all the columns (in the order you defined them), and all the data values, in the natural, default sequence.

  A *view* is an alternate representation of a list. It may not contain all the columns; the columns may be in a different order; the rows may be in a different order, and the rows may be filtered to include or exclude certain data values. A SharePoint view is similar to an Access query.

That said, here's the procedure for accessing a SharePoint list or view from Access.

1 Start Access and open a new or existing database.

2 If you want to import a copy of the SharePoint list or view, choose Get External Data from the File menu, and then choose Import.

   To establish a link to the SharePoint list or view, choose Get External Data from the File menu, and then choose Link Tables.

3 When the Import or Link dialog box appears, select Windows SharePoint Services in the Files Of Type drop-down list. This opens the Link To Windows SharePoint Services Wizard.

4 On the Select A Site wizard page shown in Figure 4-25, specify the SharePoint site where the list or view resides. If this URL doesn't appear in the drop-down list, type it in.

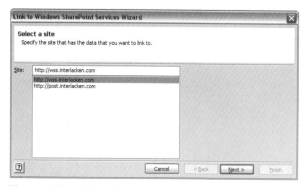

Figure 4-25. This wizard page prompts for the URL of a SharePoint site that contains data you want to process in Access.

125

5 Click Next to display the Select Lists wizard page shown in Figure 4-26. There are two ways to use this page:

- If you want to import or link to one or more lists, select Link To One Or More Lists, and then select as many lists as you want. To select more than one list, press Ctrl and click the ones you want.

- If you want to import or link to one or more views of the same list, select Link To One Or More Views Of A List and then select the list that contains those views.

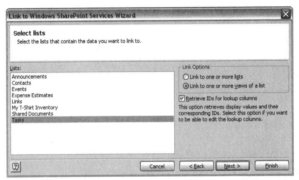

Figure 4-26. On this wizard page, specify whether you want data from SharePoint lists or SharePoint views. Then, in either case, select the list or lists providing the data.

6 By default, the Retrieve IDs For Lookup Columns check box should be selected. This is almost always the best choice, because then Access can modify the value of any lookup columns the view or list contains.

If you clear this check box, Access can't maintain the lookup relationship. Therefore, any lookup columns will be read-only in Access.

When you're finished with this wizard page, click Next.

7 If the Select Views wizard page shown in Figure 4-27 appears, select the view or views you want to import or link. To select more than one view, press Ctrl and click the ones you want.

When you're finished with this wizard page, click Next.

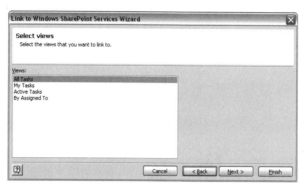

Figure 4-27. If this wizard page appears, select the views you want to process in Access.

8 If the Select Related Lists wizard page shown in Figure 4-28 appears, its Related Lists box will display all the lists that control lookup columns within the lists or views you selected. If for some reason you don't want to import or link to any of these tables, deselect them. However, the associated lookup columns will then be read-only.

When you're finished with this wizard page, click Next.

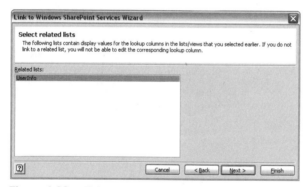

Figure 4-28. This wizard page offers to include SharePoint lists that have relationships to the lists you first selected.

9 When the Finish wizard page shown in Figure 4-29 appears, review the contents of the List/Views box. If these aren't the lists or views you want, click the Back button and correct your input. Otherwise, click Finish.

Chapter 4

Figure 4-29. The last page of the wizard summarizes the actions it will take.

Troubleshooting

Some list fields are read-only in Access

You may encounter situations where you select the Retrieve IDs For Lookup Columns check box on the Select Lists wizard page, and you select all the lists in the Select Related Lists wizard page, but some fields in the Access tables are nevertheless read-only. There are two possible reasons for this.

- One or more tables that appeared in the Select Related Lists wizard page themselves contain lookup fields. To correct this situation, link to those tables separately.

- Windows SharePoint Services may have sole control of the column. For example, you can't update the Created, Created By, Modified, or Modified By columns of a table linked to a SharePoint Tasks list. Windows SharePoint Services will update those columns automatically when you create or update records in the list.

Once you've linked to a SharePoint list, it will appear in Access as shown in Figure 4-30. The [...] links in the Edit column display the SharePoint list item in your browser. The arrows in front of the table icons indicate SharePoint links. Normal Access table icons identify lists you import.

Here's the procedure for exporting an Access table or query to a SharePoint list.

1 In Access, select the table or query you want to export.

2 Choose Export from the File menu.

3 When the Export dialog box appears, select Windows SharePoint Services in the Files Of Type drop-down list. This opens the Export To Windows SharePoint Services Wizard.

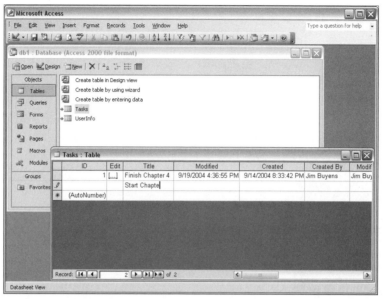

Figure 4-30. This is how linked SharePoint lists appear in Access.

4   On the Specify Site And List Information wizard page, fill in these fields:

■   **Site**   Specify the URL of the SharePoint site where you want the list or view to reside. If the URL doesn't appear in the drop-down list, type it in.

■   **List Name**   Review the proposed name for the new SharePoint list, and correct it if necessary. This name must not already exist in the SharePoint site you selected. The default name is the Access table name.

■   **Description**   Review the proposed description and correct it if necessary. By default, this will be the Access table description.

■   **Open The List When Finished**   By default, this check box will be selected. When the export process completes, the new list will therefore appear in your browser. To bypass this display, clear the check box.

5   Click Finish to create the SharePoint list.

An Export always *copies* the data from Access to a new SharePoint list. You can't upload the data and link to it in one operation. If you want the one and only copy of your data to reside in a SharePoint site:

1   Export the data to a new SharePoint list.

2   Delete or rename the original Access table.

3   Link the original Access table name to the new SharePoint list.

The SharePoint browser interface also provides commands for exchanging list data with Access. To locate these commands, display the SharePoint list in your browser, and then click Edit In Datasheet and Task Pane. This produces a display like the one shown previously in

129

Figure 4-23. The first two Access commands appear in the bottom right corner. In fact, three commands are available:

- **Export To Access**   Copies the current view into Access, just as if you'd imported the view in Access with all defaults.

- **Create Linked Table In Access**   Creates an Access link to the current view with all defaults.

- **Report With Access**   Copies the current view into Access (the same as Export To Access) and then creates an Access report that displays the data.

In each case, the Web page command provides less flexibility and control than the corresponding commands in Access. However, if the Web page commands meet your needs and seem more convenient, don't hesitate to use them.

Using SharePoint with InfoPath

The Microsoft Office System 2003 includes a new program called InfoPath, designed primarily for information gathering. Basically, InfoPath is a Windows desktop program that displays fill-in forms, captures form input, and saves the resulting data. Figure 4-31 shows InfoPath displaying a typical form.

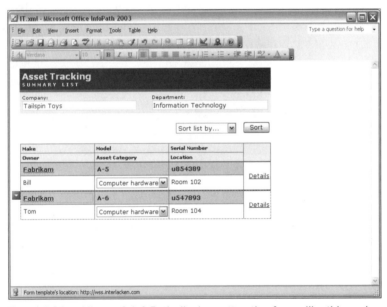

Figure 4-31.   Microsoft InfoPath displays attractive forms like this and saves the submitted data as XML.

Unlike more traditional forms programs, InfoPath uses XML for both the form templates and the saved form data. It also supports many kinds of network and database connectivity.

Windows SharePoint Services supports InfoPath with a special type of document library called, logically enough, a *form library*. Figure 4-32 shows a simple form library named Asset Forms. This library collects submissions from the Asset Tracking form shown in the previous figure.

Figure 4-32. The list view for a SharePoint form library shows one record for each submitted form. The view can include submitted form data.

The default document template for a form library is an InfoPath template. When a team member displays the library and clicks the Fill Out This Form button, the SharePoint site downloads the template and the team member's PC starts InfoPath. When the team member saves the form, the default location is the form library.

Each record in the form library represents a different XML file—a different form submission. Knowing the format of the submitted XML files (which it gleans from the form template), the form library can extract the content of submitted form fields and display it as list columns. From there, you can display the list data in additional SharePoint views, export or link it to Excel or Access, or process it as raw XML.

You can create a new form library through the SharePoint browser interface or directly in InfoPath. To create a new form library using a browser, proceed as follows.

1 Open the SharePoint site that will host the form library.

2 Click the Create link on the top navigation bar and then, under document libraries, choose Form Library.

3   When the New Form Library page appears, fill in the following fields.

■ **Name**   Give the form library a one-line name.

■ **Description**   Enter a few sentences describing the library.

■ **Display This Form Library On The Quick Launch Bar?**   Choose Yes or No.

■ **Create A Version Each Time You Edit A File In This Form Library?**   Choose Yes or No.

■ **Form Template**   Select a form template. Unless your administrator has provided more choices, the only option will be Blank Form.

4   Click Create to create the form library.

5   When the view page for the new form library appears, click Modify Settings And Columns.

6   Under General Settings, Template, click the Edit Template link to download the form template to InfoPath for editing.

In many cases, the Blank Form template isn't the best starting point for a new form. When you start from nothing, you have to create everything. As a result, you might prefer to start from another form within your company or one of the sample forms that come with InfoPath. Typically, you would design such a form offline, and then, when the design is complete, you would create the form library directly within InfoPath.

Here, therefore, is the procedure for creating a SharePoint form library directly within InfoPath.

1   In InfoPath, open your form, choose Design A Form from the File menu, and then design the form.

Designing InfoPath forms is a relatively complex task involving both visual and technical issues. If this task falls to you, consider purchasing *Introducing Microsoft Office InfoPath 2003* from Microsoft Press.

2   Choose Save As from the File menu and then, when the Microsoft Office InfoPath dialog box shown below appears, click Publish.

3   When the Publishing Wizard appears, click Next to advance past the welcome page.

4   When the second page of the wizard prompts, "Where do you want to publish this form?" select To A SharePoint Form Library and then click Next.

5   When the third page of the wizard appears, choose one of these options:

■ Create A New Form Library (Recommended).

■ Modify An Existing Form Library.

6 The fourth page will prompt, "Enter The Location Of Your SharePoint Site." Enter the URL, and then click Next.

7 When the fifth page appears, enter a one-line name and a one-paragraph description of the new form library, and then click Next.

8 The next page of the wizard appears at left in Figure 4-33. It shows which form fields InfoPath proposes to make visible as columns when the SharePoint site displays the form library.

- To add a field, click Add and then make a selection in the resulting Select A Field Or Group dialog box shown at right in Figure 4-33. If the field is repeating (such as line item data in an invoice), you'll also need to select a function to use for aggregating it, such as first, last, sum, average, min, max, or count. This is because the SharePoint form library listing can display only one value for each field on a form.

- To remove a field, click the Remove button.

- To change a field, click the Modify button and then use the Select A Field Or Group dialog box just as you would for an addition.

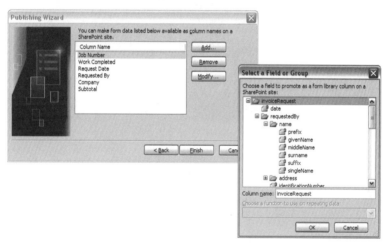

Figure 4-33. This wizard page from InfoPath specifies which form fields will be available as SharePoint form library columns.

9 Click Finish to create the form library.

If you display the contents of a form library (or if you look back to Figure 4-32), you'll notice that the Select A View section include a Merge Forms command. This command displays a view of the form library that has a check box for each form and a Merge Forms toolbar button.

If you select one or more of these check boxes and click the Merge Forms button, the SharePoint site will download all the data from those forms, and your PC will load the data into InfoPath. This may be useful as a viewing and reporting mechanism.

Chapter 4

133

Working with Pictures in Picture Manager

Microsoft Office Picture Manager is a new utility program that comes with Office 2003 and, like all Office programs, it integrates nicely with Windows SharePoint services.

When you want to add several pictures to a SharePoint picture library, Picture Manager can save you the work of uploading each picture individually. Here's the procedure:

1 Display the SharePoint picture library in your browser.

2 Click the Add Picture button.

3 When the Add Picture Web page appears, click the Upload Multiple Files link.

4 When Picture Manager starts, locate and select all the pictures you want to upload. Figure 4-34 shows this operation in progress.

Figure 4-34. Microsoft Office Picture Manager can upload as many pictures to a SharePoint library as you want.

5 To add the pictures to your SharePoint picture library, click the Upload And Close button.

Picture Manager is also useful for performing simple edits on pictures in a SharePoint picture library. Here's the procedure.

1 Display the picture library in your browser.

2 Select the check boxes for one or more pictures.

3 Click the Edit Pictures toolbar button.

4   The SharePoint site will download a file that starts Picture Manager and instructs it to display the pictures you specified. Figure 4-35 shows the results.

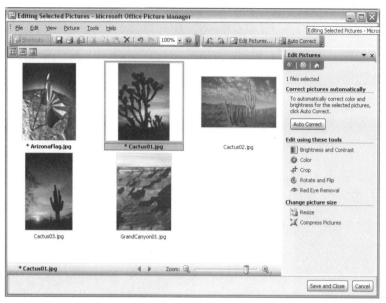

Figure 4-35.   Picture Manager can also download multiple pictures for editing.

5   To edit any displayed picture, select it and then click a tool in the Edit Pictures task pane.

6   To upload the edited pictures and close Picture Manager, click the Save And Close Button.

Supporting Project Web Access

Microsoft Project Server 2003 is a flexible platform that supports portfolio management, resource management, and collaboration capabilities for project planners and participants. Typically:

● Project managers use Project Professional 2003, a desktop program, to upload project plans.

● Project participants can use Project Web Access, a Windows SharePoint Services application, to check for assigned tasks, to report time and completion status, and to perform other tasks that aren't project planning.

Project Web Access is a custom SharePoint application unrelated to Team Sites.

Chapter 4

135

In Summary...

Every program in Office System 2003 has features that integrate its functions with those of Windows SharePoint Services. This demonstrates Microsoft's commitment not only to Office, but to SharePoint Products and Technologies as well.

The next chapter begins Part III, which explains how to create SharePoint sites and Web pages using only a browser.

Chapter 5

Creating SharePoint Sites and Pages

Within a Windows SharePoint Services server, a *site* is the basic unit for organizing content. Sites contain groups of pages what work closely together, as well as libraries and lists that store documents and other kinds of information. Sites are also the basic unit of language, security administration, disk space management, and visual appearance. Any change to those settings generally affects an entire site.

Fortunately, creating a SharePoint site is a very easy process. The previous chapter explained the convenience of creating Document Workspace and Meeting Workspace sites from within Microsoft Office System 2003 programs, and Chapter 7 will explain the power of creating SharePoint sites with Microsoft FrontPage 2003. Even so, the most common way of creating new SharePoint sites is through the browser interface, and that's the approach this chapter explains.

You can also create and modify conventional Web pages and Web Part Pages using only a browser. This doesn't match the power and flexibility you get with FrontPage, but it's always available, always handy, and it's adequate for many situations.

Planning a SharePoint Site Structure

As with any other Web server, a server running Windows SharePoint Services has a folder tree that organizes its content. On a SharePoint server, certain of these folders mark the beginning of a new SharePoint *site*.

A site, in this sense, is a group of Web pages that work closely together and that you can manage as a unit. Team Sites, document workspaces, and meeting workspaces are all examples of SharePoint sites. In most respects, any security settings you configure apply uniformly to all the pages in the site.

Windows SharePoint Services can accommodate thousands of SharePoint sites running on a single Web server, but it provides very little assistance in organizing and later finding those sites. This section, therefore, provides some guidance on how to organize the sites on a SharePoint server.

> **Note** The Areas and Topics features on a SharePoint Portal Server are quite useful for organizing thousands of Web sites, even if those sites reside at random or haphazard locations. However, not all organizations run SharePoint Portal Server, and even those that do will be better off with a well-organized collection of individual sites.

Planning SharePoint Sites

SharePoint servers typically contain a *lot* of sites. For starters, each department, product group, and employee in your organization will probably have a site. Within each of those sites, team members will create dozens more. These could be document workspaces, meeting workspaces, or specialized sites of any kind. With very little effort, you can end up with five or ten times as many sites as employees.

Having this many sites makes it imperative that you also have a way of organizing them. In most cases, this means having a logical, preplanned folder tree starting at the Web server's root. You might, for example, create folders named *depts*, *empls*, and *prods*, and then create all departmental sites, all employee sites, and all product sites within those folders.

Windows SharePoint Services has several features that help preserve and manage the site structure you or your server administrator have planned.

- You can have sites within sites. For example, within the */depts/marketing* site, you could have another site at */depts/marketing/sales.* Then:
  - The *sales* site would be a *subsite* of the */depts/marketing* site.
  - The */depts/marketing* site would be the *parent* of the *sales* site.
- To create a subsite, you must be an administrator of the parent site. An administrator, in this sense, isn't someone who controls the whole physical server, or even the virtual Web server. Each SharePoint site can have its own list of administrators.

  So, if you want someone to be capable of creating sites within */products/shovels*, make them an administrator of the */products/shovels* site. If you don't, don't.
- When you create a new site, you can initialize its permissions in either of two ways:
  - **Use Same Permissions As Parent Site**   The new subsite won't have its own set of permissions. Instead, it will *inherit* the permissions of its parent. If you later change the permissions of the parent, those changes will apply to the subsite as well. This is the default and most common choice.
  - **Use Unique Permissions**   Initially, the site will have only one member: the person who created it. That person will also be the site's first administrator, and will therefore be capable of adding additional members as required.

  The fact that most sites inherit the permissions of their parents makes security for a group of sites much easier to administer.

Planning Site Collections and Top-Level Sites

SharePoint *site collections* provide another facility for managing groups of sites with one command. A site collection begins with a so-called *top-level site* and includes every normal site that lies within the top-level site's folder tree.

Certain top-level site settings affect every site in the collection. This includes, for example:

- The gallery of Web Parts available to all sites in the collection
- The gallery of list templates available to all sites in the collection
- The gallery of site templates available to all sites in the collection
- The connection, if any, to a SharePoint Portal Server
- The maximum amount of disk space the collection may contain
- Cross-Site Groups, which are lists of members that any site in the collection can use when configuring security
- Top-level site deletion, which deletes all the sites in the collection

Planning Self-Service Site Creation

Normally, only the administrator of an entire SharePoint virtual server can create top-level sites, and therefore site collections. The administrator creates the top-level site and (usually) grants administrator privileges to a key team member. That member, in turn, authorizes the other team members who will use the top-level site and its site collection.

A server administrator can choose, however, to enable a feature called Self-Service Site Creation. With this feature enabled, any member with the Use Self-Service Site Creation right can create as many top-level sites as they want and, by default, all members (even Readers) have this right.

Managing Self-Service Site Creation

With Self-Service Site Creation activated, team members tend to create many spurious top-level sites. Cleaning up these spurious sites can be a lot of work, but Windows SharePoint Services has three features that often help.

- **Quota Templates**   Are predefined model settings for controlling the maximum amount of space a site collection can use. An server administrator can configure a virtual server so that all new top-level sites receive disk quotas based on a default quota template.
- **Site Collection Use Confirmation and Auto-Deletion**   Sends periodic warning messages to owners of any site collection that has no activity for a given period. To keep the site online, the owner must reply to one of these messages. If the owner fails to reply to, say, four messages in a row, Windows SharePoint Services will automatically delete the collection.

Chapter 5

● **Secondary Contacts**   Require that when someone creates a new top-level site, they provide the user account and e-mail address of a second person who will also administer the collection. This is primarily so the two owners can share the work and function in each other's absence, but it also creates visibility for anyone who tries to overcome low default disk quotas by creating multiple top-level sites.

For more information on these features, refer to Chapter 17, "Administering Your SharePoint Site."

A common scenario for Self-Service Site Creation involves employees creating their own personal sites. In such a case, it's often useful to dedicate a separate virtual server for this purpose. That way, you can enable Self-Service Site Creation, default quota templates, and Site Collection Use Confirmation. and Auto-Deletion for the personal sites and use different settings for departmental, product, and project sites (which would be on a different virtual server).

Planning Managed Paths

Regardless of who creates a top-level site, the top-level site's parent folder must be a SharePoint *managed path* with both the *include* and *wildcard* options in effect. This, of course, begs the question, "What's a managed path?"

As previous chapters have mentioned, all the files and folders that make up a SharePoint site reside not in the Web server's file system, but in a SQL Server or WMSDE database. Even so, a SharePoint server accepts normal-looking URLs. When a team member requests a Web page, a picture, a library document, or any other sort of file, Windows SharePoint Services:

● "Captures" the request.

● Translates the URL to a database location.

● Retrieves the database content at that location.

● Runs any executable content, such as Web Parts and Web Part Pages.

● Sends the content to the team member.

Note that the SharePoint server never matches the URL path against the server's file system. Even though files and folders seem to exist when you browse the SharePoint site, you won't find them in the Web server's file system. They're only in the database.

Sometimes, however, you might prefer that certain folder trees reside in the server's file system, and otherwise behave like normal Web sites. To accommodate such needs, Windows SharePoint Services provides *managed paths*.

A *managed path* is a folder location where Windows SharePoint Services either starts to manage or ceases to manage a Web server's folder tree: that is, where it starts or stops redirecting Web requests into the SharePoint content database. Figure 5-1 shows the page a server administrator uses to set up a managed path.

Creating SharePoint Sites and Pages

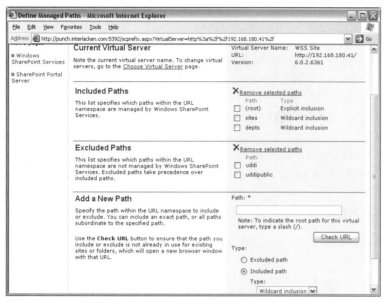

Figure 5-1. This is the page a server administrator uses to create and modify managed paths.

On this page:

- **An Excluded Path**   Specifies a location where Windows SharePoint Services *stops* managing folders and files. This means any files and folder within that location:

  - Would reside in the Web server's normal file system.

  - Wouldn't have the usual SharePoint capabilities and restrictions. For example, ASP and conventional ASP.NET pages could run.

- **An Included Path**   Specifies a location where Windows SharePoint Services *starts* to manage folders and files. If an administrator configured */depts* as a managed include path, any files and folder within that location:

  - Would reside within the SharePoint content database.

  - Would have SharePoint capabilities and restrictions. SharePoint sites could reside there, for example, but ASP and ASP.NET pages wouldn't run.

In addition, an included managed path can be *wildcard* or *explicit*.

- **Wildcard Inclusion**   Means that SharePoint manages all paths subordinate to the specified path.

- **Explicit Inclusion**   Means that SharePoint manages only the specific path you specify.

If you look closely at the Included Paths section of Figure 5-1, you'll see that the *sites* and *depts* folders are both managed paths, even though they reside within the root path (which is always included). Windows SharePoint Services would manage these paths anyway, but declaring them as managed paths makes it possible to create top-level sites there.

Microsoft Windows SharePoint Services Inside Out

A new SharePoint server has two managed paths: the root path and */sites/*. A server administrator can delete the */sites/* managed path and create others based on need. Keep in mind, however, that Windows SharePoint Services needs to check every incoming request against the list of managed paths. Setting up too many managed paths can lead to a noticeable loss of performance.

Creating a New SharePoint Site

Earlier chapters have explained how Microsoft Office programs can create certain kinds of sites, such as document workspaces and meeting workspaces. This section explains the more general procedure for using a browser to create SharePoint sites of any kind.

Displaying the New SharePoint Site Page

The first step in creating a new SharePoint site is to display the New SharePoint Site page. There are several ways of doing this, and here's the first:

1 Open the existing SharePoint site that will be the new site's parent.

2 Choose Create on the parent site's top navigation bar.

3 Scroll to the bottom of the Create page as shown in Figure 5-2. Then, under Web Pages, click the Sites And Workspaces link. This will display the New SharePoint Site page that the next section describes.

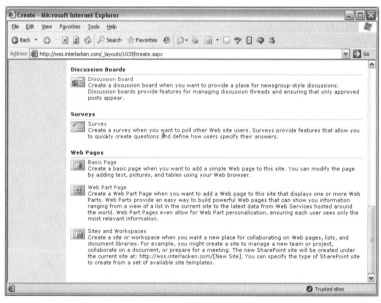

Figure 5-2. To create a new site, click the Create link on any page in its parent, and then click the Sites And Workspaces link shown here.

Creating SharePoint Sites and Pages

If you prefer, you can also use the site's administration pages to display the New SharePoint Site page. Here's that procedure.

1 Open the existing SharePoint site that will be the new site's parent.

2 Click the Site Settings link in the top navigation bar of any page.

3 On the Site Settings page, under Administration, click Manage Sites And Workspaces. This displays the Manage Sites And Workspaces page shown in Figure 5-3.

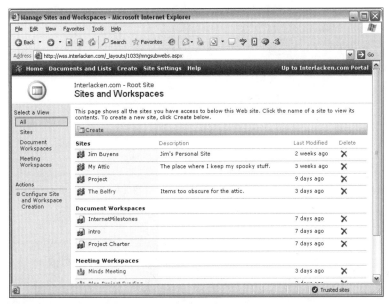

Figure 5-3. This page displays a list of all sites and workspaces located just below the current site, and which you have permission to access.

4 Click the Create button in the Sites And Workspaces toolbar. This will display the New SharePoint Site page that the next section describes.

Completing the New SharePoint Site Page

The previous section explained how to display the New SharePoint Site page shown in Figure 5-4. This is the page that actually creates the new site.

Microsoft Windows SharePoint Services Inside Out

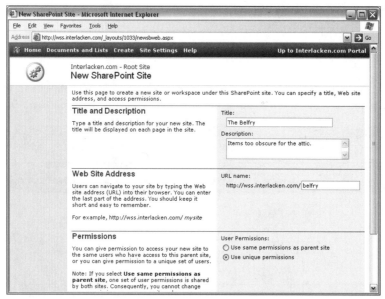

Figure 5-4. This Web page creates a new SharePoint site.

When this page appears, fill in these fields.

- **Title**   Enter the name of the site, as you want it to appear at the top of each page.

- **Description**   Briefly explain the site's intended use or purpose. This field is optional.

- **URL Name**   Enter the folder name that will appear in the site's URL. SharePoint will provide the server name and the parent path. If you want a different parent path, return to the previous section and open the parent site you want.

- **Use Same Permissions As Parent Site**   Select this option if you want the new site to admit all the same team members (and grant them all the same permission) as the parent site.

- **Use Unique Permissions**   Select this option if you want the new site to have different permissions from the parent site. Initially, you'll be the only team member, and you'll be an administrator.

Once these entries are complete , click the Create button. This will create the site and display the Template Selection page. For help in working with that page, refer to the section titled "Selecting a Site Template" later in this chapter.

Creating a New Top-Level Site

You can create a new SharePoint top-level site in either of two ways: using Self-Service Site Creation or using privileges as a server administrator. The next two sections explain these methods.

Creating a Top-Level Site via Self-Service Site Creation

If your SharePoint site permits Self-Service Site Creation, you can create your own top-level site by proceeding as follows.

1 Click the link in the Self-Service Site Creation announcement that appears on the root site's home page. Figure 5-5 illustrates this announcement and its link.

   If this announcement is no longer visible, get the URL from your administrator, or try *http://<servername>/_layouts/1033/scsignup.aspx,* where *<servername>* is the name of your server and 1033 is its locale id. (1033, for example, signifies US English.)

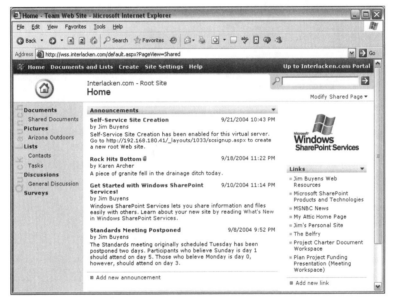

Figure 5-5. When a server administrator enables Self-Service Site Creation, an announcement like the first one shown here appears in the root site.

2 When the New SharePoint Site page shown in Figure 5-6 appears, fill in the fields as follows.

   ■ **Title** Type one line of text. This will be the site name that appears on the new top-level site's home page.

   ■ **Description** Type a few sentences that describe the new top-level site's function or purpose. This will also appear on the home page.

   ■ **URL Name** Choose a managed path from the drop-down list, and then type the folder name within that path where you want the new top-level site to reside.

   ■ **E-mail Address** Type your e-mail address.

   ■ **Secondary Owner** If this section of the form appears, type the username and e-mail address of the secondary owner of the new Web site collection.

Microsoft Windows SharePoint Services Inside Out

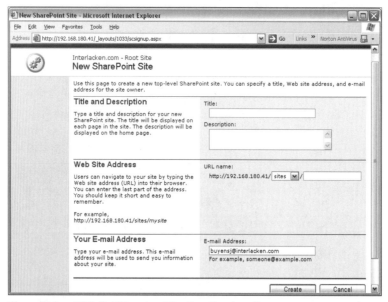

Figure 5-6. With Self-Service Site Creation in effect, any team member can create a top-level site by using this page.

3 Click Create to create the new site.

4 When the Template Selection page appears, jump forward to the section titled "Selecting a Site Template" later in this chapter.

For a list of regional and language settings, including locale IDs, browse *http://www.microsoft.com/resources/documentation/wss/2/all/adminguide/en-us/stsk09.mspx.*

Creating a Top-Level Site as an Administrator

If you're a server administrator, use the following procedure for creating a new top-level site.

1 Display the Windows SharePoint Services Central Administration page. This is usually at *http://<servername>:<port>/default.aspx,* where *<servername>* points to the server computer's first IP address and *<port>* is a random value chosen at installation time.

If you don't know this port number, you can find it by viewing the properties of the SharePoint Central Administration site in IIS Manager on the server computer.

2 Under Virtual Server Configuration, click the Create A Top-Level Web Site link.

3 When the Virtual Server List page appears, click the name of the virtual server where you want the new top-level site to reside.

Creating SharePoint Sites and Pages

4 When the Create Top-Level Web Site page shown in Figure 5-7 appears, specify these values:

- **Web Site Address** Click Create Site Under This URL, and then choose a folder path and type a folder name. Or, click Create Site At This URL, and then choose a location from the drop-down list.

- **Site Collection Owner** Type the username and e-mail address of the primary owner of the Web site collection that will start at the new top-level site.

- **Secondary Owner** If the new Web site collection will have a secondary owner, type that person's username and e-mail address.

- **Quota Template** Select a quota template from the drop-down list. This places a limit on the amount of disk space the new site collection can use.

- **Site Language** Select the spoken language in which page within the new collection will appear. This must be a language already installed on the server.

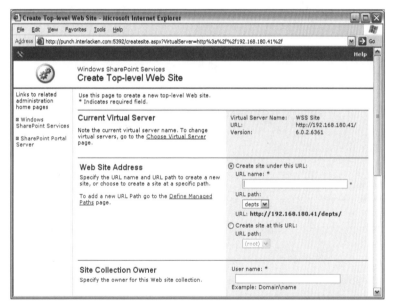

Figure 5-7. This is the top half of the page a server administrator uses to create a new top-level site.

5 Click OK to create the top-level site.

6 When the Top-Level Site Successfully Created page appears, either:

- Click the link provided for the new top-level site, and then choose a template as the next section directs.

- Notify the primary and secondary site owners that the site exists, and send them the URL. The first time one of them browses the new URL, that person can choose a template, as the next section explains.

> For information about creating and managing quota templates, refer to "Managing Quotas and Locks" in Chapter 15, "Administering a SharePoint Server."

Selecting a Site Template

Initially, every new site displays the Template Selection page shown in Figure 5-8. This page customizes the new site's Web pages and capabilities.

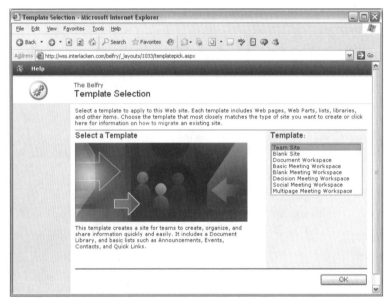

Figure 5-8.   This is the first page to appear for any new SharePoint site. Each template populates the site with a different set of the Web pages and features.

When this Web page appears, you have two choices:

- Select the template you want and click the OK button. If you need help in selecting a template, select each choice in turn and read the description that appears below the large graphic.
- Close your browser, do any other work you need to do, and then get advice from your co-workers or administrator. When you browse the new site again, the Template Selection page will reappear. Select the template you want and click OK.

> **Tip**   Until you select a template, Template Selection is the only page a new SharePoint site will display.

Applying a Theme

Once a site exists, anyone with the Apply Themes And Borders right can customize its appearance by applying a new theme. By default, members of the Administrator and Web Designer groups have this right.

A SharePoint theme is a predesigned combination of colors, fonts, and background pictures. To choose a theme:

1 Display the site whose appearance you want to modify.

2 If the site is a meeting workspace, open the Modify This Workspace drop-down list and choose Site Settings.

   For any other type of site, click Site Settings in the navigation bar at the top of the page.

3 When the Site Settings Web page appears, under Customization, click Apply Theme To Site.

4 When the Apply Theme Web page shown in Figure 5-9 appears, use the list box to select the theme you want, and then click Apply.

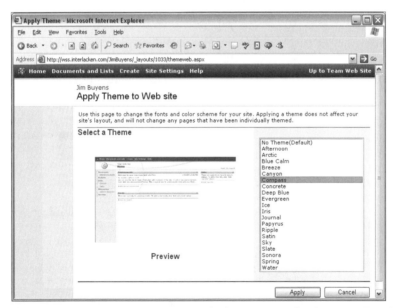

Figure 5-9. This page selects a graphical appearance for the pages in a SharePoint site.

Inside Out

Be cautious in choosing themes

Many of the themes that come with Windows SharePoint Services have dark backgrounds that make pages hard to read, or hyperlink colors that provide poor contrast when the mouse is over the link. Be sure to check these aspects of any theme you select.

For information about modifying themes or creating new ones, refer to "Creating and Customizing Frontpage Themes" in Chapter 8, "Creating and Formatting Web Part Pages."

Navigating Among SharePoint Sites

Despite its capability to host Web sites by the thousands, Windows SharePoint Services offers surprisingly few features that help team members navigate among sites. Principally:

- An Up To *<parent site name>* link appears in the top navigation bar of every site in a collection, except for the top-level site itself. This links to the home page of the current site's parent.
- If a top-level site is configured with the address of a portal site, an Up To *<portal site name>* link appears in the top navigation bar of each page.

The remaining topics in this section describe some more indirect ways of building links among SharePoint sites. In addition, you may wish to consider these choices, which are outside the Windows SharePoint Services browser interface.

- Adding SharePoint sites to an area on a SharePoint Portal Server. The section titled "Managing Areas" in Chapter 2 briefly explained this concept.
- Using FrontPage 2003 to add links directly to the Web pages in the SharePoint site. For more information on this approach, refer to Chapter 9, "Creating and Modifying Basic Site Features."

Finding Links on the Sites And Workspaces Page

The Sites And Workspaces page shown previously in Figure 5-3 displays a list of subsites that are directly subordinate to the current site, and that the current team member has permission to access. However, this is two clicks away from the home page (Site Settings, Manage Sites And Workspaces), and neither of those clicks is intuitive for general browsing.

Finding Links on the View Site Hierarchy Page

The page shown in Figure 5-10 displays a clickable list of all the sites in the current collection. However, this page is available only to top-level site administrators.

Creating SharePoint Sites and Pages

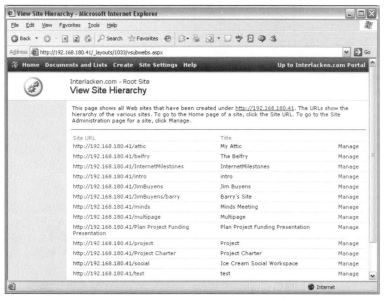

Figure 5-10. Using this page, a top-level site administrator can view the contents of an entire site collection. In addition, the administrator can browse or manage any listed site.

To display this page:

1 Click Site Settings in the top navigation bar of any page in the collection.

2 On the Site Settings page, under Administration, click Go To Site Administration.

3 If the current site isn't the top-level site, then under Site Collection Administration, click Go To Top-Level Site Administration.

4 On the Top-Level Site Administration page, under Site Collection Administration, click View Site Hierarchy.

Unfortunately, this is hardly the kind of procedure you'd want to use for everyday site navigation. And again, you must be a top-level site administrator to use it.

Displaying a List of Top-Level Sites

The method for displaying all the top-level sites on a virtual server is among the most obscure of all. If, and only if, you're a server administrator, proceed as follows.

1 Open a command window on a server running Windows SharePoint Services.

2 Change to the directory that contains the stsadm.exe program. By default, this is *C:\Program Files\Common Files\Microsoft Shared\web server extensions\60\BIN*

3 Run the following command, where *<ip address>* is the IP Address of the virtual server you want to know about.

```
stsadm -o enumsites -url http://<ip address>
```

Chapter 5

Here's a sample command and results, slightly formatted with extra line breaks for easy reading:

```
stsadm -o enumsites -url http://192.168.180.41

<Sites Count="5">
  <Site Url=http://192.168.180.41
       Owner="INTERLACKEN\jim" />
  <Site Url=http://192.168.180.41/sites/buyensj
       Owner="INTERLACKEN\jim" />
  <Site Url=http://192.168.180.41/sites/ed
       Owner="INTERLACKEN\ed"
       SecondaryOwner="INTERLACKEN\jim" />
  <Site Url=http://192.168.180.41/sites/fieldsvc
       Owner="INTERLACKEN\jim"
       SecondaryOwner="INTERLACKEN\olaf" />
  <Site Url=http://192.168.180.41/sites/karen
       Owner="INTERLACKEN\karen" />
</Sites>
```

Configuring a Links Web Part

Any Web Part Page can display a Links Web Part configured with any links you want. This displays links to subsites, parent sites, the server home page, and so forth. If you wish, it can also display links to SharePoint sites you use frequently.

If the page where you want the list of links to appear doesn't already have a Links Web Part, proceed as follows:

1 Identify the Links list you want to use. This could be either:

- A Links list that a template created when it initialized your site.

- A new list that you create by clicking the Create command at the top of any page and then, in the Lists section of the Create Page, clicking Links.

2 Display the page where you want to add a Links Web Part.

3 Open the Modify This Page drop-down list and choose the view you want to modify.

- **Shared View** Applies to all team members who view the page and haven't selected Personal View. To modify this view of a site-level page, you must have the Add And Customize Pages right. By default, only members of the Administrator and Web Designer groups have this right.

- **Personal View** Is a page layout unique to each team member. Each member can create or modify their own personal view, but only if they have the Add/ Remove Private Web Parts right. By default, the Administrator, Web Designer, and Contributor groups have this right.

Creating SharePoint Sites and Pages

4   Open the Modify This Page drop-down list again , and choose Add Web Parts and Browse.

5   When the Add Web Parts task pane appears within the Web page, click Team Web Site Gallery and then, under Web Part List, click Links. Figure 5-11 shows this operation in progress.

If the Web Part List doesn't display the Links Web Part, scroll to the bottom of the task pane and click Next or Previous until it appears.

If you still can't find the Links Web Part, click the Create button in the top navigation bar and create a Links list.

Figure 5-11.   Here a team member is adding a Links Web Part to a Web Part Page.

6   Set the Add To drop-down list to the name of the Web Part Zone where you want the links to appear.

7   Click Add to incorporate the Web Part into the page layout.

Once the Links Web Part is visible, use the following procedure for populating it with links.

1   Click the Add New Link hyperlink in the Links Web Part.

2   When the Links: New Item page shown in Figure 5-12 appears, fill in these fields and then click Save And Close.

   ■   **URL**   Enter the complete URL of the target page, including the protocol and site name (for example, *http://www.example.com/sites/alejandro*).

Microsoft Windows SharePoint Services Inside Out

- **Description**   Enter a one-line description for the page. This will become the hyperlink text.

- **Notes**   Enter any additional information you want to remember about the link. The Links Web Part won't display this.

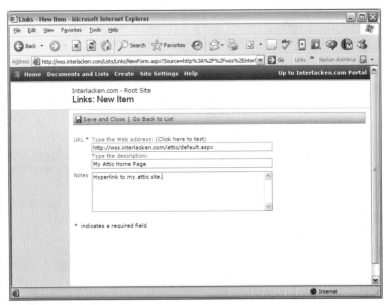

Figure 5-12.   This is the Web page for adding a new hyperlink to a Links list.

Using a Links Web Part requires only one click, not two or three or four like some of the other methods. However, it requires that you build the links manually, and remove them manually when they fall out of use. Also, this is an awkward way to manage hundreds of links, which the Web Part always lists in order of addition.

Using a Custom Web Part to Display Links

The Sites And Workspaces page shown in Figure 5-3 and the View Site Hierarchy page shown in Figure 5-10 prove that Windows SharePoint Services is well aware of the sites within a collection. Unfortunately, Microsoft provides no Web Part or other component that displays a convenient, clickable list of these sites. You can, however, create or purchase custom Web Parts that do this job. The Web Part shown in Figure 5-13, for example, displays links to:

- All subsites of the current site.
- The current site's home page
- Any sites between current site and the current collection's top-level site.
- The top-level site and the portal site (if any) to which it connects.
- The server's home page and the portal site (if any) to which it connects.

Creating SharePoint Sites and Pages

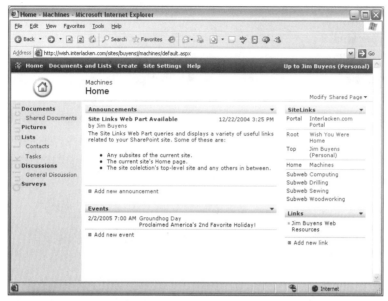

Figure 5-13. This custom Web Part displays links to site above and below the current site in the server's URL hierarchy.

The \WebParts\WssIso folder on the companion CD contains a Visual Studio .NET project that creates this Web Part and two others. The \WebParts\WssIso\debug\bin folder contains the compiled DLL. For more information about creating and installing such Web Parts, refer to Part VII of this book, "Developing Web Parts in Visual Studio.NET."

Commercial Web Parts of this type are also available. One of these is the ADVIS Site Navigator Web Part, which is available from *http://sharepoint.advis.ch*

You can search for additional components at Microsoft's SharePoint Products and Technologies Web Component Directory at *http://www.microsoft.com/sharepoint/downloads/ components/*.

Creating and Configuring Web Pages

Using nothing more than a browser, you can create and configure a surprising variety of Web pages that reside in a SharePoint site. This facility has its limitations, and it's certainly no replacement for programs like FrontPage 2003. Nevertheless, the combination of a browser and Windows SharePoint Services may be all you need for certain kinds of applications.

The procedures for working with pages in meeting workspaces is different from the procedure for any other SharePoint site. For procedures that apply to meeting workspaces, refer to the last topic in this section.

Creating Simple Web Pages

The simplest kind of page to create is an ordinary, "flat" page that contains no Web Parts or other special features. Here's the procedure.

1   Open the SharePoint site where the new Web page will reside.

2   Make sure the site has a document library. If not, create one.

3   Click the Create command in the top navigation bar of any page in the site.

4   When the Create page appears, scroll down to the Web Pages section and click the Basic Page link. This will display the New Basic Page form shown in Figure 5-14.

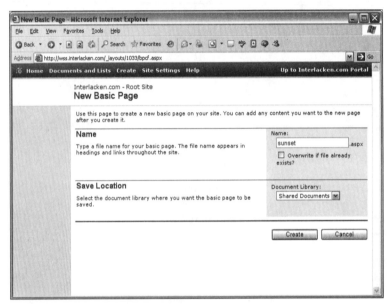

Figure 5-14.   By submitting this form, you can create a Web page designed for ordinary HTML content.

5   On the New Basic Page form, configure these settings.

   ■   **Name**   Type the filename base you want the Web page to have.

   ■   **Overwrite If File Already Exists?**   Select this check box to overwrite an existing file with the same name, should such a file exist.

   ■   **Document Library**   Select a document library where the new page will reside. This must be an existing library in the same site.

6   Click Create to create the page and start the Microsoft Rich Text Editor as shown in Figure 5-15.

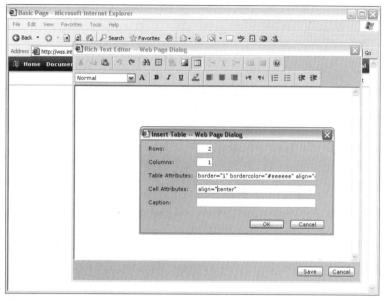

Figure 5-15. The Rich Text Editor is rudimentary compared to stand-alone HTML editors, but it can create simple content.

7 Type whatever content you like into the Rich Text Editor dialog box. In addition, you can use the toolbar buttons to apply colors, fonts, text styles, alignment, and so forth. The three buttons in the middle of the upper toolbar insert hyperlinks, pictures, and tables.

8 Click Save to save the rich text content into your new Web page. Windows SharePoint Services will supply the standard top navigation bar and apply the site's default theme.

Links to the new page will appear in all standard views of the document library where it resides. To provide additional links, add the page URL to one or more Links lists, and then display the Links list on any Web Part Page (such as the site's home page).

You should be aware of two special precautions when using the Rich Text Editor to create a Web page.

To change an existing page you created this way, click the Edit Content link that appears in the top right corner.

- If you insert any pictures or hyperlinks, be sure to specify fully qualified HTTP URLs. In the case of pictures, for example, you might want to specify the full path of a picture in a SharePoint picture library.

- Once you insert a table, you can insert rows, columns, or cells, and you can merge or split cells. However, you can no longer modify table and cell attributes such as cell spacing, cell padding, and borders. If you make a mistake, you'll need to delete the table (and its contents), and then recreate it from scratch. Plan accordingly.

> For a more flexible way of adding pages to a SharePoint site, refer to Part IV, "Creating and Designing Sites Using FrontPage 2003."

Creating Web Part Pages

Using only a browser, you can create new Web Part Pages as easily as you can create flat Web pages. With Web Part Pages, however, you don't have to fight the limited editing capability of the Rich Text Editor. Instead, Web Parts provide all the page content, and Web Parts are much more flexible and easier to configure.

To create a new Web Part Page using only a SharePoint site's browser interface, proceed as follows:

1   Browse to the SharePoint site where you want the new Web Part Page to reside.

2   Click the Create button in the top navigation bar of any page in the site.

3   When the Create page appears, scroll down to the Web Pages section and click Web Part Page. This will display the New Web Part Page form shown in Figure 5-16.

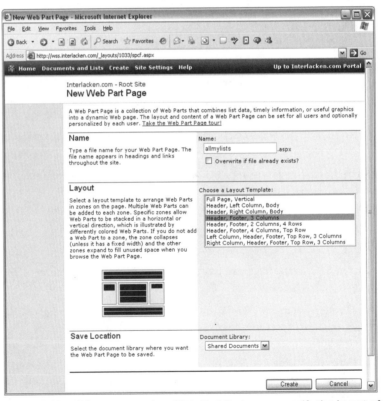

Figure 5-16.   When you create a Web Part Page, you specify the layout of Web Part Zones and not the Web Parts themselves.

Creating SharePoint Sites and Pages

4   Fill out these fields on the New Web Part Page form:

- ■ **Name**   Type a filename base for the new Web Part Page.
- ■ **Overwrite If File Already Exists?**   Select this check box to permit overwriting an existing file.
- ■ **Choose A Template Layout**   Select a layout template that appears in the list box. After you click any template, the preview graphic in the Layout section will change to show that template's arrangement of Web Part Zones. Choose the template that offers the arrangement you want.

    When making your selection, keep in mind that you can add any number of Web Parts to a single Web Part Zone, and that empty Web Part Zones take up no space when a team member views the page.

- ■ **Document Library**   Select a document library where the Web Part Page will reside. The drop-down list will include all document libraries in the same site.

5   Click Create to generate the new Web Part Page and display it in editable mode.

> **Note**   By default, a Web Part Page can contain only 50 Web parts. If this is insufficient, a server administrator can add a MaxZoneParts setting to the server's web.config file.

As with flat Web pages you create using a browser, you can find links to the new page in all standard views of the document library where the page resides, and you can add the page's URL to any Links lists you like.

The next section will explain how to modify not only a new empty Web Part Page, but existing Web Part Pages as well.

Modifying Web Part Pages

Using only a browser, you can add, reconfigure, and remove Web Parts in many SharePoint pages. This includes, for example, the home page of a Team Site and any Web Part Pages you created yourself, as described in the previous section.

Web Parts are independent units of content designed to occupy part of a Web page. Web Parts have code that executes on the Web server, much like the code in an ASP or ASP.NET page, but they don't usually display page banners, signature lines, and other aspects of a complete Web page design. The page that contains the Web Part usually provides these elements.

To display a Web Part, you put it in a Web Part Page. Whenever the Web server delivers a Web Part Page, it runs any Web Parts the page contains, and merges the resulting HTML into the surrounding Web Part Page. A single Web Part Page can contain as many Web Parts as you want. Similarly, the same Web Part can appear in many different Web Part Pages.

A Web Part Zone reserves space within a Web Part Page for one or more Web Parts.

- ● If you're using a browser to design Web Part Pages, you can add only Web Parts to Web Part Zones.

Chapter 5

- If you're using FrontPage 2003 to design Web Part pages, you can add Web Parts without using Web Parts Zones, but this sacrifices flexibility.

Windows SharePoint Services can "remember" two different views of a Web Part Page:

- **Shared**   This is the view that team members receive by default. To modify this view, a team member must hold the Add And Customize Pages right. By default, only the Administrator and Web Designer groups have this right.

- **Personal**   This is a view that each team member can customize. If a site has a hundred team members, Windows SharePoint Services could conceivably store a hundred different personal views, one for each member.

  To add, remove, or modify Web Parts in a personal view, team members need the Add/Remove Private Web Parts right. For custom lists, team members need the Manage Personal Views right as well. By default, the Contributor, Web Designer, and Administrator groups have these rights, but not the Reader group.

To determine which Web pages you can modify in a browser, look for a Modify Shared Page or Modify My Page link in the top right corner. Clicking this link will display a menu with these choices:

- **Add Web Parts**   Displays options to browse for, search for, or import Web Parts.
    - Browsing for a Web Part means selecting it from a list.
    - Searching for a Web Part means typing part of its name and then clicking a Go button.
    - Importing a Web Part means uploading a special XML document file from some other source (such as your hard disk). Web Part files have a filename extension of .dwp (deployable Web Part).

- **Design This Page**   Shifts the page into an editable view where you can rearrange Web Parts by dragging.

- **Modify My/Shared Web Parts**   Displays a submenu with one choice for each Web Part on the page. Selecting any Web Part displays a task pane where you can modify the Web Part's appearance and layout.

- **Shared View**   Displays the Web Part Page as configured for the SharePoint site as a whole.

- **Personal View**   Displays the Web Part Page using your personal settings.

- **Reset Page Content**   This option appears only if you're in Personal view and have personalized content on the page. It resets all personal settings to the shared view.

The Design This Page command displays the page as shown in Figure 5-17. This is also the view in effect after you create a new Web Part Page as described in the previous section. The two gray rectangles labeled Left and Right show the boundaries of two Web Part zones named Left and Right. These are just names, and not positions. Whoever designed this page could just as easily have named these zones East and West, Dog and Cat, Hither and Yon, or anything else.

Creating SharePoint Sites and Pages

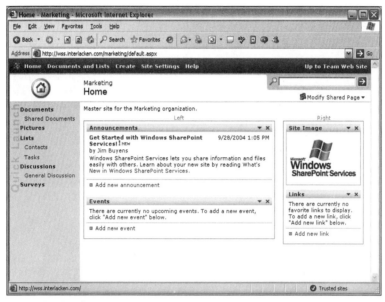

Figure 5-17.   This page is in SharePoint design mode. The Web Part Zones are visible, and you can drag Web Parts from place to place.

The page in the figure has four Web Parts: Announcements, Events, Site Image, and Links. You can rearrange these Web Parts (or any others that may be present) by drag-and-drop. To do this:

1   Move the mouse pointer over the title bar of any Web Part.

2   Press and hold down the mouse button.

3   Drag the mouse pointer to a spot above or below any other Web Part on the page. A blue bar will indicate the receiving location.

4   Release the mouse button.

Adding Web Parts to a Page

Rearranging Web Parts is a useful function, but in many cases you'll want to modify the page by adding Web Parts. Here's the necessary procedure:

1   To add Web Parts to the shared view of a page, first make sure that a Modify Shared Page link appears in the top left corner. If not, click the Modify My Page link and choose Shared View from the resulting menu.

To add Web Parts to the personal view of a page, make sure that a Modify My Page link appears in the top left corner. If not, click Modify Shared Page and choose Personal View.

2   Click the Modify My Page or Modify Shared Page link, and then choose Add Web Parts and Browse from the menu. The page will then resemble Figure 5-18.

Chapter 5

163

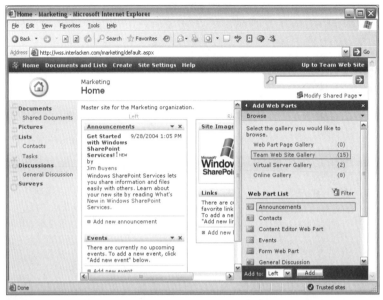

Figure 5-18. This is the interface for adding Web Parts to a Web Part Page using Internet Explorer.

3 In the Add Web Parts task pane, search each gallery for the Web Part you want. In other words, click a gallery name and then scroll through the name in the Web Part List section. If a gallery contains more than ten Web Parts, either:

- Click the Next or Previous link at the bottom of each group of ten.

- Click the Filter link, and then choose All Items, Web Parts, Lists, or Libraries, depending on the type of Web Part you want. This may reduce the list to less than ten.

Table 5-1 lists the source and function for each Web Part Gallery.

4 To add the Web Part you want to the page, either:

- Drag it from the Add Web Parts task pane and drop it into the zone you want.

- Select the Web Part, select a zone in the Add To drop-down list, and then click Add.

If browsing the four galleries one at a time seems laborious, or if the galleries are large, you may prefer searching for Web Parts by name. To do this:

1 Display the Add Web Parts search form in either of two ways:

- Choose Add Web Parts from the Modify Shared Page or Modify My Page drop-down menu, and then choose Search.

- Click the down arrow on the Add Web Parts toolbar, and then choose Search.

2 Type all or part of the Web Part name into the Search Text box.

3 Click the Go button.

Creating SharePoint Sites and Pages

Table 5-1. Web Part Galleries

Gallery	Description
Web Part Page	Contains Web Parts assigned to the page, but not currently visible in browse or design view. Every Web Part Page has its own gallery. Developers can add optional Web Parts to this gallery without adding them to the page. In addition, closing a Web Part removes it from the Web Part Page and adds it to the page's Web Part Page Gallery.
<top-level site>	Contains Web Parts a server administrator has decided are safe, and has therefore made available to all sites in a collection. The name of this gallery is the name of the collection's top-level site.
Virtual Server	Contains Web Parts a server administrator has made available to all site collections on a single virtual server..
Online	Contains Web Parts available from Microsoft or other software manufacturers and vendors.

This will again display the four galleries, but instead of a Web Parts listing, each gallery will have Search Results. Hopefully, only one gallery will have "hits" and the number of hits will be few.

You can also add a Web Part to a page by importing a configuration you received from another team member. To make this work, the team member who has the Web Part already configured must first perform these tasks:

1 Display the page that contains the Web Part.

2 Click the Modify Shared Page or Modify My Page link on that page.

3 Once the page is in design mode (as shown previously in Figure 5-17), click the down arrow in the title bar of the Web Part you want to transfer, and then choose Export from the drop-down menu.

4 If a File Download dialog box appears, click Save.

5 When the Save As dialog box appears, choose a file location, a file name, and a filename extension of .dwt. Then, click the Save button.

6 Send the resulting .dwt file to the person who wants to install the Web Part with a configuration identical to yours.

The team member who want to add the Web Part would then follow this procedure:

1 Browse to the page where you want the pre-configured Web Part to appear.

2 Display the Add Web Parts import form in either of two ways:

■ Choose Add Web Parts from the Modify Shared Page or Modify My Page drop-down menu, and then choose Import.

■ Click the down arrow on the Add Web Parts toolbar, and then choose Import.

3 Type in the name and path of the .dwp file you received, or click the Browse button and use the resulting Choose File dialog box to locate the file.

4 Click the Upload button.

5 When the Web Part appears under the Uploaded Web Part heading, Set the Add To drop-down list to the Web Part Zone you want, and then click Import.

To close the Add Web Parts task pane, click its close box.

Configuring Web Parts

Every Web Part has a drop-down arrow near the right edge of its title bar. Clicking this arrow reveals these four options:

- **Minimize**   Shrinks the Web Part so that only its title bar is visible. The command then changes to Restore, which expands the Web Part so that it displays data.

- **Close**   Removes the Web Part from the page, but keeps it in the Web Part Page gallery. This preserves the Web Part, in case you ever add it back to the page.

- **Modify My/Shared Web Part**   Displays a task pane that controls a Web Part's view, toolbar, appearance, layout, and advanced settings.

- **Help**   Displays helpful information about the Web Part.

Choosing Modify My Web Part or Modify Shared Web Part displays a Web Part task pane like the one at the right of Figure 5-19.

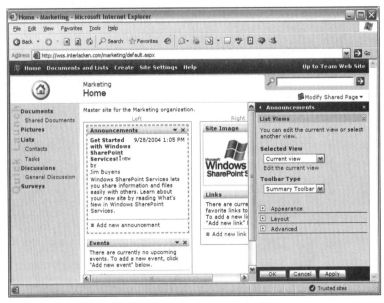

Figure 5-19.   When the Add Web Parts task pane is visible, you can drag Web Parts from the task pane to any Web Part Zone.

The properties on this task pane vary widely depending on the Web Part. For most Web Parts, however, there are a *lot* of properties. This explains why the task pane displays them in expandable sections. For most Web Parts:

- **The Appearance Section**   Controls the Web Part's title, height, width, frame state (Minimized Or Normal), and frame style (Default, None, Title Bar And Border, or Title Bar Only).

  A frame, in this case, means the area a Web Part occupies, and not part of an HTML frameset.

- **The Layout Section**   Controls whether or not the Web Part is visible, its layout direction (Default, Left To Right, or Right To Left), its Web Part Zone, and its order within that zone.

- **The Advanced Section**   Specifies whether or not team members can minimize, close, or move the Web Part to another zone. It also specifies the target location for the link on the Web Part's title bar, the location of the Web Part's help files, its icon files, and so forth.

Modifying Meeting Workspace Pages

Because meeting workspaces have a narrower focus than most other kinds of SharePoint sites, they use a simpler, file-tab model for organizing pages. The Basic meeting workspace shown in Figure 5-20 has exactly one of these file-tabbed pages; its tab title is Home.

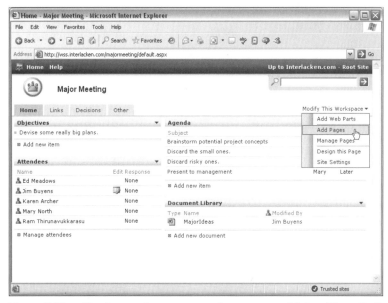

Figure 5-20.   Meeting workspaces organize pages and links differently than other types of SharePoint sites.

Chapter 5

> **Note** A new installation of Windows SharePoint Services offers five types of meeting workspace: Basic, Blank, Decision, Multipage, and Social.

To modify a meeting workspace, click the Modify This Workspace link near the top right corner of the page. This displays a menu with five choices:

- **Add Web Parts** Displays the Add Web Parts task pane shown in Figure 5-21. This task pane is similar to the one shown in Figure 5-18, but it has an additional view—Create Lists—that it displays by default.

  To create any sort of standard list and add it to the current page, either:

  - Drag it from the Create Lists view of the Add Web Parts task pane and drop it into the Web Part Zone you want.

  - Select the type of list, choose a Web Part Zone in the Add To drop-down list, and then click Add.

  To display the Browse, Search, and Import views of the Add Web Parts task pane, click the down arrow to the right of Create Lists, and then select the view you want.

Figure 5-21. With the Add Web Parts task pane in Create Lists view, you can create lists and add them to a page with one drag-and-drop motion.

- **Add Pages** Displays an Add Pages task pane with one input field: Page Name. Type in the file tab title you want, and then click Add. This will create a new page, add it to the file tab navigation system, and display the page ready to receive Web Parts.

● **Manage Pages**   Displays a Pages task pane that has four views.

■ **Order**   Appears by default, as illustrated in Figure 5-22. To change the order of any file tab except Home, select the tab name you want to move, and then click the up and down arrows until the tab is in the position you want.

■ **Add**   Displays the same view as choosing Add Pages from the Modify This Workspace menu, as described just above.

■ **Delete**   Displays a list of pages you can delete. To actually delete a page, select its name and then click the Delete button.

■ **Settings**   Displays the name of the current page so that you can change it.

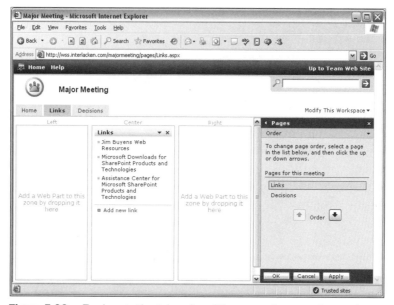

Figure 5-22.   To change the tab order of the pages in a meeting workspace, use the Order view of the Page task pane. Empty Web Part Zones are no concern; in the normal view of a page they occupy no space.

● **Design This Page**   Displays the page with its Web Part Zones visible, and with its Web Parts in a state where you can drag and drop them from place to place. This works exactly like the Design This Page command explained earlier in the section titled "Modifying Web Part Pages" (see Figure 5-17).

● **Site Settings**   Displays essentially the same page as choosing Site Settings from the top navigation bar of a Team Web Site. From that page, you can administer and customize the site, change your personal information, manage your alerts, or view information about site users.

In Summary...

This chapter explained the basics of organizing content on a server running Windows SharePoint Services. This included planning a site structure, creating sites and site collections, choosing a visual appearance, and linking among sites once they exist. It then explained how to create your own Web Part Pages, and how to add and arrange Web Parts that display your information the way you want.

The next chapter will explain how to create, modify, and display SharePoint lists and libraries using only a browser.

Chapter 6

Designing Lists, Libraries, and Pages

Lists and libraries are the repositories of almost anything you want to keep in a SharePoint site. Instead of typing your content into "flat" HTML pages, you store the content in lists and libraries. Then, you configure Web Part Pages to include Web Parts that display the lists and libraries.

Although this may seem indirect at first, as you'll soon discover, it's much easier than handcrafting a never-ending series of Web pages, and certainly easier than designing your own databases and document libraries. This chapter explains how to create your own lists and libraries, including not only the standard types that come with Windows SharePoint Services, but also custom types you design yourself.

This chapter concentrates exclusively on using a browser to create, modify, and display lists and libraries. Microsoft FrontPage 2003 also can perform these tasks, and Part IV, "Creating and Designing Sites Using FrontPage 2003," will explain that approach.

Creating Lists

Whenever you want to add data to a SharePoint site (or whenever you want others to do so), you should first locate the proper list. For example, don't store names and addresses in an Events list, and don't store hyperlinks in an Announcements list.

But what if your site doesn't contain a list that seems just right for the type of information you need to record? What if it needs two or three or five contact lists, or a completely new type of list to store data for a special application? In that case, you need to create a new list, and these two sections provide the necessary guidance.

Creating Built-In Lists

To begin creating a SharePoint list of any kind, open the site where you want the list to reside, and then click the Create link in the top navigation bar of any page. This displays the Create Page page shown in Figure 6-1.

Microsoft Windows SharePoint Services Inside Out

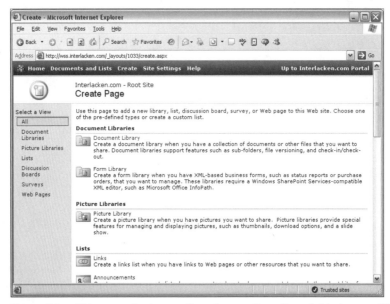

Figure 6-1. This page displays options for creating all available types of SharePoint lists, libraries, and pages.

The simplest lists to create are the built-in types that appear under the Lists heading. Table 6-1 lists these types.

Table 6-1. Built-In SharePoint List Types

Type	Description	Interface to Outlook
Links	Stores links to Web pages or other resources that you want to share.	
Announcements	Stores news, status, and other short bits of information.	
Contacts	Stores information about people your team members work with, such as customers or partners.	Yes
Events	Stores a calendar-based view of upcoming meetings, deadlines, and other important events.	Yes
Tasks	Stores work items that you or your team members need to complete.	
Issues	Stores a set of issues or problems. You can assign, prioritize, and follow the progress of issues from start to finish.	

Designing Lists, Libraries, and Pages

Although many aspects of working with these and other list types are the same, each built-in list type has properties that you can't change. For example:

- You can't change the icon assigned to a built-in list.
- Each type of list has certain required fields that you can't delete. For example, you can't delete the Title and Begin fields in an Events list.
- You can't reconfigure Contacts and Events lists not to exchange data with Outlook, and you can't reconfigure other types of lists to gain these capabilities.

This makes it important to use the correct type of built-in list for your application. Here's the procedure for creating any of the built-in list types:

> **Caution**   To create a list in a Meeting Workspace site, follow the instructions in the section "Modifying Meeting Workspace Pages" in Chapter 5.

1. Open the site that you want to contain the new list.
2. Click the Create link in the top navigation bar of any page.
3. When the Create Page page shown in Figure 6-1 appears, scroll down to the Lists section and click the type of list you want.
4. When the New List page shown in Figure 6-2 appears, configure these settings:
   - **Name**   Type a name that will identify this list throughout the SharePoint site.
   - **Description**   Optionally describe the list's content or purpose.
   - **Display This List On The Quick Launch Bar?**   Select Yes if you want the Quick Launch bar of the site's home page to display a link to this list.

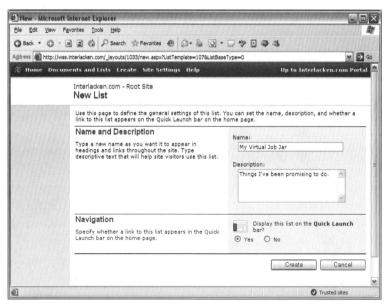

Figure 6-2.   Use this page to name and describe a new SharePoint list.

5 Click the Create button to create and display a new empty list. Figure 6-3 illustrates some typical results.

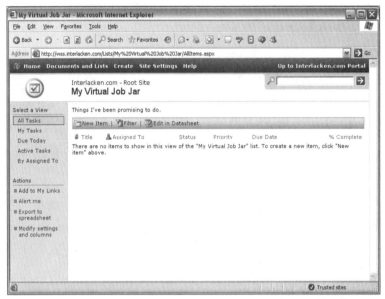

Figure 6-3. This new list has no items yet.

Once the list exists, you can enter data, create new views, display views in Web pages, or even modify the list's data fields and features. Sections later in this chapter will explain these procedures.

Creating Custom Lists

For maximum flexibility when creating a new list, choose one of the links under the Custom Lists heading. Here's how these links work.

- **Custom List**   This option displays the New List page shown in Figure 6-2, and then creates and displays a list with only one column: Title.

  In almost every case, you would use the instructions in the next section—"Modifying Lists"—to modify this starting point with additional fields and features.

- **Custom List In Datasheet View**   Like the previous option, displays the New List page and creates a list with Title as the only column. This option, however, opens the new list in Datasheet View so you can view and modify list items in a tabular interface.

  For more information about using Datasheet View, refer to the section titled "Working with Lists in Datasheet View" later in this chapter.

- **Import Spreadsheet**   Creates a list from data contained in a spreadsheet.

Designing Lists, Libraries, and Pages

Here's the procedure for creating a new list from a spreadsheet.

1 Open the site that will contain the new list.

2 Click the Create button on the top navigation bar of any page in the site.

3 Scroll down to the Custom Lists section, and then choose Import Spreadsheet.

4 When the New List page shown in Figure 6-4 appears, fill in these fields:

- **Name**   Give the new list a name.

- **Description**   Enter a few sentences describing the new list.

- **File Location**   Type the full path and filename of the spreadsheet that contains the data you want in the list. Alternatively, click the Browse button and select the file you want.

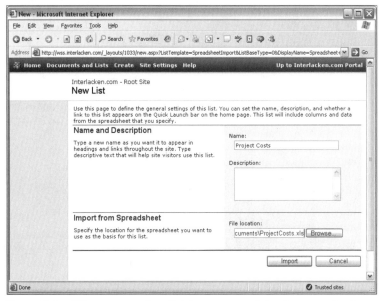

Figure 6-4. When you create a list from a spreadsheet you must, of course, specify the spreadsheet filename.

5 Click Import. This will download a file to your computer that starts Excel and displays the prompt shown in Figure 6-5.

6 Specify the following options in the Import To Windows SharePoint Services List dialog box:

- **Range Type**   Select the way you want to specify what cells to import. The choices are Range Of Cells, List Range (an Excel list), and Named Range (an Excel named range).

- **Select Range**   Specify or select the range of cells you want.

> To learn more about exchanging data between Excel and SharePoint lists, refer to "Setting Up Linked Lists from a SharePoint Site" in Chapter 4

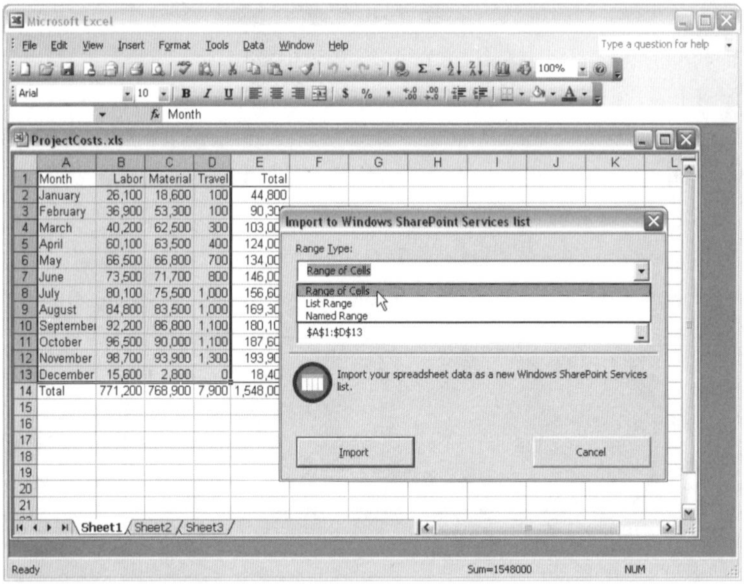

Microsoft Windows SharePoint Services Inside Out

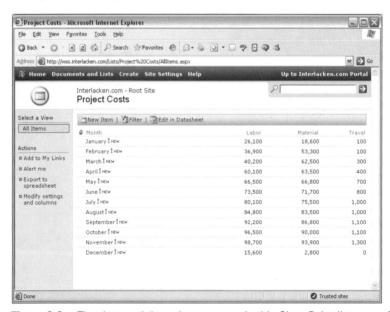

Figure 6-5. This dialog box specifies the range of the cell values that the new SharePoint list will contain.

7 Click Import to create the new SharePoint list. Figure 6-6 shows the result of the settings shown in Figure 6-5.

Figure 6-6. The data and the column names in this SharePoint list came from the spreadsheet in Figure 6-5.

Modifying Lists

Nothing is ever perfect and even if it were, the world around it would change. Such is the case with lists. Therefore, the topics in this section explain how to modify an existing list.

Modifying List Settings and Columns

SharePoint lists are very flexible: you can change their properties, behavior, security, appearance, and fields at will. To begin, display the list you want to modify, and click the Modify Settings And Columns link near the left side of the window to display the Customization page, shown in Figure 6-7.

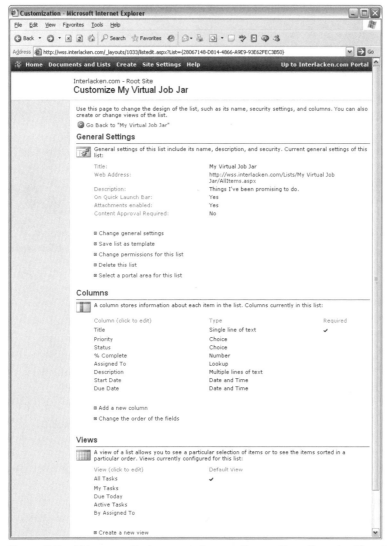

Figure 6-7. This page displays and changes the configuration of a SharePoint list.

The next few sections explain how to use each command on the Customization page.

Updating General Settings

To change the general settings for the list, click the Change General Settings link that appears below the General Settings heading. This displays the List Settings page shown in Figure 6-8.

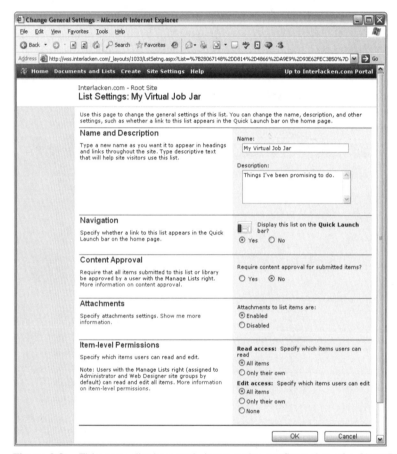

Figure 6-8. This page displays and changes the configuration of a SharePoint site list.

Once the List Settings page is on display, make any changes you like to the following fields:

- **Name**   Type a name that will identify this list throughout the site.
- **Description**   Briefly describe the list's content or purpose.
- **Display This List On The Quick Launch Bar?**   Select Yes if you want the Quick Launch bar on the site's home page to display a link to this list.
- **Require Content Approval For Submitted Items?**   Click Yes if you want to hide any new items from public view until an administrator or list manger approves them.

Clicking Yes also provides two new views of the list: one for administrators and list managers to review all Pending, Rejected, and Approved items, and one where a team member can check the status of items he or she submitted.

For more information about content approval, refer to the section titled "Using Content Approval" in Chapter 3, "Using SharePoint Built-In Features."

- **Attachments To List Items Are** Click Enabled if it's all right for team members to attach a file to each list item. Otherwise, click Disabled.

- **Read Access** Specify which items team members other than administrators and list managers can view.

  - **All Items** Select this option to make all items visible to all team members.

  - **Only Their Own** Select this option if each team member should see only items he or she submitted.

  Administrators and list managers can always view all items.

- **Edit Access** Specify which items team members other than administrators and list managers can modify.

  - **All items** Select this option if any team member can modify any item in the list.

  - **Only Their Own** Select this option if team members can modify only items they themselves submitted.

  - **None** Select this option to stop team members from editing any items.

  Administrators and list managers can always edit all items.

Saving a Template

Clicking the Save List As Template link displays a Save List As Template Web page. That page saves a copy of the current list as a template that team members can use to create more lists with the same structure and, optionally, the same initial content. The saved template will appear as an option on the Create page for any site within the current site collection

When the Save List As Template Web page appears, fill in these fields and then click OK. This will save the template in the current site collection's List Template Gallery.

- **File Name** Type a filename base for the template. Normally, this should be a shortened form of the full list name. Windows SharePoint Services will supply a filename extension of .stp

- **Template Title** Supply a one-line name that will identify the template.

- **Template Description** Type a few sentences that describe the template and its use.

- **Include Content** Select this check box if you want the template to include the content of the current list. Clear it if you want a new list based on this template to be empty.

Chapter 6

Microsoft Windows SharePoint Services Inside Out

> **Warning** Templates neither save security settings nor apply them to new lists. Take this into account before including confidential content in a template.

Changing List Permissions

To change the permissions in effect for a list, display the Customization page shown in Figure 6-7, and then click the Change Permissions For This List link. This will display the Change Permissions page shown in Figure 6-9.

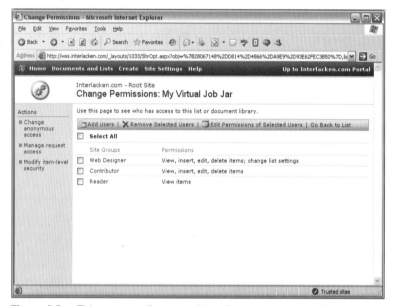

Figure 6-9. This page configures a SharePoint list to have different security than the site where it resides.

The figure shows the default groups for a new SharePoint site and the default rights assigned to each group. The Administrators group doesn't appear because administrators can always do everything.

To add users or groups and assign them permissions, follow this procedure.

- Click the Add Users toolbar button on the Change Permissions page.
- When the Add Users page shown in Figure 6-10 appears, fill in the Users box with any combination of the following, separated with semicolons:
  - E-mail addresses
  - Windows accounts (for example, domain\name)
  - Cross-site group names
  - Group names defined within the current site.

Designing Lists, Libraries, and Pages

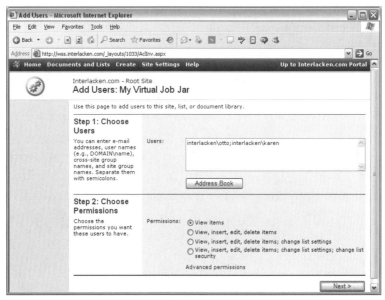

Figure 6-10. This page grants permission for additional members to access a SharePoint list or library.

● Select the permissions you want and click Next. This will display the second Add Users page shown in Figure 6-11.

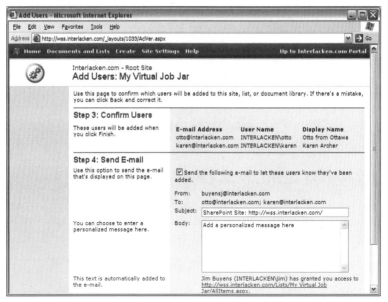

Figure 6-11. After you click the Next button in Figure 6-10, this page confirms the members you specified and offers to send them mail.

● Review the user information listed in the Confirm Users section. If any of these are incorrect or show up as invalid, click the Back button and correct your input.

● To send mail to the newly authorized team members, make sure the Send The Following E-Mail To Let These Users Know They've Been Added check box is selected, and then update the Subject and Body boxes if you wish. However, the message will always contain the message fragment that appears below the Body box.

● Click Finish to add the new team members and send the message.

To remove the access permissions for any team member or group listed on the Change Permissions page, select their check boxes and then click the Remove Selected Users toolbar button.

To change the permissions assigned to any team member or group listed on the Change Permissions page

1 Select their check boxes on the Change Permissions page.

2 Click the Edit Permissions Of Selected Users toolbar button. This displays a Modify Permissions page offering these combinations of rights.

■ View items

■ View, insert, edit, delete items

■ View, insert, edit, delete items; change list settings

■ View, insert, edit, delete items; change list settings; change list security

If you need to set more detailed permissions, click the Advanced Permissions link and then select or clear the individual check boxes.

3 Choose the permissions you want for the selected team members or groups, and then click OK.

Deleting a List

To delete a list, click the Delete This List link on the Customization page shown previously in Figure 6-7. Then, when a dialog box prompts, "Are You Sure You Want To Delete This List," click OK.

Selecting a Portal Area for a List

This command is available only if the top-level site that defines the current site collection is configured with the URL of a portal server. If it's present, clicking it displays a portal site Add Listing page with the title, description, and address of the current list filled in.

Specify a portal location and, if you wish, a portal group, image, or audience. Then, click the OK button.

> For more information about organizing content in SharePoint Portal Server, refer to "Reviewing SharePoint Portal Server" in Chapter 2.

Adding List Columns

Referring again to Figure 6-7, the Columns section of the Customization page lists all the columns (fields) in the current list. For the most part, you can add, modify, or delete these columns at will. There are just a few columns in the built-in list types that you can't delete. Here's the procedure for adding a column to an existing list.

1 Click the Add A New Column link. This will display the Add Column page shown in Figure 6-12.

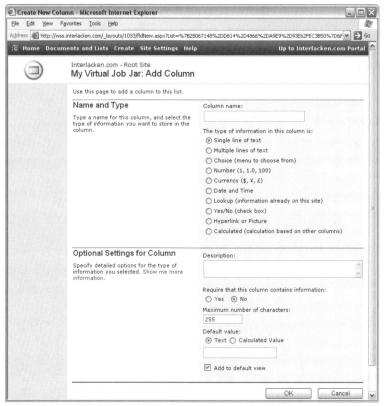

Figure 6-12. This page adds a new column to a SharePoint list. The Optional Settings For Column section changes depending on the type of information you specify.

2 In the Column Name box, give the new column a name. This will appear in all listing and input forms that display the column, so be careful with spelling and case.

3 Select one of the choices under the heading The Type Of Information In This Column Is. Table 6-2 lists the available choices and the type of control each choice will display on input forms.

Table 6-2. SharePoint List Column Types

Type of Information	Input Form
Single Line Of Text	Text box
Multiple Lines Of Text	Text area box
Choice (Menu To Choose From)	Drop-down menu, radio buttons, check boxes, or fill-in choices
Rating Scale	A list of choices that team member rate on a numeric scale, such as 1 (low) to 5 (high).
Number (1, 1.0, 100)	Text box
Currency ($, ¥, £)	Text box
Date And Time	Combination of text box (for date) and drop-down lists (for hour and minute)
Lookup (Information Already On This Site)	Drop-down list
Yes/No (Check Box)	Check box
Hyperlink Or Picture	Two text boxes: Web address and description
Calculated (calculation based on other columns)	(none)

4   Under Optional Settings for Columns, fill out these fields.

■ **Description**   Type a few sentences describing the new column. This field is optional.

■ **Require That This Column Contains Information**   This field appears for all information types except Calculated. Select Yes if whoever adds a list item must supply a value. Select No if the column value can be empty.

■ **Add To Default View**   This is always the last field under Optional Settings for Columns. Select it if you want the column to appear when, for example, a team member selects the list from the Documents And Lists page. Clear it to suppress the column from that view.

The middle of the Optional Settings for Columns section varies depending on the information type you selected. Figure 6-12, for example, shows the configuration for a Single Line Of Text column. It contains these two settings:

● **Maximum Number Of Characters**   Type the maximum length of values in this column.

- **Default Value** Type the value that will initially appear in the text box for this column when a team member displays the New Item form for this list. You can specify this value in either of two ways:

    - **Text** The characters you type in the Default Value text box will appear verbatim on the input form.

    - **Calculated Value** The characters you type in the Default Value text box are a formula that Windows SharePoint Services will evaluate. The results of this evaluation will then appear in the text box on the new item form. The formula =TEXT(Today+7, "short date") for example, will initialize a single-line-of-text column value to a date seven days in the future.

Calculating Column Values

Windows SharePoint Services can perform calculations to determine the value of a column in a given row. You can invoke such calculations in two situations:

- When initializing the form that will add a new list item.

- Every time you retrieve the list item. In this case, the column occupies no physical storage; instead, Windows SharePoint Services calculates the value every time you request data from the column.

Calculations use formulas very much like those in Excel. Of course, there are no row and column locations as there are in Excel; instead, the input for calculations generally comes from system functions such as *today* or from other columns in the list.

If there's any ambiguity as to the name of a function or column, or if the name contains any special characters, enclose the column name in square brackets. For example:

- The expression *today* refers to a function.

- The expression [today] refers to a column named today.

- The expressions FirstName and [FirstName] both refer to a column named FirstName because there's no function named *FirstName*.

For the most part, all the functions and operators from Excel are available. For example, to add the Number Present and Number Absent columns, you would code:

```
=[Number Present] + [Number Absent]
```

To combine text from two columns, use the ampersand operator. Here's an example:

```
=[Last Name] & ", " & [First Name]
```

You can also use functions in formulas. This formula, for example, returns the text weekday for the date in the Date Due column.

```
=TEXT(WEEKDAY([Date Due]), "dddd")
```

The equal sign prefix, by the way, seems to be optional.

Chapter 6

185

Microsoft Windows SharePoint Services Inside Out

Two information types deserve special mention: Lookup and Calculated.

The Lookup choice populates a drop-down list with all values that occur in a given list and column within the SharePoint site. For example, this could include all Full Name values in the User Information list, all Title values in the Shared Documents library, all E-Mail Address values in the Contacts list, and so forth. Figure 6-13 shows the Optional Settings For Column section for a typical lookup field.

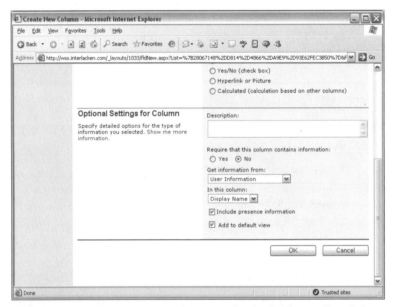

Figure 6-13. When you create a Lookup column, the Create New Column page prompts for the list and column that contain the permissible values.

To configure the Lookup column, configure these settings:

- **Get Information From**   Select the list that will provide the permissible values.
- **In This Column**   Select the column that will provide the permissible values.
- **Include Presence Information**   This setting appears only when you set Get Information From to User Information. In that case, it specifies whether a Windows Messenger icon should appear next to the data value in list views.

> **Note**   User Information is a built-in list that provides information about a site's team members.

Figure 6-14 shows how the Optional Settings For Column section looks for a calculated field.

Designing Lists, Libraries, and Pages

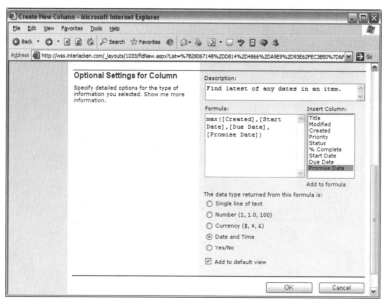

Figure 6-14. When you create a calculated column, you specify a formula like this. Thereafter, you can treat the calculated column as if it were physically in the table.

Here's how to configure a calculated column value:

- **Formula**   Type the formula in this box.
- **Insert Column**   This list works like a typing aid. Instead of typing in a column name in the formula box, you can double-click any name in the Insert Column box, or select a column name and click the Add To Formula link.
- **The Data Type Returned From This Formula Is**   Select the type of data you want the formula to return. This gives you the flexibility, for example, to add numeric column values and return the result either as a number or as a single line of text.

Changing and Deleting List Columns

To change or delete a column, click its name in the Columns section of the Customization page. This will display a Change Column page very much like the Add Column page shown in Figure 6-12, except that your options under The Type Of Information In This Column Is may be absent or limited.

- To change any other aspect of the column, correct the setting and click OK.
- To delete the column and all its data, click the Delete button at the bottom of the page.

Tip   Once a list column exists, you can only change its type of information to a format that Windows SharePoint Services can convert.

Reordering List Columns

Although a List view can display a list's columns in any left-to-right order, the list itself stores the columns in a "natural" or default order. This determines, for example, the order of the fields in the list's New Item form. To change the order of columns in a list:

1 Display the list's Customization page.

2 In the Columns section, click the Change The Order Of The Fields link. This displays the Change Field Order page shown in Figure 6-15.

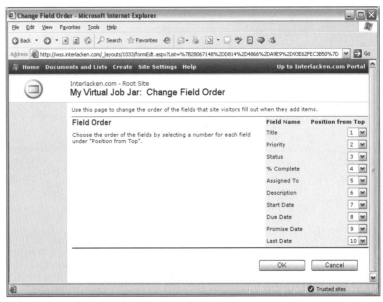

Figure 6-15.   To change the order of any field, change its Position From Top value.

3 To change the position of any field, change the selection in its Position From Top drop-down list. This will move the corresponding field into that position and force other fields up or down to accommodate it.

4 When all the fields are in the order you want, click OK.

Creating and Modifying List Views

Once you have data in a list, it's almost inevitable you'll want to view it in several different ways. For example, you may want it in a different sequence, in a different format, omitting certain columns, omitting certain data values, or showing totals. Windows SharePoint Services calls these alternate views of your data just what you'd expect: it calls them *views*.

Creating List Views

A list *view* presents any combination of list columns you want, sorted in any order you want, filtered or not filtered based on data value, with or without grouping and totals, and in various display formats. To create a new view, proceed as follows.

1 Display the list's Customization page.

2 Click the Create A New View link in the Views section. This displays the Create View page shown in Figure 6-16.

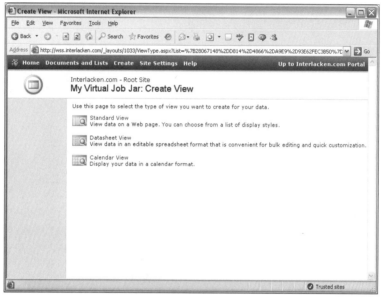

Figure 6-16. A view presents all or part of a list in other than its natural order or appearance.

3 Click one of the following links:

- **Standard View** Click this link if you want the view to display the data in a report-like format.

- **Datasheet View** Click this link if you want the view to display the data in a spreadsheet-like grid that permits in-place editing.

- **Calendar View** Click this link if you want the view to display the data in a calendar format.

Clicking one of these links will display a Create View, Create Datasheet View, or Create Calendar View page like the one shown in Figure 6-17. As you might suspect, it takes a very long Web page to configure all options in a view; the figure therefore shows all possible sections collapsed. To expand or contract each section, click the plus or minus icon that precedes the section name.

Chapter 6

189

Microsoft Windows SharePoint Services Inside Out

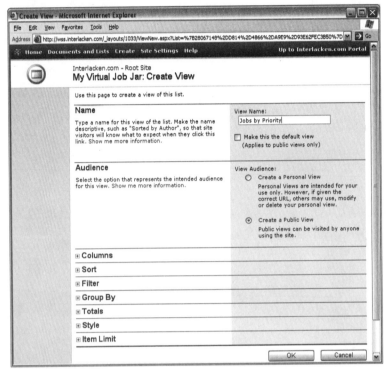

Figure 6-17. To specify the properties of a SharePoint view, expand or collapse the options on this page.

As Table 6-3 illustrates, the sections that appear on the Create View page will vary depending on the link you checked on the Create View page.

Table 6-3. SharePoint List View Settings

Section	Standard View	Datasheet View	Calendar View
Name	●	●	●
Audience	●	●	●
Columns	●	●	●
Calendar Settings			●
Sort	●	●	
Filter	●	●	●
Group By	●		
Totals	●	●	
Style	●		
Item Limit	●	●	

Here's how to fill out each possible section.

Designing Lists, Libraries, and Pages

- **Name**   Enter the following settings.
    - **View Name**   Type a name that briefly describes the view. This is the name that will appear, for example, under Select A View when you browse the list.
    - **Make This The Default View**   Select this check box if you want this view to be the one that appears when you first browse the list. If you select the check box, however, then you must also set View Audience (the next field) to Create A Public View.
- **Audience**   Choose one of these options.
    - **Create A Personal View**   Select this option if you don't want the new view to appear under Select A View for anyone but you. Contrary to the information that appears on the Create View page, only the person who creates a personal view can access it or modify it. Other users can't, even if given the URL.
    - **Create A Public View**   Select this option if you want the new view to appear under Select A View for everyone.
- **Columns**   For Standard and Datasheet views, this section contains a line for each column in the list. Each line, in turn, contains these options.
    - **Display**   Select this check box if you want the column to appear in the view.
    - **Column Name**   This column is informational. It identifies the column by name.
    - **Position From Left**   Select the drop-down list for any column to specify the position where you want the column to appear. This works very much like the drop-down lists on the Change Field Order page described earlier in this chapter. For Calendar views, the Columns section contains these two options.
    - **Base Calendar On**   Select this option if you want list items to appear for a single calendar date. Then, pick the date field to use when displaying each item.
    - **Base Calendar On The Following Interval**   Select this option if you want list items to appear on the calendar every day, beginning at some date from the list and ending on another date from the list. Then, select the fields that will provide the two dates.
- **Calendar Settings**   In this section, choose the format in which the calendar should first appear: Month View, Week View, or Day View. However, regardless of which view appears first, team members can display the other views at will.
- **Sort**   Figure 6-18 shows the expanded view of this section. Select either one or two fields to use for sorting the list, and specify whether each sort should be ascending or descending.

Chapter 6

191

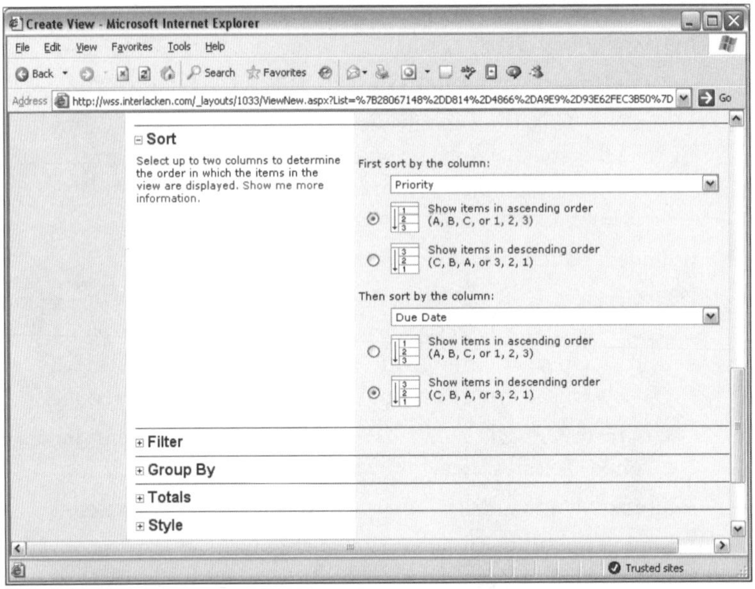

Microsoft Windows SharePoint Services Inside Out

Figure 6-18. A SharePoint view can sort items on zero, one, or two columns, in ascending or descending sequence. To sort on zero columns, set both drop-down lists to None.

- **Filter** Figure 6-19 presents a typical view of this section. Select:
  - **Show All Items In This View** To disable filtering, that is, to display all the items in the list.
  - **Show Items Only When The Following Is True** To restrict the display to certain items, based on data values. For each filtering action, select a column name, select a comparison operator, and then specify a value. The value [today] represents the current date, and only works for date columns. The value [Me] identifies the team member who requests the display, and only works for lookup columns based on the User Information list..

- **Group By** Visually, this section closely resembles the Sort section shown in Figure 6-18. However, when you specify Group By fields:
  - Windows SharePoint Services will sort first by the Group By fields, and then by the regular sort fields.
  - A dividing line will appear between every group of items having the same values in the Group By fields.

- **Totals** This section controls calculations of totals and other calculations based on the value of a column. Figure 6-20 shows a typical configuration in progress: simply choose the calculation you want, if any, from the drop-down list.

  The list view page shown in Figure 6-21 illustrates both grouping and totals. The totals appear at the top of the entire report, and again at the top of each group.

Designing Lists, Libraries, and Pages

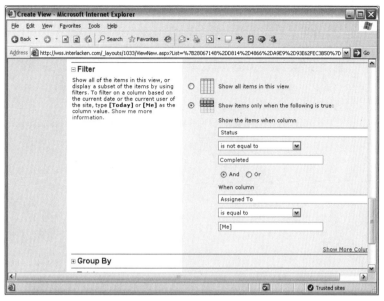

Figure 6-19. A SharePoint view can filter on any number of columns. As when sorting, you can set the drop-down lists to None.

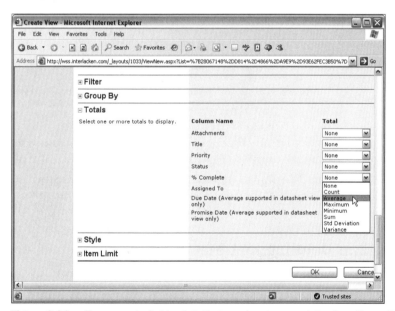

Figure 6-20. For numeric fields, totaling can invoke a variety of mathematical functions. For text fields, the only option is a record count.

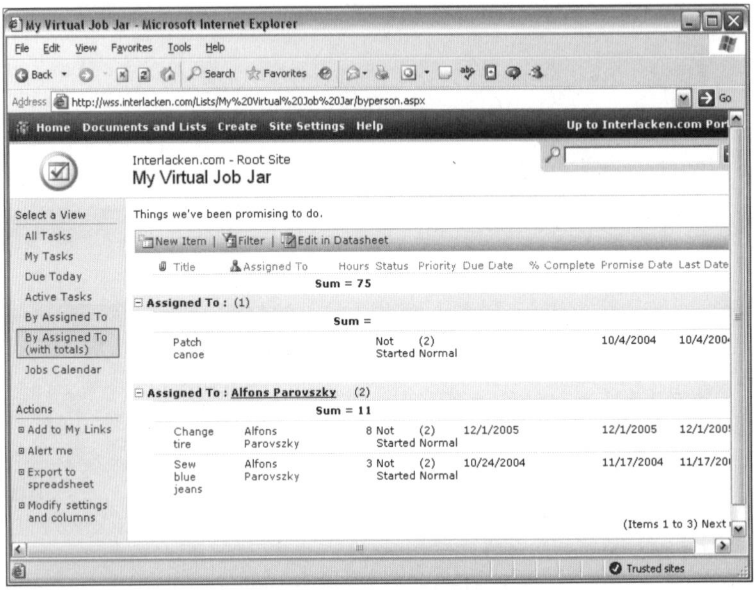

Microsoft Windows SharePoint Services Inside Out

Figure 6-21. This view illustrates both grouping and totaling in effect.

- **Style** This section of the Customization page displays a list box that controls the visual appearance of the list. Because there are no preview graphics, you may have to select a style and then display the view until you find the style you like best.

- **Item Limit** This section controls the number of list items that can appear in the browser at once. Specify the fields this way:

  - **Number Of Items To Display** Specify the maximum number of items that can appear on a Web page displaying this view.

  - **Display Items In Batches Of The Specified Size** Select this option if, when the current list view page doesn't display the last item in the sorted list, you want a Next link to appear. That link would display the next batch of items.

  - **Limit The Total Number Of Items Returned To The Specified Amount** Select this option if you don't want any Next links to appear. In this case, the view would never display more than the first batch of items.

Modifying and Deleting List Views

If you display the Customization page for any list and then, under Views, click any listed view, Windows SharePoint Services will display an Edit View page that has all the same options as the Add View page save one: you can't change the Audience setting for an existing view. In all the other cases, however, you can change any settings you like, just as if you were creating the view in the previous section.

To delete a view, click its name in the Views section of the Customization page, and then click the Delete button at the bottom of the Edit View page.

Working with List Content

Windows SharePoint Services provides a variety of ways to work with lists and views, all requiring no effort or programming to set up. This includes displaying attractive input forms and reports. This section explains how these features work.

Working with List Content in Standard View

After a list contains all the fields you want, team members can view it or update it by:

- Clicking its entry in the Quick Launch bar (provided, of course, that you chose to display this list on the Quick Launch bar when you created or later modified the list).
- Clicking the Documents And Lists link on the top navigation bar of any page in the SharePoint site. Then, under Lists, click the list name.
- Adding the list to a Web Part Page.

To add an item, proceed as follows:

1 Display the list view page using any of the methods listed above.
2 Click the New Item link.
3 When a New Item page like the one in Figure 6-22 appears, enter some data.

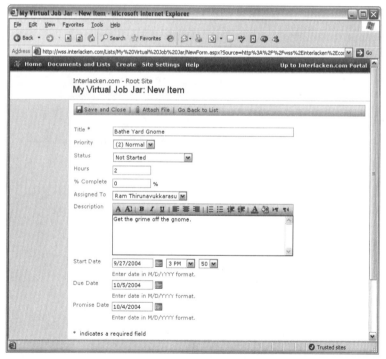

Figure 6-22. A SharePoint site automatically creates a data entry page like this for each custom list.

4 To save the data you entered, click the Save And Close link.

5 To enter more data, click the New Item link again.

> **Note** The Assigned To field in Figure 6-22 is a lookup field based on a User Information list that the SharePoint site provides. This is the list of authorized team members.

To change or delete the content of a list item:

1 Click on the item's title (which should be a hyperlink).

2 When the item appears on its own page, click the Edit Item or Delete toolbar button.

Alternatively, move the mouse pointer over the item's title, click the drop-down arrow, and then choose Edit Item or Delete Item from the shortcut menu as shown below.

Working with Lists in Datasheet View

If a team member's computer has Excel 2003 installed, it's also possible to create, modify, and delete list items using the Datasheet View shown in Figure 6-23. To invoke this view, display the usual list view page and then click the Edit In Datasheet toolbar button.

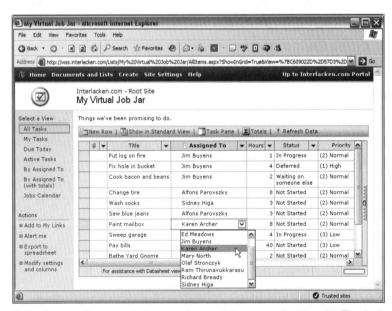

Figure 6-23. Datasheet view displays a list as an editable grid. The ActiveX control that makes this possible comes with Excel 2003.

Designing Lists, Libraries, and Pages

Here are the procedures for some common operations involving Datasheet View.

- To add an item (that is, a *row*), use any of these steps:
  - Click the New Row toolbar button.
  - Right-click the grid and choose Add Row.
  - Scroll to the bottom of the grid.

  Any of these methods will reveal a blank row, marked with an asterisk at the left. Click any field in this row and start typing the new row content.

- To modify the value in any row or editable column, just click it. This opens the value to editing, whether by typing, by drop-down list, or some other method.

  You can't edit columns that Windows SharePoint Services maintains. Created, Created By, Modified, Modified By, for example, fall into this category.

- To delete an item, right-click its row and choose Delete.

- To delete several adjacent items, select their rows, right-click, and choose Delete Rows.

- To sort or filter on any column, click the drop-down arrow at the right of its column name. This displays a selectable list of sorting and filtering options.

- To return to standard view, click the Show In Standard View toolbar button.

- To add a new column, right-click anywhere in the datasheet, and then choose Add Column from the shortcut menu. This displays the Create New Column page shown previously in Figure 6-12.

- To modify or delete a column, right-click the column heading, and then choose Edit/ Delete Column from the shortcut menu. This displays the Change Column page.

  For more information about using the Change Column page, refer to the section titled," Changing and Deleting List Columns," earlier in this chapter.

- To create a new list directly in Datasheet view:
  1. Click the Create link at the top of any page.
  2. Click Custom List In Datasheet View.
  3. Fill out the New List page shown previously in Figure 6-2.
  4. Click OK to display the list in Datasheet View. Initially, the list will have only a Title field. To add, modify, and delete columns, right-click and choose from the shortcut menu, as described in the two bullet points just above.

Creating Built-In Libraries

To create a document library, form library, or picture library, proceed as follows:

1. Click the Create link in the top navigation bar of any page in the site.
2. Click the Document Library, Form Library, or Picture Library link. This will display a New Library page like the one shown in Figure 6-24.

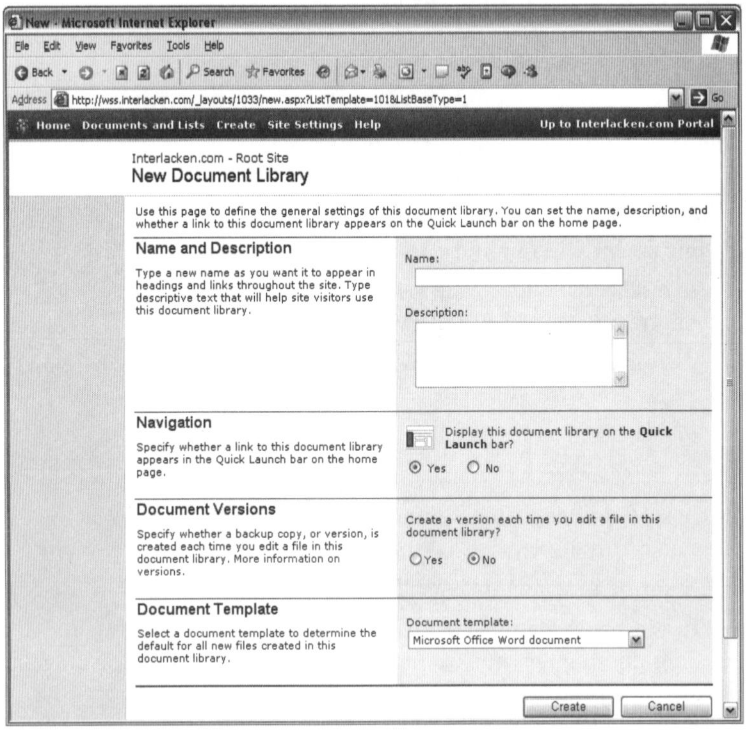

Microsoft Windows SharePoint Services Inside Out

Figure 6-24. When you create a document library, you need to decide whether to put versioning in effect, and which template to use for new documents.

Of course, for a form library, the word *Form* will replace the word *Document* everywhere on the page. For a picture library, *Picture* will replace *Document*.

3 Fill in the form as follows.

- **Name**   Assign a one-line name to the library. This name will identify the library throughout the site.

- **Description**   Type a few sentences describing the library and its intended use.

- **Navigation**   Select Yes if you want a link to the new library to appear in the Quick Launch bar on the home page.

- **Document Versions**   Select Yes if you want to Windows SharePoint Services to save a backup copy (a version) each time someone replaces a file in this library.

- **Document Template**   If you're creating a document or form library, select a document or form from the list box. This will be the basis for all new files created directly from the library. If you're creating a picture library, this setting will be absent.

4 Click OK to create the library and display its default view.

5 To modify the library columns and view, click Modify Settings And Columns on the library view page, and then proceed just as you would to modify a list.

For more information on modifying lists, refer to the section titled "Modifying Lists" earlier in this chapter.

Creating and Using Surveys

Surveys are a particularly interesting type of list. Creating a survey requires four basic steps:

1 Decide what questions you want to ask.

2 Design a form that people can use to record their answers.

3 Let the survey population fill out the form.

4 Analyze the results.

Although a SharePoint site can't choose questions for you, it does most of the work for the three remaining steps. Here's the procedure:

1 Open the site where team members will complete the survey.

2 Click the Create link on the top navigation bar of any page in the site. This displays the Create Page page, shown previously in Figure 6-1.

3 Click the Survey link on the Create Page page. This displays the New Survey page shown in Figure 6-25.

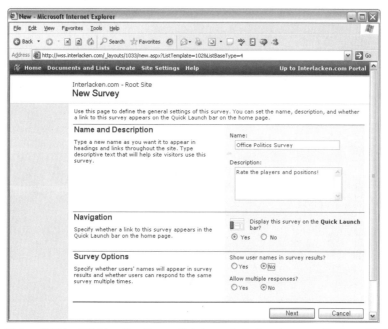

Figure 6-25. Clicking the Survey link in a site's Create page displays this Web page for creating a new survey.

Fill out the options on this form as follows:

- **Name**   Give the survey a short, descriptive name.
- **Description**   If you want, enter some text that explains the survey and its purpose.
- **Display This Survey On The Quick Launch Bar?**   Select Yes if you want all Quick Launch bars in the current site to contain a link to this survey.
- **Show User Names In Survey Results?**   Select Yes if displays of survey results should include the name of each respondent. This, however, doesn't stop the survey from recording the name of each respondent. An administrator could still look up those names.
- **Allow Multiple Responses?**   Select Yes if the same person can fill out the survey multiple times.

Click the Next button when these entries are complete.

4   The Create New Question page shown in Figure 6-26 constructs the first (or next) survey question.

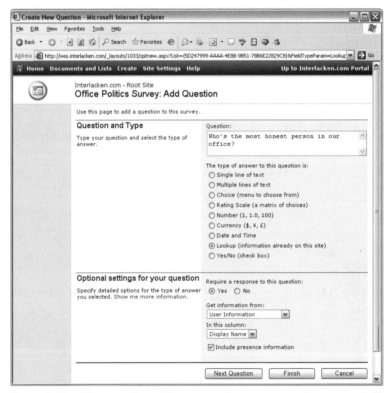

Figure 6-26.   The page for adding a question to a survey is very much like the one for adding a column to a list. Survey results, after all, are lists.

Designing Lists, Libraries, and Pages

- **Question**   Type the text for the survey question.
- **The Type Of Answer To This Question Is**   Indicate what type of data constitutes the survey answer. Table 6-2 summarized the result of each choice.

5   The bottom half of the Edit Question page changes depending on the type of answer you specify. Figure 6-26 shows the format that appears if you choose Lookup (Information Already On This Site). Configure each option as follows:

- **Require A Response To This Question**   Select Yes if the survey respondent must answer the question before proceeding. Select No if answering the question is optional.
- **Get Information From**   Select the table that contains the list of valid choices.
- **In This Column**   Select the column that contains the list of valid choices.
- **Include Presence Information**   Select this check box to place an icon showing the selected person's Windows Messenger status next to the displayed field. (This check box appears only if the lookup table is User Information.)

For assistance in filling out the Optional Settings For Your Question section for other types of answers, refer to the section titled "Adding List Columns" earlier in this chapter.

6   If this is the last question in the survey, click Finish. Otherwise, click Next Question, and go back to step 4.

Clicking Finish displays the Customization page shown in Figure 6-27.

Review the following links in the General Settings area, and modify them as necessary:

- **Change General Settings**   Displays a Change General Settings page very similar to the one shown in Figure 6-25. This provides a way to update these settings without re-creating the survey.
- **Save Survey As Template**   Saves a copy of the survey for use in creating additional surveys in the future.
- **Change Permissions For This Survey**   Controls who can complete, modify, and view the survey.
- **Delete This Survey**   Removes the survey forms, links, and data from the SharePoint site.

All these links work very much like those for lists, as described earlier in this chapter.

Chapter 6

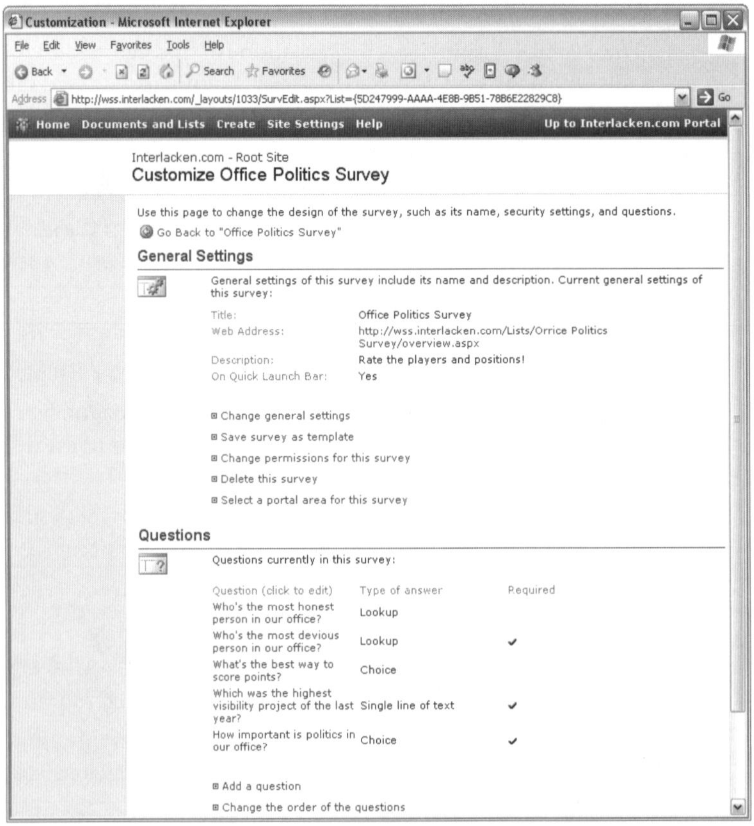

Microsoft Windows SharePoint Services Inside Out

Figure 6-27. This page modifies the overall properties of a survey.

7 Under the Questions heading, review these settings and make any necessary changes.

- **Question (Click To Edit)** Click the text of any question listed under this heading to change the text or format of that question, or to delete the question completely. You can't change a question in such a way that data would be lost.

- **Add A Question** Adds new questions to the survey. Basically, you must click this link and then repeat steps 4 and 5 once for each question.

- **Change The Order Of The Questions** Displays a list of current questions and question numbers. The question numbers appear in drop-down lists that you can manipulate to put the questions in any order.

Figure 6-28 shows how the Office Politics survey appears to a survey respondent. This is a custom survey created by using the procedure just described; it's not a standard element of every new SharePoint site.

Designing Lists, Libraries, and Pages

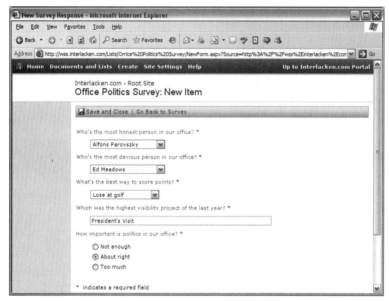

Figure 6-28. This is how the survey looks to a survey respondent. The survey itself is just a list with a column for recording each answer.

Here's how to display this page:

1 Click the Documents And Lists link on the top navigation bar of any page in the site.

2 Click the survey's list title or icon to display the Overview page, shown in Figure 6-29.

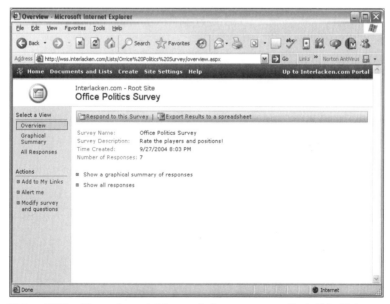

Figure 6-29. The entry point for analyzing survey results is this Web page.

Microsoft Windows SharePoint Services Inside Out

The body of a survey Overview page presents the following choices:

- **Respond To This Survey** Opens the survey so that you can answer the questions.
- **Export Results To A Spreadsheet** Downloads an Excel Web Query (.iqy) file that displays the survey data into a spreadsheet.

> For more information about downloading list data, refer to "Setting Up Linked Lists from a SharePoint Site" in Chapter 4.

- **Show A Graphical Summary Of Questions** Displays a graphical summary of survey responses similar to the one shown in Figure 6-30.

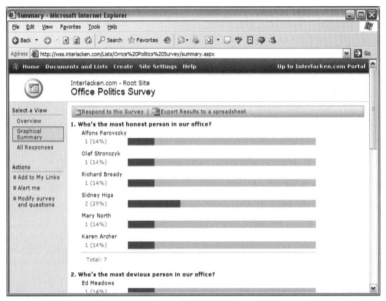

Figure 6-30. The graphical summary of survey responses looks like this.

- **Show All Responses** Displays a textual listing of survey responses similar to the one shown in Figure 6-31.

Designing Lists, Libraries, and Pages

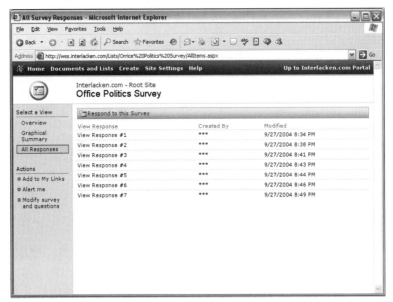

Figure 6-31. This Web page displays all responses to a survey.

The Select A View area provides access to three views:

- **Overview**   Displays the initial view shown in Figure 6-29.
- **Graphical Summary**   Displays the same view as the Show A Graphical Summary Of Responses link in the main body (as shown in Figure 6-30).
- **All Responses**   Displays the same view as the Show All Responses link in the main body: the view shown in Figure 6-31.

The Actions area provides these three choices:

- **Add To My Links**   This choice appears only if the site collection's top-level site is configured with the location of a portal site. In that case, it displays an Add Link page that updates the current user's personal site with a link to the survey.
- **Alert Me**   Click this link if you want to receive e-mail notification whenever someone completes or changes the survey.
- **Modify Survey And Questions**   Displays a page that can change the properties of the survey. This includes the survey name, description, questions, and other settings. In short, it displays the Customization page shown in Figure 6-27.

Creating Discussions

A SharePoint discussion board is a list that supports newsgroup-style dialogue. Discussion boards can be as open as you like, but they also have features for managing discussion threads and ensuring that only approved posts appear. The procedure for creating a discussion board offers no surprises.

1   Open the SharePoint site where the discussion board will reside.

2   Click the Create link in the top navigation bar of any page.

3   When the Create page appears, scroll down to Discussion Boards and click the Discussion Board link. This will display the New Discussion Board page shown in Figure 6-32.

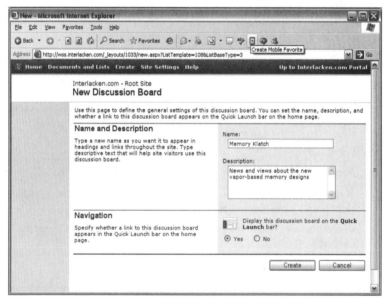

Figure 6-32.   The form for creating a discussion board is very much like that for creating any other list.

4   Fill in the fields on the New Discussion Board page as usual.

   ■   **Name**   Give the Discussion Board a short, descriptive name.

   ■   **Description**   If you want, type some text that explains the discussion board and its purpose.

   ■   **Display This Discussion Board On The Quick Launch Bar?**   Select Yes if you want all Quick Launch bars in the current SharePoint site to contain a link to this discussion board.

5   Click OK to create the discussion board and display its main page.

A discussion board is just a SharePoint list. Its Threaded and Flat views are list views. If you want to change any of a discussion board's properties, click the Modify Settings And Columns link on its main page and work with the Customization page just as you would for any other list.

For more information about using discussion boards, refer to the section titled "Using Discussion Boards" in Chapter 3. For more information about customizing SharePoint lists, refer to the section titled "Modifying Lists" earlier in this chapter.

In Summary...

This chapter explained how to create, modify, display, and delete lists and libraries. This included the standard list and library types that come with Windows SharePoint Services, as well as custom lists and libraries you design yourself.

The next chapter begins Part IV, which explains how to create and modify SharePoint using Microsoft FrontPage 2003. Using a Web design program like FrontPage involves some extra complexity, but it also provides much more power and flexibility than you can possibly get with a browser interface.

Chapter 6

Creating and Designing Sites Using FrontPage 2003

Opening, Creating, and Copying SharePoint Sites

If the SharePoint facilities for using a browser to create and modify sites don't meet your needs, you may find Microsoft FrontPage 2003 a much better match. FrontPage 2003 has powerful features for creating and modifying SharePoint sites, HTML pages, Web Part Pages, lists, libraries, and views, all with much more power and flexibility than the browser interface can provide.

FrontPage 2003 can also modify the visual aspect of your site. For example, you can add pictures, hyperlinks, and ordinary text anywhere you want, apply additional Themes, and even design new Themes.

All this power will, of course, take several chapters to describe. This chapter addresses the first and most global operations a designer or developer typically undertakes: opening a site, creating a site, and copying a site from place to place.

This series of chapters is *not* an introduction to FrontPage itself. It presumes you're reasonably proficient in using FrontPage to create and modify conventional Web sites. If you need help getting up to speed with FrontPage, the recommended reading is *Microsoft Office FrontPage 2003 Inside Out*, by Jim Buyens.

Opening a SharePoint Site

The normal procedure for opening a SharePoint site in FrontPage 2003 is the same as that for opening any other server-based Web site. Specifically:

1 Start FrontPage 2003.
2 Choose Open Site from the File menu.

3 When the Open Site dialog box shown in Figure 7-1 appears, do either of the following:

- Click My Network Places in the My Places bar. Then, find your SharePoint server or site in the large list box and double-click it.

- Type in your site's URL in the Site Name text box, and then click Open.

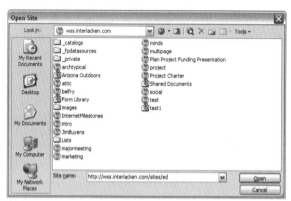

Figure 7-1. You can open a SharePoint site in FrontPage much as you would any other server-based Web site.

There's only one catch: the Open Site dialog box never displays managed paths, and this makes it impossible to point and click your way into any site collection other than the one that starts at the Web server's root. In such cases, you'll need to type the URL.

There are, of course, ways of opening a Web site without using the Open Site dialog box. For example:

- Start FrontPage. This usually reopens the site that was open the last time you quit FrontPage. If that isn't happening:
  1 Choose Options from the Tools menu.
  2 On the General tab, select Open Last Web Site Automatically When FrontPage Starts.

- Choose Recent Sites from the File menu, and click one of the sites on the submenu. (Unfortunately, this shows only the last four sites, and there's no way of increasing that.)

- Browse the site in Internet Explorer, and then click the Edit button on the standard toolbar. This opens both the current page and the site that contains it.

  If your computer has several HTML editors installed, the default editor for SharePoint pages might not be FrontPage. If so, click the Edit button's drop-down arrow and choose Edit With Microsoft FrontPage. Figure 7-2 shows this operation in progress.

- If you've already opened the parent of the site you want (for example, the top site for your site's collection), double-click the subsite icon in the parent site.

  In Figure 7-3, for example, *ProjectPlan* is a subsite of *http//wss.interlacken.com/sites/ed*. To open the *ProjectPlan* subsite, double-click its icon either in the Folder List at the left or in Folders View at the right.

212

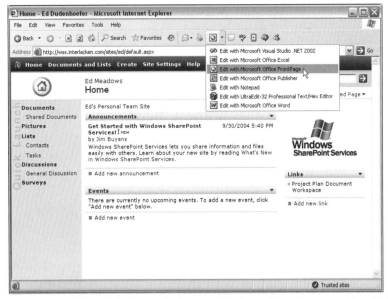

Figure 7-2. If the Edit button in Internet Explorer doesn't open a SharePoint page in the editor you want, click the drop-down arrow and make your own selection.

Figure 7-3. FrontPage displays the files in a SharePoint site as if they were in the Web server's file system. However, they're actually in a SharePoint content database.

Figure 7-3 also illustrates some unique features of a SharePoint site. Specifically:

- The files look like ordinary disk files, despite the fact that they actually reside in a SharePoint content database. Windows SharePoint Services complies with all of the normal FrontPage file handling protocols despite redirecting them into its content database.
- The site's *Lists* folder contains a special subfolder for each list. This subfolder, however, doesn't contain the list data. Instead, it contains:
  - The Web Part Pages that display the list.
  - A subfolder named *Attachments* that stores any attached files.
- SharePoint library folders reside directly in the site's root folder. The *Shared Documents* folder, for example, stores:
  - All files and folders that comprise the content of the library. In the figure, for example, the documents *ProjectPlan.doc* and *ProjectPlan.xls* are items in the *Shared Documents* library.
  - A *Forms* folder contains the Web Part Pages that display the various library views.
- The database tables used by both SharePoint lists and libraries aren't visible in Folder List or Folders View. These tables reside only in the SharePoint content database. This has implications when you want to copy a SharePoint site from place to place.

  It's perfectly all right, however, to add, change, or delete SharePoint library files or folders in FrontPage. Windows SharePoint Services will keep the library contents listing up to date, and even store document versions (provided, of course, that the library has versioning in effect).

For instructions to reliably copy a SharePoint site from one location to another refer to the sections titled, "Exporting SharePoint Packages," and "Importing SharePoint Packages," later in this chapter.

If you have any doubt whether a given site is a SharePoint site or a FrontPage server extension site, choose Site Settings from the Tools menu and make sure the General tab is selected.

- If the third setting contains the words *FrontPage Server Extensions Version* followed by a version number that begins with 5 or lower, the server is running the FrontPage Server Extensions. No features of Windows SharePoint Services will be available.
- If the third setting contains the words *SharePoint Services Version* followed by a version number that begins with 6 or higher, the server is running Windows SharePoint Services.

Figure 7-4 shows examples of both cases.

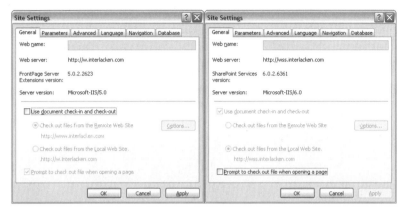

Figure 7-4.   The third line of settings in this dialog box shows what kind of Web server hosts the current site.

Avoiding Compatibility Issues

The Web pages that control a SharePoint Team Site are complex and contain many special elements that Windows SharePoint Services uses. You should therefore exercise extreme care when making changes to these pages. Change the appearance of the pages if you want, but not their underlying structure.

The following sections will address some specific precautions.

> Additional precautions apply when you use FrontPage 2003 to modify sites and pages unique to SharePoint Portal Server. For more information, browse Microsoft Knowledge Base article 831612: "Considerations that apply when you use FrontPage 2003 to edit SharePoint Portal Server 2003 sites." The URL is *http://support.microsoft.com/default.aspx?kbid=831612*.

Avoiding Older Versions of FrontPage

Microsoft created and tested FrontPage 2003 in unison with Windows SharePoint Services and SharePoint Portal Server. FrontPage 2003 is therefore safe for use with those products.

If, however, you edit your SharePoint site with an earlier version of FrontPage (such as FrontPage 2002), the earlier version of FrontPage may actually break some features or remove some functionality from SharePoint pages. This occurs because some features of SharePoint Web sites, such as Web Parts and data views, didn't exist when Microsoft developed and tested those earlier versions of FrontPage.

Avoiding Managed Areas

Be particularly careful of page areas that Windows SharePoint Services updates from time to time. One such area, for example, is the Quick Launch bar that appears on the home page of many sites. The Quick Launch bar isn't a Web Part; it's just an HTML table cell marked with the attribute id="webpartpagenavbar". You can edit the Quick Launch bar by hand, but Windows SharePoint Services is likely to overwrite your change or not work properly the next time someone clicks Yes to Display This List On The Quick Launch Bar? on the Settings page for some list or library.

This makes it best not to edit an area like the Quick launch Bar at all. If you want to add links or other content to a page, do so in an unused area.

Avoiding ASP and ASP.NET Pages

A Web server running Windows SharePoint Services won't run ASP pages, ordinary ASP.NET pages, or other common server-side programs. There are four primary reasons for this:

- A server running Window SharePoint Services doesn't provide a normal operating environment for ASP and ASP.NET pages. Instead of using normal Windows, IIS, and .NET Framework program interface for certain operations, a page running on a SharePoint server needs to read and manipulate a special SharePoint object model.

- Microsoft presumes that if you want to run Windows SharePoint Services, you want to develop Web Parts and deploy them in Web Part Pages.

- SharePoint servers are heavily locked down from a security point of view. To develop and deploy a Web Part, for example, you must use a special Visual Studio .NET template, digitally sign your code, and then register the signed module on the SharePoint server.

- A so-called Safe Mode parser examines all ASP and ASP.NET pages and prevents any server-side code they contain from executing.

If, in fact, you want to run ordinary ASP or ASP.NET pages, you should pursue one of these alternatives:

- Run the pages on an ordinary (non-SharePoint) Web server, possibly with the FrontPage 2002 Server Extensions installed. This could be a different virtual server on the same computer that runs your SharePoint site.

- Create an unmanaged (i.e. excluded) path within your SharePoint server, and then install the conventional ASP.NET application within that path.

> For more information about unmanaged (i.e. excluded) paths, refer to, "Planning Managed Paths," in Chapter 5.

Avoiding FrontPage Database Features

The following FrontPage database components don't work under Windows SharePoint Services.

Save Results To Database   Saves form results into a database table.

Database Results Wizard   Displays information from a database in various formats.

216

Database Interface Wizard   Uses the preceding components to construct a general-purpose set of Web pages for viewing, adding, changing, and deleting database records.

In most cases, the loss of these components isn't as tragic as you might think. You just need to use SharePoint lists, views, and Web Parts instead. Here are some helpful references.

- For more information about creating and processing SharePoint lists using only a browser, refer to Chapter 6, "Designing Lists and Libraries."

- For more information about integrating SharePoint lists with Access and Excel, refer to the following topics in Chapter 4.

  - "Creating and Using Lists in Access"

  - "Creating and Using Lists in Excel"

- For more information about creating and processing SharePoint lists in FrontPage, refer to:

  - Chapter 10, "Creating Data Sources and Data Views."

  - Chapter 11, "Working with List Views and Data Views."

  - Chapter 12, "Using Advanced Web Part Features."

Creating a SharePoint Site

You can use FrontPage to create new SharePoint sites in much the same way as it creates any other type of site. You just need to consider a few extra details. To begin:

1 Choose New from the File menu, and when the New task pane appears, click any link under New Web Site.

   Alternatively, on the Standard toolbar, click the down arrow on the Create A New Normal Page button, and then choose Web Site.

2 When the Web Site Templates dialog box shown in Figure 7-5 appears, choose the tab that displays the type of Web site you want.

   - **General**   This tab lists templates and wizards that FrontPage has supported over several releases. In addition, it has an option to create a SharePoint Team Site.

   - **Packages**   Each template on this tab is a Windows SharePoint Services application bundled with FrontPage 2003. These applications run only on a Web server running Windows SharePoint Services.

   - **SharePoint Services**   Each template on this tab physically resides on a Web server running Windows SharePoint Services. You can use these templates only on the SharePoint server where they reside.

217

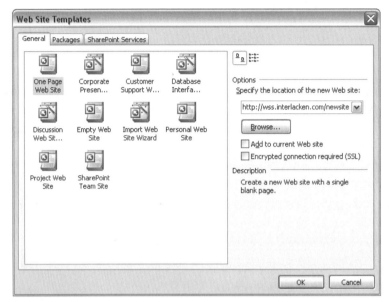

Figure 7-5. FrontPage provides this collection of templates and wizards for creating new Web sites.

Creating General Purpose Sites

The templates listed in Table 7-1 all appear on the General tab of the Web Site Templates dialog box, and they all work on servers running Windows SharePoint Services.

Table 7-1. FrontPage Web Site Templates Compatible with Windows SharePoint Services

Web Site Template	Result
Empty Web Site	A Web site with nothing in it.
One Page Web Site	A Web site with a blank home page.
Import Web Site Wizard	Adds an existing set of pages to a new or existing Web site.
Corporate Presence Wizard	A typical set of Web pages for representing a company on the Internet.
SharePoint Team Site	A specialized Web site that coordinates the activities of a project or workgroup. Your Web server must be running Microsoft Windows SharePoint Services for this feature to work.

The first four templates in Table 7-1 work on any type of Web server, SharePoint or not.

A SharePoint Team Site, of course, *requires* a server running Windows SharePoint Services. If you try to create a SharePoint Team Site on any other kind of server, you'll get an error message like the one below.

The templates listed in Table 7-2 also appear on the General tab, but they *won't* work on a server running Windows SharePoint Services. If you try to create such a site on a SharePoint server, you'll get an error message like this:

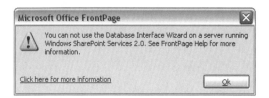

In each case, however, Windows SharePoint Services offers comparable (and in fact superior) features. These alternatives appear in the SharePoint Alternative column of Table 7-2.

Table 7-2. FrontPage Web Site Templates Incompatible with Windows SharePoint Services

Web Site Template	Result	SharePoint Alternative
Customer Support Web Site	A Web site for a company offering customer support on the Internet. This template is designed particularly for computer software companies	Team Web Site
Personal Web Site	A Web site that represents an individual, with pages for interests, favorite sites, and photos.	Team Web Site
Project Web Site	A Web site that members of a project team might use.	Team Web Site
Discussion Web Wizard	A special Web site designed for interactive discussions.	SharePoint Discussion Board
Database Interface Wizard	A Web site that includes pages to add, view, and optionally update a new or an existing database.	SharePoint List

219

Creating Web Sites from Packages

Physically, a SharePoint package is a single file that contains any number of logical files in compressed format. In this respect, a package is somewhat like a ZIP or Windows CAB file. Packages have two characteristics that ordinary templates lack:

- They consist of a single file, which is easy to transport.
- They can create libraries, lists, and other database objects as well as ordinary Web content such as Web pages and picture files.

Just as Microsoft provides the Web site templates listed previously in Table 7-1 and Table 7-2, it provides two SharePoint packages that you can deploy in a new or existing SharePoint site:

- **News and Reviews Site**   Deploys a news site complete with previews and reviews, discussions, and voting.
- **Web Log**   Deploys a blog site complete with log search, hot topics, discussions, and favorite links.

These packages appear as options on the Packages tab shown in Figure 7-6.

> **Note**   There are as many kinds of blog sites as people in the world, but the basic concept is that of a personal Web site that includes an online diary of musings, adventures, investigations, and results. The terms *blog*, *Web log*, and *weblog* are synonymous, except that *blog* is trendier and the term *Web log* can also mean a server's log files.

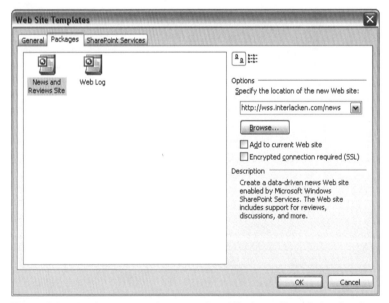

Figure 7-6.   Packages contain a complete Windows SharePoint Services site or application, complete with Web pages, ancillary files, and databases.

Figure 7-7 shows the home page that results from installing the News and Reviews Site package that comes with FrontPage 2003.

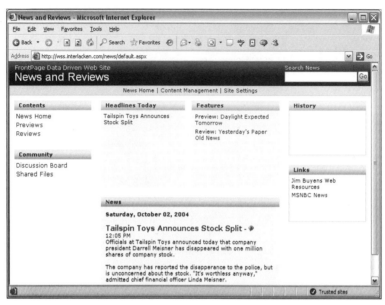

Figure 7-7. Installing a News and Reviews Site package creates a Windows SharePoint Services site with a home page like this. This isn't a SharePoint Team Site, but it uses many of the same Web Parts.

Despite some visual similarities, this site differs considerably from an ordinary SharePoint Team Site:

- The Contents and Community areas provide ordinary Web content through a Dynamic Web Template.

  For more information about Dynamic Web Templates, refer to, "Using Dynamic Web Templates," in Chapter 9.

- The Headlines Today, Features, News, History, and Links areas are Data View Web Parts. They all display information, in various levels of detail, that resides in SharePoint lists.

- The Content Management link on the menu bar jumps to a page where you can add, modify, or delete articles or features.

- Each article in the News Web Part contains a "bubble" icon that jumps to a page where visitors can enter discussion comments about that article.

Figure 7-8 shows the home page of a site that FrontPage can build from its Web Log package. This is a sort of online diary that you update, and that Web visitors can read and comment upon. This page differs visually from a standard SharePoint Team Site not only because it uses a different arrangement of Web Parts, but also because it uses a non-default theme.

Figure 7-8. This home page shows another type of SharePoint site that FrontPage can create from a package.

Here's the procedure for creating a News And Reviews Site, a Web Log, or any other type of site for which FrontPage provides a package:

1. If you want to add the application to an existing Web site on the SharePoint server, open that site in FrontPage.

2. Display the Web Site Templates dialog box using one of these techniques:
   - Click the Web Site Templates link in the New task pane.
   - Click the Create A New Normal Page down arrow on the Standard toolbar, and select Web Site.

3. In the Web Site Templates dialog box, click the Packages tab, and then select the application you want to install.

4. In the Specify The Location Of The New Web Site section, do either of the following:
   - Enter the URL where you want the new site to reside. The host name must specify a server running Windows SharePoint Services, and the path should specify a new folder on that server.
   - Select the Add To Current Web Site check box.

5. Click OK to process the package. When the Import Web Package dialog box appears, jump forward to the section "Specifying Package Import Settings," later in this chapter.

You can also create a new SharePoint site by installing a package you obtain as an .fwp file. For more information on this method, refer to the section titled, "Importing SharePoint Packages" later in this chapter.

Creating Windows SharePoint Services Web Sites

Chapter 7

This method of creating a SharePoint site occurs almost completely on the SharePoint server. FrontPage merely sends the server a command to create a site from a template already on the server. These might be Microsoft templates that come with SharePoint or custom templates an administrator provides for widespread use.

The SharePoint Services tab of the Web Site Templates dialog box shown in Figure 7-9 lists the templates available on the server that appears in the Options area of the same dialog box.

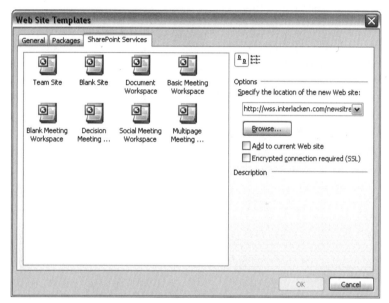

Figure 7-9. SharePoint Services templates reside on and create Web sites on a remote server running Windows SharePoint Services.

The procedure for using these templates is very much the same as that for using any other template. The main differences are that:

- FrontPage itself doesn't do the work of building the Web site; instead, FrontPage issues a command that tells the server to do the work. (This is also true of the SharePoint Team Site template on the General tab.)
- The list of templates can vary from one server to another. Whoever administers the server can add, change, or remove templates at will.

Follow these steps to create a SharePoint site from a template on the server:

1. Display the Web Site Templates dialog box, as you did in the previous sections.
2. Click the SharePoint Services tab, and then specify the new site's location in the box titled Specify The Location Of The New Web Site.
3. Select a template, and then click OK to create the site.

Troubleshooting

SharePoint Services tab is empty

When attempting to create a SharePoint site, you might find that the SharePoint Services tab of the Web Site Templates dialog box is empty.

This occurs because the list of templates comes from the server you specify in the Specify The Location Of The New Web Site box. If that server isn't running Windows SharePoint Services, no list of SharePoint templates will be available.

In most cases, you can correct this situation by entering your SharePoint server URL in the Specify The Location Of The New Web Site box, and then tabbing to another field. If that fails, try this workaround:

1 Select the General tab.

2 Enter the correct server name in the Specify The Location Of The New Web Site box.

3 Select the Packages or SharePoint Services tab.

Similarly, if the list of templates doesn't include the one you want, you may be looking at the wrong server. The solution is once again to correct the server name in the Specify The Location Of The New Web Site box, and then tab to another field.

Adding New Site Pages to an Existing Site

The same templates and wizards that add pages to new Web sites can add pages to existing sites as well. To do this:

1 Open the existing Web site.

2 Display the New task pane.

3 Choose Web Site Templates, and select a template or wizard for the pages you want to add.

4 Select the Add To Current Web Site option, and click OK.

If the template or wizard attempts to create a Web page with the same name as an existing page, FrontPage displays the Confirm Save dialog box, shown in Figure 7-10. Click Yes to overwrite the existing file with the template or wizard file. Click No to discard the new file and keep the existing one.

Figure 7-10. When you use a template or wizard to add pages to an existing Web site, FrontPage displays this prompt before overwriting an existing page.

Exporting SharePoint Packages

Since its first release, FrontPage has had a Publish command that copies the content of one Web site to another. In general, this has been the fastest and most accurate way of publishing a Web site.

In the case of SharePoint sites, however, the FrontPage Publish command has a fatal weakness: it copies only file content. It *doesn't* copy the columns, settings, and content of SharePoint libraries and lists.

To resolve this deficiency, FrontPage 2003 provides two new ways of copying content between SharePoint Team Services sites:

- **Packages** Packages copy any or all the of the following content from a SharePoint site:
  - Ordinary Web pages, Web Part Pages, and associated files such as pictures and style sheets.
  - The Web Part pages that display lists and libraries.
  - Any documents or attachments in lists and libraries.

  If you choose to package only some of the files in a site, the package feature can identify and include *associated* files. This means, for example, that adding a Web page to the package can automatically add all pictures and other files that the page needs to operate correctly on the destination Web site.

  A package, however, *doesn't* include the database contents of lists and libraries. This means that on the new site, all lists will be empty and all libraries will have only the default properties for each document they contain.

- **Backup/Restore** A backup copies everything out of an existing site, including the database content of lists and libraries, and stores it in a single backup file. A restore copies everything out of the backup file and adds it to an existing (generally empty) SharePoint site.

Whether you export a package or create a backup, the result is a single file that resides on your local disk or file share. If necessary, you can transport this file to another computer on a compact disc, or use any other method that's handy. (USB flash memory key fobs are trendy.) Then, you once again use FrontPage 2003, this time to import or restore the content.

225

Creating a Package File

Here's the detailed procedure for creating a package file:

1 Open the source Web site in FrontPage.

2 Choose Packages, Export from the Tools menu.

3 When the Export Web Package dialog box shown in Figure 7-11 appears, use the Files In Web Site list to select the content you want to send.

4 After each selection, click the Add >> button. The files you selected will then appear in the Files In Package list to the right. In all probability, some additional files will appear in the Files In Package list as well.

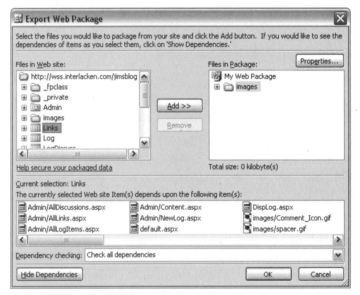

Figure 7-11. Use this dialog box to include files from the current Web in a package.

These extra files appear because whenever you add a Web page to a package, FrontPage automatically adds any pictures, style sheets, or other files that the Web page uses. This is very cool, and a major advantage of using packages.

Chapter 7

5 If FrontPage is adding more or fewer dependent files than you want, proceed as follows:

5.1 Look for a Show Dependencies button in the bottom left corner of the dialog box. If you find it, click it. The Show Dependencies button will change to Hide Dependencies.

If the Hide Dependencies button already appears, just go to the next step.

5.2 Locate the Dependency Checking drop-down list (just above the Hide Dependencies button). Use this list to specify the type of dependency checking you want. Table 7-3 lists the available options.

5.3 To preview the effect of the new Dependency Checking selection, click one or more files or folders in either the Files In Web Site or the Files In Package list. The list box titled The Currently Selected Web Site Item(s) Depends Upon The Following Items(s): will list the files FrontPage would add to the package along with the files you selected.

5.4 Changing the Dependency Checking option doesn't remove any files from the package. To remove files, you must select them in the Files In Package list and then click the Remove button.

6 Click the Properties button to add identifying information to the package. This button displays a Web Package Properties dialog box with text boxes for entering title, description, author, and company information. Click OK to close this dialog box.

7 When the package contains all the files you want, click the OK button in the Export Web Package dialog box.

8 FrontPage will display a standard Save As dialog box. Choose a file name and folder, and then click OK to create the package file. The customary file extension is .fwp.

Table 7-3. Import Package Dependency Checking Options

Dependency Checking	Description
Check All Dependencies.	Whenever you add a file to the Files In Package list, FrontPage will add every other file that your file uses. This includes pictures, style sheets, hyperlinks, and so forth (but only files in the same Web site).
Check All Dependencies, Except Hyperlinks.	This works almost exactly like the previous option, except that FrontPage won't add files that your file mentions only in hyperlinks.
Do Not Check Dependencies.	FrontPage won't add any files to the package automatically. You're completely in control.

227

Importing SharePoint Packages

As you might expect, the process of importing a package is similar to that of exporting one. The next two sections will explain the importing process.

Opening a Package

Here are the exact steps you need to perform when opening a SharePoint site saved as a package:

1. Open the destination Web site in FrontPage. If necessary, use the Empty Web Site template to create a new site as described in the earlier section titled "Creating General Purpose Sites."

2. Choose Packages from the Tools menu, and then choose Import from the submenu.

3. When the File Open dialog box shown in Figure 7-12 appears, select the package file, and then click OK.

Figure 7-12. FrontPage displays a standard File Open dialog box to find files that contain a Web package.

> **Tip** The Import Package command won't accept files that the Backup command created. However, the Restore command *will* accept files that the Export Package command created.

Specifying Package Import Settings

Once you've opened a saved SharePoint package, the Import Web Package dialog box shown in Figure 7-13 will appear.

228

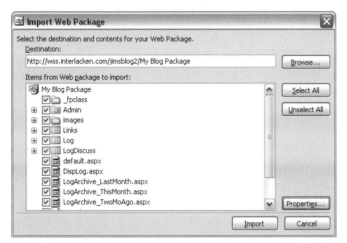

Figure 7-13. When you import a package, you have considerable flexibility in choosing which parts of the package you want.

To continue, verify the URL that appears in the Destination box and type any corrections. Alternatively, click Browse to locate the Web server where you want the imported content to reside.

Tip The default destination for a package is the site currently open in FrontPage. The path within that site defaults to the package's filename base.

Review and respond to the following settings in the Import Web Package dialog box:

- **Items From Web Package To Import**   Confirm each item in the package you want to import. If the check box to the left of an item is selected, SharePoint will import it. Normally, you should import all the items in the package.

  If a plus sign precedes an item, clicking the plus sign shows dependent items. In the case of lists, for example, the pages that process the list are dependent on the list itself. If you don't import a list, you don't import the pages that process it either.

- **Select All**   Click this button to select every item in the Items From Web Package To Import list.

- **Unselect All**   Click this button to clear the selection for every item in the Items From Web Package To Import list.

- **Properties**   Click this button to view the Title, Description, Author, Company, Size, and External Dependencies of the package.

  An *external dependency* is a file that the package requires but doesn't include. Usually these are files that appear in the root Web site when an administrator installs SharePoint.

- **Destination**   Specify the folder where you want the imported package to reside. This is a folder within the Web site you specified in step 5.

229

If, for example, several people are going to have Web logs in the same site, you would import the package once for each person, specifying a different folder location each time.

To import the package in the site's root location, delete this field.

Note In Figure 7-13, Links, Log, and LogDiscuss are SharePoint lists rather than files.

After completing these entries, click the Import button in the Import Web Package dialog box. If you get any security warnings or other prompts, respond to them. FrontPage will display an Importing Package dialog box that contains a progress bar and that might seem to freeze occasionally. Be patient—eventually, you'll receive this confirmation message:

Caution Importing a SharePoint package *doesn't* import security settings. Any items you import will have the new site's default permissions. If this isn't correct, open the site in a browser and use site, list, or library settings to configure the permissions you want.

Backing Up a SharePoint Site

A backup of a SharePoint site copies everything in the site, including the database content of lists and libraries, to a single backup file. If this is what you want, proceed as follows:

1 In FrontPage, open the SharePoint site you want to back up.

2 Choose Server from the Tools menu, and then choose Backup Web Site. This will display the Backup Web Site dialog box shown below.

3 If you want to back up the entire folder tree of Web sites starting at the current site, select the Include Subsites In Archive check box.

4 Click OK to display a File Save dialog box, and then select the folder where you want the backup file to reside.

5 In the File Name box, type a name for the backup file.

6 Click Save. FrontPage will write the backup file and then display a dialog box stating Backup Completed Successfully.

Restoring a SharePoint Site

To restore a SharePoint site from a backup you took in FrontPage, proceed as follows:

1 In FrontPage, open the site that will receive the backup. In most cases, this should be a new empty Web site.

2 Choose Server from the Tools menu, and then click Restore Web Site.

3 When the File Open dialog box appears, type or select the folder or filename where you saved the Web site backup. Then, click Open.

4 When the Restore Web Site dialog box below appears, click OK.

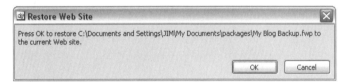

5 When the restore is complete, FrontPage will display the message: Web Site Restore Completed Successfully.

Keep the following points in mind when using FrontPage to restore any SharePoint backup.

● When FrontPage restores a SharePoint backup, it doesn't erase any files, folders, or database content. In case of name conflicts, however, the restore will overwrite existing content without warning.

● Restoring a SharePoint backup *doesn't* restore security settings. Any items you restore will have the new site's default permissions. If this isn't correct, open the site in a browser and configure the permissions you want.

● Backups you take in FrontPage are compatible with the smigrate.exe command-line program.

> **For more information about smigrate.exe, refer to the topics, "Backing Up a Site with smigrate.exe," and "Restoring a Site with smigrate.exe," in Chapter 14.**

In Summary...

This chapter explained how FrontPage 2003 can open existing SharePoint sites, create new SharePoint sites, and copy SharePoint sites from place to place.

The next chapter will explain how to modify SharePoint lists, libraries, site navigation, and Themes, all using FrontPage 2003.

Chapter 8

Creating and Formatting Web Part Pages

Although you can create and configure Web Part Pages in a browser, that experience certainly lacks the flexibility and control that most Web designers demand. Uniformity is a key attribute of all successful Web sites, but successful designers want to choose their own uniform, whether it applies to a single site or to thousands.

To meet this need, Microsoft Office FrontPage 2003 has features that create and configure Web Part Pages with great flexibility, with or without the standard SharePoint menus, and formatted any way the designer wants.

Furthermore, SharePoint themes and FrontPage themes use the same technology. As a result, you can apply FrontPage themes to SharePoint sites, even FrontPage themes you've created or modified yourself.

This chapter will explain how to work with both Web Parts and themes in FrontPage. Like the previous chapter, however, it assumes you have a basic working knowledge of FrontPage itself.

Working with Web Part Pages and Web Part Zones

A Web Part Page is basically any page that meets three conditions:

- It resides on a Web server running Windows SharePoint Services.
- It has a filename extension of .aspx.
- It contains one or more Web Parts or Web Part Zones.

> **Note** Programmers or Web designers create each Web Part independently, often without knowing which Web Part Pages—or even how many Web Part Pages—will display it. Web designers and in some cases even team members later decide what Web Part Pages a site will contain, and which Web Parts those pages will display.

As a practical matter, the vast majority of pages you create for a SharePoint site are likely to be Web Part Pages. At a high level, you:

- Find the Web Parts you need.
- Add them to a Web Part Page.
- Configure the newly placed Web Parts with settings that meet your needs.
- Save, enjoy, and refine.

Creating Web Part Pages

Once you've opened a SharePoint site in FrontPage, the Page Templates dialog box will contain a special Web Part Pages tab. Figure 8-1 shows an example of this tab.

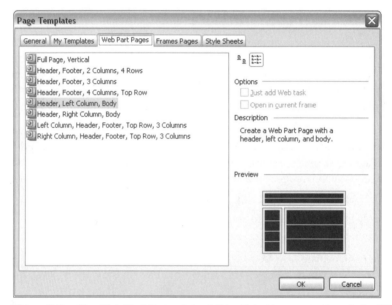

Figure 8-1. The Web Part Pages tab of this dialog box appears only for Windows SharePoint Services Web sites.

Using the Web Part Pages tab on the Page Templates dialog box is easy enough: just find the page layout that's closest to what you need, select it, and click OK. Here's the basic procedure:

1. Open the site that will contain the Web Part Page. Remember that this site must reside on a server extended with Windows SharePoint Services.

2. Choose New from the File menu. Then, in the New task pane, under New Page, click More Page Templates.

3. When the Page Templates dialog box appears, click the Web Part Pages tab.

234

4 Single-click each template listed on the Web Part Pages tab, observing the template's effect in the Preview area at the lower right. The outer rectangles with light backgrounds represent Web Part Zones. The dark, inner rectangles represent any Web Parts you might add.

5 Select the page template that provides the arrangement closest to what you want, and then click OK.

> **Tip** No matter how you create a Web Part Page, you must give it the file extension .aspx when you save it.

One advantage of using FrontPage's Web Part Page templates is that they automatically supply the same title bar, menu bar, and color scheme as a normal SharePoint Team Site page.

Another, even more flexible way of creating Web Part Pages is to first create a perfectly normal page (that is, a Normal page from the General tab) and then use Design view to add some Web Part Zones. The next section explains how to do this.

 ## Inside Out

Web Part Zones and Web Parts needn't be 1:1

As you review the templates on the Web Part Pages tab, keep in mind that a single Web Part Zone can accommodate any number of Web Parts. If you want your page to display six Web Parts, you needn't look for a template with six zones. Remember too that you can add or remove Web Part Zones once the new page is open in Design view.

Creating and Configuring Web Part Zones

Adding a Web Part Zone to any Web page is extremely simple. Here's the procedure:

1 In FrontPage, open the Web page that should contain the Web Part Zone.

2 Set the insertion point where you want the zone to appear (but not inside any other Web Part or Web Part Zone).

3 Display the Web Parts task pane by doing either of the following:
   - Choose Web Part from the Insert menu.
   - Click the drop-down arrow in the title bar of any other task pane, and then choose Web Part Gallery.

4 Click the New Web Part Zone button at the bottom of the task pane.

Figure 8-2 shows a new Web page that contains nothing but a heading and a new Web Part Zone. The title FullPage identifies the zone.

Figure 8-2. The area titled FullPage is a Web Part Zone ready to receive Web Parts.

To inspect or modify the zone's properties, take one of the following actions. They all display the Web Part Zone Properties dialog box, shown in Figure 8-3.

- Right-click the zone, and choose Web Part Zone Properties from the shortcut menu.
- Select the zone, and choose Web Part Zone Properties from the Data menu.
- Select the zone, click the drop-down arrow on its Quick Tag Selector icon ("<WebPartPages:WebPartZone>"), and then choose Tag Properties.

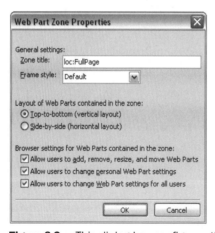

Figure 8-3. This dialog box configures the properties of a Web Part Zone.

Here's how to configure the settings in the Web Part Zone Properties dialog box:

- **General Settings**   Specify these overall properties for the current zone:
  - **Zone Title**   Assign a short but descriptive name that will identify the zone.
  - **Frame Style**   Choose a style. Table 8-1 itemizes your choices.
- **Layout Of Web Parts Contained In The Zone**   Specify how SharePoint should arrange multiple Web Parts in the current zone:
  - **Top-To-Bottom (Vertical Layout)**   Select this option if, when the zone contains more than one Web Part, they should appear one below another.
  - **Side-By-Side (Horizontal Layout)**   Select this option if multiple Web Parts within the zone should appear side by side.
- **Browser Settings For Web Parts Contained In The Zone**   Specify the extent that team members can reconfigure Web Parts in the current zone:
  - **Allow Users To Add, Remove, Resize, And Move Web Parts**   Select this check box to let team members add, remove, resize, and rearrange Web Parts.
  - **Allow Users To Change Personal Web Part Settings**   Select this check box to let team members change personal settings for Web Parts.
  - **Allow Users To Change Web Part Settings For All Users**   Select this check box to let any team member change Web Part settings that apply to all members.

Table 8-1. Table 8-1 Web Part Zone Frame Styles

Frame style	Description
Default	Web Parts in the zone default to the standard frame style. This is normally Title Bar And Border.
None	No visible frame will surround Web Parts in the zone.
Title Bar And Border	A visible frame will surround the title bar and contents of each Web Part in the zone.
Title Bar Only	A visible frame will surround the title bar of each Web Part in the zone.

To move a Web Part Zone to a different area of a page, drag it by its title tab.

To reconfigure a Web Part Zone, select it, right-click it, and choose Web Part Zone Properties.

To delete a Web Part Zone (and any Web Parts it contains) select it and then press the Delete key.

Chapter 8

237

Adding Web Parts to Zones

Once your page contains a Web Part Zone, you'll no doubt want the zone to contain one or more Web Parts. There are two ways to begin:

- If the zone contains no Web Parts, it will display a link titled Click To Insert A Web Part. Click this link to set the insertion point inside the zone, and to display the Web Parts Gallery task pane.
- If the zone already contains one or more Web Parts:

    1 Set the insertion point inside the zone, making sure that neither the zone nor any existing Web Part is selected.

    2 Choose Web Part from the Insert menu, or choose Web Part Gallery from the drop-down menu on any other task pane's title bar.

Inside Out

Setting the insertion point inside a Web Part Zone can be tricky

Clicking an existing Web Part selects the Web Part, as indicated by an orange border.

Clicking a Web Part Zone selects the Web Part Zone, as indicated by a blue border.

If either of these objects is selected when you insert a Web Part, the new Web Part will replace the selection. To avoid this, press the arrow keys until the insertion point is inside the Web Part Zone, but no blue or orange border appears.

To continue inserting the Web Part, proceed as follows:

1 In the Web Parts task pane, under Browse, select a gallery. If in doubt, try the *<site name>* Gallery first.

2 Under Web Part List, find the Web Part you want to insert. Notice that the task pane displays only ten Web Parts at a time:

- To view and potentially select additional Web Parts, you might need to click the Next link that appears after the tenth item.
- To view the tenth item and the Next link, you might need to scroll down the Web Part list.

3 Take either of these actions:

- Select the Web Part you want and then click the Insert Selected Web Part button.
- Drag the Web Part you want into the Web Part Zone you want.

Within a few moments, the Web Part you selected should appear, complete with current data. Web Parts that display lists might appear blank if the list is empty.

Chapter 8

To inspect or modify the Web Part's properties, use any of the following methods to display the Web Part's properties dialog box, shown in Figure 8-4. This dialog box has no title other than the name of the Web Part.

● Right-click the Web Part, and choose Web Part Properties from the shortcut menu.

● Select the Web Part, and choose Web Part Properties from the Data menu.

● Select the Web Part, click the drop-down arrow on the Web Part's Quick Tag Selector icon (such as <WebPartPages:ListViewWebPart>), and then choose Tag Properties.

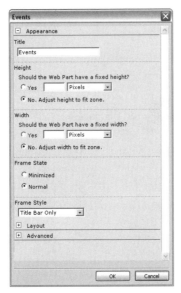

Figure 8-4. This dialog box configures the properties of a Web Part.

The properties dialog box for a Web Part contains three or more collapsible sections. Three of these—Appearance, Layout, and Advanced—appear for every Web Part. Figure 8-4 shows the Appearance section, which exposes these settings:

● **Title**   Type the text that should appear in the Web Part's title bar.

● **Height. Should The Web Part Have A Fixed Height?**   If you want the Web Part to always appear with the same height, select Yes, type a value, and select a unit of measure. Otherwise, select No, Adjust Height To Fit Zone.

● **Width. Should The Web Part Have A Fixed Width?**   If you want the Web Part to have a constant width regardless of conditions, select Yes, type a value, and select a unit of measure. Otherwise, select No. Adjust Width To Fit Zone.

● **Frame State**   Select Minimized if only the title bar should be visible when the Web Part first appears. Otherwise, select Normal.

● **Frame Style**   Choose one of the settings shown previously in Table 8-1. Default inherits the frame style of the surrounding Web Part Zone; the remaining values override it.

239

Expanding the Layout section of a Web Part's properties dialog box exposes the following settings:

- **Include On Page**   Select this check box if you want the Web Part to remain active. Clear it to disable the Web Part (that is, to retain the Web Part in Design view but bypass all processing and transmission to the team member).

- **Visible On Page**   Select this check box to make the Web Part visible to the team member. Clear the check box to process the Web Part on the server but suppress its display.

- **Direction**   Overrides the reading order of elements in the Web Part's text and frame. Choose Default, Left To Right, or Right To Left.

Controls to inspect and modify the following properties appear after you expand the Advanced section:

- **Allow Minimize**   Select this check box if it's all right for team members to switch the Web Part display between minimized and normal. Generally, a minimized view displays only the title bar.

- **Allow Close**   Select this check box if it's all right for team members to close the Web Part display. This removes the Web Part completely from view.

- **Allow Zone Change**   Select this check box if it's all right for team members to move the Web Part to a different zone on the same page. They do this by changing the Web Part's Zone ID property, or by dragging the Web Part from zone to zone.

- **Detail Link**   Specify a URL that displays a full-page view of the information in the Web Part. Clicking the title bar title jumps to this location. This is optional.

- **Description**   Explain what the Web Part does. This text often appears in search results or Web Part catalog views.

- **Help Link**   Specify the URL of a page containing information that helps the team member interact with the Web Part. This is optional.

- **Icon File (Large)**   Specify the URL of a large icon that will represent the Web Part. This is generally a GIF file no larger than 32 by 32 pixels.

- **Icon File (Small)**   Specify the URL of a small icon that will represent the Web Part. This icon is usually 16 by 16 pixels.

- **Missing Assembly Error**   Specify an error message that will appear if Windows SharePoint Services can't locate the run-time files for the Web Part. If you leave this field blank, a system message will appear.

240

Controlling the Appearance of Web Parts

Without a doubt, using Web Parts somewhat constrains your decisions as a Web designer. You can decide:

- Which Web Parts appear on each page.
- The size and placement of Web Parts on each page.
- The configuration of each Web Part, which often includes options that affect the number and arrangement of items that the Web Part displays in the browser.

But you have no direct access to the HTML tags that the Web Part sends the browser. Instead, all Microsoft Web Parts (and most third-party Web Parts) identify each type of element in a Web Part with a standard cascading style sheet (CSS) *selector*.

A selector, in this sense, is the name of a style. For example:

- **.ms-toolbar**   Is the name of the style that controls the appearance of text in the toolbars for SharePoint lists.
- **table.ms-toolbar**   Is the name of the style that controls the gradient background in the toolbars for SharePoint lists.

Fortunately, the definition of these style names resides outside the Web Part, usually in a style sheet file that's linked into the Web page that displays the Web Part. To change the appearance of a list toolbar, you don't change the HTML that the list view Web Part creates. Instead, you change the definition in the linked style sheet file. For example, here's the default configuration for the two styles mentioned above:

```
.ms-toolbar {
    font-family: verdana;
    font-size: .68em;
    text-decoration: none;
    color: #003399;
}
table.ms-toolbar {
    background-image: url("/_layouts/images/toolgrad.gif");
    background-repeat: repeat-x;
    border: 1px solid #95b7f3;
    background-color: #9ebff6;
}
```

Physically, these definitions reside in a file named ows.css, located on the SharePoint server at this path:

<drive>\Program Files\Common Files\Microsoft Shared\web server extensions\60\TEMPLATE\LAYOUTS\1033\STYLES

Windows SharePoint Services maps the start of this path, up to and including the LAYOUTS folder, to a virtual folder named /_layouts and located at the Web server's root.

241

Do You Believe in Ghosts?

Windows SharePoint Services doesn't store most Web pages, picture files, and other page components in the Web server's file system. Instead, it stores them as records in a content database. FrontPage—and, for the most part, the browser—makes it appear that these files reside in a file system, but this is an illusion.

Certain files, however, are exceptions. They appear to be in the content database, but reside instead in the server's file system. In SharePoint terminology, these files are *ghosted*.

Most SharePoint sites have a _layouts folder and, as it turns out, this entire folder tree is ghosted. Windows SharePoint Services makes one physical copy of this folder tree appear to reside locally in each Web site. This has two advantages:

- It saves a *lot* of disk space. If you have 10,000 Web sites, you don't have 10,000 copies of the _layouts folder in your content database. You have one copy on disk.
- It simplifies the task of making global changes to Web sites. Any change you make to the *<drive>*\Program Files\Common Files\Microsoft Shared\web server extensions\60\TEMPLATE\LAYOUTS folder in the server's file system instantly shows up in every Web site.

If you modify a ghosted file through FrontPage or a browser, Windows SharePoint Services *un-ghosts* that instance of the file: that is, it saves the modified version directly in the content database. That way, the site you edited uses the modified version, and all other sites continue to use the ghosted version.

Most ghosted files and folders, however, aren't accessible via FrontPage. This is why you might see the _layouts folder in the browser's address bar, but not in the FrontPage Folder List or Folders view.

In a site that uses the default SharePoint theme, each page will contain a linked stylesheet tag like this:

```
<link REL="stylesheet" Type="text/css" HREF="/_layouts/1033/styles/ows.css">
```

By using this scheme, every list toolbar in the site will get its appearance from the .ms-toolbar and table.ms-toolbar style rules in the ows.css file. And since they all get their appearance from the same rule, they all look alike. Very cool.

If you don't like the appearance that the ows.css files give your site, you can choose a different file or create a new one. Any such file, however, needs to include over *three hundred* style rules like .ms-toolbar and table.ms-toolbar. As a result, most SharePoint designers use one of these approaches.

- Use the default theme.
- Use a theme that comes with Windows SharePoint Services. To do this:
    1 Open the site in your browser.

   2 Click Site Settings and, under Customization, choose Apply Theme To Site.

   3 Choose the theme you want and then click Apply.

● Use a theme that comes with Microsoft FrontPage. The section titled "Using FrontPage Themes" later in this chapter will explain how to do this.

● Use FrontPage to modify a theme, save it with a new name, and apply it to a site.

● Purchase a third-party theme. However, if this seems attractive, make sure you buy a theme specifically designed for Windows SharePoint Services. Older themes typically contain only a fraction of the selectors a SharePoint site requires.

> For a list of all Windows SharePoint Services style selectors—including descriptions and examples—refer to the online document titled Cascading Style Sheets Class Definitions for Microsoft Windows SharePoint Services and located at *http://msdn.microsoft.com//library/en-us/spptsdk/html/tsovcssstyles.asp*

Don't Modify the OWS.CSS File

Many organizations will wish to change the default SharePoint theme so that it uses standard company colors and logos. However, it's not good practice to change the ows.css file itself. Because ows.css is a system file, service packs and patches may overwrite it unexpectedly and your updates will be lost.

Instead, save your changes in new file, and then modify a file named ONET.XML to make the new file the SharePoint default. To do this:

1 Log on to the Web server and display the following folder in Windows Explorer: *<drive>*\Program Files\Common Files\Microsoft Shared\Web Server Extensions\60\TEMPLATE\1033\STS\XML.

2 Open the ONET.XML file in Microsoft Notepad or any other text editor.

3 Find the <Project> tag and add an AlternateCSS attribute. For example, change:

```
<Project Title="Team Web Site" ListDir="Lists" xmlns:ows="Microsoft
SharePoint">
```

to

```
<Project AlternateCSS="/_layouts/1033/styles/local.css" Title="Team Web
Site" ListDir="Lists" xmlns:ows="Microsoft SharePoint">
```

Where *local.css* is the name of your alternate default style sheet file.

If you're operating a farm of SharePoint Web servers, you'll need to make this change on each one.

There is, however, a catch to all this. Because ONET.XML is a system file, service packs and patches may overwrite it unexpectedly and, once again, your updates will be lost. To guard against this, always keep backup copies of ows.css, onet.xml, or any other SharePoint system file you modify.

243

Introducing FrontPage Themes

The idea of themes isn't new to Window SharePoint Services. For years, FrontPage has provided themes as a way of automatically and uniformly formatting pages and sites. The designer picks the theme and FrontPage does the rest.

Windows SharePoint Services uses the same theme technology as FrontPage. In many cases, therefore, you can solve SharePoint design issues by opening the SharePoint site in FrontPage and modifying its theme. For example, you could choose a different theme, modify the existing theme, or create and apply a new theme.

There are, however, some differences in the way FrontPage and Windows SharePoint Services approach themes.

- Originally, FrontPage themes had just a few dozen style rules. A theme compatible with Windows SharePoint Services has over three hundred style rules.

- The FrontPage user interface for modifying themes is heavily slanted toward FrontPage features. For example, all the preview and WYSIWYG displays show FrontPage components, not SharePoint components.

- FrontPage addresses themes one site at a time. Designers responsible for a SharePoint server that supports hundreds or thousands of team members usually want to control themes on a server or top level site basis.

- FrontPage has no features for modifying the themes that SharePoint team members can apply through the SharePoint browser interface. In fact, neither does Windows SharePoint Services, except that by using a text editor you can manipulate configuration files directly on the SharePoint server.

Despite these issues, FrontPage 2003 remains the best graphical environment for working with themes used in a SharePoint site. The next few sections walk you through the process of applying themes to existing pages or Web sites, and then cover the mechanics of customizing themes and creating new ones.

Using the Themes Task Pane

FrontPage can apply themes to a single page or to an entire Web site. Figure 8-5 shows the Theme task pane, the focal point for applying, customizing, and removing themes. To display this task pane, choose Theme from the Format menu or from the drop-down list in the title bar of any other task pane.

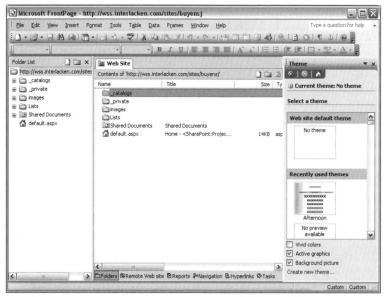

Figure 8-5. The Theme task pane imparts professional-looking designs to individual Web pages or an entire Web site.

The Current Theme heading at the top of the task pane displays which theme, if any, is currently in effect for a page or Web site:

- If the current selection is a page open for editing or a page in the Folder List or Folders view, the Current Theme heading shows the theme in effect for that page.

- If the current selection is a folder, the Current Theme heading shows the theme in effect for the entire Web site. This is the Web site's *default theme*.

If you click the plus sign icon to the left of the Current Theme heading, FrontPage will display specific settings in effect for that theme.

The Select A Theme section contains the controls that actually apply a theme. The scrolling list shows a thumbnail preview of each available theme, organized into three categories:

- **Web Site Default Theme** Displays a preview of the default theme for the current Web site. If no default theme is in effect, FrontPage displays a plain outline containing the words *No theme*.

- **Recently Used Themes** Displays previews of themes you recently applied.

- **All Available Themes** Displays previews of all available themes.

The three check boxes below the scrolling list control optional aspects of any theme you apply. The Create New Theme link starts a special editor for creating new themes. Later sections will explain these options.

As you'd expect, a Web site's default theme applies by default to each page in that Web site. Any theme that you apply to an individual page, however, overrides the Web site default.

245

If you change the Web site's default theme, any themes you applied to individual Web pages will remain in effect. The next section will explain in detail how to apply themes at either level.

Tip **Apply themes consistently throughout a site**

Themes exist to give a Web site a professional and consistent look. Applying an assortment of themes to individual pages can make your Web site appear disjointed and confusing.

Applying a theme to an entire Web site is a somewhat irrevocable action. As indicated by the warning shown in Figure 8-6, the theme replaces all the default fonts, colors, bullets, and lines in every page in a Web site, with no possibility of undoing. If you later change your mind and remove the theme, FrontPage can't restore all the colors, fonts, and other formatting your pages used to have. Instead, these properties will revert to their HTML defaults. Of course, you can always apply a different theme.

Figure 8-6. This message box warns you that applying a theme to an entire Web site overwrites formatting information that can't be restored.

Themes in FrontPage 2003 are less rigid than in past versions of FrontPage, but applying a theme is still a rather heavy-handed action. For example:

- FrontPage will dim the color and formatting options on the Page Properties dialog box.
- The order of evaluation for styles is:
  - Any style sheet files you add via Format, Style Sheet Links.
  - Any page-level styles you define.
  - FrontPage Theme styles.
  - In-line styles that you apply to individual elements.

  Thus, styles in a theme may override those you set up manually.
- You can change the theme itself, but you can't make it control fewer page elements.
- Any change you make to a theme affects *every* page that uses that theme.

If these restrictions seem severe but you like the idea of centrally controlling page appearance, consider these alternatives:

- **Dynamic Web Templates**   A type of "master" Web page that you can link to other pages in the same Web site. Those other pages then inherit the appearance and designated content of the template.

- **Linked Cascading Style Sheet Files** Files that control the appearance—and optionally the position—of standard HTML elements and other items you designate. Any number of Web pages can link to the same style sheet file, thereby achieving a standard appearance. Compared to themes and Dynamic Web Templates, this alternative has the most flexibility.

Applying Themes in FrontPage

To apply an existing theme, open a Web site in FrontPage, and choose Theme from the Format menu. This displays the Theme task pane, shown in Figure 8-5. The scrolling list in the center of the task pane shows a thumbnail preview of each available theme.

You can apply a theme to a single Web page, to a group of pages you select, or to an entire site. Here's the procedure:

1 Take one of these actions:

- To affect a single page, either open it in Design view or select it in the Folder List or Folders view.

- To affect multiple pages, select their file or folder icons in the Folder List or Folders view.

- To affect the entire site, you needn't select anything.

Regardless of how many files you plan to affect, there's some merit to opening one of them in Design view. That way you get immediate feedback as to results.

2 In the Theme task pane, find the preview thumbnail for the theme you want.

3 Modify the following optional settings if you want. They appear below the list of theme previews:

- **Vivid Colors** Select this check box to preview and apply the vivid set of colors from a theme that provides both muted and vivid colors.

- **Active Graphics** Select this check box to activate animated pictures if a theme contains them. Tread carefully here: The novelty of flashing lights can wear off quickly.

- **Background Picture** Select this check box if you want pages to display a background picture. A background picture is a small graphic, usually with some sort of pattern, that's tiled across the entire background of the page. Most themes substitute a solid background color if you clear this check box.

4 To apply the theme, first take one of these actions:

- Click the down arrow that appears when you hover the mouse over the thumbnail preview, the Folder List, or Folders view.

- Right-click the thumbnail preview.

Then, continue as follows:

- To affect a single or selected page, choose Apply To Selected Page(s).

- To affect the entire site, click Apply As Default Theme.

247

Chapter 8

> **Caution** After you apply a theme, there's no Undo command that restores your Web page (or Web site) to its prior appearance. Removing a theme returns pages to their default HTML state. Always back up your Web site first or work from a copy.

The following shortcut menu appears when you right-click a preview thumbnail or click its down arrow. An explanation of each command follows.

- **(Theme Name)** A title bar displays the name of the theme you're about to apply, customize, or delete. Make sure that this is the theme you want.
- **Apply As Default Theme** Choose this command if the theme you selected should become the default theme for all pages in the current Web site. This means that the theme will apply to all pages except those that have individual theme assignments.
- **Apply To Selected Pages(s)** Choose this command to apply the theme individually to one or more Web pages you've selected. This could be the current page open in Design view, or any number of pages you selected in the Folder List or Folders view. Themes you apply using this option override themes you apply with Apply As Default Theme.
- **Customize** Choose this command to modify the appearance of the theme itself. Any changes you make will affect all pages using that theme.
- **Delete** Choose this command to delete the theme from your computer. This, however, is subject to two cautions:
    - You can't use this command to delete themes that came with FrontPage or Microsoft Office.
    - This isn't the proper command to remove a theme from your Web site.

The process for removing a theme is almost identical to that for applying one. Instead of selecting a thumbnail preview, select the No Theme option at the top of the preview list.

After applying a theme, you might be surprised to find your Web pages less elaborate than the preview. This happens because the preview includes page banners, link bars, hover buttons, dividers, and other FrontPage components your pages don't necessarily contain. Alas, there's no solution but to edit each page and insert the desired elements.

If an element on the page had a style applied to it before a theme was applied—a Heading 1 style, for example—that element takes on the Heading 1 style of any theme you apply.

If your Web site has pages that attach Dynamic Web Templates, you'll find that FrontPage won't apply themes to those pages. This is because the Dynamic Web Template already controls the appearance of such pages. In such cases, you should apply the theme to the Dynamic Web Template and then, when you save the template, let FrontPage update the attached pages. This will propagate the theme appearance to the attached pages.

248

Creating and Customizing FrontPage Themes

The process of creating a new theme and that of customizing an existing one differ only in one step. Here's an overview of the process:

1 Display the Theme task pane. For example, choose Theme from the Format menu.

2 To create a new theme, click the Create New Theme link at the bottom of the task pane. To customize an existing theme, right-click its thumbnail preview, and choose Customize from the shortcut menu. Either action will display the Customize Theme dialog box, shown in Figure 8-7.

Figure 8-7. This dialog box provides the starting point for creating or customizing a theme.

3 Use the Colors, Graphics, and Text buttons to set the theme properties you want. The next three sections will provide more detail about this process.

4 Click the Save or Save As button to save your changes.

> **Note** If you make a change to a theme and click OK without choosing Save or Save As first, FrontPage displays a warning asking whether you want to save the changes to the current theme.

Customizing Theme Colors

Clicking the Colors button shown in Figure 8-7 displays the Customize Theme dialog box shown in Figure 8-8.

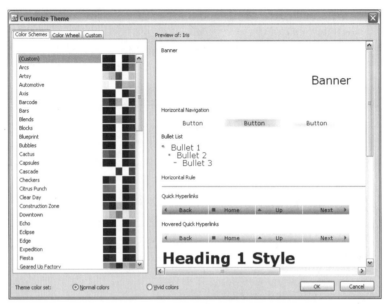

Figure 8-8. Clicking a named color scheme on the left applies a set of colors to the current theme.

The Theme Color Set option buttons at the bottom of the dialog box control which set of colors you're configuring: normal or vivid. By default, a theme's normal and vivid colors are the same. The vivid color set, should you care to define it, is usually similar to the normal set but brighter or more vibrant. A designer can switch between color sets by selecting or clearing the Vivid Colors check box in the Theme task pane.

The three tabs at the upper left offer three ways to choose a color scheme. The next three topics will explain each approach.

Choosing a Color Scheme

The first of these is the Color Schemes tab shown in Figure 8-8. This tab presents preselected sets of colors grouped to look good together. To try out a given color scheme, just select its entry in the list and view the results in the Preview Of area.

> **Note** Although there's considerable overlap, the list of color schemes and the list of themes are different. Figure 8-8 shows Automotive and Downtown color schemes, for example, but the Theme task pane shows no corresponding themes. The color schemes that share a name with a theme show the colors in that theme.

Choosing Color Values

To use the second way of choosing a color scheme, click the Color Wheel tab, shown in Figure 8-9.

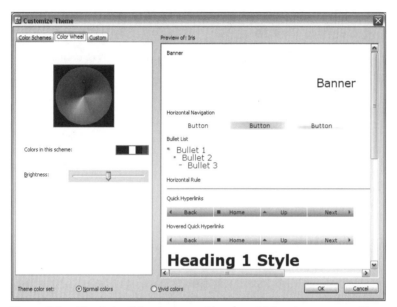

Figure 8-9. The Color Wheel tab provides an additional way to specify a color scheme.

Notice the tiny white dot superimposed on the color wheel inside the black square. Dragging this dot around the circle changes the hue and saturation of a base color for the theme. The Color Wheel tab uses the Hue, Saturation, Brightness (HSB) color model. Here's how this works:

- **Hue**   Refers to a true, pure color value. The color wheel represents hue as degrees of rotation around the wheel inside the black square. Red, blue, and green, for example, are at nine o'clock, one o'clock, and five o'clock, respectively.

- **Saturation**   Measures the purity of a color (that is, the lack of neutral colors diluting it). To increase saturation, drag the white dot closer to the center of the circle. To decrease saturation, drag it closer to the edge.

- **Brightness**   Measures the intensity of a color. If brightness is zero, for example, the result is black. The Brightness slider on the Color Wheel tab controls brightness. To increase brightness, drag the slider to the right; to decrease brightness, drag the slider to the left.

The Colors In This Scheme bar shows the colors FrontPage uses to build the theme. These change as you drag the white dot around the color wheel. The Preview Of display changes only when you *stop* dragging (that is, when you release the mouse button).

> **Caution** Be careful when you change the colors in a theme. Modifying colors changes only the colors of HTML elements such as text and backgrounds; it doesn't change graphics colors for elements such as buttons and banners.

Choosing Custom Colors

The Custom tab, shown in Figure 8-10, is the third and final way of choosing a color scheme.

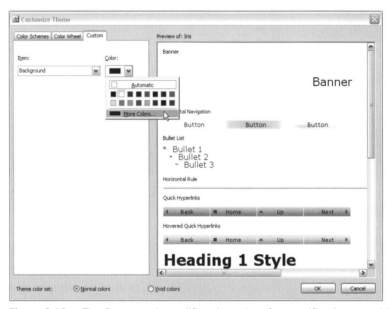

Figure 8-10. The Custom tab modifies the color of a specific element within a theme.

This tab provides direct control over seventeen Web elements that a theme controls. These elements appear as items in the Item drop-down list. To change the color of any item:

1 Select it from the Item drop-down list.

2 Click the Color drop-down arrow, and choose the exact color you want.

As you change the colors assigned to any item, the Preview Of display changes accordingly.

Customizing Theme Graphics

Clicking the Graphics button in the main Customize Theme dialog box produces the Customize Theme dialog box shown in Figure 8-11. This dialog box specifies the background pictures and fonts that the theme will apply to ten kinds of elements. Most of these elements pertain to FrontPage Link Bar components.

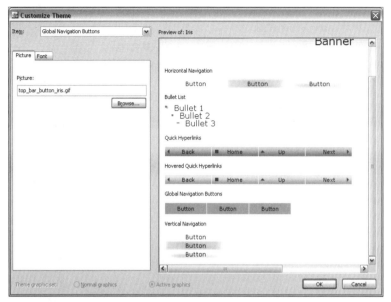

Figure 8-11. The Picture tab of this dialog box specifies the picture files FrontPage uses on pages controlled by a specific theme.

Choosing Background Pictures

To begin customizing a graphic element, select it from the Item drop-down list at the top of the dialog box. Figure 8-11, for example, shows Global Navigation Buttons ready for modification. The three most common choices are these:

- **Background Picture**   Controls the picture that fills the background of the page.
- **Banner**   Controls the picture that appears behind the page title.
- **Bullet List**   Controls the picture that marks each item in a bullet list.

The remaining seven picture types (Global Navigation Buttons, Horizontal Navigation, Quick Back Button, Quick Home Button, Quick Next Button, Quick Up Button, and Vertical Navigation) all apply to FrontPage Link Bar components.

To specify a picture the current theme should use:

1 Select an element from the Item drop-down list.

2 In the corresponding box(es), enter or browse to the picture you want FrontPage to use:

- **Picture**   Specify the graphic that will normally appear for an element.
- **Hovered Picture**   Specify an alternative picture that will appear when the mouse pointer is over the element.
- **Selected Picture**   Specify an alternative picture that will appear after the team member has clicked the element.

253

■ **List Bullet 1, 2, and 3** Specify the pictures you want to appear as bullets in the first three levels of a list.

3 View the effect of your choices in the Preview Of area.

Choosing Banner and Button Fonts

The Font tab of the Customize Theme dialog box, shown in Figure 8-12, specifies the fonts FrontPage will use for superimposing text on page banners and link bar buttons.

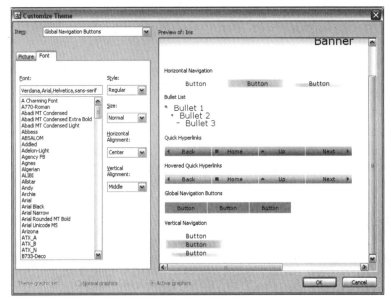

Figure 8-12. The Font tab controls the appearance of text that appears in page banners and link bars.

> For more information about fonts for normal text and headings, refer to "Customizing Theme Text," later in this chapter.

To specify the font for a given element:

1 Select an element from the Item drop-down list.

2 Specify one or more fonts in the Font box. Clicking a font name in the provided list makes it the one and only suitable font. To specify additional fonts, type their names by hand. You must separate individual font names with a comma.

> **Tip** There's no guarantee that a given font will be available on the team member's computer. That's why it's best to specify multiple fonts, and to use common ones at that.

3 In the Style drop-down list, select any font variations you want, such as Bold or Italic.

4 In the Size drop-down list, select a font size.

5 In the Horizontal Alignment drop-down list, specify how to position the text laterally over the picture: left, right, or center.

6 In the Vertical Alignment drop-down list, specify how to position the text vertically within the picture: at the top, middle, or bottom.

Customizing Theme Text

Clicking the Text button in the main Customize Theme dialog box displays the Customize Theme dialog box, shown in Figure 8-13. This dialog box specifies the font for body and heading text that appears on pages the theme controls.

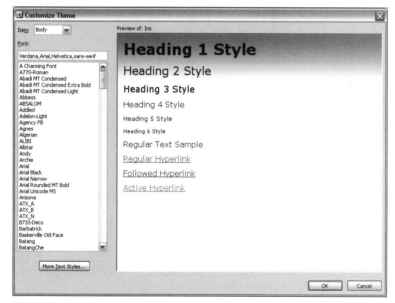

Figure 8-13. This dialog box controls the appearance of body and heading text.

Here's the procedure for modifying these properties:

1 Select the element you want to control from the Item drop-down list.

2 Select the desired font in the Font list. The selected font name appears in the Font box.

3 To specify multiple fonts in order of preference, type the second and each subsequent font into the Font box by hand, using the list as your guide. Be sure to separate the font names with commas.

As you select new fonts from the Font list, the Preview Of area changes to reflect your selection.

Clicking the More Text Styles button displays the Style dialog box shown in Figure 8-14. The More Text Styles button provides access to more CSS properties. This is a very important dialog box because it's the *only* way FrontPage can control the styles that appear in SharePoint sites, but not in FrontPage sites that run on ordinary Web servers.

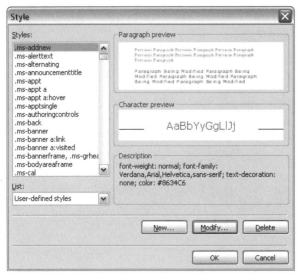

Figure 8-14. This dialog box displays all the style names (selectors) in a FrontPage or SharePoint theme.

The Style dialog box displays these controls:

- **Styles**   Displays the list of style names (selectors) that the theme you're editing currently contains.

- **List**   Determines the type of styles that appear in the Styles list. The options are:

  - **HTML Tags**   These styles share the names of HTML tags. The style named *body*, for example, controls the appearance of elements that appear between <body> and </body> tags.

  - **User-Defined Styles**   These styles don't have the same names as HTML tags. They apply to HTML elements that invoke the style by means of class= or id= attributes.

- **Paragraph Preview**   Displays a reduced size paragraph formatted in accordance with the style you select in the Styles list.

- **Character Preview**   Displays some full-sized text formatted in accordance with the style you select in the Styles list.

- **Description**   Displays the CSS code for the style you select in the Styles list.

- **New**   Displays a New Style dialog box for creating a new style.

- **Modify**   Displays a Modify Style dialog box for changing the style you select in the Styles list.

- **Delete**   Deletes the style you select in the Styles list.

256

Clicking the New or Modify button displays a dialog box like the one shown at left in Figure 8-15.

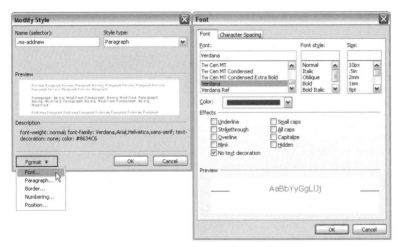

Figure 8-15.   In the dialog box at left, clicking the Format button reveals a menu of style property categories. Each choice displays a different dialog box, such as the Font dialog box at right.

This dialog box is notable because it's the only way you can modify *all* the selectors that a SharePoint Theme uses. The controls function as follows.

- **Name (Selector)**   Displays the name or the existing style, or accepts the name of a new one.

- **Style Type**   Specifies whether the style operates in paragraph (block) mode or character (inline) mode. However, when you define styles in themes, this setting has no effect.

- **Preview**   Displays a reduced size paragraph formatted in accordance with the current style.

- **Description**   Displays the CSS code for the current style.

- **Format**   Displays the drop-down menu shown at left in Figure 8-15. Click the menu item for the type of formatting you want to apply.

Clicking the Font menu choice displays the Font dialog box shown at right in Figure 8-15. The Font tab modifies the attributes shown; the Character Spacing tab controls vertical alignment and the amount of padding between characters.

The Paragraph, Border, Numbering, And Position menu choices work similarly. The Border choice actually controls both borders and spacing, and the numbering choice controls both numbering and bullets.

When you're finished modifying the style, click OK twice. This will return you to the Customize Theme dialog box shown in Figure 8-13.

Saving Modified Themes

When you've configured a theme to your satisfaction, click the Save button to save your theme under the same name, or click Save As to save it under a new name. If you click Save As, FrontPage displays the Save Theme dialog box shown in Figure 8-16, which prompts you for a theme name.

Figure 8-16.   Enter a name for a newly created theme in the Save Theme dialog box.

Some themes, such as those FrontPage supplies, are flagged read-only. In these cases, the Save button will be dimmed, and you'll have to use Save As. After you've saved a theme, you can use it in any Web pages you create.

Distributing Themes for Individual Sites

When FrontPage saves a modified theme, it saves it in a compressed format at a location on your hard disk. Then, when you apply the theme, FrontPage adds the uncompressed files to a folder in your Web site. As a result, there are two ways of distributing themes to other FrontPage designers: by copying the disk folder or by copying the Web folder. The next two sections will explain these options.

Distributing Themes by Copying a Disk Folder

You can distribute a theme to computers other than your own by copying the folder where the theme resides. For FrontPage 2003, the themes that come with FrontPage reside at:

C:\Program Files\Common Files\Microsoft Shared\THEMES11\<theme name>

and any custom themes you create reside at:

C:\Documents and Settings\<user>\Application Data\Microsoft\Themes

Where *<user>* is the name of your windows logon account.

The folder, the theme, and three of the files generally have similar names. For example, the Afternoon theme resides in the afternoon folder and contains the following files:

- **aftrnoon.elm**   Contains compressed versions of all the pictures and CSS files in the theme.
- **aftrnoon.inf**   Contains settings global to the entire theme, and titles in various languages.

- **aftrnoon.utf8**   Contains the same information as the aftrnoon.inf file, but in UTF-8 format.
- **preview.gif**   Contains sample pictures of the buttons in the theme.
- **thmbnail.png**   Contains the thumbnail pictures that FrontPage displays in the Theme task bar.

> **Note**   UTF-8 is an alternate method for encoding all the characters in the Unicode character set. However, instead of all characters occupying two bytes, some characters occupy one byte, some two, some three, and some four. The original, 7-bit ASCII characters 0-127 are all one byte in size, and retain their original values.

To copy a theme from one computer to another, copy its folder (and the files it contains) to an intermediate location—such as a disk, a file server, or an FTP location—and then copy it from there into the Themes folder on the other computer.

Distributing Themes over the Web

Applying any theme to a Web site—whether to individual pages or to the entire Web site—copies the theme into a hidden folder named, not surprisingly, _themes. This makes the theme available to anyone who opens that Web site, and overrides any like-named themes on that designer's hard disk. Distributing a theme to your entire design team is therefore as simple as applying that theme to any page in the Web site.

In fact, whenever a FrontPage designer opens a Web site, their Themes list contains two kinds of entries:

- Themes residing on their local system.
- Themes residing in the current FrontPage-based Web site.

If a designer applies a theme that resides only on the FrontPage-based Web site, FrontPage offers to download the theme and install it locally. This is an efficient way of distributing themes to those who need them.

Adding Custom Themes to a SharePoint Server

A server administrator can add new themes to a SharePoint server or customize existing ones. Here's the procedure.

1. In Windows Explorer, browse the following folder location on the SharePoint server: <*drive*>\Program Files\Common Files\Microsoft Shared\Web Server Extensions\60\TEMPLATE\THEMES.
2. Either:
    2.1 Copy an existing Theme folder.

2.2 Give the new folder a short version of the theme name. Typically, this would be six to twelve alphanumeric characters. Remember this folder name as the TemplateID.

2.3 Make any change you want. Most often, this will involve updating the largest CSS file.

or

2.1 Create or choose a theme in any FrontPage site, and apply it to at least one page.

2.2 Open the FrontPage site in Windows Explorer. For example, open c:\inetpub\wwwroot\myweb. If the Web site resides on a SharePoint Server, publish it to a disk location and then open the disk-based version.

2.3 Open the _themes folder in Windows Explorer, and locate the folder for your theme. Its name may be slightly different from the name that appears in FrontPage, but remember it as the TemplateID.

2.4 Copy the folder that contains your theme to the location in step 1.

2.5 Open the new folder and delete the _vti_cnf subfolder.

3 Open the new folder you created by copying, find the .inf file, and rename it so the filename base equals the TemplateId.

4 Open the .inf file from step 2 in Notepad or any other text editor. This file uses standard.ini format.

4.1 In the [info] section, set title= to the TemplateId.

4.2 In the [Titles] section, set 1033= to the name of the theme in English (where 1033 is the locale ID for US English). You can enter titles for any locales (and as many locales) as you like.

Then, save and close the file.

5 Create a thumbnail file and a preview file.

- **A thumbnail file** This file must be in .png format, 340 pixels wide and 130 pixels high. It actually contains eight images, each 85 pixels wide and 65 pixels high, arranged in a two rows of four. Its name is usually th< *TemplateId* >.png.

- **A preview file** This file must be in GIF format, 300 pixels wide and 179 pixels high. It usually contains a reduced screen shot without the browser borders. Its name is usually th< TemplateId >.gif.

Save both these files to the <*drive*>\Program Files\Common Files\Microsoft Shared\Web Server Extensions\60\TEMPLATE\IMAGES folder on the SharePoint server.

1 Open the <*drive*>\Program Files\Common Files\Microsoft Shared\Web Server Extensions\60\TEMPLATE\LAYOUTS\1033 folder on your SharePoint server, where 1033 is the code for your locale.

2 Using Notepad or any other text editor, open the SPTHEMES.XML in that folder, and add a <Templates></Templates> section. The following example specifies a template for the custom theme.

```
<Templates>
   <TemplateID>CpnyColors</TemplateID>
   <DisplayName>Company Colors</DisplayName>
   <Description>Description</Description>
   <Thumbnail>../images/thCpnyColors.png</Thumbnail>
   <Preview>../images/ thCpnyColors.gif</Preview>
</Templates>
```

Where CpnyColors is the TemplateId from step 2.

> **Tip** Windows SharePoint services doesn't sort the list of themes before displaying it to team members. Therefore, arrange the <Templates> sections in the SPTHEMES.XML file in the order you want.

The new theme should now appear in the list of options on the Apply Theme To Web Site page. Anyone using the same server can therefore apply it to any SharePoint site they want.

> **Caution** When you install updates, service packs, or new versions of Windows SharePoint Services, the setup program may overwrite the SPTHEMES.XML file. To guard against this, keep a second copy on hand.

You may find Theme folders that contain only five files, having the extensions .elm, .gif, .inf, .png, and .utf8. The .elm file, in this case, is a compressed library of all the files in the theme. Unfortunately, Windows SharePoint Services makes no use of .elm files. That's why the procedure above recommends using the theme in a Web site (even if it's a throwaway site) and getting the uncompressed files from its _themes folder.

If you'd rather get the files by unpacking an .elm file, refer to Microsoft Knowledge Base Article 295409, Unpacking And Repacking Files In FrontPage Themes, at *http://support.microsoft.com/default.aspx?scid=kb;en-us;295409*

> **Tip** The largest CSS file in a theme suitable for Windows SharePoint Services is usually about 30 KB in size. If you encounter a theme with a largest CSS file that's much less than 30 KB, it's probably not suitable for use on SharePoint sites.

In Summary...

This chapter explained how to create Web Part Pages in Microsoft Office FrontPage 2003, and how to work with themes that apply to both FrontPage and SharePoint sites.

The next chapter will explain how to integrate FrontPage components with pages in a SharePoint site.

Chapter 9

Creating and Modifying Basic Site Features

Once you have a SharePoint site and know how to create blank pages, the next steps are to provide content and navigation. If your content consists entirely of SharePoint lists and libraries, and if the default page layouts are acceptable, you can use the site and workspace templates that come with Windows SharePoint Services. But what if your needs exceed those limitations?

This is where Microsoft Office FrontPage 2003 really comes into play. With FrontPage you can certainly open and modify sites that use the standard SharePoint templates, but you can also create any sort of site you want, from scratch, and give it the look and feel you want. In addition, you can create sites that use a mixture of SharePoint, FrontPage, and hand-crafted techniques. The decision is entirely yours.

This chapter describes several ways of using FrontPage to customize the look and feel of a SharePoint site. Windows SharePoint Services supports nearly every feature of FrontPage, and of non-extended IIS Web servers. As such, there are few limits to what you can accomplish.

Windows SharePoint Services, however, doesn't support the legacy database features in FrontPage: Save Results To Database, Database Results Wizard, and Database Interface Wizard. Instead, you should plan on using SharePoint lists or data sources. Chapters 10, 11, and 12 will explain how to do this.

In addition, Windows SharePoint Services lacks the capability to run conventional ASP and ASP.NET pages. In many cases, Windows SharePoint Services will help you accomplish the same results without writing ASP or ASP.NET code. And if that's not possible, Part VII will explain how you can write your own Web parts.

The primary focus of this chapter, however, is navigation and appearance.

Editing Site Navigation

One of the oldest and best-known features of FrontPage involves these three components working together:

- **Navigation View** records a hierarchical diagram of the pages in a site.
- **Link Bar Based On Navigation Structure** displays a set of hyperlinks from the current page to its neighbors in the Navigation view diagram.
- **Page Banner** displays the name of the current page as entered in the Navigation view diagram.

Figure 9-1 shows a typical Navigation view diagram. To display this view, open a site, click the Web Site tab above the main editing window, and then click the Navigation tab at the bottom.

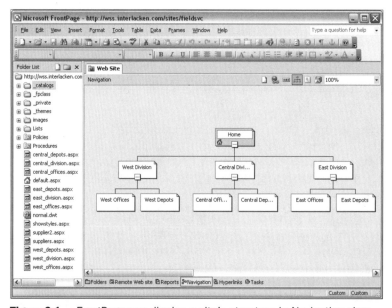

Figure 9-1. FrontPage can display a site's structure in Navigation view.

FrontPage can't construct the Navigation view diagram automatically. You have to draw it yourself by either:

- dragging pages from the folder list and dropping them in position below the parent you want, or
- adding new pages to the diagram by right-clicking an existing page and clicking New, Page. The next time you apply changes, FrontPage creates a new physical page as well.

In either case, if FrontPage doesn't give the page the name you want to appear in page banners and link bars, select the node, press F2, and type the name you want.

Tip To apply changes you've made to the Navigation view diagram, either right-click the diagram and choose Apply Changes, or simply switch to another FrontPage view.

Figure 9-2 shows the Central Division page that appears near the center of the diagram that appeared in Figure 9-1.

Figure 9-2. The heading Central Division on this page is a FrontPage Page Banner component that displays the page's name in the Navigation view diagram. The hyperlinks just below comes from FrontPage Link Bar components, also based on the Navigation view diagram.

A single Link Bar component displays the two links titled Central Offices and Central Depots. To see why this is so, inspect the Link Bar Properties dialog box shown in Figure 9-3.

Tip **Add a Link Bar Based On Navigation Structure to a page.**
First choose Web Component from the Insert menu. Then, when the Insert Web Component dialog box appears, click Link Bars in the Component Type list at the left, and Bar Based On Navigations Structure from the Choose A Bar Type list at the right.

Note that under Hyperlinks To Add To Page, the Child Level option is selected. Referring again to Figure 9-1, the children of the Central Division page are Central Offices and Central Depots. The Link Bar on the Central Division page therefore displays hyperlinks to those two pages. The hyperlink text comes from the Navigation view name of each target page.

Figure 9-3. This is the property sheet for the Link Bar component in Figure 9-2. It specifies that the Link Bar should display the children of the current page, as diagrammed in Figure 9-1.

If you changed the Navigation view diagram to show a third child under the Central Division page, the link bar on the Central Division page would automatically change to include the new, third link. You wouldn't have to open the Central Division page and add the link manually.

The page title Central Division comes from a FrontPage Page Banner component. This component displays the Navigation view name of the current page. Using this component assures that both the page and all hyperlinks that point to it use exactly the same text.

Tip Add a Page Banner component to a page.

Choose Page Banner from the Insert menu, choose the type of banner you want (graphic or text), then click OK. The current theme, if any, determines the graphic style.

The entire Navigation view, Link Bar Based On Navigation View, Page Banner approach is often appealing to new FrontPage designers for two reasons:

- It provides a way of structuring a site first, and then "filling in the blanks" for each page.
- When a FrontPage Theme is in effect, the Link Bar hyperlinks can be graphical buttons with rollover effects.

If these factors are important to you, by all means diagram your site and use Link Bar and Page Banner components. Windows SharePoint Services fully supports them. You should know, however, that most designers eventually outgrow this approach. Here are some reasons:

- As the number of pages increases, the Navigation view diagram grows unwieldy.

- Not all pages fit cleanly into a hierarchical structure.
- The same page can't appear more than once in the same Navigation view diagram.
- The designer wants more control over the spacing and arrangement of Link Bar buttons than FrontPage provides.
- Database-driven Web sites tend to collapse or supersede simple structures of flat Web pages. If, for example, your SharePoint site had a hundred products to sell, you wouldn't design and diagram a hundred Web pages. Instead, you would create a custom Products list and give the Web visitors Search pages.

To understand this last point further, consider the SharePoint approach to providing a list of administrative offices and parts depots in three divisions. Most likely, this would involve:

- A Division list with one item for each valid division.
- A Location Types list with one item for each valid location type.
- A Contacts list modified to carry:
  - A location name rather than a person's name.
  - A lookup field for Division
  - A lookup field for Location Type.

Armed with these components and a little advance knowledge from Chapter 12, you could construct a Web Part page like the one in Figure 9-4.

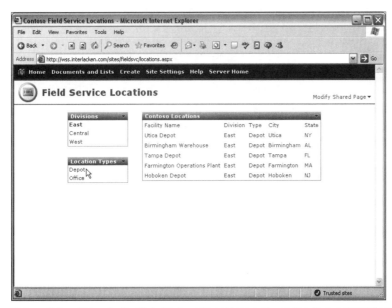

Figure 9-4. This single Web Part page replaces six pages in a conventional site: East Depots, East Offices, Central Depots, and so forth. Rather than following hyperlinks, the team member sets search parameters.

267

In this page:

- The areas headed Divisions, Location Types, and Contoso Locations are each Data View Web Parts that display the contents of their respective lists.
- The Divisions Web Part is *connected* to the Contoso Locations in such a way that:
  - The Divisions Web Part *provides data values to* the Contoso Locations Web Part.
  - The Contoso Locations Web Part is configured to *filter view using data values from* the Divisions Web Part.
- The Location Types Web Part is *connected* to the Contoso Locations in such a way that:
  - The Location Types Web Part *provides data values to* the Contoso Locations Web Part.
  - The Contoso Locations Web Part is configured to *filter view using data values from* the Location Types Web Part.

To view locations for any Division and Location Type, a team member needs only to click that Division and that Location Type. Instead of six data pages and three menu pages, the application now requires only one Web Part page! What's more, if you ever need to add another Division or another Location Type, you *don't* need to create any new Web pages. You just add an entry to the Divisions or Location Types list.

For more information about Connecting Web Parts, refer to the section "Connecting Web Parts," in Chapter 12.

The point of mentioning all this now—rather than waiting for Chapter 12—is that with a data-driven Web site, you should:

- Think more about organizing your data into lists and libraries,
- Think more about designing effective queries and search tools, and
- Think less about elaborate structures among Web pages than you would in an ordinary "flat" HTML site.

This way of thinking reduces or eliminates the need to create elaborate structures in Navigation view, and to implement them using Link Bars.

Using the Link Bar With Custom Links Component

FrontPage provides a second type of Link bar whose usefulness increases rather than decreases under Windows SharePoint Services. This is the Link Bar With Custom Links, and it actually involves two different objects.

- **Link Bar With Custom Links**   This is a component that occupies space in a Web page and displays a list of links.
- **Custom Link Bar**   This is a Navigation view object that stores a list of links for use in one or more pages. Figure 9-5 provides an example.

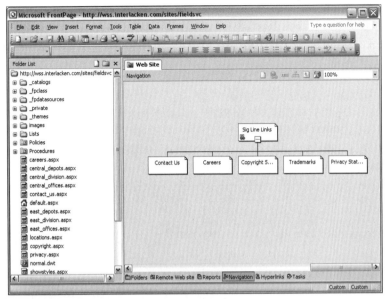

Figure 9-5. This Navigation view diagram shows a Custom Link Bar. The top node isn't a Web page; it just identifies the Link Bar.

A Custom Link Bar isn't a link bar

The Custom Link Bar object that appears in Navigation view has no physical appearance in a Web page; it's only a list of hyperlinks.

To display the links from a Custom Link Bar object, you have to add a Link Bar With Custom Links component to a Web page, and configure that component to use the set of Custom Link Bar links you want.

You have a choice of two different procedures for using Custom Link Bars (the Navigation view objects) and Link Bar With Custom Links (the Web page objects):

- You can first create the Custom Link Bar in Navigation view, and then later display it by adding a Link Bar With Custom Links to a Web page.
- You can add a new Link Bar With Custom Links to a Web page, and then use it to create a Custom Link Bar that will appear in Navigation view.

Here's the procedure for creating a Custom Link Bar in Navigation View.

1 In FrontPage, open the site you want and switch to Navigation view.

2 Either click the New Custom Link Bar button on the Navigation view toolbar.

or

Right-click the Navigation view background, and choose New and Custom Link Bar.

269

As shown previously in Figure 9-5, the new Custom Link Bar node will have a special icon in its lower left corner.

3   To add a link to the new Custom Link Bar, first right-click it, and then choose New and Page. Then, with the node for the new link selected, press F2 and type whatever text you want to appear in the finished hyperlink.

4   If you want the link to specify an existing page, right-click the new node and choose Properties. This will display an Edit Hyperlink dialog box where you can type or select the URL you want.

Otherwise, for each node you add to Navigation view, FrontPage will, by default, create a new empty Web page the next time you switch away from Navigation view or choose Apply Changes. FrontPage will base the file name on the Navigation view name you assigned, and will always use the filename extension .htm. You can change this to .aspx in the Folder list or in Folders view.

5   Repeat steps 3 and 4 for each additional link.

Here's the procedure for adding a Link Bar With Custom Links to a Web page. If Navigation view doesn't contain a Custom Link Bar with the correct links, this procedure creates one.

1   In FrontPage, open the page that should display the Link Bar With Custom Links component, and set the insertion point where you want the component to appear.

2   Choose Insert, Navigation. This displays the Insert Web Component dialog box shown in Figure 9-6.

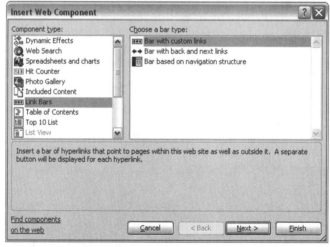

Figure 9-6.   The Insert Web Component dialog box appears with the Link Bars and Bar With Custom Links options already selected.

3   Make sure that Link Bars is selected in the Component Type list on the left, and that Bar With Custom Links is selected in the Choose A Bar Type list on the right.

4   Click Next to display the wizard page shown in Figure 9-7. Then, choose any of the bar styles listed in the Choose A Bar Style list.

270

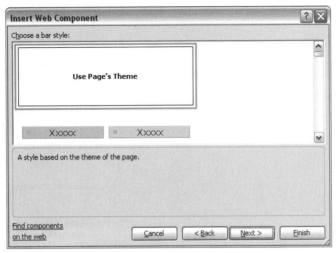

Figure 9-7. When FrontPage displays this wizard page, you can choose to use the same theme as the rest of the current page, any other theme, or various text formats.

- The first entry in the list uses the same theme as the Web page that will contain the Link Bar With Custom Links component.
- The following options use graphical buttons from any other FrontPage theme.
- Various text-based options appear at the end of the list.

5 Click Next to display the wizard page shown in Figure 9-8. Choose an orientation—horizontal or vertical—and then click Finish.

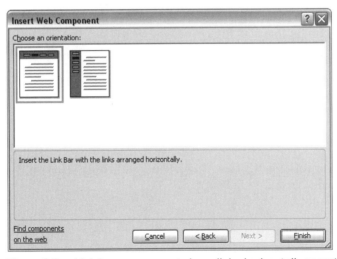

Figure 9-8. Link bars can arrange hyperlinks horizontally or vertically.

6 After you click Finish, FrontPage displays the Link Bar Properties dialog box shown in Figure 9-9.

271

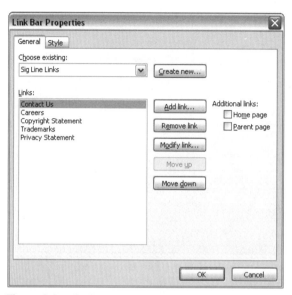

Figure 9-9. Options in this dialog box configure a Link Bar With Custom Links component. Navigation view automatically reflects any Custom Link Bars you create or modify with this dialog box.

The General tab of this dialog box configures the hyperlinks that the Link Bar With Custom Links component will display.

- To use the links from an existing Navigation view Custom Link Bar, select its name in the Choose Existing list.

- To create a new Navigation view Custom Link Bar, click the Create New button to display the Create New Link Bar dialog box shown here. Give the new Custom Link Bar a name, and click OK.

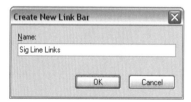

FrontPage displays this dialog box automatically if the current Web contains no Navigation view Custom Link Bars.

7 Use the following buttons to modify the links associated with the Custom Link Bar you specified in step 6. These changes will affect all Link Bar With Custom Links components—regardless of page—that use the same Custom Link Bar:

■ **Add Link** Displays the Add To Link Bar dialog box shown in Figure 9-10. In the Text To Display box near the top, type the text you want the hyperlink to display. In the Address box near the bottom, type the hyperlink location. Click OK.

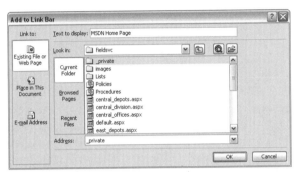

Figure 9-10. A Custom Link Bar can include locations within the current page, within the current Web, or anywhere in the world.

■ **Remove Link** Deletes the selection in the Links list.

■ **Modify Link** Displays a Modify Link dialog box that strongly resembles the Add To Link Bar dialog box shown in Figure 9-10. Update the Text To Display and Address boxes as required, and then click OK.

■ **Move Up** Moves the selection in the Links list one position higher in the list.

■ **Move Down** Moves the selection in the Links list one position lower.

8 Use the following check boxes to add links to the current Link Bar With Custom Links component. These settings will affect only the current instance of the component:

■ **Home Page** Adds a link to the current Web site's home page.

■ **Parent Page** Adds a link to the parent of the page that contains the Link Bar With Custom Links component.

9 Click OK.

Link Bar With Custom Links components are particularly useful in a SharePoint site because Windows SharePoint Services automatically adds the following Custom Link Bar components to Navigation view for you.

● **SharePoint Top Navbar** Contains the links that appear at the top of most default Windows SharePoint Services pages: Home, Documents And Libraries, Create, Site Settings, and Help.

● **Documents** Contains a link to each document library flagged for inclusion in the site's Quick Launch bar.

● **Pictures** Contains a link to each picture library flagged for inclusion in the site's Quick Launch bar.

- **Lists**   Contains a link to each list flagged for inclusion in the site's Quick Launch bar. A list, in this sense, means other than a document library, picture library, discussion, or survey.

- **Discussions**   Contains a link to each discussion flagged for inclusion in the site's Quick Launch bar.

- **Surveys**   Contains a link to each survey flagged for inclusion in the site's Quick Launch bar.

> **Tip**   To flag a list, library, discussion, or survey for inclusion in the site's Quick Launch bar, first display any view, then click Modify Settings And Columns, click Change General Settings, and set Display This List On The Quick Launch Bar? to Yes.

The links in the Documents, Pictures, Lists, Discussions, and Surveys Custom Link Bars all display the default view of the corresponding object. If, for example, the site contains a list named Relatives, and the settings for that list specified Display This List On The Quick Launch Bar? as yes, then the Lists custom link bar will contain a link to the default view of the Relatives list.

If you decide to give your SharePoint site a custom look, you can use these custom link bars to create equivalents of the top navigation bar and the quick launch bar that appear in a standard SharePoint site. The Central Division page shown previously in Figure 9-2, for example, uses Link Bar With Custom Links components to display the Documents, Lists, and SharePoint Top Navbar custom link bar objects.

Using Dynamic Web Templates

Even if you decide to give your SharePoint site a custom look, you'll probably want to propagate the *same* custom look to each page. FrontPage 2003 has a new feature called Dynamic Web Templates that does that very well.

The process of using a Dynamic Web Template begins, of course, with creating a sample page. This is your template. The unique aspect of how a Dynamic Web Template works is that you designate some parts of the template as *editable*, leaving the rest of the page *non-editable*.

- An *editable region* is an area where pages using the template can place unique content.

  If you open the template and the change the content of an editable region, FrontPage *won't* propagate that change to pages that use the template.

- A *non-editable region* is an area that remains under control of the template.

  If you open the template and change the contents of a non-editable region, FrontPage will offer to propagate that change to every page that uses the template.

The terms *editable* and *non-editable*, by the way, reflect behavior in pages that *use* the template. When you open such a page, FrontPage won't let you change the non-editable regions in Design view. When you open the template itself, however, you can edit either type of region. Table 9-1 illustrates these concepts.

Table 9-1. Effect of Dynamic Web Template Editable Regions

Type region	Editable in template	Editable in created page	Propagates template changes
Editable	Yes	Yes	No
Non-editable	Yes	No	Yes

Table 9-1 also illustrates that only non-editable areas receive new content when you update the template. In effect, all copies of a non-editable region remain in sync with the template. If any copies of editable regions remain in sync, however, it's simply a happy accident.

You can *attach* a Dynamic Web Template to any new or existing page. This is how a page begins using the template. If the page has existing content, FrontPage prompts for the name of the editable region that will receive it.

Attaching a Dynamic Web Template dims most options on the General, Formatting, Advanced, and Language tabs of the Page Properties dialog box. It also dims the Style, Style Sheet Links, Shared Borders, and Background tabs on the Format menu. If you want to change these settings, modify the template and let FrontPage update the attached pages. If this would affect more pages than you want, you probably need two Dynamic Web Templates—one for each set of appearance settings—instead of one.

If you include Page Banner components, Link Bar components, themes, styles, or linked styles sheets in a Dynamic Web Template, and then you attach the template to one or more Web pages, those components will behave as if you'd added them directly to the Web page.

If, for example, a Dynamic Web Template includes a Page Banner component, and then a Web page attaches that template, the Page Banner component will display the Web page's Navigation view name, and *not* the template's Navigation view name. The same is true for Link Bar Based On Navigation View components.

This provides a way of globally propagating the location and style of a site's navigation links into each page, but controlling the content of those links externally.

Creating Dynamic Web Templates

Before using a Dynamic Web Template you must, of course, create it. Here's the procedure:

1 Open a new or an existing page in Design view.

2 Add or modify any content you want, but concentrate on the content that will appear in every page that attaches the template.

In a new Dynamic Web Template, the entire page is, by default, non-editable.

3 Select the first area in the page you want to designate as editable. If the area you want contains no other content, add an empty paragraph so that you can select it.

4 Choose Dynamic Web Template from the Format menu, and then Click Manage Editable Regions. If FrontPage offers to save the page as a new Dynamic Web Template, click Yes.

Chapter 9

275

5 When the Editable Regions dialog box shown in Figure 9-11 appears, choose a name for the new editable region and type it into the Region Name box.

Figure 9-11. This dialog box marks the current Design view selection as an editable region and gives the region a name.

6 Click Add to make the region part of the template, and then click Close to close the Editable Regions dialog box. An orange border will surround the new editable region.

7 Repeat steps 3 through 6 for each additional editable region.

You can create as many, or as few, editable regions as you want. Presumably you'll want at least one so that each page using the template can present its own unique content. At the same time, there's usually no advantage in creating lots of small editable regions that touch each other. A single, larger editable area would work just as well.

Here's the procedure for saving a Dynamic Web Template:

1 Choose Save As from the File menu.

2 When the Save As dialog box appears, select Dynamic Web Template (*.dwt) in the Save As Type box.

3 In the File Name box, specify a short, easy-to-remember name—the same sort of name you'd give any other Web page. The filename extension must be .dwt.

4 Click Save to save the template and close the dialog box.

Chapter 9

Attaching Dynamic Web Templates

The procedure for using a Dynamic Web Template isn't difficult, but it does require a different approach than using static templates, like the ones that appear in the Page Templates dialog box. Here's the way to do it:

1 Select the page or pages you want the template to control. In the Folder list or in Folders view, you can select any combination of files and folders you want, or in Design view, you can highlight the page that's currently open. To select your entire site, select the top entry in the Folder list.

2 Choose Dynamic Web Template from the Format menu, and then choose Attach Dynamic Web Template.

3 When the Attach Dynamic Web Template dialog box shown in Figure 9-12 appears, locate and double-click the template you want to use.

Figure 9-12. Use this dialog box to associate existing editable regions with those on a different Dynamic Web Template.

4 If a Web page has any existing content, FrontPage will display the large Choose Editable Regions For Content dialog box shown in the background in Figure 9-13. By default, this will associate the existing page content—designated *(Body)*—with the first editable region in the template.

If, as in Figure 9-13, the page already uses a Dynamic Web Template and you attach a different template, FrontPage will try to match up editable regions in the old and new templates based on name. If an existing editable region name in the old template doesn't exist in the new template, FrontPage matches it up with the first editable region in the new template.

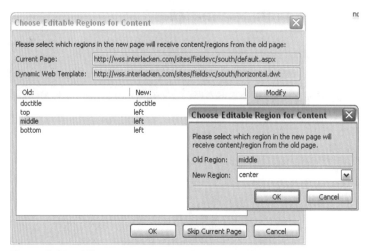

Figure 9-13. When a page uses a Dynamic Web Template and then you attach a different template, you must map content in the old editable regions to the editable regions in the new template.

If FrontPage doesn't propose the editable region matchups you want, select any line that's incorrect, and click the Modify button. This displays the small Choose Editable Region For Content dialog box that appears in the foreground of Figure 9-13. Select the new region you want from the drop-down list, and then click OK.

> **Note** The *doctitle* editable region appears in the Choose Editable Region For Content dialog box by default. It designates the title of the Web page as editable. (This is the title you enter in Design view after choosing Properties from the File menu.)

5 Click OK to close the dialog box and apply the template. FrontPage will display the following dialog box to confirm the operation:

6 To save the updated Web page, choose Save from the File menu.

Designating a Dynamic Web Template region as non-editable isn't fool-proof. In pages that attach the template, designers can modify non-editable regions in Code view, or by opening the page in any editor other than Design view. However, FrontPage will overwrite such changes the next time it propagates changes from the template.

278

Chapter 9

Maintaining Dynamic Web Templates

When you edit and save a Dynamic Web Template, FrontPage displays a confirmation prompt similar to this:

If you click Yes, FrontPage will propagate your template changes to each attached page. If you click No, FrontPage will bypass the updates. Clicking No might be useful if you're saving the template to guard against loss of work, and not because the changes are complete.

The commands that appear after you choose Dynamic Web Template from the Format menu are frequently available even when no template or page is open in Design view. This provides a capability for making global changes within a site. Table 9-2 summarizes which commands are available this way, and when.

Table 9-2. Dynamic Web Template Commands

Command	When Available	Description
Attach Dynamic Web Template	Web page(s) selected	Applies a template you specify to the selected Web page(s)
Detach From Dynamic Web Template	Web page(s) selected	Disconnects the current page from the template, but leaves the template's content in place and editable.
Open Attached Dynamic Web Template	Web page(s) selected	Opens each template file attached to one or more selected pages
Update Selected Page	Web page(s) selected	Propagates template changes to the selected pages
Update All Pages	Always	Propagates template changes to all pages that attach any template in the current site
Update Attached Pages	DWT selected	Propagates template changes to all pages that attach the current template
Manage Editable Regions	DWT open in Design view	Creates, removes, or positions to editable regions in the current template

Integrating CSS Styles with FrontPage

Cascading Style Sheets (CSS) is a technology for controlling typography and positioning in Web pages. CSS statements, however, look nothing like HTML. They serve a different purpose, and therefore have a different syntax as well. The next few sections will provide a brief introduction to CSS.

Understanding Style Sheet Terminology

This section introduces the basic syntax and mindset of CSS. If you're confident of your knowledge in this area, you can safely skip ahead. Otherwise, have a look at these definitions:

- **CSS style** This is a collection of property names and values such as font name, font size, font weight, color, background color, border type, border width, and so forth. Here's how a CSS style looks in code:

  ```
  font-family: Arial, sans-serif; color: red;
  ```

  A colon separates each property name from its value(s). Commas separate multiple values assigned to the same property. Semicolons indicate the end of a property setting and permit the beginning of the next.

- **Selector** This is the name of a CSS rule. It specifies (that is, *selects*) the page elements to which the rule will apply.

- **CSS rule** This is a statement that assigns properties to one or more selectors.

Three kinds of selectors are in common use: Type, Class, and ID. Here's a description of each type:

- **Type selector** This selector has the same name as an HTML tag (that is, the name of an HTML element *type*). Assigning properties to a type selector modifies all text controlled by the corresponding HTML tag. The *h1* selector, for example, controls the appearance of Heading 1 text. The *b* selector controls the appearance of boldface text, and so forth.

  Type selectors are among the best features of CSS. With one statement, you can change the appearance of your whole Web page or of all elements that use a given HML style.

- **Class selector** This selector has any name you choose to give it, except that the name must begin with a period and shouldn't be the name of an HTML tag. Here are some examples:

  ```
  .errmsg   {color: #990000; font-weight: bold; }
  .shaded   {background-color: #EEEEEE; }
  .firedept {color: #FF0000; }
  ```

  Unlike type selectors, class selectors don't apply automatically to all similar elements of a Web page. Instead, to apply the rule, you add a class="*class-name*" attribute to the

280

HTML tag that surrounds your content. Within the class= attribute, however, you omit the leading period. Here are some examples:

```
<p class="errmsg">Record not found.</p>
<td class="shaded">Front porch</td>
The vehicle was a <span class="firedept">red</span> fire engine.
```

In short, a class selector is one you invoke with a *class=* attribute.

● **ID selector**   This selector works somewhat like a class selector, except that it applies to a named element in your Web page. When you define the rule, you begin the name of an ID selector with a pound sign (#), like this:

```
#sigline {font-size: 80%; text-align: center; }
```

This rule would then apply to the following paragraph tag.

```
<p id="sigline">Copyright © 2005 Jim Buyens</p>
```

Because the *id* attribute also identifies the tag for use by scripts and other processes, you should never give two elements in the same page the same ID. This makes class selectors preferable for most uses.

Coding Style Sheet Rules

The syntax of CSS statements is different from that of HTML. The following is a CSS rule that assigns two properties (font family and color) to the selector *h1*:

```
h1 { font-family: Arial, sans-serif; color: red; }
```

Note that in this example:

● The selector is the first item on the line.

● Curly braces enclose the entire list of properties.

● Each property consists of a property name, a colon, and then one or more values.

● Commas separate multiple values for the same property.

● A semicolon indicates the end of a property definition.

Rules and styles are many-to-many. A single rule can apply to any number of styles, and any number of rules can affect a single style. In combination, for example, the two rules shown below tell the browser to display all text within <th> and </th> tags in green and with small caps.

```
th { color: #00FF00; }
th { font-variant: small-caps; }
```

This is perfectly equivalent to coding

```
th { color: #00FF00; font-variant: small-caps; }
```

281

The following rule makes all Heading 1 and Heading 2 text appear in boldface:

```
h1, h2 { font-weight: bold; }
```

The comma between the two selectors implies an *or* condition, meaning that the rule applies whenever the HTML tag is *h1* or *h2*. Lack of a comma implies an *and* condition. The following rule applies only to italic text located within table cells:

```
td i { color: rgb(153,0,0); }
```

When coding a rule that specifies a type selector and a class selector, it's common to omit the space between the two selectors. The following rule, for example:

```
a.menu { background-color: #FFCCCC; color: black; }
```

would apply only to hyperlinks coded class="menu." Here's an example:

```
<a class="menu" href="http://www.microsoft.com">Microsoft</a>
```

Significantly, the preceding rule would *not* apply to either of these tags.

```
<a href="http://www.interlacken.com">Jim Buyens</a>
<p class="menu">Hasty pudding</p>
```

The first tag isn't coded class="menu," and the second tag isn't a hyperlink.

Pseudo-classes are another variation you may encounter (or use yourself). Pseudo-classes pertain to the state of an element rather than the element itself. When you define them, their names begin with a colon. Here are some examples:

- **:link**   applies to a hyperlink for which no record of a previous visit is available.
- **:visited**   applies to a hyperlink for which record of a previous visit *is* available.
- **:hover**   applies while the Web visitor holds the mouse pointer over an element without activating it.
- **:active**   applies while the Web visitor is activating an element: for example, while pointing to an element and holding down the mouse button.
- **:focus**   applies while an element has the focus: that is, while it accepts keyboard events or other forms of text input.

The most common use of pseudo-classes involves hyperlinks. The following rules, for example, produce a hyperlink rollover effect:

```
a.menu       {background-color: #FFEEEE; color: #000000}
a:hover.menu {background-color: #0000FF; color: #FFFF00}
```

The following hyperlink, for example:

```
<a class="menu" href="http://www.microsoft.com">Microsoft</a>
```

would appear pink with black text except when the mouse is over it. When the mouse passes over it, it would switch to blue with yellow text.

> **For more information about the features and use of CSS, browse these locations:**
> **Microsoft:** *msdn.microsoft.com/workshop/author/*
> **W3C:** *www.w3.org/Style/*

Locating Style Sheet Styles

You can specify CSS style information in the three general locations (or, if you prefer, the three levels) listed here:

- **Attached to a specific page element** You can assign CSS style properties to individual HTML elements. Styles applied this way are called *inline styles*. The following tag, for example, contains an inline style. The style= attribute can contain any valid CSS attributes, in CSS syntax.

```
<p style="margin:0"> </p>
```

If you display the Properties dialog box for any element on a Web page, and if that dialog box contains a Style button, clicking that button displays another dialog box that applies CSS properties (font, paragraph, border, numbering, and position) to that element. In Figure 9-14, for example, the Style button in the lower left corner controls CSS properties for whatever table cells the designer selected before displaying the Cell Properties dialog box.

New Web designers often find inline styles easier to use than styles sheets, because they can apply styles directly to the text they want to affect. Experienced designers appreciate uniformity and ease of maintenance throughout a site; as a result, they usually prefer linked style sheet files.

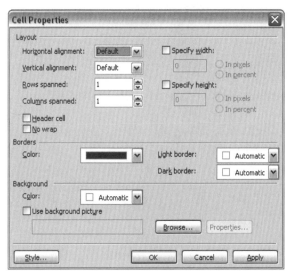

Figure 9-14. The Style button in this dialog box controls CSS properties for the selected page element.

- **In a style sheet located within a Web page**   Whenever you have a Web page open in FrontPage, choosing Style from the Format menu displays the Style dialog box shown in Figure 9-15. This dialog box can create, modify, and delete CSS rules applicable to the current page. These style rules reside in the <head> section of the page, between a pair of <style> and </style> tags.

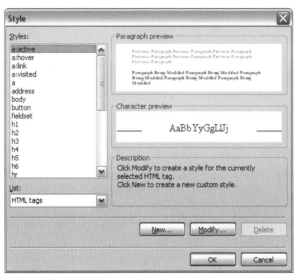

Figure 9-15.   This is the launch point for creating or modifying CSS rules.

- **In a style sheet located in another file**   Centrally controlling the appearance of similar elements in the same Web page is all well and good, but what if you want similar elements in an entire collection of Web pages to look alike? You could set up identical style sheets within each page, but that would be boring, mundane, error-prone, and difficult to maintain. Linked style sheet files provide a welcome alternative. Using linked style sheet files involves these steps:

  1   Create a CSS file, most likely based on one of the CSS templates mentioned in Chapter 8.

  2   Open the CSS file in FrontPage, choose Style from the Formatmenu, configure whatever styles you want, and save the page.

  Skip step 3 if you want to apply your style sheet to an entire Web site.

  3   Select one or more Web pages that should use styles from the file you just saved. You can select an open Web page by leaving the insertion point in it, or you can select groups of files or folders in the Folder List or in Folders view.

  4   Choose Format, Style Sheet Links. This displays the Link Style Sheet dialog box shown in Figure 9-16. If the file you saved in step 2 doesn't appear in the URL list, click Add to add it.

Chapter 9

5 To apply the style sheet to every file in the current Web, select All Pages, and then click OK.

6 To apply the style sheet to pages you selected in step 3, select Selected Page(s), and then click OK.

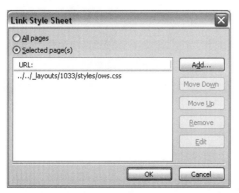

Figure 9-16. This dialog box links files containing CSS rules to selected Web pages or an entire Web site.

Tip To link a style sheet file to a page open in Design view, drag the CSS file from the FrontPage Folder list and drop it on the open Web page.

Combining Styles and Themes with FrontPage and Windows SharePoint Services

Microsoft FrontPage has supported themes since its earliest release. However, it's method of supporting themes has gradually changed.

● Up to and including FrontPage 98, FrontPage implemented themes by adding <font> and other now-deprecated HTML tags to each page. In addition, for each hyperlink on a graphical link bar, it created two button pictures and some JavaScript code. The JavaScript code swapped the pictures as the mouse passed over and away from the button.

● In FrontPage 2000 and 2002, the Web designer could choose whether FrontPage hard-coded themes into the HTML (i.e. using <font> tags) or whether it used a linked style sheet file. The practice of creating button pictures, however, remained.

● FrontPage 2003 always implements themes using linked style sheet files. However, it continues to create and swap individual button pictures.

285

Windows SharePoint services also implements themes by using linked style sheet files. However:

- If you apply a theme using the Site Settings page of a SharePoint site, you choose from a list of themes installed on the Web server, and you get the theme's CSS file from the Web server.

- If you apply a theme using FrontPage, you choose from a list of themes installed on your computer, and you get the theme's CSS file from your computer as well.

Normally, these differences don't present a problem, because FrontPage 2003 and Windows SharePoint Services ship with all the same versions of all the same themes. However, differences can occur, such as when you purchase a third-party theme and install it on your computer.

To understand the pattern of all this, it's useful to categorize the pages in a SharePoint site into three groups:

- **Site Settings Pages**   These are the pages that appear after you choose Site Settings from the main menu bar of most pages in a Team Web Site. These pages don't physically reside in each SharePoint site; instead, Windows SharePoint Services maps a single physical copy into the _layouts_ folder of each managed Web site. In fact, however, these pages actually get their formatting from two sources:

  - First the default Windows SharePoint Services stylesheet.

  - Then, as an override, the theme (if any) you applied to the site using either FrontPage commands or Site Settings pages.

- **Generated Pages**   These are pages that Windows SharePoint Services creates and physically stores within a site. The default pages for viewing and updating lists and libraries fall into this category.

  Like Site Settings pages, these pages get formatting from two sources: first the default Windows SharePoint Services stylesheet, and then any theme you applied using either FrontPage commands or Site Settings pages.

- **Custom Pages**   These are pages you create yourself using FrontPage. If you apply a theme to a site containing custom pages, the custom pages get only the theme you apply. This may result in the loss of some attributes—particularly font sizes—that are present only in the default Windows SharePoint Services stylesheet.

To ensure that your custom pages, generated pages, and Site Settings pages look alike, you should add the following tag immediately after the <head> tag of each custom page you create:

```
<link rel="stylesheet" type="text/css" href="/_layouts/1033/styles/ows.css">
```

This is the statement that Site Settings pages and generated pages use to establish the default SharePoint style as the baseline for other styles. While you're at it, you should also add the following statements right after the one above.

```
<script language="javascript" src="/_layouts/1033/owsbrows.js"></script>
<script language="javascript" src="/_layouts/1033/ows.js"></script>
```

These statements bring in script code that various buttons on the page may invoke. For example, the Help link on the SharePoint Top Navbar won't work unless these statements are present.

> **Tip** Dynamic web templates are a great way of replicating the <link> and <script> statements shown above into multiple pages within a SharePoint site.

You can apply any FrontPage theme to a SharePoint site. This includes themes not included in the SharePoint server's list of available themes. This is the list that appears after you click Site Settings and Apply Theme To Site.

If, however, you apply such a theme in FrontPage and then, in the Web interface, click Site Settings and Apply Theme To Site, you'll find that the Apply Theme page shows the theme as being No Theme (Default). This isn't a major error; it simply occurs because the current theme isn't in the Web server's list. Ignore it and move on to other work.

Locating SharePoint Selector Descriptions

When creating custom Web pages, assigning the correct CSS class selectors can be a nuisance. Ideally, you should assign the same selectors that Site Settings and generated pages use; that way, if you ever change themes, all the colors and type styles will stay in sync throughout the site. One helpful resource in this respect is the Web page at

http://msdn.microsoft.com/library/en-us/spptsdk/html/tsovcssstyles.asp

which lists and describes all the selectors in a SharePoint style.

Analyzing Styles in an Existing Web Page

Another valuable resource is the *TagWalker* script shown working in Figure 9-17. This script displays the tag name, CSS class, ID, and inline style properties of each tag that appears below the mouse pointer.

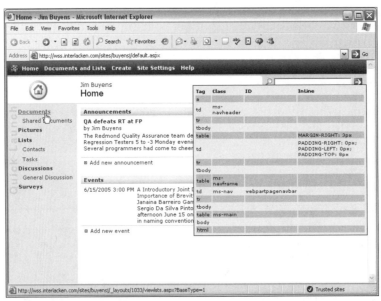

Figure 9-17. A custom script generates the box that overlays the right side of this Web page. The box continuously displays all the CSS selectors and inline styles that affect the spot under the mouse pointer.

In the example, the "current" tag is a hyperlink: that is, an <a> tag. Reading down, a <td> tag encloses the hyperlink, a <tr> tag encloses the <td> tag, and so forth. Each of these tags can have type selectors, class selectors, ID selectors, or inline style attributes.

The browser starts with a default set of style properties at the <html> level and then, working upward, overlays properties one-by-one each time it encounters another style rule. The end result determines the appearance of the element as Web visitors will see it. The *TagWalker* script can't simplify this process, but it *can* help you trace it.

To use the *TagWalker* script yourself, copy the lines below (or the same lines from the companion CD) and paste them into your Web page just above the </body> tag.

```
<script language="jscript">
function TagWalker() {
  elm =  window.event.srcElement;
  tagInfo = "<table style='font-size:10px'><tr>" +
            "<td><b>Tag</b></td>" +
            "<td><b>Class</b></td>" +
            "<td><b>ID</b></td>" +
            "<td><b>InLine</b></td></tr>";
  rsty = "";
  while (elm != null){
    if (rsty == "") {
      rsty = "style='background-color: #cccccc;'";
    }else{
      rsty = "";
    }
    tagInfo += "<tr " + rsty + ">" +
      "<td>" + elm.tagName.toLowerCase() + "</td>";
    if (elm.className == null) {
      tagInfo += "<td></td>";
    }else{
      tagInfo += "<td>" + elm.className + "</td>";
    }
    if (elm.id == null) {
      tagInfo += "<td></td>";
    }else{
      tagInfo += "<td>" + elm.id + "</td>";
    }
    if (elm.style.cssText == null){
      tagInfo += "<td></td>";
    }else{
      tagInfo += "<td>" + elm.style.cssText + "</td>";
    }
    tagInfo += "</tr>"
    elm = elm.parentElement;
  }
  tagdump.innerHTML = tagInfo + "</table>";
}
window.document.body.onmouseover = TagWalker;
</script>
<div style="border: 1px solid black; padding:3px;
position: absolute; left: 400px; top: 50px; z-index:15;
background-color:#EEEEEE">
<p id="tagdump" style="font-size:10px"> </p>
</div>
```

On the CD   To find the TagWalker script on the Companion CD, browse to the folder \utils\TagWalker.

Displaying Class Selector Samples

Figure 9-18 shows another Web page that may be helpful when working with SharePoint themes. It displays an example of each class selector in a standard SharePoint theme.

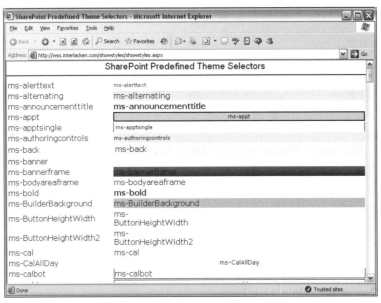

Figure 9-18. This Web page displays a sample of each selector in a SharePoint style sheet. There are over three hundred such selectors.

The following procedure may help when choosing the class selectors for a custom page:

1 Add the showstyles.aspx page and the SharePoint.gif file to your Web site.

2 Update the showstyles.aspx page to use the same shared style sheets and themes as the rest of the site.

3 Display the showstyles.aspx page in your browser.

4 Scroll through the page and find the selector that creates the appearance you want.

5 If more than one selector meets your needs, choose a name that most closely reflects the use you have in mind. The selectors Windows SharePoint Services uses for buttons have the word *Button* in their name; those it uses for calendars have Cal in their name, and so forth.

 On the CD To find the showstyles.aspx page on the Companion CD, browse to the folder \utils\ShowStyles.

Using Interactive Buttons

Graphical buttons are among the most popular user interface elements on the Web. Unlike the plain, gray buttons that HTML provides, these are actually picture files. When the mouse pointer passes over them a different picture appears, and when the mouse moves away the original picture appears. Such buttons may also change appearance when the Web visitor clicks them.

FrontPage 2003 has a new component called Interactive Buttons that makes it very easy to create such buttons. Figure 9-19 shows a Web page that uses five of these components. Each button looks like a file tab, and the button under the mouse pointer is darker. The button gets even darker if the Web visitor clicks it.

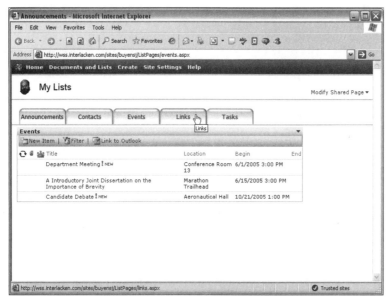

Figure 9-19. Each file tab in this Web page is actually a FrontPage Interactive Button component.

Here's the procedure for adding an Interactive Button component to any Web page. It assumes that you've already opened the page in Design view.

1 Set the insertion point where you want the Interactive Button component to appear.

2 Choose Interactive Button from the Insert menu.

3 When the Interactive Button dialog box shown in Figure 9-20 appears, select the entries in the Buttons list until you find your favorite. As you click each choice, a sample button appears in the Preview area.

Figure 9-20. The Button tab configures the most essential properties of an Interactive Button component.

4 Enter the button title in the Text box.

5 Enter a hyperlink location in the Link box, or click the Browse button to find one by pointing and clicking.

To gain more control over the font that appears on the button face, continue as follows.

1 Click the Text tab in the Interactive Buttons dialog box. This displays the fields shown in Figure 9-21.

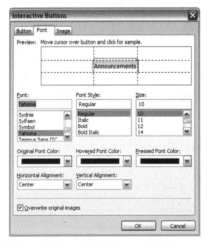

Figure 9-21. This tab controls the appearance of an Interactive Button component's text.

2 Use the Font, Font Style, and Size boxes to specify the typographical properties of the button text.

3 Use the following buttons to specify the color of the button text:

- **Original Font Color** the button's normal text color
- **Hovered Font Color** the button's text color when the mouse pointer is over it
- **Pressed Font Color** the button's text color after the Web visitor clicks the button

4 Use the Horizontal Alignment and Vertical Alignment controls to position the text where you want it.

As before, the Preview area near the top of the dialog box shows the effects of your changes; you can click OK to save them. However, you might prefer to first modify the button properties that appear on the Image tab shown in Figure 9-22.

Figure 9-22. The Image tab controls an Interactive Button component's size and effects.

If so, proceed as follows:

1 Use the Width and Height boxes to stretch or shrink the button picture.

- To change these values proportionately, make sure that the Maintain Proportions check box is selected.
- To change Height without changing Width (or vice versa) make sure that the Maintain Proportions check box is cleared.

2 Select the Create Hover Image check box if you want the button's appearance to change when the mouse pointer passes over it. Clear the check box if you don't want this effect.

293

3 Select the Create Pressed Image check box if you want the button's appearance to change when the Web visitor clicks it. If you don't want this effect, clear this check box.

4 Select the Preload Button Images check box if you want the browser to load all the button pictures into memory when it first displays the page. Otherwise, clear this check box.

Tip **Preload your button images**

Preloading button images ensures that changes to a button's appearance occur smoothly. If you don't preload images, the browser retrieves hovered and pressed images only when it first needs them, and this may incur a time delay. Preloading is usually the best choice, but it does have a drawback: The browser has to download all the button images even if it never displays them.

---

5 To specify the button background, select one of these options:

- **Make The Button A JPEG Image And Use This Background Color.** Select this option if you want the button to have a solid color background. Use the nearby color drop-down list to specify the color you want.

- **Make The Button A GIF Image And Use A Transparent Background.** Select this option if you want the button to have a transparent background.

If you're creating a new Interactive Button, the Overwrite Original Images check box will be dimmed. If you're modifying an existing Interactive Button, make sure this check box is checked.

When you save a page that includes interactive buttons, FrontPage might display the Save Embedded Files dialog box. This occurs because FrontPage needs to save the three picture files each Interactive Button might display. It's best if you save the pictures for each Web page in a different folder; otherwise, the pictures from one page might overwrite those for another.

To modify an existing button, display the Interactive Button dialog box using any of these methods:

- Double-click the Interactive Button component.
- Right-click the Interactive Button component, and then choose Button Properties from the shortcut menu.
- Open the drop-down menu on the Interactive Button component's Quick Tag Selector icon, and then choose Tag Properties. (The Quick Tag Selector icon will show an <img> tag.)
- Select the Interactive Button component, and press Alt+Enter.

Then, configure the three tags as you would for a new button.

294

Scripting DHTML Behaviors

Many popular Web page features require Dynamic HTML programming; that is, JavaScript programming that runs on the browser. Fortunately, FrontPage 2003 provides a new Behaviors task pane that handles most such requirements without making you work with programming code at all. Figure 9-23 shows an example of this task pane. When the mouse passes over the Announcements link, an *onmouseover* Behavior will display an informative message in the gray-edged box to the right. The *onmouseover* behavior clears the box when the mouse moves elsewhere.

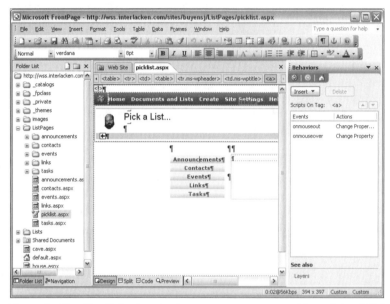

Figure 9-23. The Behaviors task pane can program a wide variety of Web page effects without exposing you to any program code.

Behaviors can take many kinds of actions. For example, they can jump to another URL, play a sound, or display a message box. In addition, an event on one page element can run a script that modifies that element, or even a different page element.

Assigning ID Properties

If you want an event on one element to modify a different page element, the modified element must have an *id* attribute. (Otherwise, the script has no way of telling the browser which element to modify.) To find or assign the *id* attribute for a page element, proceed as follows:

1 Make sure that the Quick Tag Selector is displayed. If it isn't, choose Quick Tag Selector from the View menu.

295

2   Select the page element you want a DHTML effect to modify. This will probably be a picture or a layer, but it could be almost anything on the page.

3   Selecting a page element will also select its Quick Tag Selector icon. Click the down arrow on this icon, and choose Edit Tag from the drop-down menu. This will display a Quick Tag Editor dialog box that looks like this:

Review the tag attributes, and make sure that one of them is an *id*. In this example, the *id* attribute is *id="LinkDesc"*.

- If you find an *id* attribute, write down or remember its value, and then click the X button on the right of the Quick Tag Editor dialog box.

- If no *id* attribute is present, set the insertion point between any existing attributes and supply one, taking care not to assign the same *id* value as any other element on the page. Record the new *id* value, and then click the check mark button on the right in the Quick Tag Editor dialog box.

> **Tip**   The X button closes the Quick Tag Editor dialog box without saving any changes you've made. The check mark button saves your changes before closing the dialog box.

For many page elements, the following procedure might be easier. However, it only works for elements that have Property dialog boxes containing a Style button.

1   Display the element's Properties dialog box.

2   Click the Style button on the Properties dialog box. (If the dialog box has no Style button, revert to the first procedure.)

3   When the Modify Style dialog box appears, type the *id* you want into the ID text box. *Don't* choose an existing *id* from the drop-down list!

4   Click OK twice to close the Modify Style dialog box and the Properties dialog box.

Configuring Behaviors

Here's the procedure to actually specify the event you want the browser to detect and the effect you want it to have:

1   Choose Behaviors from the Format menu.

2   Select the page element that will trigger the Behavior. To do this, either:
- Click the element in Design view.
- Click the element's tag icon in the Quick Tag Selector.

In the Behaviors task pane, a message above the central list box will confirm the tag you selected. In the current example, the message *Scripts On Tag: <a>* confirms that you're working on an <a> tag.

3   Click the Insert button in the Behaviors task pane, and then select the type of action you want the browser to take. Some of these choices include:

- **Call JavaScript**   Runs a JavaScript function you coded elsewhere in the page.

- **Change Property**   Modifies the properties of some page element.

- **Check Browser**   Jumps to another page depending on what browser the Web visitor has.

- **Go to URL**   Unconditionally jumps to another page.

- **Swap Image**   Replaces one picture with another.

Selecting any listed action displays a dialog box in which you configure the details of what you want to occur. If the name of an action doesn't clarify what it does, the fields on the resulting dialog box probably will. If not, consult the FrontPage Help files.

To construct the example in Figure 9-23, suppose you want a message to appear in a <div> tag named *LinkDesc* whenever the mousse passes over the Announcements hyperlink. After displaying the Behaviors task pane and selecting the hyperlink, you would continue as follows:

1   Click the Insert button in the Behaviors task pane, and then choose Change Property.

2   When the Change Property dialog box shown in Figure 9-24 appears, select the Select Element option. This tells FrontPage that you want to select which element the Behavior will modify.

Figure 9-24.   This dialog box specifies a list of property changes that a Behavior action will make.

297

Specifying Current Element means that the script will modify the element that triggers the Behavior.

3   In the Element Type drop-down list, select the type of element you want to modify. In order for an element type to appear, it must be present in your Web page and have an *id* attribute.

4   In the Element ID drop-down list, select the *id* of the element you want to modify. This list will display only elements of the type you specified in step 3, and that have *id* attributes.

5   To modify the textual content of an element, click the Add button at the right edge of the dialog box.

The Font, Position, Borders, and Visibility buttons display dialog boxes for modifying those properties of the element you specified in step 4.

6   When the Insert Property dialog box shown in Figure 9-25 appears, specify a Property Name of *innerText* and a Property Value consisting of the text you want to display.

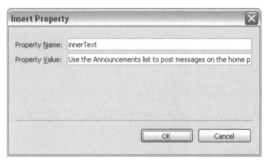

Figure 9-25.   This dialog box can control any DHTML property of any element.

Specifying attribute names in this dialog box is somewhat tricky because you must specify the exact, case-sensitive attribute names that programmers use. These aren't the same names you'd use in ordinary HTML or CSS code. For the most part, they're the same as CSS names except that initial capping replaces hyphens. The attribute name for *font-family*, for example, would be *styles.fontFamily*.

The property name *innerText* refers to the text between an element's opening and closing tags. If you want to supply any HTML tags along with the text, use the *innerHTML* property.

7   Without leaving the Change Property dialog box, you can specify changes to as many properties as you want. The list in the center of the dialog box will continue to show more entries. To change an existing attribute entry, select it, and click Modify. To remove an attribute, select it, and click Remove.

8 When a script appears for the first time in the Behaviors list box, it usually has an event type of *onclick*. This is fine if you want a mouse click to trigger the script, but unfortunate in any other case. To recover:

8.1 Click the incorrect event name (for example, *onclick*).

8.2 Click the down arrow that appears next to the incorrect event name.

8.3 Select the event you want from the resulting list. For example, *onmouseover* events fire when the mouse passes over the trigger element, even if the Web visitor takes no other action.

Troubleshooting

Behaviors affecting one element disappear when you configure another

One thing the Change Property dialog box can't do is specify changes to more than one element. If you specify changes to one element, and then change the selection in the Eement Type or Element ID list, the dialog box will *erase* your entries for the first element! This argues strongly for the following rules:

● Once you've specified property changes for an element, don't modify the Element Type or Element ID selections unless you want to discard the existing changes.

● To change the properties of more than one element, finish configuring the changes for the first element, and then click the Insert button on the Behaviors task pane and configure changes to the second element. Repeat until satisfied.

Figure 9-26 shows the finished page as it appears in a browser. As the mouse passes over each hyperlink, the text in the gray-edged box changes to provide guidance about that list. Because this is a Web Part page, it could also contain any Web Parts you decided to add.

The Behaviors task pane generally creates results that work well in Internet Explorer 4 and later, and in Netscape Navigator 6 and later. Even so, you should test your results in each browser you care about. If a script failure produces obnoxious error messages or leaves visitors with no way to navigate the site, you might need to develop alternative pages and use Check Browser scripts to switch among them.

Figure 9-26. The text inside the gray box on this page changes as the mouse pointer passes over each button at the left. This is just one of the effects you can create using FrontPage behaviors. .

In Summary...

This chapter described a variety of ways you can use Microsoft Office FrontPage 2003 to customize the look and feel of a SharePoint site. This included use of Navigation view, Link Bars, Page Banners, Cascading Style Sheets, Interactive Buttons, and Behaviors.

The next chapter will explain how to create and modify SharePoint Data Sources and Data Views. These provide the means for Web Part pages to access SharePoint lists, SharePoint libraries, and external databases.

Chapter 10

Creating Data Sources and Data Views

Chapter 6 described how you can design your own SharePoint lists and libraries, how you can create multiple views of any list and library, and how you can choose to display different views, all using only a browser. These capabilities are impressive but, like any other technique, they have limits.

One way of gaining more flexibility is, of course, to write your own Web Parts in Visual Studio .NET. Part VII will explain the basics of writing and deploying such Web Parts, but that approach requires significant programming skills.

If you need more power than the Web-based design tools provide and less complexity than writing program code in Visual Studio, Microsoft FrontPage 2003 may provide just the balance you need. FrontPage 2003 has some great new features for working with data in SharePoint lists, SharePoint libraries, external databases, and Web services accessible through Windows SharePoint Services. Learning about these features is a three-step process.

- In this chapter, you learn how to establish connections—called *data sources*—from a SharePoint site to SharePoint lists and libraries, non-SharePoint databases, XML files, Web sites, and Web services.

- In Chapter 11, you explore creating Data View Web Parts, which format and display the contents of these data sources.

- In Chapter 12, you become familiar with more advanced features of Data View Web Parts.

Best of all, none of this requires writing any program code at all. FrontPage provides all the commands and configuration you need within its graphical interface.

> **Note** Throughout this chapter, and unless otherwise stated: The term *library* means a SharePoint document library, form library, or picture library. The term *list* means a SharePoint list, survey, or discussion board.

Designing Lists and Libraries

FrontPage can create and modify SharePoint lists and libraries with all the same capabilities that the browser interface provides. The advantage is that you don't have to leave FrontPage to make such changes, and you don't have to refresh the FrontPage display afterward.

As shown in Figure 10-1, SharePoint lists and libraries appear in FrontPage as if they were folders with special icons.

- List folders contain the list view pages and forms that support the parent list. If a list permits attachments, it also has an Attachments subfolder that contains the attached files.

- Library folders contain a folder tree of library documents, plus a Forms subfolder that contains list view pages and forms. Picture Libraries also have a _t folder that contains thumbnails of each picture, and a _w folder that contains intermediate-sized versions of each picture.

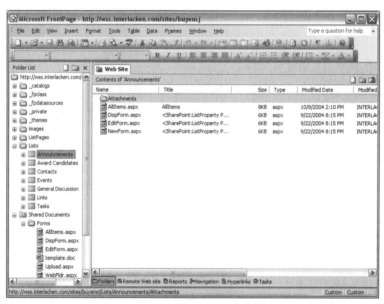

Figure 10-1. SharePoint lists and libraries appear almost like folders in FrontPage.

You can delete a list or library just as if it were an ordinary file. For example, you can right-click it and choose Delete, select it and press the Delete key, or select it and choose Delete from the Edit menu. The usual methods for renaming files and folders apply, as do the Copy and Cut commands. Curiously, you can't paste a SharePoint list or library into its own site. You can, however, copy a list or library from one site and paste it into another.

Modifying SharePoint Lists and Libraries

To modify a SharePoint list or library in FrontPage, display its properties just as you would for a normal file or folder. For example:

- Right-click it and choose Properties from the shortcut menu.
- Select it and choose Properties from the File menu.

If the object is a SharePoint list, either of these actions displays the List Properties dialog box shown in Figure 10-2. For libraries the dialog box title will be Document Library Properties, and for surveys Survey Properties.

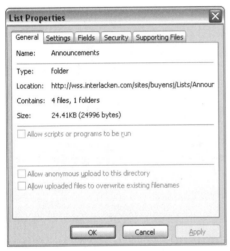

Figure 10-2. The FrontPage property sheet for a SharePoint list or library has special Settings, Fields, Security, and Supporting Files Tabs, each with update capabilities.

Configuring List and Library Settings

Clicking the Settings tab changes the dialog box so it resembles Figure 10-3. Here you can configure the following settings.

- **Name** This text identifies the list or library.
- **Description** This is a sentence or two that describes the list's purpose.
- **Hide From Browsers** Selecting this option stops Web visitors from discovering and displaying the list. This might be appropriate when a list is part of some larger application, and the standard list pages aren't appropriate for viewing or updating the data.
- **Enable Attachments** Selecting this option allows team members to attach documents to list items. This field doesn't appear for surveys.
- **Require Content Approval For New Items** Selecting this option hides new list items from team members until an administrator or list manager approves the item. Again, this field is absent for surveys.

303

● **Use A Template For New Documents**   This field appears only for document and form libraries. If you select the check box and enter a file name, that file will be the starting point for team members who click the New Document button for a document library, or the Fill Out This Form button for a form library.

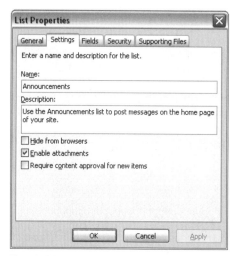

Figure 10-3.   The Settings tab controls a list or library's highest-level attributes.

Configuring List and Library Fields

To add, remove, or modify the list of fields SharePoint maintains for each item in a list or library, click the Fields tab. The dialog box will then resemble Figure 10-4.

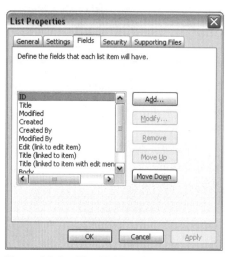

Figure 10-4.   The Fields tab controls which fields the list or library will have.

For surveys, click the Questions tab, which looks and works almost the same. In the following instructions, just think *question* whenever you read the word *field*.

To change the fields assigned to the list or library, use the following buttons.

- **Add**   Displays an Add Field dialog box that adds a new field to the list.
- **Modify**   Displays a Modify Field dialog box that changes an existing field. This button is dimmed for certain fields that Windows SharePoint Services itself controls.
- **Remove**   Deletes a field and all its values from the list. This button is dimmed for system-maintained fields and for certain fields that specific list types require.
- **Move Up**   Moves the selected field one position higher in the list. This option and the next affect the order of the input fields on New Item and Edit Item forms.
- **Move Down**   Moves the selected field one position lower in the list.

If you click the Add button, an Add Field dialog box like the one at the left side of Figure 10-5 appears. If you click the Modify field button, a similar Modify Field dialog box results. In either case, supply these values:

- **Field Name**   Enter the text that will identify the field.
- **Description**   Enter a sentence or two that explains what kind of data the field contains.
- **Information Type**   Choose the physical format of the data: Single Line Of Text, Multiple Lines Of Text, Number, and so forth. This affects which data values are valid, what kind of control appears on input forms, and how the data is sorted.
- **Add To Default View**   Select this check box if you want the field to appear in the view that team members receive when they first browse the list. (This field isn't present on the Modify Field dialog box.)

Figure 10-5.   Adding or modifying a field is a two-step process. The information type you choose in the first step determines the options you must specify in the second step.

When you're done making these entries, click the Next button. The dialog box then changes to resemble the one shown at the right side of Figure 10-5. The exact controls available, however, will vary depending on the Information Type setting you chose in the previous step.

As an example, the figure illustrates the following controls, which appear if you set Information Type to Choice (Menu To Choose From).

305

- **Choices**   Enter each permissible field value on a separate line.
- **Default Value**   If you wish, enter one of the values you listed under Choices.
- **Display As**   Choose the type of multiple-choice control you want input forms to display: Drop-Down Menu, Radio Buttons, or Checkboxes.
- **Allow Fill-In Choices**   Select this check box to have input forms display a text box in which team members can enter values other than those you specified under Choices.
- **Allow Blank Values**   Select this box if it's all right for team members not to supply a value for the field.

When you're done with these entries, click the Finish button. The new field should appear in the Fields (or Questions) tab of the Properties dialog box.

Configuring List and Library Security

The security tab shown in Figure 10-6 controls the security rules that apply to team members who are authorized to use a list. For all types of libraries, however, it's dimmed.

Figure 10-6.   The options on the Security tab determine whether security applies at the list level or at the item level.

Configure the fields on this tab as follows:

- **Specify Which Items Users Can Read**   Choose one of these settings:
  - **All Items**   If any team member authorized to view the list can view all of its items.
  - **Only Their Own**   If authorized team members can only view items they created.
- **Specify Which Items Users Can Edit**   Choose one of these settings:
  - **All Items**   If a team member authorized to edit the list can edit any and all items.

- **Only Their Own**   If authorized team members can only edit items they created.
- **None**   If only administrators and list managers can edit items.

Configuring List and Library Supporting Files

Clicking the Supporting Files tab changes the appearance of the Properties dialog box to that shown in Figure 10-7.

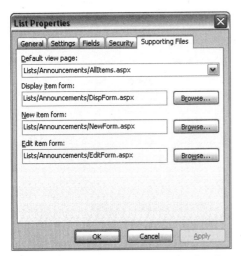

Figure 10-7.   Windows SharePoint Services normally maintains the fields on this tab.

Windows SharePoint Services normally maintains the URLs on this tab automatically. However, you can override the following settings if necessary.

- **Default View Page**   Select the Web page that appears when team members initially choose to view the list or library. This is the URL that represents the list or library in places like the site's Quick Launch Bar and its Documents And Lists page.
- **Display Item Form**   Specify the URL of the page that displays individual items in the list. This field doesn't appear for libraries.
- **New Item Form**   Specify the URL of the page that adds new items to the list.
- **Edit Item Form**   Specify the URL of the page that modifies existing list items. This field is absent for all types of libraries.

Tip   **Test Data Sources by Creating Data Views.**

To test a new or modified list, library, or data source, drag it onto a new, empty Web page. This displays the object's fields and content, even in FrontPage design view. What this does, by the way, is create a new Data View Web Part that you can add to your site and offer to your team members. The next chapter will explain much more about Data View Web Parts.

307

Creating a New List or Library

To create a SharePoint list or library in FrontPage, first display the SharePoint List dialog box. There are three ways of doing this:

> **Tip** To create a list or library while browsing a SharePoint site, click Create on the top navigation bar of any page.

- From the New task pane:
    1 Choose New from the File menu.
    2 When the New task pane appears, under New Page, click SharePoint List.
- From the Standard toolbar:
    1 Click the drop-down arrow on the Create A New Normal Page button.
    2 Select SharePoint list from the resulting menu.
- From the Data Source Catalog task pane:
    1 Display the Data Source Catalog task pane.
    2 Open the entry for the current site.
    3 Open either the entry for SharePoint Lists or SharePoint Libraries.
    4 Click either the Create New SharePoint List or the Create New SharePoint Library link at the bottom of the category listing.

All of these procedures ultimately display the SharePoint List dialog box shown in Figure 10-8.

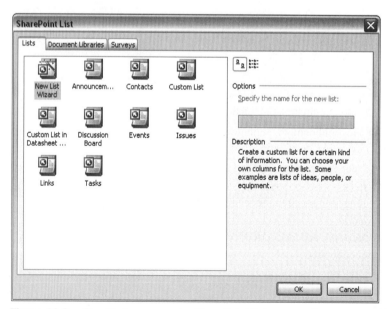

Figure 10-8. FrontPage can create SharePoint lists as easily as normal Web pages, but with more flexibility.

Chapter 10

To create a standard SharePoint list or library in the current site, proceed as follows.

1 Select the Lists, Document Libraries, or Surveys tab in the SharePoint List dialog box.

2 Select any entry except New List Wizard, New Library Wizard, or New Survey Wizard.

3 Under Options, on the right side of the dialog box, give the new list or library a name.

4 Click OK.

Tip   **Create the right kind of list or library**

Certain SharePoint lists have "locked-in" attributes you can only specify by creating a new list. For example, you can't convert some other type of list into a Contacts list that can exchange date with Microsoft Outlook. Similarly, you can't convert a list into a library, or one type of library into another. Therefore, when you create a list or library, be sure to create the type you really need.

To run a wizard that creates a custom SharePoint list or library in the current site, follow these instructions:

1 Select the Lists, Document Library, or Survey tab in the SharePoint List dialog box.

2 Select New List Wizard, New Document Library Wizard, or New Survey Wizard, and then click OK.

3 When the opening page of the wizard appears, click Next.

Figure 10-9 shows the second page of the wizard, which contains the same settings as the Settings tab in the List Properties dialog box.

For instructions on configuring the Settings tab in the List Properties dialog box, refer to the section titled "Configuring List and Library Settings," earlier in this chapter.

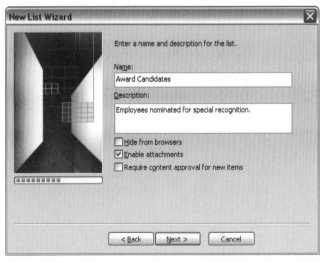

Figure 10-9.   When you create a new list or library by a wizard, this page prompts for the list or library name, and for other global settings.

309

4   If you're creating a document or form library, the next page in the wizard will resemble Figure 10-10. This page configures the library's default document template. To specify a template:

4.1   Make sure the template file resides within the current Web site. If it doesn't, import it. For example, drag it from Windows Explorer and drop it in the FrontPage Folder list.

4.2   Select the check box titled Use A Template For New Documents.

4.3   Either type the template's URL (relative to the site's root folder) into the text box, or click the Browse button and select the file you want.

5   Click the Next button when you're done with this page of the wizard. The next page of the wizard appears in Figure 10-11.

- For lists and document libraries, it configures the fields the list or library will contain. Initially, it displays all the fields Windows SharePoint Services captures automatically, plus a Title field.

- For surveys, it configures the questions the survey will ask. Initially, there are no questions.

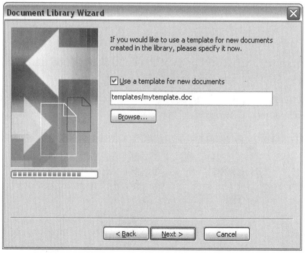

Figure 10-10.   This wizard page appears only for document and form libraries. Picture libraries and lists have no use for a template file.

The procedure for configuring this tab is the same as that for the Fields or Questions tab in the List Properties dialog box. For instructions on configuring the Fields tab in the List Properties dialog box, refer to the section titled "Configuring Lists, Fields, Library Fields, and Survey Questions" earlier in this chapter.

For libraries, this is the last page of the wizard. When you're done with it, click Finish. For lists and surveys, click Next.

Chapter 10

Figure 10-11. For lists and libraries, the wizard creates only the Title field and the standard system-maintained data fields. You can create more fields by clicking the Add button. This wizard page is blank when creating a survey, but the wizard does create the standard system-maintained data fields.

6 Configure the options on the last page of the wizard. This page appears in Figure 10-12 and works like the Security tab on the List Properties or Survey Properties dialog box.

For instructions on configuring the Security tab in the List Properties or Survey Properties dialog box, refer to the section titled "Configuring List and Library Security," earlier in this chapter.

7 Click Finish to create the new SharePoint list.

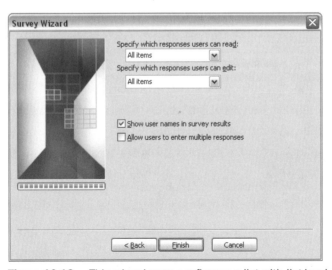

Figure 10-12. This wizard page configures a list with list-level or item-level security. It doesn't appear for libraries.

Managing the Data Source Catalog

After opening a SharePoint site in FrontPage 2003, you can easily view and maintain a list of locations from which that site can retrieve data. FrontPage calls this list the *Data Source Catalog* and it appears, logically enough, on a Data Source Catalog task pane. To display this task pane, either:

- Choose Insert from the Data menu, and then choose Data View, or
- Click the drop-down arrow in the title bar of any other task pane, and then choose Data Source Catalog.

This displays the Data Source Catalog task pane shown in Figure 10-13.

Figure 10-13. The Data Source Catalog lists all data sources available within a Windows SharePoint Services site.

Because a single site can have many data sources, the task pane displays them in an indented, expandable list. The top level of this list contains:

- A Recent node that shows the last few data sources you've worked with, and
- A node for each SharePoint site whose Data Source Catalog is accessible from the current site. By default there's only one such entry, and it names the current site.

If necessary, you can add additional SharePoint sites to the Data Source Catalog. This provides a means for one site to access lists, libraries, and other data sources that reside in other sites. Here's the procedure.

1 Click the Manage Catalog link at the bottom of the Data Source Catalog task pane.

2 When the Manage Catalog dialog box shown in Figure 10-14 appears, click the Add button.

Figure 10-14. Clicking the Manage Catalog in the Data Source Catalog task pane displays this dialog box, where you can specify additional sites whose catalogs you'd like to use.

3 When the Collection Properties dialog box shown below appears, enter these settings:

■ **Display Name**   Enter the name of the site, as you want it to appear in the Data Source Catalog.

■ **Location**   Enter the URL of the site's root folder.

4 Click OK to save your entries, and then click OK to close the Manage Catalog dialog box.

Whenever you add other SharePoint sites to your Data Source Catalog, recall these important points:

● SharePoint lists and libraries will only be available from sites on the same Web server. If you add a site that resides on a different Web server, only non-SharePoint data sources will be available.

Chapter 10

313

- To access another site's Data Source Catalog in FrontPage, you must have permission to edit that site in FrontPage.

- To access the data using a browser, a team member will need permissions on both sites: the one presenting the data, and the one where the data resides.

To view the data sources within a site, click the plus sign that precedes the site name. This will display entries for six general categories, namely:

- **SharePoint Lists**   Lists in the current SharePoint site, such as Announcements, Events, Links, and custom lists.

- **SharePoint Libraries**   Document, form, and picture libraries in the current SharePoint site.

- **Database Connections**   Databases tables located outside the current SharePoint site. These can reside in SQL Server databases at any accessible network location, or in any other database accessible by OLEDB. Examples in this latter category include Microsoft Access and Oracle.

- **XML Files**   Files that store data in XML format.

- **Server-Side Scripts**   Web locations that return data in XML format.

- **XML Web Services**   Online services that use Simple Object Access Protocol (SOAP) to handle information requests.

To view the data sources within each category, click the plus sign that precedes the category name.

To search for a data source by name:

1 Display the Find A Data Source task pane.

2 Use the Search drop-down list to select the site that contains the data source. To search all the sites in your catalog, select My Entire Catalog.

3 In the For box, enter any string of characters that the name of the data source contains.

4 Click the Search Now button.

5 To work with any data source that appears in the Search Results list, right-click it, and choose a command from the shortcut menu.

> For more information about the commands that appear after you right-click a data source name, refer to the section titled "Accessing Data Source Details," later in this chapter.

If, as in Figure 10-15, the Find A Data Source task pane finds ambiguous results, hold the mouse over each one until the tool tip displays its complete URL.

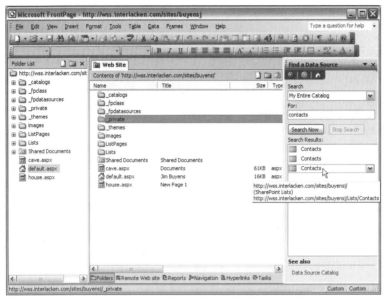

Figure 10-15. If ambiguous entries appear in the Data Source Catalog task pane, hover the mouse over each one until a tool tip appears.

The following sections explain how to create and modify data sources in each of the six categories.

Configuring SharePoint Lists and Libraries

The Data Source Catalog task pane automatically displays SharePoint lists and libraries in their respective categories. Surveys appear under the SharePoint Lists category.

> **Tip** If you need a new list or library, you can create it using either a browser or FrontPage.

Creating a SharePoint list or library automatically creates a corresponding data source. To view all the properties of any list or library and change some of them:

1 Right-click the list or library, and then choose Properties from the shortcut menu. This will display the Data Source Properties dialog box shown in Figure 10-16.

2 Click the List Properties button to display the List Properties dialog box shown previously in Figure 10-2. Then, view or update the list or library properties as instructed earlier in this chapter.

Chapter 10

315

Figure 10-16.   You can't modify the data sources that Windows SharePoint Services creates automatically for lists and libraries. One option is to modify the list or library. Another is to create a new, modifiable data source that points to the same list.

If you find that you can't modify the data source property you want to change, you might need to create a new data source that accesses the existing list or library in a new way. To pursue this approach, click the Copy And Modify button in the Data Source Properties dialog box. This displays the Data Source Properties dialog box shown in Figure 10-17.

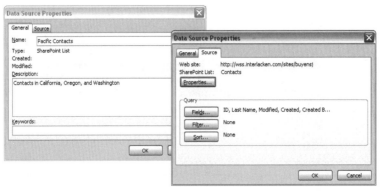

Figure 10-17.   This figure shows both tabs in the Data Source Properties dialog box. The General tab provides identifying information, and the Source tab provides entry to detailed configuration.

Note   **Data Sources Aren't Lists or Libraries**

In the case of database, XML file, server-side script, and Web service data sources, it's fairly obvious that the data source is simply a pointer to the actual data.

Because Windows SharePoint Services always creates data sources when it creates lists or libraries, and because it uses the same name for both objects, the distinction may be less obvious. But in fact, the data source is only a pointer to its list or library.

316

Initially, the Source tab will be selected. The Properties button displays the List Properties dialog box shown previously in Figure 10-2. The Fields, Filter, and Sort buttons display dialog boxes that specify which fields and which records the data source will provide, and in what order.

> For more information on using the Fields, Filter, and Sort buttons, refer to the section titled "Configuring Data Source Query Settings," which appears next in this chapter.

When you've finished configuring these settings, click the General tab shown previously in Figure 10-17, give the new data source a name, enter any description or keywords you want, and click OK.

> **Tip**   The Name field on the General tab of the Data Source Properties dialog box shows the name of the data source. The SharePoint List field on the Source tab shows which SharePoint list or library actually contains the data.

You can also perform a Copy And Modify operation by clicking any data source in the Data Source Catalog and then choosing Copy And Modify from the shortcut menu.

Data sources you create by using either Copy And Modify method don't appear as lists or libraries when Web visitors browse the site. They're strictly for use in development environments like FrontPage.

Of course, the data is fully visible on any Web pages you create using the data source. The next chapter will explain how to do this.

Configuring Data Source Query Settings

For SharePoint lists, SharePoint libraries, and database connections, the Source tab of the Data Source Properties dialog box (shown previously in Figure 10-17) contains three buttons for configuring the fields, selection criteria, and sequence of the records the data source will deliver: Fields, Filter, and Sort. The next three sections will explain how to use these buttons.

Field selection, filtering, and sorting aren't available for XML file, Server-Side Script, and XML Web Service data sources. These data sources have no query language like SQL that can perform these functions. Instead, you specify field selection, filtering, and sorting when you configure the Data View Web Part that displays the data

> For information on selecting fields, filtering data, and sorting data in a Data View Web Part refer to "Modifying List Views and Data Views," in Chapter 11.

Configuring Data Source Fields

Clicking the Fields button on the Source tab of the Data Source Properties dialog box displays the Included Fields dialog box shown in Figure 10-18.

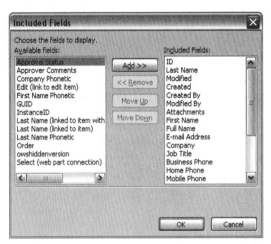

Figure 10-18. This dialog box determines which fields from a list, library, or database will actually be available through a given data source.

This dialog box specifies which fields from the original list or library will be available in the new data source.

- To include a field from the original list, library, or database, select it in the available fields list, and click the Add button. To exclude a field from the original list, library, or database, select it in the included fields list, and click the Remove button.

- To move an included field higher in the list, select it, and click the Move Up button. To move an included field lower in the list, select it, and click the Move Down button.

Note that you can't create or modify fields in this dialog box. To do that, you have to modify the original list, library, or database because that's where the fields actually reside.

Configuring Data Source Filtering

Clicking the Filter button on the Source tab of the Data Source Properties dialog box displays the Filter Criteria dialog box shown in Figure 10-19.

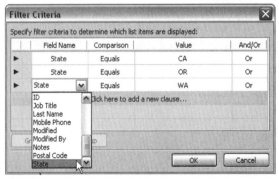

Figure 10-19. This dialog box can stop a data source from delivering records that have (or lack) certain data values.

318

This dialog box specifies criteria for displaying some records and bypassing others. To establish a filter:

1 Select the Field Name field in the first empty row, and select a field name from the drop-down list.

2 Select the Comparison field in the same row, and select a comparison operator from the drop-down list. The choices will vary depending on the type of field, but typical choices are Equals, Not Equals, Greater Than, Contains, Begins With, and so forth.

3 Click the Value field in the same row and type a comparison value. If the value is a date, you can also open a drop-down list and specify the current date.

4 Click the And/Or field in the same row and set the drop-down list to And or Or.

5 If you enter a mixture of And and Or conditions, you might be concerned about the order of evaluation. In this case, select rows for the comparisons you want made first, and then click the Group button. This has the effect of putting parentheses around those comparisons. To remove such a grouping, select the rows involved and click the Ungroup button.

Configuring Data Source Sorting

Clicking the Sort button on the Source tab of the Data Source Properties dialog box displays the Sort dialog box shown in Figure 10-20.

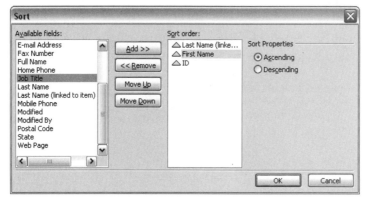

Figure 10-20. Use this dialog box to specify which fields, if any, will determine the order of the records from a data source.

This dialog box specifies which fields control the order of the records the data source will deliver.

- To use a field for sorting, select it in the Available Fields list, and click the Add button.
- To stop using a field for sorting, select it in the Sort Order list, and click the Remove button.
- To move a field higher in the sort order, select it, and click the Move Up button.
- To move a field lower in the sort order, select it, and click the Move Down button.

● To switch a field between ascending and descending sequence, select it in the Sort Order list, and then click the Ascending or Descending option button.

> **Tip** As the next chapter will explain, you can also specify a sort order when you create a Data View Web Part to display information from a data source. Generally, there's no merit to specifying a sort order in both places.

Configuring Database Connection Data Sources

The Database Connections section of the SharePoint Data Source Catalog provides access to data that resides in databases outside of Windows SharePoint Services. Such databases might be part of mission-critical or *ad hoc* systems within your organization. They can also provide a "middle ground" where several SharePoint sites can share data.

Initially, a SharePoint site won't contain any database connections. To use such a connection, you or someone else with sufficient privileges must explicitly create it. Here's the procedure:

1 Open the site in FrontPage, and display the Data Source Catalog task pane.

2 Scroll down to the Database Connections section, and then click the Add To Catalog link.

3 When the Data Source Properties dialog box shown in Figure 10-21 appears, click the Configure Database Connection button. This displays the Configure Database Connection dialog box shown in Figure 10-22.

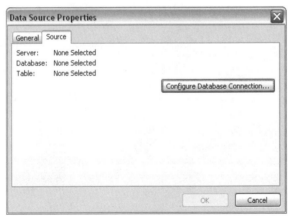

Figure 10-21. Notice the difference between this Source tab and the one on the right in Figure 10-17. This tab creates a new database connection. The Properties button and Query frame won't appear until you create the connection.

Figure 10-22. To configure a connection to a SQL Server database, fill in the Server Name and Authentication areas. To create an OLEDB database connection, click the Edit button, and fill in the Edit Connection String dialog box on the right.

4 To access a SQL Server database, make the following entries:

- **Server Name** Enter the name of the server where the database resides and, if necessary, a backslash and the instance name.

  Typically, you need to specify an instance name when two or more copies of SQL Server, MSDE, or WMSDE are running on the same computer. The syntax in that case is *<server-name>\<instance-name>*. By default, SharePoint Setup installs a WMSDE database with the instance name *SharePoint*.

- **Authentication** Choose one of the options described in Table 10-1.

Table 10-1. Data Source Authentication Options

Option	Description
Don't Attempt To Authenticate	Attempts an anonymous connection, or one using the SharePoint site's application pool account. (This option is only available for XML files, server-side scripts, and XML Web Services.)
Save This Username And Password In The Data Connection	Uses the user name and password in the User Name and Password boxes, no matter which team member accesses the database.

321

Chapter 10

Table 10-1. Data Source Authentication Options

Option	Description
Use Windows Authentication	Uses the current team member's user name and password. However, this only works when the database and Windows SharePoint Services are running on the same machine.
Use Single-Sign-On Authentication (Requires SharePoint Portal Server)	Instructs SharePoint Portal Server to supply the user name and password for accessing the database.

5 To access a non–SQL Server database, take these steps:

5.1 Select the Use Custom Connection String option, and click the Edit button.

5.2 When the Edit Connection String dialog box shown in Figure 10-23 appears, enter the OLEDB connection string required to access the database. This figure shows a typical connection string for a Microsoft Access database. The general format for an Oracle connection string is shown here:

```
Provider=SDAORA;Data Source=<service-name>;
User ID=<username>, Password=<password>
```

5.3 Click OK to close the Edit Connection String dialog box.

Figure 10-23. To use an external database other than SQL Server as a data source, you must enter an OLEDB connection string in this dialog box.

6 Click Next to display the Configure Database Connection dialog box shown in Figure 10-24, and then configure these options:

- **Database** Select the database that contains the data you want. (For Access databases, root will be the only choice.)

- **Use Custom Query** Select this check box and click the Edit button to enter a SQL statement that returns the data you want. This option and the next are mutually exclusive.

- **Table, View, Or Stored Procedure** Select the listed item that contains the data you want.

7 Click Finish to return to the Data Source Properties dialog box shown previously in Figure 10-21. Configure the Fields, Filter, and Sort options if you want.

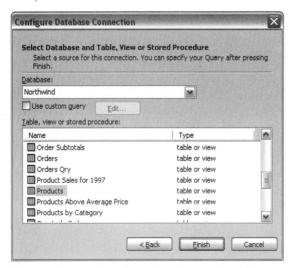

Figure 10-24. Selecting a database and a table or query is the last step in creating a database connection.

> For information about filtering and sorting information in a data source, refer to the section titled "Configuring Data Source Query Settings," earlier in this chapter.

8 Click the General tab of the Data Source Properties dialog box (shown previously in Figure 10-16). Enter at least a name—and possibly a description and keywords—and then click OK to add the connection to the Data Source Catalog.

For Oracle databases, the computer running your SharePoint site must contain both the Microsoft Oracle driver and the client software that Oracle provides (that is, SQL*NET).

For Access databases, the connection string must specify a file location accessible to the Web server. This must be:

- A file location on the physical server, complete with drive letter, full pathname, filename base, and .mdb.

- A UNC file name: that is, one beginning \\\<*servername*>\\<*sharename*>\.

  Locations within a SharePoint site won't work because the Access database—even if you could upload it—would end up as raw bits inside the site's content database, and therefore be totally inaccessible to Access itself.

A further problem is that by default, the Jet OLEDB driver that works with Access databases isn't enabled within the SharePoint data retrieval service. This results in the following dialog box after you type the connection string and click OK and Next:

323

To correct this, a server administrator must:

1 Log into a command window on the server running the virtual Web server.

2 Change to the directory where stsadm.exe resides. By default, this is:

C:\Program Files\Common Files\Microsoared\web server extensions\60\BIN\

3 Run the following command to get a list of drivers currently enabled within the data retrieval service.

```
stsadm -o getproperty -propertyname data-retrieval-services-oledb-providers
```

This will produce three lines of output such as:

```
<Property Exist="Yes"
Value="DB2OLEDB;IBMDADB2;MSDAORA;OraOLEDB.Oracle;SQLOLEDB"
 />
```

4 Enable the Jet OLEDB driver by entering the following command, all on one line, replacing the portion in bold with the value from step 3.

```
stsadm -o setproperty -propertyname data-retrieval-services-oledb-providers
-propertyvalue
DB2OLEDB;IBMDADB2;MSDAORA;OraOLEDB.Oracle;SQLOLEDB;Microsoft.Jet.OLEDB.4.0
```

As shown, the commands in steps 3 and 4 affect the default data retrieval service settings for the entire physical server. To affect only one virtual server, add a –url switch to each command. For example, the command in step 3 would be:

```
stsadm -o getproperty -propertyname data-retrieval-services-oledb-providers
-url http://192.168.180.41
```

where 192.168.180.41 is the virtual server's IP address or IIS host header value.

Once you enable the Jet OLEDB driver, team members can connect to any Access database that resides on the Web server, and for which they have NTFS permissions. The server administrator should therefore put each Access database (or group of Access databases with like permissions) in its own folder, and make sure that the permissions for those folders include no more team members than necessary.

> For more information about configuring the SharePoint data retrieval service, refer to "Configuring Data Retrieval Service Settings" in Chapter 15.

Configuring XML File Data Sources

If your SharePoint site has access to suitably formatted XML files, you can add the files to the Data Source Catalog and display their contents almost as if they were databases. Here's the procedure:

1 Display the Data Source Catalog of the SharePoint site that needs access to the data.

2 Scroll down to the XML Files portion of the catalog, and then click its Add To Catalog link.

3 When the Data Source Properties dialog box shown in Figure 10-25 appears, either hand-type the URL of the XML file you want to access, or click the Browse button to locate it.

Figure 10-25. An XML file data source can reside in the current site or at a file location.

4 If accessing the XML file requires logon credentials beyond those of the SharePoint site, select the Login tab shown in Figure 10-26, and choose one of the options described previously in Table 10-1.

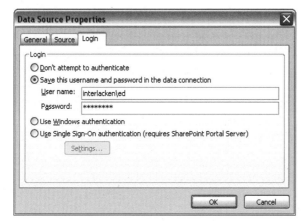

Figure 10-26. Use the Login tab to specify any special credentials required to access a data source.

5 Select the General tab, give the data source a name, and click OK to save it as you did for the preceding data source types.

Chapter 10

325

Troubleshooting

The XML file, server-side script, or XML Web service data source appears empty

When you define a data source that refers to an XML file, a server-side script that delivers XML, or an XML Web service, the data source might fail to operate and might seem empty, even though data exists. This could occur for any of the following reasons:

- The XML source contains (or is delivering) invalid XML. For example, the data might contain some malformed or mismatched tags.
- The XML source doesn't include a schema section, and the data is too inconsistent for the receiving XML document object to infer a schema.
- The XML source contains both a schema section and a data section, but
    - The schema section doesn't conform to the W3C's XML-Data specification.
    - The data in the data section fails to conform with the schema in the schema section.

Here are two ways of creating acceptable XML files. Unfortunately, both require programming skills:

- Use the .NET Framework *XMLWriter* class to save the contents of a .NET Framework *DataTable* object as XML.
- Save the contents of a classic ADO *Recordset* object by using its *Save* method with a *PersistFormat* of *adPersistXML*.

Configuring Server-Side Script Data Sources

The Server-Side Script section of a Data Source Catalog identifies Web-based programs that send XML rather than HTML in response to a Web visitor's request. Such programs might be ASP or ASP.NET "pages," but the results are essentially useless for human interpretation.

To configure a data source of this type, open the Data Source Catalog, scroll down to Server-Side Scripts, and click the Add To Catalog link. Yet another variation of the Data Source Properties dialog box will appear, this time resembling Figure 10-27.

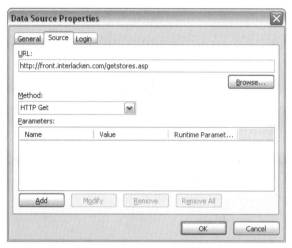

Figure 10-27. When retrieving XML from a server-side script, you might also need to specify an HTTP request method and parameters.

Configure these options:

- **URL** Specify the URL of the server-side script. To do this by pointing and clicking, click the Browse button.

- **Method** Specify the type of request the server-side script expects to receive. The GET method appends any parameter names and values to the URL, whereas the POST method sends them in the body of the request.

- **Parameters** Use the Add, Modify, and Remove buttons to specify any parameters that the server-side script needs to operate. These might be key values, for example.

As before, use the Login tab to specify access credentials and the General tab to give the data source a name and save it.

Configuring XML Web Service Data Sources

An XML Web Service is a specialized program on a Web server that both receives requests and transmits responses in XML format. To configure such a service, click the Add To Catalog link in the XML Web Services section of the Data Source Catalog to display the version of the Data Source Properties dialog box shown in Figure 10-28.

To use this dialog box, you must know the URL that requests the Web Service Description Language (WDSL) description of the XML Web service. This is a description, in XML format, of the Web service's capabilities. For Web services running on a Microsoft server, it's usually the address of the Web service plus *?WDSL*. For services running on other operating systems, it might be a URL with a .wsdl file extension. Armed with this information, continue as follows:

Figure 10-28. This figure is a composite. The portion above the Connection Info area appears before you click Connect Now, and the portion below appears after.

1 Enter the WSDL URL in the Service Description Location box, and then click Connect Now.

The URL shown in Figure 10-28 is available on any SharePoint server: just change the host name.

2 Within a moment or two, the title on the Connect Now button should change to Disconnect, and various controls in the Connection Info area will change from dimmed to enabled. Configure these settings:

- ■ **Port**   Select the application protocol you want to use for accessing the Web service. The choices listed are those that the Web service's WSDL claimed will work. If there's a choice that involves SOAP (such as the WebsSoap choice in this figure), that should be your preference.

- ■ **Operation**   Select what you want the Web service to do. Again, the choices listed are those that the Web service's WSDL identified.

- ■ **Parameters**   The dialog box will automatically display the name of any parameter the Web service requires or accepts for the operation you specified. Again, this information comes from the Web service's WSDL. To configure the permanent or default value of any parameter, select it and click the Modify button near the bottom of the dialog box.

3 As before, use the Login tab to specify access credentials, and use the General tab to give the data source a name and save it.

Chapter 10

If a Web Service has required parameters, FrontPage will flag them with an asterisk. You must follow the procedure below for each such parameter. In addition, you'll need to follow the same procedure for any optional parameters you want to use.

1   On the Source tab of the Data Source Properties dialog box, select the parameter you want to configure in the Parameters list box.

2   Click the Modify button.

3   When the Parameter dialog box shown in Figure 10-29 appears, configure these settings:

   ■ **Default Value**   Enter the fixed or default value you want this parameter to have. You can either hand-type a value or select a system-provided value from the drop-down list.

   ■ **The Value Of This Parameter Can Be Set At Runtime**   Select this check box if Web Parts using this data source will specify a parameter value every time they make a request. Clear it if the parameter value swill be constant.

4   Click OK to save your input.

If you specify that a Web service parameter can be set at runtime, you'll probably need to configure a Web Part Connection to supply that value. For more information about Web Part Connections, refer to the section titled "Connecting Web Parts" in Chapter 12.

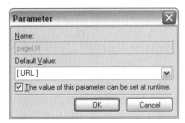

Figure 10-29.   Use this dialog box to configure parameters that Windows SharePoint Services will send to a Web service.

The URL shown in Figure 10-28 warrants a bit of additional explanation. As you may have noticed, it specifies the exact SharePoint server that most of the SharePoint examples in this book use.

In fact, every installation of Windows SharePoint Services provides Web services that can interact with almost any aspect of a SharePoint server, site, list, library, survey, or Web page. To appreciate the power of these Web services, look no further than FrontPage itself. When you create, modify, or delete a list or library in FrontPage, FrontPage does the work by means of SharePoint Web services.

The security on these Web services is the same as that for performing the equivalent action using the browser interface. As a result, not only FrontPage, but Web Part Pages, Web Parts you write yourself, and even non-SharePoint programs can use them.

329

For more information about Windows SharePoint Services Web Services, browse *http://msdn.microsoft.com/library/en-us/spptsdk/html/soapnsMicrosoftSharePointSoapServer.asp*

For an XML Web service to work as a SharePoint data source, it must return data in the same specific XML format that SharePoint sites require for XML file and server-side script data sources. If you configure an XML Web service data source without error and yet receive no data, this is probably the reason.

Accessing Data Source Details

To modify and test a data source, locate and right-click its entry in the Data Source Catalog task pane. Then, choose one of these commands from the shortcut menu:

- **Insert Data View**   Adds a Data View Web Part to the current Web page—a Web Part that displays information from the current data source. For more information about using Data View Web Parts, refer to the next chapter.

- **Show Data**   Displays a Data View Details task pane that summarizes the properties of the data source and displays the contents of one record. Figure 10-30 provides an example. Notice the row that reads roughly *Row [3/77] <>*. In that notation, *[3/77]* means that the current row is number 3 of 77. Clicking the arrows moves the display forward or backward one record.

Figure 10-30.   The Data View Details task pane summarizes the settings for one view of a data source. It can also query and display the underlying data one record at a time.

> **Tip** The Show Data command provides a quick and easy way to test any data source. Just right-click the data source, choose Show Data from the shortcut menu, and see whether any data results. Then verify that the data is what you expect.

- **Copy And Modify**   Create a new, modified version of the data source.
- **Move To**   Moves the data source definition to another SharePoint site. However, the receiving site must already be listed in your data source catalog. If it isn't, display the Data Source Catalog task pane, click the Manage Catalog link and add it.
- **Save As**   Saves a copy of the data source definition as an XML file. However, this isn't possible for SharePoint lists and libraries.
- **Mail Recipient**   Starts Microsoft Outlook and creates an e-mail message that includes the data source definition as an attachment. To complete the operation, enter the recipient's e-mail address, compose a message body, and click Send. Again, this isn't possible for SharePoint lists and libraries.
- **Remove**   Deletes the data source definition but not any lists, libraries, databases, XML files, server-side scripts, or XML Web services it refers to.
- **Properties**   Displays the Data Source Properties dialog box so that you can review and modify the data source definition.

In Summary...

This chapter explained how to configure the Data Source Catalog for a Windows SharePoint Services site. The Data Source Catalog is a list of data locations that the site can use to fulfill its purpose. These locations can be SharePoint lists, SharePoint libraries, external databases, XML files, server-side scripts, and Web services.

The next chapter will explain how to create List View Web Parts and Data View Web Parts that access the Data Source Catalog, retrieve the data, and display it with great flexibility.

Chapter 10

331

Working with List Views and Data Views

Creating lists, libraries, and data sources is satisfying and necessary work, but the payback usually comes on output. Fortunately, Windows SharePoint Services provides not one, but two great ways of displaying data: List View Web Parts and Data View Web Parts.

Superficially, these Web Parts work and behave so much alike that many new SharePoint designers get them confused. Nevertheless, and despite some overlapping capabilities, these two Web Parts are fundamentally different. Each has capabilities the other lacks.

To highlight the similarities and differences between these two Web Parts, this chapter will present them in parallel. That way, you only have to learn the common features once, and you'll clearly understand the differences.

Introducing List Views and Data Views

The next two sections will introduce List View Web Parts and Data View Web Parts, respectively.

> **Note** Generally, the term List View is synonymous with List View Web Part. Similarly, the term Data View is synonymous with Data View Web Part.

Introducing List View Web Parts

A List View Web Part displays the contents of a SharePoint list or library. As such, it's the main component of a List View Page. This is the type of page that appears when you select a list or library from the Documents And Lists page in a SharePoint Team Site.

Windows SharePoint Services creates a List View Web Part whenever you create a list or library. To display the list or library in another page, you add its List View Web Parts to that page, using either the Add Web Parts Task Pane in the browser interface or the Web Parts task pane in FrontPage. Significantly, List View Web Parts make *no* use of the Data Source Catalog.

333

Figure 11-1 shows a typical List View page. The List View Web Part begins at the top left corner of the of the toolbar that displays the New Item and Filter buttons, and occupies the rest of the Web page down and to the right.

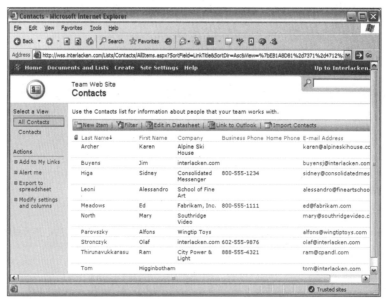

Figure 11-1. The large display in the middle of this Web page comes from a List View Web Part. Notice the specialized toolbar buttons.

Introducing Data View Web Parts

Data View Web Parts can *only* display data from the Data Source Catalog. This, however, is a strength. It means they can display not only lists and libraries, but also data from external databases, XML files, server-side scripts, and Web services.

Windows SharePoint Services never creates Data View Web Parts automatically, nor can the browser interface create them. If you want a Data View Web Part, you have to create it in FrontPage. Fortunately, doing so is child's play; you drag the Data Source icon and drop it on a Web page.

No matter the type of Data Source, a Data View Web Part always gets its data from a part of Windows SharePoint Services called the Data Retrieval Service. If the data isn't already in XML format, the Data Retrieval Service converts it. Then, the Data View Web Part uses a technology called XSLT (eXtensible Style Sheet Transformation) to transform the XML data into HTML for display in FrontPage or the browser. By taking this approach, FrontPage lays claim to being the world's first WYSIWYG XSLT editor.

Figure 11-2 shows a Data View Web Part displaying the same contacts list as the List View Web Part shown in Figure 11-1. In this case, the Data View Web Part begins at the top left corner of the title bar titled Contacts and extends to the bottom right corner of the page.

Compared to a List View, however, you have many more options for formatting the data, and you aren't limited to displaying lists and libraries. There are no toolbar buttons for the functions New Item, Edit In Datasheet, Link To Outlook, or Import Contacts, but if the current data source is a SharePoint list or library, you can hyperlink any displayed data item to these functions.

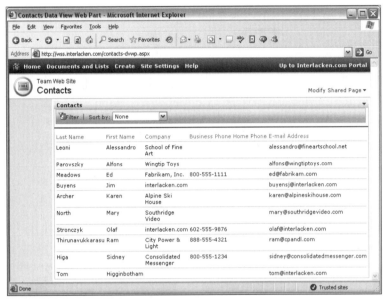

Figure 11-2. The display in the middle of this Web page comes from a Data View Web Part. The display is more generic but also more flexible than that of a List View Web Part.

Creating List View Pages

FrontPage provides two ways of creating pages that use List View Web Parts. The first is to create a new List View Web page. Here's the procedure.

1   In the FrontPage Folder list or Folders view, right-click the list or library you want to display.

2   Choose New, and then Document Library View Page or List View Page (whichever appears.)

3   When the New View Page dialog box shown below appears, type the name you want the new page to have, and then click OK.

The name you assign in the New View Page dialog box is the name that will appear in the Select A View section of other pages for the same list, in the Views section of the list's Customize page, and so forth. It will also become the Web Part Page's filename base. If you decide later you chose the wrong name, try one of these procedures:

To change the Web Part Page's filename base:

1 Select it in the FrontPage folder list or folders view.
2 Press F2.
3 Type the new name.

To change the page's display name:

1 Switch to code view and look for a DisplayName= attribute inside a <ListViewXml> tag.
2 Change the attribute value.
3 Save the page.
4 Return to Design view and press F5 to refresh the display.

To change either the filename or the display name using a browser:

1 Display the list's Customize page.
2 Click the old display name under Views.
3 Update the View Name field, the Web Address Of This View field, or both.

> **Tip**   Before using a browser to change any lists, libraries, or pages in a site, always close any pages from that site you have open in FrontPage.

The second method involves adding a List View Web Part to a new or existing page. Here are the details:

1 Open any new or existing page in FrontPage Design view. If you want a new page to have the default SharePoint look, choose one of the templates on the Web Part Pages tab of the Page Templates dialog box.
2 Display the Web Parts task pane. For example, choose Insert Web Part from the Data menu.
3 Within the Web Parts task, under Web Part List, locate the list or library you want to display.
4 Drag the list or library Web Part from the Web Parts task pane, and drop it on the open Web page.

Figure 11-3 shows the FrontPage window after a designer created a List View Web Part that displays the site's Contacts list.

Chapter 11

Figure 11-3. List View Web Parts display data even in Design view. This makes it easy to visualize what a team member would see.

Regardless of how you created the List View (and even if you used a browser) you can change its style, included fields, sort order, and other properties in FrontPage. A section titled "Modifying List Views And Data Views," later in this chapter, will explain this.

Creating Data View Pages

Here's the procedure for adding a Data View Web Part to a page in the simplest possible way:

1 Open your SharePoint site.

2 Open a new or existing Web page.

   To take maximum advantage of the styles built into a Data View Web Part, this page should use one of the templates from the Web Part Pages tab of the Page Templates dialog box. The Full Page, Vertical template is usually a good choice.

3 If no task pane is displayed, choose Insert Data View from the Data menu.

   If some other task pane is on display, select Data Source Catalog from the drop-down menu in the task pane's title bar.

4 Either:

   4.1 Drag the data source you want from the Data Source Catalog task pane.

   4.2 Drop it wherever you want in the open Web page.

   or

337

4.1 Click the spot where you want the displayed data to appear.

4.2 Right-click the data source you want to display, and then choose Insert View from the shortcut menu.

Within a few seconds, Design view should display your new Web Part, complete with a representative amount of data. The task pane also changes to show the Data View Details task pane for the data source you selected. Figure 11-4 shows the FrontPage window after a designer created a Data View Web Part that displays the site's Contacts list.

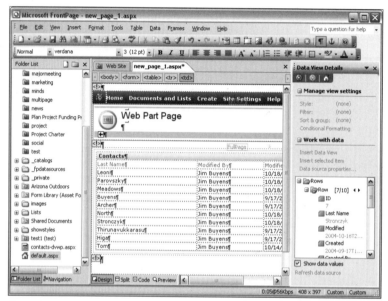

Figure 11-4. This is how a new Data View Web Part looks in FrontPage. The designer can now add, remove, rearrange, or format columns, change the overall display style, and configure filtering, sorting, and grouping options.

You can also create Data View Web Parts directly from the Data View Details task pane. This method is interesting because is provides more control over the initial results. Proceed as follows.

1 In the Data Source Catalog task pane, right-click the data source you want to use, and then choose Show Data from the shortcut menu.

2 When the Data View Details task pane appears, in the Data View list box, select the columns you want to appear in the Web page:

- To select all the columns, click either the Rows or the Row line.

- To select specific columns, click the first one, and then Ctrl+click each additional column in the order you want them to appear.

3 In the open Web page, set the insertion point where you want the Data View Web Part to appear.

4 In the Data View Details task pane, click the Insert Data View link just under the Work With Data heading.

If you want to create a Web Part that looks like a List View but uses features available only to Data Views, a third way of creating Data Views may suit your needs. Here's the procedure.

1 Create the List View in the usual way, and refine it as much as you like.

2 In FrontPage Design view, right-click the List View, and choose Convert To XSLT Data View.

Once this is complete, the Web Part will be a full-fledged Data View Web Part in every way. None of the commands unique to List View Web Parts will be available, but all the commands available for Data View Web Parts will be at your disposal. Keep in mind, however, that your options for going back are limited. To convert what was once a List View back to a List View:

1 In FrontPage, open the page that contains the List View Web Part.

2 Right-click the List View Web Part and choose Revert To SharePoint List View from the shortcut menu.

The drawback to this operation is that you lose all custom layout, formatting, and Web Part Connections in effect for the Web Part. In short, you end up with a generic List View Web Part.

To refresh the data in a Data View Web Part that appears in Design view, select it, and then choose Refresh from the Data menu.

Modifying List Views and Data Views

The Data View Details task pane serves as the property sheet for both Data Views and List Views. For example:

- If you right-click a *Data View* Web Part and choose *Data View* Properties, you get the *Data View* Details task pane. No surprise there.

- If you right-click a *List View* Web Part and choose *List View* Properties, you get (surprise!) the Data View Details task pane!

The Data View Details task pane displays a somewhat different collection of controls depending on what kind of Web Part it's configuring. Figure 11-5 shows both versions side by side for comparison.

Chapter 11

339

Figure 11-5. For a List View Web Part, the Data View Details task pane appears as shown at the left. The view at the right is for Data View Web Parts.

- **Fields** This link is only present for List View Web Parts. It displays a Displayed Fields dialog box that looks and acts very much like the Included Fields dialog box that the section titled "Configuring Data Source Query Settings" in Chapter 10 described for data sources.

- **Style, Filter, and Sort & Group** These links appear for both List Views and Data Views.

  - **Style** Displays a dialog box that controls the overall visual style of the Web Part, the presence or absence of toolbars, headers, and footers, and the maximum number of records to display at once.

  - **Filter** Displays a Filter Criteria dialog box very similar to the one Chapter 10 described for data sources in the section titled "Configuring Data Source Filtering."

  - **Sort & Group** Displays a Sort And Group dialog box somewhat similar to the Sort dialog box Chapter 10 described for data sources in the section titled "Configuring Data Source Sorting."

- **Conditional Formatting** This link appears only for Data View Web Parts, and it's only enabled if one or more content fields are selected. If available, clicking it displays a conditional formatting task pane where you can configure conditions such as negative numbers displaying as red, zero values being blank, values outside a certain range being displayed as bold, or pictures (such as an Order More icon) appearing or nor appearing based on data values (like UnitsInStock < 10).

- **Work With Data** Everything in this part of the task pane is dimmed or missing unless a Data View Web Part is selected in Design view. If active, it provides

  - Options to add subviews or fields to the Data View Web Part.

  - A link to view or modify the data source that provides data to the Web Part.

340

- A display of the data source's XML structure.
- Controls that display or hide data values in the structure view, and that refresh the display.

Another view of the Data View Details task pane appeared in the previous chapter. For details on that view, refer to the section titled "Accessing Data Source Details," in Chapter 10.

The next five sections explain how to perform all these options but one, for both List Views and Data Views. The one exception is Conditional Formatting, which the next chapter will address.

Modifying List View Fields

To modify the fields that appear in a List View Web Part, proceed as follows.

1 In FrontPage, open the page that contains the List View Web Part.

2 Right-click the List View Web Part and choose List View Properties from the shortcut menu.

3 When the Data View Details task pane appears, click the Fields link that appears under Manage View Settings.

4 When the Displayed Fields dialog box shown in Figure 11-6 appears, use the following controls to make changes.

- **Add** To make the List View Web Part display one or more additional fields, select those fields in the Available Fields list, and then click the Add button.

- **Remove** To make the Web Part stop displaying one or more fields, select those fields in the Displayed Fields list, and then click the Remove button.

- **Move Up** To make a field appear sooner in the display, select it in the Displayed Fields list, and then click Move Up.

- **Moved Down** To make a field appear later in the display, select it in the Displayed Fields list, and then click Move Down.

Note that this dialog box can't add, rearrange, or delete fields in the SharePoint list itself, nor can it change the information type of any field. To make those kinds of changes, you have to work directly with the list.

For more information about modifying lists using a browser, refer to the section titled "Modifying Lists" in Chapter 6. For more information about using FrontPage to modify lists, refer to the section titled, "Modifying SharePoint Lists and Libraries," in Chapter 10.

Chapter 11

341

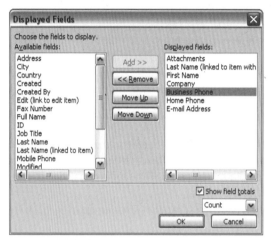

Figure 11-6. This dialog box specifies which fields a List View Web Part will display.

Modifying Data View Fields

To add, remove, or rearrange the fields that a Data View Web Part displays, you work directly with the Design view display and the Data View Details task pane. Here are some examples:

- To delete a column, select all of its cells, and then choose Delete Columns from the Table menu.

- To relocate a column, select all of its cells, and then drag it to the location you want.

Notice that these are the same commands you would use to rearrange the columns in an ordinary HTML table.

The procedure for adding a new column is a little more complicated. Proceed as follows:

1 Open the page that contains the Data View Web Part.

2 Display the Data View Details task pane.

For example, right-click the Data View Web Part, and then choose Data View Properties from the shortcut menu.

3 Create a blank column where you want the new column values to appear. Any command that would add a column to a conventional HTML table will do.

For example, right-click the column to the right of where you want the new column to be, and then choose Insert Columns from the shortcut menu.

4 Set the insertion point inside any repeating cell in the new column. Don't set the insertion point inside the header row.

5 To display data from any column as text, select the column name in the Data View Details task pane, and then click the Insert Selected Item link in that task pane.

6 To specify a format for the column data, right-click the column name in the Data View Details task pane, and then choose the command you want from the shortcut menu.

342

An Incredibly Brief Introduction to XSLT

Extensible Stylesheet Language Transformation (XSLT) is a language that transforms one XML document into another. The rules for this transformation reside in a so-called *template* file, which is also in XML format.

A template rule has two parts: a pattern that XSLT matches against the input fields, and a template that XSLT uses to construct part of the output file.

In a Data View Web Part, the pattern matches each record in the data source (subject, of course, to any filtration the pattern may specify). When the Web Part uses the Basic Table style, which is the default, the template creates an HTML table consisting of one header row plus one row for each record in the data source.

Although FrontPage Design view displays the output of the XSLT transformation, manipulating that display updates the XSLT transformation *rules*. When you add a column to the displayed table, for example, FrontPage actually adds the column to the XSLT template, and then regenerates and displays the output. Viola! The new column appears.

When you update any repeating row of a Data View table display (that is, any row but the header) you update the template that creates all such rows, and the change then propagates to all such rows. To see this in action, try selecting one cell value and making it bold.. The whole column (except for the cell in the header row) will turn bold.

When you drag a data value from cell to cell (or from the Data Source Details task pane to a cell) you're actually moving an XSL tag that looks like this:

```
<xsl:value-of select="@JobTitle"/>
```

This tag retrieves the value of the *JobTitle* field from the current input record and inserts it into the output file. A sequence such as this:

```
<xsl:value-of select="@LastName"/>, <xsl:value-of select="@FirstName"/>
```

displays names in the format Lee, Andrea.

FrontPage stores the XSLT rules for each Data View Web Part inside the tags that delimit the Web Part itself. This code is complex but clearly visible. With a certain amount of care and knowledge, you can change it by hand to achieve special effects.

For more information on XSLT, browse *http://www.w3.org/TR/xslt*.

Chapter 11

343

When you select a Data View Web Part in Design view and then right-click a column name in the Data View Details task pane, the commands on the shortcut menu vary depending on the field's information type. Here are the possibilities.

- **Insert As Text**   Formats the data as ordinary text.
- **Insert As Rich Text**   Formats the data as rich text (that is, with features such as boldface, italics, and fonts intact).
- **Number**   Formats the data as numeric.
- **Currency**   Formats the data as money.
- **Date & Time**   Formats the data as a date and a time.
- **Insert As Boolean**   Formats the data as True or False.
- **Insert As Hyperlink**   Formats the data as a hyperlink. This normally requires that the data itself be a URL. The template for a hyperlink field looks like this:

```
<a><xsl:attribute name="href">
<xsl:value-of select="@WebAddr"/></xsl:attribute>
<xsl:value-of select="@WebAddr"/></a>
```

If the *WebAddr* field contains *http://www.microsoft.com*, the template creates HTML that looks like this:

```
<a href="http://www.microsoft.com">http://www.microsoft.com</a>
```

If you want the hyperlink location and the hyperlink location to come from different fields, you'll need to either:

- First insert the field that contains the hyperlink text you want. Then select the displayed value, choose Hyperlink from the Insert menu, and click the Parameters button. Finally, click the Insert Field Value button and use the drop-down list to select the field that contains the target URL.

- Manually find and modify the template code. To find the appropriate templates tags, for example, you might search for @ followed by the field name. You could then change the field names in one of the <xsl:value-of> tags.

- **Insert As Picture**   Displays the data as a picture. However, this only works if the data contain the URL of a picture. The resulting HTML looks like:

```
<img border="0" src="{@PicLoc}"/>
```

where the value of the *PicLoc* field will replace {@PicLoc}.

The following commands are available only if the data source is a SharePoint list or library.

- **Insert As Hyperlink To New Form**   Wraps the data value in a hyperlink that displays the New Item form for the list or library.
- **Insert As Hyperlink To Edit Form**   Wraps the data value in a hyperlink that displays the Edit Item form for the current list or library item.
- **Insert As Hyperlink To Display Form**   Wraps the data value in a hyperlink that displays the view page for the current list or library item.

The following commands are always available.

- **Insert As Indexed Value**   Inserts the field value from the row number that the Data View Details task pane currently has on display.

  For example, if the task pane displays *Row [20/77] <>*, this command would specify that the field value from row 20 would appear in every row of the Data View Web Part Display.

- **Insert As Full XPath**   This works the same as Insert As Indexed Value, except that it refers to the data using a full path relative to the root of the data source. This resolves (or creates) certain problems depending on the structure of your XML file and that of your Data View Web Part. Basically, if Insert As Indexed Value doesn't produce the results you want, try Insert As Full XPath.

- **Copy Item XPath**   Copies the XML path of the data source item to the clipboard. Typically, this is a string like

  ```
  /dsQueryResponse/Rows/Row/@Modified
  ```

  This might be useful if you need to paste a field reference into XSLT code you're modifying by hand.

If you find that you've chosen the wrong formatting option, or if you want more detailed control over formatting, try this procedure:

1   Right-click one or more of the repeating values you want to reformat.

2   Choose Format Item As from the resulting menu.

3   Choose the format you want from the resulting submenu.

If you use this procedure and choose Currency, Number, or Date & Time, one of the dialog boxes shown in Figure 11-7 appears. Use the controls on this dialog box to format the data the way you want.

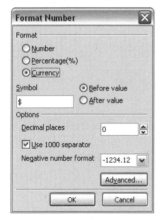
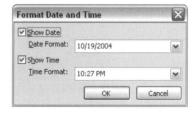

Figure 11-7.   The dialog box at the left configures the appearance of Number and Currency fields. The one at the right configures the appearance of Date & Time fields.

The choices in the Format Number and Format Date And Time dialog boxes vary depending on the page language. In a German page, for example, the default date format would follow European conventions and the currency symbol would default to €.

You can apply FrontPage formatting to Data View Web Parts just as you do to ordinary HTML content. For example, you can select a column value and then use a button on the Formatting toolbar to apply the properties you want: bold, italic, left-justified, right-justified, centered, and so forth. You can also apply fonts and CSS styles, table and cell borders, and other common formats.

The next chapter will explain how to apply conditional formatting, which changes the Web Part display based on data values.

Modifying List View and Data View Styles

To modify the general appearance of a List View or Data View Web Part, first select it, and then take one of these actions:

- Click the Styles link in the Data View Details task pane.
- Choose Style from the Data menu.

This displays the View Styles dialog box shown in Figure 11-8. Note that the dialog box is slightly different for List Views and Data Views.

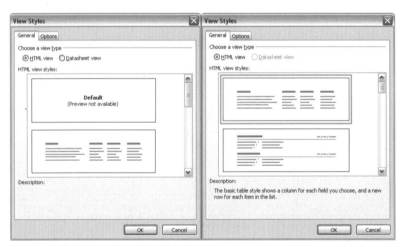

Figure 11-8. For a List View Web Part, clicking the style link on the Data View details task pane displays the options shown at the left. For Data View Web Parts, the same link displays the options shown at the right.

The General tab of the View Styles dialog box controls the visual aspect of the data display. To use this tab, select a Choose A View Type option as follows.

- **HTML View**   Select this option if you want to display the data as HTML. Then, to continue, choose a style from the HTML View Styles list box. Note that this list box offers different choices for List Views and Data Views. Clicking any preview displays a verbal description near the bottom of the dialog box.

- **Datasheet View**   This option is available only for List Views. If you select it, the data will appear in an Excel-like table. However, this view requires that team members have Office Professional Edition 2003 installed on their computers. Office supplies an ActiveX control that runs in the team member's browser and actually creates the display.

The Options tab also appears somewhat differently for List Views and Data Views. Figure 11-9 makes this apparent,

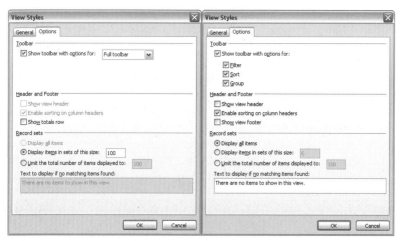

Figure 11-9.   The tab at the left configures the toolbar, header, footer, and paging technique for List Views. The one at the right is for Data Views.

Here are the instructions for setting the options on the Options tab.

- **Show Toolbar With Options For**   Select this check box to display a toolbar between the Web Part's title bar and its column headings. For List View Web Parts, a drop-down box provides these choices:
  - **Full Toolbar**   Displays a full set of toolbar buttons, including New Item, Filter, Edit in Datasheet, and so forth.
  - **Summary Toolbar**   Displays an abbreviated list of toolbar buttons, an Insert Item link that appears at the bottom of the Web Part, or, in the case of many lists, no toolbar at all.

347

For Data View Web Parts, check boxes provide these options.

- **Filter**   Displays a toolbar button that team members can use to restrict the records on display.

- **Sort**   Displays a drop-down list of column names. When the team member selects a column name, the Web Part sorts the data on that column.

- **Group**   Displays another drop-down list of column names. When the team member selects a column name, the Web Part sorts and groups the data on that column. If the team member chooses both a group field and a sort field, the Web Part sorts first on the group field, and then on the sort field.

● **Header And Footer**   Use these controls to modify the arrangement of header and footer lines:

- **Show View Header**   This check box is always dimmed for List Views. For Data Views, selecting it provides an extra line above the column headings. This line can contain whatever text you want—just enter it in Design view.

- **Enable Sorting On Column Headers**   For List Views, this check box is always dimmed but always in effect. For Data Views, selecting it changes the column heading into hyperlinks that sort the display on the given column.

- **Show Totals**   This option appears only for List Views. Selecting it displays a row of totals after the last row of data.

- **Show View Footer**   This option appears only for Data Views. Selecting it displays an extra line after the last row of data. Again, this line can contain whatever text you want. To insert record counts or totals, drag a field from the data view details task pane, drop it in the footer area, click the Paste Options drop-down arrow, and select the function you want: Sum, Count, Average, Max, Min, or Filter.

● **Record Sets**   Use these settings to control the number of records available for display:

- **Display All Items**   Select this check box to display all available records at once.

- **Display All Items Together And Limit The Number To**   Select this check box to display a given number of records in one continuous list. Use the accompanying text box to specify the maximum number of records. A team member will have no option for displaying additional records.

- **Display Items In Sets Of This Size**   Select this check box to display a fixed number of records at a time. A Data View Web Part provides Next and Previous links to scroll through all the records, but a List View Web Part provides only a Next link.

- **Text To Display If No Matching Items Found**   Enter a message that informs the team member if no records are available. This is only available for Data View Web Parts.

Filtering List Views and Data Views

To restrict the display to records having certain data values, select the List View or Data View Web Part, and then take one of these actions:

- Click the Filter link in the Data View Details task pane.
- Choose Filter from the Data menu.

This displays the Filter Criteria dialog box shown in Figure 11-10.

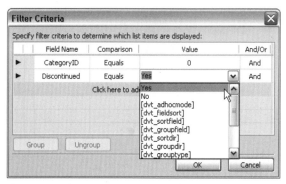

Figure 11-10. To configure criteria, specify a field name, comparison, and value for each comparison. The value can be a constant or any field name from the drop-down list.

This dialog box displays any number of filter clauses (that is, any number of comparisons). Here's the procedure for adding a filter clause:

1. Click the Click Here To Add A New Clause line. This will appear in the first line of the grid that doesn't already contain a clause.

2. FrontPage will add a line to the grid and display a drop-down list in the Field Name column. Select a field name from the drop-down list.

3. Selecting a field name will set the Comparison column to Equals. If this isn't acceptable, click the cell in the Comparison column, and choose a different condition from the resulting drop-down list. The possibilities include Equals, Not Equals, Is Null, Not Null, Less Than, Greater Than, and so forth.

4. Click the cell in the Value column, and then hand-type a value or choose one from the drop-down list.

5. Choose a grouping condition from the And/Or column.

The effect of multiple clauses is fairly obvious if you join them all with And conditions or join them all with Or conditions. The effect of mixing And and Or conditions is much less obvious.

Chapter 11

349

For Data View Web Parts, you can avoid any confusion by selecting two or more criteria you want SharePoint to evaluate first, and then click the Group button. In Figure 11-11, for example, the designer entered all three conditions, then selected the last two (by Shift+click-ing their arrows), and then clicked the Group button. This makes it fairly obvious that SharePoint should display only records with a *UnitPrice* value greater than 10, and a *CategoryId* value of 0 or 1.

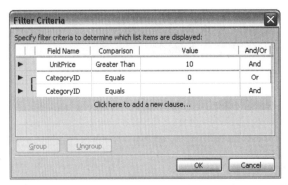

Figure 11-11. To group a series of comparisons, as if surrounding them in parentheses, select all of the comparisons, and then click Group. This view shows the result of grouping two comparisons.

Sorting and Grouping List Views and Data Views

Figure 11-12 shows how a Data View Web Part appears to the team member when common grouping options are in effect.

- Because this page groups by *SupplierID*, it sorts by *SupplierID* as well.
- A gray bar called the *group header* denotes the start of each group.
- Another gray bar called the *group footer* denotes the end of each group.
- The Team member can expand or collapse the group (that is, display or suppress the individual records) by clicking a plus or minus sign in the group header.
- Within each group, the records appear in *ProductName* order.

Grouping for List View Web Parts creates essentially the same effect.

To configure options such as these, select the List View or Data View Web Part, and then take either of these actions:

- Click the Sort & Group link in the Data View Details task pane.
- Choose Sort And Group from the Data menu.

Chapter 11

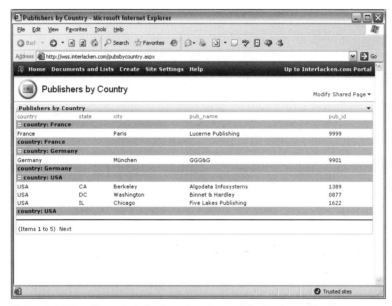

Figure 11-12. Grouping displays header and footer bars like these around all records with equal values in designated fields.

This displays the Sort And Group dialog box shown in Figure 11-13.

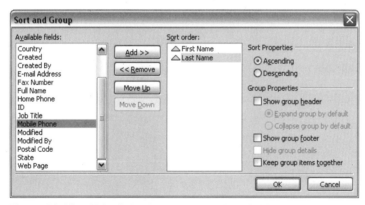

Figure 11-13. This dialog box controls which fields participate in sorting and grouping.

351

Here's how to use the controls in this dialog box:

- **Available Fields**   This list itemizes all fields not currently involved in sorting or grouping. To involve a field in sorting or grouping, either double-click it or select it and click the Add button.
- **Sort Order**   This list itemizes all fields currently involved in sorting or grouping:
  - To remove a field, select it, and click the Remove button.
  - To increase the significance of a field, select it, and click the Move Up button. This moves the field one position higher in the list.
  - To decrease the significance of a field, select it, and click the Move Down button.
- **Sort Properties**   Use these options to change the direction of sorting:
  - **Ascending**   To sort on a field in increasing order, select the field in the Sort Order list, and then select this option.
  - **Descending**   To sort on a field in decreasing order, select the field in the Sort Order list, and then select this option.

> **Tip**   Double-clicking any field in the Sort Order list toggles its Sort property between Ascending and Descending.

The settings in the Group Properties section apply individually to each field in the Sort Order list. To view or modify the settings for a specific field, first select that field. Then, apply these settings:

- **Show Group Header**   Select this check box to display a gray bar at the beginning of each group:
  - **Expand Group By Default**   Select this option if you want each record in a group to be visible when the display first appears.
  - **Collapse Group By Default**   Select this option if you want each record in a group to be hidden when the display first appears.

The next three options are only available for Data View Web Parts. If you're working with a List View Web Part, they won't appear.

- **Show Group Footer**   Select this check box to display a gray bar at the end of each group.
- **Hide Group Details**   Select this check box to display group headers only, with no possibility of viewing the individual records in each group.
- **Keep Group Items Together**   Select this check box to display all records in the same group on the same Web page. In Figure 11-12, for example, five records appear on the page because the View Styles dialog box says to display records in sets of five.

352

In fact, however, there are three more records in the USA group. To view these records, the team member would have to click the Next link at the bottom of the Web Part.

If the designer had clicked Keep Group Items Together, the page in the figure would have displayed all six records for USA, and therefore eight items in total. This would occur despite the View Styles dialog box specifying five records as the maximum.

In Summary...

This chapter explained how to use List View Web Parts and Data View Web Parts. At least one of these Web Parts can satisfy almost any data reporting requirement you may have, even if it involves data outside Windows SharePoint Services.

The next chapter will address two more facets of these Web Parts: Conditional Formatting and Web Part Connections.

Chapter 11

353

Using Advanced Web Part Features

Previous chapters described a variety of techniques for using List View and Data View Web Parts to retrieve and display data from a variety of data source types. Those techniques will satisfy a high percentage of everyday requirements, but they don't exhaust the limits of what Microsoft FrontPage and Windows SharePoint Services can do.

This chapter describes three advanced features that extend the capabilities of your SharePoint site. These are:

- **Web Part Connections**   A facility whereby events (such as mouse clicks) in one Web Part can modify the display in another Web Part. For example, you could make clicking an order number in one Web Part display items for that order in another Web Part.

- **Conditional Formatting**   A facility that can format data differently depending on values in the same row. For example, you could make negative account balances appear in red.

- **Subviews**   A facility that can display nested repeating regions within an XML file. This is useful if, for example, your XML file has repeating nodes (records) for each class at a school, and each class node has repeating nodes for each enrolled student.

Because these aren't entry-level features, the examples in this chapter presume that you're fully capable of creating Web Part Pages, Web Parts, Lists, Libraries, List Views, data sources, and Data Views without detailed instructions. When it comes to those operations, the procedures will describe only generally how to proceed. The chapter will, however, present detailed instructions for the three advanced features listed above.

Connecting Web Parts

Normally, developers construct Web Parts as freestanding units of content. This means that Web Parts have no dependencies and place no requirements on the page that contains them (other than, of course, the ability to display Web Parts). Windows SharePoint Services does, however, provide a connections facility through which Web Parts can interact.

355

Note The ability for two Web Parts to connect and interact obviously requires the cooperation and compatibility of both. There's no guarantee that any two Web Parts can interact at all, let alone in the way you want. However, the possibility of connecting Web Parts is still worth investigating, and FrontPage provides a wizard that makes this easy.

To illustrate how this works, suppose that you want to create an application that finds and displays orders in the ubiquitous Northwind database that comes with every copy of Microsoft SQL Server. This will involve three Web pages:

The first page displays a list of countries where customers reside and a list of customers in any country a team member selects. This page appears in Figure 12-1.

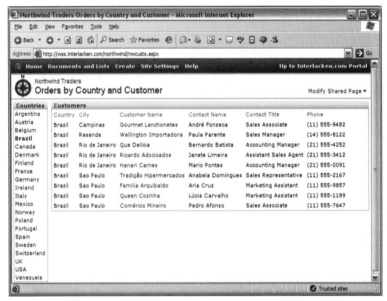

Figure 12-1. Clicking a country in the Data View at left sends that country name through a Web Part connection to the Customers Data View at right. The Customers Data View then filters on that country name.

This page contains two Web Parts:

- The Country Web Part displays a custom query that returns one record for each country that occurs in the Northwind Customers table. When a team member clicks one of these countries, a Web Part connection passes that Country name to the Customers Web Part on the same page.

- That Customers Web Part displays records from the Northwind Customers table, filtered by country. It has a Web Part connection that passes a Customer ID to the Customer Web Part on the second page.

Clicking a customer name in the Customers Web Part activates a connection to a Customer Web Part on a second page. Figure 12-2 shows some typical results.

Chapter 12

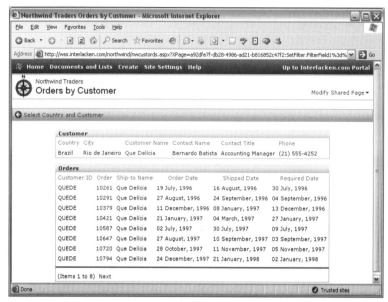

Figure 12-2. Clicking a customer name in Figure 12-1 displays the customer information and corresponding list of orders on this page. Once again, Web Part connections provide the technology.

This second page also contains two Web Parts.

- The Customer Web Part displays the same information as the Customers Web Part on the first page, but only for the customer the team member selected.

  This is the Web Part that receives data from the Customers Web Part on the first page. When a team member activates a connection in the source (sending) Web Part, Windows SharePoint services automatically displays the page that contains the target (receiving) Web Part.

  The receiving Web Part, in turn, is configured to filter its display based on the incoming value (in this case, a Customer ID).

  The Customer Web Part also has a connection to the Orders Web Part on the same page. As a result, whenever the Customer Web Part receives a Customer ID from the first page, it forwards that ID to the Orders Web Part.

- The Orders Web Part displays records from the Northwind Orders table, filtered by Customer ID. This, of course, is the Customer ID it receives from the Customer Web Part. This configuration assures that the Customer Web Part and the Orders Web Part always display information for the same customer.

  The Orders Web Part has a second connection that passes an Order ID to the Order Header Web Part on the third page. This connection, however, requires a click to activate it.

Clicking an order number in the Orders Web Part displays yet another page: one that repeats the order header information from the second page and also shows the order details. This third page appears in Figure 12-3.

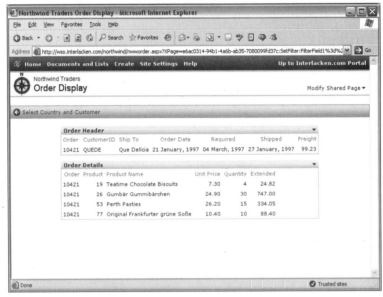

Figure 12-3. This is another page that uses Web Part connections. Clicking an order number in Figure 12-2 displays this page showing the header and detail information for that order.

This third Web page also contains two Web Parts:

- The Order Header Web Part displays records from the Northwind Orders table, filtered by the Order ID it receives from the Orders Web Part on the second page. It also has a Web Part connection that passes the Order ID to the Order Details Web Part.

- The Order Details Web Part displays records from the Northwind Order Details Extended query. This is a query that comes with the Northwind database. It returns all the fields in the Order Detail table, plus a calculated field named ExtendedPrice.

Using Web Part Connections with Data View Web Parts

To reproduce the example from the preceding section, you would need to follow these high-level steps:

1 Make sure you have a copy of the Northwind database available.

2 Open your SharePoint site and create data sources for the following tables and queries:

- The following custom query:

```
select country from Northwind.dbo.customers group by country;
```

  This is the query that returns one record for each country that appears in the Northwind customer table. Figure 12-4 shows it being configured. Name this data source Northwind Customer Countries.

  For such queries to work, a setting called Enable Update Query Support must be enabled on the virtual server that hosts your Web site. This setting appears on the Data Retrieval Service Settings page located within the Central Administration site for your server.

  The Enable Update Query Support setting for a virtual server is somewhat misnamed. It blocks or permits custom SQL statements of all kinds, including SELECT.

- The Customers table in the Northwind database. Name this data source Northwind Customers.

- The Orders table in the Northwind database. Name this data source Northwind Orders.

- The Order Details Extended query in the Northwind database. Name this data source Northwind Order Details Extended.

If you need detailed instructions for creating a Database Connection data source, refer to the section titled "Configuring Database Connection Data Sources" in Chapter 10.

Figure 12-4. Because the Northwind database has no table of valid Countries, obtaining a list of countries requires a custom query like this.

Chapter 12

Creating the Orders by Country and Customer Page

To create the first Web Part Page and the first Web Part connection, proceed as follows.

1 Create a new Web Part Page named nwcusts.aspx.

For more informational about creating Web Part pages in FrontPage, refer to the section titled "Creating Web Part Pages" in Chapter 8.

2 Add two Data View Web Parts to the nwcusts.aspx page. One should use the Northwind Customer Countries data source, and one should use the Northwind Customers data source. Configure these Web Parts to display the columns you see in Figure 12-1.

For more information about creating and configuring Data View Web Parts, refer to the section titled "Creating Data View Pages" in Chapter 11.

3 Right-click the Web Part that displays the Northwind Customer Countries data source, and then choose Web Part Properties. Open the Appearance section, change the Title field to Countries, and click OK.

4 Similarly, change the title of the Web Part that displays the Northwind Customers data source to Customers.

5 Right-click the Countries Web Part and choose Web Part Connections from the short-cut menu.

Alternatively, select the Countries Web Part and choose Web Part Connections from the Data menu.

6 When the Web Part Connections Wizard page shown in Figure 12-5 appears, open the drop-down list titled Choose The Action On The Source Web Part To Use For This Connection.

Because you're working with a Data View Web Part, the available actions are:

■ **Filter Using Data Values From**   When the current Web Part receive a value from another Web Part, you want the current Web Part to filter its display based on that value.

■ **Modify View Using Parameters From**   When the current Web Part receives a value from another Web Part, you want the current Web Part to pass that value to its data source as a parameter.

■ **Provide Data Values To**   When an event such as a click or a value change occurs on the current Web Part, the Web Part will send a value to another Web Part.

In this example, clicking an entry in the Countries Web Part will provide a data value to the Customers Web Part. Therefore, select Provide Data Values To.

Figure 12-5. Use this wizard page to specify the action a Web Part should take when a mouse click or other event occurs.

7 Figure 12-6 shows the second page of the wizard. Because:

- The Countries Web Part will connect to the Customers Web Part, and
- Both of these Web Parts are on the same page.

Select Connect To A Web Part On This Page, and then click Next.

Figure 12-6. Use this wizard page to specify where a Web Part connection should send data.

8 Figure 12-7 shows the third page of the wizard. Review these two settings, and then click Next:

- **Target Web Part**   Select the Web Part that should receive the data value. In this example, you should specify the Customers Web Part.

- **Target Action**   Choose the action you want the target Web Part to perform. The wizard will show only actions that the target Web Part can perform when it receives a value from the Web Part you specified in step 2. In this example, Filter View Using Data Values From is the only choice. Take it.

Figure 12-7.   Use this wizard page to specify which Web Part should receive data from the connection, and what action it should take.

9 Click Next to display the fourth page of the wizard, which will resemble Figure 12-8. To complete this page, you must associate a field from the source Web Part to a field in the target Web Part. Therefore:

- In the Columns In Countries list, select *country*.

- In the Columns In Customers list, select *Country*.

This specifies that the source Web Part (Countries) will send its country field, and the target Web Part (Customers) will use that value to filter on Country.

Figure 12-8. This wizard page specifies which elements from one Web Part should filter the contents of another Web Part.

10 Click Next to display the next page of the wizard, which appears in Figure 12-9. This is where you specify the field in the source Web Part that will activate the connection. Configure these settings:

- **Create A Hyperlink On** Open this drop-down list and choose the column team members will click to send the value you specified on the previous wizard page. This can be any visible column, and it *doesn't* need to be the same column you're sending. The source Web Part in the example has only one visible field—country—so that's the only choice. Take it.

- **Indicate Current Selection Using** Select this check box if, when a team member triggers the connection, you want the Web Part to visually identify the row that sent the data. In Figure 12-1, for example, bolding shows that the last country the team member clicked was Brazil. If you do select this check box, a Modify Key Columns dialog box will display a list box that contains a check box for each field in the data source. Select the check boxes for the fields you want, and then click OK.

11 Click Next to display the last page of the wizard, which appears only for confirmation. If the page contains the following information, click Finish. Otherwise, click the Back button and correct your work.

- **Source Web Part** Countries
- **Source Action** Provide Data Values To
- **Target Web Part** Customers
- **Target Action** Filter View Using Data Values From

12 Click Finish to close the wizard and apply your changes.

Chapter 12

363

Figure 12-9. This page of the wizard specifies which field should contain the hyperlink that triggers a Web Part connection.

Format the page any way you want, and then save it, taking care to use the .aspx file extension. Then choose Preview In Browser from the File menu, test, and refine.

Formatting Web Part Pages

Without repeating details presented earlier in the book, here are the primary techniques that resulted in the look and feel of the Web pages in this section.

- The page template was the Full Page, Vertical template that appears in the Web Part Pages tab of the FrontPage 2003 Page Templates dialog box.

- To customize the Title, Caption, Description, or Image that appears in the page's main title bar, right-click the title bar and choose Web Part Properties. This will display a Web Part Page Title Bar dialog box where you can customize these settings.

- Normally, Web Parts specify their width as 100%, which makes them expand to fit the browser window. To compact Web Parts horizontally, enclose them (or the Web Part Zone that contains them) in an ordinary HTML table that isn't sized to 100%. This minimizes the horizontal space into which the Web Part can expand.

- To center Web Parts or Web Part zones, enclose them in an ordinary HTML table, and then center that table. This can be the same table that the previous bullet item suggested you create.

- To reproduce the look of a SharePoint toolbar, first create a one-celled table with a width of 100%, and assign a CSS class of ms-toolbar. Then, within that table, create a second, one-rowed table with a cell for each icon, hyperlink, or divider bar. Apply the same CSS class—ms-toolbar—to each hyperlink and to each cell that contains a divider bar ("|").

Several facts about Web Part connections may not be obvious from the procedure just above, but are nevertheless worth noting.

- When you configure a Web Part connection, you affect two Web Parts (the source and the target) even though you only run the wizard once.
- The following operations:
  1. Right-click the Web Part that will send the data value, and then chose Web Part Connections.
  2. Choose Provide Data Values To on the first page of the wizard.
  3. Choose Filter Using Data Values From on the third page.

  Are equivalent to these:
  1. Right-click the Web Part that will receive the data value, and then chose Web Part Connections.
  2. Choose Filter Using Data Values From on the first page.
  3. Choose Provide Data Values To on the third page of the wizard.
- Web Part connections can only filter based on equality. For example, you can't filter records based on greater than, less then, or not equal conditions.

  If you need to use comparisons other than equality, consider adding a computed field to the data source: one that makes an equality comparison possible.

  Suppose, for example, that you want a Web Part connection to filter products by price range. You can't configure the connection to filter based on comparisons like:
  Price < 10
  (Price >= 10) and (Price < 20)
  Price >= 20
  You can, however, configure it to filter on a computed Price Range field that always contains exactly 0, 10, or 20 (the lower bound of each price range).
- If you configure a single Web Part to filter based on more than one Web Part connection, all those filters will remain continuously in effect. Furthermore, all must be true for the Web Part to display a given record. This is frequently the cause when Web Parts mysteriously display zero records.

Creating the Orders by Customer Page

Once you've got the nwcusts.aspx working, proceed as follows to create the second page in the application.

1. Create and save a new Web Part Page named nwcustords.aspx.
2. Add two Data View Web Parts:
   - Arrange for one to use the Northwind Customers data source, and title it Customer.
   - Arrange for the other to use the Northwind Orders data source, and title it Orders.

365

3 Select the Customer Web Part, and then:

   3.1 Click Style in the Data View Details task pane.

   3.2 Click the Options tab.

   3.3 Select Limit The Total Number Of Items Displayed To, and then set the accompanying value to 1.

4 Right-click the Customer Web Part, Choose Web Part Connections, and configure the connection as follows:

- **Source Web Part**   Customer
- **Source Action**   Provide Form Field Data To
- **Connect To A Web Part On**   This Page
- **Target Web Part**   Orders
- **Target Action**   Filter View Using Data Values From
- **Choose Two Columns That Contain Matching Data**   CustomerID and CustomerID
- **Create hyperlink on:**   CompanyName

5 Open the nwcusts.aspx page (the first page you created).

6 Right-click the Customers Web Part, Choose Web Part Connections, and configure the connection as follows:

- **Source Web Part**   Customers
- **Source Action**   Provide Form Field Data To
- **Connect To A Web Part On**   Another page in this web; for Page, specify nwcustords.aspx
- **Target Web Part**   Customer
- **Target Action**   Filter View Using Data Values From
- **Choose Two Columns That Contain Matching Data**   CustomerID and CustomerID
- **Create hyperlink on:**   CompanyName

7 Save both pages, browse the nwcusts.aspx page, and click a customer name. This should display the nwcustords.aspx page.

> **Note** Clicking a customer name in the first page's Customers Web Part sends the corresponding Customer ID to the second page's Customer Web Part. The Customer Web Part then sends the same Customer ID to the Orders Web Part. This is how the two Web Parts on the second page display data for the same customer.

Both the Customer Web Part and the Orders Web Part should display information about the customer whose name you clicked. If not, recheck your Web Part connection properties.

For more information about reviewing and correcting Web Part connection properties, refer to the section titled "Reviewing and Correcting Web Part Connection Properties" later in this chapter.

Creating the Order Display Page

The drill for creating the order display page is very much like that for creating the Orders by Customer Page. Here it is.

1 Create and save a new Web Part Page named nworder.aspx.

2 Add two Data View Web Parts:

- Arrange for one to use the Northwind Orders data source, and title it Order Header.
- Arrange for the other to use the Northwind Order Details Extended data source, and title it Order Details.

3 Select the Order Header Web Part, and then:

3.1 Click Style in the Data View Details task pane.

3.2 Click the Options tab

3.3 Select Limit The Total Number Of Items Displayed To, and then set the accompanying value to 1.

4 Right-click the Order Header Web Part, Choose Web Part Connections, and configure the connection as follows:

- **Source Web Part**   Order Header
- **Source Action**   Provide Form Field Data To
- **Connect To A Web Part On**   This Page
- **Target Web Part**   Order Details
- **Target Action**   Filter View Using Data Values From
- **Choose Two Columns That Contain Matching Data**   OrderID and OrderID
- **Create hyperlink on:**   OrderID

5 Open the nwcustordss.aspx page (the second page you created).

6 Right-click the Orders Web Part, Choose Web Part Connections, and configure the connection as follows:

- **Source Web Part**   Orders
- **Source Action**   Provide Form Field Data To
- **Connect To A Web Part 0n**   Another page in this web; for Page, specify nworders.aspx
- **Target Web Part**   Order Header
- **Target Action**   Filter View Using Data Values From
- **Choose Two Columns That Contain Matching Data**   OrderID and OrderID
- **Create hyperlink On**   OrderId

367

7 Save both pages, and then:

    7.1 Browse the nwcusts.aspx page, and click a customer name.

    7.2 When the nwcustords.aspx page appears, click an order number.

    This should display the nwcustords.aspx page.

Both the Order Header Web Part and the Order Details Web Part should display information about the order name you clicked. If not, recheck your Web Part connection properties.

Reviewing and Correcting Web Part Connection Properties

Once a Web Part is either the source or the target of a connection, right-clicking it and choosing Web Part Connections displays the Web Part Connections dialog box, shown in Figure 12-10.

● To add a new connection, click the Add button. This starts the Web Part Connections Wizard.

● To modify an existing connection, select it, and then click the Modify button. This reruns the Web Part Connections Wizard.

● To delete an existing connection, select it, and then click the Delete button.

Figure 12-10. This dialog box configures Web Part connections for Web Parts that have one or more connections already.

When you display the Web Part Connections dialog box, it may contain more connections than you expect. This is usually because of connections to or from other Web Parts. Remember that establishing a connection between two Web Parts modifies both of them.

Connecting Form, List, and Image Web Parts

Because all the preceding examples used Data View Web Parts, you might suspect that Web Part connections work only with Web Parts of that type. This, however, would be an error. List View Web Parts, the Form Web Part, and the Image Web Part all support connections, as may others that you encounter from time to time.

The page in Figure 12-11, for example, has a connection from the Form Web Part near the top of the page to the List View Web Part in the middle.

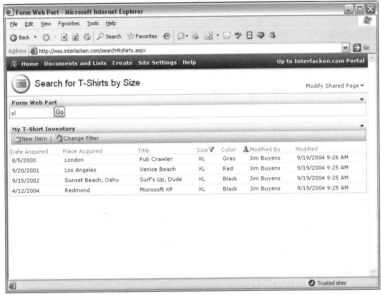

Figure 12-11. A Web Part connection transfers data from the Form Web Part in this page to the My T-Shirt Inventory List View Web Part. Typing a value in the text box and clicking Go causes the List View to filter for that value in the Size column.

The Web Part Connection settings in this page are:

- **Source Web Part** Form Web Part
- **Source Action** Provide Data Values To
- **Target Web Part** My T-Shirt Inventory
- **Target Action** Get Sort/Filter From
- **Columns That Contain Matching Data** size = Size

To create such a page yourself, you would:

1 Use the Web Parts task pane to add a Form Web Part and a List View Web Part to the page.

2 Use the normal FrontPage commands for adding, removing, and configuring the form fields within the Form Web Part, just as you'd configure the elements of an HTML form in an ordinary Web page.

Initially, a Form Web Part contains a text box named T1 and push button named Go. The example renamed the text box *size* but you can design as complex a form as you like.

3 Right-click the Form Web Part, choose Web Part Connections, and configure the connection in the usual way.

Figure 12-12 shows a Web page that connects a Data View Web Part with an Image Web Part. The Data View at the left displays the contents of a picture library named Arizona Outdoors. The Image Web Part at the right receives a picture URL by means of a Web Part connection configured like this:

- **Source Web Part** Arizona Outdoors
- **Source Action** Provide Data Values To
- **Connect To A Web Part** On This Page
- **Target Web Part** Image Web Part
- **Target Action** Get Image From
- **Choose A Column In The Source Web Part To Match** URL Path
- **Create A Hyperlink On** Name (for use in forms)
- **Indicate Current Selection Using** Name (for use in forms)

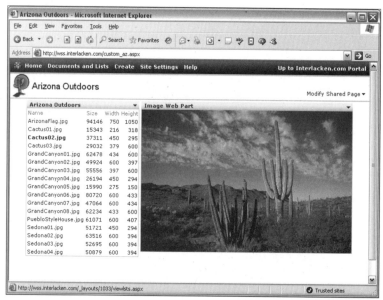

Figure 12-12. A Data View Web Part on the left lists the contents of a SharePoint picture library. When a team member clicks a picture name, a Web Part connection transfers the full URL path to the Image Web Part, which then displays it.

Conditionally Formatting a Data View

This feature changes the appearance of a Data View Web Part field based on its own value or that of other fields in the same row. For example, you can make negative numbers appear in red, specified values appear in boldface, or values outside a certain range invisible. To make use of conditional formatting:

1 In any Data View Web Part, take one of these actions:

- Right-click any instance of the field that you want to format, and then choose Conditional Formatting from the shortcut menu.

- Select any instance of the field you want to format, and then display the Conditional Formatting task pane.

- Select any instance of the field you want to format, and then choose Conditional Formatting from the Data menu.

Don't try any of these procedures with a column heading; that won't work.

2 When the Conditional Formatting task pane shown in Figure 12-13 appears, click the Create button and choose one of these commands from the menu:

- **Show Content**   Choose this command to specify conditions under which column values will be visible.

- **Hide Content**   Choose this command to specify conditions under which columns values will appear empty.

- **Apply Formatting**   Choose this command to specify when values should have an alternative appearance.

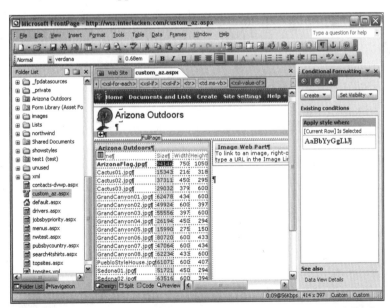

Figure 12-13.   The Conditional Formatting task pane creates and displays formatting rules that depend on data values.

371

3   When the Condition Criteria dialog box shown in Figure 12-14 appears, configure the condition or conditions you want to detect. You can base conditional formatting of one field on the value of the same field, a different field, or several fields. The dialog box itself works very much like the ones that configure filters for a data source, Data View, or List View.

For more information about filtering a data source, refer to "Configuring Data Source Filtering" in Chapter 10.

For more information about filtering a List View or Data View, refer to "Filtering List Views and Data Views" in Chapter 11.

For even more advanced conditions, click the advanced button in the condition criteria dialog box and edit the XSLT code for the condition.

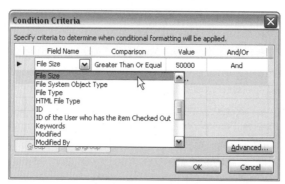

Figure 12-14.   Setting criteria for conditional formatting involves the same process as setting filtering criteria.

4   Click OK. If you chose the Apply Formatting command in step 2, FrontPage will display the Modify Style dialog box, shown in Figure 12-15. To apply styles, click the Format button, and then choose Font, Paragraph, Border, Numbering, or Position.

Figure 12-15.   Conditional formatting can apply any CSS style attribute to the data on display.

Chapter 12

This dialog box works exactly like the Modify Style dialog box that configures CSS styles for a normal HTML element, except that you can't apply named styles such as type selectors, class selectors, and ID selectors. You can only configure inline styles.

5 When you've finished applying styles, click OK.

The Conditional Formatting task pane will display each conditional formatting rule that applies to the current Web Part. Figure 12-16, for example, shows the display for two rules:

● The first rule applies bolding to the Name field when the current row is selected. This rule came from running the Web Part Connection Wizard.

● The second rule applies bolding and a red color to the file size field for values of 50,000 bytes or more.

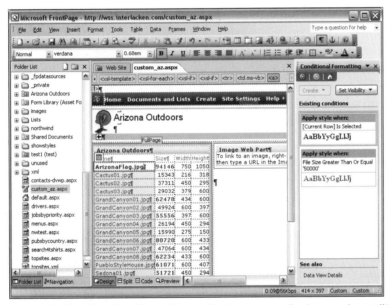

Figure 12-16. The Conditional Formatting task pane displays each conditional formatting rule in effect for a Web Part.

Any data that Design view displays will reflect the rules in effect, as will the entire Web page if you view it in your browser. To see which column a style affects, click the Apply Style When title at the top of that rule. FrontPage will then highlight the relevant column.

A single Data View Web Part can contain as many conditional formatting rules as you want. To create more, just repeat the preceding procedure. However, if you create multiple rules for the same field, try to avoid overlaps. It's fine, for example, to create two rules on the same field, one for values of 0 to 10 and another for values of 11 to 50. But if you create one rule for 0 to 10 and another for 0 to 50, the Web Part might not apply them in the order you expect.

Chapter 12

373

Clicking any rule displays a drop-down menu with six commands. Here are the first three:

- **Edit Condition**   Redisplays the Condition Criteria dialog box so that you can modify the criteria for the rule.
- **Modify Style**   Redisplays the Modify Style dialog box so that you can modify the styles that an Apply Formatting rule assigns.
- **Delete**   Eliminates the rule.

The next three commands override or restore the rule's condition or effect. This can be helpful for seeing the effect of a rule even if no matches occur in the current data, and for checking the values of a field that a rule hides. The exact commands vary according to the type of rule.

For Show Content rules, the three commands are:

- **Show: Default**   The rule will display data in accordance with the condition you specified.
- **Show: All**   The rule will ignore the condition you specified and display data in all cases.
- **Show: None**   The rule will ignore the condition you specified and hide data in all cases.

For Hide Content rules, the following commands will appear:

- **Hide: Default**   The rule will hide data in accordance with the condition you specified.
- **Hide: All**   The rule will ignore the condition you specified and hide data in all cases.
- **Hide: None**   The rule will ignore the condition you specified and show data in all cases.

For Apply Formatting rules, the following commands will appear:

- **Apply: Default**   The rule will format the data in accordance with the condition you specified.
- **Apply: All**   The rule will ignore the condition you specified and apply the formatting you specified in all cases.
- **Apply: None**   The rule will ignore the condition you specified and never apply the formatting you specified.

The Set Visibility button at the top of the Conditional Formatting task pane provides more global control over the visibility of rules. To use this facility, click the button, and then choose one of these commands from the resulting drop-down menu:

- **Default**   All rules will operate in accordance with their current settings.
- **All Formatting Hidden**   No rules will apply. The Web Part will display data as if no rules existed.
- **All Formatting Visible**   All rules will apply, regardless of conditions.

374

> **Note** The Set Visibility button on the Conditional Formatting task pane temporarily controls the visible effect of rules, and not the ongoing visibility of data.

Again, these options are for testing. It's difficult, for example, to verify that a Hide rule is working properly when you can't see the data. To see what data the Hide rule is suppressing, you could choose either All Formatting Hidden from the Set Visibility menu or Hide: None from the rule's menu. Afterward, of course, you would choose Default from the same menu so that the rule would resume normal operation.

Inserting Subviews

Normally, each row of a Data View Web Part displays one value in each column. In most cases, this is quite adequate, but it presents a problem if your data source contains repeating regions of XML data within other repeating regions. Consider, for example, the following XML data, which contains only one repeating level: *driver*.

```
<drivers>
    <driver>
        <firstname>Ed</firstname>
        <lastname>Meadows</lastname>
    </driver>
    <driver>
        <firstname>Karen</firstname>
        <lastname>Archer</lastname>
    </driver>
</drivers>
```

If you created a data source that pointed to a file containing this data, the Data View Details task pane would indent the *firstname* and *lastname* fields equally. This changes, however, if each driver node itself contains a repeating node, such as the *car* nodes shown below in bold.

```
<drivers>
    <driver>
        <firstname>Ed</firstname>
        <lastname>Meadows</lastname>
        <cars>
            <car>
                <make>Ford</make>
                <model>Galaxy 500</model>
                <modyr>1965</modyr>
            </car>
            <car>
                <make>Chevrolet</make>
                <model>Biscayne</model>
                <modyr>1962</modyr>
            </car>
        </cars>
    </driver>
```

375

Chapter 12

```
<driver>
    <firstname>Karen</firstname>
    <lastname>Archer</lastname>
    <cars>
        <car>
            <make>Hudson</make>
            <model>Model L Brougham</model>
            <modyr>1933</modyr>
        </car>
    </cars>
</driver>
</drivers>
```

This structure shows that Ed Meadows drives two cars, a 1965 Ford Galaxy 500 and a 1962 Chevrolet Biscayne. Karen Archer apparently drives one car: a 1933 Hudson Model L Brougham.

Confronted with such data, the Data View Details task pane displays the additional repeating groups with further indentation. Figure 12-17 provides an example of this.

- The notation *driver [1/3] <>* informs you that this is driver node one of three.

- The notation *car [1/2] <>*, which is further down the task pane and indented further right, informs you that this is car node one of two *within* the driver node.

Figure 12-17. This data source has nested repeating groups. Each driver record can have multiple car groupings.

Chapter 12

Displaying Single Values from a Repeating Region

When a subordinate repeating region (such as the *car* region in this case) exists, you can display the data in an ordinary Data View Web Part, provided you only want to display one value per column. Just use one of these commands.

- **Insert As Text, Number, Boolean, Hyperlink, or Picture**   If you right-click a repeating column (such as *make, model,* or *modyr* in this example) and then choose one of the commands, the Data View will always display the *first* value from the repeating group.

- **Insert As Indexed Value**   If you right-click a repeating column and then choose this command, the Data View will always display the instance that corresponds to the current node position.

  If, for example, the Data View Details task pane displays *car [2/3] <>*, and then you right-click the *make, model,* or *modyr* field and choose Insert As Indexed Value, the Web Part will always display the second instance of that field.

- **Insert As Full XPath**   This works the same as Insert As Indexed Path, except that it refers to the data using a full path relative to the root of the data source. Most of the time, Insert As Indexed Value will produce the results you want, and is preferable. But if that's not working, you should definitely try Insert As Full XPath.

Displaying Multiple Values from a Repeating Region

None of the preceding commands can display multiple rows from one repeating group within another. To do that, you need to use the *Subview* feature of Data View Web Parts. A Subview is essentially a Data View Web Part that appears inside one cell of another Data View Web Part. To display repeating data in a Subview, proceed as follows:

1   Open a new or an existing Web Part Page.

2   Add a Data View Web Part that displays the ordinary columns from the data source. (*Ordinary columns*, in this sense, are those that contain a single data value in each row.)

3   Right-click the existing Data View Web Part, and choose Data View Properties from the shortcut menu. This displays the Data View Details task pane.

4   Add a new column to the Data View Web Part. For example, right-click anywhere in an existing column, and then choose Insert Columns from the shortcut menu.

5   Set the insertion point inside the new column, but not inside the header row.

6   Select the field or fields you want the Subview to display, and then, under the Work With Data heading, click the Insert Subview link. Within a few moments, Design view will display data in the Subview column.

Chapter 12

377

If the Insert Subview link is dimmed, the Data View Details task pane is probably displaying a different data source than the current Data View Web Part. A Subview and the Data View Web Part that contains it must use the same data source. Try repeating step 3.

7 To change the appearance of the Subview, select any column value and then choose Style from the Data menu. This displays the same View Styles dialog box that configures an entire Data View.

For instructions on using the View Styles dialog box for a Data View, refer to "Modifying List View and Data View Styles" in Chapter 11.

Figure 12-18 shows a Web Part Page displaying a Data View Web Part that includes a Subview.

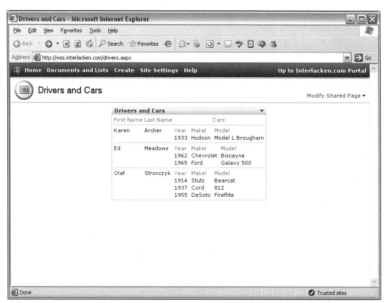

Figure 12-18. The data in the three leftmost columns of this Data View Web Part come from a Subview. There are zero to many Subview items for each main item at the left.

The fact that a Subview must use the same data source as the Web Part that contains it is a major limitation. It prevents you, for example, from displaying header and detail data from separate tables. If this is what you want to do, proceed as follows:

1 Add separate Data View Web Parts for the header and detail tables.

2 Set up a Web Part connection from the header Web Part to the detail Web Part.

In Summary...

This chapter explained how to use Web Part connections, conditional formatting, and Subviews, three features that add to the functionality of List View, Data View, Form, and Image Web Parts. Web Part connections capture events that occur in one Web Part and send data to another Web Part. Conditional formatting changes the appearance of designated data items depending on the value one or more fields in the same data row. Subviews display nested repeating data structures that exist in an XML data source.

The next chapter begins Part V, "Installing Windows SharePoint Services at the Server." Chapter 13 explains installation, while Chapter 14 explains configuration, and Chapter 15 details migration of data from earlier SharePoint products.

Part V

Installing SharePoint at the Server

Chapter 13

Planning and Installing Windows SharePoint Services

Most people who use Windows SharePoint Services never install it. They simply connect as clients, using either a browser or a Microsoft Office 2003 program.

If you're a server administrator, however, then installation and system administration lie squarely in your corner. This is just as true for part-time administrators in small businesses as it is for enterprise administrators in large organizations.

If your needs are simple, so is the task of installing Windows SharePoint Services. You make sure Internet Information Services (Microsoft's Web server) is running on a copy of Windows Server 2003, and then you download one file, run it, and click Next a few times. Voilà! Windows SharePoint Services is running at your organization.

If your needs are more complex, the task of installation will be more complex as well. This should come as no surprise. Fortunately, however, none of the additional tasks is onerous. You may need to configure some settings in SQL Server, configure some settings in IIS, create some domain user accounts, create an Active Directory organization unit, or run a few command-line programs. Individually, none of these tasks is difficult, and this chapter will provide the background and step-by-step instructions to perform each one.

Planning Your Installation

Windows SharePoint Services supports a wide variety of system configurations. If you want, you can run all the required components on a single computer. But if you need more capacity or performance, you can distribute these components across several computers, or even dedicate multiple computers to share the load of a single function. If you need more reliability, you can run redundant Web servers or clusters of SQL servers.

Even if you don't need these advanced configurations immediately, it's good to plan for them. Your needs, after all, are likely to increase over time. In addition, Windows SharePoint Services has numerous configuration parameters, some of which you must choose at initial installation and then live with.

The topics in this section, therefore, provide information and guidance on the major choices you'll need to make during installation.

If your only interest is to install Windows SharePoint Services for limited, small-scale use, you probably don't need all the information in the following topics. As a result, you may prefer skipping forward to the section titled "Installing Windows SharePoint Services with WMSDE," later in this chapter.

Choosing a Database Type and Location

Every server running Windows SharePoint Services has at least two virtual Web servers:

- A Central Administration server that server administrators use to configure settings that affect the entire physical server or an entire virtual server.
- One or more content servers that host and deliver SharePoint sites.

Windows SharePoint Services stores all the data and most of the Web pages for these virtual servers in databases. You choose which type of database to use when you install Windows SharePoint Services. Windows SharePoint Services can work with either of two databases: Microsoft SQL Server 2000 Desktop Engine (Windows), or the full Microsoft SQL Server 2000. The next two sections will discuss the advantages of each.

Choosing Microsoft SQL Server 2000 Desktop Engine (Windows) (WMSDE)

This is a limited version of SQL Server that provides only a small subset of the features in the full product. For example:

- WMSDE doesn't include enterprise management tools such as SQL Enterprise Manager. To backup, restore, or otherwise manage the database you must use command line tools that come with Windows SharePoint Services.
- WMSDE doesn't accept network connections except from the local machine. This blocks both remote data access and remote administration. (In some cases, this may be a security advantage.)
- WMSDE doesn't support full-text search. Searching a SharePoint site for given text therefore isn't possible
- You can't deploy WMSDE in a Web farm or clustered configuration. This limits scalability and presents a single point of failure.
- WMSDE requires Microsoft digital signatures on all database schemas. This prevents you from using it for anything other than Windows SharePoint Services.

Nevertheless, by choosing all the default options during setup, you can install Windows SharePoint Services, install WMSDE, and create a working SharePoint site in minutes. This is the easiest way to get Windows SharePoint Services up and running.

Planning and Installing Windows SharePoint Services

If you install Windows SharePoint Services on a single server with WMSDE, anticipating only light usage of your Web sites, and later find that you require more database power, you can migrate your data to a SQL Server database.

Choosing Microsoft SQL Server

Microsoft SQL Server includes many tools for managing database processes, such as backup and restore. It also supports the use of multiple back-end database servers, each storing a portion of the total Web content. If necessary, you can cluster these back-end database servers for high availability.

You can install Windows SharePoint Services to work with an existing installation of SQL Server. This is more complex than installing it for use with WMSDE, but it provides higher capacities and more room for growth.

The size and performance of your database server obviously depend on the number, size, and activity of the Web sites your server supports. A SQL Server installation, however, will definitely support more sites and more activity than a WMSDE configuration.

Consider using SQL Server instead of WMSDE if you anticipate supporting more than ten large, active Web sites. If necessary, you can improve capacity and performance by installing SQL Server and Windows SharePoint Services on separate computers.

The primary disadvantages of SQL Server are license costs and increased complexity during installation. The complexity is due to some manual steps you need to perform so that SQL Server and Windows SharePoint Services can work together securely.

In two situations, you must always use SQL Server databases. WMSDE databases won't work in these circumstances.

- Your operating system is Windows Server 2003, Web Edition.
- You want to run Windows SharePoint Services in Active Directory Account Creation mode. In this mode, team members don't use ordinary domain accounts to access SharePoint sites. Instead they use accounts stored in a specified organizational unit within Active Directory.

> **Note** All references to SQL Server in this chapter refer to Microsoft SQL Server 2000 Service Pack 3 or later. This is the first release of SQL Server that Windows SharePoint Services supports.

Troubleshooting

Windows Server 2003 doesn't support SQL Server 2000

When you install SQL Server 2000 on a Windows Server 2003 computer, the message shown in Figure 13-1 may appear.

Figure 13-1. You can install SQL Server 2000 on Windows Server 2003 even though this message appears. However, you should apply SQL Server Service Pack 3 when setup completes.

This occurs because Windows Server 2003 supports only SQL Server 2000 Service Pack 3 or later, and your installation media doesn't include that service pack.

To work around this problem, keep installing SQL Server 2000, and then immediately apply SQL Server 2000 Service Pack 3.

Choosing an Authentication Type for SQL Server

If you choose to use SQL Server with Windows SharePoint Services, you must also choose the authentication method to use for connections between Windows SharePoint Services and the SQL Server databases. You can use either Windows authentication or SQL Server authentication for these connections.

● **Windows authentication** Is more secure, because it uses an encrypted challenge/response protocol. This makes it extremely difficult to sniff credentials over a network. The account that accesses the database is that of the IIS application pool that runs the SharePoint site.

For more information about IIS application pools, refer to the section titled "Choosing an IIS Application Pool Configuration" later in this chapter.

Chapter 13

● **SQL Server authentication**   Is less secure, because when you connect to the database, the database username and password travel from server to server in a weakly encrypted format. Administrative Web pages specify the SQL Server account and password that each virtual server will use.

You make the database authentication choice after installation, when you connect a virtual server to the SQL Server database for the first time.

About WMSDE and Authentication Types

When you install Windows SharePoint Services with the default settings, the setup program also installs WMSDE to provide database support. By default, the authentication for connections between Windows SharePoint Services and WMSDE is Windows authentication.

The setup program sets the password for the WMSDE system administrator (sa) account to a random string, and then continues without storing or logging that password in any way. Therefore, if you want to use SQL Server authentication or mixed authentication with WMSDE, and you want to use the sa account, you'll need to change the sa password.

Because the setup program doesn't store the sa password, you can't log in as the sa account to change the password. Instead, you must log in as a member of the WMSDE system administrator (sysadmin) role.

By default, the sysadmin role for WMSDE includes the sa account and all administrators of the local computer. All these accounts therefore have full administrative access to WMSDE, including the ability to change the sa password.

Caution   Take care not to remove the local administrators from the WMSDE sysadmin role, or you won't be able to change the sa password. If you remove all users except sa from the sysadmin role, without first changing the sa password, the WMSDE instance will be unusable.

Planning Virtual Servers

Small to medium sized Web sites typically require only a fraction of the computing power available on modern server hardware. As a result, it's very common to run several or many Web servers on one physical server. Each of those Web servers is then a *virtual server*. Internet Information Services provides three methods for routing incoming requests to the correct virtual server.

● **IP Address**   In this method, each virtual Web server listens for requests sent to a different IP address. The operating system, of course, must listen on all those addresses.

- **Port Number**   Just as virtual servers can listen on different IP addresses, they can also listen on different port numbers. This cuts down on the number of IP addresses a server uses, but requires Web visitors to know each virtual server's port number.

- **Host Header**   In this method, each virtual server watches for requests that have a given host header value.

  A host header is a line that browsers add to each HTTP request, indicating the host-name portion of the requested URL. If a Web visitor typed:

  ```
  http://wss.interlacken.com/sites/buyens/default.aspx
  ```

  the browser would send:

  ```
  GET /sites/buyens/default.aspx
  ```

  ```
  Host: wss.interlacken.com
  ```

  plus a variety of other headers. By keying off the host header, a physical server configured with a single IP address can support many virtual servers.

A server running Windows SharePoint Services always runs at least two virtual servers: one SharePoint Central Administration server listening on a randomly-chosen port number, and one or more content servers listening on port 80.

Unfortunately, because of a design problem discovered late in its development cycle, Windows SharePoint Services 2003 provides only limited support for multiple virtual servers acting as content servers. Specifically:

- You should never bind a SharePoint virtual Web server to a specific IP address. Microsoft doesn't support this configuration. If you view the virtual server's properties in IIS Manager, the Web Site tab should *always* display IP Address: (All Unassigned).

- If you choose to implement a virtual server by using host headers (that is, by clicking Advanced on the Web Site tab, and then clicking Edit and entering the virtual server's DNS name in the Host Header Name box), you should never install custom Web Parts in that virtual server's /bin folder. Instead, you should install them in the server's Global Assembly Cache (GAC).

> For more information about installing custom Web Parts, refer to, "Deploying Custom Web Parts," in Chapter 19.

Windows SharePoint Services won't stop you from violating these restrictions, and the resulting site will probably work correctly in most regards. Eventually, however, you'll encounter one of these problems:

- When you add an Online Library Web Part to a page, you receive the error message:

  Cannot retrieve properties at this time.

- When you try to edit a Web Part page in FrontPage 2003, or when you try to export a Web Part, you receive this message:

Planning and Installing Windows SharePoint Services

The server could not complete your request. Contact your Internet service provider or Web server administrator to make sure that the server has the FrontPage Server Extensions or SharePoint Services installed.

- When you install a custom Web Part, it doesn't show up on the Web Part Gallery: New Web Parts page (NewDwp.aspx).

> For more information about the Web Part Gallery: New Web Parts page, refer to "Managing the Web Part Gallery," in Chapter 17.

These restrictions apply at least through Windows SharePoint Services 2003 Service Pack 1. To determine the status of these issues in later releases, consult the release notes or monitor the status of the following Microsoft Knowledge Base article:

"Soap:Server Exception of Type Microsoft.SharePoint.SoapServer.SoapServerException" message when you try to edit a portal by using FrontPage 2003, or when you try to export a Web part (*http://support.microsoft.com/Default.aspx?id=830342*)

The next section describes an effective, fully-supported way of hosting multiple root-level SharePoint sites on a single virtual server.

Choosing a Hosting Mode

Windows SharePoint Services provides a choice of two hosting modes; that is, a choice of two ways it can deliver content from the server image that a request specifies.

- **Nonscalable hosting mode**   Is the default. In this mode, Windows SharePoint Services uses separate content databases and virtual servers for each root-level site.

  If, for example, you had a site named *http://antelopes.example.com* and wanted to create a new site named *http://gnus.example.com*, you would have to create at least one new virtual server and one new content database dedicated exclusively to the new site.

  Despite its name, this mode is highly scalable when hosting a single large site. For example, you can keep adding front-end Web servers and back-end database servers almost without limit. However, it's not scalable in the direction of hosting many independent sites, each with its own root folder.

- **Scalable hosting mode**   In this mode, a single instance of Windows SharePoint Services inspects the host header of each incoming request, and responds with content for that host name.

  In this scenario, creating a new root-level site requires no new virtual servers and no new content databases. Instead, you run the stsadm.exe command-line program and identify the new host name.

  On servers or server farms hosting a single server image, choosing scalable hosting mode would simply add overhead. Scalable hosting mode, however, is the best way of supporting multiple server images on one physical server or farm. A server that might support a few hundred virtual Web servers could probably support images of several thousand servers in scalable hosting mode.

389

If you wish, you can deploy scalable hosting mode across a farm of front-end Web servers and back-end database servers. This provides high availability and performance for hundreds or even thousands of small sites that otherwise couldn't afford redundant hardware support.

> **Note** Some documentation refers to scalable hosting mode as *host header mode*, or as *multiple host names deployment*.

You can only specify scalable hosting mode when you create a new configuration database. After that, it applies to the entire server or server farm and remains in effect permanently.

To create a configuration database that uses scalable hosting mode, you must use the stsadm.exe command-line program. The SharePoint Central Administration Web pages don't provide the necessary options.

> For instructions on using stsadm.exe to create a configuration database that uses scalable hosting mode, refer to the section titled "Installing Windows SharePoint Services from the Command Line," later in this chapter.

Choosing a User Account Mode

When you install Windows SharePoint Services, you must choose a mode for working with user accounts. Windows SharePoint Services supports two user account modes:

- **Domain Account mode**   Uses existing domain logon accounts; the same accounts that team members use for file sharing, print sharing, and other applications in a Windows domain.

  If a SharePoint site administrator tries to grant access to an account that doesn't exist, an error results.

  This mode is most common on intranets, where team members already have domain accounts. It presumes that team members will change their passwords when logging into those resources, and therefore provides no way for team members to change their passwords via Windows SharePoint Services.

- **Active Directory Account Creation mode**   Uses Active Directory accounts located in an organizational unit reserved for this purpose, and which probably has no other privileges.

  This mode is most useful when most of the team members who will use a SharePoint server don't have—and shouldn't have—accounts on a local Windows domain. This occurs most frequently on public Internet sites. In addition, Active Directory Account Creation mode replaces the local account creation feature in SharePoint Team Services 1.0.

  If a site administrator displays the Add Users page and tries to authorize an account that doesn't exist, Windows SharePoint Services creates an account with the given name. It then sends the new team member an e-mail message that provides a temporary password and invites him or her to access the site.

Planning and Installing Windows SharePoint Services

Active Directory accounts created this way have no use other than accessing SharePoint sites. Therefore, team members on a site using Active Directory Account Creation mode can use the page _layouts/1033/password.aspx (relative to the root URL of any site) to change their password. If the site's locale is other than US English, replace 1033 with the site's locale ID.

Inside Out

Active Directory Account Creation mode isn't a self-registration system where Internet visitors provide an e-mail address, choose a password, receive validation mail and validate themselves. A site administrator must create each team member's account in advance.

The choice of user account mode affects the way Windows SharePoint Services creates the configuration database for your server or server farm. As a result:

- You can't change user account modes after creating the configuration database, and this step is part of initial installation.

- You can't mix account modes in a single configuration database. Therefore, the physical server or server farm must run entirely in Domain Account mode or entirely in Active Directory Account Creation mode.

Before choosing Active Directory Account Creation mode, you should be aware of these restrictions:

- To run Active Directory Account Creation mode, the computer running Windows SharePoint Services must be a member server in an Active Directory domain.

- It takes at least two computers to run Active Directory Account Creation mode. One is a member server that runs Windows SharePoint Services., The other must be a domain controller. You can't combine these functions on a single computer.

- Any application pool that runs Windows SharePoint Services must use a Windows account that can add, create, and delete accounts in the Active Directory organizational unit that supports Active Directory Account Creation.

- On the domain controller, the group policy for Minimum Password Age must be 0 days. Otherwise, the only team members who can change their own password will be those with administrator rights on the server.

- Active Directory Account Creation mode requires a SQL Server database.

- When using Active Directory Account Creation mode, you can't perform the following actions from Web pages in the SharePoint Central Administration site:

  - Create the configuration database.
  - Create a top-level Web site.
  - Enable Self-Service Site Creation.

■ Add a user to a site. (However, you *can* add users by using the Site Settings pages in individual sites.)

To perform these actions in Active Directory Account Creation mode, you must use the stsadm.exe command-line program or write your own program that manipulates the Windows SharePoint Services object model.

Choosing an IIS Application Pool Configuration

The architecture of IIS 6.0 isolates Web sites and applications into self-contained processes called application pools. Application pools provide:

● Increased reliability because errors in one application pool can't cause another application pool, or the server itself, to fail.

● Increased security because each application pool can run under a different user account. This provides a way to control which applications can perform which actions.

Windows SharePoint Services provides great flexibility in the way you assign virtual servers to application pools.

● You can run all virtual servers on the same machine in a single, default application pool.

● You can run each virtual server in its own application pool.

● You can group any number of virtual servers into a smaller number of application pools. If you had five virtual servers, for example, you could run three in one application pool and two in another.

● You can run the application pools under the same account, or all under different accounts, or any combination.

When you install Windows SharePoint Services on a physical server and set the configuration database, you specify the application pool that the Central Administration virtual server will use.

● If you choose an existing application pool, the pool will continue to run under its existing account.

● If you choose to create a new application pool, you can have it run under a predefined account or under a so-called *configurable* account.

  ■ The predefined accounts are Network Service, Local Service, and Local System.

  ■ A configurable account is a local or domain account that you've, uh, *configured* with the properties and privileges you want.

If this seems rather vague, refer to Figure 13-2, which shows IIS Manager running on a Windows Server 2003 computer that supports one SharePoint Central Administration server and one SharePoint content server named Whoosh #1.

Planning and Installing Windows SharePoint Services

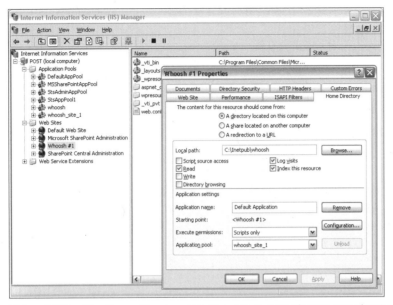

Figure 13-2. The Home Directory tab of a virtual server's property sheet server displays its assigned application pool.

Opening POST (local computer) and then Application Pools reveals that the server currently has six application pools.

- **DefaultAppPool** The default pool that installing IIS creates. It's also the default application pool for any new virtual servers an administrator creates.

- **MSSharePointAppPool** Runs the Microsoft SharePoint Administration site, which administers the FrontPage 2002 Server Extensions.

- **StsAdminAppPool** The application pool that a default (WMSDE) installation creates for the SharePoint Central Administration server.

- **StsAppPool1** The default application pool for the first SharePoint content server.

- **Whoosh** A custom application pool for the SharePoint Central Administration server. It runs under a domain account named interlacken\whoosh.

- **Whoosh_site_1** A custom application pool for the first SharePoint Content server. It runs under a domain account named interlacken\whoosh_site_1.

IIS Manager can also show which application pool a virtual server is using. If this seems interesting, proceed as follows:

1 Right-click the server name.

2 Choose Properties from the shortcut menu.

3 Click the Home Directory tab. This is the tab that appears in the foreground of Figure 13-2.

The Application Pool drop-down list near the bottom of the dialog box shows the currently assigned pool.

IIS Manager can also show what account an application pool is using. To get this information, follow these steps:

1   Right-click the name of the application pool.

2   Choose Properties from the shortcut menu.

3   Click the Identity tab.

As shown in Figure 13-3, this tab displays the current account.

Figure 13-3.   The Identity tab of an application pool's property sheet displays its assigned security account.

The user account you assign to an application pool has special significance in two situations.

●   If you choose to run Windows SharePoint Services with a SQL Server database:

■   The application pool that runs the Central Administration server must use an account granted the Database Creators and Security Administrators roles in SQL Server.

■   The application pool that runs each content server must use an account that has authority to read and update the SharePoint content databases.

Note that these accounts must be valid on both the Web server and the SQL Server. If these are (or might someday be) different computers, best practice is to use domain accounts. However, you can also use the Network Service account on the content server, and then grant the Web server's machine account the necessary roles in SQL Server.

Planning and Installing Windows SharePoint Services

- If you choose to run Active Directory Account Creation mode, every application pool that runs a SharePoint site must use an account that has authority to create, read, and update accounts in the Active Directory organization unit that you configure Account Creation to use.

> For instructions on granting SQL Server rights for an application pool account to read, update, and create databases, refer to the section titled "Granting Database Creation Rights in SQL Server," later in this chapter.

> For instructions on delegating authority so an application pool account can create, read, and update accounts in an Active Directory organization unit, refer to the section titled "Delegating Permissions to the Organizational Unit," later in this chapter.

Note that this account must be valid on both the Web server and the domain controller. Therefore, it must be a domain account.

Whenever you decide to have your application pools use domain accounts, it's generally best to follow these practices:

- Create a new domain account for each use. If you use the same domain account for two different purposes, the account usually has excess privileges in both cases.
- Configure the account with a non-expiring password that can't be changed.
- Restrict use of the account to the computers that truly need it.
- On each computer that has application pools using the account, grant the account the Log On As A Service user right.

> For instructions on granting the Log On As A Service user right, refer to the section titled "Granting the Log On As A Service User Right," later in this chapter.

Planning for Heavy Load

In situations of extremely heavy load and large numbers of simultaneous users, you should consider the following special configuration steps for the content virtual servers.

Using a Specially-Configured Domain Account for the Application Pool Account

When you create the domain account for an application pool, configure it with the host name of the virtual server (for example, http://my.corp.net or http://virtualserver) and register the host name as a Service Principal Name (SPN) for the account on the Kerberos domain. If there are multiple host names represented by this virtual server, you must register each host name as a Service Principal Name with this account.

> For more information about registering Service Principal Names for specific accounts in a Kerberos domain, see the topic "Delegating Authentication," in the Windows Server 2003 Help system.

Microsoft Windows SharePoint Services Inside Out

Changing the IIS Authentication Method to Negotiate/NTLM

By default, Windows SharePoint Services configures virtual servers with Integrated Windows authentication. Note that you must be using Active Directory to use Negotiate/NTLM.

The following procedure uses a script to configure a virtual server for Negotiate/NTLM authentication.

1　Open a command window on the physical server.

2　Change to the \inetpub\adminscripts directory.

3　Run the following command:

```
cscript adsutil.vbs get w3svc/##/NTAuthenticationProviders
```

Where ## is the virtual server ID number (1 for the default virtual server) to verify the current authentication setting. This should return following string:

```
ntauthenticationproviders: (STRING) "NTLM"
```

4　Run the following command to change to Negotiate/NTLM:

```
cscript adsutil.vbs set w3svc/##/NTAuthenticationProviders
"Negotiate,NTLM"
```

Where ## is the virtual server ID number (1 for the default virtual server).

Preserving Existing Web Content

A single physical server can support any combination of virtual servers running in the following modes:

- Extended with Windows SharePoint Services
- Extended with the FrontPage 2002 Server Extensions
- Not extended

However, when you extend a virtual server with Windows SharePoint Services, the server's physical content tree (such as C:\InetPub\wwwroot for the default server) becomes inaccessible by Web browsing. This is because:

- Windows SharePoint Services intercepts incoming Web requests and satisfies them by referring to its content databases. The Web server never gets a chance to satisfy requests by looking in its physical content tree.
- Extending a server with Windows SharePoint Services doesn't add the server's previous content to the SharePoint content databases.

This argues strongly for extending virtual servers with Windows SharePoint Services only if those servers are new or empty.

Chapter 13

Planning and Installing Windows SharePoint Services

> **Note** Extending a virtual server with Windows SharePoint Services doesn't delete the server's existing content; it just makes the content inaccessible to Web browsers. You can still view, move, copy, or otherwise retrieve the old content through the physical server's file system.

Preserving Ordinary Web Content

If you need to extend a virtual server in place but save the server's existing content, your choices are to:

- Copy the existing content to a new virtual server, and then extend the original server with Windows SharePoint Services.
- Extend a new virtual server with Windows SharePoint Services, and then configure the existing server and the new SharePoint server with the host names you want.
- Define a managed exclude path for the file system content you want the server to deliver.

> For more information about defining a managed exclude path, refer to "Planning Managed Paths," in Chapter 5.

Preserving FrontPage-Based Content

If the FrontPage Server Extensions are installed on a virtual server that you want to extend with Windows SharePoint Services, the situation becomes slightly more complicated. This is because you can't extend the same virtual server with *both* Windows SharePoint Services *and* the FrontPage 2002 Server Extensions.

By default, the Windows SharePoint Services setup program extends the computer's first (that is, default) virtual Web server with Windows SharePoint Services. If, however, that virtual server is already extended with the FrontPage Server Extensions, you'll get the message shown in Figure 13-4.

Figure 13-4. Windows SharePoint Services setup won't extend a virtual server configured to use the FrontPage Server Extensions.

Microsoft Windows SharePoint Services Inside Out

A similar message appears if you use the SharePoint Central Administration pages to extend a virtual server with Windows SharePoint Services, and the FrontPage Server Extensions are present on that virtual server.

To avoid such problems, it's best to check for the existence of the FrontPage Server Extensions before installing Windows SharePoint Services. To do this:

1 Open IIS Manager on the computer that hosts the virtual web server.

2 Open the Computer and Web Sites entries.

3 Right-click the virtual server you want to extend, and then choose All Tasks from the shortcut menu.

4 If the following commands appear on the resulting shortcut menu, the FrontPage Server Extensions are installed.

- Check Server Extensions 2002

- Recalculate Server Extensions 2002 Web

- Remove Server Extensions 2002

Figure 13-5 illustrates this choice.

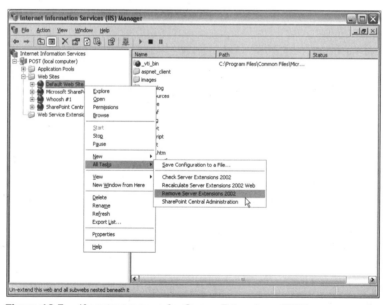

Figure 13-5. If context menus for Server Extensions 2002 are present, so are the FrontPage Server Extensions.

When the FrontPage Server Extensions are present, you have these choices:

- Extend a different virtual server (a new one, perhaps) with Windows SharePoint Services.

If you're running initial setup, you can do this by clicking OK when the message in Figure 13-4 appears, and then jumping forward to the section titled "Extending a Virtual Server with Windows SharePoint Services and Connecting It to SQL Server" later in this chapter.

- Remove the FrontPage Server Extensions from the server you want to extend with Windows SharePoint Services, and then extend the same server with Windows SharePoint Services. This, however, masks the server's previous content.

  If you're at the point of running initial setup, it's easiest to do this before running the setup program. But if you're already running setup, click Cancel when the message shown in Figure 13-4 appears, remove the FrontPage Server Extensions, and then restart setup.

- Move the existing FrontPage content to a new virtual server, freeing up the original one. This involves the following steps.

  1 Create a new virtual server.

  2 Extend the new server with the FrontPage 2002 Server Extensions.

  3 Publish all the FrontPage content from the old server to the new one.

  4 Remove the FrontPage Server Extensions from the original server.

  5 Extend the original server with Windows SharePoint Services.

  If you're running initial setup, click Cancel when the message shown in Figure 13-4 appears, perform the steps above, and then restart setup.

> **Note** If you upgraded from Windows 2000 to Windows Server 2003, FrontPage 2002 Server Extensions were installed by default to port 80.

If the FrontPage Server Extensions are present because the virtual server has been running SharePoint Team Services 1.0 from Microsoft, the upgrade path is as follows:

1 Install Windows SharePoint Services.

2 Extend a virtual server with Windows SharePoint Services.

3 Use a command-line utility to import the SharePoint Team Services 1.0 sites.

> For more information about migrating sites from SharePoint Team Services 1.0, refer to Chapter 15, "Migrating Data from Earlier SharePoint Products."

Preparing the Server

Before installing Windows SharePoint Services on a server, you should verify that the computer meets these requirements:

- The computer must be running Microsoft Windows Server 2003. The Standard, Enterprise, Datacenter, and Web editions are all acceptable.

- The computer must be running Internet Information Services (IIS) in IIS 6.0 Worker Process Isolation mode.

- The computer must be running ASP.NET 1.1 or later.
- The computer must be using the NTFS file system.
- The client computers must be running Microsoft Internet Explorer 5.01 or later or Netscape Navigator 6.2 or later to use Windows SharePoint Services features. Of course, the most recent release available of Internet Explorer will get the best results.

> **Note** Windows Server 2003 includes a utility named convert.exe that converts an existing file allocation table (FAT) volume to NTFS without loss of data.

Configuring the Server as a Web Server

IIS is an integral part of Windows Server 2003, but it isn't installed by default. Instead, you must follow this procedure:

1 On the Windows Start menu, choose All Programs, Administrative Tools, and Manage Your Server.

2 When the Manage Your Server page appears, click Add Or Remove A Role. This will start the Configure Your Server Wizard.

3 When the Preliminary Steps wizard pane appears, click Next.

4 When the Server Role pane shown in Figure 13-6 appears, select Application Server (IIS, ASP.NET) and then click Next.

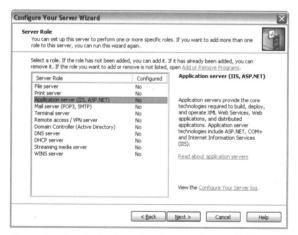

Figure 13-6. Adding the Application Server Role to Windows Server 2003 installs Internet Information Services, Microsoft's flagship Web server.

5 When the Application Server Options pane shown in Figure 13-7 appears:

   5.1 Make sure the FrontPage Server Extensions box is cleared.

   5.2 Select the Enable ASP.NET box.

   5.3 Click Next.

Planning and Installing Windows SharePoint Services

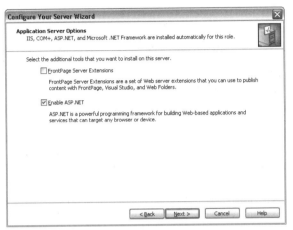

Figure 13-7. Windows SharePoint Services requires the absence of the FrontPage Server Extensions, but the presence of ASP.NET.

6 When the Summary of Selections pane appears, make sure these four selections are present:

- Install Internet Information Services (IIS)
- Enable COM+ for remote transactions
- Enable Microsoft Distributed Transaction Coordinator (DTC) for remote access
- Enable ASP.NET

and then click Next.

7 At this point, the wizard will install IIS, and may ask for your Windows Server 2003 installation CD. When the wizard displays the message:

`This server is now an application server.`

click Finish.

> **Tip** After installing IIS (or any Windows Server component) you should reapply the latest service pack and run Windows Update to apply the latest patches.

Checking the IIS Isolation Mode

By default, a new installation of IIS will run its application pools in IIS 6.0 Worker Process Isolation mode. This is the mode Windows SharePoint Services requires.

If, however, IIS was previously installed on the computer, you should verify that it's *not* running in IIS 5.0 Isolation mode. To do this:

1 On the Windows Start menu, choose All Programs, Administrative Tools, and then Internet Information Services (IIS) Manager.

Microsoft Windows SharePoint Services Inside Out

2 When the Internet Information Services (IIS) Manager window appears, make sure the entries below the server name are visible.

3 Right-click the Web Sites folder, and then select Properties.

4 In the Properties dialog box, click the Service tab.

5 In the Isolation Mode section, make sure the Run WWW Service In IIS 5.0 Isolation Mode check box is cleared. Figure 13-8 shows the correct setting.

6 Click OK.

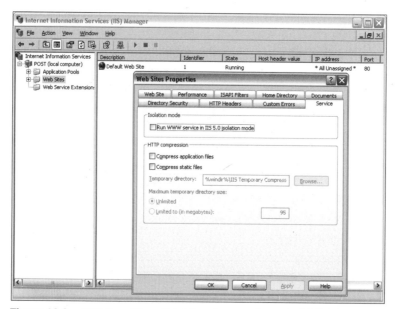

Figure 13-8. Windows SharePoint Services can't run in IIS 5.0 Isolation Mode.

If you find that the Run WWW Service In IIS 5.0 Isolation Mode check box is selected, it could be for either of two reasons.

- The server previously ran Windows 2000 and IIS 5.0, and was upgraded to Windows 2003 and IIS 6.0. For compatibility, this upgrade preserves IIS 5.0 Isolation mode.

- The Web server needs to run applications that are incompatible with IIS 6.0 Worker Process Isolation mode. ASP.NET 1.0 is one such application.

If the server is currently running applications that require IIS 5.0 Isolation mode, you'll need to choose one of these options:

- Upgrade the incompatible applications so they run in IIS 6.0 Worker Process Isolation mode.

- Move the incompatible applications to a different computer.

- Run Windows SharePoint Services on a different computer.

Creating Application Pool Accounts

In IIS 6, each virtual Web server runs in an application pool, and each application pool runs with a user account. The privileges of this account determine what the application pool, and therefore the virtual server, can do.

> For more information about application pool accounts, refer to "Choosing an IIS Application Pool Configuration," earlier in this chapter.

Application pools can run with either predefined or configurable accounts. A predefined account is one like Network Service that comes with the operating system. A configurable account is more secure, because you create it yourself and grant it only the permissions it needs.

Creating an Application Pool Account

Here's the procedure for creating a configurable application pool account for Windows SharePoint Services processes:

1 Log on to the domain controller console.

2 On the Windows Start menu, choose Programs, Administrative Tools, Active Directory Users And Computers.

3 Open the entry for your domain, right-click the Users Entry, and then choose New and User from the shortcut menus.

4 When the New Object – User dialog box appears, specify at least a Last Name, Full Name, and User Logon Name. For example, set all of these to SharePoint_admin.

5 Click Next to display the second page of the wizard. Then:

    5.1 Specify a password (twice) for the new account.

    5.2 Select User Can't Change Password.

    5.3 Select Password Never Expires.

6 Click Next and Finish to create the account.

The account must be a member of the Domain Users group, which is the default group for new accounts. For more information about creating an account on your domain controller, see the Windows Server 2003 Help system.

Application pool accounts for Windows SharePoint Services require the Log On As A Service user right privileges on the front-end Web server. The next section explains how to configure this. The account also requires specific permissions on the database server.

> For information on granting an application pool account privileges in SQL Server, refer to "Granting Database Creation Rights in SQL Server," later in this chapter.

Granting the Log On As A Service User Right

Here's the procedure for granting the Log On As A Service user right to a domain account on a Windows Server 2003 computer:

1 Open a console session and log on to the Windows Server 2003 computer as an administrator.

2 From the Windows Start Menu, click Administrative Tools and then Local Security Policy.

3 When the Local Security Settings window appears, open Local Policies and select User Rights Assignment.

4 In the Policy listing that appears at the right, double-click Log On As A Service.

5 When the Log On As A Service Properties dialog box appears, click the Add User Or Group button.

6 When the Select Users, Computers, Or Groups dialog box appears, type the name of the domain account that an application pool will use, and then click OK. Figure 13-9 shows this operation in progress.

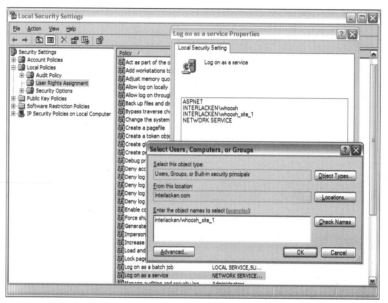

Figure 13-9. User accounts you assign to an application pool require the Log On As A Service right on the computer where the application pool runs.

Preparing Active Directory for Account Creation Mode

If you plan to run a SharePoint server in Active Directory Account Creation Mode, you'll need to create an active directory organizational unit where the accounts can reside, and delegate permissions for the application pool accounts to update it. The next two sections explain how to perform these tasks.

Creating an Organizational Unit (OU) for the User Accounts

When using Active Directory account creation mode, you need to define an organizational unit where Windows SharePoint Services can create new user accounts. All Windows SharePoint Services user accounts from the same server or server farm will reside in this organizational unit.

Conversely, no accounts other than SharePoint user accounts should reside in the organizational unit that Account Creation mode uses. For example, none of the following accounts should reside there:

- Server administrator accounts.
- Application pool accounts.
- Domain user accounts.

Accounts such as these need significantly greater privileges than SharePoint user accounts. Keeping these account types in different organization units makes it much easer to control group policy and privileges.

> **Tip** Never add accounts manually to the organizational unit you designate for use by Active Directory Account Creation mode. Only allow the accounts that Windows SharePoint Services creates.

Here's the procedure for creating an Active Directory organizational unit where Account Creation user accounts can reside.

1 If Active Directory Users and Computers isn't already running, go to the Windows Start menu and then choose Programs, Administrative Tools, Active Directory Users And Computers.

2 Right-click the Active Directory domain name, and then choose New and Organizational Unit from the shortcut menus.

3 When the New Object – Organizational Unit dialog box appears, type a name for the organizational unit. For example, type sharepoint_ou.

4 Click OK.

Delegating Permissions to the Organizational Unit

In order for Windows SharePoint Services to have permissions to create accounts in the sharepoint_ou organizational unit, you must delegate the correct permissions to the application pool accounts for the content server and for the SharePoint Central Administration server. To do this, proceed as follows.

1 If Active Directory Users and Computers isn't already running, go to the Windows Start menu and then choose Programs, Administrative Tools, Active Directory Users And Computers.

2 Right-click the new organizational unit, and then choose Delegate Control from the shortcut menu.

3 When the Delegation Of Control wizard opens, click Next to bypass the Welcome pane.

4 When the Users and Groups pane appears, click Add.

5 In the Enter The Object Names To Select box, type the user name you plan to use for the application pool.

6 Click OK to close the dialog box, and then Next to advance past the Users and Groups pane.

7 In the Tasks to Delegate pane, select:

- The Create, Delete, And Manage User Accounts check box
- The Read All User Information check box

and then click Next.

8 Click Next and then Finish .

If your content server and your SharePoint Central Administration server are using different application pool accounts, repeat this procedure once for reach account.

Installing Windows SharePoint Services

This section explains how to install Windows SharePoint Services in the most common scenarios.

Installing Windows SharePoint Services with WMSDE

The simplest way of installing Windows SharePoint Services is on a single server, and using the WMSDE database. To do this, you simply run the setup program with all defaults. You should, however, be aware of these precautions:

- During setup, in a default installation, Windows SharePoint Services extends the default virtual server with Windows SharePoint Services. This doesn't delete or overwrite the server's existing content, but it does make that content inaccessible through the Web server.

- If, however, the FrontPage 2002 Server Extensions are running on the default virtual server on port 80, running setup with all defaults *won't* extend that server with Windows SharePoint Services.

- By default, the WMSDE database will reside at:
  C:\Program Files\Microsoft SQL Server\MSSQL$SHAREPOINT

Downloading and Unpacking the Installation Files

The first step in installing Windows SharePoint Services is to download and unpack the installation files. Proceed as follows.

1 Download the setup program, STSV2.exe, to your computer.

You can download STSV2.exe from the Downloads for SharePoint Products and Technologies page at *http://www.microsoft.com/technet/downloads/sharepnt.mspx*

Planning and Installing Windows SharePoint Services

2 Run STSV2.exe to extract the installation files and start the installation.

3 If you want your installation of Windows SharePoint Services to deviate in any way from the default, click Cancel when the End User License Agreement window appears.

Whether or not you click Cancel, a complete set of unpacked installation files will now reside at C:\Program Files\STS2Setup_1033, where 1033 is the Locale ID for your version of the setup program; 1033, for example, indicates US English.

Installing Windows SharePoint Services with Default Settings

To install Windows SharePoint Services with all defaults in effect, proceed as follows:

1 If you downloaded and ran stsv2.exe as directed in the previous section, and never clicked Cancel, proceed to the next step.

Otherwise, switch to the C:\Program Files\STS2Setup_1033 folder that stsv2.exe created, and start the setupsts.exe program.

2 When the End-User License Agreement page appears, carefully review the terms and conditions. If you agree, select the check box titled I Accept The Terms In The License Agreement check box, and then click Next.

3 When the Type Of Installation page shown in Figure 13-10 appears, select Typical Installation and then click Next.

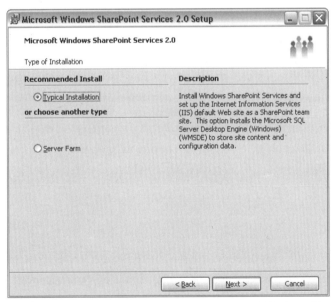

Figure 13-10. A server farm installation installs Windows SharePoint Services and a Central Administration server. A typical installation also installs WMSDE, creates configuration and content databases, and extends the default Web server.

Microsoft Windows SharePoint Services Inside Out

4   When the Summary Page appears, click Install. (Back and Cancel are the only other alternatives.)

5   The setup program will then:

- Install Microsoft Windows SharePoint Services.

- Install WMSDE.

- Create a new virtual server named SharePoint Central Administration, running on a randomly selected port number. This Web site configures SharePoint settings that apply to entire virtual servers or the entire computer.

- Extend the default virtual server with Windows SharePoint Services and configure it to use the WMSDE database.

- Create a Team Site in the root folder and open it in Internet Explorer.

When this is complete, you can begin using or modifying the new Team Site, creating additional sites, and so forth.

Specifying the Location of the WMSDE Database

By default, the Windows SharePoint Services setup program will install the WMSDE database at the following location:

C:\Program Files\Microsoft SQL Server\MSSQL$SHAREPOINT

If you want the database to reside elsewhere, perform the installation like this:

1   Download and unpack the Windows SharePoint Services installation files as directed in the section titled "Downloading and Unpacking the Installation Files," earlier in this chapter. However, click Cancel when the End User License Agreement wizard page appears.

2   Open a command prompt and change to the C:\Program Files\STS2Setup_1033 folder, replacing 1033 with your Locale ID if it's other than US English.

3   Start the setup program by typing a command such as:

```
setupsts.exe /datadir="<path>"
```

making sure that the path ends in a backslash. For example, to install the WMSDE database to the D:\SharePointDb\ directory, type the command:

```
setupsts.exe /datadir="D:\SharePointDb\"
```

The full path to the database will then be D:\SharePointDb\MSSQL$SHAREPOINT\.

4   Continue with the installation as directed in the previous section.

Specifying Command-Line Options for setupsts.exe

Table 13-1 summarizes all the command-line options for setupsts.exe, the Windows SharePoint Services setup program.

Table 13-1. setupsts.exe Command-Line Options

Property	Description
remotesql=yes/no	No, the default, specifies that setupsts.exe should install Windows SharePoint Services, install WMSDE, provision the SharePoint Central Administration server, and extend the first virtual server. Yes specifies that setupsps.exe should install Windows SharePoint Services and provision the SharePoint Central Administration server, but shouldn't install WMSDE or extend any virtual servers. Instead, you will manually extend virtual servers with Windows SharePoint Services and specify one or more existing SQL Server installations for each virtual server.
provision=yes/no	Yes specifies that setupsts.exe should provision the SharePoint Central Administration server. However, it won't extend the default virtual server or create a top-level Web site. No specifies that setupsts.exe won't perform any of these actions. Instead, you will later use the Stsadm.exe command-line tool.
/datadir="<path>"	Specifies where to install WSMDE databases. Set this property to a path on your local server.
/q or qn	Run setupsts in quiet mode (unattended setup with no user intervention).
/qb	Run setupsts in basic mode (limited user intervention). Includes a progress bar.
/qf	Run setupsts in full mode: the administrator must fill in options during setup. This is the default option.
/qr	Run setupsts in reduced mode. This means it displays a reduced user interface.
qn+	Run setupsts in quiet mode (unattended setup with no user intervention). Displays a Setup Complete dialog box at the end of the installation.
/qb+	Run setupsts in basic mode (limited user intervention). This includes a progress bar and, if the installation completes, a Setup Complete dialog box.
/qb-	Run setupsts in basic mode (limited user intervention). No Setup Complete dialog box will appear.
/x	Uninstall Windows SharePoint Services.

Note that the setupsts.exe program doesn't support all the standard setup options for Microsoft Windows Installer programs. For example, there's no /a option that creates an administrative installation point for Windows SharePoint Services.

You can, however, share a copy of the stsv2.exe program or the C:\Program Files\STS2Setup_1033 folder on a file server.

Although setupsts.exe accepts the /fulluninstall switch, it has no bearing, The /x switch does perform an uninstall, but Microsoft recommends using the Add Or Remove Programs control panel to uninstall Windows SharePoint Services.

Installing Windows SharePoint Services to Use SQL Server

Before installing Windows SharePoint Services to work with SQL Server, you must ensure that SQL Server is installed, up to date, and ready to host Windows SharePoint Services data. This includes not only the SQL Server software, but also the correct authentication method and the necessary privileges for the account that will run the Windows SharePoint Services application pools.

Enabling Windows Authentication for SQL Server

To ensure that the connection from Windows SharePoint Services to your SQL Server database is secure, Microsoft recommends configuring the database to use Windows authentication. Here's the necessary procedure.

1 Log on to the computer running SQL Server.

2 From the Windows Start menu, choose All Programs, SQL Server, and then Enterprise Manager.

3 When the SQL Server Enterprise Manager window appears, open the SQL Servers entry (click the plus sign that precedes it).

4 Within SQL Servers, open the SQL Server Group entry.

5 Right-click the SQL Server name, and then click Properties.

6 When the Properties dialog box appears, click the Security tab.

7 Under Authentication, select Windows Only. Figure 13-11 illustrates this selection.

8 Click OK.

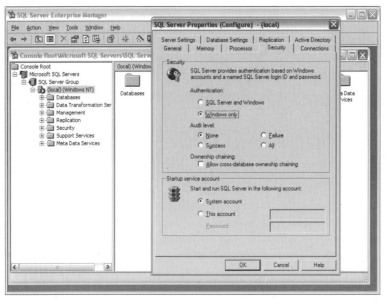

Figure 13-11. For maximum security, Microsoft recommends running SQL Server in Windows-Only authentication mode.

Granting Database Creation Rights in SQL Server

Any account that you assign to an application pool that runs Windows SharePoint Services must have certain rights on the SQL Server installation that hosts the SharePoint databases. To assign these rights, proceed as follows.

1 Log on to the computer running SQL Server.

2 From the Windows Start menu, choose All Programs, SQL Server, and then Enterprise Manager.

3 When the SQL Server Enterprise Manager window appears, open the SQL Servers entry (click the plus sign that precedes it).

4 Within SQL Servers, open the SQL Server Group entry.

5 Within SQL Server Group, open the entry for your server.

6 Within the entry for your server, open the Logins entry.

7 Right-click the Logins entry, and click New Login.

8 When the SQL Server Login Properties – New Login dialog box appears, make sure the General tab is selected. Then, in the Name box, type the account in the form domain\name. The left side of Figure 13-12 provides an illustration.

Microsoft Windows SharePoint Services Inside Out

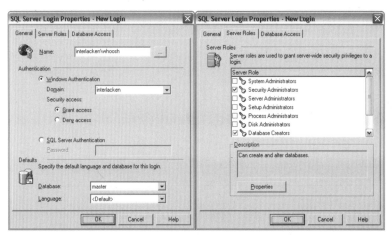

Figure 13-12. Security accounts you assign to application pools that run SharePoint virtual servers require these rights in SQL Server.

9   Click the Server Roles tab and then, as shown at the right side of Figure 13-12, select the following check boxes in the Server Role list box:

- Security Administrators
- Database Creators

10   Click OK to save your changes and close the dialog box.

After you configure the administrative virtual server (and grant SQL Server rights to the new application pool account, if necessary), you must restart Internet Information Services (IIS) by typing iisreset at the command line. When that completes, you can continue configuring your server.

Installing Windows SharePoint Services without Installing WMSDE

By default, the Windows SharePoint Services setup program installs WMSDE. To avoid installing WMSDE, you must override the setup program's Typical Installation option. Here's the procedure for doing this:

1   If this is your first installation, download and run the stsv2.exe program as directed in the section titled "Downloading and Unpacking the Installation Files" earlier in this chapter.

If you previously downloaded and ran stsv2.exe, open the C:\Program Files\STS2Setup_1033 folder (where 1033 is your Locale ID) and double-click setupsts.exe.

2   When the End-User License Agreement wizard page appears, carefully review the terms laid forth. If you agree, select the check box titled I Accept The Terms In The License Agreement and then click Next.

3   When the Type of Installation wizard page shown previously in Figured 12-4 appears, make sure Server Farm is selected, and then click Next.

Planning and Installing Windows SharePoint Services

If you want Server Farm to be the default, run setupsts.exe from the command line and specify remotesql=yes as shown below.

```
setupsts.exe remotesql=yes
```

4 When the Summary page appears, make sure that only Windows SharePoint Services will be installed, and then click Install.

5 The setup program will then:

- ■ Install Microsoft Windows SharePoint Services.

- ■ Create a new virtual server named SharePoint Central Administration, running on a randomly selected port number. This Web site configures SharePoint settings that apply to entire virtual servers or the entire computer.

- ■ Open the Configure Administrative Virtual Server page shown in Figure 13-13. This is a page in the new SharePoint Central Administration site.

As setupsts.exe performs these steps, the screen will occasionally be devoid of SharePoint-related dialog boxes. In addition, command line windows will occasionally open and close. Your role in all this is to wait patiently until the Configure Administrative Virtual Server page appears in your browser.

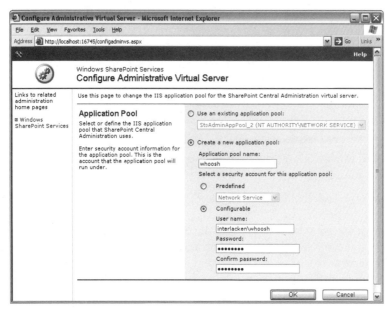

Figure 13-13. This page creates or assigns the application pool for the SharePoint Central Administration virtual server. If you choose to create a new application pool, you must give it a security account that has the privileges the virtual server needs.

After setupsts.exe completes, you must still perform the following tasks:

- Configure your administrative virtual server.
- Connect the administration site to a configuration database.
- Extend one or more virtual servers with Windows SharePoint Services.

The next three sections will explain how to perform these tasks.

Configuring the Administrative Virtual Server

The first step in configuring the SharePoint Central Administration server is to specify an application pool and, as a consequence, a user account. To begin, make sure the Configure Administrative Virtual Server page is displayed in your browser. Its URL is:

http://<server>:<port>/configadminvs.aspx

where *<server>* is the Web server's DNS name or IP address, and *<port>* is a random number that setupsts.exe assigns during installation.

> **Tip** If you don't know the port number for a SharePoint Central Administration server, start IIS Manager and view the server's properties. The port number appears on the Web Site tab.

The most secure (and therefore recommended) approach is to run the SharePoint Central Administration server in a new application pool using a dedicated account (that is, an account that serves no other purpose). To do this, proceed as follows:

1 In the Configure Administrative Virtual Server page shown previously in Figure 13-13, select the Create A New Application Pool option.

2 Type the name to use for the new application pool.

3 Specify whether to use a predefined or configurable security account for the application pool.

■ If you selected Predefined, select the security account to use.

If you want Windows SharePoint Services to run under a predefined account but use SQL Server running on a different machine, chose the Network Service account for Windows SharePoint Services and grant the Web server's machine account the Security Administrators and Database Creators roles in SQL Server.

■ If you selected Configurable, type the user name and password to use.

The account you use must be valid on the computer running Windows SharePoint Services *and* on each SQL Server computer that will host configuration or content databases. For that reason, it will usually be a domain account. In addition, that account must be a member of the Security Administrators and Database Creators roles on each of those SQL Servers.

Planning and Installing Windows SharePoint Services

> For instructions on granting the Security Administrators and Database Creators roles, refer to the
> section titled "Granting Database Creation Rights in SQL Server," earlier in this chapter.

If you decide to use an existing application pool, any other Web applications using that pool
will run under the same account as your Central Administration Server. This means they'll
have authority to modify the Windows SharePoint Services databases, and this poses a
security risk. If, nevertheless, you prefer to use an existing application pool, follow this
procedure:

1 Select the Use An Existing Application Pool option button.

2 Select the pool you want from the drop-down box.

Once you've specified a new, Predefined, or existing application pool, continue as follows:

1 Click OK to display the Application Pool Changed page shown in Figure 13-14.

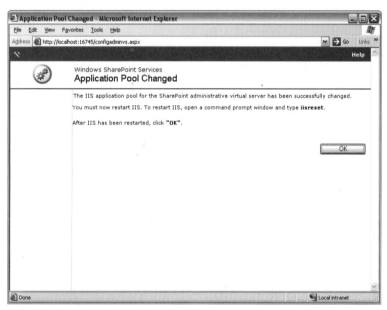

Figure 13-14. This page reports that a change to an application pool was
successful, and reminds you to restart IIS before proceeding.

2 If there are any error messages, click the browser's Back button and correct your
entries. Otherwise, open a command window and run the command:

```
iisreset
```

3 When the iisreset command finishes, click OK. This will display the Set Configuration
Database Server page. The next section will explain how to configure that page.

Connecting the Administration Site to a Configuration Database

This section explains how to configure the Set Configuration Database Server page shown in Figure 13-15. This page connects the SharePoint Central Administration site to a new or existing configuration database.

Figure 13-15. This Web page connects a Central Administration server to its configuration database. If necessary, it will also create that database.

This page cannot, however, create a configuration database that supports scalable hosting mode. If that's the mode you want, you'll need to create the configuration database by using the stsadm.exe command-line program.

> For instructions on using stsadm.exe to create a configuration database that supports scalable hosting mode, refer to the section titled "Creating the Configuration Database," later in this chapter.

To connect a SharePoint Central Administration server to a new configuration database that doesn't use scalable hosting mode, or to an existing configuration database, enter the following fields:

- **Database Server**   Type the network name and, if necessary, the instance name of the SQL Server installation that will host the configuration database that the SharePoint Central Administration server will use.

Planning and Installing Windows SharePoint Services

- **SQL Server Database Name**   Type the name of the configuration database.
- **Database Connection Type**   Select the type of authentication the SharePoint Central Administration server should use when connecting to the SQL server.

  - **Use Windows Authentication**   Select this option to use Windows authentication (and the application pool's username and password) when connecting to the database. Microsoft recommends this option.

  - **Use SQL Authentication**   Select this option to use SQL Server authentication when connecting to the database. Then, specify the SQL Server username and password to use. Microsoft doesn't recommend this approach because the username and password travel over the network with little or no encryption.

- **Connect To Existing Configuration Database**   Select this option if the database server and name you specified identify an existing SharePoint configuration database.

  If you intend to create a new configuration database, make sure this check box is cleared.

- **Users Already Have Domain Accounts**   Select this option if the team members who'll be using SharePoint sites on the current server already have accounts on the same Windows domain as the server, or on a trusted domain.

  This is the most common option for intranet installations of Windows SharePoint Services, because team members can use their existing Windows logon accounts.

- **Automatically Create Active Directory Accounts For Users Of This Site**   Select this option if the SharePoint team members don't already have domain or trusted accounts. Windows SharePoint Services will then create an account for each member as the need arises. If you select this option, you must also fill in the following boxes:

  - **Active Directory Domain**   Type the fully qualified name of the Active Directory domain where the SharePoint accounts will reside.

  - **Organizational Unit**   Type the Organizational Unit where the SharePoint accounts will reside.

  This is the most common option for installations accessible via the public Internet. Typically, you would store the accounts in an organizational unit that has no system logon privileges.

When all these entries are complete, click OK. This completes configuration of the SharePoint Central Administration server.

Extending a Virtual Server with Windows SharePoint Services and Connecting It to SQL Server

Once your Central Administration server is up, running, and connected to SQL Server, you can configure virtual Web servers to host Windows SharePoint Services sites. That is, you can *extend* virtual servers with Windows SharePoint Services.

Microsoft Windows SharePoint Services Inside Out

> **Tip** Before extending two or more virtual servers with Windows SharePoint Services on the same computer, refer to the precautions mentioned in "Planning Virtual Servers," earlier in this chapter.

To extend a virtual server, proceed as follows.

1 Browse the server's SharePoint Central Administration site. The URL will be:

   http://<server>:<port>/default.aspx

   where *<server>* is the server's DNS name or IP address, and *<port>* is a random number that setupsts.exe assigns during installation.

2 When the Central Administration page shown in Figure 13-16 appears, click Extend Or Upgrade Virtual Server.

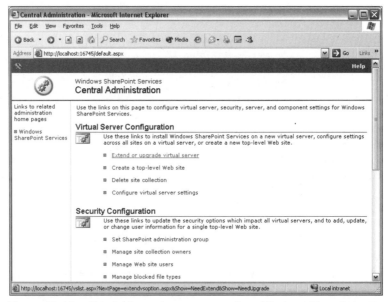

Figure 13-16. This is the main menu page for a Windows SharePoint Services Central Administration server. The Extend Or Upgrade Virtual Server link begins the process of extending a virtual server with Windows SharePoint Services.

3 When the Virtual Server List page shown in Figure 13-17 appears, click the name of the virtual server you want to extend.

Planning and Installing Windows SharePoint Services

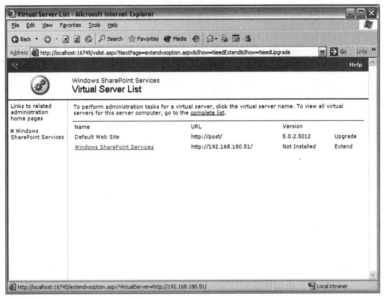

Figure 13-17. This page lists the virtual servers you can extend or upgrade with Windows SharePoint Services.

Note **SharePoint Version 5 Indicates FrontPage Server Extensions**

In Figure 13-17, the Virtual Server List page shows the Default Web Site server as having a SharePoint version of 5.0.2.5012, and proposes an action of Upgrade.

In fact, any version number beginning with 5 or lower indicates the FrontPage Server Extensions, a configuration you can't directly upgrade.

For more information about installing Windows SharePoint Services on a virtual server currently running the FrontPage Server Extensions, refer to the section titled "Preserving FrontPage-Based Content" earlier in this chapter.

---

4 When the Extend Virtual Server page shown in Figure 13-18 appears, under Provisioning Options, click Extend And Create A Content Database.

The Extend And Map To Another Virtual Server link extends the virtual server but connects it to another virtual server's content database. Both virtual servers will then deliver the same content.

Microsoft Windows SharePoint Services Inside Out

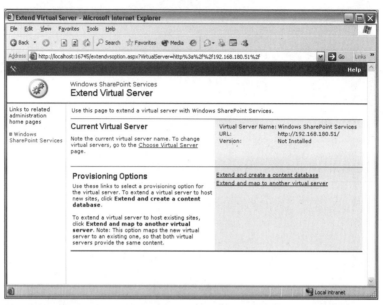

Figure 13-18. This page connects a virtual server to its content database.

5 The Extend And Create A Content Database page shown in Figure 13-19 will be next to appear. When it does, in the Application Pool section, select either of the following:

- **Use An Existing Application Pool** The newly extended virtual server will run in the same pool with other processes. This means your new SharePoint virtual server will share security and crash exposure with those processes.

   Other processes may have access to resources within your site.
   If another process brings down the pool, the SharePoint server you're extending will go down as well.

- **Create A New Application Pool** The newly extended virtual server will run in its own pool. This is the recommended setting.

   However, if you choose this setting, you'll need to specify the name of the application pool, plus the user name and password that the pool will use. This user name is typically a domain account that has the Run As A Service right on the computer. However, it doesn't need to have database creation rights in SQL Server. The Central Administration server will create any necessary databases.

Planning and Installing Windows SharePoint Services

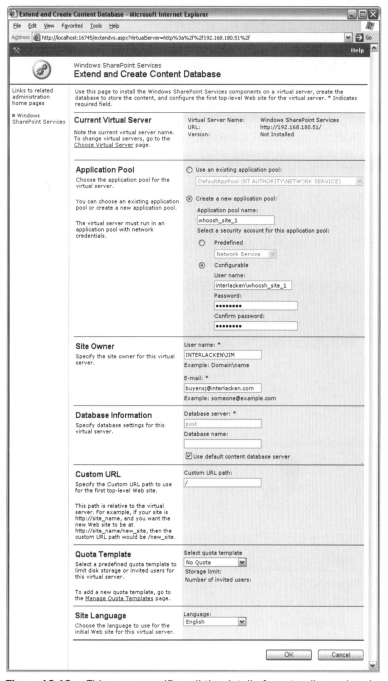

Figure 13-19. This page specifies all the details for extending a virtual server.

6 In the Site Owner section, type the site owner's username into the User Name text box. If this username belongs to a Windows domain, use the DOMAIN\username format.

Microsoft Windows SharePoint Services Inside Out

7 Type the site owner's E-mail address in the E-Mail box.

8 In the Database Information section take one of these actions:

- Select the Use Default Content Database Server check box.

- Clear the Use Default Content Database Server check box, and then type the database server name and database name to use for a new content database. For a WMSDE database, this will be the computer name followed by the word "SharePoint." For example: POST\SHAREPOINT.

9 In the Custom URL Path box, specify the location of the server's top-level Web site. The default (and normal choice) is to create the top-level Web site at the virtual server's root.

10 If you're using quotas, specify the quota template you want in the Quota Template section.

11 In the Site Language section, select the language you want to use.

12 Click OK. After a few moments, the Virtual Server Successfully Extended page shown in Figure 13-20 should appear.

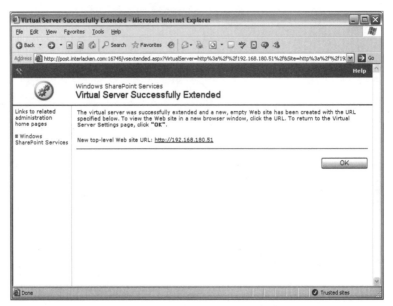

Figure 13-20. This page informs you that the extending a virtual server was successful.

Clicking the New Top-Level Web Site URL link on the Virtual Server Successfully Extended page will display the same Template Selection page that appears when you create a new SharePoint site any other way.

> For more information about using the Template Selection page, refer to the section titled "Selecting a Site Template," in Chapter 5.

Installing Windows SharePoint Services from the Command Line

In some situations, you may prefer to install Windows SharePoint Services using the command-line program stsadm.exe. from the command line. This might be attractive if, for example:

- You want to use scalable hosting mode. The SharePoint Central Administration Web pages don't provide all the options you need to complete this type of installation.
- You want to develop a batch file or script that repeats the installation on multiple computers.

The steps for installing Windows SharePoint Services from the command largely parallel those for installing it using the Web pages. Subsequent sections will explain each of these steps:

1 Install Windows SharePoint Services without WMSDE.
2 Create the Central Administration server application pool.
3 Configure SQL Server with permissions for Windows SharePoint Services.
4 Create the configuration database.
5 Specify the e-mail server settings.
6 Extend a virtual server.
7 Specify the host name for the first site (scalable hosting mode only).
8 Create a site.

Installing Windows SharePoint Services without WMSDE

To use Active Directory Account Creation mode, you must install Windows SharePoint Services without installing WMSDE. To do this, follow the procedure in the section titled "Installing Windows SharePoint Services Without Installing WMSDE" earlier in this chapter. However:

- When creating the administrative virtual server's application pool, specify that its application pool run under the account you created when you prepared the domain controller.
- Don't continue into the subsequent sections, such as, "Configuring the Administrative Virtual Server."

Instead, return to this point and continue by using the command-line operations that next few sections will describe.

Creating the Administration Virtual Server Application Pool

Unfortunately, the Web pages in the Central Administration site don't provide all the options you need to configure a physical server to operate in Host-Header (that is, Scalable Hosting) mode. Instead, you must do the job using a command-line utility named stsadm.exe. The Windows SharePoint Services setup program, setupsts.exe, installs stsadm.exe in the following folder:

C:\Program Files\Common Files\Microsoft Shared\web server extensions\60\BIN\

To use this program you should either change to that folder or add the folder name to your path environment variable.

> **Tip   Modify Your Path Setting**
>
> To change your path environment variable on Windows Server 2003, click Start, Control Panel, System, Advanced, Environment Variables, and then create or modify a path variable in the User Variables frame. Windows will append the user path to the system path the next time you log on.

To create the Central Administration server, assign a new application pool, and specify an application pool account and password, you run stsadm.exe with the -o setadminport option. The complete syntax appears below. Of course, to actually run the command, you would type it as one long line.

```
stsadm.exe -o setadminport
-port <port>
-admapcreatenew
-admapidname <apppoolid>
-admapidtype configurableid
-admapidlogin <domain\account>
-admapidpwd <password>
```

The variable arguments for this form of the stsadm.exe command are:

- *<port>*   The port on which the SharePoint Central Administration server will listen.
- *<apppoolid>*   The name of the application pool where the administration server will run.
- *<domain\account>*   The domain name and account name under which the Central Administration server will run.
- *<password>*   The password for the account you specified.

The following command, for example, creates a Central Administration server with these options in effect:

- The server will listen on port *2000*.
- The server will run in a new application pool named *whoosh*.
- The whoosh application pool will run under the user account *interlacken\whoosh*.
- The password for the interlacken\whoosh account is *password*.

```
Stsadm.exe -o setadminport -port 2000 -admapcreatenew -admapidname whoosh
-admapidtype configurableid -admapidlogin interlacken\whoosh -admapidpwd password
```

If you specified a application pool account that doesn't already have the Security Administrators, and Database Creators roles in SQL Server, you'll need to assign those roles now.

> For instructions on granting the Security Administrators, and Database Creators roles to an application pool account, refer to the section titled "Granting Database Creation Rights in SQL Server," earlier in this chapter.

Creating the Configuration Database

The next step is to create to the configuration database. To do this, you run stsadm.exe with the -o setconfigdb switch.

To create the configuration database in nonscalable hosting mode, use the following syntax:

```
stsadm.exe -o setconfigdb
-ds <dbserver>
-dn <dbname>
-adcreation
-addomain <domain>
-adou <ou>
```

The variable arguments are:

- *<dbserver>* The network name of the database server that will host the configuration database.
- *<dbname >* The name that you want the configuration database to have.
- *<domain>* Specifies the NETBIOS name of the domain (or the domain controller) where the team member accounts will reside. Don't specify a fully qualified domain name such as *ad.example.com*.
- *<ou>* Specifies the name of the organizational unit where the team member accounts will reside.

For example, the following command creates and assigns a configuration database with these properties:

- The database will reside in the SQL Server installation running on the computer *post*.
- The database name will be *whoosh*.
- The NETBIOS name of the active directory domain is *interlacken*.
- The user accounts will reside in an organizational unit named *sharepoint_ou*.

```
Stsadm.exe -o setconfigdb -ds post -dn whoosh -adcreation -addomain interlacken
-adou sharepoint_ou
```

To create the configuration database in scalable hosting mode, use the following syntax. This is identical to the previous syntax, except that the –hh switch is present.

```
stsadm.exe -o setconfigdb
-ds <dbserver>
-dn <dbname>
-hh
-adcreation
-addomain <domain>
-adou <ou>
```

Specify the E-Mail Server Settings

When using Active Directory Account Creation mode, you must specify an SMTP server, e-mail account, and codepage to use for sending invitation e-mail to new users. Figure 13-21 shows a typical invitation message.

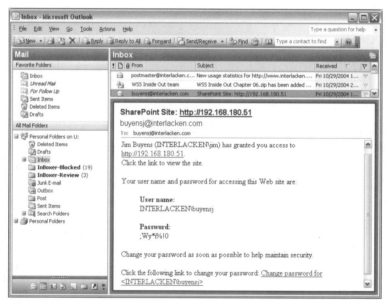

Figure 13-21. A message like this invites a new Active Directory Account Creation member to start using a SharePoint site, and provides an initial password for doing so.

This is the only way new users can get their initial, system-generated password. To specify e-mail server settings, you run stsadm.exe with the -o email switch. Here's the complete syntax.

```
stsadm.exe -o email
-outsmtpserver <SMTPserver>
-fromaddress <fromaddr>
-replytoaddress <replyaddr>
-codepage <codepage>
```

Planning and Installing Windows SharePoint Services

The variable arguments are:

- *<SMTPserver>*   The DNS name of your SMTP mail server.
- *<fromaddr>*   The e-mail address that will appear as the send of any invitation mail the server sends.
- *<replyaddr>*   The e-mail address that will appear in the To: field if a new team member replies to an invitation e-mail message.
- *<codepage>*   Identifies a translation from the Unicode character set that Window uses to an ANSI character set acceptable in e-mail. For example, 1252 is the code page for Windows 3.1 US (ANSI).

The command below configures these settings for sending invitation e-mail messages to new account holders.

- The SMTP mail server's DNS name is *smtp.west.cox.net.*
- The mail will appear to be from *buyensj@interlacken.com.*
- If a recipient clicks the Reply button, the mail program should address the message to *buyensj@interlacken.com.*
- The code page (that is, the characters set) for outgoing messages should be Windows 3.1 US (ANSI): that is, *1252.*

```
stsadm.exe -o email -outsmtpserver smtp.west.cox.net -fromaddress
buyensj@interlacken.com -replytoaddress buyensj@interlacken.com -codepage 1252
```

Extending a Virtual Server

Once you have a Central Administration server and a configuration database, you're ready to extend virtual servers with Windows SharePoint Services. To do this, you run stsadm.exe with the -o extendvs switch. In addition:

- If you're going to run the server in scalable hosting mode, you must specify a –donotcreatesite switch. This stops the extendvs operation from creating the first top-level Web site.

   Eventually, of course, you'll still need to create a top-level Web site. The section titled "Create a Site," which follows shortly, will explain how to do this.

- If you're not using scalable hosting mode, the –donotcreatesite switch is optional. However, if you omit it, you'll need to specify –ownerlogin to specify the site owner's logon account and –owneremail to identify the site owner's e-mail address.

Chapter 13

Here's the syntax for using the stsadm.exe program to extend a virtual server with Windows SharePoint Services:

```
stsadm.exe -o extendvs
-url <url>
-ds <dbserver>
-dn <dbname>
-donotcreatesite
-apcreatenew
-apidname <apppoolid>
-apidtype configurableid
-apidlogin <domain\account>
-apidpwd <password>
-ownerlogin <ownerlogin>
-owneremail <owneremail>
```

The variable arguments are:

- *<url>*   The new site's network location, such as http://whoosh.interlacken.com.
- *<dbserver>*   The network name of the database server that will host the content database.
- *<dbname >*   The name that you want the content database to have.
- *<apppoolid>*   The name of the application pool where the virtual server will run.
- *<domain\account>*   The domain name and account name to use for running the virtual server's application pool will run. Type this account in the format DOMAIN\name. Microsoft recommends using a different account from the one you used for the application pool for the administration virtual server.
- *<password>*   The password for the account you specified.
- *<ownerlogin>*   The login account of the site owner.
  - If you specify –donotcreatesite, don't specify –ownerlogin or –owneremail.
  - If you omit –donotcreatesite, you must specify –ownerlogin or –owneremail.
- *<owneremail>*   The e-mail address of the site owner.

The following command extends an existing virtual server with Windows SharePoint Services and creates a top-level site, putting these settings into effect.

- The virtual server's URL is *http://192.168.180.51.*
- The content database will reside in a SQL server instance on the computer *post.*
- The name of the content database will be *whoosh_site_1.*
- The virtual server will run in a new application pool named *whoosh_site_1.*
- The new application pool will run under an account named *interlacken\whoosh_site_1.*

  This account must also have permission to create, delete, and manage accounts in the organizational unit for Windows SharePoint Services.

Planning and Installing Windows SharePoint Services

- The password for the interlacken\whoosh_site_1 account is *password.*
- The e-mail address of the new root site's owner is *buyensj@interlacken.com.*

```
Stsadm.exe -o extendvs -url http://192.168.180.51 -ds post -dn whoosh_site_1
-apcreatenew -apidname whoosh_site_1 -apidtype configurableid -apidlogin
interlacken\whoosh_site_1 -apidpwd password -ownerlogin interlacken\karen
-owneremail buyensj@interlacken.com
```

Specifying a Host Name for the First Site (Scalable Hosting Mode Only)

For scalable hosting mode, you must create the first host-named site for each virtual server. To specify the host name for the site, open the \WINDOWS\system32\drivers\etc\hosts file and add an entry for the site. For example:

xxx.xxx.xxx.xxx www.example.com

where the x's are the IP address of the server. After the host name is configured, you can create a site.

Creating a Site (Scalable Hosting Mode Only)

You can create a site in either scalable or nonscalable hosting mode by running stsadm with the –o createsite switch. Here's the required syntax:

```
stsadm -o createsite -url http://www.example.com -owneremail
buyensj@interlacken.com
```

Be sure to supply a valid e-mail address after the owneremail switch. Windows SharePoint Services will use this address to when addressing account credentials to new team members.

Working with Your New Site

After setup finishes, your default Web site is extended with Windows SharePoint Services. Your browser window opens to the home page of your new Web site, and you can start adding content right away, or you can customize the site or set administrative options by using HTML Administration pages. Some actions you can take to get users working with your site are:

- Adding users to the site.
- Customizing the home page and other pages in the site.
- Setting up version control.

If you have more virtual servers to extend with Windows SharePoint Services, use the Web pages in the SharePoint Central Administration site.

> For more information about Configuring Windows SharePoint Services, refer to Chapter 14, "Configuring Windows SharePoint Services."

As always, be sure to reapply any recent service packs, and to run Windows Update to identify, download, and install the latest patches and fixes.

Addressing Further Scenarios

Microsoft designed Windows SharePoint Services to suit a truly wide range of environments. It supports such a wide range of installation scenarios, in fact, that this chapter can't describe all of them.

If your requirements fall outside the scenarios that do appear in this chapter, you may want to review the following scenarios on Microsoft's Web site.

- **Server Farm with Multiple Host Names Deployment**   In this configuration, a server farm can host several sites on the same virtual server, using the same IP address, but with multiple site names and separate content for each. For instructions on configuring this option browse:

  http://www.microsoft.com/resources/documentation/wss/2/all/adminguide/en-us/ stsc03.mspx

- **Configuring Two Virtual Servers to Host the Same Content**   In this configuration, a server farm provides the same content to two sites. Both sites share a single copy of the content: there's no duplication. For example, you could set up Internet and intranet servers that deliver the same content. For more information on this configuration, browse:

  http://www.microsoft.com/resources/documentation/wss/2/all/adminguide/en-us/ stsc04.mspx

- **Performing a Quiet Installation**   In this scenario, Windows SharePoint Services setup runs without any user intervention. The setupsts.exe program logs any messages or other output to a file in the Windows temp folder. This is useful for developing scripts that deploy Windows SharePoint Services across several servers. For more information browse:

  http://www.microsoft.com/resources/documentation/wss/2/all/adminguide/en-us/ stsd02.mspx

Chapter 13

Installing Language Template Packs

Windows SharePoint Services can create Team Sites and standard workspaces in over thirty languages. There are just two precautions to keep in mind:

- You must specify a language when you create a site, and then the language never changes. This means, for example:
    - You *can* create English sites for English-speakers and Lithuanian sites for Lithuanian-speakers, but
    - You *can't* create a site that switches languages automatically based on the language preference in the team member's browser.
- You must download and install a language pack for each language you want to use for creating sites.

To download and install a Windows SharePoint Services language pack, proceed as follows.

1 Browse the Microsoft download center at *http://www.microsoft.com/downloads/*.

2 In the Search For A Download section of the page:

   2.1 Select Windows SharePoint Services in the Product/Technology drop-down list.

   2.2 Type **language** in the Keywords box.

   2.3 Click the Go button.

3 When the Microsoft Download Center Search Results page appears, click Windows SharePoint Services 2.0 Language Template Pack.

4 When the Download Details page shown in Figure 13-22 appears, select the language you want from the drop-down list, and then click Go.

5 The Download Details page will now appear in the language you selected. Click the Download button (or, in the case of Polish, the Pobierz button) and save the resulting file in a convenient file share, or in a place on your SharePoint server.

6 Log on to the physical server running Windows SharePoint Services and run the file you downloaded in the previous step.

Microsoft Windows SharePoint Services Inside Out

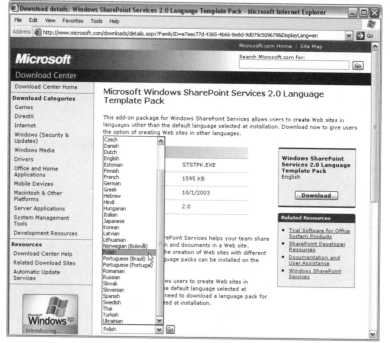

Figure 13-22. By using the language packs available from this Web page, you can create SharePoint sites in over thirty languages.

Inside Out

Keeping track of language packs

Unfortunately, Microsoft gives all SharePoint language packs the same file name: STSTPK.EXE. To avoid confusion after downloading you should rename them using some convention, such as STSTPK-Arabic.EXE, STSPK-Bulgarian.EXE, STSTPK-Polish.EXE, and so forth.

To use the new language capabilities, use your browser to create a new SharePoint site as usual. However, when you get to the New SharePoint Site page, specify the language you want in the Select Language dialog box. From that point on everything—including the template selection page—will appear in the language you specified. Figure 13-23, for example, shows a Team Site created in Polish.

Planning and Installing Windows SharePoint Services

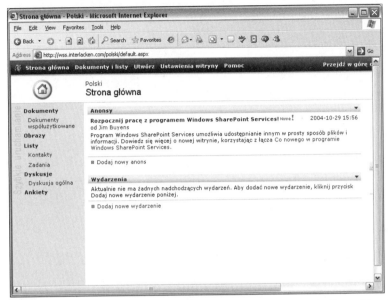

Figure 13-23. With the Polish language pack, you can create Team Sites like this.

In Summary...

This chapter explained the factors and choices you should review before installing Windows SharePoint Servers, and then explained how to install the product in the most common and likely scenarios.

The next chapter will explain how to backup and restore SharePoint sites, and how to migrate from SharePoint Team Services 1.0.

Backing Up, Restoring, and Migrating SharePoint Sites

For most people, every day brings its share of little surprises. An accountant in the Finance department hits a wrong key. A supervisor in Manufacturing deletes a wrong file. A sales representative in Marketing overwrites a critical document version. An engineer in Product Development needs a document from someone who left the company. A forklift driver from Shipping impales the SharePoint server. Oh well. That which does not kill us makes us stronger (Nietzsche).

On such occasions, no one was ever sorry to have a backup. This is such a known fact that Windows SharePoint Services provides three ways of making backups and, even better, restoring them. This chapter describes all three.

Backup/restore is also the best method of moving sites from one server to another, and for upgrading from SharePoint Team Services v1.0. Therefore, this chapter will address those situations as well.

Choosing a Backup Option for Windows SharePoint Services

Backing up a Windows SharePoint Services server is inherently more complex than backing up an ordinary Web server. This isn't an oversight; rather, it's because Windows SharePoint Services makes such heavy use of databases. Database are more complex than flat files—it's as simple as that.

Fortunately, you have a choice of approaches. You can back up and restore data for Windows SharePoint Services using any combination of these four methods:

- **Microsoft SQL Server 2000 Tools** If your SharePoint server is using a SQL Server database, you can use the backup tools that come with SQL Server 2000 to get a full-fidelity, complete backup of your SharePoint databases. Full-fidelity, in this case, means that a restore resurrects all Web pages, data, settings, and permissions that were present at the time of the backup. Here are the merits and drawbacks of this approach:

- Of the four backup and restore options, this is the most secure.

- To use this method, you must have a local administrator account on the server computer running SQL Server.

- This option isn't very granular. The smallest unit you can back up and restore is one configuration database, with all the content databases from sites using that configuration database. In other words, you have to back up or restore a whole server or server farm at once.

- This method doesn't work with WMSDE—Microsoft SQL Server 2000 Desktop Engine (Windows)—because WMSDE doesn't include the necessary backup tools.

- **The stsadm.exe Command-Line Tool**   This program has –o backup and –o restore options that can back up and restore one site collection at a time. Here are the advantages and disadvantages of this method.

   - You get a full-fidelity, complete backup or restore of an entire site collection.

   - This method doesn't require SQL Server 2000. It also works with WMSDE.

   - Because this is a command-line program, you can use it in batch files. Furthermore, you can run the program itself or the batch files from Windows Scheduler.

   - As with the previous method, you must have a local administrator account on the database server.

   Methods are available to run stsadm.exe –o backup automatically for every collection on a server, or for every collection that changed since the last backup, within the previous day, or within the pervious week.

- **The Microsoft SharePoint Migration Tool (smigrate.exe)**   This is a command-line program that can back up one site or tree of sites at a time. This method isn't full-fidelity; you may lose some customizations or settings in the process. For example, it doesn't restore security settings such as membership in site groups. However, it does offer these advantages.

   - To use this method, you don't need a local administrator account on the server. You only need to be in the Administrator group for the site or subsite.

   - You can use this method remotely. By running smigrate.exe on your PC, for example, you can back up and restore any sites you administer, regardless of the server's location.

- **Microsoft Office FrontPage 2003**   Choosing Server from the Tools menu in FrontPage 2003 reveals Backup Web Site and Restore Web Site commands that essentially duplicate the functions of the smigrate.exe command-line program. Using FrontPage for backup/restore offers these advantages:

   - The FrontPage GUI is more intuitive for team members unfamiliar with a command-line interface.

Backing Up, Restoring, and Migrating SharePoint Sites

- FrontPage will prompt you to supply missing or incorrect additional login credentials when there's a problem with the network connection. Smigrate.exe simply quits and makes you restart from scratch.

Smigrate.exe, however, has strong points as well.

- Network or site administrators can run smigrate.exe without installing or learning to use the FrontPage desktop software.

- Site administrators can use smigrate.exe in batch files and scripts that perform backups or restores.

In any event, the FrontPage and smigrate.exe backup file formats are identical. This means you can backup with smigrate.exe and restore with FrontPage, or vice versa, or any other combination.

> For more information about using FrontPage 2003 to backup and restore SharePoint sites, refer to the topics, "Backing Up a SharePoint Site," and, "Restoring a SharePoint Site," in Chapter 7.

Table 14-1 summarizes the scope, fidelity, and necessary permissions for each backup and restore method.

Table 14-1. Windows SharePoint Services Backup/Restore Methods

Method	Scope	Fidelity	Required permissions
SQL Server 2000 Backup and Restore	Entire server or farm	Full	Administrator on local server
stsadm.exe Backup and Restore	Site collection	Full	Administrator on local server
smigrate.exe SharePoint Migration Tool FrontPage 2003	Site or subsite	Some customizations or settings may not migrate. Doesn't migrate security settings.	Administrator of site or subsite

Backups are more difficult and expensive to run than you might suspect. Here are some of the reasons:

- In many cases, backups are the most resource-intensive processes that run on your server. Nothing else is likely to exercise your file system, your database, your CPU, and your network connection as hard as a backup program striving to access 100 percent of your data in minimum time.

- Secondary storage systems—whether tape or secondary disk—are expensive and labor-intensive. Being exposed to air and dust, tapes and tape drives are prone to physical error. In addition, tapes require operator handling, at least for off-site storage. Secondary disk systems require monitoring, management, and maintenance.

- Unless you back up directly to tape, each backup will probably require more physical disk space than the original data.

  If, for example, you have 4 GB of data, each full backup you keep online will probably consume another 5 GB of space.

To balance these factors you must consider the time importance of your data. For example:

- If you only back up once a week—on Saturday night, perhaps—how much would it cost your company if a failure or error occurred on Thursday and your restoration lacked three or four days activity?

- If the server became unusable and you had to rebuild it from scratch, what would be the cost per hour or cost per day of having the server unavailable?

These factors will, of course, vary from one organization to the next. Even within a single organization, they'll vary over time. As a result, no one backup schedule can possibly be right for every case. For starters, however, consider this approach:

- Take SQL Server backups every week or month, primarily for disaster recovery.

- Once a week, probably over the weekend or during some other period of minimal use, run stsadm –o backup for every site collection.

- Once a day, run stsadm –o backup for site collections that have changed.

When you run stsadm –o backup for a site collection, the result is a single flat file. Another factor, then, is whether you want to keep a week's worth of these flat files online. If some other process is backing up the server's file system, there may be no point in keeping multiple backups on the original server.

The next three sections will describe each backup method in more detail.

Backing Up and Restoring Databases Using the SQL Server 2000 Tools

If you're running Windows SharePoint Services on Microsoft SQL Server 2000, you can use the tools that come with SQL Server to back up and restore your SharePoint databases. However, the smallest unit you can back up or restore is an entire server or server farm.

To understand why this is so, remember that Windows SharePoint Services uses databases in two ways:

- **A Configuration Database** Stores all server and site configuration information. Most of the data you maintain in the Central Administration server goes into a configuration database. There's one configuration database per server or server farm.

- **Content Databases** Store the unique contents of each virtual server. However, if data volumes or activity levels warrant, a virtual server may spread its content across several content databases.

When you back up a SharePoint server or farm, you must back up its configuration database and all its content databases.

Backing Up WMSDE Databases

The WMSDE database that Windows SharePoint Services installs by default has no built-in capabilities for backup and restore. Instead, you must choose one of these approaches:

- Stop your SharePoint Web servers, stop WMSDE, copy the database files, and then restart WMSDE and your SharePoint Web servers.
- Use the stsadm.exe program described later in this chapter.
- Use the smigrate.exe program also described later.
- Investigate third-party backup agents.

If you install the client tools for SQL Server 2000 on the same server as WMSDE, the client tools can take backups. However, using the client tools this way requires a full SQL Server 2000 license, so you may as well upgrade to SQL Server.

If you want to upgrade from WMSDE to SQL Server, refer to the section titled "Upgrading a WMSDE Database to SQL Server" later in this chapter.

Backing Up Databases

A SharePoint Central Administration server and its configuration database needn't reside on the same physical server. To find the location of this database, proceed as follows:

1 Open the Home Page of the Central Administration virtual server.

If you don't know your Central Administration server's URL or port number, follow this procedure:

  1.1 Log on to the physical server.

  1.2 Open IIS Manager.

  1.3 Right-click the SharePoint Central Administration virtual server and choose Properties.

  1.4 Click the Web site tab. This will display the server's IP address and port number.

2 If a SharePoint Portal Server Central Administration page appears, click the Windows SharePoint Services link that appears at the left of the page, under Links To Related Administration Home Pages.

3 Under Server Configuration, click Set Configuration Database Server.

4 When the Set Configuration Database Server page shown in Figure 14-1 appears, the contents of the Database Server box and the SQL Server Database Name box will identify the configuration database. Write down these values.

Chapter 14

Microsoft Windows SharePoint Services Inside Out

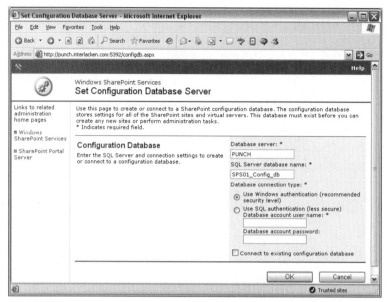

Figure 14-1. This Web page specifies and displays the configuration database for a Windows SharePoint Services server.

To find out which content databases the site is using, you need to inspect the configuration of each SharePoint virtual server that uses the given configuration database. Here's the procedure:

1 On the Central Administration home page, under Virtual Server Configuration, click Configure Virtual Server Settings.

2 When the Virtual Server List page shown in Figure 14-2 appears, take note of which virtual servers are acting as Windows SharePoint Services content servers. In the figure, for example:

   ■ Default Web Site and WSS site are SharePoint content servers. You can recognize this by their version numbers, which begin with a 6, and by the fact that they're not Central Administration servers.

   ■ Microsoft SharePoint Administration is a Central Administration server. That's why, after its version number, the message Not Administrable appears.

   ■ FrontPage Site is a server running the FrontPage Server Extensions. You can recognize this by its version number, which is lower than 6.

   ■ Vanilla is a virtual server running neither Windows SharePoint Services nor the FrontPage Server Extensions. That's why Not Installed appears rather than a version number.

3 Click the server name of first content server. For example, in Figure 14-2, click Default Web Site.

4 When the Virtual Server Settings page appears, under Virtual Server Management, click Manage Content Databases.

Backing Up, Restoring, and Migrating SharePoint Sites

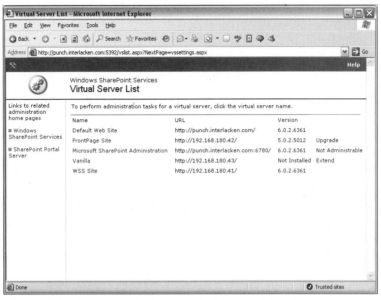

Figure 14-2. This page displays a clickable list of virtual servers that a Central Administration site controls.

5 When the Manage Content Databases page shown in Figure 14-3 appears, click the first name that appears in the Database Name column.

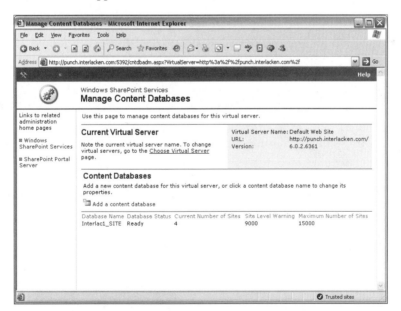

Figure 14-3. This page displays and modifies the list of content databases assigned to a SharePoint virtual server.

6 When the Manage Content Database Settings page appears, the contents of the Database Server box and the SQL Server Database Name box will identify the content database. Write down these values.

7 Click the browser's Back button, and then repeat steps 5 and 6 for each additional database name.

8 Click the browser's Back button twice more, to get the Virtual Server List page, and then repeat steps 3 to 7 for each additional content server.

When you finish this procedure, you'll have a list of all the SQL Server databases you need to back up. For instructions on actually performing these backups, consult your SQL Server documentation. Other than backing up all the right databases, backing up SharePoint SQL Server databases involves no special procedures or precautions.

Keep in mind, however, that SharePoint sites contain preference and other personal data about team members. Backup files therefore contain such data as well. You must ensure that backup files don't fall into the wrong hands. In addition, team members should be aware that the data will be on retention, and that administrators—bound by company policy—will have access to it.

Restoring from a Backup

Restoring a SQL Server backup for Windows SharePoint Services is a fairly major operation. Basically, you must recreate (or overwrite) the entire original operating environment. At a high level, this involves the following steps.

1 On one or more servers, as appropriate, install IIS and create as many virtual Web servers as you need to host your SharePoint content.

The number of physical and virtual servers you need to create will vary depending on the reason for the restoration. If you're moving a site for performance reasons, the new environment may have more or fewer servers than the old one. If you're restoring just to get a few sites back, a single server may be adequate to restore a site that required many servers in production.

2 Using the SQL Server restore tools, restore the databases from the backups. Again, the assignments of databases to database servers may be different than in production.

3 Create one or more Windows domain accounts for use by application pools. Then, make sure these accounts are members of the Security Administrators and Database Creators roles in SQL Server.

4 Install Windows SharePoint Services, thus creating a Central Administration server. Be sure to install the version of Windows SharePoint Services, with all the same options, that was in effect at the time of the backup. For example, you must choose the same account mode, the same hosting mode, and you must install any language packs that were in use.

You must also reapply any local changes you made to the Web server or Windows SharePoint Services. This might include, for example:

- Custom style sheets
- Custom site templates
- Content areas that you flagged as excluded paths

In short, reproduce the SharePoint environment as it was at the time of the database backup.

5 Extend each content server with Windows SharePoint Services. On the Extend Virtual Server page:

- First try choosing the Extend And Map To Another Virtual Server option. Then, under Server Mapping, choose the site whose content you want the virtual server to deliver.
- If that command won't complete, use the Extend And Create A Content Database option, and let it create a new empty database.

In either case, specify the application pool account that you created for this server in step 3.

If you're still not connected to the correct content databases:

5.1 Display the Manage Content Databases page previously shown in Figure 14-3.

5.2 Click Add A Content Database and add the content database you want.

5.3 Click the name of any content database you don't want. Then when the Manage Content Database Settings page appears, select Remove Content Database and click OK.

When you've completed these steps, your restoration is complete. All sites included in your backup should be functioning again, complete with the site content, users, and settings as they were when the sites were backed up.

If you restored the SharePoint site to an offline or temporary server, and now you need to transfer one or more sites back to the production environment, you can do so using:

- **FrontPage 2003**   For information on this approach, refer to these topics in Chapter 7:
  - Exporting SharePoint Packages
  - Importing SharePoint Packages
  - Backing Up a SharePoint Site
  - Restoring a SharePoint Site
- **stsadm.exe or smigrate.exe**   The next two sections explain how to use these tools.

Backing Up and Restoring Sites with stsadm.exe

Windows SharePoint services comes with a command-line program that can back up and restore one site collection at a time. There are several advantages to using this program:

- It works with any kind of database.
- Each backup file represents one site collection. This divides the backup into manageable units of content.
- Each backup creates a single file in the server's file system. This file retains all the sites in the collection, including all Web pages, all files in document libraries, all lists, and all security, permission, and feature settings.
- A restored backup can replace the original collection, or create a new one.
    - Replacing a collection is more appropriate if someone accidentally deleted it, or the collection became hopelessly corrupted.
    - Restoring to a new location is more appropriate if you only want to recover selected content. Team members will be able to access both the original and restored sites, and therefore recover just the information they need.
- Because stsadm.exe is a command-line program, you can run it in batch files or scripts. In addition, you can run the program itself, batch files that call it, or scripts that call it from Windows Scheduler.

Of course, there are limitations to the stsadm.exe backup/restore method as well. They are:

- Each time you run stsadm.exe, you must back up or restore exactly one site collection: that is, exactly one top-level site and all its subsites. You can't back up or restore an entire server, nor can you back up or restore a single subsite.

    Of course, if your server contains 10, 100, or 1000 top-level sites, you can run stsadm.exe 10, 100, or 1000 times to take all the backups.

- Backup and restore operations are inherently memory-intensive, processor-intensive, and disk-intensive. If you choose to schedule automatic backups, make sure they run during periods of least usage.
- To perform backups or restores using the stsadm.exe program, you must have an account that's one of the following:
    - A member of the physical server's Administrators group
    - A member of the SharePoint Administrators group
- Stsadm.exe backup and restore is generally the best method for moving a Windows SharePoint Services site from one server to another. However:
    - To migrate a SharePoint Team Services 1.0 site to Windows SharePoint Services, or to create backup files compatible with FrontPage 2003, use the Microsoft SharePoint Migration Tool, smigrate.exe.
    - To back up or restore team or personal sites on a machine running SharePoint Portal Server 2003, you should use the spsbackup.exe utility for disaster recovery or portal-specific needs, and smigrate.exe to export, import, or migrate personal or team sites.

Backing Up, Restoring, and Migrating SharePoint Sites

- The stsadm.exe program won't restore a like-named collection from a different server. Suppose, for example, that:
    - Servers Budapest and Djakarta both contain site collections named *sites/bart.*
    - You run stsadm.exe and back up *http://budapest.example.com/sites/bart.*
    - You run stsadm,exe again and try to restore *http://djakarta.example.com/sites/bart.*

    The restore won't replace the *sites/bart* collection on Djakarta because the *sites/bart* collection in the backup file came from a different server.

- To successfully restore a site, the receiving server must provide the appropriate language packs. Otherwise, team members who browse the collection will receive a File Not Found error.

- If you back up a collection on a server that's running in Active Directory Account Creation mode, you must restore it to a server that's running in Active Directory Account Creation mode. The converse is also true. If you back up a collection from a server that's *not* running in Active Directory Account Creation mode, you can't restore it to a server that *is* running in Active Directory Account Creation mode.

- If you restore a collection to a different location on the same server, be very careful running both collections simultaneously. This is because:
    - Team members who have access to the original site have equal access to the restored site.
    - Any user management you perform on one site will apply to the other site.

- When deleting either the original or restored collection from a site running in Active Directory Account Creation mode, use the stsadm.exe program and specify the -deleteadaccounts false option. Otherwise, as the second sub-bullet just above warned you, all the team members will disappear from both sites. Here's an example:

```
stsadm.exe -o deletesite -url http://budapest.example.com/restores/bart
-deleteadaccounts false
```

Checking for Active Directory Account Creation Mode

To determine if a SharePoint server is running in Active Directory Account Creation mode, open a command prompt on the server, type the following command, and then press Enter:

```
stsadm.exe -o getproperty -pn createadaccounts
```

- A response of <Property Exist="Yes" Value="Yes" /> indicates that Windows SharePoint Services is in Active Directory Account Creation mode.

- A response of <Property Exist="Yes" Value="No" /> indicates that Windows SharePoint Services is not in Active Directory Account Creation mode.

Backing Up Individual Site Collections

To back up a site collection, you use the backup operation with the stsadm.exe command-line tool. The backup operation takes the parameters listed in Table 14-2.

Table 14-2. Stsadm.exe Backup/Restore Parameters

Parameter	Required	Description
-filename	Yes	The name of the backup, such as backup.spb.
-url	Yes	The URL of the site collection. For example, *http://server_name/site*.
-overwrite	No	If this parameter is absent, backups won't overwrite existing files, and restores won't replace existing collections. Instead, the operation will stop. If the parameter is present, backups will overwrite existing files and restores will replace existing collections.

The -filename parameter can specify a name for the output file in any of three ways.

- As a filename, such as backup.spb
- As a path on the local hard disk, such as c:\backups\backup.spb
- As a path on a network share, such as \\share\folder\backup.spb

The following command backs up a site collection at *http://budapest.example.com/sites/bart* and saves the result in a new file named C:\backups\budapest_bart.spb.

```
stsadm.exe -o backup -url http://budapest.example.com/sites/bart -filename
c:\backups\budapest_bart.spb
```

To back up the same site and overwrite an existing backup file, you would use this command:

```
stsadm.exe -o backup -url http://budapest.example.com/sites/bart -filename
c:\backups\budapest_bart.spb -overwrite
```

Troubleshooting

Stsadm.exe doesn't recognize DNS names

The stsadm.exe program doesn't look up host names in DNS; it only looks for them in the local IIS metabase. As a result, it will only resolve hostnames you've configured in IIS as a host header value. To configure a hostname as a header value:

1 In IIS Manager, right-click the virtual server and choose Properties.

2 On the Web Site tab, click Advanced.

3 In the Advanced Web Site Identification dialog box, click Add.

4 In the Add/Edit Web Site Identification dialog box, specify the virtual server's IP address, its port, and the name you want to use in the stsadm.exe command.

Selecting Site Collections for Automatic Backup

To use the stsadm.exe program and back up an entire SharePoint server, you must run the program once for each top-level site. In order to prepare for that, you'll need a list of all the top-level sites on the SharePoint server. Fortunately, stsadm.exe has an enumsites operation that can display this information. Simply log on to the server and run a command such as this:

```
stsadm.exe -o enumsites -url http://192.168.180.41
```

This produces output such as the following, which is in XML format.

```
<Sites Count="5">
  <Site Url="http://192.168.180.41" Owner="INTERLACKEN\jim" />
  <Site Url="http://192.168.180.41/sites/buyensj" Owner="INTERLACKEN\jim" />
  <Site Url="http://192.168.180.41/sites/ed" Owner="INTERLACKEN\ed" />
  <Site Url="http://192.168.180.41/sites/fieldsvc" Owner="INTERLACKEN\jim" />
  <Site Url="http://192.168.180.41/sites/karen" Owner="INTERLACKEN\karen" />
</Sites>
```

If you wanted, you could use this information to create five stsadm.exe –o backup commands, put them in a batch file, and configure Windows Scheduler to run the batch file every night, or twice a week, or at some other frequency.

Running an stsadmin Backup Script

Unfortunately, keeping that batch file up to date will likely be difficult. First, any administrator who creates a top-level site must remember to update the batch file as well. And second, if you've turned on self-service site creation, anyone with a logon account can create top-level sites.

Microsoft Windows SharePoint Services Inside Out

To solve such problems, you can run a script like the one below. In fact, a copy of this script appears on the companion CD. The location is <*drive*>:\utils\WssBackup\wssbackup.vbs, where <*drive*> is the letter of your CD-ROM drive.

```
01 Option Explicit
02 Const BU_FOLDER = "C:\wssbackup\files\"
03 Const BU_SERVER = "http://192.168.180.41"
04 Const STSADM_PATH = "C:\Program Files\Common Files\Microsoft Shared\Web
   server extensions\60\BIN\stsadm"
05 Dim objFso
06 Dim objFolder
07 Dim objFiles
08 Dim objFile
09 Dim objShell
10 Dim objExec
11 Dim strResult
12 Dim objXml
13 Dim objSc
14 Dim objUrl
15 Dim strUrl
15 Dim strFileName
17 Dim strCmd
18 Dim tstLog
19
20 Set objFso = CreateObject("Scripting.FileSystemObject")
21 Set objFolder = objFso.GetFolder(BU_FOLDER)
22 Set objFiles = objFolder.Files
23
24 Set tstLog = objFso.OpenTextFile(BU_FOLDER & "log.txt", 8, true)
25 tstLog.WriteLine vbCrLf & Now() & " " &  "Backup starting."
26
27 ' Delete all backup files currently present in the backup folder.
28 For Each objFile in objFiles
29   If objFile.Name <> "log.txt" Then
30     objFile.Delete(True)
31   End If
32 Next
33
34 ' Retrieves all site collections in XML format.
35 Set objShell = CreateObject("WScript.Shell")
36 Set objExec = objShell.Exec(STSADM_PATH & _
37                 " -o enumsites -url " & BU_SERVER)
38 strResult = objExec.StdOut.ReadAll
39 tstLog.WriteLine String(50, "-")
40 tstLog.WriteLine vbCrLf & Now() & " enumsites:" & strResult
41
42 ' Load XML in DOM document so it can be processed.
43 Set objXml = CreateObject("MSXML2.DOMDocument")
44 objXml.LoadXML(strResult)
45
46 ' Loop through each site collection and call stsadm.exe to make a backup.
47 For Each objSc in objXml.DocumentElement.ChildNodes
48     strUrl = objSc.Attributes.GetNamedItem("Url").Text
49     strFileName = BU_FOLDER & _
```

Backing Up, Restoring, and Migrating SharePoint Sites

```
50          Replace(Replace(strUrl, "http://", ""), "/", "_") & ".spb"
51       strCmd = STSADM_PATH & " -o backup -url """ & strUrl & _
52                """ -filename """ & strFileName & """"
53       tstLog.WriteLine vbCrLf & Now() & " " & strCmd
54       objShell.Exec(strCmd)
55  Next
56
56  tstLog.WriteLine vbCrLf & Now() & " " &  "Backup successful."
57  tstLog.close
```

To use this script, proceed as follows:

1 Copy the wssbackup.vbs file from the \utils\WssBackup\ folder on the companion CD to a folder on your SharePoint server. For example, create a WssBackup folder on the server and copy the file there.

2 In Windows Explorer, right-click the wssbackup.vbs file and choose Properties. If the Read-Only check box on the General tab is selected, clear it.

3 Open the wssbackup.vbs file in Microsoft Notepad (or any other text editor). Then, on lines 2 to 4, change the values of these constants:

- **BU_FOLDER**   Specify the folder location where you want the backup files to appear. Don't forget the trailing backslash, and make sure the folder already exists. The script won't create it.

- **BU_SERVER**   Specify the URL of the virtual server you want to back up. This must be the name of the site as registered in the configuration database. Don't specify a trailing slash.

- **STSADM_PATH**   Specify the full pathname of the stsasm.exe program. The default value is usually correct.

Here are the major functions that each section of this script performs.

- Lines 5 to 18 define variables that the rest of the script uses.

- Lines 20 to 22 create an object that can perform file operations, create an object that represents the folder you specified in the BU_FOLDER constant, and create an object that represents the files in that folder.

- Lines 24 and 25 open a log file in append mode and write a message stating that the script has started.

- Lines 27 to 32 delete any existing files in the backup folder. If you'd rather retain those files, you can delete these lines.

- Lines 34 to 40 run the stsadm –o enumsites command and capture the output XML in a string named *strResult*.

- Lines 42 to 55 load the XML in the *strResult* variable into an XML Document object, extract each top-level site URL, and run stsadm.exe –o backup for each URL.

The name of the backup file will be that of the top-level site's URL, minus the http:// prefix, plus the backup folder prefix, changing all other slashes to underscores, and adding a .spb filename extension. Thus, the backup file for

http://budapest.example.com/sites/bart

would be

C:\wssbackup\files\budapest.example.com_sites_bart.spb

Note specifically that lines 51 and 52 construct the stsadm.exe –o backup command. If you deleted lines 27 to 32, you should probably append the –overwrite switch here, as shown below.

```
51      strCmd = STSADM_PATH & " -o backup -url """ & strUrl & _
52                  """ -filename """ & strFileName & """ -overwrite"
```

Figure 14-4 shows how to configure the Windows Task Scheduler to run the script.

Figure 14-4. The Scheduled Tasks control panel applet can run batch files or scripts that back up SharePoint sites.

In this figure:

- cscript is the console version of the Windows Scripting Host processor.
- C:\wssbackup\wssbackup.vbs is the full pathname of the script.
- In the Start In box, C:\wssbackup specifies the current folder when the script starts.
- Run As specifies the account under which the script will run. This account doesn't need to be an administrator on the local server, but it must meet these requirements:

    - Be a member of the Administrators group for the SharePoint server.
    - Be a member of the Users group on the local computer.
    - Have Read permission to the folder where the script resides.

Backing Up, Restoring, and Migrating SharePoint Sites

- Have Change permission to the folder where the log files will appear.
- Hold the Log On As A Batch Job user right. You configure this in the Local Security Policy administrative tool.

The Schedule tab, of course, controls the dates and times when the script will run.

Backing Up Changed Collections

If backing up all the SharePoint sites on your server is too resource-intensive or excessive in some other way, you may prefer taking incremental backups. This means backing up only those sites that had changes in the past day or week.

To do this, you need another command-line program called spbackup.exe. This program comes with the Microsoft SharePoint Products and Technologies Resource Kit. The program doesn't make backups itself, but it creates a batch file of stsadm.exe –o backup commands for all site collections that match criteria you specify.

 On the CD The spbackup.exe program is also available from the companion CD. The location is *<drive>*:\utils\SPBackup\, where *<drive>* is the letter of your CD-ROM drive.

To install spbackup.exe, you copy it into the same folder as stsadm.exe. Then, to run it, you use this syntax.

```
spbackup {-a | -d | -w} [-f <filename>]
```

where

- You must specify one of these switches:
  - -a To create a file that backs up all site collections.
  - -d To create a file that backs up all site collections that had changes in the past day.
  - -w To create a file that backs up all site collections that had changes in the past week.
- The -f *<filename>* argument optionally specifies the name of the output batch file. The default is SPBakOut.Bat.

Here, for example, is a typical spbackup command. It creates a batch file named weekly.bat that backs up all SharePoint collections on the local physical server that changed during the preceding seven days.

```
spbackup -w -f weekly.bat
```

Running the weekly.bat file would then create all the backup files, in whatever folder was current at the time.

To automate daily incremental backups, you would write a batch file similar to the one shown below.

```
C:
cd \spbackup\files\
"C:\Program Files\Common Files\Microsoft Shared\Web server
extensions\60\BIN\spbackup.exe" -d
spbakout.bat
```

This presumes that the batch file itself resides in the C:\spbackup folder, and that you want the backup files to go in the C:\spbackup\files folder. You could run this batch file from Windows Scheduler using the techniques—including the user account privileges—that the previous section described.

Restoring Site Collections

To restore a site collection, you run stsadm.exe with the –o restore option. Just as for backups, you must also specify these arguments:

- **-filename**   Specifies the name of the backup file you want to restore.
- **-url**   Specifies the location of the top-level site where the restoration will appear.
- **-overwrite**   If present, replaces the entire contents or the site collection that begins at the URL you specified.

When you specify the top-level site URL, you have a choice of three scenarios. These are:

- You can replace the contents of an existing site collection with the contents of the backup.

  This is a dangerous approach because it completely deletes the existing site collection. It *doesn't* somehow merge the backup and the live site. The top-level site and all its subsites revert to their state at the time of the backup.

- You can restore a collection to a new collection on the same server.

  This is usually the best option, especially if you're restoring the collection to recover a few data items, because it doesn't overwrite anything After the restore, you or the site owner can simply copy the necessary data out of the restored collection.

  When restoring collections to a new location, you must ensure that the new location has included and excluded paths similar to the old location. If, for example, you backed up the /sites/carnival collection and want to restore it as /restores/carnival, you'd have to ensure that /restores/ is a managed include path.

- You can restore a collection to a separate virtual or physical server. That server, however, must use the same configuration database (or a copy) as the server that hosted the backed-up collection.

  This is a more complicated scenario because it requires configuring a second server identical to the one where you took the backup. However, it does reduce the risk of accidentally overwriting data, and you can use the Site Use Confirmation And Automatic Deletion feature to automatically remove the collection after a specified time period.

> The Site Use Confirmation And Automatic Deletion feature is configurable only at the virtual server level. For more information about this feature, refer to "Configuring Virtual Server Settings" in Chapter 15.

To restore the backup file backup.spb and create a new collection at *http://nairobi.example.com/sites/beach*, you would code the stsadm.exe command like this:

```
stsadm.exe -o restore -filename backup.spb -url http://nairobi.example.com/sites/
beach
```

To restore the same file and replace an existing collection at *http://algiers.example.com/sites/oasis*, you would code:

```
stsadm.exe -o restore -filename backup.spb -url http://algiers.example.com/sites/
oasis -overwrite
```

Migrating and Upgrading Web Sites

Microsoft provides a second tool that can back up and restore SharePoint sites, namely the SharePoint Migration Tool, smigrate.exe. This tool differs from the backup and restore operations in stsadm.exe in that:

- You can back up and restore sites over the network. For example, running smigrate.exe on a Windows XP workstation, you can back up a site on one SharePoint server and restore it to another.

- You can back up a single site or any tree of sites. It makes no difference whether the starting site is a top-level site or not.

- With smigrate.exe, you can back up SharePoint Team Services v1.0 sites (such as the one shown in Figure 14-5) as well as Windows SharePoint Services sites. This provides a way to migrate SharePoint Team Services v1.0 sites to Windows SharePoint Services sites.

- You needn't be a server administrator to run smigrate.exe. You only need to be a site administrator for the source and destination sites.

> **Tip** You can run the SharePoint Migration Tool on any computer running Microsoft Windows 2000 Service Pack 3 or later, even if Windows SharePoint Services isn't installed.

You should consider using the Microsoft SharePoint Migration Tool (smigrate.exe) in either of the following situations.

- You're the administrator of a server that's been running SharePoint Team Services v1.0 for some time, and now you want to move the content to a server running Microsoft Windows SharePoint Services.

Microsoft Windows SharePoint Services Inside Out

- You're not a server administrator, but you *are* the administrator of one or more sites Running Windows SharePoint Services. Furthermore, you want to back up or relocate one or more SharePoint sites yourself. For example:

  - You might want to back up a Windows SharePoint Services Team Site at some critical point in a project.

  - You might be moving a Windows SharePoint Services site from one Internet Service Provider to another.

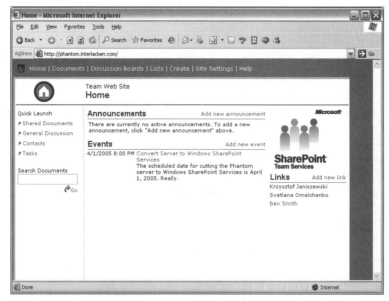

Figure 14-5. This is the home page of a SharePoint Team Services v1.0 site, ready for migration to Windows SharePoint Services.

> To perform large-scale migrations from one Windows SharePoint Services server to another, the backup and restore operations in stsadm.exe will generally be simpler and more robust. For more information on this approach, refer to the section titled "Backing Up and Restoring Sites with stsadm.exe" earlier in this chapter.

As when using stsadm.exe, migrating a site using the SharePoint Migration Tool involves two separate operations.

- First, you back up the site to a file. In so doing, you specify:

  - The URL of the starting Web site.

  - The name of the backup file to create.

  - The scope of the backup. You can back up either a single site or a starting site and all its subsites.

Backing Up, Restoring, and Migrating SharePoint Sites

- Then, you restore the file to a new site. This time you specify:

  - The name of the backup file to restore.
  - The URL of the target Web site.
  - Parameters that specify which security and site settings the restore should try to preserve.

Using smigrate.exe to back up and restore a site may result in some loss of fidelity. Usually, this is a result of two factors.

- SharePoint Team Services v1.0 and Windows SharePoint Services have somewhat different security models. Therefore, some permissions you had in effect for SharePoint Team Services may appear differently or be absent in Windows SharePoint Services.

- A smigrate.exe backup stores user names as text strings. If:

  - The target SharePoint server *isn't* using Active Directory Account Creation mode, and
  - Windows SharePoint Services can't locate a migrated username,

  then the username in the target site will either:

  - Be blank (for example, in lookup fields), or
  - Be the username of the person who performed the migration (as in the owner name of library document).

  Such issues usually arise when you migrate from SharePoint Team Services (which often used local server accounts rather than domain accounts) or when you migrate from one Windows domain to another.

Table 14-3 summarizes the parameters you can specify when running the smigrate.exe program.

Table 14-3. smigrate.exe Backup/Restore Parameters

Parameter	Description	Type	Explanation
–w	Web site URL.	Required	A valid URL, such as http://kathmandu.example.com/taxis or https://kathmandu.example.com/banks.
–f	The name of the backup file.	Required	A simple filename, the full path to a filename, of a UNC name such as \\kathmandu\folder\backup.fwp. If you don't supply an extension, smigrate will append .fwp.
–r	Restores a site to a new location.	Optional	Valid only for restores.
–e	Excludes subsites during backup.	Optional	Valid only for backups.

Table 14-3. smigrate.exe Backup/Restore Parameters

Parameter	Description	Type	Explanation
–x	Excludes security during restore.	Optional	Valid only when migrating from SharePoint Team Services v1.0 to Windows SharePoint Services.
–y	Overwrites an existing backup file.	Optional	Valid only for backups.
–u	The user name of a Web site administrator.	Optional	A valid user name, in the form DOMAIN\name.
–pw	The password for the Web site administrator.	Optional	A valid password. Use "*" to be prompted to type a password.

The –u and –pw parameters warrant some additional explanation.

- If you're running smigrate.exe on a server that has Internet Explorer Enhanced Security in effect, you must specify the -u and -pw parameters.
- You must also specify -u and -pw if the virtual Web server is configured to use Basic Authentication only.
- In any other case, if the account you logged on with has sufficient rights to perform the backup or restore, smigrate.exe will ignore the –u and –pw parameters. If you want to perform the migration using a specific account, do one of these:
  - Log on with that account before migrating.
  - Change your Internet settings to avoid automatic logon, that is, so your computer doesn't automatically try to use your Windows logon account.

When performing large-scale migrations, you may wish to create and use an account dedicated to that purpose. That way, if the SharePoint Migration Tool can't validate an author or last-modified-by account, it will substitute the name of the dedicated account rather than yours. For example, if you create an account named *SharePoint Migration* and then use that account to restore a site, team members will see *SharePoint Migration* as the author of list items whose author was unavailable.

Backing Up a Site with smigrate.exe

The Windows SharePoint Services setup program installs smigrate.exe in the same folder as stsadmin.exe, that is, in the \Program Files\Common Files\Microsoft Shared\Web Server Extensions\60\Bin folder on your server's system drive.

> You can also download the SharePoint Migration Tool from Microsoft's Web site. To find it, browse *http://www.microsoft.com/downloads*, leave Product/Technology set to All, type **SharePoint migrate** in the Keywords box, and click the Go button.

Backing Up, Restoring, and Migrating SharePoint Sites

To back up a site, use smigrate.exe with the following parameters:

```
smigrate.exe -w <Web_site_URL> -f backup_<filename> [-e -y -u <username> -pw
<password>]
```

For example, to back up a site at *http://kathmandu.example.com/taxis* as a file named c:\backup.fwp, without including any subsites, you would type the following:

```
smigrate.exe -w http://kathmandu.example.com/taxis -f c:\backup.fwp -e
```

If the site's URL contains any spaces, enclose the URL in quotation marks ("). For example, to backup *http://kathmandu.example.com/hotel deals*, type:

```
-w "http://kathmandu.example.com/hotel deals"
```

Restoring a Site with smigrate.exe

You can migrate a site to a new virtual server, to a new top-level Web site on an existing virtual server, or to a subsite under an existing top-level Web site.

Before you restore a site, however, you must create a blank site at the destination. That is, you must create the site *without* applying a site template. To do this, use your browser to create a site in the usual way, but when the Template Selection page appears, simply close the browser window without applying any template (not even the Blank Site template). Otherwise, the restore operation will fail.

> For more information about creating a new virtual server, refer to "Extending Or Upgrading a Virtual Server" in Chapter 15. For more information about creating sites, refer to "Creating a New SharePoint Site" in Chapter 5.

Before you migrate a site, make sure that all the settings in the destination site are correct. Remember that if smigrate.exe can't verify a domain user account, and you're not using Active Directory Account Creation mode, smigrate.exe won't restore the account.

To actually restore a site, you run smigrate.exe with the following parameters:

```
smigrate.exe -r -w <Web_site_URL> -f <backup_filename> [-u <username> -pw
<password>]
```

For example, to restore the above site to *http://kingston.example.com/taxi*, you would type the following:

```
smigrate.exe -r -w http://kingston.example.com/taxi -f c:\backup.fwp
```

If you're logged on with an account that doesn't have specific permissions to the destination Web site, you can specify a site administrator user name and password that has the appropriate permissions. For example, to restore a site and specify the administrator user name and password, you would use the following syntax:

```
smigrate.exe -r -w <Web_site_URL> -f <backup_filename> -u <admin_account> -pw
<password>
```

After running any restore, you should view the smigrate.log file to see which items migrated successfully and which didn't. The smigrate.log file is stored in the %temp% directory for your user account. If a log file already exists from a previous backup or restore, a log file will be created using the next available name (such as smigrate_1.log, smigrate_2.log, and so on).

Upgrading from SharePoint Team Services

If you're using the SharePoint Migration Tool to migrate and upgrade a site from SharePoint Team Services v1.0 or FrontPage 2002 Server Extensions to Windows SharePoint Services, be aware that several features or types of customizations supported in those environments won't migrate properly or won't work in a migrated site.

> For a list of items that you must re-create or work around, see "Upgrade Considerations" in the Windows SharePoint Services Administrator's Guide. This page is available online at *http://www.microsoft.com/resources/documentation/wss/2/all/adminguide/en-us/stsb04.mspx*.

If you're upgrading from SharePoint Team Services v1.0 to Windows SharePoint Services, you can also specify whether to migrate the security settings for the site. Security settings, in this sense, means all of the following:

- The list of user roles and associated rights
- The list of user accounts and role membership
- The anonymous access settings
- The setting for inherited or unique permissions for the site

If you backed up a SharePoint Team Services v1.0 site, and you want to restore it to a server running Windows SharePoint Services, and you want to exclude security information such as user accounts and site groups, run smigrate.exe with the –x parameter as shown below:

```
smigrate.exe -r -w <Web_site_URL> -f <backup_filename> -x
```

If the site you're backing up or restoring is large, backups and restores can take a long time to run. A typical rate for either operation is 1.5 gigabytes (GB) per hour. In addition, the more files in a site, the longer backups and restores will take.

In general, you'll get the best backup/restore performance by using separate computers for each task. Here's a sample configuration:

- One computer running smigrate.exe
- One or more computers running as front-end Web servers
- One or more computers running as SQL back-end servers

Figure 14-6 shows the result of migrating the SharePoint Team Services v1.0 site shown in Figure 14-5 to Windows SharePoint Services.

Backing Up, Restoring, and Migrating SharePoint Sites

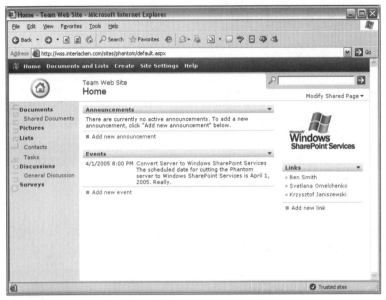

Figure 14-6. This is how the SharePoint Team Services v1.0 site shown in Figure 14-5 appears after migration to Windows SharePoint Services.

Accommodating Large Upgrades

The following sections will address various performance and configuration issues that might arise when using smigrate.exe, and especially when migrating large SharePoint Team Services v1.0 sites. Some of the steps in these sections require changing settings in Microsoft Internet Information Services (IIS) or Microsoft SQL Server.

- To complete the steps that use IIS:
  - You must be logged on as a member of the Administrators group on the local computer, or
  - You must be logged on using an account that's a member of the SharePoint administrators group, *and* that has permissions to administer IIS.
- To complete the steps that use SQL Server, you must be logged on using an account that's a member of the db_owner role in SQL Server.

Accommodating Temporary Files during Backup and Migration

When backing up a site, the SharePoint Migration Tool creates temporary files in the same folder as the backup file. Before starting a backup, therefore, you should ensure that folder has 25 percent more free space than the backup files alone will require.

When restoring, the migration tool creates temporary files in the Temporary Internet Files folder of the computer running the tool. Therefore, before starting a restore, make sure that folder has free space equal to 20 percent of the data and files from the original Web site.

Migrating a Windows SharePoint Services Site to Another Server

If you use the SharePoint Migration Tool to migrate a Windows SharePoint Services site to another server (also running Windows SharePoint Services), the tool won't migrate the following information:

- Security settings. This includes rights, site groups and memberships, cross-site groups, anonymous access setting, and inheritance of permissions from the parent site.
- SharePoint Central Administration settings for the server or virtual server.
- Personalizations, including personal views.
- Web Part customizations team members have made through Modify My Web Part. (However, it *will* migrate customizations members have made through Modify Shared Web Part.).

Migrating Sites to Windows SharePoint Services in Active Directory Account Creation Mode

When you migrate a site from SharePoint Team Services v1.0 to a server running Windows SharePoint Services in Active Directory Account Creation mode, the migration will automatically create Active Directory accounts for team members that existed in the original site. If you don't want to migrate user information this way, specify the -x switch when you run smigrate.exe.

The migration will name these user accounts based on the team member's e-mail address. Therefore:

- If a team member doesn't have an e-mail address in the existing site, the migration can't create an account for that member.
- Each team member should have a unique e-mail address.
- If two team members have the same e-mail address, the result will be a single user account that has all the rights held by any of the original team members. In addition, this e-mail address will appear as the creator of any items that members who were using the shared address created.

> **Tip**   Before migrating a site, make sure each existing team member has a unique, full e-mail address, including domain, such as roscoe@example.com.

When the migration creates user accounts, it doesn't send the usual e-mail messages informing new members of their usernames and passwords. Therefore, you must manually reset the passwords for any new user accounts, and then notify the team members personally.

Using a Secure Sockets Layer (SSL) Connection to Migrate a Site

The SharePoint Migration Tool can migrate sites over an Secure Sockets Layer (SSL) connection, but only if the following conditions are true:

- The computer that runs the migration tool must trust the certificate authority that issued the SSL certificate.
- The hostname you provide when running the SharePoint Migration Tool must match the hostname on the SSL certificate.
- The certificate must be valid. For example, it can't be expired.

If the computer running the migration tool doesn't trust the certificate authority that issued the SSL certificate, proceed as follows:

1   Browse to the destination https site. This will display the Security Alert window, indicating that you don't currently trust the authority that issued the certificate.

2   In the Security Alert window, click View Certificate.

3   When the Certificate window appears, click the Certification Path tab.

4   On the Certification Path tab, click the parent certificate of the selected certificate. The parent certificate will have a red and white "X" through it.

5   Click the View Certificate button.

6   When a second Certificate window appears, click the Install Certificate button.

7   When the Certificate Import Wizard appears, click Next.

8   When the Certificate Store window appears, choose either of these options:

- **Automatically Select The Certificate Store Based Upon The Type Of Certificate**   Choose this option if you want the new certificate to be kept in the default store for that kind of certificate.

- **Place All Certificates In The Following Store**   Choose this option if you want to specify the store in which the new certificate will be kept. After choosing this option, click the Browse button and specify the store you want.

9   Click Next, and then Finish.

10   In the Root Certificate Store window, click Yes.

Migrating Sites by Using Proxy Server Connections

Problems can occur if the SharePoint Migration Tool must migrate a site over a proxy server connection. If, for example, the proxy server requires different credentials than the destination Web server does, then no single username/password combination will satisfy both, and the migration will inevitably fail.

One solution in such a case is to get a temporary network connection that bypasses the proxy server. Another is to run the backup, the restore, or both on computers local to relevant server.

Migrating Sites across Domains

Issues can arise when migrating a site to a destination Web server in a different Windows domain, even if you use the -u and -pw parameters to supply the necessary user name and password. If this happens to you, configure the computer running smigrate.exe to prompt for user authentication. Here's the procedure:

1 On the Windows Start menu, click Control Panel.

2 When the Control Panel; window appears, double-click Internet Options.

3 When the Internet Options window appears, click the Security tab.

4 Select the Internet zone that lists the destination site, and then click the Custom Level button.

5 When the Security Settings dialog box appears, scroll down to the User Authentication heading and then, under Logon, click Prompt For User Name And Password.

6 Click OK.

Preparing to Migrate Sites to Windows SharePoint Services

Before using smigrate.exe to migrate a site, you should review the following configuration settings:

1 If the original site is running SharePoint Team Services v1.0, the SharePoint Migration Tool will fail unless you download and install Office XP Service Pack 3 for SharePoint Team Services. To obtain this service pack, browse *support.microsoft.com/ ?kbid=833845*.

   To install this service pack, you must be a member of the local Administrators group on the server.

2 If you expect the migration to take a long time, you can ensure consistency by setting the original site to read-only. This stops team members from making changes after the migration has passed their site.

   When you make a SharePoint Team Services v1.0 server read-only, the change affects the entire server. If this is what you want, proceed as follows.

   2.1 On the original server, open the Windows Start menu and then choose All Programs, Administrative Tools, and Microsoft SharePoint Administrator.

   2.2 On the Server Administration page, click Set List Of Available Rights.

   2.3 When the Set List of Available Rights page appears, clear all the check boxes except for Browse, View Lists, and View Web Document Discussions.

   2.4 Click Submit.

   If you're migrating a site based on Windows SharePoint Services to a new location, you can set the site to read-only by locking the site. For more information about locking a site, refer to "Managing Quotas and Locks" in Chapter 15.

Chapter 14

Backing Up, Restoring, and Migrating SharePoint Sites

3 If the original site is running Windows SharePoint Services, disable blocked file types so that smigrate.exe can include all site files in the backup. To do this:

3.1 Browse the Central Administration home page on the original server.

3.2 Under Security Configuration, click Manage Blocked File Types.

3.3 When the Manage Blocked File Types page appears, copy the list of blocked file types and save it in a text file. For example, click anywhere in the list, press Ctrl+A, press Ctrl+C, start Notepad, press Ctrl+V, and then choose Save As from the file menu.

3.4 In the list of blocked file types, delete the file types you want to include in the backup.

3.5 Click OK.

The list of blocked file extensions affects every site on the server or in the server farm, not just the site you're migrating. After migrating, you should restore the blocked file settings to protect any sites that remain on the server or server farm.

4 If you're migrating a large Web site and need additional virtual memory, increase the paging file size to at least 1 GB. This is especially true if you're running the SharePoint Migration Tool directly on a front-end Web server. For detailed instructions on doing this, refer to the section titled "Increasing a Server's Paging File Size" later in this chapter.

5 Change the following server settings on the destination server:

- Increase the IIS timeout settings to 65,000 seconds. For instructions, refer to the section titled "Increasing IIS Timeout Settings" later in this chapter.

- If you want to migrate anonymous access settings, you must turn on anonymous user access in IIS. For more details, refer to the section titled "Turning On Anonymous User Access in IIS" later in this chapter.

- If you're using quotas for the destination virtual server, and the site you're migrating is close to the quota limit for the virtual server, double the quota limit. For instructions, refer to "Doubling a Quota Limit" later in this chapter.

- Turn off blocked file extensions on the destination server. This requires essentially the same procedure as in step 3 above, but on the destination server.

- If the destination server is using a Microsoft SQL Server 2000 database, disable full-text search before migrating. This step can decrease the amount of time required to restore by as much as 40 percent in some cases.

6 Change the following virtual server settings on the destination virtual server:

- Change the maximum file size temporarily from 50 MB to 500 MB (or to the maximum upload limit for your hardware configuration).

- Set the maximum number of allowed alerts to Unlimited.

For instructions on making these changes, refer to the section titled "Changing Virtual Server Settings for Maximum Uploads And Alerts" later in this chapter.

7   Create a destination collection, top-level Web site, or site and don't apply a template. For example, create the site in your browser and then, when the Template Selection page appears, close the browser window or choose another site from your Favorites list.

After you've finished migrating your sites to Windows SharePoint Services, don't forget to reconfigure both servers back to their normal operating modes.

Increasing a Server's Paging File Size

If you're migrating a large site or running the SharePoint Migration Tool directly on a front-end Web server, you may need to increase the server's paging file size to 1 GB or more. To do this, proceed as follows.

1   On the Windows Start menu, select All Programs, Administrative Tools, and then Computer Management.

2   When the Computer Management window appears, right-click Computer Management (Local), and then select Properties.

3   Click the Advanced tab and then, under Performance, click Settings.

4   When the Performance Options dialog box appears, under Virtual Memory, click Change.

5   When the Virtual Memory dialog box appears, in the Drive list, click the drive that contains the paging file you want to change.

6   Under Paging File Size For Selected Drive, select Custom Size, and then type 1024 in the Initial Size (MB) box.

7   Specify a larger number in the Maximum Size (MB) box, and then click Set.

Increasing IIS Timeout Settings

To prevent long-running migration steps from timing out in IIS, proceed as follows.

1   On the Windows Start menu, select All Programs, Administrative Tools, and then Internet Information Services (IIS) Manager.

2   Double-click the name of the physical server where the destination Web site will reside, and then double-click Web Sites.

3   Right-click the destination virtual server, and then choose Properties from the shortcut menu.

4   When the virtual server's Properties dialog box appears, click the Web Site tab and then, in the Connection Timeout box, specify 65,000 seconds.

5   Click OK.

Turning On Anonymous User Access in IIS

If you want to migrate the anonymous user access settings to the destination server, you must enable IIS anonymous user access on that server. If this is what you want, proceed as follows.

1 On the Windows Start menu, select All Programs, Administrative Tools, and then Internet Information Services (IIS) Manager.

2 Double-click the name of the physical server where the destination Web site will reside, and then double-click Web Sites.

3 Right-click the destination virtual server, and then choose Properties from the shortcut menu.

4 On the Directory Security tab, under Authentication And Access C\ontrol, click Edit.

5 Select the Enable Anonymous Access check box, and then click OK twice.

Doubling a Quota Limit

The following procedure doubles the maximum amount of disk space a SharePoint site may consume.

1 Browse the Central Administration home page on the destination server.

2 Under Component Configuration, click Manage Quotas And Locks.

3 When the Manage Quotas and Locks page appears, click Manage Site Collection Quotas And Locks.

4 Enter the URL of the site collection, and then click View Data.

5 When the Manage Site Collection Quotas and Locks page appears, in the Site Quota Information section, double the value that appears in the box titled Limit Site Storage To A Maximum Of.

6 Click OK.

To reverse this change after the migration, perform the same steps but in step 5, type the original value in the box titled Limit Site Storage To A Maximum Of.

Disabling Full-Text Searching in SQL Server 2000

By default, SQL Server 2000 will begin indexing a newly migrated site even before the migration finishes. This, of course, reduces the system resources available to the migration, which in turn increases migration time. To avoid this effect, proceed as follows.

1 Browse the Central Administration home page on the destination server.

2 On the SharePoint Central Administration page, under Component Configuration, click Configure Full-Text Search.

3 When the Configure Full-Text Search page appears, clear the Enable Full-Text Search And Index Component check box.

4 Click OK.

Of course, you should reverse this change after the migration is complete.

Changing Virtual Server Settings for Maximum Uploads And Alerts

In order to successfully complete a large migration, you may need to increase the following settings on the destination virtual server:

- The maximum file upload size. This is necessary to accommodate any large files that exist in the original site.

- The number of alerts. Setting this to Unlimited ensures that the destination site can accommodate all the alerts team member have in effect.

When IIS receives an uploaded file, it temporarily stores the entire file in memory. When a large file consumes a significant portion of the server's physical memory, this creates a severe strain that can stall or crash the entire physical server. The point at which this occurs depends on the number of such requests occurring simultaneously and on your hardware. Here, nevertheless, are some general guidelines.

- An installation that includes a front-end Web server with 512 MB of RAM and a back-end server with 1 GB of RAM may be able to handle file sizes up to about 128 MB.

- As an upper limit, such as during a migration, it's generally safe to set the maximum upload size to one-quarter of the size of the server's physical memory.

By default, Windows SharePoint Services enforces a maximum file upload size of 50 MB. In practice, not many files exceed this limit and if possible, you should encourage team members with larger files to store them elsewhere. Of course, during a migration, the objective is usually to ignore past mistakes and just migrate whatever you've got.

> **Tip** When you increase the maximum permissible size of file uploads, you may need to increase the virtual server's timeout value as well.

In any event, here's the procedure for increasing the Maximum Upload Size and Maximum Number Of Alerts for a SharePoint server.

1. Browse the Central Administration home page on the destination server.
2. Under Virtual Server Configuration, click Configure Virtual Server Settings.
3. When the Virtual Server List page appears, click the name of the virtual server that contains the destination site.
4. When the Virtual Server Settings page appears, under Virtual Server Management, click Virtual Server General Settings.
5. When the Virtual Server General Settings page appears, find the Maximum Upload Size section. Then, in the Maximum Upload Size box, type the maximum size you want to allow.
6. In the Alerts section, under Maximum Number Of Alerts That A User Can Create, select Unlimited Number.
7. Click OK.

Upgrading a WMSDE Database to SQL Server

If you've outgrown WMSDE but want to continue using a single server for Windows SharePoint Services, you can simply upgrade your database instance from WMSDE to SQL Server. Because this process requires your sites to be offline while the databases are upgraded, you should perform these steps when usage is generally low, and you should notify team members that their sites will be offline for a time.

> **Note** Before you upgrade your databases, it's a good idea to back them up. If you first install only the SQL Server client tools on your server, you can use them to back up a WMSDE database. Otherwise, stop WMSDE and make a copy of the database files before installing SQL Server.

Upgrading WMSDE in Place

Here's the procedure for installing SQL Server and upgrading your databases:

1. Log on to the server running WMSDE, and then run the SQL Server 2000 SP3 Setup program. This occurs automatically when you insert the SQL Server installation CD.

2. When the Autorun panel appears, click SQL Server 2000 Components.

3. Click Install Database Server and then, on the Welcome panel, click Next.

4. In the Computer Name box, select Local Computer and then click Next.

5. hen the Installation Selection pane appears, select Upgrade, Remove, Or Add Components To An Existing Instance Of SQL Server, and then click Next.

6. When the Instance Name pane appears, clear the Default check box. Then in the Instance name box, select SHAREPOINT, and click Next.

7. When the Existing Installation pane appears, verify that Upgrade is selected, and then click Next.

8. When the Upgrade pane appears, verify that the Yes, Upgrade My Programs check box is selected, and then click Next.

9. When the Licensing Options pane appears, select your licensing options and then click Next.

10. When the Select Components pane appears:

    10.1 If you want to enable full-text searching, click Server Components, and then select the Full-Text Search.

    10.2 In the left pane, select Management Tools.

    10.3 In the right pane, select Enterprise Manager and Query Analyzer.

    10.4 Select any other components you want.

    10.5 Click Next.

11. When the Start Copying Files pane appears, click Next, and then click Finish.

After the upgrade to SQL Server 2000 is complete, your SharePoint sites should work as usual.

Migrating SharePoint Databases to a Server Farm

The process of upgrading a SharePoint site to use a remote instance of SQL Server rather than a local copy of WMSDE is inherently more complex than that for upgrading WMSDE in place. At a high level, and assuming you want to keep using the existing Web server, here are the required steps:

1 Install the SQL Server client tools on the original server running WMSDE. This is so that you can use the client tools to back up and restore the SharePoint content and configuration databases. As you do so, keep these facts in mind:

   ■ The version of WMSDE that comes with Windows SharePoint Services doesn't accept network connections, except from the local computer. This includes network connections from the SQL Server client tools.

   ■ Using the SQL Server client tools to manage WMSDE on an ongoing basis violates the SQL Server license agreement. To comply, you'd need to purchase an additional, full SQL Server license.

2 If necessary, install SQL Server 2000 Service Pack 3 (SP3) on the remote server.

3 In IIS, stop any virtual servers that are hosting SharePoint sites. This is so that team members can't change any sites or content.

4 Disconnect the WMSDE content databases from the virtual server, and then remove Windows SharePoint Services from that virtual server.

5 Get or create domain accounts for the SharePoint Central Administration virtual server and the content virtual servers. Then, update the SharePoint Central Administration virtual server to use a domain account.

6 Register the local instance of WMSDE in SQL Server Enterprise Manager, and then back up the content and configuration databases.

7 Copy the backup files to the destination server and restore the content and configuration databases.

8 In SQL Server, change the database ownership and permissions for the configuration and content databases. This makes them accessible to the SharePoint site.

9 Connect the SharePoint Central Administration to the migrated copy of the configuration database.

10 Extend the content virtual server, specifying the migrated copy of the content databases.

11 Update the default content database server so that it creates any future content databases on the new server.

Backing Up, Restoring, and Migrating SharePoint Sites

For the most part, instructions earlier in this chapter or in Chapter 15 explain how to perform each of these steps. If, however, you'd like a detailed procedure for the entire process, consult the following Web page from the Administrator's Guide for Windows SharePoint Services:

http://www.microsoft.com/resources/documentation/wss/2/all/adminguide/en-us/stsf17.mspx

In Summary...

This chapter explained three ways of backing up and restoring a Windows SharePoint Services site. It also explained how to upgrade from SharePoint Team Services v1.0, and how to upgrade from WMSDE to SQL Server 2000.

The next chapter begins Part VI, which explains how to administer and manage existing SharePoint servers and sites.

Chapter 14

Part VI

Administering SharePoint Services

Administering a SharePoint Server

Once you've installed Windows SharePoint Services, you'll undoubtedly want to change settings to suit your environment, extend servers, create sites, assign permissions, and perform a myriad of other tasks, all in the context of site administration. That's what the chapters in this part explain how to do.

This chapter explains how to administer servers and virtual Web servers running Windows SharePoint Services. You can do this through Web pages on a so-called Central Administration server or at the command line. Most administrators use the Web pages for most of their work, so that's the chapter's primary focus. However, there's also a brief introduction to command-line administration. To use any of these tools, you must be a member of the Administrator group on the local server, or a member of a designated SharePoint administration group.

Chapters 16 and 17 will explain how to administer individual sites. The functions in those chapters all reside in the Site Settings link in each site, and using them requires special permissions only for the site in question. In short, Chapter 15 is for server administrators, while Chapters 16 and 17 are for the owners of individual sites.

Finding the Central Administration Server

When you install Windows SharePoint Services, the setup program always creates a new virtual Web server called SharePoint Central Administration. The Web pages on this server provide high-level SharePoint administrative functions such as extending new virtual servers, controlling security, and managing disk quotas and virus scanning. To access this Web server, you must use an account that belongs to the SharePoint administrators group, or to the local Administrators group for the server computer.

> **For more information on the SharePoint administrators group, refer to "Setting the SharePoint Administration Group" later in this chapter.**

During installation, the setup program assigns the Central Administration server a random port number. If you don't know that port number, the following procedure will help you find it.

1 Start IIS Manager. For example, choose Start, Administrative Tools, Internet Information Services (IIS) Manager.

2 If you started IIS Manager on a remote computer:

2.1 Right-click Internet Information Services.

2.2 Choose Connect from the shortcut menu.

2.3 Type the computer name where Windows SharePoint Services is running.

2.4 Click OK.

3 Open the following entries in IIS Manager:

- Internet Information Services
- The name of the computer running Windows SharePoint Services
- Web Sites

4 In the right pane, read the port number of the Central Administration server. In Figure 15-1, for example, the Central Administration server is listening on port 5392.

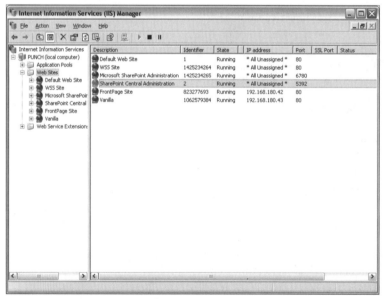

Figure 15-1. IIS Manager reveals the port number of a SharePoint Central Administration server.

> **Note** Don't be confused by the Microsoft SharePoint Administration server in Figure 15-1. Despite its name, it manages the FrontPage Server Extensions, and not Windows SharePoint Services.

474

Browsing the Central Administration site will display the Central Administration home page shown in Figure 15-2. The remainder of this chapter will explain the options on this page.

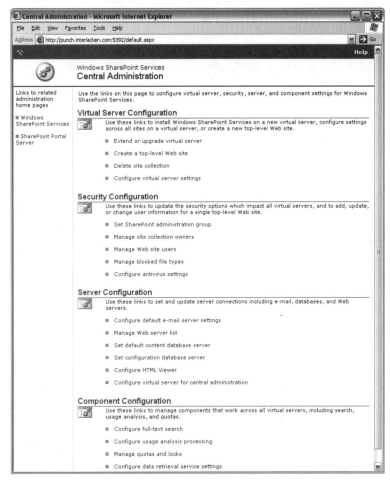

Figure 15-2. This is the home page of a SharePoint Central Administration server.

Administering an Entire Server

This section will explain how to configure the Central Administration settings that affect the entire server running Windows SharePoint Services.

Configuring a Virtual Server for Central Administration

The first step in configuring a Central Administration server is to give it a proper application pool, running under a suitable logon account. To configure the application pool for the Central Administration server, proceed as follows.

475

1 On the SharePoint Central Administration home page, under Server Configuration, click Configure Virtual Server For Central Administration. This will display the Configure Administrative Virtual Server page shown in Figure 15-3.

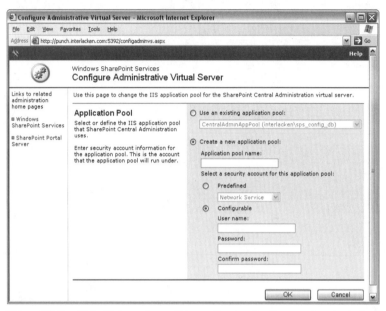

Figure 15-3. This Web page configures the application pool and application pool account for a Central Administration server.

2 Enter or update these fields on the Configure Administrative Virtual Server page.

- **Use An Existing Application Pool** To run the Central Administration server in an existing IIS application pool, select this option, and then select a pool from the drop-down list. Be sure to select a pool that runs with a user account having all the necessary database permissions.
  If you choose this option, the remaining options on the page are irrelevant.

- **Create A New Application Pool** To create a new IIS application pool for the Central Administration server, select this option and then complete the remaining settings on the page.

- **Application Pool Name** Give the new application pool a name that will help you remember its purpose.

- **Predefined** Select this option if you want the application pool to run under a standard account that the operating system provides. The choices are Network Service, Local Service, and Local System.
  If you choose this approach, make sure the account you choose has sufficient rights in SQL Server. Also, keep in mind that none of these accounts has rights extending beyond the local computer. For example, you can't give them rights to an instance of SQL Server running on a different computer.

- **Configurable**   Select this option if you want the application pool to run under an account you create and configure. This is usually a Windows domain account.

- **User Name**   Specify the name of the configurable account you want the application pool to use.

- **Password**   Type the password for the user account you specified.

- **Confirm Password**   Repeat the password for the user account you specified.

3   Click OK to save any changes, or click Cancel to quit without saving.

> **For more information about IIS application pools, refer to the section titled "Choosing an IIS Application Pool Configuration" in Chapter 13.**

Configurable application pool accounts are usually Windows domain accounts with non-expiring, non-changeable passwords, restricted to be valid only on known computers. They don't need Administrator status, but they do need the Log On As A Service user right. The advantage of domain accounts is that they're valid on multiple computers, such as an application pool running on one server and SQL Server running on another.

> **Tip**   If you specify a configurable application pool account, make sure you specify the correct password. Windows SharePoint Services will check the Password and Confirm Password values against each other, but not against Active Directory. If you specify a wrong password, you won't know it until the application pool fails to start.

The concept of least privilege generally dictates creating a separate account for each purpose. Using the same account for two, three, or a dozen services results in each of those services having permissions it doesn't need, and that's an open door to trouble.

> **Tip**   Keep careful records of each service account you create, what services and computers use it, and what password you assign. You should also have a procedure for changing those passwords occasionally, and for updating the necessary services.

Setting the Configuration Database Server

Every server running Windows SharePoint Services needs a configuration database. This is where it stores the settings for each SharePoint virtual server. Without a configuration database, the capabilities of a Central Administration site are greatly limited. You certainly can't extend any virtual servers or create any sites, because there's nowhere to store their configurations.

Chapter 15

477

One administrative task you *can* perform without having a configuration server is, logically enough, specifying a configuration database. To do this, proceed as follows:

1   On the Central Administration home page, under Server Configuration, click Set Configuration Database Server. This will display the Set Configuration Database Server page shown in Figure 15-4.

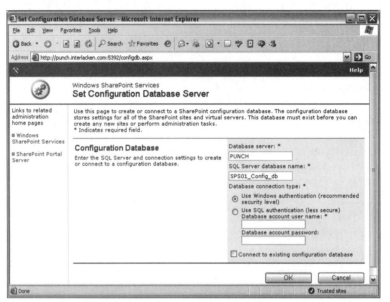

Figure 15-4. This page specifies the configuration server for a SharePoint server or farm.

2   Enter or update these fields on the Set Configuration Database Server page.

- **Database Server**   Type the name of the database server that will host the new configuration database, or that already hosts an existing one.

- **SQL Server Database Name**   Type the database name for the new or existing configuration database.

- **Use Windows Authentication**   Select this option if you want the Central Administration server to use a Windows user account and Windows authentication protocols when authenticating itself to the database server. This is the more secure—and recommended—option.

- **Use SQL Authentication**   Select this option if you want the Central Administration server to use a SQL Server account when authenticating itself to the database server. This is less secure than using Windows authentication, and therefore not the recommended option.

- **Database Account User Name**   Type the name of a SQL Server account that has the Security Administrators and Database Creators roles on the database server you specified. This field and the next apply only if you've chosen SQL Server authentication.
- **Database Account Password**   Type the password for the account you specified.
- **Connect To Existing Configuration Database**   Select this box if you want to connect to an existing configuration database. Clear it to create a new database.

3   Click OK to save any changes, or click Cancel to quit without saving.

Here are two common reasons for connecting to an existing configuration database:

- For performance reasons, you're moving the database to a different server. You've already backed up the existing database and restored it to the new server, and now you're ready to start using it.
- You want to add a front-end Web server to a server farm. That is, you want a new SharePoint server to start delivering exactly the same content as one or more existing SharePoint servers. This requires that the new SharePoint server use the same configuration and content database as the existing servers.

Setting the Default Content Database Server

Whenever you extend a virtual server with Windows SharePoint Services, you must identify the database server that will host the new virtual server's content databases. To specify a default database server, proceed as follows.

1   On the Central Administration home page, under Server Configuration, click Set Default Content Database Server.

2   When the Set Default Content Database Server page appears, type the server name you want into the database server box. This is the only input field on the page.

3   Click OK to save any changes, or click Cancel to quit without saving.

The server name you specify on this page has no relevance after you create a virtual server. It only controls the default value that appears on the Extend And Create Content Database page.

For more information about extending a virtual server with Windows SharePoint Services, refer to "Extending a Virtual Server with Windows SharePoint Services" later in this chapter.

Managing the Web Server List

When you're managing a farm of front-end Web servers, you'll frequently need to switch from one Central Administration server to another. To ease this task, the Central Administration site provides the Manage Web Server List page shown in Figure 15-5.

479

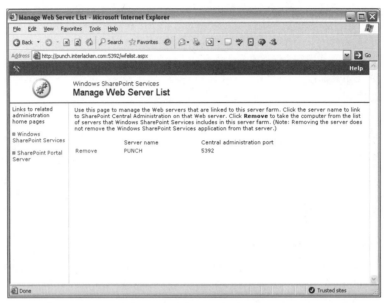

Figure 15-5. This page lists all the SharePoint servers using the same configuration database as the current Central Administration site.

To display this page, click the Manage Web Server List link in the Server Configuration section of the Central Administration home page. Then:

- To display the Central Administration home page for another server, click the server name.
- To remove a server from the farm, click the Remove link.

A farm, in this sense, is two or more SharePoint servers all configured to use the same configuration database. Here are two common reasons to do this:

- You want two or more servers to deliver exactly the same content. Then, you would use DNS, a load-sharing router, or some other solution to distribute requests across the available servers.
- You want to distribute Web sites across several servers, but manage all the servers as a unit.

Removing a front-end Web server from such a farm doesn't affect the front-end Web server in any way. The server continues to use the same configuration and content databases as before, and continues doing productive work.

The Central Administration server and its configuration database, however, "forget" that the front-end Web server exists. If you make a configuration change that affects all front-end Web servers, the front-end server you removed won't receive that change. Furthermore, the server you removed will no longer appear on the Manage Web Server List page.

To reconnect a front-end Web server that you removed, browse the Central Administration site on that server, and reconnect it to the original configuration database.

For instruction on connecting a front-end Web server to a configuration database, refer to the section titled "Setting the Configuration Database Server" earlier in this chapter.

Setting the SharePoint Administration Group

Members of the physical server's Administrators group always have full permission to administer Windows SharePoint Services. Sometimes, however, you might want to delegate SharePoint administration to someone other than a server administrator. In such a case, you can simply add the person to the SharePoint administration group.

You can configure any Windows group you like as the SharePoint administration group. To do this, or to find out what group is currently assigned, proceed as follows.

1 On the Central Administration home page, under Security Configuration, click Set SharePoint Administration Group.

2 When the Set SharePoint Administration Group page shown in Figure 15-6 appears, note or retype the contents of the Group Account Name box. The group you specify must already exist, and you must specify it in domain\name format.

3 Click OK to make a change, or Cancel to quit without saving.

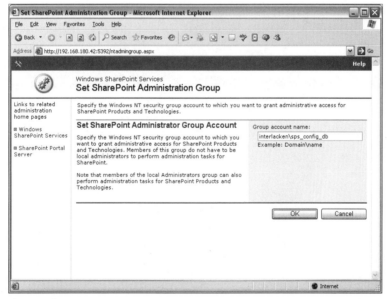

Figure 15-6. Use this page to specify the Windows security group that identifies SharePoint administrators.

The group you specify as the SharePoint administration group is a perfectly ordinary Windows domain group. To add or remove members, use the usual Windows administration tools.

Managing Blocked File Types

Windows SharePoint Services typically refuses to honor upload and download requests for files with certain file name extensions. For the most part, these are executables or other kinds of program files. Blocking these extensions stops team members from downloading software they shouldn't have, and from putting software on the server that the server shouldn't run.

To add a filename extension to (or remove an extension from) the prohibited list, proceed as follows.

1 On the Central Administration home page, under Security Configuration, click Manage Blocked File Types.

2 When the Manage Blocked File Types page shown in Figure 15-7 appears, add or remove any items you want from the text box titled Type Each File Extension On A Separate Line. Because this is a text box:

   ■ To add a new extension, you set the insertion point at the beginning or end of an existing line, press Enter, and then type extension you want to block.

   ■ To remove an extension, you set the insertion point at the beginning of the line and press Delete until the line disappears.

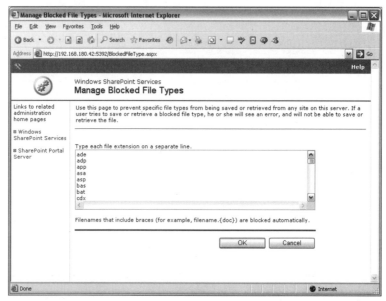

Figure 15-7.   Windows SharePoint Services will block upload or download of any file having an extension listed on this page.

3 Click OK to make a change, or Cancel to quit without saving.

Configuring Antivirus Settings

Windows SharePoint Services can submit documents to a third-party virus scanning program whenever a team member uploads a document to a library or list, whenever a team member downloads a document, or both. If the virus scanner finds an infection, Windows SharePoint Services can also request that the document be cleaned, and it can also block the upload or download.

This assumes, of course, that you have a third-party, SharePoint-compatible virus scanner installed on the computer running Windows SharePoint Services. In a server farm, you must have the virus scanner installed on each front-end Web server.

> **Note**   To locate a virus scanner that works with Windows SharePoint Services, first consult your normal antivirus vendor. If they don't have a suitable product, another vendor will.

Antivirus protection is configurable only at the server level. That is, whatever settings you choose apply to all SharePoint virtual servers on the same physical computer. If you have a farm of front-end Web servers, you need to configure virus scanning on each one.

Once you have the third-party virus scanner installed, configure Windows SharePoint Services as follows:

1   On the Central Administration home page, under Security Configuration, click Configure Antivirus Settings. This will display the Configure Antivirus Settings page shown in Figure 15-8.

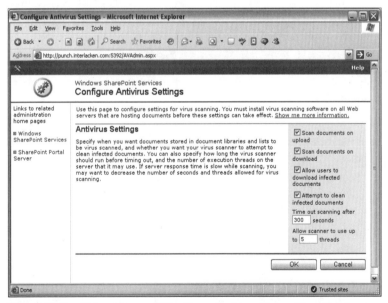

Figure 15-8.   This page specifies the extent to which a SharePoint server scans for viruses. You must, however, install a third-party SharePoint-compatible virus scanner.

483

2 Configure the following antivirus settings:

- **Scan Documents On Upload**   Select this box if you want to scan documents when team members upload them.

- **Scan Documents On Download**   Select this box if you want to scan documents when team members download them.

- **Allow Users To Download Infected Documents**   Select this box if you want team members to have the capability of downloading infected files. Presumably, a virus scanner on the team member's PC would then handle the virus.

- **Attempt To Clean Infected Documents**   Select this box if you want the virus scanner to try removing any viruses it finds.

- **Time Out Scanning After <seconds> Seconds**   Type the number of seconds to allow before terminating the scanning process. The default time of 300 seconds (5 minutes) is normally sufficient. Smaller values conserve server resources, and larger values permit scanning larger documents.

- **Allow Scanner To Use Up To <threads> Threads**   Type the maximum number of threads you want the scanning process to use. The default is five threads, which is usually sufficient. Smaller values conserve server resources. Larger values permit scanning more documents at once.

3 Click OK to make a change, or Cancel to quit without saving.

If no virus scanner is installed on your server and you activate SharePoint virus scanning anyway, no error message appears when you click OK, and no error messages appears when team members upload or download documents. To verify that virus scanning is working, you need to monitor statistics in the virus scanning software.

Configuring Default E-Mail Server Settings

Windows SharePoint Services sends e-mail to team members in a number of circumstances. A few of these are:

- Alerts that notify team members of changes to lists or libraries.

- Invitation messages that new team members receive when an administrator grants them access to a site.

- Request Access messages that Windows SharePoint Services sends to an administrator after it denies access to a team member, and the team member clicks a Send Request button on the error page.

- Site Collection Use Confirmation messages the optional Site Collection Use Confirmation and Auto-Deletion feature sends to owners of unused sites.

- Over-Quota messages that site owners receive when their site exceeds a warning or maximum amount of disk space.

To configure the default settings for sending all this mail, proceed as follows.

484

1 On the Central Administration home page, under Server Configuration, click Configure Default E-Mail Server Settings. This will display the Configure E-Mail Server Settings page shown in Figure 15-9.

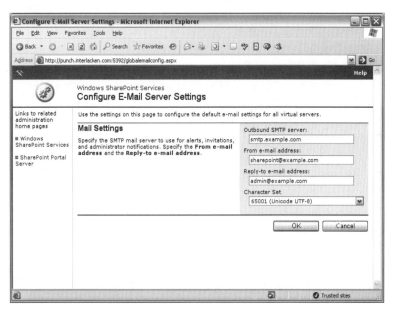

Figure 15-9. The e-mail settings on this page serve as defaults when you extend a new virtual server.

2 Configure the following e-mail settings:

- **Outbound SMTP Server** Specify the DNS name or IP address of the SMTP mail server to use for sending the mail. This doesn't need to be a Microsoft Exchange server; it can be any SMTP server that relays mail.

- **From E-Mail Address** Specify the e-mail address that will appear in the From Address field of each message.

- **Reply-To E-Mail Address** Specify the e-mail address that will appear in the To Address if a team member replies to mail from the SharePoint server.

- **Character Set** Specify the character set to use in the body of each mail message. The default character set is 65001 (Unicode UTF-8), a standard character set that works well for most languages. If you choose a specific language code, such as 1256 (Arabic (Windows)), the text is less likely to appear correctly in mail readers configured for other languages.

3 Click OK to make a change, or Cancel to quit without saving.

The values you enter on this page are the defaults that take effect when you extend a new virtual server with Windows SharePoint Services. Once the virtual server is extended, you manage these properties at the virtual server level.

Finding a Usable Mail Server

It's your responsibility to find and specify a server that accepts mail from Windows SharePoint Services. Because of efforts to control unsolicited e-mail (spam), this may be more difficult than you suspect. Very few mail servers, especially on the Internet, accept and relay (that is, forward) mail from unidentified senders. Here are some typical policies that SMTP administrators enforce:

● The sender's computer must have an address on the organization's network. The organization, in this sense, may be a company, a government agency, or a public DSL or cable modem provider.

● The From address, or at least the domain portion of the From address, must be known to the service provider.

● The mail server may require authentication before accepting mail.

The first two policies are relatively easy to accommodate; just make sure your SharePoint server has an acceptable IP address, and that you specify a suitable From address. The third is more difficult because Windows SharePoint Services doesn't have a way to config-ure a username and password for outgoing mail. If your provider won't relax this policy, you may need to find another provider.

Internet Information Services (IIS) includes an SMTP server that works with Windows SharePoint Services. However:

● It's not part of the default configuration. You must specifically install it.

● You must configure it to allow anonymous access, which isn't the default.

● You must configure it to permit e-mail relaying, which isn't the default.

For more information about the IIS SMTP service, refer to the Help system for IIS Manager.

Configuring an HTML Viewer Service

If your SharePoint server has Web visitors who don't have Microsoft Office 2003 installed on their computers, but who need to view the content of Office 97 or later Word, Excel, or PowerPoint files, the HTML Viewer service may provide an answer. This service:

1 Receives Office 97 or later documents over the network.

2 Translates them to HTML using filters that come with Office 2003.

3 Sends the resulting HTML version back to the originating server for retransmission to the Web visitor.

To perform these translations, the HTML Viewer service uses translation filters that come with Office 2003. Therefore, a copy of Office 2003 must be installed on the computer running the HTML Viewer service. Microsoft recommends installing the HTML Viewer service on a computer running Windows XP Professional, with the .NET Framework installed. However, it also runs acceptably on Windows Server 2003.

486

Here's how to obtain and install the HTML Viewer service:

1 Browse *http://www.microsoft.com/dowloads.*

2 When the Microsoft download center page appears, enter the following settings and then click Go:

- **Product/Technology** Windows SharePoint Services.
- **Keywords** Viewer.

3 When the Search Results page appears, click HTML Viewer Service for Windows SharePoint Services.

4 When the Download Details page appears, click the Download button.

5 When the file download dialog box appears, choose to save the file.

6 Run the downloaded file (that is, htmlview.exe) to extract the files for the installation.

7 Look among the extracted files for a document named "html viewer whitepaper.doc." Open this file to get detailed installation instructions. Basically, you run a special installation of Office 2003, and then you install the viewer service.

Be sure to read the entire documentation file, including the security precautions, and configure your environment accordingly.

> **Tip** Translating Office documents to HTML can be a resource-intensive process. To avoid slowing down other processes, Microsoft recommends running the HTML Viewer service on a dedicated computer.

Once you have the HTML Viewer service running, you must configure Windows SharePoint Services to use it. Proceed as follows.

1 On the SharePoint Central Administration home page, under Server Configuration, click Configure HTML Viewer. This will display the Configure HTML Viewer page shown in Figure 15-10.

2 Enter or update these fields on the Configure HTML Viewer page.

- **Allow HTML Viewing** Select this check box to activate use of the HTML Viewer service for document libraries on the current server.
- **Path To HTML Viewer Server** Specify the network path to the HTML Viewer service. This is normally http:// followed by the computer name and port 8093.
- **Maximum Cache Size** Enter the maximum size for the HTML Viewer cache in megabytes (MB).
  Upon receiving a translated document from the HTML Viewer service, Windows SharePoint Services stores it in a content database. Then, if a second request for the same document arrives, Windows SharePoint Services delivers the saved translation rather than requesting a new one.
  The default value for this setting is 5000, which is 5 gigabytes (GB).

Chapter 15

487

■ **Maximum File Size**   Specify the maximum file size, in whole kilobytes (KB),
for translating a document to HTML. A setting of 3000 means that Windows
SharePoint Services won't submit documents larger than 3000 kilobytes (3 MB)
for translation.

■ **Timeout Length**   Specify the maximum number of seconds the SharePoint
server should wait for the HTML Viewer service to translate a document to
HTML.

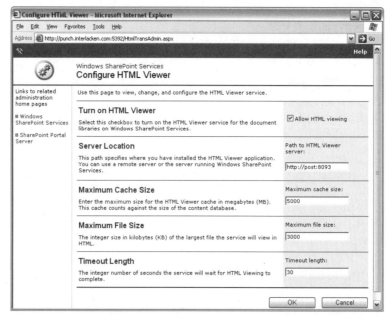

Figure 15-10.   An HTML Viewer service converts Office documents to HTML so
that team members who don't have Office installed can view them.

3   Click OK to save any changes, or click Cancel to quit without saving.

> **Tip**   To verify that the HTML Viewer Service is running on a computer, make sure that the
> Office HTML Viewer Load Balancing Service and the Office HTML Viewer Service appear
> under Control Panel, Services and are running. To verify or modify the port number, follow
> the instructions in the Changing Default Port Assignments section of the html viewer white-
> paper.doc that comes with the software.

To test your results, log on to a computer that *doesn't* have Microsoft Office installed, browse
to a SharePoint document library, and click a Word, Excel, or PowerPoint document. The
result should be a Web page like the one in Figure 15-11. Clicking the View In HTML button
should, after a slight delay, result in a viewable version of the document. Choosing Source
from the View menu will reveal the HTML.

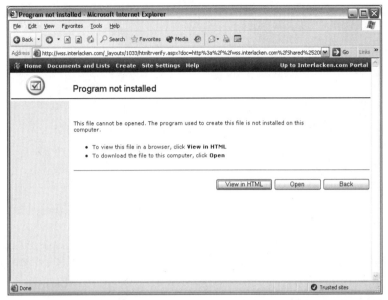

Figure 15-11. This page appears when a team member doesn't have Microsoft Office installed, but tries to view an Office document in a SharePoint list or library. Clicking View In HTML sends the document to an HTML Viewer service for translation.

Configuring Full-Text Search

If your SharePoint server is using a SQL Server database, you can activate full-text searching of lists and libraries. Such searches find matching text in the list or library index, as well as in list or library documents, but only within the current SharePoint site.

> **Note** If you want to search, index, and categorize documents in multiple sites, investigate the Search Service in SharePoint Portal Server.

To use the full-text search that Windows SharePoint Services provides, you must first install the full-text searching feature for SQL Server 2000. To do this:

1 On the computer running SQL Server, start the SQL Server 2000 Setup program.
2 When the opening setup screen appears, click SQL Server 2000 Components, and then click Install Database Server.
3 When the Welcome page of the Microsoft SQL Server 2000 Installation Wizard appears, click Next.
4 When the Computer Name page appears, select the computer type, and then click Next.
5 On the Installation Selection page, select Upgrade, Remove, Or Add Components To An Existing Instance Of SQL Server, and then click Next.

489

6 When the Instance Name page appears:

    6.1 Clear the Default check box.

    6.2 In the Instance Name box, select the SQL Server instance you're using with Windows SharePoint Services.

    6.3 Click Next.

7 Select Add Components To Your Existing Installation, and then click Next.

8 When the Select Components panel appears, select Full-Text Search in the Sub-Components list, and then click Next.

9 Click Next to begin the installation, and then click Finish.

To configure Windows SharePoint Services to use full text searching, proceed as follows:

1 On the SharePoint Central Administration home page, under Component Configuration, click Configure Full-Text Search.

2 The Configure Full-Text Search page, when it appears, will have only one configurable option: a check box titled Enable Full-Text Search And Index Component. Select this check box.

3 Click OK to save any changes, or click Cancel to quit without saving.

Once this configuration is complete, a search control box should appear on the on the home page of each SharePoint site. This box doesn't appear if Full-Text Search isn't configured.

The search function may not return a complete list of documents immediately after installation. This is because it takes some time to build the full-text search catalog.

Configuring Usage Analysis Processing

Windows SharePoint Services can accumulate statistics on activity levels and disk space within each site. Two processes make use of these statistics:

- **View Site Usage Data Pages**   A link titled View Site Usage Data appears on the Site Administration page of every SharePoint site. This link displays a Site Usage Report page that shows not only Web page hits, but list and library document hits as well. In addition, it provides statistics on activity by user, client operating system, and browser.

- **Disk Space Quotas And Locks**   This process sends warning messages to the owners of sites that are near a preconfigured amount of disk space. If a site exceeds its limit, viewing and deleting will become the only available options.

To gather these statistics, Windows SharePoint Services must continually create log files and then analyze them once a day. This, however, isn't the default. To activate usage analysis, and thereby start gathering statistics, proceed as follows:

1 On the SharePoint Central Administration home page, under Component Configuration, click Configure Usage Analysis Processing. This will display the Configure Usage Analysis Processing page shown in Figure 15-12.

490

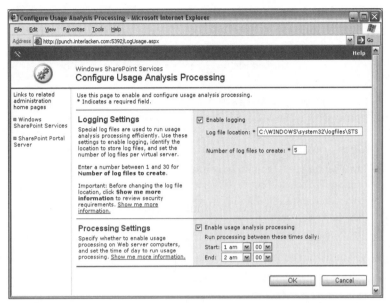

Figure 15-12. Use this page to configure creation and analysis of SharePoint activity logs.

2 Configure these settings on the Configure Usage Analysis Processing page:

- **Enable Logging** Select this check box if you want Windows SharePoint Services to create log files for usage analysis.

- **Log File Location:** Specify the folder where you want the log files to reside. The STS_WPG user group must have Read, Write, and Update permissions to this folder. The default location is C:\WINDOWS\system32\logfiles\STS.

- **Number Of Log Files To Create** Enter the number of log files per day you want to create. If you type 2, each log file will contains twelve hours of activity. If you type 4, each log file will cover 6 hours, and so forth.

- **Enable Usage Analysis Processing** Select this check box if you want Windows SharePoint Services to analyze its log files every day.

- **Start** Select the earliest time you'd like Windows SharePoint Services to start analyzing its log files.

- **End** Select the latest time you'd like to start analyzing log files. If, for some reason, daily usage analysis hasn't started by this time, it won't run until the next day.

3 Click OK to save any changes, or click Cancel to quit without saving.

You should also be aware of these facts regarding Windows SharePoint Services usage analysis.

- Each Web request (each hit) to a SharePoint server generates about 200 bytes of log information. The log file for a server receiving a million hits a day would therefore be about 200 MB in size.

  The daily usage analysis process reads each log file entirely into memory. Therefore, processing a 200 MB log files would briefly consume 200 MB of server RAM. This is the incentive for creating multiple log files per day. Processing ten log files of 20 MB each would consume only 20 MB of RAM at any given time.

- In a server farm, you must configure usage analysis to run on each front-end Web server. Each front-end Web server, however, will store the resulting statistics in the shared content database. This aggregates the statistics for all servers delivering the same content.

- Daily usage statistics remain in the content database for 31 days.

- Monthly usage statistics remain in the content database for 31 months.

- Usage analysis never deletes the original log files. Therefore, you may want to develop your own process for deleting log files past a certain age.

- The log files that Windows SharePoint Services creates and uses are distinct from the log files IIS creates.

- Usage analysis uses the SharePoint Timer service to schedule log processing. Therefore, when you activate usage analysis, you should verify that this service is running, and that it will start automatically whenever the server boots.

Managing Quotas and Locks

By assigning quotas, you can limit the amount of disk space a given site collection can use. For ease in management, this is a multi-step process.

- At the Central Administration level, you define one or more *quota templates*. A quota template is a named object that specifies:

  - The number of megabytes that will trigger a warning message to the top-level site owner.

  - The number of megabytes that will lock a top-level site. Locking means permitting only Read and Delete access.

- At the virtual server level, you specify the default quota template for new top-level sites on that sever.

- When an administrator uses the Central Administration server to create a new top-level site, he or she can assign a different quota template. But if someone with lesser privileges (someone using Self-Service Site Creation, for example) creates a new top-level site, the default quota template will always apply.

● Changing a quota template (or the default quota for a virtual server) has no effect on existing sites. To change the quota for an existing site, you must edit the properties of that site.

To create or modify a quota template, proceed as follows:

1 On the SharePoint Central Administration home page, under Component Configuration, click Manage Quotas And Locks.

2 When the Manage Quotas And Locks page appears, click Manage Quota Templates. This will display the Manage Quota Templates page shown in Figure 15-13.

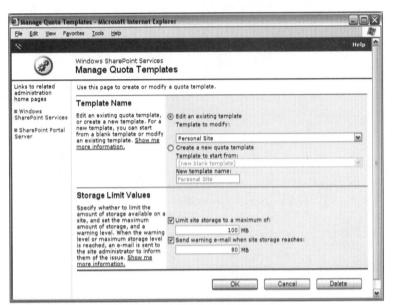

Figure 15-13. This page configures named sets of predefined quota settings.

3 Configure the following settings:

■ **Edit An Existing Template**   Select this option if you want to modify a quota template that already exists. Then, select the existing template from the Template To Modify drop-down list.

■ **Create A New Quota Template**   Select this option if you want to create a new template. Then, if you want to use an existing template as a base, select a template from the Template To Start From drop-down list. Finally, type a name in the New Template Name text box.

■ **Limit Site Storage To A Maximum Of**   If you want the quota to strictly limit the amount of disk space a top-level site consumes, select this check box and type the number of megabytes in the accompanying text box.

493

- **Send Warning E-Mail When Site Storage Reaches**   If you want the quota to notify the top-level site administrator when disk space reaches a warning level, select this check box and type the number of megabytes in the accompanying text box.

4 Click OK to save any changes, or click Cancel to quit without saving.

To modify a Web site collection by changing its quota template, changing its quota values, or clearing a lock, proceed as follows:

1 On the SharePoint Central Administration home page, under Component Configuration, click Manage Quotas And Locks.

2 When the Manage Quotas And Locks page appears, click Manage Site Collection Quotas And Locks.

3 When the Manage Site Collection Quotas And Locks page appears, type the URL of the collection's top-level site in the box titled URL Of Top-Level Web Site, and then click the View Data button. The page should then display all the fields shown in Figure 15-14.

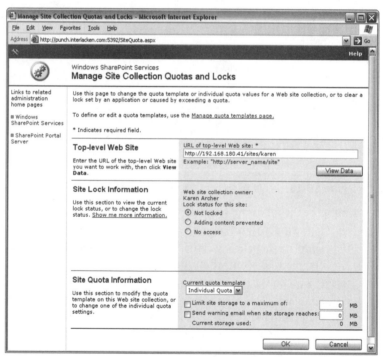

Figure 15-14.   This is the page that manages disk quotas for a site collection.

4 Configure the following settings.

- **URL Of Top-Level Web Site**   To work with quotas and locks for a different collection, type the top-level site's URL and click View Data.

- **Lock Status For This Site**   Select Not Locked, Adding Content Prevented, or No Access.

- **Current Quota Template**   From the drop-down list, choose either Individual Quota or a predefined quota template. If you choose Individual Quota, you can specify the limits you want. If you choose a predefined template, the limits for that template will apply.

- **Limit Site Storage To A Maximum Of**   If you chose a predefined quota template, this check box will reflect the lock setting in that template. If you click the check box, the template will revert to Individual Quota so that you can disable and specify, or disable, a disk limit.

- **Send Warning Email When Site Storage Reaches**   This check box works like the preceding one, except that it affects warning messages rather than locks.

5 Click OK to save any changes, or click Cancel to quit without saving.

When you use the Manage Site Collection Quotas And Locks page to display the properties of a collection, and that collection uses a named template, the current template values will appear as Site Quota Information. These are not, however, the current values in effect for that collection. To update the values in effect, you must click the OK button.

Configuring Data Retrieval Service Settings

Among its many other features, Windows SharePoint Services serves as the platform for data retrieval services. These are services through which data consumers and data sources can communicate using the Simple Object Access Protocol (SOAP) and XML. In the simplest terms, data retrieval services retrieve data from various sources and present it as XML.

Client applications (such as FrontPage) and data-bound Web Parts (such as Data View Web Parts and the Spreadsheet Web Parts) can use a data retrieval service to query an available data source.

To enable, disable, or configure access to the data retrieval services on a SharePoint server, take these steps.

1 On the SharePoint Central Administration home page, under Component Configuration, click Configure Data Retrieval Service Settings. This will display the Data Retrieval Service Settings page shown in Figure 15-15.

Chapter 15

495

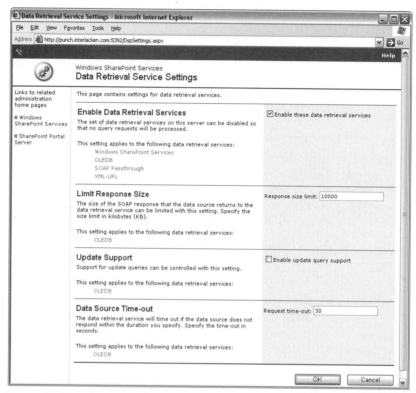

Figure 15-15. Data Retrieval Services present data from various sources in a standard, XML-based way.

2 Configure these settings on the Data Retrieval Service Settings page:

- **Enable These Data Retrieval Services** Select this check box to enable access to the data retrieval services running on the server. By default, these are Windows SharePoint Services, OLEDB, SOAP Passthrough, and XML-URL.

- **Response Size Limit** Specify the maximum size (in kilobytes) of the SOAP response that the data source can return to the data retrieval service. This guards against an application's trying to retrieve an entire, large database by mistake.

- **Enable Update Query Support** Select this box to give applications the authority to submit SQL statements for processing. (In practice, this applies to SELECT statements as well as to INSERT, UPDATE, and DELETE.)

- **Request Time-Out** Specify the maximum number of seconds the data retrieval service should wait for the data source to respond.

3 Click OK to save any changes, or click Cancel to quit without saving.

In a default configuration, the Response Size Limit, Enable Update Query Support, and Request Time-Out settings apply only to OLEDB.

> The Spreadsheet Web Part runs a subset of Microsoft Excel 2003 in a Web Part Page. To use it, you must install the Microsoft Office 2003 Web Parts and Components on your SharePoint server, and have the Microsoft Office 2003 Web Components installed on each client computer. For information on obtaining and installing these components, refer to, "Installing the Microsoft Office 2003 Web Parts and Components," in Chapter 18.

If you want the data retrieval service to connect to a remote Microsoft SQL Server database that uses Windows authentication, all of the following must be using Kerberos authentication:

- The server running the data retrieval service
- The remote server running SQL Server
- The client initially making the request

> For more information about setting up Kerberos authentication, see the Help system for Internet Information Services (IIS) 6.0 and Microsoft Knowledge Base article 832769, "How to configure a Windows SharePoint Services Virtual Server To Use Kerberos Authentication," at *support.microsoft.com/?id=832769*.

Administering Virtual Servers

This section explains how you can extend, maintain, and delete virtual Web servers extended with Windows SharePoint Services.

Extending a Virtual Server with Windows SharePoint Services

Chapter 13 explained the procedure for extending the first virtual server on a computer running Windows SharePoint Services. The procedure for extending the second and all subsequent servers is the same, even if the server is running WMSDE. It assumes you've already:

- Created a folder that will serve as the virtual server's root.
- Started IIS Manager, right-clicked the Web Sites entry for the computer, chosen New and Web Site from the shortcut menus, and completed the Web Site Creation Wizard.
- Chosen a new port number to use, or configured IIS to filter traffic to the new virtual server based on Host headers. At least through Service Pack 1, Windows SharePoint Services doesn't support virtual servers bound to a specific IP address.

> For instructions on extending a virtual server with Windows SharePoint Services, refer to "Extending a Virtual Server with Windows SharePoint Services and Connecting It to SQL Server" in Chapter 13.

Configuring Virtual Server Settings

A Central Administration site can configure a variety of settings for each virtual server extended with Windows SharePoint Services. To reach the main menu page for all these settings, proceed as follows:

1 On the SharePoint Central Administration home page, under Virtual Server Configuration, click Configure Virtual Server Settings. This displays the Virtual Server List page shown in Figure 15-16.

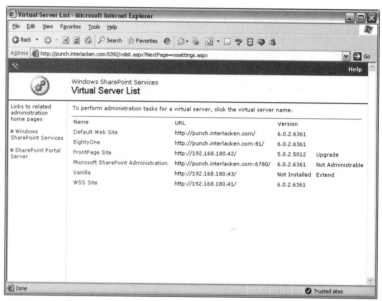

Figure 15-16. This page displays a list of all the virtual Web servers on a computer, SharePoint servers or not.

2 When the Virtual Server List page appears, click the name of the SharePoint Virtual Server you want to configure.

■ The server titled Microsoft SharePoint Administration Server is the Central Administration server. That server name won't respond to mouse clicks.

■ If a virtual server's version begins with a 5 or lower, it's running the FrontPage Server Extensions. You can't manage such sites through the Central Administration server.

■ If a virtual server's version is Not Installed, clicking its name displays the Extend Virtual Server page explained in Chapter 13.

■ If a virtual server's version begins with a 6, clicking it name displays the Virtual Server Settings page shown in Figure 15-17.

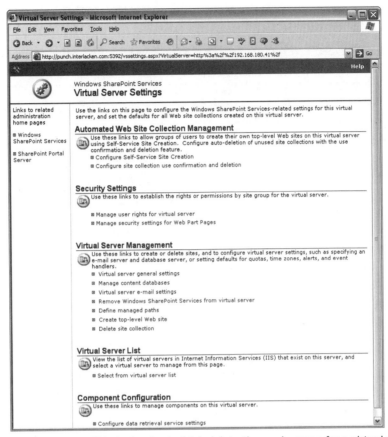

Figure 15-17. This is the Central Administration main menu for a virtual server.

Once the Virtual Server Settings page is on display, you can return to the Central Administration page by clicking the Windows SharePoint Services link under Links To Related Administration Home Pages in the top left corner of the page.

To administer a different virtual server, click the Select From Virtual Server List link under Virtual Server List. This again displays the Virtual Server List page shown in Figure 15-16.

The remaining topics in this section explain how to configure the settings available on the Virtual Server Settings page.

Specifying Virtual Server General Settings

To configure the most global and most common settings for a virtual server extended with Windows SharePoint Services, proceed as follows.

1   On the Virtual Server Settings page, under Virtual Server Management, click Virtual Server General Settings. This will display the Virtual Server General Settings page shown in Figures 15-18 and 15-19.

499

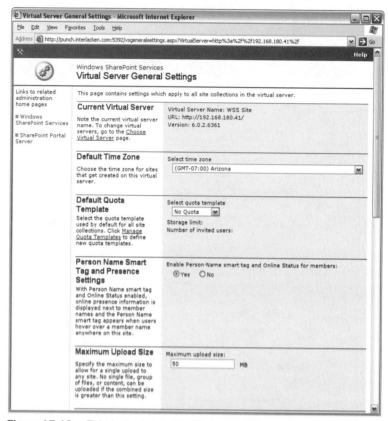

Figure 15-18. This is the top half of the page that configures the most common settings for a SharePoint virtual Web server.

2 Configure these settings on the Virtual Server General Settings page:

- **Select Time Zone** Select the time zone to use when displaying times throughout the virtual server. Times appear in the server's time zone, and not in the team member's time zone.

- **Select Quota Template** Select the quota template that will apply by default to all new site collections. To define a new quota template, click the Manage Quota Templates link.

- **Enable Person Name Smart Tag And Online Status For Members** Click Yes of you want sites on the virtual server to display online presence information (that is, a Windows Messenger icon) next to member names, and if you want a Person Name smart tag to appear when team members pass the mouse over a member name.

- **Maximum Upload Size** Specify the maximum number of megabytes a team member can upload to the server in a single operation. If the member is uploading multiple files at once, the limit applies to the total of all those files. This is important because file uploads reside briefly in memory until the server saves them.

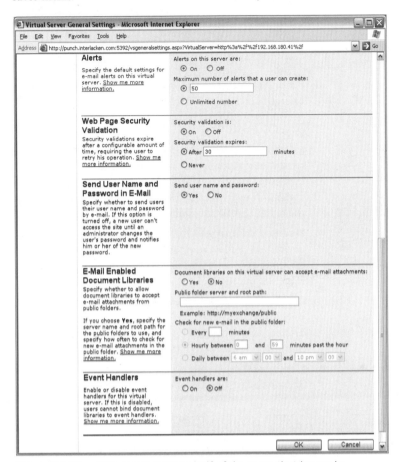

Figure 15-19. This is the bottom half of the page that began in Figure 15-18.

- **Alerts On This Server Are** Specify On to give team members the option of receiving e-mail messages when changes occur to lists, libraries, or other aspects of the site. This is the default. Specify Off to suppress this feature.

- **Maximum Number Of Alerts That A User Can Create** Specify the greatest number of alerts a team member can have in effect at once, or select Unlimited Number.

■ **Security Validation Is** Select On if you want the virtual server to display an error page when a team member submits information to the server after a period of inactivity. This is in addition to any logon/password prompts that may occur. To recover, the team member must refresh the original page and then resubmit the information.

■ **Security Validation Expires** If you chose Security Validation Is On, either select the After Minutes box and specify a timeout period, or select Never.

■ **Send User Name and Password** This option has meaning only if the server is operating in Active Directory Account Creation mode. In that mode, the first time a site administrator grants permission to a user name not in Active Directory, Windows SharePoint Services adds the name to Active Directory with a random password.

In that case, select Yes if you want Windows SharePoint Services to send the new username and password to the team member by e-mail. Select No if an administrator will reset the new member's password to a known value, and then notify the team member personally.

■ **Document Libraries On This Virtual Server Can Accept E-Mail Attachments** Select Yes if you want SharePoint libraries on the virtual server to accept documents sent by e-mail.

■ **Public Folder Server And Root Path** If you chose Yes in the previous setting, specify the HTTP address of the Exchange public folder that will receive the mail. This should be in the format http://exchange.example.com/public, where exchange.example.com specifies a Microsoft Exchange 2000 or later server and public specifies a designated public folder.

■ **Check For New E-Mail In The Public Folder** Specify how often Windows SharePoint Services should check the Exchange public folder for messages containing new library documents. Then specify either a number of minutes, a certain time past the hour, or a certain time of day.

After configuring this setting, you must also configure public folder settings on the Exchange server and Advanced settings for each SharePoint library that you want to receive documents. For more information, consult the article "Integrating Exchange Server 2003 with SharePoint Products and Technologies," at http://www.microsoft.com/technet/prodtechnol/sppt/reskit/c4161881x.mspx#EBAA

■ **Event Handlers Are** Select On if you've obtained or written software that responds to document library events and performs programmed actions. A programmer could use this, for example, to send a series of InfoPath forms to a team member. Submitting each form would trigger the download of the next.

3 Click OK to save any changes, or click Cancel to quit without saving.

Managing Managed Paths

A managed path is a spot in a SharePoint server's URL tree where Windows SharePoint Services starts or stops managing content.

- An *Include Managed Path* is a URL folder were Windows SharePoint Services starts managing content. Content within an include managed path resides (or at least appears to reside) within a SharePoint content database. In addition:
  - A top-level site must begin at an include managed path. For example, if */sites/* is an include managed path, you could create a top-level site at */sites/summit*.
  - Any site you create just inside an include managed path *must* be a top-level site. So again, if */sites/* is an include managed path, you couldn't create a subsite at */sites/flatlands*.
- An *Exclude Managed Path* is a URL folder where Windows SharePoint Services stops managing content. Content within an exclude managed path resides in the Web server's normal file system.

Chapter 5 explained the procedure for creating and removing both kinds of managed paths.

> For more information about using the Central Administration server to define managed paths, refer to "Planning Managed Paths" in Chapter 5.

On common reason for setting up exclude managed paths is to permit conventional ASP.NET applications and Windows SharePoint Services to run on the same virtual server. This, however, requires more than just the exclude managed path.

> For information on configuring a SharePoint server to run conventional ASP.NET pages, refer to Microsoft Knowledge Base article 828810, "How to Enable an ASP.Net Application to Run on a SharePoint Virtual Server," at *http://support.microsoft.com/?id=828810*.

Configuring Self-Service Site Creation

By default, only SharePoint administrators can create top-level Web sites. However, if you want to give team members the right to create their own top-level sites (and consequently their own site collections), proceed as follows.

1. On the Virtual Server Settings page, under Automated Web Site Collection Management, click Configure Self-Service Site Creation. This will display the Configure Self-Service Site Creation page shown in Figure 15-20.

2. When the Configure Self-Service Site Creation page appears, configure these settings:
   - **Self-Service Site Creation Is**   Select On to give team members the capability of creating their own top-level sites. Otherwise select Off.
   - **Require Secondary Contact**   Select this check box to require that any team member who creates a top-level Web site must designate a second team member as the site's co-owner.

503

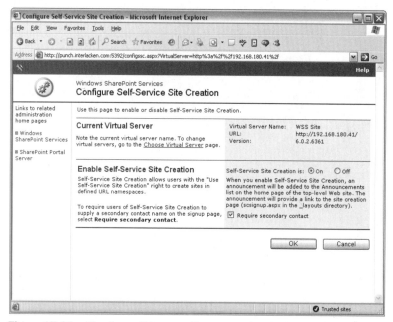

Figure 15-20. Configure this page if you want (or don't want) SharePoint team members to create their own top-level sites.

3 Click OK to save any changes, or click Cancel to quit without saving.

> For guidance on planning for Self-Service Site Creation, refer to "Planning Self-Service Site Creation" in Chapter 5. To learn about the procedure team members use to create their own top-level Web sites, refer to "Creating a Top-Level Site via Self-Service Site Creation" in Chapter 5.

Configuring Site Collection Use Confirmation and Deletion

No matter how heavily trafficked at the onset, most Web sites eventually fall out of use. Projects mercifully complete; departments realign; individuals change positions. And unfortunately, very few sites left behind achieve the status of true historic landmarks.

To root out and retire these remnants of days gone by, Windows SharePoint Services provides a Site Collection Use Confirmation and Deletion feature. This feature:

● Periodically sends the owner of each site an e-mail message, asking if the site is still necessary.

● In the absence of any response to repeated messages, deletes the site.

By default, this feature is inactive. To configure it and get it running, proceed as follows.

1 On the Virtual Server Settings page, under Automated Web Site Collection Management, click Configure Site Collection Use Confirmation And Deletion. This will display the Configure Site Collection Use Confirmation And Auto-Deletion page shown in Figure 15-21.

504

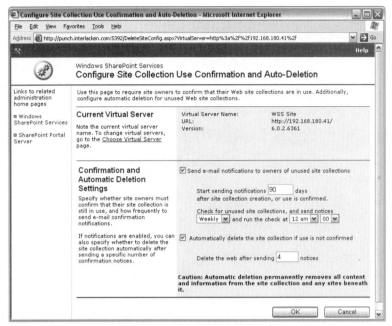

Figure 15-21. This page configures a process that detects, reports, and potentially deletes unused site collections.

2 Configure the following settings:

- **Send E-Mail Notifications To Owners Of Unused Site Collections**   Select this check box if you want Windows SharePoint Services to send notifications to owners of unused site collections.

- **Start Sending Notifications <interval> Days After Site Collection Creation Or Use Is Confirmed**   If you selected the preceding check box, type the period of inactivity, in days, that will cause notifications to start.
  Windows SharePoint Services starts a timer when it creates the top-level site, and resets it when the site owner receives a notification message and clicks a link indicating the site is still in use.

- **Check For Unused Site Collections, And Send Notices**   Select the interval between repeated message to the owners of unused sites collections, and the time of day for sending such messages. (Unused, in this sense, means unconfirmed by the site owner, regardless of hit counts or other activity measures.)
  If, for example, you specify Weekly and 12:00 AM, each owner of an unused site collection would receive a notice once a week, dated at or slightly after midnight.

- **Automatically Delete The Site Collection If Use Is Not Confirmed**   Select this check box if you want Windows SharePoint Services to automatically delete unconfirmed collections after sending a certain number of notifications and getting no response.

An owner responds to an unused site collection notice by clicking a hyperlink in the body of the notification message. This counts as a "use" and resets the timer.

- **Delete The Web After Sending <count> Notices**   Specify the number of notifications that a collection owner must ignore before Windows SharePoint Services deletes an unused collection.

3   Click OK to save any changes, or click Cancel to quit without saving.

Managing User Rights for a Virtual Server

Windows SharePoint Services takes a multi-layered approach toward controlling which actions a given team member may perform.

- A site administrator assigns each team member to one or more site groups.
- The site administrator also configures each site group with a set of rights. (Windows SharePoint Services provides some default groups with default rights, but a site administrator can override these.)
- Each right grants permission to perform certain actions.

Tables 15-1, 15-2, and 15-3 list the nineteen rights that each site group can potentially have, along with the capabilities each right confers.

Table 15-1. Windows SharePoint Services List Rights

User Right	Capabilities
Manage List Permissions	Grant, deny, and change user permissions to a list.
Manage Lists	Approve content in lists, add or remove columns in a list, and add or remove public views of a list.
Cancel Check-Out	Check in a document without saving the current changes.
Add Items	Add items to lists, add documents to document libraries, and add Web discussion comments.
Edit Items	Edit items in lists, edit documents in document libraries, edit Web discussion comments in documents, and customize Web Part Pages in document libraries.
Delete Items	Delete items from a list, documents from a document library, and Web discussion comments in documents.
View Items	View items in lists, documents in document libraries, view Web discussion comments, and set up e-mail alerts for lists.

Table 15-2. Windows SharePoint Services Site Rights

User Right	Capabilities
Manage Site Groups	Create, change, and delete site groups, including adding users to the site groups and specifying which rights are assigned to a site group.
View Usage Data	View reports on Web site usage.
Create Subsites	Create subsites such as Team Sites, Meeting Workspace sites, and Document Workspace sites.
Manage Web Site	Grants the ability to perform all administration tasks for the Web site as well as manage content and permissions.
Add and Customize Pages	Add, change, and delete HTML pages and Web Part Pages, and edit the Web site using a Windows SharePoint Services-compatible editor.
Apply Themes and Borders	Apply a theme or borders to the entire Web site.
Apply Style Sheets	Apply a style sheet (.CSS file) to the Web site.
Browse Directories	Browse directories in a Web site.
View Pages	View pages in a Web site.

Table 15-3. Table 15-3 Windows SharePoint Services Personal Rights

User Right	Capabilities
Manage Personal Views	Create, change, and delete personal views of lists.
Add/Remove Private Web Parts	Add and remove private Web Parts on a Web Part page.
Update Personal Web Parts	Update Web Parts to display personalized information.
Create Cross-Site Groups	Create a group of users who can be granted access to any site within the site collection.

In addition, a server administrator can enable or disable these rights for an entire virtual server. If, for example, an administrator wants to make sure that no one but a server administrator could view usage data, the administrator could disable the View Usage Data right for the entire server. To take such an action, proceed as follows:

1 On the Virtual Server Settings page, under Security Settings, click Manage User Rights For Virtual Server.

2 When the Manage User Rights For Virtual Server page shown in Figure 15-22 appears:

■ Clear the check box for any user right you don't want any team member to have.

507

- Select the check box for any user right team a team member could have, provided the team member belongs to a site group having that right.

- To enable all rights on the virtual server (which is the default), select the Select All check box.

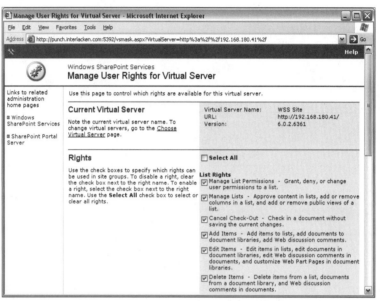

Figure 15-22. This page enables and disables rights for an entire virtual server. Team members must also have rights in individual sites.

3 Click OK to save any changes, or click Cancel to quit without saving.

After you disable a user right at the server level, that right will no longer be present in the Edit Site Group page that appears in each site. This is the page that assigns user rights to site groups.

If, at the server level, you enable a user right that you previously disabled, that right will appear once again in all Edit Site Group pages, with all prior settings intact.

Managing Security Settings for Web Part Pages

This section explains how to control two of the ways team members can customize Web Parts. As usual:

1 On the Virtual Server Settings page, under Security Settings, click Manage Security Settings For Web Part Pages. This will display the Manage Settings For Web Part Pages page shown in Figure 15-23.

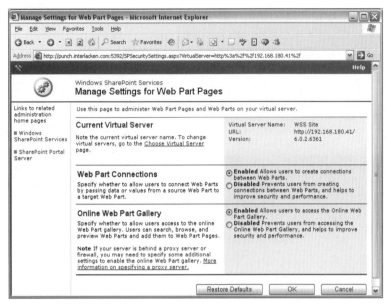

Figure 15-23. By using this page, you can limit the way team members acquire and configure Web Parts.

2 Configure these settings on the Manage Settings For Web Part Pages page:

- **Web Part Connections** Click Enabled if it's all right for team members to create connections among Web Parts. Click Disabled to prevent this activity.

- **Online Web Part Gallery** Click Enabled if it's all right for team members to retrieve and install Web Parts from the Online Web Part Gallery. To prevent this, click Disabled.

3 Click OK to save any changes, or click Cancel to quit without saving.

The Online Web Part Gallery offers a collection of Web Parts team members can download and install from Microsoft's Web site. The content may vary over time, but typically it offers news, weather, and sports from MSNBC.

For more information about Web Part Connections, refer to "Connecting Web Parts" in Chapter 12

Managing Content Databases

Every SharePoint virtual server has at least one content database. This is where all the lists, libraries, documents, customized Web pages, users lists, group memberships, site settings, and other aspects of each site reside.

Content databases can reside on the same computer as a SharePoint Web server or—in the case of SQL Server—on a different server. If you have a server farm with multiple front-end Web servers, they can all access the same content database. This guarantees that all Web visitors get the same content, no matter which front-end server handles their request.

To view or modify the content databases a virtual server is using, proceed as follows:

1 On the Virtual Server Settings page, under Virtual Server Management, click Manage Content Databases.

2 When the Manage Content Databases page shown in Figure 15-24 appears, the Current Virtual Server section identifies the current virtual server, and the Content Databases section lists the current content databases.

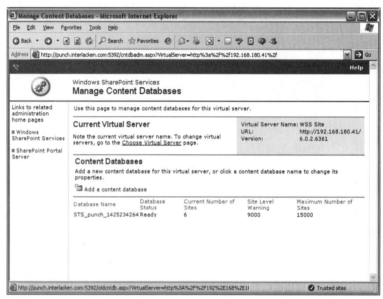

Figure 15-24. Each SharePoint virtual server has one or more content databases. This Web page maintains the list.

3 To add a content database, click the Add A Content Database link in the Content Databases section. Then, when the Add Content Database page shown in Figure 15-25 appears, fill in these fields:

■ **Use Default Content Database Server**   Click this option if you want to create a content database on the default database server configured for your server or server farm. The name of this server will appear—dimmed—in the Database Server box just below.

> For information about configuring the default content database server, refer to "Setting the Default Content Database Server" earlier in this chapter.

■ **Specify Database Server Settings**   Click this option if you want to create a content database on a server other than the default. Then, specify the server name in the Database Server box, and a database name in the Database Name box.

If you choose this approach, make sure that virtual Web server's application pool account belongs to the server roles Security Administrators and Database Creators in the database server you specify.

- **Number Of Sites Before A Warning Event Is Generated**   Specify the number of sites the database can accommodate without sending a warning message to an administrator.

- **Maximum Number Of Sites That Can Be Created In This Database**   Specify the number of sites the database can accommodate before refusing requests to create more sites.

When these entries are complete, click OK to create the database, or click Cancel to quit without saving. Both actions return you to the Manage Content Databases page.

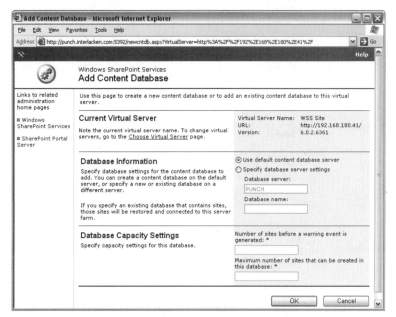

Figure 15-25.   Clicking the Add A Content Database link in Figure 15-24 displays this page, which adds a new or existing content database to a virtual server.

4   To modify or delete a content database, click its name in the Database Name column on the Manage Content Databases page. Then, when the Manage Content Database Settings page shown in Figure 15-26 appears, fill in these fields:

- **Database Status**   Select Ready if it's all right for Windows SharePoint Services to continue adding sites to this database. Click Offline to block creation of new sites.

- **Number Of Sites Before A Warning Event Is Generated**   Specify the number of sites the database can accommodate without sending a warning message to an administrator.

- **Maximum Number Of Sites That Can Be Created In This Database**   Specify the number of sites the database can accommodate before refusing requests to create more sites.

- **Remove Content Database**   Select this check box to remove a content database from its virtual server or server farm. When you select the Remove Content Database check box and click OK, the database is no longer associated with this virtual server. This removes any sites in that content database from the server farm, but the site data remains in the database.

When these entries are complete, click OK to modify the database, or click Cancel to quit without saving. Both actions return you to the Manage Content Databases page.

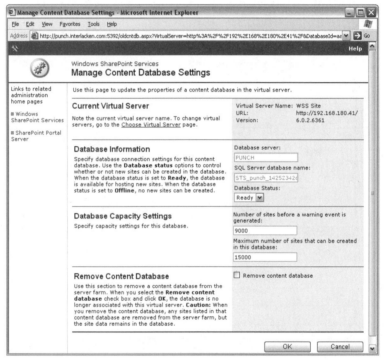

Figure 15-26.   This page modifies the properties of a content database and can also remove it from a virtual server.

5   When you're finished using the Manage Content Databases page, click the Windows SharePoint Services link under Links To Related Administration Home Pages.

When you use the Manage Content Database Settings page to delete a content database, any sites in that database will instantly become unavailable. However, those sites remain in the content database, and will reappear if you connect the same (or another) virtual server to that database.

Specifying Virtual Server E-Mail Settings

After you extend a virtual server with Windows SharePoint Services, the new virtual server's e-mail settings will be the defaults that were in effect for the entire server. To override these, proceed as follows.

1 On the Virtual Server Settings page, under Virtual Server Management, click Virtual Server E-Mail Settings.

2 When the Virtual Server E-mail Settings page appears, it will display the same fields as the Configure E-Mail Server Settings page described earlier in this chapter. Modify these fields as you wish.

3 Click OK to save any changes, or click Cancel to quit without saving.

> For instructions on setting the default e-mails settings for an entire server, refer to the section titled "Configuring Default E-Mail Server Settings" earlier in this chapter.

Configuring Data Retrieval Service Settings for a Virtual Server

An earlier section in this chapter briefly explained the concepts of a data retrieval service, and then explained how to configure data retrieval service settings for an entire server.

If the need arises, you can configure a SharePoint virtual server to have data retrieval service settings different from the default for the server. To do this:

1 On the Virtual Server Settings page, under Component Configuration, click Configure Data Retrieval Service Settings.

2 When the Data Retrieval Service Settings page shown in Figure 15-27 appears, either:

- Select the Inherit The Global Settings check box to use the settings in effect for the entire server.

- Clear the Inherit The Global Settings check box to specify unique settings for the current virtual server. Then, configure the rest of the page as you would the server-level data retrieval service settings, modifying any values you choose.

3 Click OK to save any changes, or click Cancel to quit without saving.

> For more information about configuring data retrieval service settings for an entire server, refer to "Configuring Data Retrieval Service Settings" earlier in this chapter.

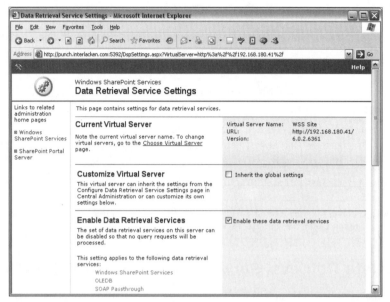

Figure 15-27. This page for virtual servers accepts or overrides the data retrieval service settings for the computer as a whole.

Removing Windows SharePoint Services from a Virtual Server

To remove Windows SharePoint Services from a virtual server, proceed as follows.

1 On the Virtual Server Settings page, under Virtual Server Management, click Remove Windows SharePoint Services From Virtual Server. This displays the Remove Windows SharePoint Services From Virtual Server page shown in Figure 15-28.

2 If you want the keep the content databases that the virtual server used, select Remove Without Deleting Content Databases. You could then reconnect those content databases to the same virtual server (after re-extending it) or to another virtual server.

If you have no further use for the content database, select Remove And Delete Content Databases.

3 Click OK to save any changes, or click Cancel to quit without saving.

If you need help connecting an existing content database to a SharePoint virtual server, refer to the section titled "Managing Content Databases" earlier in this chapter.

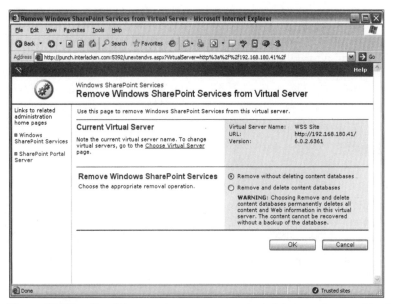

Figure 15-28. Use this page to remove a content database from a virtual server.

Administering SharePoint Sites

Site administrators (including the site owner) generally perform most administration on individual SharePoint sites. Nevertheless, the Central Administration site does have a few options that maintain individual sites. The next few sections explain these options.

Creating a Top-Level Web Site

Chapter 5 has already explained the procedure for using the Central Administration server to create a top-level Web site. For details on that procedure, refer to Chapter 5.

Deleting a Site Collection

Deleting a site collection removes all its lists, libraries, Web pages, and configuration settings from the server. There's no undo, other than restoring from a backup. If this is what you need to do, proceed as follows.

1 On the SharePoint Central Administration home page, under Virtual Server Configuration, click Delete Site Collection.

2 When the Delete Site Collection page appears, it will contain only one input field: URL Of The Site To Delete. Type the full URL of the Top-Level Web site that starts the collection.

Be sure to type a full URL such as *http://wss.fabrikam.com/sites/toledo*.

3 Click OK to save any changes, or click Cancel to quit without saving.

Managing Site Collection Owners

Every top-level Web site—and therefore every site collection—must have an owner, and may have two. If an administrator creates a top-level Web site, the administrator assigns the primary owner—and optionally the secondary owner. If a team member uses Self-Service Site Creation to create a top-level Web site, the creator is the primary owner and may designate a secondary. In either case, each owner automatically becomes a site administrator.

Site owners receive any quota or auto-deletion notices, and they're automatically site collection administrators. They can't, however, reassign ownership. Instead, a server administrator must proceed as follows.

1 On the Central Administration home page, under Security Configuration, click Manage Site Collection Owners.

2 When the Manage Site Collection Owners page shown in Figure 15-29 appears, type the top-level site's URL in the Web Site URL box and then click View.

   ■ If this displays an error page, click the browser's Back button and correct the URL.

   ■ If this displays the top-level site's current owners, proceed to the next step.

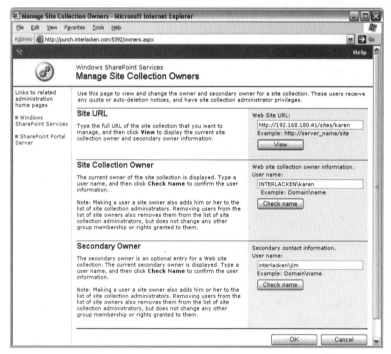

Figure 15-29. This Central Administration page can update the owner information for a site collection.

3 Under either Site Collection Owner or Secondary Owner, type a new user name in User Name box, and then click the nearby Check Name button.

- If a red error message such as, "Error in checking owner name: User cannot be found," appears at the top of the page, correct your entry.

- If there's no message, check the other owner name or proceed to the next step.

4 Click OK to apply your changes or Cancel to quit without saving.

Managing Web Site Users

Normally, the administrator of each SharePoint site controls which team members can access that site. If, however, that person isn't available, a server administrator can add, modify, or delete users by means of this procedure:

1 On the Central Administration home page, under Security Configuration, click Manage Web Site Users. This displays the Manage Web Site Users page shown in Figure 15-30.

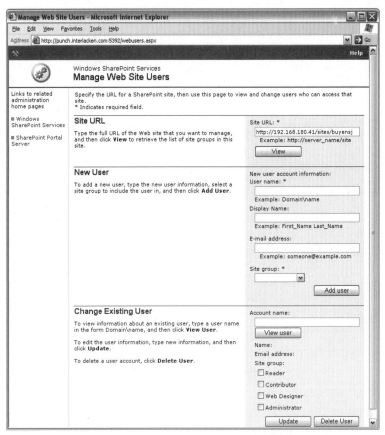

Figure 15-30. By using this page, administrators can add and authorize team members, or remove from individual sites.

2 Type the site's URL in the Site URL box and then click View.

3 To add a new team member, specify values for these fields in the New User section:

- **User Name**   Type the team member's domain or Active Directory account, in domain\name format.

- **Display Name**   Type the new team member's full name, such as Hung-Fu (Tony) Ting.

- **E-Mail Address**   Type the team member's e-mail address, such as hungfu@litwareinc.com.

- **Site Group**   Select a site group that the new team member will join, such as Reader, Contributor, Web Designer, or Administrator.

  When these entries are complete, click the Add User button.

4 To change a team member's group membership, follow these steps:

4.1 In the Change Existing User section of the page, type the team member's domain account in the Account Name box, and then click View User. If this results in a message like, "User cannot be found," correct your entry and retry.

4.2 If the Name and E-Mail Address fields display the values you expect, select the check box for each site group the team member should belong to, and clear the rest.

4.3 Click the Update button.

5 To delete all site privileges for a team member, proceed as follows:

5.1 As in the previous step, type the team member's domain account in the Account Name box, and then click View User.

5.2 If the Name and E-Mail Address fields display the values you expect, click the Delete User button.

6 To return to the Central Administration menu, click the Windows SharePoint Services link under Related Administration Home Pages, in the top left corner of the page.

Using the Command-Line Administration Program

You can administer a SharePoint server from the command line as well as through the Central Administration Web pages. This is useful not only for certain commands that have no equivalent in the Central Administration pages, but also for running commands in scripts and batch files.

A program named stsadm.exe is the launch point for all Windows SharePoint Services command-line functions. By default the setup program installed this program at:

C:\Program Files\Common Files\Microsoft Shared\web server extensions\60\BIN\

The first argument when running stsadm.exe is always an operation code, which you prefix with an –o switch. Here's an example:

```
stsadm.exe -o getadminport
```

After the operation code, you type any additional switches and values in much the same way. For example, the following command adds a team member named Karen Archer to a site at http://192.168.180.41/sites/ed. Of course, you would type it all on one line.

```
stsadm -o adduser
        -url http://192.168.180.41/sites/ed
        -userlogin interlacken\karen
        -useremail karen@interlacken.com
        -role contributor
        -username "Karen Archer"
```

To get the full syntax for any operation code, type stsadm –help followed by the operation code. Here's an example:

```
stsadm -help adduser
```

Table 15-4 lists all the possible operation codes.

For a more detailed explanation of the stsadm commands, refer to the section titled "Command-Line Operations," in the Administrator's Guide for Windows SharePoint Services. You can view this section online at: *http://www.microsoft.com/resources/documentation/wss/2/all/adminguide/en-us/ stsk01.mspx*

Table 15-4. stsadm.exe Operations

Operation	Description
addpath	Adds a defined path (inclusion or exclusion) to a virtual server.
addtemplate	Adds a site template to the template gallery.
adduser	Adds a user account to a site and assigns the account to a site group.
addwppack	Adds a Web Part package to a server Web Part gallery.
backup	Backs up a site at the specified URL.
binddrservice	Registers a data retrieval service so it appears on the Data Retrieval Services Settings page.
createadminvs	Creates the Central Administration virtual server.
createsite	Creates a site at a specified URL.
createsiteinnewdb	Creates a site at a specified URL and creates a new content database with the username and password you specify.
createweb	Creates a subsite at a specified URL.
deleteadminvs	Deletes the Central Administration virtual server.
deleteconfigdb	Deletes the configuration database.
deletepath	Removes an included or excluded managed path.
deletesite	Deletes a site.
deletetemplate	Deletes a site template.

Chapter 15

519

Table 15-4. stsadm.exe Operations

Operation	Description
deleteuser	Deletes a user.
deleteweb	Deletes a subsite.
deletewppack	Removes the Web Parts in a Web Part package from a virtual server.
disablessc	Disables Self-Service Site Creation for a virtual server.
disablestsisapis	Disables the Windows SharePoint Services ISAPI extensions.
email	Sets the e-mail configuration settings for a server, or for a specific virtual server.
enablessc	Enables Self-Service Site Creation for a virtual server.
enablestsisapis	Enables the Windows SharePoint Services ISAPI extensions.
enumroles	Lists the site groups that are available for use in a site or subsite.
enumsites	Lists all of the sites that have been created under a virtual server.
enumsubwebs	Lists the subsites that have been created under a site.
enumtemplates	Lists the site templates that are available.
enumusers	Lists the users of a site or subsite.
enumwppacks	Lists the Web Part Packages currently in a server Web Part gallery.
extendvs	Extends a virtual server with Windows SharePoint Services and creates a new content database.
extendvsinwebfarm	Extend a virtual server with Windows SharePoint Services for use in a server farm.
getadminport	Returns the Central Administration port.
getproperty	Returns the property value for a property name.
removedrservice	Removes a data retrieval service.
renameweb	Renames a subsite.
restore	Restores a Web site from a backup file.
setadminport	Sets the port number for the administration virtual server.
setconfigdb	Connects to a new or existing configuration database.
setproperty	Sets a property with a value.
siteowner	Sets the owner or secondary owner of a site collection.
unextendvs	Removes Windows SharePoint Services from a virtual server.
uninstall	Uninstalls Windows SharePoint Services from the default virtual server at port 80.
upgrade	Upgrades a server or virtual server.
userrole	Specifies the site group membership for a user.

520

Using the SharePoint Configuration Analyzer

The SharePoint Configuration Analyzer is an unsupported Microsoft application that detects a wide range of configuration errors, and also copies log files, configuration files, and other data to a results folder for further analysis or archiving. Figure 15-31 shows some results, including two configuration errors.

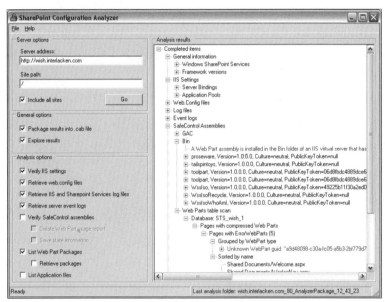

Figure 15-31. Running the SharePoint Configuration Analyzer on a SharePoint server checks for and reveals a variety of common configuration problems.

For information about downloading and using this tool, refer to "Using SharePoint Configuration Analyzer," in the Administrator's Guide for Windows SharePoint Services. This is available online at *http://www.microsoft.com/resources/documentation/wss/2/all/adminguide/en-us/stswp04.mspx.*

In Summary...

This chapter explained how server administrators and SharePoint administrators can create, maintain, and delete physical servers and virtual Web servers running Windows SharePoint Services. For the most part, this involves using pages in a restricted Central Administration Web site, but you can also do administration at the command line.

The next two chapters will explain how site owners and site administrators can maintain their own SharePoint sites.

Chapter 16

Managing Site Settings

This chapter and the next explain how to administer and control existing SharePoint sites. Much of this involves security settings, such as who can access the site and what functions they can perform, but other aspects control the site's overall appearance and capabilities, as well as personal information about each team member.

In a default installation, none of the commands in this chapter or the next requires that you be a server administrator, or even an administrator of the entire SharePoint installation. At most, you need to be an administrator of the one SharePoint site you want to modify. And for some commands, you need only be part of that one site's Web Designer, Contributors, or even Readers group. As a result, most team members will use at least some of these commands at one time or another.

This chapter explains the commands that appear on the Site Settings menu of most sites. These are the most-used and least-restricted commands. Chapter 17 will explain the commands on the Site Administration menu, which are geared more directly towards site administrators.

Displaying the Site Settings Menu

To manage settings and team member information for the current site, click the Site Settings link in the top navigation bar of any page in the site. This displays the Site Settings page shown in Figure 16-1.

The remaining sections in this chapter will explain how to use all but one of the links on this page. The one exception is the Go To Site Administration link (under Administration), which the next chapter will explain.

Each of these functions requires some level of security, but the exact level is subject to variation. Generally:

- Functions that control user accounts and user rights require membership in the Administrator site group.

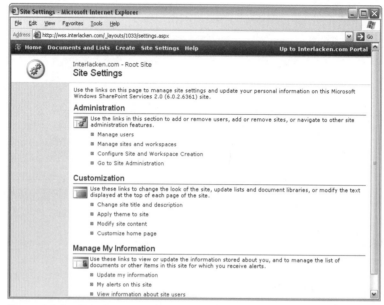

Figure 16-1. The links on this page provide access to the administrative commands most often used in a SharePoint site.

- Functions that control the site's appearance require membership in the Web Designer site group.

- Functions that involve updating site content require membership in the Contributors site group.

- Functions that involve accessing site content require membership in the Readers site group.

Of course, your site may be using a different number of site groups, differently named site groups, or a different assignment of rights to site groups. The best rules are:

- If you find yourself blocked out of a function you believe you need to perform, contact the site administrator.

- If you're the site administrator, look up the site groups that the complaining team member belongs to, and then review the rights assigned to those groups.

Managing Users

Most SharePoint sites permit access only by registered team members. There are several reasons for this:

- It denies access by people outside your team.

- It's the only way you can assign different privileges—such as Reader, Contributor, Web Designer, and Administrator—to different people.

- It's also the only way you can keep a history of who performed various actions, such as who updated a library document, who posted to a discussion board, and who responded to a survey.

A SharePoint site can get its list of authorized team members from either of two sources:

- It can maintain its own list of team members. All top-level sites must operate in this mode, and so can subsites if the need arises.
- It can inherit the team members of its parent site. This is the default for subsites, but you can easily override it.

If your site is inheriting its list of team members from its parent, the following commands won't appear on the Site Settings page.

- Manage Users
- Configure Site and Workspace Creation

To learn how to configure a subsite so it uses its own list of team members, refer to "Managing Permission Inheritance" in Chapter 17.

If these commands *do* appear, you must be a site administrator to use them.

To maintain the list of authorized team members (and their site groups, which determine permissions), proceed as follows.

1. On the Site Settings page, under Administration, click Manage Users. This displays the Manage Users page shown in Figure 16-2.

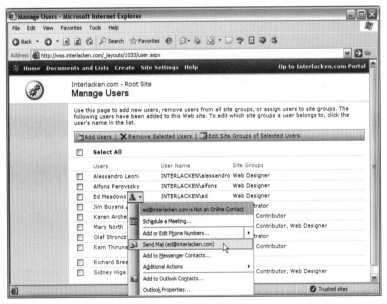

Figure 16-2. This page displays, adds, modifies, and deletes team members authorized to access a site.

525

2   If the client computer is using Internet Explorer and Office 2003 is installed, hovering the mouse over any team member's name and clicking the resulting drop-down arrow displays a menu of Windows Messenger and Outlook functions for that team member. This menu is typical of those that appear throughout Windows SharePoint Services and Office 2003.

Chapter 4 first described the commands on such menus. For more information, refer to the section titled "Using the Shared Workspace Members Tab" in Chapter 4.

3   To add a new team member, click the Add Users toolbar button on the Manage Users page. This will display the Add Users page shown in Figure 16-3.

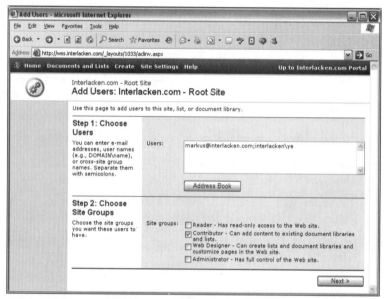

Figure 16-3.   This is the first of two pages you must submit to add a new team member.

To add the new team member, continue as follows:

3.1   In the Users box, type one or more e-mail addresses, usernames, domain group names, or cross-site group names separated with semicolons. Specify any domain users or domain groups in *domain\accountname* format. To add e-mail addresses from your Outlook address book, click the Address Book button.

3.2   In the Site Groups section, select the check box for each site group you want to assign. To place some new team members in different groups than others, either add them in separate transactions, or add them all with the same groups and correct the exceptions later.

3.3   Click the Next button to display the Add Users page shown in Figure 16-4.

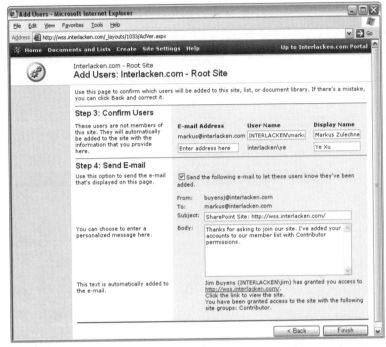

Figure 16-4.   This is the second page you submit to add a new team member.

3.4   Review the E-Mail Address, User Name, and Display Name values for each team member or group you specified on the previous page. If any of the information in text boxes is missing or incorrect, correct it on this page. If any of the values you entered on the previous page are incorrect, click the Back Button to correct them.

3.5   To send an e-mail message to the new team members, select the check box titled Send The Following E-Mail To Let These Users Know They've Been Added, and then update the Subject and Body fields if you want.

3.6   Click Finish to add the new team members.

4   To disable access to the site by one or more team members, select their check boxes on the Manage Users page, and then click the Remove Selected Users toolbar button.

5   To modify the site groups to which one or more team members belong, take either of these actions on the Manage Users page:

■   Select the check boxes for the team members you want to administer, and then click the Edit Site Groups Of Selected Users toolbar button.

■   Click the name of the team member you want to administer.

Both of these actions display an Edit Site Group Membership page that provides a check box for each available site group.

Select the check box for each site group you want to assign, and then click OK to apply your change, or Cancel to quit without saving.

527

Managing Sites and Workspaces

To create, delete, or browse a direct subsite of the current site, complete the following procedure.

1 On the Site Settings page, under Administration, click Manage Sites And Workspaces. This displays the Sites And Workspaces page shown in Figure 16-5.

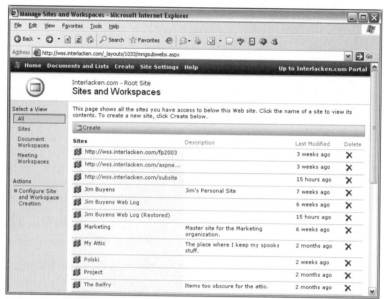

Figure 16-5. This page lists all subsites of the current site. In addition, it can create and delete subsites.

2 To create a site, click the Create toolbar button. This displays a New SharePoint Site page.

For more information about using the New SharePoint Site page, refer to "Creating a New SharePoint Site" in Chapter 5.

3 To delete a site, click its Delete icon (at the far right of the page).

4 To browse a site, click its name.

Configuring Site and Workspace Creation

By default, only the administrators of a site can create subsites. To relax this restriction, proceed as follows.

1 On the Site Settings page, under Administration, click Configure Site And Workspace Creation. This displays the Modify Site And Workspace Creation page shown in Figure 16-6. This page displays a check box for each site group that has enough privileges to update the current site, but not enough privileges to create a subsite.

In essence, the page displays the site groups that are candidates to receive the privileges necessary to create a subsite.

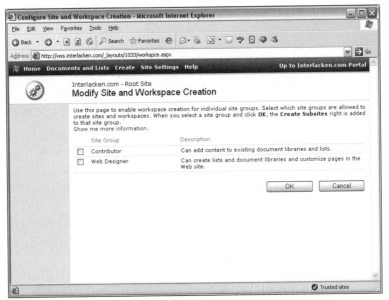

Figure 16-6.   This page adds the Create Subsites right to any site groups you select. Members of those groups can then create subsites.

2   Select the check box for each site group that needs the ability to create subsites.

3   Click OK to apply your changes, or Cancel to quit without saving.

Changing Site Title and Description

Every SharePoint site has a title and may have a description. This text appears on the standard SharePoint home page and in various other contexts that identify the site. To change these values, proceed as follows.

1   On the Site Settings page, under Customization, click Change Site Title And Description.

2   When the Change Site Title And Description page shown in Figure 16-7 appears, update the Title and Description fields as you want.

3   Click OK to apply your changes, or Cancel to quit without saving.

Chapter 16

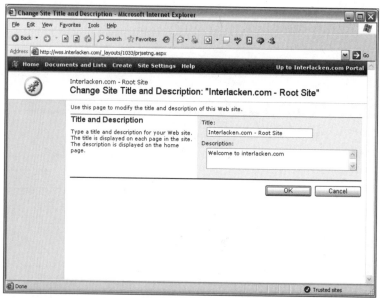

Figure 16-7. This page changes the title and description of the current site.

Applying a Theme to a Site

A Theme applies a uniform set of colors and fonts to a Web site. Windows SharePoint Services comes with a number of predesigned themes you can apply.

> For instructions on changing the Theme that applies to a site, refer to "Applying a Theme" in Chapter 5. For information about using FrontPage 2003 to apply, customize, and deploy themes, and about adding custom themes to a SharePoint server, refer to the material in Chapter 7 starting with "Introducing FrontPage Themes."

Modifying Site Content

As Chapter 6 explained, all standard view pages for SharePoint libraries and lists contain a Modify Settings And Columns link. This link displays a Customize page that can change the general settings, columns, or views for that library or list.

To display one of these Customize pages without first displaying the list, proceed as follows.

1   On the Site Settings page, under Customization, click Modify Site Content.

2   When the Modify Site Content page shown in Figure 16-8 appears, click the link titled "Customize *<listname>*", where *<listname>* identifies the list or library you want to modify.

3   Use the Customize page as Chapter 6 explained.

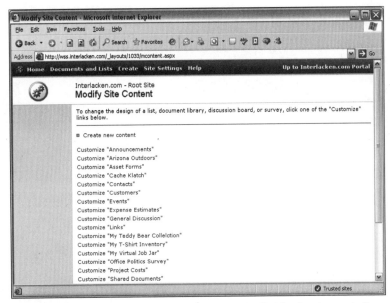

Figure 16-8. The links on this page connect to the Customize page for each list and library in the current site.

Customizing a Home Page

Chapter 5 explained how you can click the Modify Shared Page link on a Web Part Page and then add, reconfigure, relocate, or remove Web Parts from that page.

To work with your site's home page this way without first displaying it, display the Site Settings page and then, under Customization, click Customize Home Page.

> For more information about Modifying Web Part Pages, refer to the topics "Modifying Web Part Pages" and "Adding Web Parts to a Page," in Chapter 5.

Updating Your Personal Information

Windows SharePoint Services doesn't store a lot of personal information about team members, but to update the information that it *does* keep about you, proceed as follows. On the Site Settings page, under Manage My Information, click Update My Information. This will display the Personal Settings page shown in Figure 16-9.

● To update the information on this page, click the Edit User Information toolbar button. This displays the Edit Personal Settings page shown in Figure 16-10.

Specify these fields on the Edit Personal Settings page.

■ **E-mail Address** Enter or correct your e-mail address.

■ **Notes** Enter or correct descriptive info you want to provide about yourself.

Chapter 16

531

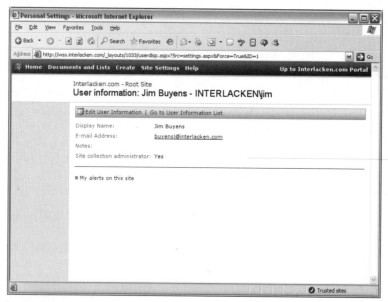

Figure 16-9. This page displays the essential information for one team member.

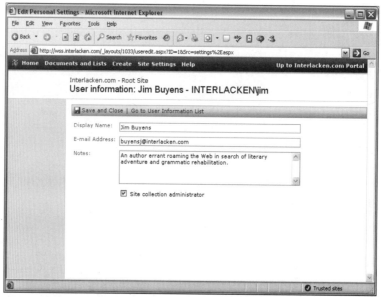

Figure 16-10. This page updates the essential information for one team member.

■ **Site Collection Administrator**   If you're currently a site collection administrator, this check box will be selected. Clearing the box relinquishes that authority.

If you're not a site collection administrator, you can't just select this check box and become one. However, a site collection administrator can display this page on your behalf, and select the box for you.

For information on how site collection administrators can display and update the User Information page for team members other than themselves, refer to "Viewing Site Collection User Information" in Chapter 17.

When you're finished making changes, click the Save And Close toolbar button.

● To display a page that lists all alerts you currently have in effect for the current site, click the My Alerts On This Site link. The next section will explain how to use the resulting page.

● To display a list of all team members that have ever accessed the current site, click the Go To User Information List toolbar button. The last section in this chapter will explain how to use the resulting page.

Managing Your Alerts

Alerts are triggers that send you an e-mail message when changes occur to lists or libraries that you've selected. To view, add, modify, or delete your alerts on a given site, first browse the site and then, on the Site Settings page, under Manage My Information, click My Alerts On This Site. The resulting My Alerts On This Site page, shown in Figure 16-11, displays all alerts you have in effect within the current site, grouped by frequency.

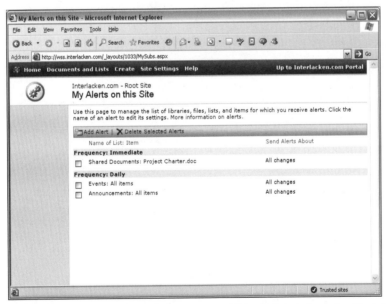

Figure 16-11.   On this page you can see which alerts you have in effect. You can also add, edit, or delete alerts.

533

● To add an alert, click the Add Alert toolbar button. This will display the New Alert page shown in Figure 16-12.

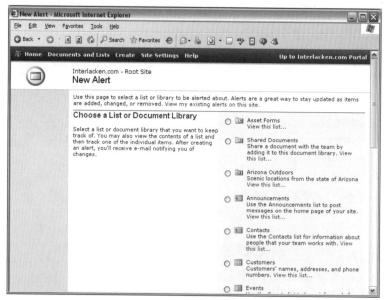

Figure 16-12. This page illustrates the first step in creating a new alert: choosing the list or library the alert will monitor.

Select the list or library for which you wish to receive an alert message, and then click the Next button at the bottom of the page. This displays the New Alert page shown in Figure 16-13.

Under Alert Me About, specify the condition that will generate an alert message:

■ **All Changes**   Whenever someone adds, changes, or deletes an item in the list or library

■ **Added Items**   Whenever someone adds an item to the list or library

■ **Changed Items**   Whenever someone changes a list or library item

■ **Web Discussion Updates**   Whenever someone comments on a document by using the Web Discussion feature. This option appears only for document and form libraries.

■ **Deleted Items**   Whenever someone deletes a list or library item

Chapter 16

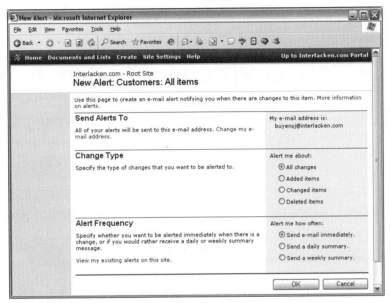

Figure 16-13. On this page you specify the conditions and frequency of the alert notifications.

If you wish, Windows SharePoint Services can summarize alert notifications into one daily or weekly e-mail message. To control this, choose one of these options under Alert Me How Often:

- **Send E-Mail Immediately** Select this option to receive alert notification individually, as they occur.
- **Send A Daily Summary** Select this option to receive summarized alerts once a day. An administrator configures the time of day when this occurs.
- **Send A Weekly Summary** Select this option to receive summarized alerts once a week. An administrator configures the day of the week and the time of day when this occurs.

Click OK to create the alert.

- To edit an existing alert, click its name in the My Alerts On This Site page. This displays an Edit Alert page that strongly resembles the New Alert page shown previously in Figure 16-13. Select the change type and alert frequency you want, and then click OK.
- To delete one or more alerts, select the check box that precedes each on the My Alerts On This Site page, and then click the Delete Selected Alerts toolbar button.

Viewing Information about Site Users

To display a list of team members who a site administrator has authorized (or who have otherwise participated in) the current site, click the View Information About Site Users link on the Site Settings page. This link appears under the Manage My Information heading, and it displays the page shown in Figure 16-14.

> **Note** Certain administrative accounts can access a SharePoint site accounts even though a site administrator never specifically authorizes them. When an administrative account "participates: in a site this way, Windows SharePoint Services creates the necessary site account, and the account then appears on the site's User Information page.

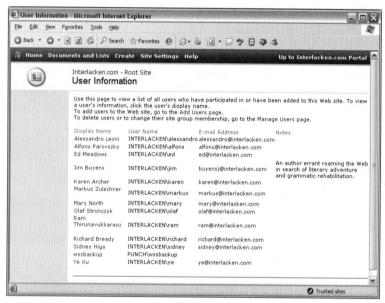

Figure 16-14. This page displays manually authorized and other participating team members in the current site.

- To add users to the Web site, click the Add Users Page link near the top of the page. This displays the Add Users page shown previously in Figure 16-3.

  For more information about using the Add Users page, refer to the section titled "Managing Users" earlier in this chapter.

- To delete users or to change their site group membership, click the Manage Users Page link that appears in the line below the Add Users Page link. This displays the Manage Users page shown previously in Figure 16-2.

  For more information about using the Manage Users page, refer to the section titled "Managing Users" earlier in this chapter.

- To change the E-mail Address, Notes, or Site Collection Administrator status of any listed team member, click the member's display name. This displays the User Information page shown previously in Figure 16-9.

  For more information about using the User Information page, refer to the section titled "Updating Your Personal Information" earlier in this chapter.

In Summary...

This chapter explained how to use the most common commands for controlling the team members, access, appearance, and capabilities of a SharePoint site.

The next chapter will explain additional configuration options, mostly of interest to administrators.

Administering Your SharePoint Site

Every SharePoint site has not only a Site Settings menu, but also a Site Administration menu. The commands on the Site Administration menu are mostly for administrators of individual sites and site collections. They cover such functions as authorizing team members, changing permissions, selecting regional settings, managing disk space, viewing activity statistics, and managing resources common to all the sites in a collection.

As you review this chapter, don't forget the concepts of site collections. A site collection consists of one, specially created *top-level* Web site, and all its subsites. The commands for managing collection resources appear in the top-level site, but the resources themselves are available in every subsite.

Displaying the Site Administration Menu

To display the Site Administration page for any site, first click the Site Settings link in the top navigation bar of any page and then, under Administration, click Go To Site Administration. This displays the Site Administration page shown Figure 17-1.

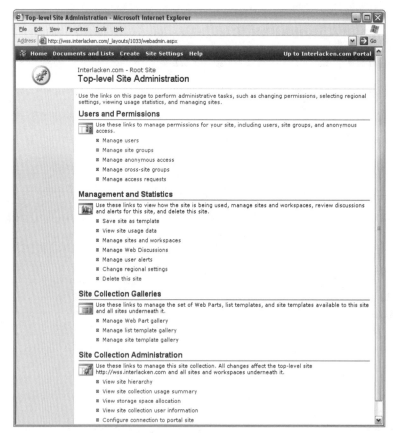

Figure 17-1. The Site Administration page provides the most global commands for site collection and site administrators.

The Site Administration page varies somewhat depending on whether the current site is:

- A top-level site using Windows domain accounts for authentication.
- A top-level site using Active Directory account creation.
- A subsite that inherits permissions from its parent site.
- A subsite that uses unique permissions.

Table 17-1 summarizes the administration commands that appear in each case.

Table 17-1. Site Administration Command Availability

Function	Top Site		Subsite	
	Domain Accounts	AD Accounts	Inheriting	Unique
Users and Permissions				
Manage permission inheritance	○	○	●	●
Manage users	●	●	○	●
Manage site groups	●	●	○	●
Manage anonymous access	●	●	○	●
Manage cross-site groups	●	●	●	●
Manage access requests	●	○	○	●
Management and Statistics				
Save site as template	●	●	●	●
View site usage data	●	●	●	●
Manage sites and workspaces	●	●	●	●
Manage Web discussions	●	●	●	●
Manage user alerts	●	●	●	●
Change regional settings	●	●	●	●
Delete this site	●	●	●	●
Site Collection Galleries				
Manage Web Part gallery	●	●	○	○
Manage list template gallery	●	●	○	○
Manage site template gallery	●	●	○	○
Site Collection Administration				
Go To Top-Level Site Administration	○	○	●	●
View site hierarchy	●	●	○	○
View site collection usage summary	●	●	○	○
View storage space allocation	●	●	○	○
View site collection user information	●	●	○	○
Configure connection to portal site	●	●	○	○

Chapter 17

541

Managing Permission Inheritance

A subsite can have its own list of authorized team members and site groups, or it can use the security configuration of its parent site. To vary this setting, proceed as follows.

1 On the Site Administration page, under Users And Permissions, click Manage Permission Inheritance.

2 When the Manage Permission Inheritance page appears, choose one of these options:

■ **Use The Same Permissions As The Parent Site** The current site will use the same user accounts and site groups as its parent Web site.

■ **Use Unique Permissions.** The current site will have its own list of user accounts and site groups. A site administrator can manage these user accounts and site groups separately from the parent Web site.

3 Click OK to apply your change, or Cancel to quit without saving.

If you change a subsite's permissions from inherited to unique, the subsite will initially receive a copy of its former parent's account list and site groups.

If you change a subsite's permissions from unique to inherited, Windows SharePoint Services discards the subsite's account list and site groups. The parent site's permissions will be in effect for both sites.

Managing Users

To view, add, modify, or delete the team members authorized to use the current site, click the Manage Users link in the Users and Permissions section of the Site Administration page.

This link displays the same Manage Users page, with the same functions, as the Manage Users link on the Site Settings page.

For more information about using the Manage Users page, refer to "Managing Users" in Chapter 16.

Chapter 17

Managing Site Groups

Site groups occupy an intermediate position between rights and team members. There are two ways of looking at this relationship.

- You assign rights to site groups, and then configure each site group to include the team members who need those rights.
- You assign team members to site groups, and then grant each site group the rights its team members need.

To view, add, or delete a site group, or to change its rights or membership, click the Manage Site Groups link in the Users And Permissions section of the Site Administration page. This displays the Manage Site Groups page shown in Figure 17-2.

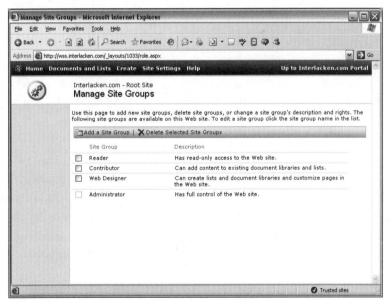

Figure 17-2. Site groups associate one or more team members with a list of specific rights. Windows SharePoint Services creates these four site groups as part of every new site, but you can add, change, or delete any site groups you want.

To create a new site group, proceed as follows:

1 On the Manage Site Groups page, click the Add A Site Group toolbar button. This displays the Add A Site Group page shown in Figure 17-3.

Chapter 17

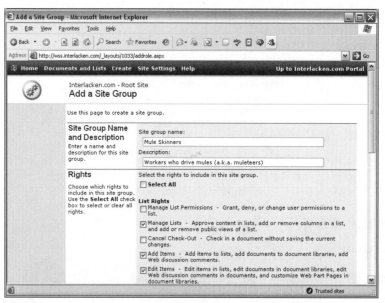

Figure 17-3. When you create a site group, you specify the rights it will confer. The list of possible rights is longer than this screen shot shows.

2   Enter the following fields:

- ■ **Site Group Name**   Type the name by which you and other team members will know the site group.

- ■ **Description**   Type a brief description of the site group or its purpose.

- ■ **Rights**   Select the check box for each right that members in this site group require. There are twenty rights in all.

3   To create the site group, click the Create Site Group button at the bottom of the page. To quit without saving, click the Cancel button.

Here's the procedure to delete one or more site groups:

1   On the Manage Site Groups page, select the check boxes for each site group you want to delete.

2   Click the Delete Selected Site Groups toolbar button.

3   When the Are You Sure confirmation prompt appears, click Yes.

To change the membership or rights of a site group, follow this procedure.

1   On the Manage Site Groups page, click the name of the site group you want to modify. This will display the Site Group Members page shown in Figure 17-4.

2   To add one or more team members, click the Add Members toolbar button on the Site Group Members page. This will display the same Add Users page that Chapter 16 described for adding users to a site. In this context, of course, the page adds team members to a site group rather than a site.

For more information about using the Add Users page, refer to "Managing Users" in Chapter 16. However, every time you read the word *site*, think *site group*.

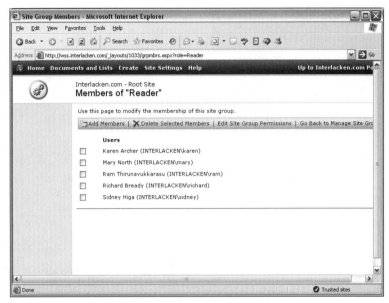

Figure 17-4. This page lists and maintains the list of team members who belong to a site group.

3 To delete team members from a site group, take these steps.

3.1 On the Site Group Members page, select the check box for each team member you want to delete.

3.2 Click the Delete Selected Members toolbar button.

3.3 When the Are You Sure confirmation prompt appears, click Yes.

4 To change the rights assigned to a group, take these steps.

4.1 On the Site Group Members page, click the Edit Site Group Permissions toolbar button. This will display an Edit Site Group page very similar to the Add A Site Group Page shown previously in figure 17-3, except that you can't change the Site Group Name field.

4.2 If you wish, change the site group's description.

4.3 Select the check boxes for any additional rights the site group requires, and clear the check boxes for any rights the site group should no longer have.

4.4 To save the modified group under a new name, click the Copy Site Group button at the bottom of the page.

4.5 To save your changes, click the Submit button.

4.6 To quit without saving, click the Cancel button

Managing Anonymous Access

By default, all SharePoint sites require team members to identify themselves by logging in. You might not even notice this if you're using domain accounts and Internet Explorer, but it happens just the same.

> When Internet Explorer encounters a Web site that's running on a Windows Web server, that's in the Web visitor's Trusted Sites zone, and that requires authentication, it tries by default to use the current Windows logon account for access. Only if that fails do you get the Username / Password prompt.

If, however, you want anyone in the world (or anyone in your company) to have access to a site, proceed as follows:

1 On the Site Administration page, under Users And Permissions, click Manage Anonymous Access. This will display the Change Anonymous Access Settings page shown in Figure 17-5.

Figure 17-5. Anonymous access means the site admits all visitors without question. Authenticated users are those with valid Windows accounts in the server's domain or a trusted domain.

2   In the Anonymous Access Section, select one of these options.

- **Entire Web Site**   The site won't require login, and all content on the site will nevertheless be available.

- **Lists And Libraries**   The site won't require login, but an administrator or list manager will designate which lists and libraries anonymous visitors can access.

- **Nothing**   The site will reject all but known team members. This is the default.

3   In the All Authenticated Users section, specify these options.

- **Allow All Authenticated Users To Access Site?**   Select Yes to open the site to anyone with a valid Windows account in the same domain as the SharePoint server, or in a trusted domain. Select No if you want to explicitly specify which team members have access.

- **Assign These Users To The Following Site Group**   Choose the site group that provides the correct security for domain-wide, trust-wide team members.

4   Click OK to apply your changes, or Cancel to quit without saving.

When anonymous access is in effect and you access a site without logging in, a Sign In button will appear in place of the usual Modify Shared Page or Modify My Page link. To log in explicitly, click that button. Otherwise, you can wait until you access a secured page, and log in at the resulting prompt.

If Anonymous Access: Lists And Libraries is in effect for a site, use the following procedure for granting access to anonymous visitors:

1   Log in to the site as an administrator or list manager, and then display the default View page for the list or library.

2   Click Modify Settings And Columns, and then Change Permissions For This List.

3   When the Change Permissions page appears, under Actions, click the Change Anonymous Actions link.

4   When the Change Anonymous Access Settings page appears, under Anonymous Users Can, select any combination of these check boxes.

- **Add Items**   You want anonymous visitors to add list items, library documents, or Web discussion comments.

- **Edit Items**   You want anonymous visitors to edit list items, library documents, Web discussion comments, or Web Part Pages in document libraries.

- **View Items**   You want anonymous visitors to view list items, library documents, or Web discussion comments. This also lets them set up e-mail alerts.

5   Click OK to apply your changes, or Cancel to quit without saving.

Chapter 17

Troubleshooting

Anonymous options Entire Web Site and Lists And Libraries are dimmed

If, under Anonymous Access, the options Entire Web Site and Lists And Libraries are dimmed, it's probably because anonymous access is disabled in IIS. To correct this, proceed as follows:

1 On the server running Windows SharePoint Services, click Start, Programs, Administrative Tools, and Internet Information Services (IIS) Manager.

2 Under Internet Information Server, open the (local computer) and Web Sites entries.

3 Right-click the virtual server that contains the site needing anonymous access and choose Properties from the shortcut menu.

4 When the virtual server's Properties dialog box appears, click the Directory Security tab and then, under Authentication And Access Control, click the Edit button.

5 When the Authentication Methods dialog box appears, select Enable Anonymous Access and then click OK.

Even though the Enable Anonymous Access setting in IIS manger affects the entire virtual server, Windows SharePoint Services will enforce security on any pages, lists, or sites you configure to require authentication.

Managing Cross-Site Groups

It's quite common for a group of team members to need the same permissions in many different sites. This is fairly easy to implement in a site collection that has no subsites with unique permissions; you just create a site group in the top-level site. Every subsite that inherits permissions from the top-level site can then use the site group you created.

If your collection has subsites with unique permissions, those subsites can't use site groups from any other site. To use a group in two or more sites, at least one of which has unique permissions, you must create a *cross-site group*.

A cross-site group doesn't belong to any one site in a collection. You can, however, add a cross-site group to any site group. This grants the members of the cross-site group the same privileges as they would have if you'd added their accounts to the site groups individually. Of course, the cross-site group is much easier to maintain over time.

To work with cross-site groups, click the Manage Cross-Site Groups link under Users And Permissions on the Site Administration page. This will display the My Cross-Site Groups page shown in Figure 17-6.

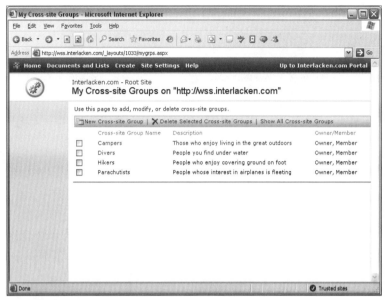

Figure 17-6. New sites and site collections have no cross-site groups by default. However, you can create any cross-site groups you need.

This page lists all the cross-site groups of which you are the owner or a member. To display a similar page that lists all site groups, click the Show All Cross-Site Groups toolbar button.

To create a cross-site group, you must have the Create Cross-Site Groups right. By default, anyone in the Contributors, Web Designers, or Administrators site group has this right. Here's the procedure:

1 Click the New Cross-Site Group button on the Cross-Site Groups page. This displays the New Cross-Site Group page shown in Figure 17-7.

2 Fill out the fields on this page as follows:

- **Name**   Give the new cross-site group a name that clearly signifies its membership or usage.

- **Description**   Type a sentence or two that describes the new cross-site group.

- **Owner**   Specify who will update the list.

   Yourself means that you will perform the updates.

   Allow Members Of This Cross-Site Group To Add And Remove Site Users means that anyone in the cross-site group can change it.

   Someone Else means that a team member other than yourself will maintain the cross-site group. To choose that team member, click the Select button.

Chapter 17

3 Click Create to create the list, or Cancel to quit without saving.

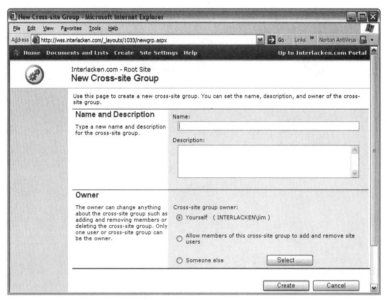

Figure 17-7. When you create a cross-site group, you must specify an owner who will maintain it.

To delete one or more cross-site groups, select their check boxes on the My Cross-Site Groups page, and then click the Delete Selected Cross-Site Groups toolbar button.

To change the membership or other properties of a cross-site group, follow this procedure:

1 Click the name of the cross-site group on the My Cross-Site Groups page. This displays the Cross-Site Group Members page shown in Figure 17-8.

2 To add a member, click the Add Members tool bar button. This displays an Add Users page that looks and works very much like the Add Users page for a site or a site group. Type a list of user accounts or e-mail addresses separated with semicolons, click Next, check for errors, and then click Finish.

3 To remove one or more members, select their check boxes, and then click the Delete Selected Members toolbar button.

4 To change the name, description, or owner of a cross-site group, click the Change Cross-Site Group Settings toolbar button. This displays a Change Cross-Site Group Settings page that looks and behaves very much like the New Cross-Site Group page shown previously in Figure 17-7.

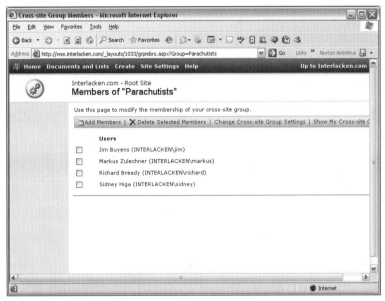

Figure 17-8. You maintain the list of members of a cross-site group much as you do for a site group.

To use a cross-site group, you specify its name on the Add Users page for a site, a site group, a list, or a library.

Managing Access Requests

When a team member gets an Access Denied error, Windows SharePoint Services can display a Request Access page whereby the team member can ask an administrator for whatever permissions they're lacking. Figure 17-9 shows how this page might look after a team member named Karen Archer, who's not a site administrator, clicked the Manage Users link on a Site Settings page.

Figure 17-10 shows the message an administrator will receive if Karen clicks the Send Request button in Figure 17-9.

Chapter 17

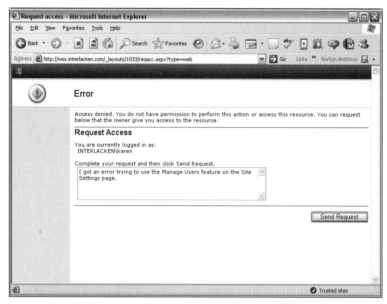

Figure 17-9. If Manage Access Requests is in effect for a site, this page offers team members who encounter security restrictions an easy way to request permission.

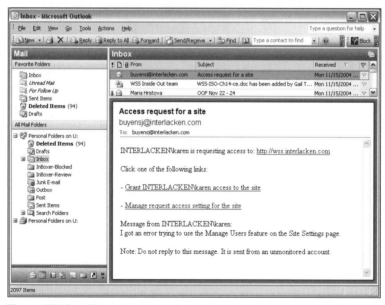

Figure 17-10. This is the type of message an administrator would receive from the Web page in Figure 17-9.

To activate this feature, proceed as follows:

1   On the Site Administration page, under Users And Permissions, click Manage Access Requests. This displays the Manage Request Access page shown in Figure 17-11.

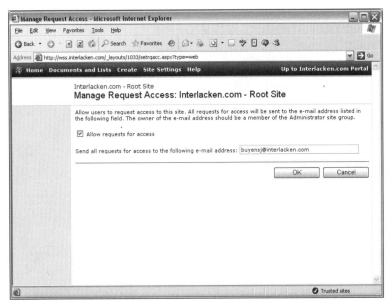

Figure 17-11.   This page enables or disables access requests for a SharePoint site.

2   Specify these fields on the Manage Request Access page.

   ■   **Allow Requests For Access**   Select this box to enable the Request Access process.

   ■   **Send All Requests For Access To The Following E-Mail Address**   Specify the e-mail address to receive the access requests. Typically, this would be a help desk or administrator.

3   Click OK to apply your changes, or Cancel to quit without saving.

Saving a Site as a Template

If you've developed a customized site that others would like to replicate, you can save your site as a template. Then, whenever someone creates a new site in the same site collection, the template you saved will appear as a choice when the Template Selection page appears.

For more information about the Template Selection page, refer to "Selecting a Site Template" in Chapter 5.

553

To create a site template based on an existing site, proceed as follows.

1 On the existing site's Site Administration page, under Management And Statistics, click Save Site As Template. This displays the Save Site As Template page shown in Figure 17-12.

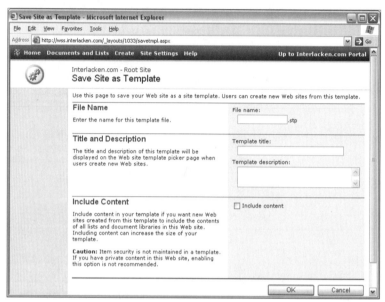

Figure 17-12. This page saves the current site as a template—with or without content—that any team member can use when creating a new site.

2 Specify these fields on the Save Site As Template page:

- **File Name**   Type a filename base that describes the template. Windows SharePoint services will append the filename extension .stp.

- **Template Title**   Type a line of text that describes the template. This is the text that will appear in the Template list box on the Template Selection page.

- **Template Description**   Type a sentence or two that further describes the template. This text also appears on the Template Selection page, but only after the team member selects the template.

- **Include Content**   Select this box to include the content of libraries and lists in the template. Clear it if you want the new site's libraries and lists to be empty.

3 Click OK to save the template, or Cancel to quit without saving.

Before selecting the Include Content check box, keep in mind that site templates don't preserve security settings. This means that, in effect, you have no control over who sees the data you saved with the template. A new site will inherit the permissions of its parent, and the site owner can grant permissions to anyone they please. *Don't* save confidential data in site templates.

When you click OK on the Save Site As Template page, Windows SharePoint services saves the template in the current collection's Site Template Gallery.

For more information about using the Site Template Gallery refer to the section titled "Managing the Site Template Gallery" later in this chapter.

Viewing Site Usage Data

To view a hit count for each page in the current site, click the View Site Usage Data link that appears on the Site Administration page under Management And Statistics. This displays the Site Usage Report page shown in Figure 17-13.

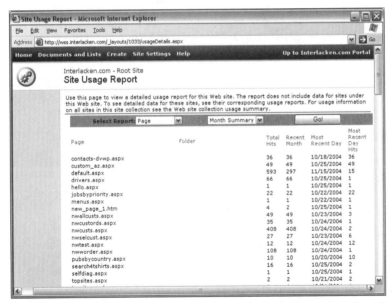

Figure 17-13. This page displays activity statistics for five categories of site usage, by month or day.

This page offers five reports and two reporting intervals. The reports are Page, User, OS, Browser, and Referrer URL. The intervals are Month Summary and Daily. Set the Select Report and Interval drop-down lists to the values you want, and then click Go.

Chapter 17

Monthly summary reports display these statistics:

- **Total Hits**   The total number of times since inception that visitors have accessed a document.
- **Recent Month**   The total number of hits for the last 31 days.
- **Most Recent Day**   The most recent day that a visitor accessed a document.
- **Most Recent Day Hits**   The total number of hits on the most recent day.

The daily reports display hit counts for each of the last 31 days.

If no usage statistics are appearing, a SharePoint or server administrator may need to configure usage analysis processing on the Central Administrations server.

> For more information about configuring usage analysis for an entire server, refer to "Configuring Usage Analysis Processing" in Chapter 15. For information about viewing summary statistics for a site collection, refer to "Viewing a Site Collection Usage Summary" later in this chapter.

Managing Sites and Workspaces

Windows SharePoint Services can display a list of subsites that reside directly below the current site, and that you have permission to access. To do this, on the Site Administration page, under Management And Statistics, click Manage Sites And Workspaces.

This displays the Sites And Workspaces page shown in Figure 17-14. Sites appear on that page within three categories: Sites, Document Workspaces, and Meeting Workspaces. The Sites category includes all sites other than document and meeting workspaces.

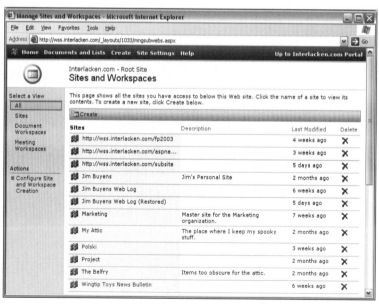

Figure 17-14. This page provides a handy way to create, delete, or browse subsites.

Starting from the Sites And Workspaces page, you can perform the following actions.

- To create a new site, click the Create toolbar button. This displays the New SharePoint Site page that Chapter 5 described.

- To browse a site, click its name in the Sites column.

- To delete a site, click its Delete icon. This displays a Delete Web Site page asking you to confirm the deletion. Click Delete to proceed with the deletion, or Cancel to leave the site in place.

> **For more information about using the New SharePoint Site page, refer to "Creating a New SharePoint Site" in Chapter 5.**

Managing Web Discussions

When a team member browses a document library, opens the drop-down menu for an item, and chooses Discuss, the result is a *Web discussion*. Windows SharePoint Services downloads the document into Internet Explorer (or an instance of an Office application running within Internet Explorer), and the team member can then enter comments as electronic sticky notes. You can also start Web discussions directly in Internet Explorer 4.0 or later, and in compatible client software such the Office 2003 system.

Any comments that arise from a Web discussion go into a SharePoint database, and not into the document itself. This design offers these advantages:

- Several people can view the document and make comments simultaneously.
- It's very easy to merge all the comments into one view.

Don't confuse Web discussions with SharePoint discussion boards, which are more like Internet newsgroups.

> **For more information about the Web discussion feature, refer to "Using Web Discussions" in Chapter 3.**

To see what Web discussions are in progress, or to clear out any old Web discussions, proceed as follows:

1 On the Site Administration page, under Management And Statistics, click Manage Web Discussions. This displays the Manage Web Discussions page shown in Figure 17-15.

557

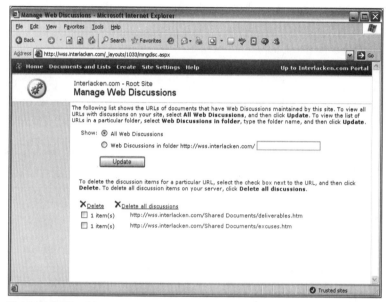

Figure 17-15. Using this page, you can identify and delete Web discussions.

2   Initially, the Manage Web Discussions page displays all Web discussions in the current site. To restrict this by folder (that is, by document library):

   2.1   Select the Web Discussions In Folder option.

   2.2   Type the folder name in the accompanying text box.

   2.3   Click the Update button.

   To restore the original full view of all Web discussions, select the All Web Discussions option and then click Update.

3   To delete Web discussion comments for one or more specific documents:

   3.1   Select the check boxes for each such document.

   3.2   Click the Delete link.

   3.3   Click OK on the resulting Are You Sure… dialog box.

4   To delete all displayed Web discussions, click the Delete All Discussions link. Then, when the Are You Sure… prompt appears, click Yes.

Managing User Alerts

Chapter 16 explained how team members can display a summary of their alerts and then add, edit, or delete any alerts that belong to them. Occasionally, however, an administrator might need to view or delete another team member's alerts.

> For more information on the way team members can maintain their own alerts, refer to "Managing Your Alerts" in Chapter 16.

To administratively view or delete alerts belonging to other team members, proceed as follows.

1 On the Site Administration page, under Management And Statistics, click Manage User Alerts. This displays the Manage User Alerts page shown in Figure 17-16.

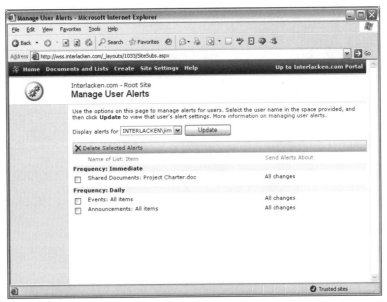

Figure 17-16. An administrator can view and delete another team member's alerts. This is particularly useful when a member leaves the team.

2 Open the Display Alerts For drop-down list, select the team member whose alerts you need to manage, and then click Update.

3 To delete any listed alert, select its check box and then click the Delete Selected Alerts toolbar button.

Chapter 17

Deleting a team member from a site *doesn't* delete that member's alerts. Therefore, if you take no other action, the former team member will continue to receive alert messages. At best, this is a nuisance for the former team member. At worst, it's a security exposure for the team, because the site is leaking information about team activities. Best practice is therefore to check for and delete alerts whenever you delete a member.

Changing Regional Settings

To change regional settings such as date format, number format, time zone, and locale for an existing site, proceed as follows.

1. On the Site Administration page, under Management And Statistics, click Change Regional Settings. This displays the Regional Settings page shown in Figure 17-17.

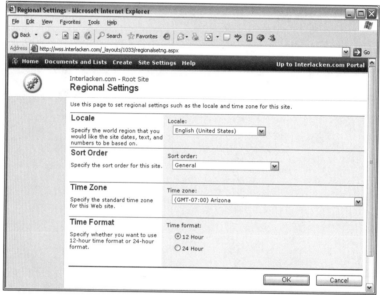

Figure 17-17. You can choose the regional format for dates, times, text, numbers, and sort order at the site level.

2. Configure the settings on the Regional Settings page as follows:

   - **Locale**   Specify the world region whose conventions you want Windows SharePoint Services to follow when it formats dates, text, and numbers.

   - **Sort Order**   Specify the sort order to use when displaying lists and libraries.

   - **Time Zone**   Specify the time zone in which the site will display all dates and times.

   - **Time Format**   Choose whether to display dates in 12-hour or 24-hour format.

3. Click OK to apply your changes, or Cancel to quit without saving.

This page can't reconfigure a site so that all its Web pages appear in another language. This is something you can specify only when you create a new site.

For information on creating SharePoint sites in various languages, refer to "Installing Language Template Packs" in Chapter 13.

Similarly, you can't configure a SharePoint site to check the culture and time zone preferences in each HTTP request and display the site accordingly. The same settings apply to all visitors.

Tip If team members from different time zones use your site, consider adding a time zone reminder such as "All times are Mountain Standard Time (GMT-07:00)," to the Description property of each list or library. The reminder will then appear at the top of the list or library's view pages.

Deleting a Site

Deleting a site deletes all its Web pages, all its security settings, and the content of all its lists and libraries. If this is what you want, display the sites Site Administration page, look under Management And Statistics, and click Delete This Site.

This will display a Delete Web Site page. Click Delete to delete the site, or Cancel to redisplay the Site Administration page.

If you delete a site by mistake, refer to Chapter 14, "Backing Up, Restoring, and Migrating SharePoint Sites," and hope it's not too late.

Managing the Web Part Gallery

The administrator of a top-level Web site can, to some extent, control which Web Parts are available for use within the site collection. To understand how this works, and its limitations, you need to know these facts about Web Parts:

- The program code for a Web Part is actually an ASP.NET custom control. This is a compiled object that serves whatever purpose its creator intended. Significantly, though, it displays output by creating HTML.
- Once compiled, ASP.NET custom controls reside in a .NET assembly. Like many other executable file types, it probably has an extension of .dll.
- In order to operate as a Web Part, the ASP.NET custom control must reside in one of two locations:
  - The physical server's global assembly cache (GAC), which is a sort of program library available to all .NET programs on the computer.
  - A virtual Web server's /bin folder. Assemblies in this location are available only on that virtual server.

Once installed, the ASP.NET custom control is accessible by means of a class name such as *Microsoft.SharePoint.WebPartPages.ImageWebPart.* Web Part Pages or other programs refer to the control by this class name, and not by its physical file location.

● In addition, any virtual server that uses the Web Part must list it as a Safe Control in its web.config file. This is an XML file that physically resides in the virtual server's root folder and configures a variety of ASP.NET and SharePoint settings.

● Finally, a Web Part Page needs a Web Part Definition (.dwp) file. This is a small XML file that describes the Web Part. Among other things, it includes the user control's class name, a friendly name for team members to use, and configuration settings.

> **Note** Windows SharePoint services will only run Web Parts that an administrator has specifically designated as safe. This protects the server from mischievous, malfunctioning, unauthorized, or inappropriate software.

When you use the browser interface or FrontPage to add Web Parts to pages, the Web Part galleries you see are actually lists of Web Part Definition (.dwp) files. Typically, there are three or four Web Part galleries:

● **Web Part Page Gallery**   Lists Web Part definitions stored in the current page. Typically, these are Web Parts the page is currently using, or has used in the past. This gallery appears in the browser interface, but not in FrontPage.

● **Site Collection Gallery**   Lists Web Part definitions associated with the current site collection. Some of these, such as the List View Web Parts that display lists and libraries, come from the current site. An administrator configures other Web Parts for the entire site collection.

● **Virtual Server Gallery**   Lists Web Part definitions associated with the current virtual server.

● **Online Gallery**   Lists Web Part definitions available from Microsoft's Web site.

As a top-level site administrator, you can't control which Web Part definitions the virtual server gallery contains, or whether the online Web Part gallery is available. You also have no control over List View Web Parts that appear in the site collection gallery; if the list or library exists, so does the List View Web Part. You do, however, have control over other kinds of Web Parts that appear in the site collection gallery.

> To install a Web Part in the virtual server gallery, an administrator must install it as a Web Part package, and using the stsadm.exe –o addwppack command. For more information about installing Web Parts, refer to "Deploying Custom Web Parts" in Chapter 19.

To begin managing the site collection Web Part gallery, take the following steps.

1   Open your collection's top-level site.

2   Display the site's Top-Level Site Administration page. For example, click Site Settings, and then Go To Site Administration.

3 Under Site Collection Galleries, click Manage Web Part Gallery. This displays the Web Part Gallery page shown in Figure 17-18.

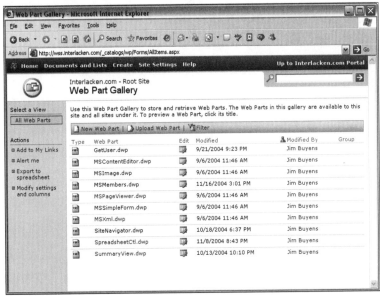

Figure 17-18. The Web Part definitions on this page will appear in the site collection's Web Part gallery.

The site collection Web Part gallery is a SharePoint list, and the Web Part Gallery page is a List View page. As such, it contains the usual links under Select A View and Actions, along the left edge of the page. The body of the page displays one line for each Web Part in your site collection gallery, other than List View and other system-provided Web Parts. To filter the listing, click the Filter toolbar button and choose filtration values from the resulting drop-down list boxes.

If your virtual server's web.config file identifies safe Web Parts that aren't yet in your gallery, the following procedure will add them:

1 Click the New Web Part toolbar button on the Web Part Gallery page.

2 When the New Web Parts page shown in Figure 17-19 appears, select the check boxes that precede the Web Parts you want to add.

3 To override the default filename of any Web Part you clicked, use the text box in the File Name column.

Chapter 17

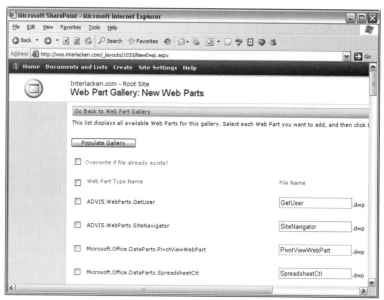

Figure 17-19. This page lists the user controls specified as safe in the virtual server's web.config file. Such controls don't appear automatically in the site collection Web Part gallery.

4   Click the Populate Gallery button to add the Web Parts you selected. To quit without making any changes, click the Go Back to Web Part Gallery toolbar button.

You can also add a Web Part definition to your gallery from a file on your computer or file server. However, any such file must refer to an ASP.NET custom control already installed on your server and registered as safe. That is, it must refer to one of the controls that appear on the New Web Parts page shown previously in Figure 17-19. Here's the procedure:

1   Click the Upload Web Part toolbar button on the Web Part Gallery page. This displays the Upload Web Part page shown in Figure 17-20.

2   Fill in the following fields:

■   **Overwrite existing file(s)**   Select this check box if, should you upload a filename already in use, you want it to overwrite the existing file.

■   **Name**   To upload a single file, type the Web Part Definition file's full drive letter, path, and filename, or click the browse button to locate it using a standard Choose File dialog box.

■   **Upload Multiple Files**   To upload several files, click this link to display a Windows Explorer–like view of your computer's file system. Then, select the check box that precedes each Web Part Definition file you want to upload.

- **Group** Select a group name from the drop-down list, or select the Specify Your Own Value option and type in the group name you want. (This field is optional. If you specify a group name for your Web Parts, a team member can search for Web Parts by group when he or she adds them to a page.)

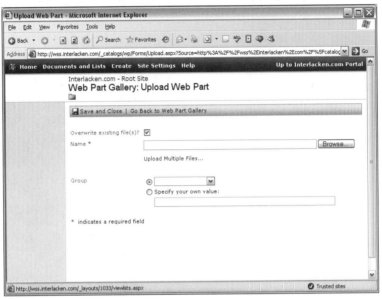

Figure 17-20. This page uploads a Web Part definition from a file on your computer.

3 Click the Save And Close toolbar button to upload your file. Click the Go Back to Web Part Gallery toolbar button to quit without making any change.

To preview the appearance of a Web Part, click its Type icon or its name in the Web Part column. This will display the Web Part in a Web Part Preview page.

To edit the properties of an existing Web Part definition, proceed as follows:

1 On the Web Part Gallery page, click the Edit icon for the Web Part definition you want to modify. This displays the Web Part Gallery page shown in Figure 17-21.
2 To modify the Web Part definition's properties, update the Name, Title, Description, and Group fields, and then click the Save And Close toolbar button.
3 To delete the Web Part definition, click the Delete toolbar button.
4 To save the Web Part definition as a file on your computer, click the Export toolbar button. This is basically the opposite of the Upload function described earlier.
5 To view the Web Part definition's XML code, click the View XML toolbar button.
6 To return to the Web Part Gallery page, click the Go Back To Web Part Gallery toolbar button.

Chapter 17

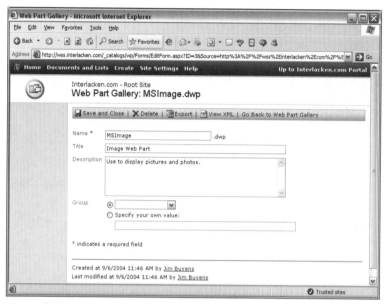

Figure 17-21. With this page you can view, modify, download, or delete a Web Part definition in your site collection gallery.

Remember that the site collection Web Part gallery is *not* a security mechanism. It simply makes Web Parts easier to find. If you remove an entry from the gallery:

- Web pages already configured to use the Web Part will keep working.
- Team members can still add the Web Part to Web Part Pages. For example, one team member can:

  1 Display a page that uses the Web Part.
  2 Click the drop-down arrow on any Web Part, click Export, and save the resulting file.

Another team member could then:

  1 Display a page where they'd like to use the Web Part.
  2 Click Modify My Page, Add Web Parts, and Import.
  3 Specify the file obtained in step b above, and then click Upload.

To completely prevent the use of a Web Part, you must ask a server administrator to remove it from the server, or to remove it from the list of safe controls in the virtual server's Web.config file.

Managing the List Template Gallery

Each site collection has a list of templates that team members can use to create new lists or libraries. Team members usually create such templates by customizing a new or existing list or library, and then saving the result as a template. The new template then belongs to the site collection's *list template gallery*, and appears as a choice on the Create page of each site in the collection.

> For instructions on saving an existing list or library as a template, refer to "Saving a Template" in Chapter 6.

To view or modify the list template gallery for your collection, proceed as follows.

1. Open your collection's top-level site.

2. Display the site's Top-Level Site Administration page. For example, click Site Settings, and then Go To Site Administration.

3. Under Site Collection Galleries, click List Template Gallery. This displays the List Template Gallery page shown in Figure 17-22.

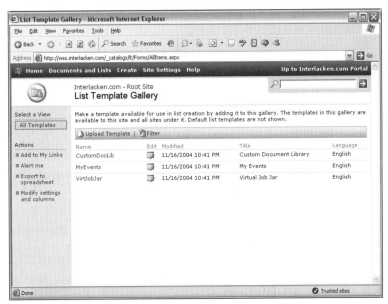

Figure 17-22. This page lists all the list templates available in your site collection.

4. To download a list definition, click its name in the Name column. This starts the usual file download dialog box. The result will be a list definition file with an .stp filename extension. An authorized member of another top-level site could add the template to that site's collection by following the instructions in the next step.

5 To upload a template from a file on your computer, click the Upload Template toolbar button. This displays an Upload Template page where you specify the name of the file on your disk, and then click the Save And Close button to upload it.

6 To manage the details of a list template, click its icon in the Edit column. This displays the List Template Gallery page for that template, shown in Figure 17-23.

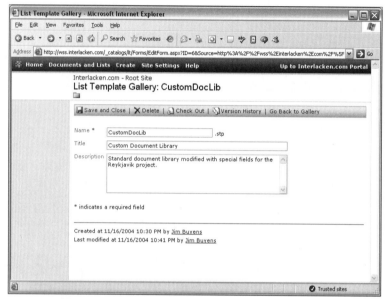

Figure 17-23. Using this page, you can manage the properties of an individual list template.

Here's how to use the toolbar buttons on this page:

■ **Save And Close** Make any changes you like to the Name, Title, and Description fields, and then click this button to save your changes.

■ **Delete** Click this button to remove the list template from the gallery.

■ **Check Out/Check In** If this button is Check Out, click it to reserve the template so that no one else can modify it. If it's Check In, click it to display a page where you can finalize your changes and release the template, finalize changes without releasing the template, or discard changes and revert to the version in effect at check-out.

■ **Version History** Click this button to display a version history of the current template, with options to delete or revert to past versions.

■ **Go Back to Gallery** Click this button to discard any changes you've made to the Name, Title, and Description fields, and to redisplay the List Template Gallery page.

> **Note** Despite having a .stp filename extensions, list definition files are actually Windows CAB files If you rename the file to have a .cab filename extension, you can open it in Windows Explorer and inspect its contents.

Managing the Site Template Gallery

Just as each SharePoint site collection has its own gallery of list templates, each collection has a gallery of site templates as well. The site template gallery works almost exactly like the list template gallery, except that:

- To create a site template, you:
  1. Create a prototype site.
  2. Click the Save Site As Template link on the prototype site's Site Administration page.

  For more instructions on how to create a site template, refer to the section titled "Saving a Site as a Template," earlier in this chapter.

- Items in the site template gallery appear in the Template Selection page the first time you browse a new site. (This is automatic when you create a new site through the browser interface.) They also appear in FrontPage, when you display the Web Site Templates dialog box and click the SharePoint Services tab.

Here's the procedure to view or modify the site template gallery for your collection:

1. Open your collection's top-level site.
2. Display the site's Top-Level Site Administration page. For example, click Site Settings, and then Go To Site Administration.
3. Under Site Collection Galleries, click Site Template Gallery.

This displays a Site Template Gallery page that looks and works almost exactly like the List Template Gallery page that the previous section described.

Viewing a Site Hierarchy

To display a clickable list of all the sites in a collection, follow this procedure:

1. Display the Top-Level Site Administration page for the collection. To do this:
   - 1.1 Open any site in the collection.
   - 1.2 Click Site Settings, and then Go To Site Administration.
   - 1.3 If the Site Collection Administration section of the Site Administration page contains a Go To Top-Level Site Administration link, click that link.

569

2 On the Top-Level Site Administration page, under Site Collection Administration, click View Site Hierarchy. This displays the View Site Hierarchy page shown in Figure 17-24.

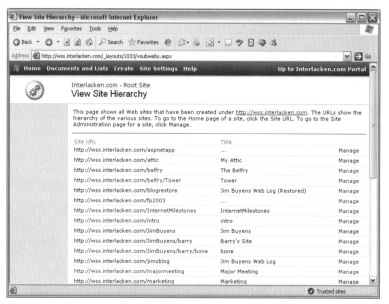

Figure 17-24. This page lists all the sites in the collection, with links to view or manage each site.

3 To view any listed site, click its Site URL.

4 To display the Site Administration page for any listed site, click its Manage link.

Viewing a Site Collection Usage Summary

To view usage statistics summarized for the entire site collection, display the Top-Level Site Administration page and then, under Site Collection Administration, click the View Site Collection Usage Summary link. This displays the Site Collection Usage Summary page shown in Figure 17-25.

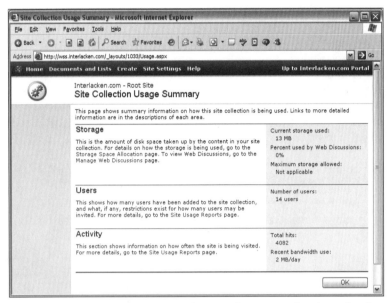

Figure 17-25. These usage statistics pertain to an entire site collection.

This page displays the following statistics.

- **Current Storage Used** The total number of megabytes that the site collection consumes.

- **Percent Used By Web Discussions** The total number of megabytes consumed by Web discussions, divided by Current Storage Used. This pertains to the feature where team members display documents in Internet Explorer and attach comments. It doesn't measure space that SharePoint discussion boards use.

- **Maximum Storage Allowed** The sum of all Web site quotas for the collection.

- **Number Of Users** The number of user accounts registered as users of any site in the collection.

- **Total Hits** The total number of HTTP requests received since inception.

- **Recent Bandwidth Use** The number of megabytes per day of network utilization attributable to sites in the collection.

Viewing Storage Space Allocation

To search for large or outdated document libraries, documents, or lists anywhere in your collection, display the Top-Level Site Administration page and then, under Site Collection Administration, click the View Storage Space Allocation link. This displays the Storage Space Allocation page shown in Figure 17-26.

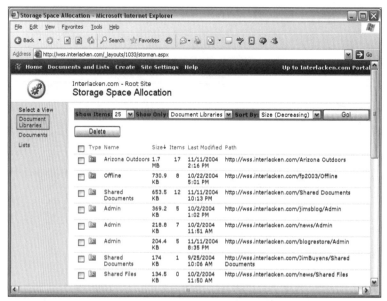

Figure 17-26. This is a great page for locating and deleting large, unused libraries, documents, or lists.

Initially, this page displays disk size, number of items, date last modified, and URL path for the largest 25 document libraries in the collection, sorted in descending order by disk size.

- To display individual documents or lists rather than document libraries, either:
  - Click one of the links under Select A View, or
  - Make a selection in the Show Only drop-down list box, and then click Go.
- To show a different number of libraries, documents, or lists, make a selection in the Show Items drop-down list and then click Go.
- To sort on any column, either:
  - Click on its column heading, or
  - Select a field name from the Sort By drop-down list, and then click Go.

Chapter 17

- To toggle the sort order between ascending and descending, click the same column heading twice in a row.

- To view a library, document, or list, click its name in the Name column

- To delete one or more libraries, documents, or lists, select their check boxes and then click the Delete button.

Viewing Site Collection User Information

To display all current or historical login accounts that have accessed the site collection, display the Top-Level Site Administration page and then, under Site Collection Administration, click the View Site Collection User Information link. This displays the Manage Site Collection Users page shown in Figure 17-27.

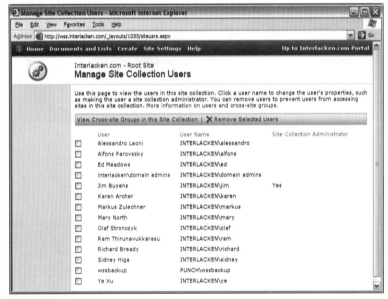

Figure 17-27. This page lists all team members who have access to any site in the collection, even if no one site includes them all.

To use this page, follow these procedures:

- To display the User Information page for any listed user, click the name in the User column.

  For information about using the User Information page, refer to "Updating Your Personal Information" in Chapter 16.

- To delete a user, select the check box that precedes the user name and then click the Remove Selected Users toolbar button.

- To display a list of cross-site groups in the collection, click the View Cross-Site Groups In This Site Collection toolbar button. This display a Cross-Site Groups page similar to the one shown previously in Figure 17-6.

  For information about managing cross-site groups, refer to "Managing Cross-Site Groups" earlier in this chapter.

Configuring a Connection to a Portal Site

If your organization operates a SharePoint portal server anywhere on your network, you can easily connect your site collection to it. Your team members can then add their lists to portal Areas, display portal server user profiles, link to portal search, and so forth. To provide this capability, proceed as follows:

1. On the Top-Level Site Administration page, under Site Collection Administration, click Configure Connection To Portal Site. This displays the Configure Connection To Portal Site page shown in Figure 17-28.

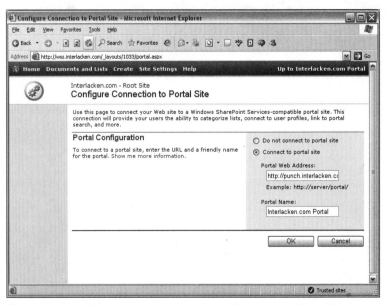

Figure 17-28. This page connects a site collection to a SharePoint portal server.

2 Fill in the following fields:

- **Connect To Portal Site**   Click this option if you want to connect your site connection to the portal site. Otherwise, click Do Not Connect To Portal Site.

- **Portal Web Address**   Type the URL of the portal's root folder.

- **Portal Name**   Type the name of the portal site. This will appear as a link in the top navigation bar of each page in your top-level site. (The Portal Web Address field provides the URL).

3 Click OK to save your changes, or Cancel to quit without saving.

In Summary...

This chapter explained how to use the links on the Site Administration page, which appears automatically in every SharePoint site. This includes commands that manage users, permissions, Web discussions, alerts, regional settings site collection resources, disk usage, and activity reports.

The next chapter will explain how to use some of the utility Web Parts and other server controls that come with Windows SharePoint Services, how to obtain and install new Web Parts on a server, and how to customize the look and features of a SharePoint site at the server level.

Chapter 18

Advanced Design Techniques

This chapter describes a number of techniques that are useful when designing SharePoint sites, but that require administrative privileges to install, enable, or deploy.

Windows SharePoint Services includes a number of built-in Web Parts that don't relate directly to lists, libraries, or data sources. In some cases, these might not even appear in your collection's Web Part gallery, and a collection administrator will need to add them. The first section in this chapter describes these Web Parts.

If you're developing Web Part Pages from scratch rather than using a predesigned template, you'll undoubtedly want your pages to include full-text search forms, Modify My Page links, Sign In buttons for anonymous sites, and "Up To" links. Windows SharePoint Services provides some ASP.NET server controls that are very useful in this regard, and this chapter explains how to use them.

The next major topic concerns the Office 2003 Web Parts and Components, a downloadable package that increases the integration between Windows SharePoint Services and Office 2003. This topic explains how a server administrator can download and install these components, and then briefly how team members can use them.

The last topic concerns site definitions, which behave in some respects like site templates but which, in fact, operate much closer to the internals of Windows SharePoint Services.

Using Built-In Web Parts

This section explains how to use some of the miscellaneous Web Parts that come with Windows SharePoint Services. None of these Web Parts makes any direct use of lists, libraries, or data sources on the server, or of ActiveX or Office 2003 components on the Web visitor's computer.

Occasionally, these Web Parts will appear with slightly different names. The Page Viewer Web Part, for example:

- Has the name Page Viewer Web Part in the site collection gallery.
- Has the name MSPageViewer.dwp on the Web Part Gallery page.
- Has the class name *Microsoft.SharePoint.WebPartPages.PageViewerWebPart* on the New Web Parts page.

577

- Has the suggested File Name PageViewerWebPart on the New Web Parts page.

Nevertheless, all these names point to the same Web Part. Similar variations in name occur for other Web Parts in this section.

Configuring the Title Bar Web Part

The Title Bar Web Part displays (what else?) the title bar of most pages having the standard SharePoint look and feel. In Figure 18-1, a Title Bar Web Part displays:

- The two light-colored lines.
- The icon.
- The caption, "Miscellaneous Web Parts."
- The title, "Title Bar, Image, Members, and Page Viewer."
- The Modify Shared Page link.

Figure 18-1. This page uses four built-in Web Parts: Title Bar, Image, Members, and Page Viewer.

Once you have a Title Bar Web Part on your page, you can configure the following properties:

- **Title** A one-line name that appears in a large font within the Web Part display.
- **Caption** One line of text that appears in a small font above the title.

- **Description**   A sentence or two that appears as a tool tip when the mouse passes over the title bar.

- **Image Link**   The URL of the icon picture that should appear just before the title.

> The URL path for all the standard SharePoint icons is /_layouts/images/, which equates on the server to the physical path C:\Program Files\Common Files\Microsoft Shared\web server extensions\60\TEMPLATE\IMAGES. However, you can locate custom icon files wherever you want.

If the page contains any Web Part Zones that the current team member can modify, the Title Bar Web Part will automatically display a Modify Shared Page or Modify My Page link. However, Title Bar Web Parts don't automatically display Search Form controls. If anonymous access is enabled and the current visitor hasn't signed in, the Web Part will also display a Sign In button

> For information on adding a Search Form control to a Web Part Page, refer to "Using the ViewSearchForm Control" later in this chapter.

A Title Bar Web Part doesn't display the top navigation bar in Figure 18-1 or, for that matter, in any other page. To construct a top navigation bar by hand, open the page in FrontPage 2003 and then:

1 Create a one-row, three-column table with a width of 100%, and with a border thickness, cell spacing, and cell padding of zero.

2 Assign the CSS class name *ms-bannerframe* to the table.

3 For each cell, set the CSS class name to *ms-banner*, no wrap to *true*, and vertical alignment to *middle*.

4 Set the width of the middle cell to 100%, and the horizontal alignment of the right cell to *right*.

5 Display an icon in the left cell. For pages in the root folder of a SharePoint site, the URL of the default icon is *_layouts/images/logo.gif*.

6 Add a FrontPage Link Bar With Custom Links component to the middle cell. Configure this component to display the link bar named SharePoint Top Nav Bar.

7 Add the following tag to the rightmost cell. This displays the Up To links.

```
<SharePoint:PortalConnection runat="server" />
```

8 Make sure the page contains this tag, before the <body> tag. Otherwise, the tag from step 7 will raise an error.

```
<%@ Register Tagprefix="SharePoint"
Namespace="Microsoft.SharePoint.WebControls" Assembly="Microsoft.SharePoint,
Version=11.0.0.0, Culture=neutral, PublicKeyToken=71e9bce111e9429c" %>
```

9 Be sure to save the page with a file name extension of .aspx.

Chapter 18

579

Displaying Pictures with the Image Web Part

This Web Part simply displays a picture file. You specify the URL of the picture file, and the Web Part wraps it in an <img> tag and the usual Web Part border. Figure 18-1 shows an example of this Web Part in a page.

You could display the same picture by editing the page in FrontPage, but using the Image Web Part has two advantages:

- You can allow Web Visitors to add, modify, or delete Image Web Parts using only a browser.
- You can build Web Part connections from other Web Parts, and thereby control which picture the Web Part displays.

When you configure an Image Web Part, you can specify these properties:

- **Image Link**   The URL of the picture you want to display.
- **Image Vertical Alignment**   The vertical position the picture will occupy within the Web Part frame: Top, Middle, or Bottom. The default is Middle.
- **Image Horizontal Alignment**   The horizontal position the picture will occupy within the Web Part frame: Left, Center, or Right. The default is Center.
- **Web Part Background Color**   The background color that will fill the Web Part's frame. The default is Transparent.

To configure the title, size, frame appearance, visibility, and configurability of the Web Part, use the Appearance, Layout, and Advanced sections of its property sheet, just as you would for any other Web Part.

Configuring the Members Web Part

This Web Part displays a list of team members who have access to the current site, grouped by Windows Messenger status. An example appears in Figure 18-1. Clicking any member name displays either:

- That member's personal site under SharePoint Portal Server or, if none exists,
- That member's User Information page from Windows SharePoint Services.

The Web Part also displays a Windows Messenger icon. Clicking this icon displays a menu with options to connect via Windows Messenger, or to perform the usual assortment of Outlook actions: schedule a meeting, add or edit phone numbers, send mail, and so forth.

When you configure a Members Web Part, you can specify these properties:

- **Number Of Items To Display**   The maximum number of members the Web Part will display.
- **Toolbar Type**   The type of toolbar to display: summary or none.

In addition, the usual options appear in the Appearance, Layout, and Advanced sections of the Web Part's property sheet.

Displaying Content with the Page Viewer Web Part

This Web Part adds an <iframe> element to a Web Part Page. The <iframe> (and therefore the Web Part Page) can then display any file, folder, or Web page the team member's computer can access. Figure 18-1 shows a Page Viewer Web Part displaying a Web page from MSN.

When you configure a Page Viewer Web Part, you can specify these properties:

- **Web Page, Folder, or File**   Select one of these options depending on the type of content you want to display.
- **Link**   Specify the URL or path of the content you want to display.

If you want the Page Viewer Web Part to display a folder or file, be sure to specify a path that's valid from each team member's computer. In most cases, this will be a UNC path such as \\<server>\<sharename>\myfolder\myfile.doc.

If you specify a path like c:\localfiles\myfile.doc, the Web Part will look for that folder and file on each team member's computer.

Adding Forms with the Simple Form Web Part

Chapter 12 briefly mentioned this Web Part in its discussion about Web Part connections. It provides a way of adding simple HTML forms to a Web Part Page, and then using any form fields you create as input to a connection to another Web Part.

> For more information about using the Simple Form Web Part, refer to "Connecting Form, List, and Image Web Parts" in Chapter 12.

Configuring the XML Web Part

This Web Part uses eXtensible Stylesheet Language Transformation (XSLT) to transform an XML file into HTML, and then adds the resulting HTML to the Web Part Page for display. To use this Web Part, you add it as usual to a Web Part Page, and then display its properties. Figure 18-2 shows how this looks in FrontPage 2003.

Chapter 18

581

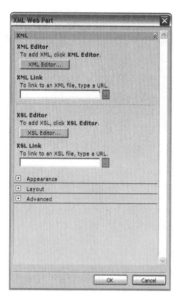

Figure 18-2. This is how FrontPage 2003 displays the property sheet for an XML Web Part

Here are the specific XML Web Part properties you can modify. All are optional.

- **XML Editor**   Click this button to display a Text Entry dialog box. This dialog box has a large text box where you can type or paste the XML input to the transformation.

- **XML Link**   Type the URL of the XML source that provides the input to the transformation. If you make an entry in this field, it overrides any XML you may have supplied after clicking the XML Editor button.

- **XSL Editor**   Click this button to display another Text Entry dialog box, this time to enter the XSLT code that will transform the source XML file.

- **XSL Link**   Type the URL of the XSLT code that will transform the source XML. Any entry in this field overrides any XSLT code you may have supplied after clicking the XSL Editor button.

If you don't specify any source XML, or if you specify an empty file, no error will occur except that the result will be empty. If you don't supply any XSLT code, no transformation will occur; the output will be identical to the input XML.

> To appreciate what the XML Web Part can do, try using it to syndicate RSS content (blogs) into a Web Part Page. To get the necessary XSLT file, download the Syndication (RSS) tool from *http://www.asaris-matrix.com/sweber/playground/default.aspx?id=15*.

Displaying HTML with the Content Editor Web Part

This Web Part displays static HTML obtained from a URL or entered by hand. Figure 18-3 shows an example in use.

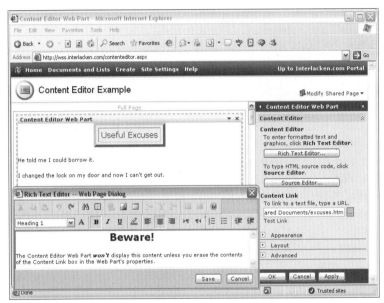

Figure 18-3. The Content Editor Web Part can display its own content or a remote URL, but it can edit only its own content.

In this figure, a Web designer:

1 Added the Content Editor Web Part to the page and configured its Content Location property to display an HTML file in a document library.

2 Browsed the page and verified that data from the Content Link location appears in the Web Part.

3 Clicked the Web Part's down arrow and chose Modify Shared Web Part.

4 Clicked the Rich Text Editor button.

If you try this yourself, you'll discover that:

● Neither the Rich Text Editor button nor its close cousin, the Source Editor button, edits the contents of the document at the Content Link location!

Instead, these two buttons modify a block of HTML code that the Web Part stores as part of its own definition. Initially, this block of code is empty, and that's why the Rich Text Editor comes up empty.

Chapter 18

583

- Clicking the Rich Text Editor's Save button *doesn't* update the document at the Content Link location, nor does it update the content editor Web Part's display.

  As long as the Content Link property contains data, the Web Part displays the data from that location, and ignores any data you may have entered through the Rich Text Editor, or by clicking the Source Editor button.

Got that? If not, here's another way of looking at the same information.

- The Content Editor Web Part displays data *either* from a content location URL *or* from its own Web Part definition.

- The Web Part displays data from its own Web Part definition *only* if the Content Location field is empty.

- The Rich Text Editor and Source Editor Buttons edit *only* the HTML stored in the Web Part definition.

- The Rich Text Editor and Source Editor Buttons *never* save data back to the document at the content location.

- The Rich Text Editor and Source Editor buttons edit the same HTML data: the data stored in the Web Part definition. You can click one, save, click the other, save, and continue in that mode as long as you like.

Adding ASP.NET Server Controls

This section describes four ASP.NET server controls that come with Windows SharePoint Services. These aren't Web Parts, so to use them you must have access to a page's HTML. For example, you must open the page in FrontPage, Visual Studio, or Notepad. Nevertheless, they're useful for adding certain common features to your pages.

Using the ViewSearchForm Control

This control displays the search form that appears on the home page of most SharePoint sites, provided that the site is using a SQL Server database with full-text searching in effect. If the database is WMSDE or if full-text searching is disabled, the control displays nothing. Figure 18-4 illustrates the control in its visible state.

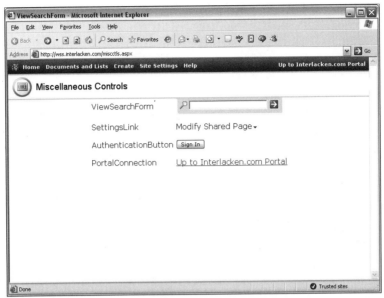

Figure 18-4. SharePoint ASP.NET server controls display all four elements in the right column of this Web Page. In practice, the SettingsLink control and the AuthenticationButton control would never both be visible.

Even if searching is available, the Title Bar Web Part doesn't display the search form. If you want your page to contain a search form, you have to add some HTML like the following to it:

```
<table cellspacing="0" cellpadding="0" border="0">
  <tr>
    <td></td>
    <SharePoint:ViewSearchForm
      id="SearchView"
      action="searchresults.aspx"
      go="Go"
      prompt="Search this site"
      runat="server" />
  </tr>
</table>
```

Chapter 18

When the ViewSearchForm control produces output, it writes four <td> tags, the second of which is coded colspan="2". It doesn't write any <table> or <tr> tags. For this reason, it's usually best to enclose the control in your own <table> and <tr> tags, plus an empty pair of <td> and </td> tags. The empty <td></td> pair avoids the illegal HTML sequence <table><tr></tr></table> in case the View Search Form control produces no output.

Like any other ASP.NET control, ViewSearchForm requires a unique id= attribute and a runat="server" attribute. In addition, you'll probably want to code these attributes:

- **Action** The name of the page in the _layouts folder that will perform the search and display the results. Typically, you code this attribute action="searchresults.aspx".

  If you omit this attribute, the ViewSearchForm will connect to each List View Web Part on the same page, and tell those Web Parts to search their respective lists.

  If you omit the Action attribute and the page contains no List View Web Parts, submitting a search creates a JavaScript error.

- **Go** The tooltip text that will appear if the team member hovers the mouse over the search button. Typical coding would be go="Go" or go="Search".

- **Prompt** The tooltip text that will appear if the team member hovers the mouse over the search terms text box. For example, this might be prompt="Search this site".

The search form itself is designed to reside immediately below a Title Bar Web Part, at the right margin of the page. This placement will ensure that the background shape blends into the rest of the page layout.

Any page that uses the ViewSearchForm control must also:

- Contain the following tag somewhere before the <body> tag. This prevents errors that occur when loading the control on the server.

  ```
  <%@ Register Tagprefix="SharePoint"
  Namespace="Microsoft.SharePoint.WebControls" Assembly="Microsoft.SharePoint,
  Version=11.0.0.0, Culture=neutral, PublicKeyToken=71e9bce111e9429c" %>
  ```

- Contain this tag in the <head> section, to avoid JavaScript errors that prevent the search from working.

  ```
  <SCRIPT language='javascript' src='/_layouts/1033/ows.js'></SCRIPT>
  ```

- Contain the following tag, also in the <head> section, so that the form appears with colors and fonts that match the rest of the page:

  ```
  <link rel="stylesheet" type="text/css" href="_layouts/1033/styles/ows.css">
  ```

Any Web Part Page that Windows SharePoint Services creates will already contain these tags. So will any page you create in FrontPage 2003 by displaying the Page Templates dialog box and choosing a template from the Web Part Pages tab.

Using the SettingsLink Control

This control displays the Modify Shared Page or Modify My Page link that team members click when they want to modify a Web Part Page through the SharePoint browser interface. It also displays the accompanying drop-down menu. Figure 18-4 illustrates this control.

> **Tip** A Title Bar Web Part displays a link identical to the one that a SettingsLink control displays. Therefore, if your page contains a Title Bar Web Part, you probably don't need a separate SettingsLink control.

A SettingsLink control displays nothing unless the current team member has sufficient rights to modify the page. If the site permits anonymous access, for example, the Modify Shared Page or Modify My Page link won't appear until the team member signs in. To permit easy sign-in, you should add an AuthenticationButton control to the page. The options on the drop-down menu, if it appears, will vary depending on the team member's permissions.

To display either a Modify Shared Page or Modify My Page link, as appropriate, simply add the following tag to your Web Part Page:

```
<WebPartPages:SettingsLink runat="server"/>
```

Any page that uses a SettingsLink control must also include the following tag preceding the <head> tag:

```
<%@ Register Tagprefix="WebPartPages"
Namespace="Microsoft.SharePoint.WebPartPages" Assembly="Microsoft.SharePoint,
Version=11.0.0.0, Culture=neutral, PublicKeyToken=71e9bce111e9429c"%>
```

However, because Web Part Zones also require this tag, it's almost certain to be present in any Web Part Pages you encounter.

Using the AuthenticationButton Control

If your SharePoint site permits anonymous access, team members who need to use secured features need a way to sign in explicitly. The Title Bar Web Part displays a Sign In button for this purpose but if necessary, you can get the same button by adding the following tag to your page.

```
<WebPartPages:AuthenticationButton runat="server"/>
```

Figure 18-4 shows a sample of the resulting button. However, the button appears only if the current team member *isn't* signed in.

Any page that uses an AuthenticationButton control must provide the <%@ Register %> tag already described for the SettingsLink control.

Using the PortalConnection Control

Within a top-level Web site, this control displays a link to the portal site, if any, specified after clicking Configure Connection To Portal Site on the site's Top-Level Site Administration page. Within a subsite, it displays a link to the parent site.

> For more information about configuring a connection to a portal site, refer to "Configuring a Connection to a Portal Site" in Chapter 17.

Figure 18-4 shows two examples of this link. One is in the top navigation bar, and the other appears in the body of the page. The top navigation bar is the usual position. To display this link, add a tag like the following to your page.

```
<SharePoint:PortalConnection runat="server" />
```

As with the ViewSearchForm control, any page that uses the PortalConnection control must also contain the following tag somewhere before the <body> tag:

```
<%@ Register Tagprefix="SharePoint" Namespace="Microsoft.SharePoint.WebControls"
Assembly="Microsoft.SharePoint, Version=11.0.0.0, Culture=neutral,
PublicKeyToken=71e9bce111e9429c" %>
```

However, as before, most Web Part Pages already contain this tag.

Installing and Using Office 2003 Web Parts and Components

Office 2003 Web Parts and Components is a collection of Web Parts and Great Plains Web Part Pages that work closely with Microsoft Office 2003 and Windows SharePoint Services 2.0.

Installing the Microsoft Office 2003 Web Parts and Components

To use the Microsoft Office 2003 Web Parts and Components, you must first obtain and install them on your SharePoint server. To do this, proceed as follows:

1 Browse *http://www.microsoft.com/downloads*.

2 In the Search For A Download section:

- Set Product/Technology to Office System.
- Set Keywords to Web Part.

Then click Go.

3 When, the Search Results page appears, click Office 2003 Add-in: Web Parts and Components.

4 When the Download Details page appears, click the Download button and save the ststpkpl.exe file in a location accessible to your SharePoint server.

5 Run ststpkpl.exe on the server running Windows SharePoint Services. (You must be a server administrator to run this step.)

6 Add the Web Parts to the Web Part gallery for your SharePoint site collection. To do this, you must be an administrator of the collection.

> Fro instructions on adding a Web Part to a site collection's Web Part gallery, refer to "Managing the Web Part Gallery" in Chapter 17.

Running setup for the Office 2003 Web Parts and Components affects all virtual servers on the same computer. It doesn't affect:

- Other servers in the same farm. To install Office 2003 Web Parts and Components on multiple servers, you must run setup on each server.
- Virtual servers you create in the future. To add the Office 2003 Web Parts and Components to a new virtual server, you must rerun the original setup program or run Reinstall or Repair from Control Panel, Add Or Remove Programs.

Installing the Office 2003 Web Components

The Microsoft Office 2003 Web Parts and Components are usable only on client computers that have Microsoft Office 2003 installed. The Web Components run within the browser window, and not on the server. You can install them as part of Office 2003, as a separate install from the Office 2003 CD, or from the Microsoft Office Online Web site. To install from the Web site, proceed as follows.

1 Browse *http://office.microsoft.com/*.

2 Click Downloads.

3 Search Downloads for, "Office 2003 Web Components."

4 Click Office 2003 Add-in: Office Web Components.

5 Download and run the owc11.exe file.

Using the PivotView, Spreadsheet, Web Capture, and Quick Quote Web Parts

The Office 2003 Web Parts and Components includes several Web Parts. For detailed information on each one, add it to a Web Part Page and then click Help on the Web Part's menu. The following is a summary description of each Web Part.

Chapter 18

589

- **PivotView Web Part** This Web Part displays, analyzes, and reports data in any of three related views: PivotTable view, PivotChart view, or Datasheet view. This data comes from a source you specify in either of two file types:

  - An Office Database Connection (*.odc) file. This connects to SQL Server and other database systems using database drivers on the Web visitor's computer.

  - An Office Data Retrieval Service Connection (*.uxdc) file. This connects to SharePoint lists and other data sources accessible via the data retrieval services on a SharePoint server.

  Significantly, these files reside on each team member's computer. This means that the same Web page could display completely different data for each team member.

  PivotView Web Parts participate in many kinds of Web Part connections, including Chart Data From, Chart Data To, Filter Data With, Get Data From, Provide Data To, and Provide Row To.

  To save any results you obtain using this Web Part, display the Web Part toolbar and click the Export To Microsoft Office Excel button.

- **Spreadsheet Web Part** This Web Part adds the Office 2003 Spreadsheet Component to a Web Part Page. Using a classic, two-dimensional spreadsheet grid, you can then import data, enter data by hand, enter formulas, and so forth.

  Like the PivotView Web Part, this Web Part imports data based on an Office Database Connection or Office Data Retrieval Service Connection file. As to Web Part connections, it supports only Chart Data To.

  You can save any result you obtain using this Web Part by displaying its toolbar and then clicking the Export To Microsoft Office Excel button.

- **Web Capture Web Part** This Web Part retrieves an entire Web page, and then displays all or selected portions within the Web Part border. For example, you can choose to display only selected tables, images, or Web Parts.

- **Quick Quote Web Part** With this Web Part, you can enter the symbol of a stock, fund, or index and retrieve a brief summary quote for that symbol. Any such information will be at least 20 minutes old.

For more information about any of these Web Parts, add the Web Part to a page and then click the Help button on its toolbar.

Previewing Microsoft Office 2003 Integration for Great Plains

The Office 2003 Web Parts and Components include a number of Web Parts that provide read-only access to information in Microsoft Business Solutions Great Plains business systems. For example, you can analyze sales, inventory, and employee earnings data.

Installing Office 2003 Web Parts and Components also installs Great Plains Site sample data, and this is what the Web Parts initially display. To access data from a production Great Plains system, you must install the following software:

- Microsoft Office 2003 Integration for Great Plains. You can download this software from the Microsoft Business Solutions Web site.
- Microsoft SQL Server 2000 with Service Pack 3 (SP3) or later.

Customizing Site Definitions

Chapter 17 described how to save an existing SharePoint site as a template, and how to manage the site template gallery for a Web site collection.

A *site definition* is a second, more fundamental way of defining and creating SharePoint sites. If fact, when you first install Windows SharePoint Services, no site templates are available. Instead, a site definition describes each type of Web site a default installation can create: a Team Site, a blank site, a Document Workspace site, and five kinds of Meeting Workspace sites. That's eight site definitions in all.

Ghosting Site Template Files

When you create a site based on a site definition, Windows SharePoint Services doesn't copy a complete set of Web pages into the SharePoint content database. Instead, it *ghosts* the pages in the site definition. This means that if, for example, you create a hundred Team Sites, those sites would behave as if the content database contains a hundred copies of the Team Site pages. But in fact, all hundred sites would share one set of pages, and that set of pages would reside in the Web server's file system. This avoids the overhead of storing, retrieving, and caching duplicated pages in the content databases.

Of course, when someone opens an individual site and uses a program like FrontPage to customize one of its pages, the SharePoint server can no longer ghost that file for that site. Instead, it saves the new file version in the content database, and that version overrides the ghosted file from disk. (This is called *unghosting* the file).

Taken as a unit, the files that make up a site definition describe every detail necessary to create a new site. A site template, however, contains only the differences between a site definition and the state of the site at some later time (with or without list and library content). When you create a site from a site template, Windows SharePoint Services:

1 Creates a site based on the site definition that created the original site.
2 Applies any changes that the site template specifies.

Working with Site Definition Files

When you first install Windows SharePoint Services, a file named WEBTEMP.XML identifies each site definition. (TEMP in this context means *template*, not *temporary*.) You can find this file at:

C:\Program Files\Common Files\Microsoft Shared\web server extensions\60\TEM-PLATE\1033\XML

where 1033 is the current locale ID. A version of this file (with greatly shortened Description values) appears below:

```
<?XML version="1.0" encoding="utf-8" ?>
<!-- _lcid="1033" _version="11.0.5510" _dal="1" -->
<!-- _LocalBinding -->
<Templates xmlns:ows="Microsoft SharePoint">
  <Template Name="STS" ID="1">
    <Configuration ID="0" Title="Team Site"
      Hidden="FALSE" ImageUrl="/_layouts/images/stsprev.png"
      Description="description">
    </Configuration>
    <Configuration ID="1" Title="Blank Site"
      Hidden="FALSE" ImageUrl="/_layouts/images/stsprev.png"
      Description="description">
    </Configuration>
    <Configuration ID="2" Title="Document Workspace"
      Hidden="FALSE" ImageUrl="/_layouts/images/dwsprev.png"
      Description="description">
    </Configuration>
  </Template>
  <Template Name="MPS" ID="2" >
    <Configuration ID="0" Title="Basic Meeting Workspace"
      Hidden="FALSE" ImageUrl="/_layouts/images/mwsprev.png"
      Description="description">
    </Configuration>
    <Configuration ID="1" Title="Blank Meeting Workspace"
      Hidden="FALSE" ImageUrl="/_layouts/images/mwsprev.png"
      Description="description">
    </Configuration>
    <Configuration ID="2" Title="Decision Meeting Workspace"
      Hidden="FALSE" ImageUrl="/_layouts/images/mwsprev.png"
      Description="description">
    </Configuration>
    <Configuration ID="3" Title="Social Meeting Workspace"
```

```
    Hidden="FALSE" ImageUrl="/_layouts/images/mwsprev.png"
    Description="description">
  </Configuration>
  <Configuration ID="4" Title="Multipage Meeting Workspace"
    Hidden="FALSE" ImageUrl="/_layouts/images/mwsprev.png"
    Description="description">
  </Configuration>
  </Template>
</Templates>
```

Each <Template></Template> block identifies a set of similar Web site definitions. Within each <Template> tag:

- The Name attribute supplies a mnemonic name.
- The ID attribute supplies a unique identifier.

Within each <Template></Template> block there's one <configuration> tag for each site definition. Within this tag:

- The ID attributes provide a unique identity within each <Template> node.
- The Title, ImageUrl, and Descriptions fields specify values that the Template Selection page will display when a team member creates a site.

Working with ONET.XML Files

Further information about each site definition appears in a file named ONET.XML. Because the WEBTEMP.XML file specified two template names (STS and MPS), there are two ONET.XML files. To find these files, first navigate to C:\Program Files\Common Files\Microsoft Shared\Web server extensions\60\TEMPLATE\1033\ and then to these locations:

STS\XML\ONET.XML
MPS\XML\ONET.XML

Each ONET.XML file defines a series of common elements for individual sites to use. This includes navigation bars such as the top navigation bar and the quick launch bar, list templates, document templates, base types, configurations, and modules.

A *configuration* is the structure that describes an individual site definition.

- The STS\XML\ONET.XML file contains one configuration structure for each ID value in the <Template Name="STS"> node of the WEBTEMP.XML file.
- The MPS\XML\ONET.XML file contains one configuration structure for each ID value in the <Template Name="MPS"> node of the WEBTEMP.XML file.

A *module* is a block of XML code that specifies all the files associated with a definition and the location of those files in the new site. In the case of a Web Part Page, for example, the module definition specifies not only the Web Part Page file, but also the specific Web Parts, List Views, and files to include on the page.

593

Working with SCHEMA.XML Files

Another XML file named SCHEMA.XML defines the views, forms, and fields for each type of list. The file for any of the standard list types resides at a location such as

C:\Program Files\Common Files\Microsoft Shared\Web server extensions\60\TEMPLATE\1033\STS\LISTS\ANNOUNCE\SCHEMA.XML

where 1033 is the culture ID, STS is the template name from the WEBTEMP.XML file, and ANNOUNCE is a mnemonic name identifying the type of list (Announcements, in this case).

Customizing Site Definitions

Making changes to the WEBTEMP.XML, ONET.XML, and SCHEMA.XML files that come with Windows SharePoint Services is generally a bad idea. Here are the two main reasons:

- Microsoft considers these to be system files. As a result, any reinstallation, repair, or upgrade to Windows SharePoint Services might replace them, overlaying any changes you've made.

- Any site created from a site definition continues to use the WEBTEMP.XML, ONET.XML, and SCHEMA.XML files indefinitely. Therefore, an incorrect change, even if it works for new sites, could break hundreds or thousands of existing sites.

The correct approach, therefore, is to create new site definitions rather than change existing ones. To do this, you create a new site definition file in the same folder as WEBTEMP.XML, and append a suffix to the filename base. Here, for example, are some possible site definition files names:

WEBTEMPIDAHO.XML
WEBTEMPLOGBOOKS.XML
WEBTEMPSALES.XML

When Windows SharePoint Services starts up, it scans the C:\Program Files\Common Files\Microsoft Shared\web server extensions\60\TEMPLATE\1033\XML folder for filenames that begin with WEBTEMP and end in .XML (both all caps) and consecutively loads them into memory. This provides a way of adding new site definitions without modifying the Microsoft-supplied WEBTEMP.XML file. The content below would be typical for a WEBTEMPSALES.XML file.

```
<?XML version="1.0" encoding="utf-8" ?>
<Templates xmlns:ows="Microsoft SharePoint">
   <Template Name="SALES" ID="10011">
      <Configuration ID="0" Title="Sales Tracking Site" Type="0"
         Hidden="FALSE"
         ImageUrl="images/salestrack.jpg"
         Description="A site for tracking new and potential
         customers, for recording customer visits and
         conversations, and for reporting orders.">
      </Configuration>
   </Template>
</Templates>
```

Chapter 18

Note that the template name SALES on line 3 matches the characters you appended to the WEBTEMP filename base. This is a good practice but not a requirement. Note as well that the template ID is greater than 10,000. Microsoft numbers its templates starting at zero and, to avoid conflicts, suggests that customers number their templates starting at 10,001.

Next, you would create the C:\Program Files\Common Files\Microsoft Shared\Web server extensions\60\TEMPLATE\1033\SALES\XML\ path and provide an ONET.XML file. Because the ONET.XML file is long and complex, you'll probably want to copy and modify an existing file rather than type one from scratch.

Finally, for each list, you'll need to create the C:\Program Files\Common Files\Microsoft Shared\Web server extensions\60\TEMPLATE\1033\SALES\LISTS\<listname>\ path and add a SCHEMA.XML file that defines that list.

Although the WEBTEMP.XML, ONET.XML, and SCHEMA.XML files provide the essence of a site definition, you'll need to supply many other files as well. For example, you'll need to provide copies of all the Web pages and associated files the site will use. To observe the type and location of these files, inspect the folder tree for any of the Microsoft-supplied site definitions.

Choosing between Site Templates and Site Definitions

With two methods of designing sites that team members can create, you need some guidelines for deciding which method is best in a particular situation. Here are some factors to consider.

- **Ease of Use** Site templates are easy to create and deploy. You can find or create a site with the features you want, save it as a template, deploy the template, and start creating new sites, all without leaving the browser interface or FrontPage 2003.

  Creating a site definition requires working with XML code in a text editor. Then, when you deploy it, you must do so on each front-end Web server in the same farm. Without a doubt, site definitions are harder to create and deploy.

- **Who Performs the Work?** Any SharePoint Web designer can create a sample site and save it as a template. Then, any site collection administrator can deploy it.

  Because site definitions require access to the Web server's file system, development requires administrative access to test Web servers, and deployment requires the cooperation of production server administrators.

- **Resource Dependence** Site templates don't include all the information required to create a site. Instead, they specify a site definition to use as a starting point, and then a list of changes to apply. If that site definition isn't present, or if it's the wrong version, the site template will fail.

  Site definitions, by contrast, completely describe the sites they create, without dependence on any other site definition. This makes site definitions more attractive to software developers, server administrators, and third-party suppliers.

Chapter 18

595

● **Extent of Modification**   A site template can override many aspects of its underlying site definition, but not all. A site template can, for example, modify logos, menus, means of navigation, and default lists and libraries, but it can't incorporate new data types, new file types, new view styles, or new drop-down edit menus.

The more your site needs to differ from any of the default site definitions, the more likely your approach should be a new site definition.

● **Maintainability**   Once you create a site from a template, modifying the template has no effect on that site. This gives you the freedom to change a template, and thereby add, remove, or modify features in future sites. Because templates reside in the configuration database or in a site template gallery, a single command deploys them for an entire server farm.

Once you've deployed a site definition, there's no safe way to delete or change its features. This is because sites created from the site definition refer to it on an ongoing and active basis, and depend on it remaining constant. If a site definition is no longer adequate, you can only add features or create a new site definition.

● **Performance**   Web pages "ghosted" from a site definition run faster than pages that reside in a content database. This is because:

■ The Web server's file system is faster than a WMSDE or SQL Server database.

■ Caching files from the Web server's file system is more efficient than caching them from a content database.

■ The fewer cache hits, the more often ASP.NET must compile any .aspx pages. Each compilation incurs a performance penalty.

When you create a site solely from a site definition, none of its pages physically resides in the content database, and performance is at peak. Thereafter, the new version of each page you customize (using, for example, a program like FrontPage) resides in the content database and incurs a performance penalty.

When you create a site from a site template, each page that differs from the underlying site definition resides in the content database, and therefore incurs the performance penalty.

Initially, a site created from a template will have one or more pages in the content database, and a site created from a site definition will have none. This often results in the templated sites running somewhat slower.

Note, however, that if you create a site from a site definition and then modify some of its pages, the modified pages then reside in the content database. Depending on the number of unghosted pages, a site created from a site definition could therefore run slower than, at the same speed as, or faster than a site created from a template.

In practice, the performance difference between sites created from a template and sites created from a site definition usually isn't noticeable. Nevertheless, these factors may be worth considering in a large-scale environment.

Chapter 18

For more information about creating and using site definitions, refer to these resources.

- Customizing SharePoint Sites and Portals: Using Templates and Site Definitions by Dino Dato-on and Jinger Zhao (*http://msdn.microsoft.com/library/en-us/odc_SP2003_ta/html/ODC_SPSCustomizingSharePointSites2.asp*)
- Customizing Templates for Microsoft Windows SharePoint Services (*http://msdn.microsoft.com/library/en-us/spptsdk/html/SPPTWSSTemplates.asp*)

In Summary...

This chapter explained four advanced techniques for creating Web Part Pages and sites: built-in SharePoint Web Parts, SharePoint ASP.NET server controls, the Office 2003 Web Parts and Components, and site definitions.

The next chapter begins Part VII, which explains how to write your own Web Parts using Visual Studio .NET.

Developing Web Parts in Visual Studio .NET

Chapter 19

Beginning Web Part Development

With the flexibility of powerful prewritten Web Parts, Web Part Pages, custom lists and libraries, browser-based editing, FrontPage-based editing, Data Sources, Data Views, Web Part connections, and connectivity to Microsoft Office applications, it's amazing how much you can do with Windows SharePoint Services without programming. Inevitably, however, no tool—or set of tools—can do everything. And with software, that's the time to think about writing your own code.

In a SharePoint environment, writing your own code usually means writing Web Parts. Web Parts integrate smoothly with the rest of your SharePoint site, leveraging its existing appearance, organization, security, and data management. What's more, Web Parts are reusable. You can write them once and use them in as many pages as you like.

Of course, these advantages come at a price. Web Parts work differently than ordinary ASP.NET pages do, and much more differently than legacy ASP pages. As a result, developing and deploying a Web Part requires a different mind-set and a somewhat different tool set than does developing other kinds of server-based Web components. With that in mind, this chapter explains the essence of how Web Parts work and what software you need to develop them. Chapters 20 and 21 will provide step-by-step instructions for creating some simple but useful Web Parts.

The purpose of these chapters is to introduce Web Part programming. They assume you already have some experience with .NET programming, and with Web-based programming in general. The examples are in Microsoft C#, but you could use Microsoft Visual Basic .NET just as effectively.

Configuring Your Development Environment

Web Parts run only within the environment of Windows SharePoint Services, which, in turn, requires Windows Server 2003 or later. As a result, you'll need a copy of Windows Server 2003. If possible, you should have your own server because:

- Software development by its very nature leads to frequent IIS resets and occasional system reboots.

- Interactive debugging works best on the local machine, and can monopolize resources.

- To get your application working (or figure out why it isn't), you'll need authority to inspect or adjust any aspect of system configuration.

You can run Windows Server 2003 in any of these modes:

- **As your primary workstation operating system**   This option uses the least hardware, but exposes your day-to-day work environment to changes or crashes caused by unfinished (and therefore unreliable) software. In addition, you may encounter issues running desktop software designed primarily for Windows XP.

- **On its own computer**   This option isolates your daily working environment from your development activities, but it does require another piece of hardware.

- **As a virtual machine under Microsoft Virtual PC**   This option saves you the expense of buying a new computer, but it's not free. You still have to buy Microsoft Virtual PC and, in all probability, some additional memory and disk space for the PC that will run it. A major advantage, however, is the ease of saving and restoring system images. If you find that some approach or some experiment isn't working out, you can revert to an earlier system image.

To create, compile, and test the code for Web Parts, you'll need a copy of Microsoft Visual Studio .NET. Any version will do, including the stand-alone products Visual C# .NET Standard Edition and Visual Basic NET Standard Edition.

Microsoft Developer Network (MSDN) subscriptions come with licenses to download, install, and run Visual Studio .NET, Virtual PC, Windows Server 2003, SQL Server, and most other Microsoft products for development use only. MSDN Universal, the top offering, includes all Microsoft Office programs and SharePoint Portal Server. For more information about this option, browse *http://msdn.microsoft.com/howtobuy/*.

If you're an independent developer, you may prefer to register as a Microsoft Partner (which is free) and then purchase a Microsoft Action Pack Subscription. This includes developer licenses for Microsoft Office, Virtual PC, Windows Server 2003, SQL Server, and many other products. For more information, browse *http://partner.microsoft.com/* and click Get An Action Pack Software Subscription.

Action Pack subscriptions don't include Visual Studio, so if you're on a budget, Visual C# .NET Standard Edition might be attractive.

How Web Parts Work

In ASP.NET terminology, a *server control* is a software component that runs on the Web server as part of one or more ASP.NET Web pages. This provides a way of breaking complex Web pages into manageable pieces, and of using the same component in multiple pages. There are two kinds of ASP.NET server controls: user and custom.

- **User Controls**   These controls consist of two parts:
  - A file that has an .ascx filename extension, and that contains sample HTML.
  - The program code that executes on the Web server. This code, plus the code for all other ASP.NET pages and user controls in the same application, is usually compiled into a single DLL that resides in the application's bin folder. However, it can also reside in source form, within the .ascx file.

  Most developers find user controls fairly easy to create. This is because the developer (or even a Web designer) can use a visual designer to create the sample HTML, and because programming a user control is very much like programming an ordinary ASP.NET page.

  User controls, however, can be difficult to deploy widely. When a change occurs, someone must:

  1   Identify each Web site that uses the control.
  2   Install the new .ascx and source code files in each Web site.
  3   Recompile all the source code in each Web site.
  4   Copy the revised .ascx file and the recompiled code to each production Web site.

  If Web Parts were user controls, deploying a new Web Part (or upgrading one) would require recompiling and reinstalling the program code for every SharePoint site that uses the Web Part. That's why Web Parts aren't user controls.

- **Custom Controls**   These controls consist entirely of program code. There's no HTML template like the .ascx file for a user control, and consequently no way of using a WYSIWYG editor to design its HTML. A programmer must write code that emits each scrap of HTML that the control needs in order to display output.

  The advantage of custom controls lies in deployment. Each custom control (or, if you choose, each logical group of custom controls) has its own DLL, and at your option you can install this once per physical server or once per virtual Web server. This is the model that Web Parts use. All Web Parts are, in fact, ASP.NET custom controls.

In practice, laying out page elements with no WYSIWYG editor and writing program code that emits HTML aren't the grueling tasks you might expect. The reason is that the output of most Web Parts is fairly simple. Many page elements—such as the top navigation bar, the page banner, any toolbars, and any link areas—are part of the Web Part Page or of other Web Parts. Any Web Parts you create need only display their specific data, and they inherit styles from the site's theme.

Windows SharePoint Services provides a base class for creating Web Parts, namely *Microsoft.SharePoint.WebPartPages.WebPart*. This class provides a base upon which you can write any type of Web Part you like. To *inherit* from this class (that is, to use it as a base), you code the following statement in the source code for your Web Part:

```
public class WebPart1 : Microsoft.SharePoint.WebPartPages.WebPart
{
// Your custom code goes here.
}
```

In addition, virtually all Web Parts override two methods in the *WebPart* class:

- *CreateChildControls*   The *WebPart* class calls this method to create child server controls that the Web Part will later convert to HTML.

- *RenderWebPart*   The *WebPart* class calls this method to render (that is, create) the HTML that the Web Part will display.

> **Note**   If you've ever written ASP.NET custom controls that aren't Web Parts, you're probably accustomed to overriding the *Render* method rather than the *RenderWebPart* method. In a Web Part, however, the *Render* method creates only the chrome (the Web Part's title bar and border, for example). The *RenderWebPart* method creates the HTML that appears in the body of the Web Part.

The reason for overriding (that is, superseding) these methods is that the versions in the *WebPart* class essentially do nothing. Overriding them means that at the proper time, the *WebPart* class will call custom methods you provide rather than its own do-nothing methods. Adding these two overrides to the previous code gives the Web Part this structure:

```
public class WebPart1 : Microsoft.SharePoint.WebPartPages.WebPart
{
//  Global declarations go here.

    protected override void CreateChildControls ()
    {
//      Code to create a list of Web or HTML server
//      controls goes here
    }
    protected override void RenderWebPart(HtmlTextWriter output)
    {
//      Code to render the list of Web or HTML server
//      controls goes here
    }
}
```

> For more information about overriding the *CreateChildControls* method, refer to the section titled "Adding Layout Controls and Content" later in this chapter.

Beginning Web Part Development

> For more information about overriding the *RenderWebPart* method, refer to the section titled "Writing Web Part Output" later in this chapter.

If you've written conventional ASP.NET pages or ASP.NET user controls, you probably made extensive use of the *Page_Load* event. A similar event occurs for custom controls, but most Web Parts never bother detecting it. There are at least two reasons for this:

- *Page_Load* normally fires when ASP.NET finishes loading the page's server controls into memory. In a Web Part, however, ASP.NET doesn't load the server controls; your own *CreateChildControls* method does that. So, you may as well put your code in the *CreateChildControls* method, or call it from within that method.

- Within a *Page_Load* event handler, programmers normally use the *IsPostBack* property to differentiate between the initial display of a page and a subsequent submission. But in the case of Web Parts, a postback also occurs when a team member uses a browser to add, remove, or reconfigure any Web Part on the page.

  This makes sense if you stop and think about it. There are many times—such as when you use a browser to add a Web Part to a page—when a round trip to the server clearly occurs. However, these aren't normal form submissions, and you shouldn't process any data that form fields might contain.

So, if you're not going to use *Page_Load* to initialize the display, and you're not going to use it for form submissions, you're probably not going to use it much at all.

As in conventional ASP.NET pages, most Web server controls have *onServerClick* or *onServerChange* events that can trigger event handlers in a Web Part. This is the normal way of detecting actual form submissions.

> For more information about using *onServerClick* and *onServerChange* events in a Web Part, refer to the section titled "Using the ASP.NET Event Model" later in this chapter.

Starting a New Web Part Project

Before starting to create your first Web Part, you need to have Windows SharePoint Services up and running, and any version of Visual Studio .NET installed on the computer you plan to use for coding and compiling.

With those items in place, you're ready to install the Web Part templates For Visual Studio .NET. This is something you need to do only once. Here's the procedure:

1 If you're not going to run Visual Studio on the SharePoint server, copy the Microsoft.SharePoint.dll file from the server to the Visual Studio machine. By default, this file resides at:

   C:\Program Files\Common Files\Microsoft Shared\web server extensions\60\ISAPI

   You can copy this file to any folder you like on the Visual Studio machine; just remember its location and don't delete it by accident.

2   On the machine where Visual Studio is installed, browse *http://www.microsoft.com/ technet/downloads/sharepnt.mspx*

3   When the Downloads for SharePoint Products and Technologies page appears, click the hyperlink titled SharePoint Products And Technologies Templates: Web Part Templates For Visual Studio .NET.

4   When the Download Details page appears, click the Download button and save the resulting file (WebPartTemplatesforVSNetSample2.exe) to a temporary location.

5   Run the file you downloaded in step 4. When the WinZip Self-Extractor dialog box appears, choose a folder for the unzipped setup files and then click Unzip.

6   Open the folder you specified in step 5 and run the setup.exe program.

7   Click Next on the opening page of the setup wizard, and then I Agree and Next on the License Agreement page.

8   On the third wizard page, select the check box for each set of templates you want to install. The choices are Visual C# and Visual Basic .NET. The examples in this book are all in C#, but feel free to install both.

9   If the wizard page shown in Figure 19-1 appears, enter the folder location where you saved the Microsoft.SharePoint.dll file you copied in step 1.

10   Click Next and Finish to perform the installation.

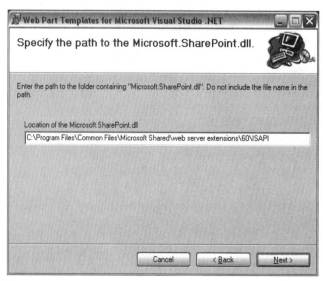

Figure 19-1.   If you install the Web Part Templates for Visual Studio .NET on a machine not running Windows SharePoint Services, you'll need to supply a local copy of Microsoft.SharePoint.dll and provide its location on this wizard page.

Beginning Web Part Development

To actually start programming a Web Part, proceed as follows.

1 Start Visual Studio, choose New from the File menu, and then choose Project.

2 When the New Project dialog box shown in Figure 19-2 appears, apply the following settings and then click OK

- **Project Types** Select either Visual Basic Projects or Visual C# Projects. This presumes, of course, that you installed the corresponding templates in the previous procedure. The examples in this book are all in C#.

- **Templates** Choose Web Part Library.

- **Name** Specify the name of the Visual Studio project. By default, this will also be the name of the DLL that deploys your Web Part. Visual Studio will also create a solution having this name.

- **Location** Specify a folder where the Visual Studio project and solution will reside.

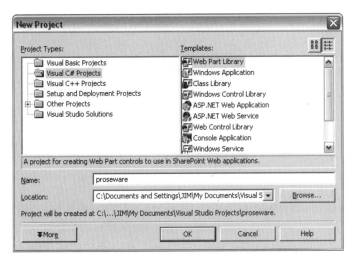

Figure 19-2. The Web Part library template initializes a project for creating Web Parts.

3 Visual Studio will create the new project and open the class file for a Web Part named WebPart1. Figure 19-3 illustrates this result.

Microsoft Windows SharePoint Services Inside Out

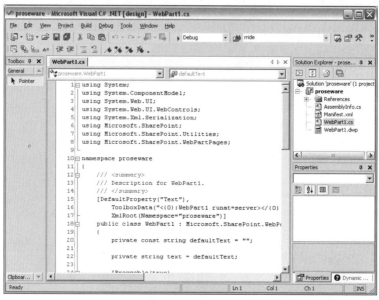

Figure 19-3. This new Web Part project is ready to receive custom code.

4   Unless you want your Web Part to be named WebPart1:

  4.1   Choose Find And Replace from the Edit menu, and then choose Replace.

  4.2   When the Replace dialog box appears, set Find What to WebPart1, Replace With to the name you want, and then click Replace All.

  4.3   Click the close box in the Replace dialog box, and then in the WebPart1.cs file. When Visual Studio prompts Save Changes To The Following Items?, click Yes.

  4.4   Right-click the WebPart1.cs file in Solution Explorer, choose Rename from the shortcut menu, and change the filename base to the name you assigned in step 4.2.

> **Tip**   If the Solution Explorer window isn't visible, press Ctrl+Alt+L or choose Solution Explorer from the View menu.

Writing Web Part Output

For an ordinary ASP.NET page or user control, the first step after creating a new file is to design the HTML. This is also true for ASP.NET custom controls (and consequently for Web Parts) but, because there's no text file that contains "raw" HTML, you need to approach this task differently.

Beginning Web Part Development

As you no doubt recall, every Web Part that creates output contains a method declaration like this:

```
protected override void RenderWebPart(HtmlTextWriter output)
{
}
```

ASP.NET runs this function automatically after all initialization functions, event handlers, and child functions have finished—in short, when all other processing is complete. To actually emit HTML, you have a choice of two approaches:

- You can call the *Write* method of the *HtmlTextWriter* object named *output*. (Note that the *RenderWebPart* method receives a pointer to this object as an argument.) For example, to write a paragraph that displays the value of a variable named *strMsg*, you would code:

  ```
  output.Write("<p>" + SPEncode.HtmlEncode(strMsg) + "</p>");
  ```

  SPEncode.HtmlEncode is a method that converts reserved HTML characters to character entity references. For example, it converts < to < and > to >.

- You can call the *RenderChildren* method, specifying the *HtmlTextWriter* object named *output* as a parameter. Here's an example:

  ```
  RenderChildren(output);
  ```

To understand the *RenderChildren* method, you should know that every ASP.NET page, user control, and custom control has a *Controls* collection. This collection contains an object for each element the page or control will display. When you're working with ASP.NET pages or user controls, ASP.NET loads the *Controls* collection from the .aspx or .ascx file as follows:

- Each tag you code runat="server" creates a corresponding object in the *Controls* collection.

- Any content that appears *between* tags coded runat="server" appears in the *Controls* collection as a single *System.Web.UI.LiteralControl* object.

Because custom controls (and therefore Web Parts) have no .aspx or .ascx file, the *Controls* collection is initially empty. You can, however, write program code that adds any controls you want to the *Controls* collection. Here's an example:

```
HtmlGenericControl prgMsg;                    // Declare variable.
prgMsg = new HtmlGenericControl("p");         // Create object.
prgMsg.InnerText = strMsg;                    // Set value inside <p> and </p>.
Controls.Add(prgMsg);                         // Add to Controls collection.
```

A single call to the *RenderChildren* method will then tell each control, in order, to emit its HTML. If you use code such as the above to create five paragraph controls, *RenderChildren* would write five sets of <p> and </p> tags, each with the content you assigned.

The choice between using *output.Write* and *RenderChildren* is entirely yours. The *output.Write* method is easier to see and understand. Loading up the *Controls* collection and calling *RenderChildren* is more abstract, but it helps modularize your program and it guards against invalid HTML.

Although there's nothing wrong with *output.Write*, the examples in this book will use the *RenderChildren* method exclusively.

Adding Layout Controls and Content

ASP.NET provides two sets of objects you can add to a *Controls* collection. They are:

- *System.Web.UI.HtmlControls* These controls correspond very closely to standard HTML elements. For a complete list, browse:
  http://msdn.microsoft.com/library/en-us/cpref/html/frlrfSystemWebUIHtmlControls.asp

  To use these controls, the source code for your Web Part should contain this statement:

  ```
  using System.Web.UI.HtmlControls;
  ```

  Otherwise, you'll need to type the entire namespace every time you refer to one of its class names.

- *System.Web.UI.WebControls* Controls in this group are either:

  - Enhanced versions of HTML server controls. Unlike the *HtmlSelect* control, for example, the *ListBox* Web server control can trigger immediate postbacks.

  - Entirely new elements, such as a calendar, an ad rotator, and the ubiquitous *DataGrid* control.

  For a list of these controls, browse:
  http://msdn.microsoft.com/library/en-us/cpref/html/frlrfSystemWebUIHtmlControls.asp

  To use these controls, the source code for your Web Part should contain this statement:

  ```
  using System.Web.UI.WebControls;
  ```

The preceding section already showed some example code for creating a paragraph tag and adding text to it. Here it is again.

```
HtmlGenericControl prgMsg;
prgMsg = new HtmlGenericControl("p");
prgMsg.InnerText = strMsg;
Controls.Add(prgMsg);
```

Beginning Web Part Development

In fact, however, not all this code is likely to appear together in one block. The second and fourth statements must appear within the *CreateChildControls* method, as shown below:

```
protected override void CreateChildControls ()
{
    prgMsg = new HtmlGenericControl("p");
    Controls.Add(prgMsg);
}
```

The second statement, however, could easily reside in the method that determines the value of the *strMsg* variable. Here's an example:

```
01 HtmlGenericControl prgMsg;
02
03 public void MsgLoad(object sender, EventArgs e)
04 {
05     string strMsg;
06     strMsg = "Help! I'm a prisoner in a Web Part!";
07     EnsureChildControls();
08     prgMsg.InnerText = strMsg;
09 }
10 protected override void CreateChildControls ()
11 {
12     prgMsg = new HtmlGenericControl("p");
13     prgMsg.Load += new EventHandler(MsgLoad);
14     Controls.Add(prgMsg);
15 }
```

In this code:

- The statement on line 13 establishes *MsgLoad* as an *onLoad* event handler for the *prgMsg* object. This means that the *MsgLoad* method on line 3 will run as soon as the *prgMsg* object finishes loading.

- The *EnsureChildControls* method on line 7 ensures that the *CreateChildControls* method has finished executing. If not, it waits for that method to complete. This avoids the embarrassing moments that occur when a method tries to manipulate an object that *CreateChildControls* hasn't created yet.

- The assignment statement on line 8 stores a value into the paragraph control created on line 12.

- The declaration of the *prgMsg* variable appears on line 1, which is outside both the *MsgLoad* method and the *CreateChildControls* method. This makes the *prgMsg* available within both of those methods.

This, by the way, plus the Web Part templates for Visual Studio .NET, is just about all the code you need to write an elementary Web Part. A Visual Studio project using this code appears in the \WebParts\proseware folder of the companion CD, and a screen shot appears in Figure 19-4.

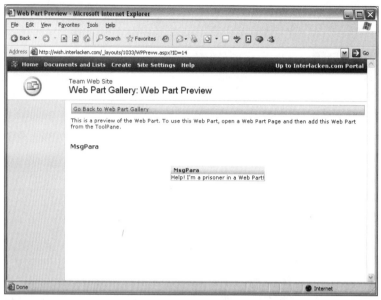

Figure 19-4. This is a very simple Web Part, and it required very little code.

Manipulating SharePoint Objects

Windows SharePoint Services provides a rich collection of objects for working with sites, lists, permissions, and other administrative objects. All these objects reside within a namespace named, logically enough, *SharePoint*. Its major classes include:

- *SharePoint.SPSite*   Represents a SharePoint site collection. Its properties and methods provide access to the collection's subsites, templates, cross-site groups, and so forth.

  Remember: an *SPSite* object doesn't represent a site. Its properties and methods pertain to an entire site collection, and not to any one Web site.

- *SharePoint SPWeb*   Represents an individual SharePoint site: either a top-level Web site or a subsite. It provides access to all the site's lists, files, folders, Web Parts, and other objects.

- *SharePoint.SPList*   Represents a SharePoint list. The term *list*, in this context, is very broad. It includes not only generic lists, but also surveys, discussion boards, document libraries, picture libraries, and form libraries.

For a complete listing and description of the objects in the SharePoint namespace, browse *http://msdn.microsoft.com/library/en-us/spptsdk/html/tsnsmicrosoftsharepoint.asp*.

Beginning Web Part Development

The statement below creates an *SPWeb* object named *spwCurr* that describes the current SharePoint Web site. In other words, it describes the site that contains the page that displayed the Web Part.

```
SPWeb spwCurr = SPControl.GetContextWeb(Context);
```

The next statement creates an *SPSite* object named spsColl that describes the site collection that contains the current site.

```
SPSite spsColl = SPControl.GetContextSite(Context);
```

Once you have these objects, you can retrieve more information about the site or its collction by using their properties and methods. For example, after you create an *SPWeb* object named *spwCurr* as described above:

- *spwCurr.CurrentUser.LoginName*   Returns the current team member's login name, such as interlacken\karen.
- *spwCurr.CurrentUser.Name*   Returns the current team member's personal name, such as Karen Archer.
- *spwCurr.Name*   Gets or sets the name of the current site.
- *spwCurr.Lists*   Returns a collection of *SPList* objects, one for each list in the site.
- *spwCurr.Delete()*   Deletes the current site.

In most cases, if a property is editable, your code can simply store a value into it. Editable, in this sense, means that Windows SharePoint Services permits direct updates to a field, and that the current user has permission to perform the operation.

To enumerate a collection, code a *foreach* loop like the one below:

```
foreach (SPList splCurr in spwCurr.Lists){
//  splCurr will point to a different list during each iteration
}
```

In addition, you can index into lists using either numbers or names. The following statement, for example, creates a *SPList* object named *splNrTwo* that points to the second list in the spwCurr.Lists collection:

```
SPList splNrTwo = spwCurr.Lists[1];
```

And this statement creates an *SPList* object that points to a Shared Documents library:

```
SPList splSharedDocs = spwCurr.Lists["Shared Documents"];
```

613

To add objects to and remove them from SharePoint collections, you use Add and Delete methods, just as you do with most other .NET collections. The following statement, for example, creates a new Contacts list named Swamp Dwellers. The second parameter supplies the list description:

```
spwCurr.Lists.Add("Swamp Dwellers",
    "Ducks, Frogs, Gators, and other creepy critters",
    SPListTemplateType.Contacts);
```

Using the ASP.NET Event Model

Web Parts experience the same lifecycle events as ordinary Web pages: *Init, Load, DataBinding, PreRender,* and *Unload.* To capture these, add a method like the following to the class for your Web Part:

```
protected override void OnLoad(EventArgs e)
{
//      Your code goes here
    base.OnLoad(e);
}
```

This example illustrates the code for the *Load* event. To capture other life cycle events, change the word *Load*—in two places—to *Init, DataBinding, PreRender,* or *Unload.*

To capture button clicks, drop-down menu changes, and other form events, you must create the control, add an event hander to it, and then code the event handler. The following code, for example, creates a *DropDownList* control, adds an event handler named *Priority_Change* for the *SelectedIndexChanged* event, and then forces the form to autosubmit whenever the team member changes the current selection.

```
lstPriority = new DropDownList();
lstPriority.SelectedIndexChanged += new EventHandler(Priority_Change);
lstPriority.AutoPostBack = true;
```

Note the += operator in the second statement. This *appends* the new event handler without discarding any others for the same event. The code for the event handler itself appears below.

```
private void Priority_Change(object sender, EventArgs e)
{
// Your code goes here.
}
```

A Visual Studio project illustrating these techniques appears in the WebParts\tailspintoys folder of the companion CD, and a screen shot appears in Figure 19-5.

Beginning Web Part Development

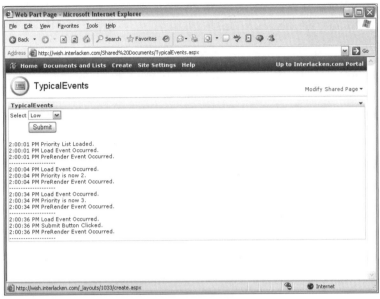

Figure 19-5. This Web Part traces and displays its lifecycle steps. The current display reflects four submissions.

This figure illustrates four executions of the Web Part Page, and therefore of the Web Part.

- The *Load* and *PreRender* event handlers display simple messages, and fire for each execution.
- The following code creates the drop-down list:

```
lstPriority = new DropDownList();
lstPriority.SelectedIndexChanged
    += new EventHandler(Priority_Change);
lstPriority.AutoPostBack = true;
```

And this code populates the list items:

```
if (lstPriority.Items.Count < 1)
{
    lstPriority.Items.Add(new ListItem("High","1"));
    lstPriority.Items.Add(new ListItem("Medium","2"));
    lstPriority.Items.Add(new ListItem("Low","3"));
    litMsgs.Text += "<br>" + DateTime.Now.ToLongTimeString()
                 + " Priority List Loaded.";
}
```

The message Priority List Loaded appears only once in figure 19-5 because the ASP.NET ViewState mechanism persists the items (and the current selection) from one execution to another.

The messages Priority Is Now 2 and Priority Is Now 3 appear because the team member changed the selection in the drop-down list box, and this caused an autopostback.

● The message Submit Button Clicked appears because the team member clicked the Submit button. The following code creates this button and specifies a *Click* event handler named *Submit_Click*.

```
btnSubmit = new Button();
btnSubmit.Text = "Submit";
btnSubmit.Click += new EventHandler (Submit_Click);
```

Here's the code for the event handler:

```
private void Submit_Click(object sender, EventArgs e)
{
    EnsureChildControls();
    litMsgs.Text += "<br>" + DateTime.Now.ToLongTimeString()
                    + " Submit Button Clicked.";
}
```

As in all ASP.NET pages, a single HTML form surrounds the content of each Web Part Page. Therefore, you needn't ever (and shouldn't ever) add your own <form> tags or *HtmlForm* objects to a Web Part. The Web Part Page will provide these.

When a Web Part Page displays several Web Parts, they *all* execute every time the Web page makes a round trip to the server. For example, your Web Part will execute:

● Every time the team member clicks the browser's Refresh button.

● Every time the team member clicks a Submit button or otherwise creates a postback from another Web Part.

● Every time the team members use browser-based design features such as:

   ■ Switching from shared view to personal view.

   ■ Entering, using, or exiting browser-based Design mode.

   ■ Displaying the Add Web Parts task pane.

   ■ Scrolling through multiple pages in a Web Part gallery.

   ■ Modifying a Web Part.

As a result, any event handlers in your Web Part that book orders, adjust account balances, or perform any other kinds of updates should only react to events that come from elements that you *know* reside in your Web Part, and not to general, page-wide events like *Page_Load*.

Beginning Web Part Development

Exposing Custom Properties

Many Web Parts expose properties that team members can change through the Modify Web Part task pane in the browser, or through the Web Part Properties dialog box in FrontPage. The Text property in Figure 19-6 provides an example. Windows SharePoint Services calls these *custom properties*.

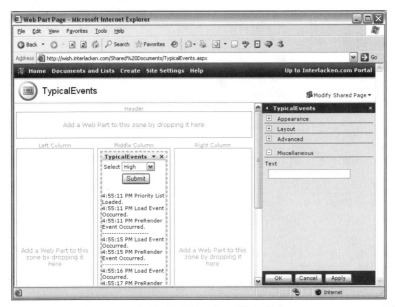

Figure 19-6. The input field titled Text is a SharePoint custom property. Windows SharePoint Services does most of the work in displaying and saving such values.

The code that appears below creates a custom property named *Text*. You put this inside the class definition for your Web Part, but not inside any method. The Web Part templates for Visual Studio .NET provide a version of this code in every new Web Part class file.

```
private const string defaultText = "";
private string text = defaultText;

[Browsable(true),
    Category("Miscellaneous"),
    DefaultValue(defaultText),
    WebPartStorage(Storage.Personal),
    FriendlyName("Text"),
    Description("Text Property")]
public string Text
{
    get { return text; }
    set { text = value; }
}
```

The first two lines define a default value and a class-wide variable for the custom property value. The last five lines are a very ordinary property definition. The middle six lines, within square brackets, actually define the custom property as it will appear in the Web Part's property pane. Table 19-1 lists and describes all the available properties.

Table 19-1. Custom Property Attributes

Attribute	Purpose
Browsable	A value of *false* stops the custom property from appearing in the Web Part's property sheet The default is *true*. Setting the *WebPartStorage* attribute to *Storage.None* has the same effect.
Category	The section title where the custom property will appear on the property sheet. If you leave this attribute empty or set it to Default, Appearance, Layout, or Advanced, the custom property will appear in the Miscellaneous section.
DefaultValue	The custom property's default value.
Description	The tool tip text that appears if a team member hovers the mouse pointer over the custom property's input control.
FriendlyNameAttribute	The caption or title that identifies the custom property. If you leave this empty, the program name for the property will appear.
ReadOnly	A value of *true* makes the custom property read-only in the property sheet. The default is *false*.
WebPartStorage	The view modes for which Windows SharePoint Services will display and save custom property values. The permissible values are: ● **Storage.Shared** Only when configuring the Web Part's shared view. ● **Storage.Personal** When configuring either the shared or personal view. ● **Storage.None** Never.
HtmlDesignerAttribute	Associates a property builder (that is, a custom Web page or module) with the property. This overrides the normal input format in Web page designers such as FrontPage.

You can define as many of these custom properties as you need. Windows SharePoint Services takes care of displaying them, and of saving the configured values as part of the Web Part definition for that page (or, in the case of personal views, for that team member). The type of input control depends on the data type of the custom property. For example, a string property will get a text box, and a Boolean property will get a check box.

Of course, it's your responsibility to write code that makes use of the custom property, once received.

If you need the capability of rejecting a custom property, choose one of these approaches:

- Raise an exception in the property's set method. This approach is simple and normally works as you want in both the SharePoint browser interface and in FrontPage. Instead of closing, the property sheet will display the error message from your exception.

  If, however, your exception occurs when the Web Part's property sheet isn't visible, then the whole page may fail. This can occur, for example, when another control tries to set the property pragmatically.

- Use a Web Part Tool Part, as the next section describes.

Using Web Part Tool Parts

If the default user interface that Windows SharePoint Services provides for custom properties doesn't meet your needs, Web Part Tool Parts may provide an answer.

Basically, a Web Part Tool Part is a class that displays and processes an HTML user interface for one or more custom properties. To use Web Part Tool Parts, the Web Part class file must override the *GetToolParts* method with code like this:

```
public override ToolPart[] GetToolParts()
{
    ToolPart[] toolparts = new ToolPart[3];
    toolparts[0] = new CustomPropertyToolPart();
    toolparts[1] = new WebPartToolPart();
    toolparts[2] = new WebPartLibrary2.ToolPart1();
    return toolparts;
}
```

Notice that this override returns an array of *ToolPart* objects.

- The first is a standard *CustomPropertyToolPart* object, which displays any custom properties just as the previous section described. If you override *GetToolParts* and omit this entry, no controls for custom properties will appear.

- The second is a *WebPartToolPart* object, which displays the standard Appearance, Layouts, and Advanced sections of the Web Part's property pane. If you omit this entry, these sections won't appear.

- The third (and each subsequent) is a custom class that you develop separately in the same project, and that inherits the *Microsoft.SharePoint.WebPartPages.ToolPart* class.

Any *ToolPart* classes you write must override four methods: *ApplyChanges*, *SyncChanges*, *CancelChanges*, and *RenderToolPart*.

> For more information about writing classes that override the *ToolPart* class, and about using Web Part
> tool tips in general, refer to the article "Creating a Web Part with a Custom Tool Part" at
> *msdn.microsoft.com/library/en-us/spptsdk/html/CreateWPToolPart.asp*

Providing a Design Time HTML Provider

If you open a Web Part Page in FrontPage, any custom Web Parts you develop are likely
to appear with the following message in place of a WYSIWYG display:

The preview for this Web Part is not available.

This is because FrontPage Design view doesn't actually run any Web Parts it displays: instead,
it calls a method called *GetDesignTimeHtml* and displays the resulting HTML. If your Web
Part doesn't override this method, the message shown above appears.

The *GetDesignTimeHtml* method is part of an interface named *IDesignTimeHtmlProvider*.
Here, then, are the steps necessary for your Web Part to appear graphically in an editor like
FrontPage.

1 To signify that your Web Part class supports the *IDesignTimeHtmlProvider* interface,
   append a comma and the interface name to the class declaration. For example, change:

   ```
   public class SimpleWebPart : Microsoft.SharePoint.WebPartPages.WebPart
   {}
   ```

   to:

   ```
   public class SimpleWebPart : Microsoft.SharePoint.WebPartPages.WebPart,
               IDesignTimeHtmlProvider
   {}
   ```

2 Add a public method such as the following to your class:

   ```
   public string GetDesignTimeHtml()
   {
       return "<p>Any HTML</p>";
   }
   ```

Of course, the *GetDesignTimeHtml* method can return any HTML you want. You might
arrange, for example, for a common method to format actual data in the *RenderWebPart*
method, and sample data in the *GetDesignTimeHtml* method.

> For more information about using the *IDesignTimeHtmlProvider* interface, refer to the article section
> titled "Implement the *IDesignTimeHtmlProvider* Interface in Your Web Part to Ensure Correct Rendering
> in FrontPage" at *http://msdn.microsoft.com/library/en-us/odc_SP2003_ta/html/
> ODC_WSSWebPartTips.asp*

Beginning Web Part Development

Assigning a Strong Name

Strong naming is a technique whereby Visual Studio uses a private key to digitally sign any assemblies (for example, any DLLs) it creates. It also stamps those assemblies with a public key that can validate the signature. This guards against any unauthorized versions of a program (such as a Web Part). If the given public key fails to validate the digital signature, or if the assembly contains an unexpected public key, Windows SharePoint Services will refuse to run the module. Instead, you get a message like the following:

A Web Part or Web Form Control on this Web Part Page cannot be displayed or imported because it is not registered on this site as safe.

As you'll learn in the next section, there are two ways of deploying Web Parts: one that requires a strong name and one that recommends one. Here is the procedure for giving a Web Part assembly a strong name:

1   Identify the folder that contains your Visual Studio Web Part project. The following is a typical path, where *<user>* is your windows logon ID and *<project>* is the name of your Visual Studio project.

    C:\Documents and Settings*<user>*\My Documents\Visual Studio Projects*<project>*

2   On the machine running Visual Studio, open a command prompt.

3   Change to the directory containing the sn.exe file. This is usually one of the following:

    C:\Program Files\Microsoft Visual Studio .NET\FrameworkSDK\Bin\

    C:\Program Files\Microsoft Visual Studio .NET 2003\SDK\v1.1\Bin\

4   Create a key pair file by running the following command:

    ```
    sn.exe -k "<path>\<project>.snk"
    ```

    where *<path>* is the path to your Visual Studio project (from step 1) and *<project>* is the name of your Visual Studio project.

5   Open your Visual Studio project, and then choose Add Existing Item from the File menu.

6   When the Add Existing Item dialog box appears, find and select the file you created in step 4, and then click Open.

7   In Video Studio, open the AssemblyInfo.cs file for your project.

8   Scroll to the bottom of the file, and change the line

    ```
    [assembly: AssemblyKeyFile("")]
    ```

    to:

    ```
    [assembly: AssemblyKeyFile("..\\..\\<project>.snk")]
    ```

    where *<project>* is the name of your Visual Studio project.

As usual in C# literals, a single backslash is an escape character. For example, \n means new line, not a backslash followed by an n. To get a backslash in the literal's value, you have to code two backslashes.

The path ..\..\ is necessary because the strong name key file resides two directory levels closer to the root than the DLL file Visual Studio creates when it builds your project.

9 Scroll about halfway up the AssemblyInfo.cs file and look for a line like:

```
[assembly: AssemblyVersion("1.0.0.0")]
```

If this line contains any asterisks, replace them with digits. This will avoid creating a new version number every time you compile the Web Part.

10 Choose Rebuild Solution from the Build menu. This (and every subsequent build) will create a strongly named assembly.

> **Tip** Whenever the name, version number, or digital signature of a Web Part changes, you have to reinstall the Web Part on each SharePoint server that uses it, and reconfigure each Web Part Page that uses it. As a result, most programmers avoid changing these properties.

Deploying Custom Web Parts

To deploy or upgrade a Web Part, you must first compile it in Visual Studio. Then, you must copy the resulting assembly (that is, the resulting .dll file) into one of two locations:

- **The SharePoint server's Global Assembly Cache (GAC)** This makes the Web Part available to all virtual servers on the same computer, with maximum privileges. However, the assembly *must* have a strong name. (You must have compiled it with a key pair file.)

  To install a Web Part this way, drag its .dll file into the C:\Windows\Assembly folder, where C:\Windows is the server's system folder.

- **The bin folder of one or more virtual servers** This makes the Web Part available only on those virtual servers where you install it. Assemblies you install this way don't need strong names, but strongly naming your assemblies is always a good idea.

  Unfortunately, at least through windows SharePoint Services Service Pack 1, this method doesn't work properly on computers running more than one SharePoint content server.

Chapter 19

Beginning Web Part Development

There are three ways to install Web Parts into the bin folder of a virtual server:

- **Install the Web Part manually.** To do this:

    1 Create your own .dwp file.

    2 Copy this .dwp file into the wpcatalog folder at the virtual server's physical root.

    3 Copy the Web Part's .dll into the bin folder at the virtual server's physical root.

    4 Update the <SafeControls> section of the virtual server's web.config file.

- **Create and install a Web Part Package.** To take this approach, create a Windows CAB file (with a .wpp filename extension) that contains:

    ▪ A mainfest.xml file describing each file you need to install.

    ▪ Each file you need to install.

- Then, run the following command to install the package:

    ```
    stsadm.exe -o addwppack -filename <filename> -globalinstall -force
    ```

    where <filename> is the name of the .cab file.

- **Use the InstallAssemblies tool.** This tool examines your .dll file, creates the required .dwp file and Web Part Package, and then runs stsadm.exe –o addwppack, all from a graphical interface. In almost every case, this is the easiest, most accurate, and overall best approach.

> To install the InstallAssemblies tool, copy the \utils\Web Part Toolkit\ folder on the companion CD to a C:\Program Files\Web Part Toolkit\ folder on your SharePoint server. Then, to run the tool, launch C:\Program Files\Web Part Toolkit\InstallAssemblies\InstallAssemblies.exe.

After you install a Web Part to either the Global Assembly Cache or a virtual server's bin folder, you can usually install new versions simply by dragging the .dll file into the same folder as its predecessor. However, this won't work if you've changed the file's name, version number, or strong key signature.

Unless you manually installed a .dwp file in the virtual server's wpcatalog folder, New Web Parts don't appear automatically in the Web Part gallery of any site collection. To make them appear, a site collection administrator will need to add them.

> For instructions on adding a Web Part to a Web Part gallery, refer to "Managing the Web Part Gallery" in Chapter 17.

If you added your Web Part to the bin folder of one or more virtual servers, and running it produces a security failure, you may need to locate the following tag in the server's web.config file:

```
<trust level="WSS_Minimal" originUrl="" />
```

and change WSS_Minimal to WSS_Medium or Full. Keep in mind, however, that this grants increased privileges to all Web Parts run from the virtual server's bin folder.

> To configure a trust level that grants privileges to a specific assembly, refer to the section titled "To Give Access To An Assembly" in the article "Microsoft Windows SharePoint Services and Code Access Security, at *http://msdn.microsoft.com/library/en-us/odc_sp2003_ta/html/ sharepoint_wsscodeaccesssecurity.asp*

After you install or update a Web Part assembly or a .dwp file, and after you modify the config.sys file, the change may not take effect until after you stop and restart the Internet Information Services (IIS) server. To do this, open a command prompt on the server and run the iisreset command.

> For more information on deploying Web Parts, refer to "Packaging and Deploying Web Parts for Microsoft Windows SharePoint Services" at *http://msdn.microsoft.com/library/en-us/odc_sp2003_ta/ html/sharepoint_deployingwebparts.asp*

For additional guidance in creating Web Parts, try browsing these resources.

- Creating a Basic Web Part
  http://msdn.microsoft.com/library/en-us/spptsdk/html/CreateABasicWP.asp

- A Developer's Introduction to Web Parts, by Andy Baron
  http://msdn.microsoft.com/library/en-us/odc_sp2003_ta/html/ sharepoint_northwindwebparts.asp

- Best Practices for Developing Web Parts for SharePoint Products and Technologies, by Susan Harney
  http://msdn.microsoft.com/library/en-us/odc_SP2003_ta/html/ ODC_WSSWebPartTips.asp

In Summary...

This chapter explained the basics of how Web Parts work, and what tools you need to create Web Parts of your own. It then explained the basic programming techniques you need to successfully create and deploy custom Web Parts.

The next chapter will provide step-by-step instructions for creating some simple but practical custom Web Parts.

Chapter 20

Creating Basic Web Parts

This chapter explains how to create, compile, install, and test three simple but useful Web Parts.

- **The Welcome Web Part** Displays the current team member's name and login account. Optionally, it can display the Notes field from the team member's user properties, and any site groups and cross-site groups to which the team member belongs.

- **The SiteLinks Web Part** Displays links to the current site's home page, its child sites, its parent sites, its top site, its server root site, and any configured portal sites.

- **The ListBrowser Web Part** Displays a drop-down list for selecting any SharePoint list or library in the current site. The Web Part then displays the selected list or library using an ASP.NET DataGrid control.

This chapter presumes that you've already satisfied the system requirements that the previous chapter described: you have Windows SharePoint Services running on a test server, you've installed Microsoft Visual Studio .NET or C# Standard Edition, and you've installed the Web Part templates for Visual Studio .NET.

> For more information about configuring your development to write Web Parts, refer to "Configuring Your Development Environment" in Chapter 19.

The chapter also presumes you have some familiarity with Visual Studio .NET and with writing .NET programs in general. It's not an introduction to programming, and it's not a keystroke-by-keystroke approach to writing Web Parts.

Creating the WssIso Project

To begin creating the three Web Parts in this chapter, you must first create a Visual Studio project. To do this, proceed as follows.

1   Start Visual Studio .NET or C# Standard Edition, whichever you have.

2   Choose New from the File menu, and then Project.

3   When the New Project dialog box appears:

   3.1   Select Visual C# Projects in the Project Types list at the left.

   3.2   Select Web Part Library in the Templates list at the right.

   3.3   Specify WssIso in the Name box and then click OK.

4   When Visual Studio finishes creating the project, it will open a file named WebPart1.cs. Proceed to the next section without closing this file, and without closing Visual Studio.

> For more information about initializing a Visual Studio project to write new Web Parts, refer to "Starting a New Web Part Project" in Chapter 19.

You can find a copy of the completed WssIso project on the Companion CD, in the \Webparts\WssIso folder. To look at these finished results rather than create them from scratch, follow this procedure:

1   Copy the WssIso folder from the CD to the *<My Documents>*\Visual Studio Projects folder on your hard disk, where *<My Documents>* is typically C:\Documents and Settings*<username>*\My Documents and *<username>* is your Windows logon account.

2   Right-click the resulting WssIso folder and choose Properties.

3   Clear the Read-Only box and click OK.

4   Open the copied WssIso\WssIso.sln file in Visual Studio .NET.

Creating the Welcome Web Part

This Web Part displays some basic information about the team member currently accessing a SharePoint site. Adding this Web Part to a site's home page is a courteous way to greet team members. An example appears at the right side of the page in Figure 20-1.

Creating Basic Web Parts

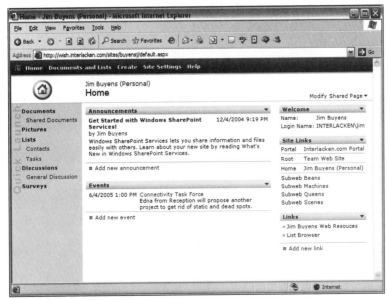

Figure 20-1. The Welcome and SiteLinks Web Parts on this page display information about the current team member and site. You can create such Web Parts yourself in Visual Studio.

If WebPart1.cs from the previous section is still open in Visual Studio, begin with these steps:

1 Right-click the WebPart1.cs file in Solution Explorer, choose Rename from the shortcut menu, and change the filename to welcome.cs.

2 In the now-renamed welcome.cs file, change all occurrences of WebPart1 to Welcome. For example:

   2.1 Press Ctrl+H.

   2.2 Set Find What to WebPart1.

   2.3 Set Replace With to Welcome.

   2.4 Click Replace All, and then Close.

If you're adding the Welcome Web Part to some other project, or if you closed the WssIso project, then open the solution that contains the project you want, and either open the existing Web Part file or create a new one. Here's the procedure to create a new one.

1 Choose Add New Item from the Project menu.

2 When the Add New Item dialog box appears:

   2.1 Select Local Project Items in the Categories list at the left.

   2.2 Select Web Part in the Templates list at the right.

   2.3 Type Welcome.cs in the Name box and then click OK.

Microsoft Windows SharePoint Services Inside Out

Writing the Custom Property Code

The Welcome Web Part will have one custom property, namely the Show All property shown in the Modify task pane in Figure 20-2. This property controls the presence or absence of the team member's e-mail address, notes, site groups, and cross-site groups.

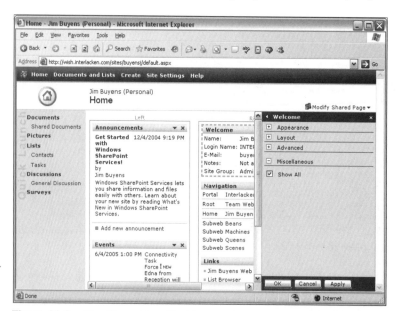

Figure 20-2. The Show All setting is a custom property of the Welcome Web Part. By configuring such properties, team members can customize the Web Part to suit their needs.

The Web Part template provides some sample code that implements one custom property: a string value named Text. To modify this code so it implements a Boolean property named Show All, proceed as follows.

1 Locate the default class definition, which consists of the following code:

```
[DefaultProperty("Text"),
    ToolboxData("<{0}:Welcome runat=server></{0}:Welcome>"),
    XmlRoot(Namespace="WssIso")]
```

and change the *DefaultProperty* attribute to *booShowAll*, as shown below in bold.

```
[DefaultProperty("booShowAll"),
    ToolboxData("<{0}:Welcome runat=server></{0}:Welcome>"),
    XmlRoot(Namespace="WssIso")]
```

2   Locate the declarations for the custom property value and its default, which look like this:

```
private const string defaultText = "";
private string text = defaultText;
```

and change them to:

```
private const bool dftShowAll = false;
private bool booShowAll = dftShowAll;
```

3   The template provides the following property attributes.

```
[Browsable(true),
    Category("Miscellaneous"),
    DefaultValue(defaultText),
    WebPartStorage(Storage.Personal),
    FriendlyName("Text"),
    Description("Text Property")]
```

Change this code to

```
[Browsable(true),
    Category("Miscellaneous"),
    DefaultValue(dftShowAll),
    WebPartStorage(Storage.Personal),
    FriendlyName("Show All"),
    Description("Choose complete or compact display.")]
```

4   Locate the template-provided *get* and *set* accessor methods for the custom property. These should appear as follows.

```
public string Text
{
    get
    {
        return text;
    }

    set
    {
        text = value;
    }
}
```

Make the changes shown below in bold.

```
public bool ShowAll
{
    get
    {
        return booShowAll;
    }

    set
    {
        booShowAll = value;
    }
}
```

This completes the changes you need to make in order to implement the Show All custom property. Windows SharePoint Services will expose the property to team members as shown in Figure 20-2, and the current property value will be available to other code via the *booShowAll* variable.

For more information about custom properties, refer to "Exposing Custom Properties" in Chapter 19.

Creating the Child Controls

An HTML table will organize the captions and data values that the Web Part displays. To create this table and provide its content, proceed as follows.

1 Include the *System.Web.UI.HtmlControls* namespace by adding the following directive after any other *using* directives at the top of the code:

```
using System.Web.UI.HtmlControls;
```

2 Declare an *HtmlTable* variable within the scope of the *Welcome* class, but outside the scope of any method or structure. For example, add this statement after the code you entered in step 2 of the previous section.

```
private HtmlTable tblOut;
```

3 Add the following code within the *Welcome* class, but outside any other method or structure. This code overrides the default *CreateChildControls* method, creates the *HtmlTable* object, and adds that object to the Web Part's *Controls* collection.

```
protected override void CreateChildControls ()
{
    tblOut = new HtmlTable();
//      Code to supply table content will appear here.

    Controls.Add (tblOut);
}
```

Chapter 20

Creating Basic Web Parts

4 To create an object that provides access to the current Web site, replace the comment in step 4 with the code shown below in bold.

```
tblOut = new HtmlTable();
SPWeb spwCurr = SPControl.GetContextWeb(Context);
Controls.Add (tblOut);
spwCurr.Close();
```

GetContextWeb is a static method of the *SPControl* object, which resides in the *Microsoft.SharePoint.WebControls* namespace. To include that namespace, add the following directive after the one you added in step 1.

```
using Microsoft.SharePoint.WebControls;
```

The *spwCurr.Close()* statement closes the *SPWeb* object named *spwCurr*, releasing any resources it has in use. It's good practice to close *SPWeb* objects when you're done with them.

5 The *spwCurr* variable from step 4 identifies an *SPWeb* object that describes the current site. The *CurrentUser* property of that object identifies an *SPUser* object that describes the current team member. That *SPUser* object, in turn, has:

■ A *Name* property that provides the member's name.

■ A *LoginName* property that provides the name of the member's login account.

To display these two properties, add the code shown below in bold.

```
tblOut = new HtmlTable();
SPWeb spwCurr = SPControl.GetContextWeb(Context);
AddTblRow(tblOut, "Name:", spwCurr.CurrentUser.Name);
AddTblRow(tblOut, "Login Name:", spwCurr.CurrentUser.LoginName);
Controls.Add (tblOut);
spwCurr.Close();
```

AddTblRow is a custom method that adds a row and two cells to an *HtmlTable* object. The first argument is a pointer to the table, the second is the value for the first cell, and the third argument is the value for the second cell. The next section explains how to write the *AddTblRow* method.

6 The Web Part won't display any more *spwCurr.CurrentUser* properties unless Show All is in effect. To determine if this is so, add the code shown below in bold.

```
tblOut = new HtmlTable();
SPWeb spwCurr = SPControl.GetContextWeb(Context);
AddTblRow(tblOut, "Name:", spwCurr.CurrentUser.Name);
AddTblRow(tblOut, "Login Name:", spwCurr.CurrentUser.LoginName);
if (booShowAll)
{
// Code to display additional properties will go here.
}
Controls.Add (tblOut);
spwCurr.Close();
```

Chapter 20

7   To conditionally display the team member's e-mail address and Notes, add the statements shown below in bold.

```
if (booShowAll)
{
    AddTblRow(tblOut, "E-Mail:", spwCurr.CurrentUser.Email);
    AddTblRow(tblOut, "Notes:", spwCurr.CurrentUser.Notes);
}
```

8   To display the team member's site groups and cross-site groups, add the loops shown below in bold.

```
protected override void CreateChildControls ()
{
    SPWeb spwCurr = SPControl.GetContextWeb(Context);
    tblOut = new HtmlTable();
    AddTblRow(tblOut, "Name:", spwCurr.CurrentUser.Name);
    AddTblRow(tblOut, "Login Name:", spwCurr.CurrentUser.LoginName);
    if (booShowAll)
    {
        AddTblRow(tblOut, "E-Mail:", spwCurr.CurrentUser.Email);
        AddTblRow(tblOut, "Notes:", spwCurr.CurrentUser.Notes);
        foreach (SPRole sprRole in spwCurr.CurrentUser.Roles)
        {
            AddTblRow(tblOut, "Site Group:", sprRole.Name);
        }
        foreach (SPGroup sprGroup in spwCurr.CurrentUser.Groups)
        {
            AddTblRow(tblOut, "Cross-Site Group:", sprGroup.Name);
        }
    }
    Controls.Add (tblOut);
    spwCurr.Close();
}
```

The first loop iterates through all the *SPRole* objects in the *spwCurr.CurrentUser.Roles* collection and displays the *Name* property of each one.

Similarly, the second loop iterates through all the *SPGroup* objects in the *spwCurr.CurrentUser.Group*s collection.

This completes the code for overriding *CreateChildControls* method.

Expanding the Layout Table

The previous section used a method named *AddTblRow* for adding rows to the table that arranges the output fields in the Welcome Web Part. This section explains how to write that method.

The *System.Web.UI.HtmlControls* namespace provides the objects listed in Table 20-1 for working with HTML tables in memory. The Equivalent HTML column shows the code you would write within an .aspx or .aspx file to load these objects for use in a conventional ASP.NET page or an ASP.NET user control.

Creating Basic Web Parts

Table 20-1. HTML Table Objects

Object	Element	Equivalent HTML
HtmlTable	Table	`<table runat="server"></table>`
HtmlTableRow	Row	`<tr runat="server"></tr>`
HtmlTableCell	Cell	`<td runat="server"></td>`

Web Parts, of course, are custom controls, and so you have to create these objects with program code like this:

```
tblOut = new HtmlTable();
rowTbl = new HtmlTableRow();
celTbl = new HtmlTableCell();
```

An *HtmlTable* object has a *Rows* collection of *HtmlTableRow* objects, and an *HtmlTableRow* object has a *Cells* collection of *HtmlTableCell* objects. Both of these collections have *Add* methods that append elements of the proper type.

All three object types (and in fact, all the object types in the *System.Web.UI.HtmlControls* namespace) have properties that correspond to normal HTML attributes. When the object is told to render its HTML, it writes attributes and expressions that correspond to any properties you set.

Here, then, is the procedure for writing the *AddTblRow* method:

1 Declare the *AddTblRow* method as follows:

```
private void AddTblRow(HtmlTable tblTable, string strTitle, string strValue)
{
// Processing code for the method will go here.
}
```

In the sample code, this code appears immediately after the *CreateChildControls* method. In fact, however, you can put it anywhere within the scope of the *Welcome* class, as long as it's outside the scope of any method or structure.

2 Replace the comment in step 1 with declarations for two variables: one that will point to an *HtmlTableRow* object, and one that will point to an *HtmlTableCell* object. Here's the required code:

```
HtmlTableRow rowTbl;
HtmlTableCell celTbl;
```

3 Immediately after the code from step 2, create an *HtmlTableRow* object and add it to the table specified in the method argument *tblTable*. Here's the code:

```
rowTbl = new HtmlTableRow();
// Code to create and append table cells will go here.
tblTable.Rows.Add(rowTbl);
```

Chapter 20

633

4   Replace the comment in step 3 with code that creates two table cells and adds them to the *rowTbl* object. This requires the code shown below in bold.

```
rowTbl = new HtmlTableRow();
celTbl = new HtmlTableCell();
// Code to populate the first table cell will go here.
rowTbl.Cells.Add(celTbl);
celTbl = new HtmlTableCell();
// Code to populate the second table cell will go here.
rowTbl.Cells.Add(celTbl);
tblTable.Rows.Add(rowTbl);
```

Notice that using the same variable for both *HtmlTableCell* table cells doesn't release the first one for garbage collection, because an entry in the *rowTbl.Cells* collection still points to it.

5   Supply the two table cells with content and formatting by adding the code shown below in bold. The first (left) cell displays the contents of the *strTitle* argument, and the second (right) displays the contents of the *strValue* argument.

```
private void AddTblRow(HtmlTable tblTable, string strTitle, string strValue)
{
    HtmlTableRow rowTbl;
    HtmlTableCell celTbl;
    rowTbl = new HtmlTableRow();    // Create a row
    celTbl = new HtmlTableCell();   // Create a cell
    celTbl.InnerText = strTitle;
    celTbl.VAlign = "top";
    celTbl.NoWrap = true;
    rowTbl.Cells.Add(celTbl);       // Add the cell to the row.
    celTbl = new HtmlTableCell();   // Create a cell
    celTbl.InnerText = strValue;
    celTbl.VAlign = "top";
    rowTbl.Cells.Add(celTbl);       // Add the cell to the row.
    tblTable.Rows.Add(rowTbl);      // Add the row to the table.

}
```

This completes the *AddTblRow* procedure.

Rendering the Web Part

The Web Part template provides the following sample code for overriding the base *WebPart* object's *RenderWebPart* method.

```
protected override void RenderWebPart(HtmlTextWriter output)
{
    output.Write(SPEncode.HtmlEncode(Text));
}
```

Creating Basic Web Parts

The *output.Write* statement is designed for writing HTML code in string format. To instead write the HTML equivalent of each object in the Web Part's *Controls* collection, change that statement to the one that appears below in bold.

```
protected override void RenderWebPart(HtmlTextWriter output)
{
    RenderChildren(output);
}
```

This completes the coding for the *RenderWebPart* method.

Creating a Strong Name Key Pair

To ensure that compiling the Web Part creates a strongly named assembly, you must:

1   Run the sn.exe command-line program with the –k switch.

2   Add the resulting file to your project.

3   Reference the file in the project's AssemblyInfo.cs file.

To perform these tasks, follow the instructions in Chapter 19.

> For more information about creating a key pair file and using it to strongly name a Web Part assembly, refer to "Assigning a Strong Name" in Chapter 19.

Installing and Testing

Before you can run the Web Part, you must, of course, compile it. To do this, choose Rebuild Solution from the Build menu. Unless you're compiling on the SharePoint server itself, the following messages may appear:

```
The dependency 'Microsoft.SharePoint.Security' could not be found.
The dependency 'Microsoft.SharePoint.Dsp' could not be found.
The dependency 'Microsoft.SharePoint.Library' could not be found.
```

These are "normal" and no cause for concern. If you get any other compilation errors, double-click the error message to position the Visual Studio editor at the offending statement.

If the compilation is successful, the resulting DLL file will be in the bin\debug or bin\release folder, depending on the build configuration in effect.

Installing the Web Part Manually

To install the Web Part by hand, copy its DLL to one of the following locations on your SharePoint server:

● The \bin folder of your SharePoint virtual server, such as C:\inetpub\wwwroot\bin. However, don't use this location if the computer is running more than one SharePoint content server.

- The server's Global Assembly Cache (GAC), which appears in the special folder C:\windows\assembly (assuming C:\windows is your system folder).

To register your Web Part as a safe control, use a text editor such as Microsoft Notepad to open the virtual server's web.config file, and add a line such as the following to <SafeControls> section:

```
<SafeControl Assembly="WssIso, Version=1.0.0.0, Culture=neutral,
    PublicKeyToken=49225b11f30a2ed0"
Namespace="WssIso" TypeName="*" Safe="True" />
```

In this code:

- **Assembly**   Specifies your DLL's filename base.
- **Version**   Specifies the version number from your AssemblyInfo.cs file.
- **Culture**   Can always be neutral.
- **PublicKeyToken**   Is the public key for the assembly's strong name.
- **Namespace**   Is the value you specified on the namespace statement of your source file, such as:

```
namespace WssIso;
```

- **TypeName**   The Web Part's class name or an asterisk ("*"). An asterisk indicates that the entry applies to all Web Part classes in the specified assembly and namespace.
- **Safe**   Should always be "True". A value of "False" deliberately stops the Web Part from working.

In most cases, it will be easiest to copy and paste an existing <SafeControl> entry, and then update its Assembly, Version, PublicKeyToken, and Namespace values.

If you copied your assembly to the virtual server's bin folder, follow this procedure to get its PublicKeyToken into the clipboard.

1   Open a command window on the server.
2   Change to the folder where the sn.exe program resides. This is usually one of the following:
    C:\Program Files\Microsoft Visual Studio .NET\FrameworkSDK\Bin\
    C:\Program Files\Microsoft Visual Studio .NET 2003\SDK\v1.1\Bin\
3   Run the command:

```
sn.exe -T "<path>\<project>\bin\debug\WssIso.dll"
```

where the –T switch specifies capital T, *<path>* is the path to your Visual Studio project, *<project>* is the project name, and bin\debug\WssIso.dll is the path and name of your DLL. This will display a line of output such as:

```
Public key token is 49225b11f30a2ed0
```

4   Choose Edit and then Mark from the command window's system menu, and then drag the mouse across the displayed public key token value and press Enter.

Creating Basic Web Parts

If you copied your assembly to the GAC, you can get the PublicKeyToken into the clipboard by following this procedure.

1 Display the server's \windows\assembly folder in Windows Explorer.

2 Right-click your assembly and choose Properties.

3 Drag the mouse across the Public Key Token value, and then right-click the selection and choose Copy.

Installing the Web Part with InstallAssemblies

As Chapter 19 mentioned, the InstallAssemblies utility is usually the easiest and most accurate way of installing Web Parts. This is part of the Web Part Toolkit you can find on the Companion CD at \utils\Web Part Toolkit. After installing this tool, proceed as follows:

1 Start the InstallAssemblies utility.

2 When the InstallAssemblies window appears, specify these settings for a typical installation:

- **Web Part Package Deployment**   Selected.

- **Install Location:**   Global Assembly Cache or Application Bin Folder.

- **Generate Safe Control Entries**   Selected.

- **Select Assemblies:**   Click this button and select the DLL file that building your project in Visual Studio created. By default, this will be in your project's bin\debug or bin\release folder.

3 Click Install. Figure 20-3 shows some typical results.

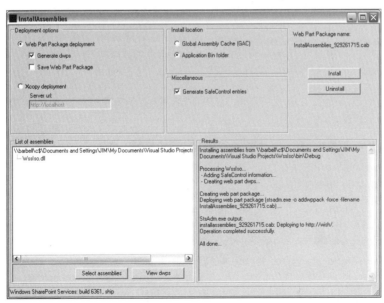

Figure 20-3. InstallAssemblies is an unsupported Microsoft program that efficiently and correctly installs Web Parts.

Testing the Web Part

Once the Web Part is installed, it should appear in the New Web Parts (_layouts/1033/ NewDwp.aspx) page for any site collection on your server. If you select its check box and click Populate Gallery, it should then appear on the Web Part Gallery page, and also in the site collection gallery that appears on the Add Web Parts task pane of any Web Part Page.

> For more information about displaying and using the Web Part gallery and New Web Parts pages, refer to "Managing the Web Part Gallery" in Chapter 17.

You can also add your new Web Part to the Web Part Gallery page (and the gallery itself) by importing a Web Part Definition file. This is a file with a .dwp filename extension and some XML content like that shown below.

```xml
<?xml version="1.0"?>
<WebPart xmlns="http://schemas.microsoft.com/WebPart/v2">
  <Assembly>WssIso, Version=1.0.0.0, Culture=neutral,
    PublicKeyToken=49225b11f30a2ed0</Assembly>
  <TypeName>WssIso.Welcome</TypeName>
  <Title>Welcome</Title>
</WebPart>
```

The variable parts of this file structure should already be familiar:

- **WssIso** Is the name of the assembly: that is, the DLL's filename base.
- **1.0.0.0** Is the version number from AssemblyInfo.cs.
- **49225b11f30a2ed0** Is the Public Key Token value.
- **WssIso.Welcome** Is the namespace and class name.
- **Welcome** Will appear in the Web Part's title bar.

Most of this information is also in the <SafeControl> entry for your Web Part. If you import the Web Part Definition files, both sets of values must agree.

 Troubleshooting

Installed Web Part doesn't appear on the New Web Parts page

If you believe you've properly installed a new Web Part on your server but it doesn't appear on the New Web Parts (NewDwp.aspx) page, investigate these possible causes:

- The Web Part may not be in the correct location. The two acceptable locations are the virtual server's bin folder and the computer's Global Assembly Cache (which Windows Explorer displays as c:\windows\assembly).
- The <SafeControl> entry for the Web Part is missing or invalid. This entry must be present in the <SafeControls> section of the virtual server's web.config file. For example, the assembly name, version, public key token, or namespace may not match the values in your DLL.

Chapter 20

- The virtual server may be bound to a fixed IP address. All SharePoint Web servers must have their IP addresses set in IIS Manager to (All Unassigned).

- The virtual server may be filtering on host headers, and you placed the Web Part in the virtual server's bin folder. When a virtual server is filtering on host headers, you must place any Web Parts in the Global Assembly Cache.

For more information about issues involving Web Parts and virtual server configuration, refer to "Planning Virtual Servers" in Chapter 12.

Displaying the Web Part

You can preview a Web Part by clicking its entry on the Web Part Gallery page, but to test it completely, you must add it to a Web Part Page. For example, it's often expedient to:

1 Choose Create from the top navigation bar of any page.

2 Choose Web Part Page when the Create page appears.

3 Type a filename base when the New Web Part Page appears, and then click Create.

4 Use the Add Web Parts task pane to add your new Web Part to the page.

5 Close the Add Web Parts task pane to start testing the Web Part.

For more information about using a browser to create Web Part Pages, refer to the material starting at "Creating Web Part Pages" in Chapter 5.

Increasing a Virtual Server's Trust Level

If running a Web Part Page that contains your new Web Part results in an error page like the one in Figure 20-4, and if you installed the Web Part in the virtual server's bin folder, you may need to increase the virtual server's trust level.

To increase a virtual server's trust level, proceed as follows.

1 Open the virtual server's web.config file in Notepad.

2 In the <system.web> section, locate the <trust /> tag.

- If the <trust /> tag specifies level="WSS_Minimal", change it to level="WSS_Medium".

- If the <trust /> tag specifies level="WSS_Medium", change it to level="Full".

3 Reset the Web server, retest, and repeat as necessary.

Chapter 20

Microsoft Windows SharePoint Services Inside Out

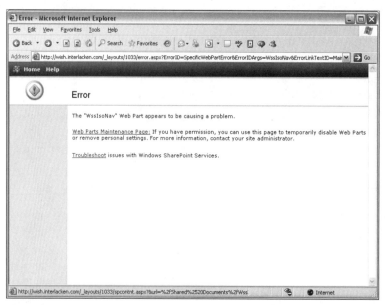

Figure 20-4. This page appears when Windows SharePoint Services detects a serious error in running a Web Part. Clicking Web Parts Maintenance Page displays a page listing the Web Parts in use and offers to remove any you select.

Keep in mind, however, that increasing this trust level grants increased privileges to every Web Part that resides in the virtual server's bin folder.

Displaying Full ASP.NET Error Messages

If your Web Part is throwing an exception and you need a more precise error message than Windows SharePoint Services provides, try this procedure:

1 On the SharePoint server, display the C:\Program Files\Common Files\Microsoft Shared\Web Server Extensions\60\TEMPLATE\LAYOUTS folder and rename the file global.asax file to global.bak.

2 In the same folder, open the web.config file in Notepad and change customErrors = "On" to customErrors="Off". (Note that this *isn't* the web.config file in the virtual server's physical root folder.)

3 Reset the Web server.

Debugging and Testing

If necessary, you can interactively debug Web Parts. This is easiest if you install Visual Studio .NET on the Web server, but also possible remotely. For more information, browse "Debugging Web Parts" by Suraj Poozhiyilat, at *http://msdn.microsoft.com/library/en-us/ odc_sp2003_ta/html/sharepoint_debugwebparts.asp*.

For a checklist of tests to perform on custom Web Parts, browse "Checklist for Testing SharePoint Web Parts" by Lana Fly and Susan Harney, at *http://msdn.microsoft.com/library/ en-us/odc_SP2003_ta/html/Office_SharePointWebPartsTestingChecklist.asp*.

Creating the SiteLinks Web Part

This Web Part appeared previously in Figure 20-1. It displays links to the home pages of:

- The Portal Site (if any) configured for the root site collection.
- The site at the server root.
- The Portal Site (if any) configured for the current site collection.
- The current collection's top-level Web site.
- Any Web sites between the current collection's top-level Web site and the current site.
- The current site.
- All subsites of the current site.

Note that in some cases, the list above may contain the same site twice. For example, the current site may *be* the top-level site in its collection, and the current collection may be the root collection. The Web Part therefore contains some logic to avoid listing duplicate links.

In terms of overall approach, this Web Part isn't much different from the Welcome Web Part. The main difference is that the SiteLinks Web Part obtains and displays site information rather than team member information

To obtain the links, the Web Part first uses the following code to get objects that point to the current site, the current collection, and the collection's top-level site.

```
SPWeb spwCurr = SPControl.GetContextWeb(Context);
SPSite spsColl = SPControl.GetContextSite(Context);
SPWeb spwTpLv = SPControl.GetContextSite(Context).RootWeb;
```

To get the root site URL, it takes the current collection's URL, up to the first slash, not counting the slashes in http://. Then, it runs this statement to create an object that points to the root site.

```
SPSite spsRoot = new SPSite(strRootUrl);
```

The site collection objects have *PortalName* and *PortalUrl* properties that provide the Name and URL of a portal site, provided one's been configured.

The following loop gets the parents of the current site. The first statement creates an object that points to the current site's parent (if any), and each iteration replaces this object with another that points to the next higher parent.

```
SPWeb spwParent = spwCurr.ParentWeb;
while (spwParent != null)
{
//      Logic to display parent site goes here.
    spwParent = spwParent.ParentWeb;
}
```

The following loop iterates through each of the current site's subwebs (if any).

```
foreach (SPWeb webSub in spwCurr.Webs)
{
    AddSiteToTable(tblGrid, "Subweb", webSub.Url, webSub.Title,
        webSub.Name, -1);
}
```

To detect duplicate sites (such as the current site also being the top site), the Web Part compares the ID property of the two site objects. This property is a GUID that Windows SharePoint Services assigns to each site. Comparing these GUIDs is much easier than comparing URLs, where differences in case and trailing slashes can occur.

Depending on the structure of the sites on your server, and on the position the current site, these two loops may detect the presence of dozens or hundreds of sites. If so, the loops will create an equal number of *SPWeb* objects, and use them to create dozens or hundreds of links. If this proves time-consuming, you may need to avoid adding the SiteLinks Web part to frequently-used Web part pages.

To create this Web Part yourself, follow the instructions in the following sections. To check your work or simply to view the finished results, open the SiteLinks.cs file in the \WebParts\WssIso project on the companion CD.

Creating the SiteLinks Class File

There's no need to create a new Visual Studio .NET project for every Web Part you write. A single project can accommodate as many Web Parts as you like. This makes it easy for related Web Parts to share code, and it simplifies deployment because the entire set of Web Parts resides in a single DLL.

To illustrate this, the instructions that follow will add the code for the SiteLinks Web Part to the WssIso project that already contains the Welcome Web Part. Proceed as follows:

1   Use Visual Studio.NET to open the WssIso project that already contains the Welcome Web Part. For example, open the WssIso.sln or WssIso.csproj file in your My Documents\Visual Studio Projects\WssIso\ folder.

2   Choose Add Class from the Project menu.

3 When the Add New Item dialog box appears, select Local Project Items in the Categories list and Web Part in the Templates list.

4 Type SiteLinks.cs in the Name box, and then click Open.

5 The SiteLinks Web Part will make no use of custom property values or custom tool parts. Therefore, delete the default class definition shown below:

```
[DefaultProperty("Text"),
    ToolboxData("<{0}:SiteLink2 runat=server></{0}:SiteLink>"),
    XmlRoot(Namespace="WssIso")]
```

and all the code within the *SiteLink* class declaration except the *RenderWebPart* method shown below.

```
protected override void RenderWebPart(HtmlTextWriter output)
{
    output.Write(SPEncode.HtmlEncode(Text));
}
```

6 As you did for the Welcome Web Part, modify the *RenderWebPart* method so it renders all the objects in the Web Part's *Controls* collection. This requires the one-line change shown below in bold.

```
protected override void RenderWebPart(HtmlTextWriter output)
{
    RenderChildren(output);
}
```

7 Append the following *using* directives to those at the top of the file.

```
using Microsoft.SharePoint.WebControls;
using System.Web.UI.HtmlControls;
```

These directives provide access to SharePoint and HTML classes, respectively, that the Web Part will use.

8 To save your work thus far, choose Save SiteLinks.cs from the File menu.

Overriding the CreateChildControls Method

Like virtually all Web Parts, the *SiteLinks* class must override the default *CreateChildControls* method with a custom method that loads any controls the Web Part uses for output. To do this, add the following declaration anywhere within the *SiteLinks* class, but not within any other structure or method.

```
protected override void CreateChildControls ()
{
    this.Title = "Site Links";
}
```

Any value you assign to *this.Title* will appear in the Web Part's title bar.

Getting Site and Site Collection Objects

The main purpose of the *SiteLinks* Web Part is to display the name, URL, and other properties of the current site and those that surround it. These properties are available from various SharePoint objects that represent those sites. To load these objects, proceed as follows.

1 Add the statements shown below in bold to the *CreateChildControls* override method you coded in the previous section.

```
this.Title = "Site Links";
SPWeb spwCurr = SPControl.GetContextWeb(Context);
SPSite spsColl = SPControl.GetContextSite(Context)
SPWeb spwTpLv = SPControl.GetContextSite(Context).RootWeb;
```

The first new statement creates an *SPWeb* object named *spwCurr* that represents the current site.

The second creates an *SPSite* object named *spsColl* that represents the current site collection.

The third creates an *SPWeb* object named *spwTpLv* that represents the top-level site at the root of the current site collection. Note that this could be identical to the current site (represented by *spwCurr*), or to the root site for the entire server. Later code will need to deal with these possibilities.

2 Get the URL of the server's root site, then create an *SPSite* object that points to the root site collection.

This is slightly tricky because to create the *SPSite* object, you must know the exact URL string by which Windows SharePoint Services knows the collection, and this might be different from the virtual server's customary DNS name. The following code therefore gets the starting URL of the current collection, and then discards any path portion (that is, anything after the first slash that follows the host name). This goes after the code from the preceding step.

```
int intFirstSlash = spsColl.Url.IndexOf("/",7);
string strRootUrl;
if (intFirstSlash > 0 )
{
    strRootUrl = spsColl.Url.Substring(0,intFirstSlash);
}
else
{
    strRootUrl = spsColl.Url;
}
SPSite spsRoot = new SPSite(strRootUrl);
```

If, for example, the current site collection starts at *http://wish.interlacken.com/sites/buyensj*, the *strRootUrl* will end up containing *http://wish.interlacken.com/*. (The argument *7* tells the *IndexOf* method where to start looking for a slash: the *w* in *wish*, in this case). The last statement creates an *SPSite* object for the collection at the resulting address (that is, in *strRootUrl*).

Displaying the Links

As Figure 20-1 illustrated, the output of the *SiteLinks* Web Part is a two-column HTML table. In most rows, the left column identifies the type of site, and the right column displays a clickable site name. For clarity, however, some rows display separator lines that span both columns. A different custom method will create each of these row types.

- **AddTblRow**   Is the method that formats normal table rows. It accepts these six arguments:
    - A pointer to the HTML table that will contain the new row.
    - The type of site, such as Portal, Root, Home, or Subweb. (Home designates the home page of the current site.)
    - The site's URL.
    - The site's title, as a team member would specify under Site Settings, Change Site Title and Description. The *AddTblRow* method uses this as the hyperlink text.
    - The site's name, which is normally the relative path from its top-level site. If the site's title is blank, the *AddTblRow* method uses this argument as the hyperlink text.
    - The position where the new row should reside. If this argument is negative, the method adds a row to the end of the table. If the argument is positive, the new row appears after the given position, and ahead of any existing rows. (Suppose, for example, that the table contains 6 rows. Inserting a row after position 4 would place it in position 5, and the former rows 5 and 6 would occupy positions 6 and 7.)
- **AddTblSeparator**   Is the method that formats separator rows. It accepts one argument: a pointer to the HTML table that will contain the new row. Furthermore, it takes care *not* to display a separator in either of these conditions:
    - The separator would be the first row in the table.
    - The separator would immediately follow an existing separator.

    Including these provisions in the *AddTblSeparator* method simplifies program logic elsewhere.

Later sections will explain how to develop the *AddTblRow* and *AddTblSeparator* methods. For now, return to the *CreateChildControls* override method and proceed as follows.

1 Create a new *HtmlTable* object named *tblGrid* that displays no cell padding. In other words, add the following statements after the code from the previous section.

```
HtmlTable tblGrid = new HtmlTable();
tblGrid.CellPadding = 0;
```

2 If an administrator has configured a site collection to connect with a portal site, the portal's URL and name will appear in the *SPSite* object's *PortalUrl* and *PortalName* properties. So, if the root collection's *PortalUrl* is non-blank, display a link to the given portal site, and then a separator line.

```
if (spsRoot.PortalUrl != "")
{
    AddTblRow(tblGrid, "Portal", spsRoot.PortalUrl,
            spsRoot.PortalName, spsRoot.PortalName, -1);
    AddTblSeparator(tblGrid);
}
```

Note that this code uses the *AddTblRow* and *AddTblSeparator* methods just explained. The code specifies *spsRoot.PortalName* for both the title and name arguments because there's no such property as *spsRoot.PortalTitle*.

3 Display a link to the virtual server's root site, but only if the root site is different from the current site. (Later code will display the current site.)

```
if (spwCurr.ID != spsRoot.RootWeb.ID)
{
    AddTblRow(tblGrid, "Root", spsRoot.Url,
            spsRoot.RootWeb.Title, spsRoot.RootWeb.Name, -1);
}
```

Recall that Windows SharePoint Services assigns a unique ID value to each site it creates. Thus, if the ID properties of two *SPWeb* objects are different, they represent different sites.

4 If the current top-level site isn't the top-level site at the server's root (that is, if the values of the *spwTpLv.ID* and *spsRoot.RootWeb.ID* properties are unequal), then display links to the current collection's portal site (if any) and to the current collection's top-level site. This requires the following code, next in sequence.

```
if (spwTpLv.ID != spsRoot.RootWeb.ID){
    if (spsColl.PortalUrl != "")
    {
        AddTblRow(tblGrid, "Portal", spsColl.PortalUrl,
                spsColl.PortalName, spsColl.PortalName, -1);
        AddTblSeparator(tblGrid);
    }
    if (spwCurr.ID != spwTpLv.ID)
    {
        AddTblRow(tblGrid, "Top", spwTpLv.Url,
                spwTpLv.Title, spwTpLv.Name, -1);
    }
}
```

The code within the *if* statement basically repeats that in steps 1 and 2, except that is specifies *spsColl* rather than *spsRoot*, and *spwTpLv* rather than *spsRoot.RootWeb*.

Creating Basic Web Parts

5 Conditionally display a separator line, then display the link to the current site's home page. To do this, append the following code to that from step 4.

```
AddTblSeparator(tblGrid);
AddTblRow(tblGrid, "Home", spwCurr.Url,
         spwCurr.Title, spwCurr.Name, -1);
```

Recall that the *AddTblSeparator* method suppresses any separator that would appear in the first row of the table, or immediately after the previous separator.

6 Calculate the table row index for any sites that are parents of the current site. Here's the code:

```
int intLayoutRow = tblGrid.Rows.Count - 2;
```

Note that at this point, the link to the current site resides in the last table row. If there are 4 rows in the table, the link to the current site resides at index 3, so the *AddTblRow* method should add any parent sites after index 2.

7 Retrieve the first parent of the current site, then retrieve each further parent until no more remains. This requires the following code, next in sequence.

```
SPWeb spwParent = spwCurr.ParentWeb;
while (spwParent != null)
{
    // Code to display a site link will go here.
    spwParent = spwParent.ParentWeb;
}
```

Note that after each iteration, the *spwParent* variable points to a SharePoint site one level closer to the server root. This continues until *spwParent* receives a null pointer, which indicates that no more parents remain. Top-level sites have no parents, even if they're not located at the server root.

8 Because this Web Part may create dozens or hundreds of *SPWeb* objects (one for each link it displays) it's important to close these objects as soon as possible. To accomplish this, add the statements shown below in bold.

```
SPWeb spwParent = spwCurr.ParentWeb;
while (spwParent !=null)
{
    // Code to display a site link will go here.
    SPWeb spePrevParent = spwParent;
    spwParent = spwParent.ParentWeb;
    spwPrevParent.Close();
}
```

The first statement saves the address of the current *SPWeb* object, and the second new statement closes that object. (In between, the existing statement from step 7 points the *spwParent* variable at a different object: one that represents the current site's parent.

Chapter 20

9 Terminate the loop from step 7 if it encounters the server root site or the top-level site in the current collection, both of which earlier code has already displayed. This requires the code shown below in bold.

```
SPWeb spwParent = spwCurr.ParentWeb;
while (spwParent != null)
{
    if ((spwParent.ID == spsRoot.RootWeb.ID)
    || (spwParent.ID == spwTpLv.ID))
    {
        break;
    }
    //  Code to display a site link will go here.
    spwParent = spwParent.ParentWeb;
}
```

10 Replace the comment in step 9 with code that displays the site that the *spwParent* object currently represents. This code appears below in bold.

```
SPWeb spwParent = spwCurr.ParentWeb;
while (spwParent != null)
{
    if ((spwParent.ID == spsRoot.RootWeb.ID)
    || (spwParent.ID == spwTpLv.ID))
    {
        break;
    }
    AddTblRow(tblGrid, "Parent", spwParent.Url,
            spwParent.Title, spwParent.Name, intLayoutRow);
    SPWeb spwPrevParent = spwParent;
    spwParent = spwParent.ParentWeb;
    spwPrevParent.Close();
}
```

Note that the call to *AddTblRow* specifies the *intLayoutRow* variable as its sixth argument, but the loop never changes its value. This ensures that each parent site pushes down (and thus appears before) its child site.

11   The *Webs* property of any *SPWeb* object points to a collection of additional *SPWeb* objects, one for each subsite. Assign this collection to a variable named *swcWebs*.

Then, if the collection contains any members, display a separator line, then display a link to each subsite. To accomplish this, add the following code after the loop you completed in step 10.

```
SPWebCollection swcWebs = spwCurr.Webs;
if (swcWebs.Count > 0 )
{
    AddTblSeparator(tblGrid);
    foreach (SPWeb webSub in swcWebs)
    {
        AddTblRow(tblGrid, "Subweb", webSub.Url,
                  webSub.Title, webSub.Name, -1);
        webSub.Close();
    }
}
```

Notice the *webSub.Close()* statement, which closes each *SPWeb* object as soon as the loop finishes with it. Because of this statement, the loop will release resources as fast as it consumes them.

12   Add the *tblGrid* table object to the Web Part's *Controls* collection, and then close the *spwCurr* and *spwTpLv* objects. These will be the last statements in the *CreateChildControls* override method.

```
Controls.Add(tblGrid);
spwCurr.Close();
spwTpLv.Close();
```

In some situations, you may prefer that the Web Part display only subsites that the current team member can access. *SPWeb* objects have a *GetSubwebsForCurrentUser* method that's useful in this regard. To take advantage of this facility, replace the first statement in step 11, namely:

```
SPWebCollection swcWebs = spwCurr.Webs;
```

with this statement:

```
SPWebCollection swcWebs = spwCurr.GetSubwebsForCurrentUser();
```

Chapter 20

Writing the AddTblRow Method

This section explains how to write the *AddTblRow* method that adds site links to an HTML table that the browser will display. Proceed as follows.

1 Add the following declaration anywhere within the *SiteLinks* class, but not within any other structure or method.

```
private void AddTblRow(HtmlTable tblAdd,
                       string strType,
                       string strUrl,
                       string strTitle,
                       string strName,
                       int intPos)
{
// Code to add a table row will go here.
}
```

2 In place of the comment from step 1, declare variables named *rowGrid*, *celGrid*, and *ancUrl*. Respectively, these will identify *HtmlTableRow*, *HtmlTableCell*, and *HtmlAnchor* objects.

```
HtmlTableRow rowGrid;
HtmlTableCell celGrid;
HtmlAnchor ancUrl;
```

3 Create a new *HtmlTableRow* object and a new *HtmlTableCell* object. Arrange for the table cell to display the type of site information from the second method argument, and to have a vertical alignment of *top*. Finally, add the *HtmlTableCell* object to the *HtmlTableRow* object's *Rows* collection. This requires the following code, next in sequence.

```
rowGrid = new HtmlTableRow();
celGrid = new HtmlTableCell();
celGrid.InnerText = strType;
celGrid.VAlign="top";
rowGrid.Cells.Add(celGrid);
```

4 Create another *HtmlTableCell* object (still named *celGrid*) and an *HtmlAnchor* object named *ancUrl*. Set the *HtmlAnchor* object's *HRef* property to the URL received as the method's third argument.

```
celGrid = new HtmlTableCell();
ancUrl = new HtmlAnchor();
ancUrl.HRef = strUrl;
```

Creating Basic Web Parts

5   If *strTitle* (the fourth method argument) contains data, displays it as the *HtmlAnchor* object's visible text. Otherwise, display the contents of *strName*, the fifth argument. But if that, too, is empty, display the URL. This requires the following code.

```
if (strTitle != "")
{
    ancUrl.InnerText = strTitle;
}
else
{
    if (strName != "")
    {
        ancUrl.InnerText = strName;
    }
    else
    {
        ancUrl.InnerText = strUrl;
    }
}
```

6   Add the *HtmlAnchor* object named *ancUrl* to the *Controls* collection of the *HtmlTableCell* object named *celGrid*. Then, add the completed table cell to the *rowGrid.Cells* collection. This goes after the code from step 5

```
celGrid.Controls.Add(ancUrl);
celGrid.VAlign="top";
rowGrid.Cells.Add(celGrid);
```

7   If the caller specified a negative position for inserting the new row, call the *tblAdd.Rows.Add* method, which adds the row to the end of the table. Otherwise, call the *tblAdd.Rows.Insert* method, which inserts the row at the specified position. Here's the code.

```
if (intPos < 0)
{
    tblAdd.Rows.Add(rowGrid);
}
else
{
    tblAdd.Rows.Insert(intPos, rowGrid);
}
```

This completes the code for the *AddTblRow* method.

Writing the AddTblSeparator Method

As you no doubt recall, this method generates the horizontal lines that the SiteLinks Web Part displays between groups of related links. These "lines" are actually thin table cells formatted to have a contrasting background color. If you coded the HTML directly, it would look like this:

```
<tr>
  <td class="ms-partline" colspan="2"><img src="/_layouts/images/blank.gif"
width="1" height="1" border="0" /></td>
</tr>
```

The CSS class *ms-partline* provides the background color, and Windows SharePoint Services provides a transparent GIF file at */_layouts/images/blank.gif*.

To develop a method that emits this HTML, and that guards against it appearing repeatedly or at the top of a table, proceed as follows.

1   Declare a class-level integer variable named *intLastSeparator* and initialize it to zero. In other words, add the following code within the *SiteLinks* class but outside any other method or structure. If in doubt, code it just before the first method declaration,

```
private int intLastSeparator = 0;
```

Each time the *AddTblSeparator* method adds a row to the HTML table of links, it will store the resulting number of rows in this variable. If, upon reentry, the method discovers that the number of table rows still matches this value, it will bypass writing an additional separator.

Initializing the variable to zero guards against adding a separator row when the table contains no data.

2   Declare a method named *AddTblSeparator*, also within the *SiteLinks* class and outside any method or structure. Code it to accept one argument, an *HtmlTable* object named *tblAdd*. Here's the code.

```
private void AddTblSeparator(HtmlTable tblAdd)
{
}
```

3   Within the curly braces from step 2, declare the following local variables:

```
HtmlTableRow rowGrid;
HtmlTableCell celGrid;
HtmlImage imgBlank;
```

4   If the table received as an argument contains no more rows than it did after adding the most recent separator, exit with no further action. This requires the following code:

```
if (intLastSeparator == tblAdd.Rows.Count)
{
    return;
}
```

5 Create a new *HtmlTableRow* object named *rowGrid*, a new *HtmlTableCell* object named *celGrid*, and a new *HtmlImage* object named *imgBlank*.

Then, set the *HtmlImage* object's *Src* attribute to */_layouts/images/blank.gif*, its *Width* and *Height* attributes to 1, its alt text to empty, and its border width to zero. Here's the code.

```
rowGrid = new HtmlTableRow();
celGrid = new HtmlTableCell();
imgBlank = new HtmlImage();
imgBlank.Src = "/_layouts/images/blank.gif";
imgBlank.Width = 1;
imgBlank.Height = 1;
imgBlank.Alt = "";
imgBlank.Border = 0;
```

6 Add the *HtmlImage* object *imgBlank* to the *Controls* collection of the *HtmlTableCell* object *celGrid*. Then, set the cell's CSS class to *ms-partline* and its *ColSpan* attribute to 2. In short, append these statements to the code from step 5.

```
celGrid.Controls.Add(imgBlank);
celGrid.Attributes["class"] = "ms-partline";
celGrid.ColSpan = 2;
```

7 Add the completed table cell to the *Cells* collection of the *HtmlTableRow* object named *rowGrid*. Then, add the *rowGrid* object to the *tblAdd* table received as an argument. Finally, store the resulting number of rows in the *intLastSeparator* variable.

```
rowGrid.Cells.Add(celGrid);
tblAdd.Rows.Add(rowGrid);
intLastSeparator = tblAdd.Rows.Count;
```

This completes the coding for the *AddTblSeparator* method, and for the *SiteLinks* Web Part.

You can find the complete code for this example in the SiteLinks.cs file in the \Web-Parts\WssIso project on the companion CD. The procedures for building, installing, and testing this Web Part are the same as those for the Welcome Web Part described earlier in this chapter.

Creating the ListBrowser Web Part

This Web Part displays an elementary (some would say crude) listing of any SharePoint list or library in the current site. Figure 20-5 shows some typical results. The drop-down list provides a choice for every list or library in the site. Also displayed are a count of items in the current list, and then a tabular display of the list items.

Microsoft Windows SharePoint Services Inside Out

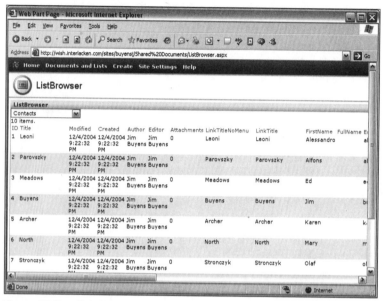

Figure 20-5. This Web Part displays the raw content of any list or library in the current site.

In a real application, you'd undoubtedly be more selective in the list columns you display, and you probably wouldn't use field names as the column headings. Displaying all the columns and the actual field names does, however, provide some insight into the structure of SharePoint lists.

This Web Part illustrates how to handle events from form fields, how to retrieve data from a SharePoint list, and how to use an ASP.NET control—specifically the DataGrid—in a Web Part. To create it, follow this procedure:

1 Open the WssIso project that the previous examples used, and then choose Add New Item from the Project menu.

2 When the Add New Item dialog box appears:

    2.1 Select Local Project Items in the Categories list at the left.

    2.2 Select Web Part in the Templates list at the right.

    2.3 Type ListBrowser.cs in the Name box and then click OK.

3 This project makes no use of custom properties or custom tool parts. You may therefore wish to delete:

    ■ The code for the Text custom property that appears just before and after the *public class proto* statement.

    ■ The commented code pertaining to custom tool parts, which appears just before the *protected override void RenderWebPart* statement.

Creating Basic Web Parts

4 Within the *ListBrowser* class, but not inside any other method or structure, declare a variable named *ddlLists* for the drop-down list, a variable named *spwCurr* for an *SPWeb* object that will point to the current site, and a method that overrides the default *CreateChildControls* method. Here's the code:

```
DropDownList ddlLists;
SPWeb spwCurr;
protected override void CreateChildControls ()
{
}
```

5 Within the *CreateChildControls* method, create an *SPWeb* object that points to the current site. Then create the drop-down list, specifying that an event handler named ListsChange should run whenever the team member changes the selected item. Finally, add the drop-down list to the Web Part's *Controls* collection. In short, add the lines shown below in bold.

```
protected override void CreateChildControls ()
{
    spwCurr = SPControl.GetContextWeb(Context);
    ddlLists = new DropDownList();
    ddlLists.SelectedIndexChanged += new EventHandler(ListsChange);
    Controls.Add(ddlLists);
}
```

To use the *SPControl* and *DropDownList* objects, you must also append the following references to the list of *using* statements at the top of the ListBrowser.cs file.

```
using Microsoft.SharePoint.WebControls;
using System.Web.UI.HtmlControls;
```

6 If the site contains any SharePoint lists but the *ddlLists* drop-down list is empty, iterate through the site's *Lists* collection and create a drop-down list item for each SharePoint list. Then, select the drop-down list's first item and configure the drop-down list to immediately submit the form whenever the visitor changes the selection. Finally, call a method named *DisplayList*, which displays the contents of the current list. All together, this requires the code shown below in bold.

```
protected override void CreateChildControls ()
{
    spwCurr = SPControl.GetContextWeb(Context);
    ddlLists = new DropDownList();
    ddlLists.SelectedIndexChanged += new EventHandler(ListsChange);
    Controls.Add(ddlLists);
    if ((spwCurr.Lists.Count > 0) && (ddlLists.Items.Count < 1))
    {
        foreach (SPList list in spwCurr.Lists)
        {
            ddlLists.Items.Add(new ListItem(list.Title));
        }
        ddlLists.SelectedIndex=0;
```

Chapter 20

```
        ddlLists.AutoPostBack = true;
        DisplayList();
    }
}
```

Once the drop-down list is loaded with list names, the ASP.NET *ViewState* mechanism will restore the values during each subsequent execution. This explains why the drop-down list might contain items immediately after you create it.

7 The *ListsChange* event handler will run whenever a team member changes the selection in the drop-down list. At that point, the event handler needs to refresh the display, using the same method that created the original display. To do this, add the following code within the *ListBrowser* class but outside any other method or structure:

```
private void ListsChange (object sender, EventArgs e)
{
    DisplayList();
}
```

8 Declare the *DisplayList* method, again within the *ListBrowser* class but outside any other method or structure. Also declare a variable that will point to an ASP.NET *DataGrid* object.

```
private void DisplayList()
{
    DataGrid grdCurList;
//  Code to create and load the DataGrid will go here.
}
```

9 Replace the comment in step 8 with code that makes sure the *CreateChildControls* method has finished running, and that creates an *SPList* object that points to the selected list.

```
EnsureChildControls();
SPList splCurList = spwCurr.Lists[ddlLists.SelectedItem.Text];
```

To understand the second statement, recall that:

- The *spwCurr* variable points to an *SPWeb* object that describes the current site.

- The *Lists* collection of an *SPWeb* object includes an *SPList* object for each list.

- By design in step 6, each item in the *ddlLists* drop-down list (including the selected item) contains the name of a list.

10 Create a generic paragraph tag with a zero margin, make it display the number of items in the current list, and add it to the Web Part's *Controls* collection for eventual output. In other words, add the following code next in sequence.

```
HtmlGenericControl parCount = new HtmlGenericControl("p");
parCount.Style.Add("margin", "0");
parCount.InnerText = splCurList.Items.Count + " items.";
Controls.Add(parCount);
```

Creating Basic Web Parts

11 If the list contains any items, establish a pointer named *licCurList* that points to the list's *Items* collection. Then, create a *DataGrid* object and set its visual properties. Finally, render the list's *Items* collection as an ASP.NET *DataTable*, assign the *DataTable* as the *DataGrid's* data source, bind the data into the *DataGrid*, and add the *DataGrid* to the Web Part's *Controls* collection. Here's the code.

```
if (splCurList.Items.Count > 0)
{
    SPListItemCollection licCurList = splCurList.Items;
    grdCurList = new DataGrid();
    grdCurList.BorderWidth = 0;
    grdCurList.CellSpacing = 0;
    grdCurList.CellPadding = 2;
    grdCurList.HeaderStyle.CssClass = "ms-vh2";
    grdCurList.ItemStyle.CssClass = "ms-vb2";
    grdCurList.AlternatingItemStyle.CssClass = "ms-vb2 ms-alternating";
    grdCurList.EnableViewState = false;
    grdCurList.DataSource = licCurList.GetDataTable();
    grdCurList.DataBind();
    Controls.Add(grdCurList);
}
}
```

The CSS class names *ms-vh2, ms-vb2,* and *ms-alternating* are all standard elements of SharePoint style sheets. This ensures that the Web Part's appearance will always match that of the surrounding site.

Because the *GetDataTable* method creates an ADO.NET *DataTable,* it needs methods from the *System.Data* namespace. Therefore, add the following reference to the list of *using* statements at the top of the source file.

```
using System.Data;
```

12 Change the template-provided *RenderWebPart* method to agree with the following. As in previous examples, this sends the browser the HTML from all the objects in the Web Part's *Controls* collection.

```
protected override void RenderWebPart(HtmlTextWriter output)
{
    RenderChildren(output);
}
```

You can find the complete code for this example in the List Browser.cs class in the \WebParts\WssIso project on the companion CD. To build, install, and test the Web Part, follow the same procedures you used earlier for the Welcome Web Part.

In Summary...

This chapter explained how to write three simple but useful Web Parts. You can use these Web Parts as the basis for those you create yourself.

The next chapter will explain how to write a Web Part that performs an administrative task. This requires using objects from a special *SharePoint.Administration* namespace.

Chapter 21

Creating Custom Administration Tools

Chapters 15, 16, and 17 explained the many ways you can administer Windows SharePoint Services at the site, site collection, virtual server, and server farm level. Inevitably, however, some organizations will prefer to design their own administrative interfaces. For example, they may wish to reduce common operations from multiple screens to one, or to synchronize member lists and other information with external systems.

In cases like these, Windows SharePoint Services comes to the rescue with a rich set of administration objects you can access from custom Web Parts or, for that matter, from any Windows program. This chapter will introduce those objects, and then show how to develop a custom Web Part that performs two simple administrative tasks: displaying and creating the top-level sites on a SharePoint server.

Why create a Web Part like this when you can use the Create Top-level Web Site page on the Central Administration server to do the same job? Here are three common reasons:

- The Create Top-Level Web Site page may have more options than you want the person who creates top-level sites to have. In other words, you want to reduce the chances of making a mistake.

- You want to automate certain corporate policies. Suppose, for example, that the same username string should appear in all logon accounts, e-mail addresses, and top-level site URLs. You could program the Web Part to display a single text box and construct the logon account, e-mail address, and top-level site URL programmatically.

- The Web Part displays a list of existing top-level sites. Windows SharePoint Services provides no Web Page that displays this information.

> For more information about the Create Top-level Web Site page, refer to "Creating a Top-Level Site as an Administrator" in Chapter 5.

Accessing Administrative Methods

The *Microsoft.SharePoint.Administration* namespace provides a rich array of objects you can manipulate to manage a SharePoint server or server farm. This is where you should look if you want to write your own Web Parts or stand-alone programs that perform administrative tasks, and if the *Microsoft.SharePoint* namespace doesn't have the properties or methods you need.

The most important classes in the *Microsoft.SharePoint.Administration* namespace are:

- *SPGlobalAdmin*   This class provides access to all server-level settings in a SharePoint deployment. It provides methods, for example, to create and delete central administration servers, create and delete configuration databases, and extend and unextend virtual servers.

- *SPVirtualServer*   This class provides access to virtual server settings, such as its collection of top-level sites, its collection of content databases, its e-mail settings, and so forth.

To create an *SPGlobalAdmin* object, you add a *using* statement such as this to your source file:

```
using Microsoft.SharePoint.Administration;
```

and then code a statement like this within any convenient method:

```
SPGlobalAdmin spgAdmin = new SPGlobalAdmin();
```

After you do this, the following expressions would, for example, return the IP address and name of the first front-end Web server using the current configuration database.

```
spgAdmin.Config.WebServers[0].Address
spgAdmin.Config.WebServers[0].Name
```

There are three ways of getting an *SPVirtualServer* object. Choose the one that best suits your application.

- Use the *VirtualServers* property of the *SPGlobalAdmin* class to get a collection of *SPVirtualServer* objects: one for each virtual server on the current computer or in the current farm. The following code, for example, creates an *SPVirtualServer* object that represents the first virtual server.

  ```
  SPGlobalAdmin spgAdmin = new SPGlobalAdmin();
  SPVirtualServer spvServer = spgAdmin.VirtualServers[0];
  ```

  And the following code iterates through the entire collection of virtual servers:

  ```
  foreach (SPVirtualServer spvServer in spgAdmin.VirtualServers)
  {
  // Code to handle each virtual server would go here.
  }
  ```

- Use the *VirtualServer* property of the *SPSiteCollection* class.

  All *SPVirtualServer* objects have a *Sites* property that points to an *SPSiteCollection* object. That object, in turn, has a *VirtualServer* property that points back to the *SPVirtualServer*.

  This might seem a bit redundant, but if all you have is the *SPSiteCollection* object, it's good to know you can get back to the virtual server if the need arises.

- Use the *VirtualServer* property of the *SPVirtualServerConfig* class.

  Again, this is circular. An *SPVirtualServer* object has a *Config* property that points to an *SPVirtualServerConfig* object, and that object has a *VirtualServer* property that points back to the virtual server. It's there if you need it.

Starting from the *SPGlobalAdmin* and *SPVirtualServer* objects, you can retrieve or modify almost any aspect of a SharePoint server or server farm. For example, the rest of this chapter will describe a Web Part that uses these objects to display and create top-level Web sites.

When you write a custom program to administer Windows SharePoint Services, the program must run under an account capable of performing the same actions using the SharePoint Central Administration pages, Top-Level Site Administration pages, or Site Administration pages.

- In the case of a Web Part, Windows SharePoint Services will display a new login prompt if the team member running the Web Part doesn't have enough privileges.

- In the case of a batch or command-line program, Windows SharePoint Services will raise an exception if the login account lacks the necessary permissions.

> For more information about the *SPGlobalAdmin* object, the *SPVirtualServer* object, and all their children, browse the article "Microsoft.SharePoint.Administration Namespace" at *msdn.microsoft.com/library/en-us/spptsdk/html/tsansMicrosoftSharePointAdministration.asp*.

Creating the TopSites Web Part

To illustrate some aspects of programmatically administering a SharePoint site, this section explains how to write a Web Part that displays and adds top-level Web sites on a virtual server. This is the Web Part that appears in Figure 21-1.

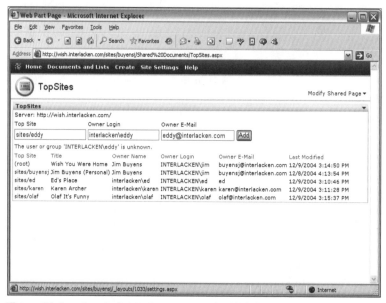

Figure 21-1. An administrator can use the Web Part in this page to display and create top-level sites.

For simplicity, this Web Part always administers the first SharePoint content server on the computer where the Web Part is running. To create a top-level site, an administrator fills in the Top Site, Owner Login, and Owner E-Mail boxes, and then clicks the Add button.

Initializing the WssIsoAdmin Project

To create a Microsoft Visual Studio .NET project for the *TopSites* Web Part, proceed as follows.

1 Start Visual Studio and create a new project named WssIsoAdmin. Specify the Web Part Library templates just as you did for the WssIso project in Chapter 20.

2 When the WebPart1.cs file appears in Visual Studio, rename it to TopSites.cs and then, within the file, change all occurrences of WebPart1 to TopSites.

Alternatively, choose Add New Item from the Project menu and use the Web Part template to create a new class named TopSites.cs.

Once you have a TopSites.cs file, delete or resolve to ignore the template code for the Text custom property, and the commented code for custom tool parts. This Web Part won't use either of those features.

You can find a copy of the completed WssIsoAdmin project on the Companion CD, in the \Webparts\WssIsoAdmin folder. To install this project on your system, copy the WssIsoAdmin folder into your Visual Studio Projects folder, clear the Read-Only attributes, and then open the WssIsoAdmin.sln file.

Creating Custom Administration Tools

Declaring Namespaces and Class Variables

The tasks in this section provide access to classes in two namespaces that the Web Part template doesn't include by default, and they declare variables used in more than one method. Proceed as follows.

1 Add the following statements just after the *using* statements that the template provides.

```
using System.Web.UI.HtmlControls;
using Microsoft.SharePoint.Administration;
```

The *System.Web.UI.HtmlControls* namespace provides classes for the HTML tables and paragraphs in the user interface. The *Microsoft.SharePoint.Administration* namespace provides objects for inspecting and modifying SharePoint sites.

2 Declare the following variables within the *TopSites* class, but not within any other method or structure.

```
SPGlobalAdmin spgAdmin;
SPVirtualServer spvServer;
SPSiteCollection sscTopLvs;
HtmlGenericControl parMsg;
TextBox txtPath;
TextBox txtLogin;
TextBox txtEmail;
HtmlInputHidden hidRepost;
```

The *spgAdmin* variable will point to an *SPGlobalAdmin* object that provides entry to the administration functions. The *spvServer* and *SPSiteCollection* variables will point to objects that represent the virtual server and its list of site collections.

The *parMsg* variable will point to an HTML paragraph that displays any error messages. The *txtPath, txtLogin,* and *txtEmail* variables will identify the three text boxes shown in Figure 21-1. The *hidRepost* variable will point to a hidden form field that differentiates between initial display and subsequent postback.

Overriding the CreateChildControls Method

Like the Web Parts in Chapter 20, Web Parts that perform administrative tasks must override the *CreateChildControls* method in order to create output controls at the proper time. To perform this task for this Web Part, proceed as follows.

1 Override the *CreateChildControls* method, just as you did in the previous chapter. In other words, add the following code within the *TopSites* class but outside any other method or structure. This code also creates the *SPGlobalAdmin* object.

```
protected override void CreateChildControls ()
{
    spgAdmin = new SPGlobalAdmin();
}
```

2 Search the *SPGlobalAdmin* object's *VirtualServers* collection, looking for the first administrable server. When you find it:

- Save a pointer named *spvServer* that points to the virtual server.
- Save a pointer named *sscTopLvs* that points to the server's list of site collections.
- Break out of the loop.

This requires the code shown below in bold.

```
spgAdmin = new SPGlobalAdmin();
foreach (SPVirtualServer spvSrv in spgAdmin.VirtualServers)
{
    if (spvSrv.State == SPVirtualServerState.Ready)
    {
        spvServer = spvSrv;
        sscTopLvs = spvServer.Sites;
        break;
    }
}
```

SPVirtualServerState.Ready is a public constant that means the server is extended with Windows SharePoint Services, that it's running, and that it isn't a SharePoint Central Administration server. Table 21-1 lists all the possible *SPVirtualServerState* values

Table 21-1. SPVirtualServerState Values

Name	Description
NeedExtend	The server needs to be extended.
NeedUpgrade	The server needs to be upgraded.
NotAdministrable	Windows SharePoint Services can't manage the server.
NotNTFS	The server doesn't use a Microsoft Windows NT file system.
Ready	The server is ready.

3 Create a generic HTML paragraph and use it to display the virtual server's URL. This requires the following code, next in sequence.

```
HtmlGenericControl parSite = new HtmlGenericControl("p");
parSite.InnerHtml = "Server: " + spvServer.Url.ToString();
parSite.Style.Add("margin","3px");
Controls.Add(parSite);
```

Notice that *spvServer* is the variable where step 2 stored the *SPVirtualServer* object that points to the first administrable virtual server. The *Url* property points to a *System.Uri* object that provides a variety of information about the server's URL.

Creating Custom Administration Tools

4 To start displaying the input form, create an HTML table, add a new row, add four new cells, and store heading text in the first three of those cells. Here's the necessary code:

```
HtmlTable tblForm = new HtmlTable();
tblForm.Rows.Add(new HtmlTableRow());
tblForm.Rows[0].Cells.Add(new HtmlTableCell());
tblForm.Rows[0].Cells.Add(new HtmlTableCell());
tblForm.Rows[0].Cells.Add(new HtmlTableCell());
tblForm.Rows[0].Cells.Add(new HtmlTableCell());
tblForm.Rows[0].Cells[0].InnerText = "Top Site";
tblForm.Rows[0].Cells[1].InnerText = "Owner Login";
tblForm.Rows[0].Cells[2].InnerText = "Owner E-Mail";
```

5 To prepare for the form fields, add another row and another four cells to the same table. This requires the following code, next in sequence:

```
tblForm.Rows.Add(new HtmlTableRow());
tblForm.Rows[1].Cells.Add(new HtmlTableCell());
tblForm.Rows[1].Cells.Add(new HtmlTableCell());
tblForm.Rows[1].Cells.Add(new HtmlTableCell());
tblForm.Rows[1].Cells.Add(new HtmlTableCell());
```

6 Instantiate the three text boxes and add them to the first three cells from step 5. In other words, append the following code:

```
txtPath = new TextBox();
tblForm.Rows[1].Cells[0].Controls.Add(txtPath);

txtLogin = new TextBox();
tblForm.Rows[1].Cells[1].Controls.Add(txtLogin);

txtEmail = new TextBox();
tblForm.Rows[1].Cells[2].Controls.Add(txtEmail);
```

7 Instantiate the form button, give it a caption of Add, and assign an event handler named *BtnAddClick* to its *Click* event. Then, after adding the button to the fourth table cell, add the entire table to the Web Part's Controls collection.

```
Button btnAdd = new Button();
btnAdd.Text = "Add";
btnAdd.Click += new EventHandler(BtnAddClick);
tblForm.Rows[1].Cells[3].Controls.Add(btnAdd);

Controls.Add(tblForm);
```

Chapter 21

Microsoft Windows SharePoint Services Inside Out

8   Create another generic paragraph, this time for any error messages that occur. Set its
    EnableViewState property to *false* so that ASP.NET doesn't restore the error message
    the next time the Web Part runs. Assign the standard SharePoint CSS class ms-error,
    override this with a paragraph margin of 3 pixels, and initialize the content to a non-
    breaking space. Finally, add the paragraph to the Web Part's *Controls* collection.

    ```
    parMsg = new HtmlGenericControl("p");
    parMsg.EnableViewState = false;
    parMsg.Attributes["class"] = "ms-error";
    parMsg.Style.Add("margin", "3px");
    parMsg.InnerHtml = " ";
    Controls.Add(parMsg);
    ```

9   Create a hidden form field named *hidRepost*, make sure its *EnableViewState* property
    is *true*, and assign an event hander named *RepostLoaded* for the *Load* event. Then, of
    course, add it to the Web Part's *Controls* collection.

    ```
    hidRepost = new HtmlInputHidden();
    hidRepost.EnableViewState = true;
    hidRepost.Load += new EventHandler(RepostLoaded);
    Controls.Add(hidRepost);
    ```

This completes the coding for the *CreateChildControls* method.

Writing the RepostLoaded Event Handler

The Web Part needs to generate the list of existing top-level sites in two distinctly different
situations:

- When the page runs for the first time.
- Whenever the team member clicks the Add button.

The TopSites Web Part uses a hidden form field to detect when it runs for the first time. On
the first execution this field will, by default, contain an empty string. When the code finds
this empty value, it changes it to a *y* and then displays the list of top-level sites. On subsequent
executions, the value of *y* keeps the Web Part from reloading the list of sites.

> **Note**   Web Parts, like any other ASP.NET control, use a multithreaded event model. This
> means that ASP.NET starts methods within the Web Part as soon as they're ready to run,
> and in no particular order. This improves the overall performance of the server.

Unfortunately, reading the values of hidden form fields (or, for that matter, any kind of form
fields) can be tricky. When you create a control in the *CreateChildControls* method, you can't
depend on values from the browser being immediately present. It may take some time for a
parallel process to insert the form field value received from the browser.

Creating Custom Administration Tools

This is why step 9, in the previous section, appended an event hander to the hidden form field's *Load* event. The *Load* event doesn't fire until the control is fully loaded, which includes receiving its value from the browser.

Fortunately, the code for this event handler is much simpler than the explanation. The complete code listing appears below.

```
void RepostLoaded(object sender, EventArgs e)
{
    if (hidRepost.Value != "y")
    {
        hidRepost.Value = "y";
        ListSites();
    }
}
```

The name of the event hander agrees with the name you specified in step 9 of the previous section. If the form field's value isn't *y*, the code sets it to *y* and runs a method named *ListSites*. This is the method that displays the current list of top level sites.

Insert this code anywhere within the *TopSites* class, but not within any other method or structure.

Writing the BtnAddClick Event Handler

The code that created the Web Part's *Button* object specified that clicking the button should run an event handler named *BtnAddClick*. To develop this event handler, proceed as follows:

1 Add the following method declaration anywhere within the *TopSites* class, but not within any other method or structure.

```
void BtnAddClick(object sender, EventArgs e)
{
}
```

2 Between the curly braces, call the *EnsureChildControls* method to ensure that the *CreateChildControls* method has completed and that all children of the Web Part's *Controls* collection have finished loading. Then, code a *try / catch* block. This requires the statements shown below in bold:

```
void BtnAddClick(object sender, EventArgs e)
{
    EnsureChildControls();
    try
    {
    }
    catch(Exception ex)
    {
    }
}
```

3 Add the code shown below in bold to the *try* block, the *catch* block, and the end of the method.

```
void BtnAddClick(object sender, EventArgs e)
{
    EnsureChildControls();
    try
    {
    SPSite newSiteCollection =
        sscTopLvs.Add(txtPath.Text, txtLogin.Text, txtEmail.Text);
    }
    catch(Exception ex)
    {
        parMsg.InnerText = ex.Message;
    }
    ListSites();
}
```

The code in the *try* block creates a new top-level site at the given path, with the given owner login account, and with the given owner e-mail address. This is the simplest form of the *Add* method for an *SPSiteCollection* object.

If Windows SharePoint Services can't create the new top-level site, it raises an exception, and the code in the *catch* block runs. That code retrieves the error message from the exception and displays it in the *parMsg* control.

The last statement runs the *ListSites* method, just as the *RepostLoaded* method did. This displays a current listing of top level sites.

This completes the code for the *BtnAddClick* event handler.

Adding Top-Level Web Sites

The *SPSiteCollection* class has several overloaded methods, all named *Add,* and each accepting a different combination of arguments. The TopSites Web Part uses the simplest form, which specifies only the top-level site's URL, primary owner account, and primary owner e-mail address.

By calling the *Add* method with different signatures, you can also specify the Web site title, description, locale identifier, site definition or site template, primary owner display name, secondary owner account, display name, and e-mail address, the name of a new database, and the user name and password of the database administrator.

For more information, browse the home page for the *SharePoint.Administration* namespace at *http://msdn.microsoft.com/library/en-us/spptsdk/html/ tsansMicrosoftSharePointAdministration.asp*, and then click the link for the *SPSiteCollection* class.

Creating Custom Administration Tools

Writing the ListSites Method

Both the *RepostLoaded* event handler and the *BtnAddClick* event handler call this method to display a current listing of top-level sites. To code the method, proceed as follows:

1 Declare a method named *ListSites*. As usual, locate this anywhere within the *TopSite* class, but not within any other method or structure. Here's the code:

```
void ListSites ()
{
}
```

2 Within the curly braces from step 1, declare an *HtmlTable* variable named *tblSites* and an *HtmlTableRow* named *rowSites*.

```
void ListSites ()
{
    HtmlTable tblSites;
    HtmlTableRow rowSites;
}
```

3 Instantiate the *HtmlTable* object. Then, to avoid sending large amounts of *ViewState* data to the browser (and receiving it back), set its *EnableViewState* property to *false*. This requires the code shown below in bold.

```
HtmlTable tblSites;
HtmlTableRow rowSites;

tblSites = new HtmlTable();
tblSites.EnableViewState = false;
```

4 Add a table row to the *tblSites* table, set a variable that points to it, and set its *class* attribute to ms-vh. This is the usual CSS class for SharePoint table headings.

```
tblSites.Rows.Add(new HtmlTableRow());
rowSites = tblSites.Rows[tblSites.Rows.Count - 1];
rowSites.Attributes["class"] = "ms-vh";
```

5 Add six cells to the row, then store the six column headings in them.

```
rowSites.Cells.Add(new HtmlTableCell());
rowSites.Cells.Add(new HtmlTableCell());
rowSites.Cells.Add(new HtmlTableCell());
rowSites.Cells.Add(new HtmlTableCell());
rowSites.Cells.Add(new HtmlTableCell());
rowSites.Cells.Add(new HtmlTableCell());
rowSites.Cells[0].InnerText = "Top Site";
rowSites.Cells[1].InnerText = "Title";
rowSites.Cells[2].InnerText = "Owner Name";
rowSites.Cells[3].InnerText = "Owner Login";
rowSites.Cells[4].InnerText = "Owner E-Mail";
rowSites.Cells[5].InnerText = "Last Modified";
```

Chapter 21

6 Set up a loop that iterates through each member of the *Names* collection in the current virtual server's *SPSiteCollection* object. The *sscTopLvs* variable points to this object. Here's the code:

```
foreach (string strTopUrl in sscTopLvs.Names)
{
}
```

Each item in the *Names* collection contains the relative URL of one top-level site.

7 *VirtualServer* objects have a *MakeFullUrl* method that converts a relative URL such as *sites/buyensj* to a fully qualified URL such as *http://wish.interlacken/com/sites/buyensj*.

Using this method, get the fully qualified URL of the current top-level site, and then use the result to create an *SPSite* object named *spsSiteColl*. This requires the code shown below in bold.

```
foreach (string strTopUrl in sscTopLvs.Names)
{
    SPSite spsSiteColl = new
            SPSite(sscTopLvs.VirtualServer.MakeFullUrl(strTopUrl));
}
```

8 Add a new row to the table you created in step 3, and then add six cells to that row. Here's the required code in bold:

```
foreach (string strTopUrl in sscTopLvs.Names)
{
    SPSite spsSiteColl = new
            SPSite(sscTopLvs.VirtualServer.MakeFullUrl(strTopUrl));
    tblSites.Rows.Add(new HtmlTableRow());
    rowSites = tblSites.Rows[tblSites.Rows.Count - 1];
    rowSites.Cells.Add(new HtmlTableCell());
    rowSites.Cells.Add(new HtmlTableCell());
    rowSites.Cells.Add(new HtmlTableCell());
    rowSites.Cells.Add(new HtmlTableCell());
    rowSites.Cells.Add(new HtmlTableCell());
    rowSites.Cells.Add(new HtmlTableCell());
}
```

9 For each of the six table cells you created in step 8, set the valign= attribute to top. This requires the following code, next in sequence.

```
foreach (HtmlTableCell celSites in rowSites.Cells)
{
    celSites.VAlign = "top";
}
```

10   Create an *HtmlAnchor* object (that is, a hyperlink). If the current top-level site's URL is empty, make the *HtmlAnchor* object display (root); otherwise, make it display the site's relative URL. Set the hyperlink's *Href* property to the fully qualified version of the top-level site's URL, and then add the *HtmlAnchor* object to the first table cell's *Controls* collection. Append this code to that from the previous step.

```
HtmlAnchor ancTopUrl = new HtmlAnchor();
if (strTopUrl == "")
{
    ancTopUrl.InnerText = "(root)";
}
else
{
    ancTopUrl.InnerText = strTopUrl;
}
ancTopUrl.HRef = spvServer.MakeFullUrl(strTopUrl);
rowSites.Cells[0].Controls.Add(ancTopUrl);
```

11   Load table cells 2 through 6 with their respective property values. Here's the code:

```
rowSites.Cells[1].InnerText = spsSiteColl.RootWeb.Title;
rowSites.Cells[0].Controls.Add(ancTopUrl);
rowSites.Cells[2].InnerText = spsSiteColl.Owner.Name;
rowSites.Cells[3].InnerText = spsSiteColl.Owner.LoginName;
rowSites.Cells[4].InnerText = spsSiteColl.Owner.Email;
rowSites.Cells[5].InnerText =
    spsSiteColl.LastContentModifiedDate.ToLocalTime().ToString();
```

Note that the *LastContentModifiedDate* will appear by default as a UTC time. The *ToLocalTime* method converts this to the server's local time zone

12   Add the *tblSites* table to the Web Part's *Controls* collection. Make sure this statement is within the *ListSites* method, but not within the loop that iterates through the *sscTopLvs.Names* collection.

```
Controls.Add(tblSites);
```

This completes the code for the *ListSites* method. A complete listing appears below.

```
void ListSites ()
{
    HtmlTable tblSites;
    HtmlTableRow rowSites;

    tblSites = new HtmlTable();
    tblSites.EnableViewState = false;
    tblSites.Rows.Add(new HtmlTableRow());
    rowSites = tblSites.Rows[tblSites.Rows.Count - 1];
    rowSites.Attributes["class"] = "ms-vh";
    rowSites.Cells.Add(new HtmlTableCell());
    rowSites.Cells.Add(new HtmlTableCell());
    rowSites.Cells.Add(new HtmlTableCell());
    rowSites.Cells.Add(new HtmlTableCell());
```

```
rowSites.Cells.Add(new HtmlTableCell());
rowSites.Cells.Add(new HtmlTableCell());
rowSites.Cells[0].InnerText = "Top Site";
rowSites.Cells[1].InnerText = "Title";
rowSites.Cells[2].InnerText = "Owner Name";
rowSites.Cells[3].InnerText = "Owner Login";
rowSites.Cells[4].InnerText = "Owner E-Mail";
rowSites.Cells[5].InnerText = "Last Modified";

foreach (string strTopUrl in sscTopLvs.Names)
{
    SPSite spsSiteColl = new
        SPSite(sscTopLvs.VirtualServer.MakeFullUrl(strTopUrl));
    tblSites.Rows.Add(new HtmlTableRow());
    rowSites = tblSites.Rows[tblSites.Rows.Count - 1];
    rowSites.Cells.Add(new HtmlTableCell());
    rowSites.Cells.Add(new HtmlTableCell());
    rowSites.Cells.Add(new HtmlTableCell());
    rowSites.Cells.Add(new HtmlTableCell());
    rowSites.Cells.Add(new HtmlTableCell());
    rowSites.Cells.Add(new HtmlTableCell());
    foreach (HtmlTableCell celSites in rowSites.Cells)
    {
        celSites.VAlign = "top";
    }
    HtmlAnchor ancTopUrl = new HtmlAnchor();
    if (strTopUrl == "")
    {
        ancTopUrl.InnerText = "(root)";
    }
    else
    {
        ancTopUrl.InnerText = strTopUrl;
    }
    ancTopUrl.HRef = spvServer.MakeFullUrl(strTopUrl);
    rowSites.Cells[0].Controls.Add(ancTopUrl);
    rowSites.Cells[1].InnerText = spsSiteColl.RootWeb.Title;
    rowSites.Cells[2].InnerText = spsSiteColl.Owner.Name;
    rowSites.Cells[3].InnerText = spsSiteColl.Owner.LoginName;
    rowSites.Cells[4].InnerText = spsSiteColl.Owner.Email;
    rowSites.Cells[5].InnerText =
spsSiteColl.LastContentModifiedDate.ToLocalTime().ToString();
}
Controls.Add(tblSites);
}
```

Overriding the RenderWebPart Method

Find the version of the *RenderWebPart* method that the Web Part template provides, and change it to read as follows.

```
protected override void RenderWebPart(HtmlTextWriter output)
{
    RenderChildren(output);
}
```

This completes the coding for the Web Part.

Building, Installing, and Testing the Web Part

Compiling and testing the TopSites Web Part involves the same tasks you performed for the Web Parts in Chapter 20. Specifically:

1   Use the sn.exe program to generate a strong key file. You need this so that Visual Studio .NET can give your assembly a strong name.

2   Add the strong key file to your project, and enter its name in the AssemblyInfo.cs file.

3   Choose Rebuild Solution from the Build menu and resolve any compilation errors. Repeat as necessary.

4   Copy the resulting DLL into your server's Global Assembly Cache, or into the bin folder for your virtual server.

5   Add a <SafeControl> entry to the <SafeControls> section of the virtual server's web.config file.

Remember that the InstallAssemblies tool can perform steps 4 and 5 for you.

6   Make sure the Web Part appears on the Web Part Gallery: New Web Parts (AllItems.aspx) page. If so, select it and click Populate Gallery.

7   Add the Web Part to a Web Part Page (probably a new one) and see what happens.

> For more detail on the process of installing and testing a Web Part, refer to the section titled "Installing and Testing" in Chapter 20.

In Summary...

This chapter introduced the high-level objects that Windows SharePoint Services provides for performing administrative tasks. It then explained how to use these objects to write a Web Part that displays the top-level sites on a virtual server and creates new top-level sites.

This book introduced and explained every major aspect of Windows SharePoint Services, including the browser interface, integration with the Microsoft Office System, advanced design with FrontPage 2003, installation on Windows Server 2003, use with Microsoft SQL Server 2000, complete administration and configuration, and custom programming with Visual Studio .NET. This is an impressive range of topics, and it clearly indicates the strategic position Windows SharePoint Services occupies among Microsoft technologies. Hopefully, this book has magnified your understanding of this important technology and provided exceptional benefit to you and your organization. Good luck with your site, and I hope we meet again.

Index to Troubleshooting and Inside Out Topics

Entries in italic are Inside Out Topics

Index

About the Author

Jim Buyens has been professionally involved with the World Wide Web since its inception, including roles as a server administrator, Web master, content developer, and system architect. He has many years of experience in the telecommunications industry, and is also an acclaimed Microsoft Most Valuable Professional (MVP) who contributes extensively to the Microsoft Online FrontPage Communities.

Jim received a Bachelor of Science degree in Computer Science from Purdue University in 1971 and a Master of Business Administration from Arizona State University in 1992. When not enhancing the Web or writing books, he enjoys traveling and attending professional sports events—especially NHL hockey. He resides with his family in Phoenix.

Other books by Jim Buyens include:

- Microsoft Office FrontPage Version 2003 Inside Out, August 2003, Microsoft Press
- Faster Smarter Beginning Programming, November, 2002, Microsoft Press
- Web Database Development Step by Step .NET Edition, June, 2002, Microsoft Press
- Troubleshooting Microsoft FrontPage 2002, May, 2002, Microsoft Press
- Microsoft FrontPage Version 2002 Inside Out, May , 2001, Microsoft Press
- Web Database Development Step by Step, June, 2000, Microsoft Press
- Running Microsoft FrontPage 2000, June, 1999, Microsoft Press
- Stupid Web Tricks, July, 1998, Microsoft Press
- Running Microsoft FrontPage 98, October, 1997, Microsoft Press
- Building Net Sites with Windows NT—An Internet Services Handbook, July 1996, Addison-Wesley Developers Press

Contacting the Author

Hearing from happy readers is always a welcome and pleasant experience, and hearing from the less-than-satisfied is important as well. Please note that I can respond only if you write in English. My e-mail address is

buyensj@interlacken.com

I'm most interested in your impressions of this book: what you liked or disliked about it, what questions it did or didn't answer, what you found superfluous and what you'd like to see added in the next edition. I'll post errors, omissions, corrections, and frequently-asked questions on my Web site at

www.interlacken.com/wss-iso/

I can accept enhancement requests only for this book, and not for the Microsoft software. To suggest product enhancements, send e-mail to:

mswish@microsoft.com

or browse the Web page at

register.microsoft.com/mswish/suggestion.asp

Please understand that I'm just one person and I can't provide technical support or debugging assistance, even for readers. Please try other channels, including the following newsgroups

microsoft.public.sharepoint.windowsservices
microsoft.public.sharepoint.portalserver
microsoft.public.sharepoint.portalserver.development

and the Microsoft Search page at

search.microsoft.com

If you're getting an error message or error number, try searching for that exact phrase or number, plus the word *SharePoint*. If you're having trouble with a specific feature or component, try searching for the name of the component plus, again the word *SharePoint*

If all else fails, please write. While I can't promise to answer each message, I'll try to provide at least a useful suggestion. Even when I can't answer your e-mail messages directly, I find it instructive to learn what problems users like you are experiencing—and therefore how I can make this and future books more useful to everyone.

What do you think of this book? We want to hear from you!

Do you have a few minutes to participate in a brief online survey? Microsoft is interested in hearing your feedback about this publication so that we can continually improve our books and learning resources for you.

To participate in our survey, please visit:

www.microsoft.com/learning/booksurvey

And enter this book's ISBN, 0-7356-2171-3. As a thank-you to survey participants in the United States and Canada, each month we'll randomly select five respondents to win one of five $100 gift certificates from a leading online merchant.* At the conclusion of the survey, you can enter the drawing by providing your e-mail address, which will be used for prize notification *only*.

Thanks in advance for your input. Your opinion counts!

Sincerely,

Microsoft Learning

Learn More. Go Further.